MMPI Patterns of American Minorities

Publication of this book was assisted
by a grant from the McKnight Foundation
to the University of Minnesota Press's program.

MMPI Patterns of American Minorities

W. Grant Dahlstrom, David Lachar,
and Leona E. Dahlstrom

with contributions by
Luther A. Diehl, Malcolm D. Gynther,
Kevin L. Moreland, and James T. Webb

University of Minnesota Press
Minneapolis

Published by the University of Minnesota Press
2037 University Avenue Southeast, Minneapolis, MN 55414.
Published simultaneously in Canada by Fitzhenry & Whiteside Limited, Markham. Printed in the United States of America.

Library of Congress Cataloging-in-Publication Data

Dahlstrom, W. Grant (William Grant)
MMPI patterns of American minorities.

Bibliography: p.
Includes index.
1. Minnesota multiphasic personality inventory. 2. Psychological tests—United States. 3. Minorities—United States—Psychology. I. Lachar, David. II. Dahlstrom, Leona E. III. Title. [DNLM: 1. Minority Groups—psychology. 2. MMPI. WM 145 D131m] BF698.8.M5D34 1986 155.2'83 86-3369
ISBN 0-8166-1530-6

The University of Minnesota is an equal-opportunity educator and employer.

To the memory of
STARKE R. HATHAWAY
in recognition of his
sustained interest in all peoples

Contributors

W. Grant Dahlstrom
Ph.D. Professor of Psychology,
University of North Carolina,
Chapel Hill, North Carolina

Leona E. Dahlstrom
M.A. Clinical Psychologist,
Chapel Hill, North Carolina

Luther A. Diehl
Ph.D. Chief Psychologist,
Spartanburg Area Mental Health Center,
Spartanburg, South Carolina

Malcolm D. Gynther
Ph.D. Professor of Psychology,
Auburn University, Auburn, Alabama

David Lachar
Ph.D. Director of Psychology Training and Research,
Institute of Behavioral Medicine,
Good Samaritan Medical Center, Phoenix, Arizona,
and Adjunct Professor, Arizona State University

Kevin L. Moreland
Ph.D. Product Development Manager,
Professional Assessment Services,
National Computer Systems,
Minnetonka, Minnesota

James T. Webb
Ph.D. Professor of Psychology,
School of Professional Psychology,
Wright State University, Dayton, Ohio

CONTENTS

PREFACE

Social scientists who seek to analyze and document the personological and behavioral characteristics associated with membership in a particular subgroup are often chided for attempting to carry out such studies on groups in which they themselves are not members. Although their preliminary efforts may often be clumsy or inopportune, these investigators should not be faulted for making the effort merely on the grounds of being outsiders. No one can know the experiences of any other person. Novelists, poets, and biographers struggle to convey to their readers the common elements of the black experience, of the Indian way, or of the Amish life; but whatever these commonalities may be, they cannot be known directly by outsiders. They can only be inferred from the observations of others, from distillations of conversations, or from perceptions of reactions indirectly felt through empathy or recipathy.

Membership in the subgroup in question, it is true, may provide an investigator with ready-made distinctions, sharper perceptions, or more acute intuitions; but out-group status may in turn provide some compensating distance and a differing perspective. In-group feelings may create strong impressions of a comforting commonality; nevertheless, the human condition is universal and inevitable: we are all victims of the inescapable solipsism inherent in our biological autonomy. We can only hope that our methods in the behavioral sciences provide us with insights that are both supplementary and complementary to those coming from intuitive writers and artists. Both approaches aim at converging on the same fundamental goals: meaningful and accurate communication, useful and productive understanding among all humans.

Personality assessment shares with other techniques in the social sciences the goal of documenting commonalities. Research on assessment strives to ascertain the shared characteristics of individuals identified by some assessment score or index so that these commonalities can be used to characterize the next individual so identified. Simple as this task may seem, it has proven to be fraught with various kinds of error and the risks of inappropriate generalization. Predicted correlates of the index may not be found when scores are obtained on new sets of subjects, or these features may turn out to be related to other characteristics as well, so that the desired specificity is lacking. Much of the empirical research on assessment is devoted to the task of bracketing for a given score or index the ranges of its valid generalization. The limits that are discovered may then be specified in terms of various background features of the subjects as well as the temporal limits within which the index (together with its associated personological features) provides a dependable guide to individual assessment. These findings may furnish the basis for establishing special norms like those for the two sexes or for different age levels or for generating corrective weights such as those for test-taking approach or attitude.

The present volume records a systematic effort to examine the evidence for the generalizability of the validity of the Minnesota Multiphasic Personality Inventory (MMPI), one of the most widely used personality tests in the world, as applied to members of various ethnic minorities in the United States. The focus of the empirical research is on the differences appearing on the MMPI between black and white men and women, but the issues involve many other subcultural groups and minorities in this country today. We hope that the approach reported here and the preliminary findings of these investigations may serve as a guide to future studies of the many other diverse subgroups needing similar examination and understanding.

ACKNOWLEDGMENTS

We are indebted to a great number of people who have helped in the various phases of this effort. We wish to thank those who aided in the collection of the data from the adult black men and women: in Michigan, Ms. Dyan Taylor and Mr. Willie Busby; in North Carolina, Dr. William H. Anderson and Mrs. Mary Thomas Tripp; in Alabama, Mr. Milton S. Hurst. Data collection in this phase of the project was funded by the National Institute of Drug Abuse (NIDA Grant H81DA01879). Additional data on the white community sample from Ohio and West Virginia were supplied by Dr. James T. Webb and Dr. Luther A. Diehl. Data from the Ohio psychiatric sample were provided by Dr. John R. Graham of Kent State University.

Statistical assistance was provided by Dr. Mark Appelbaum and Mr. Jeffrey Brooks of the Department of Psychology at the University of North Carolina and by Dr. James L. Grisell of the Lafayette Clinic. Preparation of the manuscript was facilitated by the assistance of Mrs. Mary Lynn Eckert and Mrs. Blanche Critcher. An early draft of the manuscript was read by Dr. Bernadette Gray-Little, who made many helpful comments. Without these many sources of advice and encouragement this volume would not have reached final publication.

The following tables and figures have been reproduced or adapted from these sources with the permission of the authors and publishers (where necessary):

from *Journal of Clinical Psychology*:

the figures in chapter 2 were adapted from Gynther, Fowler, and Erdberg (1971); table G-13 in the appendix was excerpted in part from table 1 in Mandelzys (1979); table G-22 was excerpted from tables 2 and 3 in McCreary and Padilla (1977).

from *Canadian Journal of Criminology*:
table G-13 was excerpted in part from table 2 in Mandelzys and Lane (1980).

from *Journal of Studies on Alcohol*:
table G-12 was adapted in part from table 1 in Uecker, Boutilier, and Richardson (1980). Reprinted by permission from *Journal of Studies on Alcohol*, vol. 41, pp. 357-362, 1980. Copyright by Journal of Studies on Alcohol, Inc., Rutgers Center of Alcohol Studies, New Brunswick, NJ, 08903.

from *Journal of Personality Assessment*:
table G-21 was adapted from table 1 in Holland (1979).

from *Psychological Reports*:
table G-25 was adapted from table 3 in Hibbs, Kobos, and González 1979). Reprinted with permission of authors and publisher from: Hibbs, B. J., Kobos, J. C., and González, J. Effects of ethnicity, sex, and age on MMPI profiles. *Psychological Reports*, 1979, 45, 591-597, table 3.

from *Journal of Consulting and Clinical Psychology*:
table G-16 was adapted in part from table 2 in Butcher, Braswell, and Raney (1983); table G-20 was adapted from table 1 in Penk et al. (1981b).

Dissertations and theses by the following individuals were also abstracted and excerpts included in appendix G: Dr. Steven Abe, Dr. J. F. Bryde, Mr. R. Warren Bull, Mr. B. S. Francis, Dr. Robin LaDue, Dr. J. R. Murphy, Dr. Grant Plemons, and Dr. Rex Selters.

Additional data and further analyses were provided by Dr. Jerry McGill, Dr. Ronald D. Page, Mr. James H. Panton, Dr. Walter Penk, Dr. Robert R. Reilley, Dr. Vitali Rozynko, Dr. James H. Shore, Dr. William Tsushima, Mr. Roberto Velásquez, Dr. Glenn White, and Dr. J. S. Wormith.

We wish to express our grateful appreciation to all of these investigators for their generous help and kind support.

MMPI Patterns of American Minorities

CHAPTER 1

Ethnic Status and Personality Measurement

W. Grant Dahlstrom

The need is compelling for objective and dependable test instruments to assess personality in both clinical practice and basic research. As the research literature on the Minnesota Multiphasic Personality Inventory (MMPI) has accumulated (Dahlstrom, Welsh, & Dahlstrom, 1975; Graham, 1977; Greene, 1980), its acceptance and utilization has grown apace. The test has been used to appraise personality and emotional status in a multitude of clinical contexts and research settings differing markedly from the psychiatric services within which the MMPI was originally developed. Many of these applications have involved individuals who differed in a number of important ways from the patients and normals who were examined as part of the derivational research at the University of Minnesota Hospitals.

As the material summarized in the next two chapters documents, the suitability of the MMPI for use with persons from such diverse backgrounds and origins has come under increasing scrutiny. This interest is by no means of recent origin, however; as early as 1944, Grace Arthur published a study of the usefulness of the MMPI in evaluating the personality characteristics of students enrolled in the twelfth grade of a federal school for American Indians that was located in Minnesota. Although the test was still in a preliminary form at the time she administered it to the members of this ethnic minority, Dr. Arthur's findings led her to conclude that it was a suitable instrument for such assessment purposes. Since that time, however, many investigators have come to question that conclusion.

The concept of ethnic membership itself has been used in personality research with a variety of meanings and connotations. Numerous attributes have been ascribed to members of these subgroups in the United States, many of them contradictory or even mutually exclusive. In addition, the bases for characteristics associated with ethnic background have been attributed to many different factors, such as genetic mechanisms; labeling processes; carry-overs from the cultures of origin; or social and economic hardships arising from systematic biases, exclusions, discriminations, and deprivations imposed upon members of American minorities. Many investigators have used tests like the MMPI in attempts to clarify these conflicting views and contentions. Thus, the suitability of these instruments for such research purposes is a central concern for these research workers.

Parameters of Ethnic Variation

Because the concept of ethnicity has been variously defined and formulated, there is no one universally accepted definition. The following view seems to be one that is sufficiently general and comprehensive to serve the present purpose:

> Ethnic status is defined as an easily identifiable characteristic that implies a common cultural history with others possessing the same characteristic. The most common ethnic "identifiers" are race, religion, country of origin, language, and/or cultural background. Ethnic status is an ascribed status—that is, unlike social class, it is attributed by others and is not easily changeable from birth. (Eaton, 1980, p. 160)

It should be quite obvious that the various characteristics serving as ethnic identifiers do not usually occur as independent features but appear in configurations (e.g., most Irish immigrants to the United States probably possessed Celtic physiques, spoke English with a Gaelic brogue, and belonged to the Roman Catholic denomination of the Christian religion). Such patternings of interrelated characteristics make it difficult, if not impossible, to carry out research that can provide clear-cut answers to questions about the possible role that any one of these features may play in the development and maintenance of human personality patterns. Additional complications in this kind of investigation arise from the transitory nature of some of these identifiers over the lifetime of particular members of an ethnic group or, especially, over the generations within families in such groups. For example, first-generation immigrants from Norway to the United States may be identifiable not only by physique and physiognomy, by speech characteristics, by Protestant church membership, or by ethnocentric social affiliations, but also by adherence to Scandinavian food preferences, work ethics, and political values. By the second or third generation, however, descendants of these Norwegian immigrants may fail to show most of these identifiable characteristics, preserving only a surname and Nordic physical features from the original ethnic configuration.

Other nationalities, racial groupings, cultural or religious patterns may be more enduring, however, and may thus constitute more meaningful bases for ethnic study, not only over the lifetime of particular individuals but even over many generations of immersion in a multicultural society like that of the United States. Such characteristics as the variations in skin color that form the broad groups of human races; the strong intragroup ties of religion, language, and cultural heritage that serve to restrict out-marriage (e.g., Jewish religion, Basque language, or the nomadism of Gypsy family groups); or the stigma of caste membership that may prevent group members from passing freely into the larger society (e.g., the Untouchables of India or the Eta of Japan) are clearly more enduring in their physical and psychological makeup as well as in the cultural practices of both in-groups and out-groups. Such characteristics come closer to meeting the general requirements put forth by Eaton as stable ethnic identifiers. Understandably, then, most of the research studies have tended to focus upon these latter features to define group membership for the study of ethnic variation in psychological attributes.

These same ethnic identifiers have also been instrumental in the other inescapable aspect of ethnic status in the United States. They have often served as a means of attributing ethnic group membership in such a way as to make these individuals stand out from the majority of Americans; it has made them members of a minority. Political, social, and economic processes in this country have combined to generate for members of various ethnic minorities special conditions that affect their living arrangements, their work patterns, and even the views they hold of themselves. To a lesser extent, perhaps, associated factors such as residential restrictions have contributed to or even accentuated these conditions. Many of the resulting patterns of self-identification and self-evaluation may by now have come to be institutionalized in child-rearing practices, values, and traditions in the families of American minorities. Social scientists of widely different training and orientation— anthropologists, economists, social psychologists, sociologists, developmental psychologists, psychiatrists, clinical psychologists—have been trying to document the results of these various converging forces and explain the ways that each affects the personality and behavior of those growing up as members of one or another of these subgroups.

Alternative Views of Ethnic Diversity

Current writing and research on personality characteristics associated with ethnic group membership in the United States reflect a variety of different explanations. Each of these views carries quite different implications for the way in which personality test differences between various subgroups in our diverse culture could be interpreted. These various explanations also pose different research issues and call for different research strategies in any effort to disentangle their relative contributions to the validity of any psychological test. Some of these competing views can be appraised in a fairly straightforward way by available methods of data gathering and analysis; other formulations require research techniques and designs beyond the range of methods available today. Few of these explanations are free of highly charged emotional overtones or risks of misunderstanding and misinterpretation.

Do ethnic differences arise primarily from genetic differences? Because some ethnic identifiers are known to have a genetic basis (various features of skin color, physique, or physiognomy), there exists a strong temptation to ascribe to genetics all other differences that may be discovered in comparisons of such groups with those groups lacking such physical features. In at least three respects, such conclusions are at best premature, and they are most probably wrong. First, very few (if any) of the studies in the vast literature on ethnic diversity use genetic techniques to assign individual research subjects to one or another of the ethnic groups under investigation. Ethnicity is ascribed through social custom or self-identification, not through procedures involving blood-typing, biochemical analyses, or other means of gene mapping. Second, although rapid advances have been made in the last few years, current behavioral genetic methods have not been applied to any sizable number of social and behavioral patterns known to differ between ethnic groups. That is, heritability estimates or other ways of documenting genetic contributions to within-group variations are not available for the vast majority of characteristics of interest in between-group studies, such as those involving ethnicity. Third, most of the genetic evidence available to date on ethnic groups points to an overwhelming commonality of the human gene pool across all racial and ethnic groupings; for only a few morphological features are large and important differences in the patterns of gene frequencies known. Loehlin, Lindzey, and Spuhler (1975) summarize these findings with respect to racial membership. The evidence that they have marshaled fails to show any very extensive genetic differentiations between the broad racial subgroups. Nor has there been reported any more convincing evidence about the role of genetic differences between other ethnic groupings.

The same misconceptions about genetic mechanisms that give rise to hasty generalizations about genetic causes of ethnic variations open this field of study to an even more pernicious bias: radical racism. Highly charged and emotional contentions of racial inferiority and superiority, based upon fallacious stereotypes, historic national rivalries, or ethnocentric pride and sensitivities may enter into such discussions. Racist bigotries tend to obscure even the most objective scientific discussions and to raise inflammatory issues of biological inferiority and racial purity. In spite of careful analyses (by such writers as Thomas & Sillen, 1972; Malina, 1973; and Loehlin et al., 1975) of the false beliefs and misconceptions that are involved, the risk of invoking such emotional reactions remains strong even today. Although there have been many significant advances in the field of behavioral genetics in the last few years, the position taken by the participants in the American Association for the Advancement of Science (AAAS) symposium nearly 20 years ago (Mead et al., 1968) is still the only scientifically defensible one. Focusing upon issues of race as the most salient of the ethnic identifiers, the members of this panel (organized by the Scientists' Institute for Public Information and assembled at the 1966 meeting of the AAAS) wrote forcefully about the lack of evidence either for the view that human races are closed Mendelian populations or for any other general, biologically based theory relevant to differences in general social or cultural achievement. These pronouncements were prompted by the lingering effects of the Nazi propagandists about racial superiority and inferiority but were addressed more broadly to counter all the various biological rationales for racial discrimination and prejudice. Although more is now known about the specific genetic mechanisms of various racially associated disorders (such as sickle-cell anemia, G6PD deficiency, or Tay-Sachs disease), no evidence for any overall inequity or disparity between racial or other ethnic groups has been forthcoming. The denunciation of racist views of human nature that was put forth by the AAAS panel under the general editorship of Margaret Mead is as relevant and, unfortunately, as needed today as it was nearly two decades ago.

Do ethnic differences arise directly from reactions to being labeled as deviant? In recent years, the study of potential effects of being identified or labeled as different from some reference group has been extended and developed by social psychologists and sociologists. Rubington and Weinberg (1973) believe that the sorts of differences that may invoke a label of some deviance (delinquent or criminal, "queer" or "peculiar," alcoholic or addicted) from members of a reference group and the subsequent reactions and effects on the individuals so labeled interact through the cascading and amplifying processes of exclusion, in-group formation, and altered self-conceptions. Within this general perspective, these writers believe that the *consequences* of the attachment of the label, in its full range of behavioral and social impacts, far outweigh the magnitude and social significance of the initial variations that provoked the label. Labeling theories of deviance, then, have been put forward to explain most of the behavioral variations between people, such as criminal career versus law-abiding conformity, homosexual versus heterosexual life-style, drug addiction or alcohol abuse versus sobriety, and, most importantly, major psychiatric aberration versus emotional stability. In these various patterns of deviance, the fact of early identification and labeling is seen as contributing most of the variance; the initial differences that these subjects may show in degree of emotional instability, substance use, sexual preference, or conformance to rules and laws are generally viewed as trivial by comparison (see Winslow, 1972).

In spite of the size of the theoretical and empirical literature now appearing on the deviance hypothesis, there is little hard evidence on the correctness of this formulation in the areas of human variation to which it has been applied. Proper testing of these assumptions will await prospective longitudinal studies of similar subjects, labeled and not labeled, that are designed to trace their subsequent careers. In any extension of this deviance formulation to ethnic groupings, the labeling process is equivalent to the ascription of ethnic group membership to particular individuals. Since an ethnic ascription is usually made at birth and by other in-group members, special properties of ethnic group labels (over and above sheer deviance) may be intrinsic to this process, properties that are probably not conveyed by the labeling of sexual preference, substance abuse, or mental health variations. Most of the formulations of the deviance labeling process assume, for example, that being identified as different has strongly derogatory implications and that most individuals strongly prefer to be accepted as fitting in with the group. Instances of ethnic pride; motivations to excel and stand out from the peer group as unusually capable, talented, or praiseworthy; and efforts to achieve distinctions in dress, adornment, or possessions all cast doubt on any oversimplified application of the deviance hypothesis to ethnic group membership.

In another way, however, this focus upon deviance per se suggests that in a complex, multicultural nation like the United States it is often possible to locate individuals who are ethnically like the majority (reference) group but who, in a particular locale, are the ones who are different. That is, white, Anglo-Saxon, Protestant individuals, who generally are members of the reference group against which various others are viewed as ethnically deviant, may be so situated in some circumscribed geographical region that they are the ones who are labeled deviant (in respect to race, language, cultural heritage, religion, or a combination of these attributes). If so, the deviation hypothesis suggests that they themselves will, under such a labeling process, manifest the characteristics more generally ascribed to members of (statistical) minority groups. Such possibilities are explicitly introduced in Braucht's (1979) model of the interaction between subject characteristics and situational circumstances in the postdiction of a very deviant form of behavior (serious suicidal attempts, whether successful or not). For each census tract in the large urban area of Denver, Colorado, ethnic majority and minority concentrations and ratios were established. Individuals in the minority for a given urban area were found to be more likely than the local majority members to make such attempts, regardless of their own ethnic group membership. Use of this kind of situational reference to define deviance may be one effective way to study the impact of sheer difference itself in the formation of behavioral and social characteristics of ethnic group members in the United States. In terms of the general deviance explanation, however, there should be a considerable degree of homogeneity across all ethnic groups that share the common circumstance of being statistically in the minority and readily identifiable as deviant by the members of the majority or reference group. This formulation would lead to the expectation that there is more commonality than diversity among the various ethnic groups in the United States, sharing as they do the consequence of being labeled as minority group members. Such an expectation runs counter to the formulation to be taken up later that attributes an important role to the special cultural histories, the different origins and backgrounds, and the values and traditions of each ethnic group in America.

Are ethnic differences attributable to an American caste system? Our American society, according to idealized egalitarian values and aspirations in the United States, is envisioned as a fundamentally individualistic one, with people being accepted for what they actually are rather than for where they come from, whom they know, or to whom they may be related. It should be obvious that many of the exclusions suffered by members of ethnic minorities in this country are directly contrary to these espoused traditions of the United States as a land of equal opportunity and that these experiences of deprivation have often been bitterly disillusioning and disenchanting. It is in this perspective, then, that some social scientists have proposed that the actual social structure of the United States bears important similarities in its intergroup patterns of relationship to those societies that have had traditional caste structures.

As used by sociologists, the concept of a caste differs from other forms of social stratification:

> A caste system may be viewed as a close approximation to a pure type of social stratification in which class membership is hereditary and the various classes are rigidly segregated by occupational

> specialization, religious and dietary taboos and by the moral belief that what is, ought to be. (Lopreato & Lewis, 1974, p. 412)

The social schema represented by a caste system differs in important ways from social stratification by social class:

> . . . a system of inequality, unlike castes or estates, [that] requires no legal or other formally institutionalized support. Since opportunities for social mobility are held out to all members of the society, changes in ascribed status through personal accomplishments frequently occur. The society has no formal restrictions on social relations or on marriage among members of different strata. Thus, social organization along class lines is minimal and class boundaries are blurred. (Roach, Gross, & Gursslin, 1969, p. 75)

In many ways, this may be one of the most debatable conceptualizations of the place of ethnic minorities in contemporary American society. It characterizes the relationship between the dominant white majority and the nonwhite minorities as forming a distinct caste system, usually with parallel hierarchies of social status within each caste. That is, the white majority and the nonwhite minorities are both ordered by levels of increasing status according to occupation, income, and differential desirability of residential and geographic location; but the general groupings are kept separate by almost impermeable social barriers that limit intergroup relationships, intermarriage, and neighborhood sharing. These barriers not only serve to exclude minorities from certain jobs and professions but provide effective ceilings to the rise of any lower caste member within business, government, or educational institutions. As a result of these broad restrictions on low-caste members, the distribution of individuals over socioeconomic levels within the various racial groupings is disproportionately skewed; thus nonwhite members are overrepresented in the lower levels of status (Haller, 1971).

In this caste formulation, then, only if nonwhite minority members can effectively mask their racial features and ancestry can they "pass" for white and enter fully into the mainstream of American social and economic life. "Passing," it is said, carries the double risk of losing all support and ties with the low-caste ethnic group of origin and of being discovered and rejected as a nonwhite by the majority group (see Costello, 1978). In this context, various ethnic characteristics (family names, hair texture, religious practices, or physiognomic features) may act as stigmas. Although some may be amenable to change (to permit racial "passing"), these characteristics may become closely tied to ethnic personality. Their stigmatizing value may accordingly produce seriously adverse effects on the self-views of particular members of these ethnic minorities. Such persons may come to devalue themselves because they possess the hated shape of the nose, the despised religious heritage, or the telltale family name. Plastic surgery, sales of hair straighteners, and legal actions to change family names are all cited as evidence to document both the existence of such a caste system and the urgent desire of some minority members to escape ethnic stigmas so as to be acceptable to the majority group. As spelled out by early psychologists and sociologists (e.g., Dollard, 1937; Davis & Dollard, 1940) and updated by Duberman (1976), the operation of the caste system in this country does not approach, either in the extensiveness of its ramifications or in its rigidity, the age-old caste system of India (although even there the ancient customs are gradually yielding to modernization). Despite its greater subtlety, however, the operation of our caste system is said to be potent and pervasive.

In terms of its implications for personality studies, one of the most important consequences of the existence of an American caste system based upon ethnic status would be in the ways in which parents caught in low-caste positions prepare their children for their eventual entry into the same caste (Proshansky & Newton, 1968). If their child-rearing practices successfully shape the child to fit comfortably into such a low status role, the child may be incorporating a variety of self-views that could be deprecatory, demeaning, or destructive of self-confidence and self-acceptance. If socialization is directed instead toward acceptance of and belief in the traditional American dream of self-betterment, fulfillment, and the winning of social acclaim, the parents' efforts may be laying the groundwork for later disillusionment, frustration, and self-betrayal when their child encounters caste barriers and limits. If the parents' own efforts are all directed toward accommodations to such a caste system but their child takes initiatives out of keeping with the family strictures, then the child may be assuming burdens of guilt and family rejection in addition to whatever rebuffs he or she may encounter in an alien and hostile society. All too little is known about the effects on the personality of the developing minority child that may be produced by these experiences while growing up in a caste-ridden society (White, 1984). Nevertheless, powerful objections have been raised during the last 30 years or so by psychologists and sociologists against various legal barriers to racial mixing and other limits to free access to resources (school segregation; exclusions from recreational facilities, social clubs, and restaurants; or restrictions on participation in various occupations, professions, and unions) because of the findings that such exclusions may injure the self-images of ethnic minority members so victimized. These lines of evidence have been summarized by writers such as Clark in *Dark Ghetto* (1965) and Baughman in *Black Americans* (1971). Although these works focus upon black groups, it can certainly be assumed that other American minorities also experience the adverse impact of castelike exclusions.

As noted above, these analyses of social stratification in American society based on a concept of caste are by no means universally accepted by contemporary sociologists. On the other hand, writers such as Duberman (1976) propose expanding these castelike descriptions to include social barriers based upon age and gender that arbitrarily limit mobility and restrict earnings. However, other research summaries raise doubts about the immutability of the relationships between various ethnic and racial groups in contemporary American society. Writers like Williams (1977) offer many kinds of evidence that social barriers are being significantly reduced and that intergroup relationships have been improving over recent decades. In addition, the research methods that served to document alleged psychological scarring of the self-images of minority members have themselves come under criticism as potential sources of misinformation (see Gray-Little & Appelbaum, 1979).

Are ethnic differences a direct reflection of the history of these groups in terms of their origins before immigration and their experiences since arriving in America? In this view, each ethnic group has developed a unique cultural pattern that is shared in part or totally by the individual members of that group. This pattern of traditions, values, and behaviors is partly a function of what each group brought here from its country (or countries) of origin and partly a result of the experiences each has encountered in adapting to this country with its particular customs, demands, and opportunities. As the sociologist Steinberg succinctly states:

> Ethnic pluralism in America has its origins in conquest, slavery, and exploitation of foreign labor. Conquest, first, in the case of native Americans who were systematically uprooted, decimated and finally banished to reservation wastelands; and second, in the case of Mexicans in the Southwest who were conquered and annexed by an expansive nation. Slavery, in the case of the millions of Africans who were abducted from their homelands and forced into perpetual servitude on another continent. Exploitation of foreign labor, in the case of the tens of millions of immigrants who were initially imported to populate the nation's land mass, and later to provide cheap labor for industrial development.
>
> To say that ethnic pluralism in America had its origin in conquest, slavery, and exploitation is not to deny that in the course of American history ethnic diversity has come to assume positive value. Nor is it to deny that minorities have often reaped the benefits of an affluent society, notwithstanding the circumstances of their origins. (Steinberg, 1981, p. 5)

That is, although there may be distinctive cultural traditions and self-views that each ethnic group has brought with it in its migration to this country, these distinctive characteristics inevitably become mixed with the effects of various local social and economic vicissitudes before being transmitted to succeeding generations here. Thus, the personality characteristics of American minority group members today may not be recognizable representations of the cultural heritages of their place of origin (see Bennett, 1975).

Three closely interrelated concepts have been proposed to characterize this evolving complex of traditional and adaptational behaviors that make up each pattern: ethnic personality, ethnic identity, and ethnic identity model. As defined and elaborated by Devereux, ethnic personality can best be viewed as:

> a conceptual scheme derived inductively from concrete data of two not very distinct types. The first consists of directly observed behavior which, as one's data become more numerous, appear to be typical of and distinctive for a particular group. . . . The second type of concrete data is directly observed verbal behavior consisting of generalizations about the ethnic personality by informants acting as self-ethnographers. . . . It is inherent in the notion of ethnic personality that members of the *ethnos* display that ethnic personality both in various ways and to a different degree . . . . Ethnic personality may be defined as a set of usually hierarchized sets of positive (positive = ego ideal) predictive statements, such as "A Spartan is brave, dour, frugal, laconic, etc." All such adjectives are attributes, even when they are negatively worded . . . [and] . . . such negative formulations often reflect historical processes. They highlight the dissociative-differentiating origins of many ethnic personality traits. (Devereux, 1975, pp. 45-47)

For Devereux, the concept of ethnic identity in its simplest and most unambiguous form is a "label or sorting device for oneself and for 'others' and sociologically, a label which can be attributed or withheld only totally" (1975, p. 49). That is, a member either of the group so designated or of some contrasted group may apply such a label and thus ascribe an ethnic identification to himself or to another. This narrow meaning of ethnic identity merely signifies that a distinction has been drawn with regard to some membership in a group formed on the basis of one or more ethnic identifiers. As Devereux goes on to elaborate this labeling step:

> Hence, it matters not at all, in this frame of reference and at this stage of the analysis, whether *A* asserts, "I am a Spartan" (with *B*

> concurring or dissenting), or whether *B* asserts, "*A* is a Spartan" (with *A* concurring or dissenting). In practice, of course, such things do matter. (Devereux, 1975, p. 49)

However, once an individual who has become aware of the personality characteristics of the ethnic group with which he or she is now identified begins to act explicitly in accord with this ethnic pattern, he or she can be said to be expressing an ethnic identity model. This kind of self-conscious behavior (the self-identification of ethnicity) that some call

> "ethnic identity," denotes *not* the pure concept (label), but the impure ethnic identity model, which is more or less congruent, in terms of what is predicated about it, with the inductively formulated ethnic personality. . . . Behavior expressing ethnic identity often disappears as soon as *A* ceases to be under the eyes of other members of his *ethnos*. . . . Behavior expressive of ethnic identity also tends to disappear when a strong upheaval brings about a state of affairs incompatible with the ethnic identity model. . . . There is often a tendency to exaggerate, with respect to foreigners, an ethnic identity trait that is less obvious in intra-ethnic relations. Spartan laconism with aliens is an example. . . . A variant of this process is the exaggeration of the tokens of one's ethnic identity during exile. (Devereux, 1975, pp. 49-53)

As Steinberg (1981) notes, membership in an ethnic minority in the United States today generally, but by no means invariably, carries with it a number of disadvantages. The minority member may encounter economic, occupational, or political limitations through denial of access to status positions; may operate under language handicaps that raise special educational barriers; and may live in geographic or residential isolation that increases the risk of criminal victimization, sanitation and housing inadequacy, dietary and nutritional deficiency, or special disease exposure and susceptibility. Many recent sociological studies have tried to document the impact that such systematic exclusions, discriminations, and deprivations over so broad an array of factors may have on the attitudes and behaviors of individual minority group members (see Simpson & Yinger, 1972). Such effects may be manifested not only in the adaptational style of people subjected to these experiences (ethnic personality) but also in the way they prepare their children for exposure to similar conditions. In other words, the impact is seen as shaping an emerging ethnic identity model for the next generation.

In this view, then, proper understanding of the personality processes of members of various ethnic groups requires knowledge of the surviving elements of the culture of origin of each group, together with some appreciation of the ways in which these values, customs, and behaviors have been modified to enable these individuals to survive and prosper on the contemporary American scene. A separate identity model may be needed to comprehend the behaviors of present-day members of each group, and quite separate norms, scales, and standards may thus be required of our psychometric instruments if these tests are to function properly.

It should be obvious that there are other barriers that may have similar psychological consequences and that may operate in the same way or combine with race to block effective access to full use of physical and cultural resources. Some of these include such biological factors as gender (as reflected in different roles in childbearing and child rearing), sensory and physical handicaps, or learning disabilities caused by brain damage. Similarly, limitations of personality may interfere, such as low self-esteem or emotional crippling. Environmental factors may play a similar role in individuals in rural isolation or in ghetto areas with associated economic deprivation. The psychological consequences of such barriers may produce adverse effects similar to those attributed to racial discrimination.

Can differences between American ethnic groups be explained in terms of differential distributions over various socioeconomic levels of the members of these minorities? Some psychologists and sociologists, unimpressed with the evidence put forth in support of the concept of an American caste system, propose to explain observed differences in behavior and personality among various groups in this country as reflecting primarily the different numbers of each group falling within each socioeconomic class or level. That is, if disproportionate numbers of these minority groups occupy positions at, say, the bottom of the socioeconomic scale in the United States, then any comparison of these groups with the dominant reference group that does not control for the socioeconomic class level is likely to reflect differences in status as well as any attributes idiosyncratic to particular ethnic status (Steinberg, 1981). If this view is correct, the same personality characteristics that emerge from comparisons between samples of individuals drawn from various ethnic groups should also appear within any one of these ethnic groups when members of that group who differ in socioeconomic class or level are compared. In this way, characteristics of socioeconomic status across American ethnic groups can be distinguished from those attributes characteristic of particular subgroups.

This socioeconomic status explanation is based on two important assumptions: first, that there is a pattern of socioeconomic stratification in the United States that is comparable within each ethnic group; and second, that individuals in these various levels or classes differ in important ways in their attitudes, personalities, and behavior. As noted earlier in the discussion of possible castelike social organization in America, most social scientists concur in characterizing the complex patterns of interrelationships among Americans as organized in respect to several levels of social standing. Although there is less agreement about the need to include in such a summary details about the power struggles, the limitations on access to goods, or the patterns of competition for limited resources, there is little dissent about the importance of class levels in controlling social contacts and interrelationships (Dohrenwend & Dohrenwend, 1969). The existence, importance, and stability of this kind of socioeconomic stratification in American society are almost universally acknowledged, although there are still a few idealists who would deny that there exists any very formal social class structure in the United States. More and more, however, Americans themselves are willing to acknowledge that they belong to some particular class. In this regard, it is interesting to note that a strong leveling action is operating recently in such self-labeling behaviors: an excessive number of self-assignments are being made to the "middle class" from both above and below (Gilbert & Kahl, 1982).

Indices of socioeconomic class or level use various background data to assign an individual a place in this hierarchy, either from facts about his or her family of origin (attributed status) or in terms of particular characteristics of the individual under study (achieved status). Primary among these data are the person's annual income, highest level of education completed, kind of occupation (if any) from which income is derived, and, sometimes, data on the area of residence and kind of dwelling in which the person's home is located (Gilbert & Kahl, 1982). Although this system of stratification is summarized as a simple vertical structure, there is ample evidence that the hierarchy is more accurately viewed as a complex, multidimensional system of interpersonal relationships. This complexity constitutes a serious challenge to social scientists in any effort to match or control for socioeconomic differences in studies of various factors that may interact with or be affected by differences in class membership (Meehl, 1967). More pressing for the current issue, of course, is the question of the comparability of the dimensional structure of socioeconomic status over the range of ethnic minorities in this country (see Warheit, Holzer, & Arey, 1975). Only a little information on this important question is yet available, primarily on socioeconomic levels in white and black groups. There is little reason to believe that the structures within some of the other American ethnic minorities will turn out to be any less complex.

One of the most recent analyses of the structure of socioeconomic status as it appears in white and black adults was carried out on data obtained in a study in 1968 in Toledo, Ohio (Stricker, 1982). Many items of information that enter into traditional socioeconomic indices were collected on black and white heads of household in Lucas County (which covers the urban area of Toledo and some of the surrounding suburban and rural areas). An even longer list of supplementary data of either "theoretical or empirical relevance" to social stratification in these groups was also collected by interviewers who were assigned to respondents of the same race. These variables covered such areas as the background and current situation of each family, child-rearing patterns, purchasing and leisure time activities, as well as political and religious involvements. The interviewers also rated the respondents on various dimensions such as social class, intelligence level, and grammatical usage.

Parallel factor analyses were carried out on these data from the two racial samples. Stricker found that the major dimensions (six in all) in the socioeconomic status (SES) data from white subjects could be matched only roughly to some of the seven dimensions in the data from the black subjects. Even the first factor of social status showed little direct correspondence in the two racial groups; only the traditional data on number of years of formal education (as scaled by Warner, Meeker, & Eells [1949] or by Hollingshead & Redlich [1958]) showed comparable loadings on this factor. Many of the other traditional indices (as well as the interviewer ratings) failed to show the expected relationships to this main factor in the data from black heads of household while showing much clearer relationships to this dimension in the data from white subjects. There was some reassurance, perhaps, in the comparability between black and white factor loadings on an apparently separate aspect of socioeconomic structure—attributed status from one's family of origin. Stricker found that the family background characteristics of the heads of household appeared on a separate factor (termed Main Support's Social Status) with very similar loadings for both racial groups on such items as their fathers' occupation and educational level, and their mothers' occupation and educational level as well. The location of these variables on a separate factor in Stricker's analyses serves to highlight the fact that different implications of status come from data about a subject's family of origin as compared with that person's own earned or achieved status. These findings from Stricker's analyses also indicate that it may not be feasible to match socioeconomic status levels within one ethnic group to levels in some other ethnic group. That is, although black and white heads of household can be directly compared on educational background characteristics (in terms of both attributed and achieved status as reflected in years of schooling), they can be less readily compared on occupational level. In terms of other data that often enter into socioeconomic scales, no support was found in these data from the Toledo study for any direct comparability between racial groups in terms of indices based on income, numbers and kinds of possessions, or residential areas (as measured by property values or levels of typical rents).

Some explanation for this lack of comparability in terms of the relevance and applicability of standard SES indices may be found in the concept of hierarchization of ethnic groups in a complex, industrialized country like the United States. In the view of van den Berghe (1967), for example, a given occupation may carry different socioeconomic status value depending upon the characteristics of the individual filling that position (e.g., male or female, white or black, Christian or Jew, old or young). Since status level is increasingly dependent upon level of income alone (see Sowell, 1978), this formulation seems consistent with current findings that there are systematic differences between sexes, races, and so on, in earnings within specific occupations. As noted earlier, these differentials are viewed by some social scientists (e.g., Duberman, 1976) as evidence in support of the operation of a castelike set of barriers to full social and economic mobility in this country. Hierarchization may be essentially equivalent to the caste theories in this context. That is, full understanding of the socioeconomic structure of the various groups in this country may require some complex combination of the concepts from these two formulations.

Implications for Personality Assessment

From this brief treatment of the various competing views about American ethnic diversity, it is all too obvious that these issues are complex and challenging. It should be quite understandable, then, that it is difficult to disentangle the effects of cultural traditions, social inequities, or personal failures in trying to understand the personality status of any one member of an American ethnic minority. Social scientists have used many concepts to characterize these various factors and equally diverse methods to study their possible contributions to human personality. At this stage in our understanding of these influences, it may be impossible to sort them out accurately or to assess their relative and conjoint impact on particular individuals. It is possible, however, to keep these alternative perspectives in mind as a framework for the interpretation of the numerous empirical studies to be summarized in succeeding chapters.

Although there is no unanimity, several of these formulations do involve an assumption that members of American ethnic minorities are likely to manifest a common set of views about contemporary society in terms of cynicism about fairness in the job market, mistrust of authority figures, skepticism about prospects for future self-betterment or for social and economic progress, and serious misgivings about their chances of being judged on their own merits rather than being viewed in stereotyped fashion by prejudiced members of the majority group. Jaundiced views of their future lives in the United States, then, may lead to defenses and coping strategies that reflect suspiciousness, guardedness, and alienation from society. Distantiation and estrangement may color many if not all of their dealings with members of the dominant group, especially if these relationships are also burdened with problems of different languages, idioms, or linguistic styles. Countering such expectations, however, are the strengths and positive self-views arising from ethnic pride, intragroup social supports, and long-standing traditions of facing adversities and overcoming hardships.

Psychological instruments designed to assess personality may reflect many of these general attributes, either in the ways that members of various ethnic minorities approach the task of completing these tests or in the component scales and measures themselves. That is, testing procedures may be viewed as part and parcel of the dominant society from which many of these individuals are deeply estranged and cut off. Or, these self-views and perceptions may be so deeply ingrained in the personality organization that they are, in fact, part of some developing psychopathology, leaving such individuals vulnerable to stress and less able to cope with life's hard knocks.

Personality Test Validity and Bias

Any present-day method of psychological measurement beyond simple counting or enumeration is based upon sets of differences. That is, nothing akin to the absolute measurement procedures in the physical sciences is yet available to behavioral scientists. Any given measurement, therefore, is a summary of observed differences between the actions of the individual under study and the comparable behaviors of one or more other individuals. Several methodological problems inherent in the process of measurement are made more difficult by this limitation in current psychometric procedures, prominent among them being the identification and reduction of error or systematic bias in these measurements. Errors of measurement are never totally irradicable, of course, but requirements of scientific method demand that unremitting effort be devoted to the appraisal of possible sources, directions, and magnitudes of constant errors in our test data and to the discovery of ways to eliminate, control, or make allowance for them in all of our measurements.

Personality inventories like the MMPI rely for their validity upon the cumulative effect of large numbers of small differences. Each endorsement, true or false, reflects several sources of variance; if only one such source is common to all items included in a particular scale, then the numerous other sources of differences in item answers tend to cancel each other out. If one or more additional sources of variance are also common to some substantial number of items in a scale, however, the effect of these extraneous sources of test item endorsement will not be eliminated and the total scores on such a scale may be adversely affected by such pervasive errors.

The way in which a particular item set is assembled through the selection of component items affects the likelihood of inclusion of substantial numbers of items with common biases. One approach to item selection relies upon expert judgment to identify the psychological basis for the item answers (face validity) and the best subset of items for the measurement purpose. Reasonable skepticism about the psychological acumen of the panel of judges who select the component items that make up a test scale requires that the accuracy of their insights be established by further study of the way in which the test scale relates to the inferred criterion characteristic, as well as to other attributes of potential test subjects. A second method uses analytical techniques (factor analysis, clustering techniques, etc.) that identify those items that tend to be answered by the same individuals, providing a basis for organizing the items into scales. Although empirical data were used to form clusters of items that constitute factor scales, further research is needed to discover the psychological basis for their common pattern of endorsements. A third method of constructing scales relies upon known differences between individuals as a basis for forming contrasting groups; items found to differ systematically (by empirical endorsement data) between these groups of subjects are identified and assembled into a tentative scale to be used to evaluate the characteristics on which the subjects were originally separated. The dependability of this collection of items to assess such characteristics must then be documented by cross-validation.

Most of the component scales in the basic profile of the MMPI were derived by the third method described above: empirical item selection based on contrasting groups known to differ in various important features of their personality or emotional status. Although care was taken by the test authors (Hathaway & McKinley, 1940) to minimize the influence of noncriterion differences between the normal subjects and each of the various pathological groups used in the selection of items for the component scales of the test, inevitably such factors as age, marital status, or educational attainment could also enter into the selection of subjects for the contrasting groups. That is, in any effort to perfect particular personality scales or instruments to enhance the correspondence between particular scale differences and known differences in the characteristics under study, it is important to know what sources of variation give rise to particular responses. In theory, all behavioral variations are of inherent interest. In a measurement task, however, with some special characteristic to be assessed, it is imperative to sort out sources of variation in terms of true score and noncriterion (error) variance.

Any of the scale construction methods described above, if properly cross-validated, should provide solutions to this multiple determination of response deviations. Inventory scales generally depend upon the accumulation of relatively small deviations or response differences that reflect one common source of variation but differ in respect to numerous other determiners. Such item sets, as noted above, when appropriately scored and combined, should form a scale that maximizes the correspondence to the criterion characteristic and, through cancellation, minimizes the distortion or error from other characteristics that are, at that moment, of no interest in regard to the individuals under study. The strategy may not always work, however, since some of the characteristics may be interrelated at some other level of analysis (Meehl, 1967). Recent research has been sobering in demonstrating that various sources of error may interact in complex ways with true variation in the given characteristic in such a way as to make it difficult to extricate true variance from error in particular responses or behavioral differences. Thus, although any bit of behavior may be psychologically significant, it is usually impossible to determine about any specified response just what that significance may actually be.

A specific example of this intermingling of criterion and (potential) error variance comes from the research leading to the first clinical scale of the MMPI. When the Hs scale was under construction by McKinley and Hathaway (1940) to assess hypochondriacal neurosis, normal men and women were examined on the same test items as the cases diagnosed as hypochondriacal. Those items that were answered markedly differently by the neurotic men and women were identified and assembled into a tentative scale for this syndrome. Since most of the neurotic individuals were unmarried and most of the normal subjects were married, there was a distinct possibility that any individual who was single could get an elevated score on this scale, not from any neurotic somatization but deriving solely from the complex of social relationships relating to his or her marital status. Accordingly, the test authors made a further comparison of item answers of the neurotic cases to a special subgroup of individuals who were younger but as yet unmarried. Neither age nor marital status per se seemed to alter the responses of individuals to this set of items. The authors did find consistent differences between men and women, however, in the ways that they endorsed these items in describing themselves on the

MMPI. Therefore, the norms on the scale for hypochondriasis were scaled separately for males and females, but no special norms were needed for subjects differing in marital status. That is, the differences noted between normals and neurotics in marital status seemed to derive from the nature of the neurotic disorder itself: neurotic men and women are less likely to enter into marriage or to maintain a stable relationship once they are married. Differences in marital status, rather than being sources of major error variation in this set of deviant responses making up the Hypochondriasis scale, are therefore actually part of the complex criterion variance for which this scale was being constructed.

It should be clear, then, that other background characteristics may also enter into the process by which particular test item answers are made. In the same way that persons with serious emotional difficulties may encounter trouble in achieving successful and enduring marriages, such individuals may also have special difficulties in meeting successively more demanding educational standards, thus ending up with fewer years of schooling. Similarly, persons in trouble with the law because of their impulsive actions tend to be younger and more frequently unmarried than the cross section of the Minnesota state population comprising the normal comparison group used for the MMPI scale derivations. The extent to which such differences as these, as well as other sources of variance, affect scores on the component scales of the MMPI has been a continuing concern, not only to the test authors themselves but to others who have been interested in the applicability of this test to a variety of practical, real-life problems. The present focus is upon the scales and patterns of the MMPI, but the same kinds of problems enter into the derivation of any personality scale designed to assess particular psychopathological attributes. The more extensive the implications may be of the psychopathological process for the social and emotional adaptation of an individual, the more difficult it will be to guarantee that such scales are free from such potential error or confounding sources of variance.

One of the most pervasive (and highly charged) of the potential sources of error in test scales, in the MMPI and in many other psychological instruments, has been ethnicity. Investigators in many different fields have come to rely upon contemporary psychological instruments to assess the personality characteristics and emotional status of individual members of various American ethnic groups. A central question in such applications, either clinical or research, of these instruments is whether the data from psychological tests and personality devices are distorted or biased to any important degree either by nonpersonality factors in the individuals involved (test subject or test administrator) or by special features of the situation in which the assessment takes place. Investigations to evaluate the possible effects of such biases are complicated; the scientific worth of the available studies is often debatable, and the results are often difficult to appraise. First, it is necessary to document the fact that particular differences do appear consistently and that they are sizable, both statistically and psychologically. Second, it is necessary to show in some convincing way that such reliable differences are artifacts and not reflections of bona fide personality variations.

Accurate assessment of personality is essential in any scientific effort to comprehend the nature of group differences, to explain the development and course of behavior of members of any group, or to intervene to ameliorate the psychopathological status of any individual so identified. Almost all current means of personality measurement, objective or projective, are dependent upon verbal or other socially mediated forms of response of the individual. They are, therefore, open to possible biases arising from the subcultural status of the respondent that may tend to alter the scale scores so seriously as to distort the measurement of the personological attribute he or she may be manifesting. An essential step in the cross-validation of any personality measure, therefore, is the careful examination of potential artifacts that may enter when the use of the instrument is extended further into new settings and applications. If the direction and extent of systematic bias can be so documented, more circumscribed interpretations would then have to be drawn from the available data or, better yet, suitable corrections be made in the construction, the scaling, or the standardization of these psychological devices. Before the completion of this kind of critical examination of our instruments, however, it is premature to draw conclusions, one way or the other, about the legitimacy of our tests or their suitability for application to assessment problems in this area of research.

CHAPTER 2

Previous MMPI Research on Black Americans

W. Grant Dahlstrom and Malcolm D. Gynther

Although other American minorities have been studied by means of the MMPI (see chapter 3), black Americans have clearly received the most attention in the research literature. For more than 35 years investigations have been carried out comparing black and white subjects who have been examined under many different circumstances and in a wide variety of settings. These studies have been reviewed and summarized from time to time in a series of publications by Gynther (1972; 1979b; 1981) and by Gynther and Green (1980). Since the dependability and generalizability of these research findings vary widely, this literature will be reviewed in some detail. It is not an easy task to summarize the conflicting conclusions about personality characteristics of black Americans that have been drawn from the MMPI. The task is important, however, for determining the implications of these conclusions for the suitability of this personality instrument as a means of assessing the personality and adjustment status of members of this ethnic group. The various conclusions found in the literature will in turn be reexamined in light of new findings to be reported later in the present volume.

The Riverbend Study

One of the most striking examples of a group of black adults who differed greatly from the MMPI normative group was published by Gynther, Fowler, and Erdberg in 1971. These investigators administered the MMPI in 1968 to members of an all-black, geographically isolated, rural community in southwestern Alabama (which was for this study termed Riverbend). Cotton farming had been the major occupation for many years, and the average family cash income was less than $1,000 per year at the time of the study. The central settlement comprised a school, a store, and several churches; however, most residents lived on farms scattered throughout the surrounding area.

Community leaders were asked to recruit normally functioning residents who had no previous history of imprisonment or of treatment for emotional problems. To minimize literacy differences, the tape-recorded version of the MMPI was used. Nearly all the subjects took the test in a large school classroom with a local teacher in charge. Each participant was paid $2. The group consisted of 32 men and 56 women with a modal education of 8 years. The age range for males was 16 to 60 years (median=20); for females, it was 15 to 66 years (median=24).

The title of the article, in part, was "False Positives Galore," and indeed every MMPI index suggested that most of these community residents were severely maladjusted. Figures 2.1 and 2.2 show the mean MMPI profiles earned by these men and women.

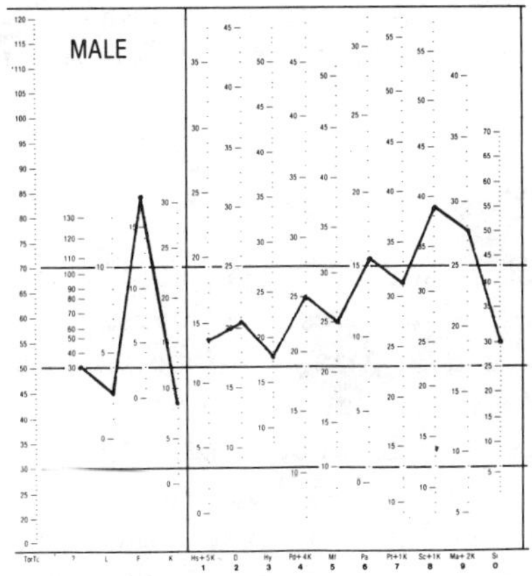

Figure 2-1. Mean profile of black male residents of an isolated rural Alabama community (N = 32; mdn. age = 20)
Code: 8″96′74-25 103/ F″-/LK

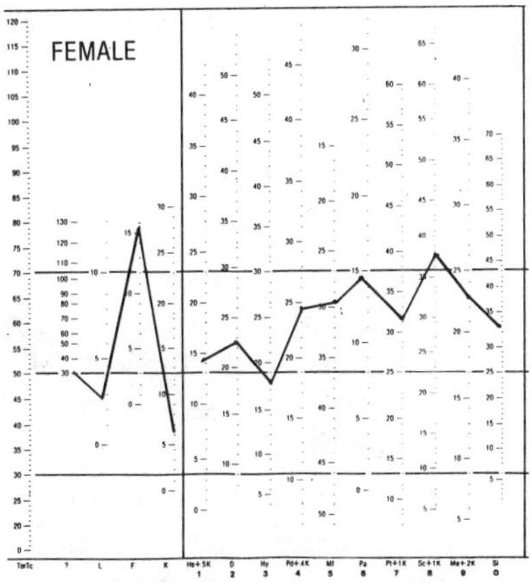

Figure 2-2. Mean profile of black female residents of an isolated rural Alabama community (N = 56; mdn. age = 24)
Code: 8′69547-021/3 F′-/L:K

Note. Adapted from Gynther, Fowler, & Erdberg (1971).

There was some question about the validity of a few of the test protocols. For example, 10 of the subjects omitted more than 60 items on their answer sheets. Forty-one of the 88 profiles had F scores greater than 16. However, the general results are dramatically deviant for a group of men and women who were making a satisfactory adjustment to a rural community life. The most frequent high point for both sexes was on scale 8 (Sc). The second most frequent peak score was scale 9 (Ma) for males and scale 6 (Pa) for females. The most frequent two-point high-point codes were 8-6 and 8-9 (tied) for males and 6-8, 8-6, and 8-9 (tied) for females. These code types are all suggestive of psychosis.

Other indices would lead to the same conclusion. Goldberg's (1965) most effective differentiator of psychotics from neurotics was (L+Pa+Sc) − (Hy+Pt). Although this index was designed to classify psychiatric patients, it was applied to this group for illustrative purposes; 84 of the 88 subjects would have been called "psychotic"! The Roche computerized interpretation system (Fowler, 1967) characterized 43 of the 88 subjects as "schizophrenic," 18 as "resembling psychiatric patients," 7 as having "severe emotional problems," 3 as questionably "within normal limits," and 7 as definitely "within normal limits" (the records with more than 60 Cannot Say responses did not have narrative printouts). In short, only about 10% of these subjects were described as normal. Analyses were also made at the item level. For example, the response to item 27 ("Evil spirits possess me at times") by the normative Minnesota white sample was 36 of 541 adults or 7% saying True to this item; in Riverbend, on the other hand, 58% endorsed the True response category.

Implications of the Riverbend Study

The results of the Riverbend survey surely raise a challenge that must ultimately be dealt with in some satisfactory way by research investigators and users of tests like the MMPI. Are there in fact sizable numbers of individuals residing quietly and unobtrusively in isolated rural areas of the country who have emotional disturbances that, in other perhaps more demanding circumstances of modern urban life, would soon bring them to the attention of mental health workers and agencies? That is, has this community survey brought to light a range of individuals who are manifesting marginal adjustment and who constitute a pool of potential clients or patients if and when they have occasion to come into contact with adequate mental health services? Or have these men and women grown up in a special subculture based in large part on religious fundamentalism, evangelical beliefs and practices, and rejection of the more general American norms, a subculture that in some fashion leads them to describe themselves and their view of the world sufficiently like various psychopathological groups as to mimic psychiatric patients on the MMPI? For example, Erdberg has reported (personal communication) that the older adolescents in Riverbend were required to absent themselves one by one from others for a few days "in the wilderness" (until some hallucinatory-like communication was received from God bestowing an identity and a new name on each wanderer), after which they then returned to rejoicing and acceptance by the congregation. Does this practice constitute an element in such a subculture that could generate in these subjects systematic differences on MMPI item endorsements that would artifactually inflate their test scores? Or, as a third possibility, has their economic deprivation amd their systematic exclusion and isolation from the mainstream of American life with its high educational and occupational aspirations resulted in feelings of estrangement, alienation, and distantiation that reflect a history of discrimination, segregation, and exclusion but not necessarily gross psychopathology? Although it is impossible to provide a definitive answer in regard to this particular study, an examination of the pertinent research literature may shed light on the variables involved.

The findings from the Riverbend study probably define the outer limits of variations from the norms for any group, but statistically significant differences on a number of MMPI scales and items have been reported in many studies involving black and white subjects. These studies are reviewed below, organized by the settings in which the individuals were examined.

As will become clearer in the following discussions, the studies reported in the MMPI research literature have been carried out for several different and often contradictory purposes. A number of these investigations have been conceived as illuminations of the nature of the different mental health problems likely to be encountered in practice with white versus black client populations, with the MMPI being used as one effective means to highlight these differential rates of disorder. In such studies, the concurrent or predictive validities of the test itself have been assumed to hold equally well for patient samples of either ethnic group. A second purpose, often based on the assumption that the true rates of psychopathology within black and white populations in this country are not in fact different, has been to try to account for the differences that have emerged by identifying sources of bias either within the mental health, criminal justice, or educational systems or within the test instrument itself. In the latter case, the internal structure of the MMPI or its mode of administration and scoring has been the focus of the investigation. A third form of research, related to the second purpose but sufficiently distinct from it to be noted separately, is the search for stable differences in the correlates of MMPI patterns obtained from black and white subjects. That is, do scores at the same T-score level on a given MMPI scale mean the same when obtained by black and white subjects? Obviously, these different purposes have led investigators to design their studies and collect their data in ways sufficiently different to make direct comparisons of research findings difficult or impossible.

Samples Drawn from the Criminal Justice System

One of the earliest investigations of MMPI differences between black and white subjects was a study by Fry in 1949 of male felons tested while in prison. A scale-by-scale analysis of the means obtained by these two ethnic groups on the basic clinical scales revealed no statistically significant difference between them (table 2.1). Black prisoners scored higher than white felons only on scale 9 (Ma); the white group was higher on the other eight scales (scale 0 [Si] was not scored), but none of these differences were found to be statistically significant. (A subsequent reanalysis of these data by Harrison and Kass [1967] revealed that the differences on scale 9 did reach the .05 level of significance.) The black inmates who volunteered to participate in Fry's study were quite comparable to the white prisoners in age, years of schooling, and tested intelligence level. (No information on the criminal histories of these men was provided.)

This degree of comparability in background characteristics was by no means achieved in several of the subsequent studies of prison inmates, however; MMPI-based findings have at times reflected some unknown mixture of other important characteristics in addition to the ethnic contrast under scrutiny. Of even greater importance, in terms of the suitability of samples of black and white felons for the purpose of characterizing general ethnic differences in personality, are studies by Bell (1973), Fitzpatrick (1974), or Davis (1976) that spell out the implications of the differing ways that black and white felons view the nature of their own behavior and the treatment they receive in the criminal justice system. Such studies document the black defendant's greater likelihood of being charged, brought to trial, convicted, and, then, given an active sentence rather than being considered for a suspended sentence or placement on probation. Thus, black and white individuals who appear in any prison cohort are not likely to be equally representative of the offenders in their ethnic group. Moreover, the differential treatment they have received while being processed through the system can leave lasting perceptions, beliefs, and expectations, particularly on the minority members, that would not have been true of their views of themselves or of the society around them before such traumas. Clearly, the attitudes with which members of these ethnic groups enter prison are likely to differ as a result.

A consistent pattern of MMPI elevations has emerged from studies of general prison populations (Dahlstrom, Welsh, & Dahlstrom, 1975), and this pattern is also reflected in the findings of the studies cited in table 2.1. The mean profiles of these felons show prominent elevations (generally at least one-and-a-half to two standard deviations) on scale 4

Table 2.1. MMPI Studies of Black and White Prisoners

Source	Subjects	*N*	MMPI Scales												
			L	F	K	Hs	D	Hy	Pd	Mf	Pa	Pt	Sc	Ma	Si
Fry (1949)	Prison inmates	B: 22M W: 76M	No differences found[a]												
Caldwell (1954)	Prison inmates (rural, youthful)	B: 34M W: 65M							WM[b]	BM[b]			BM[b]		
Panton (1959)	Prison inmates	B: 342M W: 910M		BM				WM			BM		BM	BM	
Flanagan & Lewis (1969)	Inmates: similar SES and education	B: 93M W: 103M												BM	
Costello et al. (1973) Sample 2	Inmates matched for IQ and education	B: 37M W: 37M	No differences found												
Sutker & Moan (1973)	Prisoners: lower SES and education	B: 56M,18F W: 80M,18F					BM		WF		BM		BM	BM	
Cooke et al. (1974)	Prisoners referred for competence evaluation; similar education	B: 34M W: 39M	No differences found												
Rosenblatt (1976)	Inmates with similar education	B: 105M W: 187M	BM	BM									BM	BM	
McCreary & Padilla (1977) Sample 1	Prisoners referred for psychiatric evaluation	B: 36M W: 236M						WM		WM					
Sample 2	Subsample matched on education and occupation	B: 36M W: 36M			WM			WM						BM	
Holland (1979)	Prisoners: similar age, SES, and education	B: 208M W: 396M		BM									BM	BM	
Holcomb et al. (1984)	Murderers equated for IQ level	B: 49M W: 111M			BM										WM

Note. In this, and in the tables following in this chapter, the letters *B, W, M,* and *F* refer to *black, white, male,* and *female*, respectively. A letter entry for a scale means that subjects in the category indicated are significantly higher ($p < .05$) on this scale than their counterparts. For example, BM means that black males were higher than white males on the scales indicated. If B or W is given without M or F, this indicates a main effect associated with race but that gender differences were not analyzed.

[a]Reanalyses of the Fry data by Harrison and Kass (1967) indicated that scale 9 (Ma) showed B > W at the .05 level.

[b]Differences in means of five or more T-score points; tests of significance not reported.

(Pd) and scale 9 (Ma), with a little lower but still an important elevation as well on scale 8 (Sc) and a comparable elevation of the F scale among the validity indicators. Penk, Woodward, Robinowitz, and Hess (1978) have noted that MMPI patterns associated with particular institutional settings may interact with ethnic subgroup attributes in such a way as to obscure the latter effects. This does not appear to be the case with prison samples. In the studies listed in table 2.1 in which black and white prisoners are compared, the most consistent differences between these ethnic groups appear on the same high-point scales. Thus, the ethnic differences serve to enhance the basic pattern of deviation found among prison inmates as a group, with the minority inmates showing the basic pattern to a more extreme degree. The deviant beliefs, the social and emotional alienation, and the marginal controls over sexual and aggressive impulses that are suggested by the basic profile configuration appear to be accentuated in the test results from black felons. In light of the selective processes noted above, as well as the adverse effects of mistreatment and prejudice encountered by black defendants in the criminal justice system as administered in various parts of the United States, it is difficult to disentangle the contributions of the differential operation of background factors, special emotional reactions to mistreatment, or the greater prevalence of characterological disorders or other psychopathological features in this minority group. In fact, the differences reported in the groups in table 2.1 probably result from some combination of these processes. In investigations in which the comparisons have been carried out on black and white felons with similar backgrounds (in family of origin, work or educational history, or academic ability), however, the number and size of the differences on the basic MMPI scales tend to be smaller.

One clear exception to this decrease in MMPI differences of black and white groups as a result of comparability in such background factors can be seen in the data reported by Sutker and Moan (1973) on prisoners from very low educational and occupational levels. The black male felons scored significantly higher than the white male prisoners on scales 2, 6, 8, and 9; only the F scale failed to demonstrate the usual statistically significant separation. The special circumstances that seem to be involved in low socioeconomic status subjects in such ethnic comparisons will be noted throughout this review. Davis, Beck, and Ryan (1973) also found the MMPI patterns to be less dependable in identifying schizophrenic disorders in black patients with lower educational achievement, despite a lack of statistically significant mean differences between their samples of less educated white and black psychiatric patients.

Samples Drawn from the Mental Health System

In 1961, Miller, Wertz, and Counts, working at a Veterans Administration center in the San Francisco Bay Area, identified a sample of 100 black psychiatric patients who had completed valid MMPI protocols. They compared their scores with data from those white patients whose names were next to each black patient alphabetically in the center's files and who also had valid MMPI records. The black patients had significantly higher scores than the white patients on scales 1 (Hs) and 9 (Ma) in the clinical profile and on the L scale in the validity indicators; the white patients were higher on scale 5 (Mf) at a statistically significant level (table 2.2). In 1968, Miller, Knapp, and Daniels augmented the analyses of these data. They demonstrated that the differences in mean profiles led to some important differences in high-point codes, and they also explored some of the ethnic differences in the item endorsements on which the scale level separations depended (see the discussion on item differences below).

In their 1961 publication, Miller et al. also summarized the findings from the Fry (1949) study of prisoners and the Hokanson and Calden (1960) study of tubercular patients at a VA hospital in Wisconsin (see the discussion on medical studies below). After considering the proposal made by Hokanson and Calden that special norms should be developed for black and white test subjects on the MMPI, Miller and her associates recommended against such a departure from standard practice. Instead, based on analyses of their own and these additional samples, they concluded that

> social factors such as occupational level, education, etc., rather than race determine most of the variance in test scores. It would appear that rather than trying to develop appropriate norms for negro and white subjects on the MMPI, we need to evaluate the MMPI findings for social and racial groups for particular settings. (1961, p. 161)

These conclusions and recommendations from Miller et al. were not readily accepted, however; further investigations of the nature and extent of ethnic differences manifested within various psychiatric settings have been published (see table 2.2), often accompanied by calls for special black norms.

In the mental health settings, the most consistent findings of statistically significant differences have also been on scales F, 8, and 9. The data summarized in table 2.2 document the fact that it has been important in these settings, as well as the prison settings, to evaluate the impact on MMPI scale scores of systematic differences in various social and educational background factors found between black and white patient samples. Where such differences are small or statistically controlled, the

Table 2.2. MMPI Studies of Black and White Psychiatric Patients

Source	Subjects	N	MMPI Scales												
			L	F	K	Hs	D	Hy	Pd	Mf	Pa	Pt	Sc	Ma	Si
Miller et al. (1961)	VA MHC patients: similar age and education	B: 100M W: 100M	BM			BM				WM				BM	
Costello et al. (1972)[a] Sample 2	Patients: stringent validity criteria	B: 58M&F W: 58M&F						No differences found							
Costello et al. (1973) Sample 1	Patients matched for age, SES, etc.	B: 49M, 117F W: 49M, 117F		BFM	WF				BF		BF		BF	BF	
Davis, et al. (1973) Sample 1	VA hospital: schizophrenics	B: 51M W: 54M		BM					BM				BM		
Sample 2	VA schizophrenics: education controlled	B: 40M W: 40M					WM								
Davis & Jones (1974)	VA patients: diagnosis and education controlled	B: 80M W: 80M						No differences found							
Hedlund (1974)	State hospital patients	B: 385M&F W: 3,000M&F		B				W		W				B	
Davis (1975)	VA patients: diagnosis and education controlled	B: 40M W: 40M						No differences found							
Genthner & Graham (1976)	State hospital patients	B: 85M&F W: 265M&F		B									B	B	
Klinge & Strauss (1976)	Adolescent patients	B: 18M, 30F W: 63M, 62F						No differences found							
RPSI survey (1978)	National sample, primarily outpatients	B: 3350M, 2819F W: 36,539M, 38,998F		BFM[b]						BF[b]			BFM[b]	BFM[b]	
Bertelson et al. (1982)	Patients matched for education, SES, etc.	B: 78M, 154F W: 78M, 154F		B						B				B	
Butcher et al. (1983)	Patients matched for education and occupation[c]	B: 60M, 37F W: 60M, 37F		B			W			W	B		B	B	

[a]Sample 1 analyses are not reported because all the black patients in this study were also used in the Sample 1 analyses reported in 1973 by the same first author.
[b]Differences in means of five or more T-score points. (Differences on all scale means were statistically significant.)
[c]When validity scale criteria were imposed, however, only the scale 9 difference remained significant.

differences on the clinical and validity scales of the MMPI tend to be small and statistically insignificant. In addition, as reflected in the data from Costello, Tiffany, and Gier (1972) and from Butcher, Braswell, and Raney (1983), in a psychiatric setting it has been particularly important to monitor the range of scores on the validity indicators to assure that the ethnic comparisons are based upon equally dependable test protocols from these patients, many of whom in both groups are too disturbed to provide an acceptable MMPI record at the time of assessment. For example, in psychiatric settings the most likely assumption should be that elevations on the F scale probably reflect a lack of ability to complete the inventory in a satisfactory fashion. Patients of either ethnic group having high scores on the F scale are most apt to be markedly confused, uncooperative, disorganized, or otherwise impaired, rather than showing an effect of some particular interpretations of the content of these items that might arise from an atypical background or some special personological attributes (Gynther, Lachar, & Dahlstrom, 1978; Smith & Graham, 1981).

As was true for MMPI data gathered in various components of the criminal justice system, so too the issue of equal likelihood of being in such settings is a major concern for investigations that are carried out in mental health settings. Investigations of the ethnic composition of various psychiatric patient populations (e.g., Mayo, 1974, or Weiss & Kupfer, 1974) or the adequacy of services that are provided by mental health agencies to various ethnic minorities (e.g., Sue, McKinney, Allen, & Hall, 1974; see also the discussion in chapter 3 of the present volume) strongly suggest that black or other minority individuals in need of treatment for emotional disorders in many American communities have to be more severely disturbed than majority white clients before they gain access to the help that they require. If this bias is operative in settings in which data for some of the investigations cited in table 2.2 were carried out, then it would be important to impose some matching of kind and degree of pathology on the patients being tested and compared before appropriate conclusions could be drawn about the accuracy of the various test patterns obtained by the men and women in the ethnic groups under study. In those studies in table 2.2 in which both socioeconomic background (including educational level) and diagnostic status are comparable, the differences in MMPI scores typically shrink to statistical insignificance (e.g., Davis, Beck, & Ryan, 1973).

Concern over such sources of variance and the ways in which they could distort conclusions about possible ethnic bias in the MMPI was raised by Pritchard and Rosenblatt (1980b) in response to an earlier commentary on the MMPI research literature on differences between black and white Americans by Gynther and Green (1980). In an effort to clarify the issue of possible sources of the differences on scales F, 8, and 9 of the MMPI that had been noted by the latter authors as most consistent in this literature, Peteroy and Pirrello (1982) gathered samples of black and white psychiatric patients from a Missouri mental health center who were comparable in age, education, acceptability of validity indicators, and, most importantly, severity of psychopathology (as reflected in hospital status, voluntary admission, and length of illness). With these appropriate constraints on subjects in the two racial groups, Peteroy and Pirrello found no statistically significant differences between black and white MMPI profiles on scales F, 8, or 9.

Two further points should be made about the material summarized in table 2.2. First, the study by Genthner and Graham (1976) is based on preliminary analyses of some of the protocols that provide the bases for much more extensive analyses to be reported here in chapters 6 and 7. The research setting and methods of data collection are discussed in those chapters (see the Ohio samples). Second, in the Roche Psychiatric Service Institute (RPSI) data, not only are the samples very large but they also represent a national sample, suggesting that special attention be paid to these findings. Accordingly, the means and standard deviations on the various MMPI scales from the RPSI survey have been summarized in Appendix G. The differences between black and white clients on scales F, 8, and 9 ranged from 4.18 to 6.72 T-score points.

Samples Drawn from Medical Settings

Three investigations have been conducted of medical patients (table 2.3). Two of these studies were quite early and did not control for educational or other socioeconomic differences. However, in the Hokanson and Calden study (1960), the medical condition of the patients was the same, namely, tuberculosis severe enough to require hospitalization. Black and white male veterans differed significantly on several validity and clinical scales. In more recent samples of veterans who were suffering some form of renal disorder as reported by Burke (1979), black and white patients were virtually indistinguishable on the MMPI. (Another study of individuals tested in a medical setting is included in a later table dealing with normal subjects because the data were gathered from normal women examined in their last month of pregnancy in a free obstetrical clinic serving low-income families in the Boston area [Harrison & Kass, 1967, 1968].)

Table 2.3. MMPI Studies of Black and White Medical Patients

Source	Subjects	*N*	MMPI Scales												
			L	F	K	Hs	D	Hy	Pd	Mf	Pa	Pt	Sc	Ma	Si
Gottlieb & Eisdorfer (1959)[a]	Medical patients					W	W	W	B				B		
Hokanson & Calden (1960)	Tuberculosis patients	B: 34M W: 84M	BM	BM					BM	BM			BM	BM	
Burke (1979)	VA patients on renal dialysis	B: 27M W: 50M					WM								

[a]Unpublished study cited by Butcher et al. (1964). Number of subjects not given.

Samples Drawn from Substance Abuse Programs

Studies have also compared groups of black and white individuals in various programs for the rehabilitation of those who have been abusing addicting substances, primarily opiates and alcohol (table 2.4). The earliest study of such ethnic differences was reported by Hill, Haertzen, and Glaser in 1960 based on groups of men who either volunteered for rehabilitation for narcotic addiction or were sentenced to the federal Addiction Research Center in Lexington, Kentucky, for various violations of laws governing controlled substances. All of these individuals were examined after the acute phase of their withdrawal from heroin had passed but while they were still enrolled in the ARC residential treatment program. The white and black former addicts were comparable in education and intelligence, but the white men were about 12 years older on the average (37.4 versus 25.6 years, respectively). The pattern of scores in the mean MMPI profiles was very similar, with elevations of scales 2, 4, 8, and 9, together with the F scale in the validity indicators. The only differences that reached statistical significance in comparisons of these two ethnic groups were higher scale 2 scores for the white men and higher scale 9 scores for the black men. These investigators also reported on a sample of teenage heroin addicts; since these younger subjects did not show the same degree of elevation on scale 9 that the black adults had shown, the authors were unwilling to ascribe the difference found between the two adult groups to sheer difference in average age. Instead, they carried out a sorting study of various profile patterns and noted the difference in prevalence of what they termed Type I: Psychopathic Personality (pure 49′) patterns in the two ethnic groups. Hill et al. also reviewed the family backgrounds and addiction histories of these men and noted that the black men showed higher frequency of residence in "fringe" localities in American metropolitan centers where there are

> sub-cultures in which family disintegration, delinquency, alcoholism, criminality, and disease are also prevalent. Thus, these subcultures not only provide the milieu for the development of deviant personalities, but they also provide availability of drug supplies and at least a semi-acceptance of experimentation with them. (1960, p. 136)

The role of an individual's subculture and the extent to which he or she deviates from that set of standards seems to be an important factor in interpreting ethnic differences found in substance abuse groups.

The pattern of differences noted in previous institutional samples between white and black adults does not appear in this kind of setting. In

Table 2.4. MMPI Studies of Black and White Problem Drinkers, Alcoholics, and Drug Abusers

Source	Subjects	N	MMPI Scales												
			L	F	K	Hs	D	Hy	Pd	Mf	Pa	Pt	Sc	Ma	Si
Hill et al. (1960)	Narcotic users (Lexington)	B: 70M W: 88M					WM							BM	
Penk & Robinowitz (1974)	Opiate users: similar education, IQ, SES	B: 61M W: 49M		WM				WM							
Patalano (1978)	Polydrug abusers: similar education	B: 40M, 40F W: 40M, 40F	B				W	W				W			W
Penk et al. (1978)															
Sample 1	VA heroin users	B: 252M W: 120M	BM		BM		WM	WM	WM	WM		WM	WM		WM
Sample 2	Subsample: age, validity, IQ, SES controlled	B: 136M W: 87M		WM			WM		WM			WM	WM		WM
Sutker et al. (1978)	Drug abusers: education level similar	B: 22M, 6F W: 38M, 18F		W			W				W	W			
Sutker et al. (1980a)															
Sample 1	Hospitalized drug abusers (Louisiana)	B: 85M, 8F W: 72M, 13F		WF				W	W					BM	
Sample 2	Hospitalized drug abusers (South Carolina)	B: 59M, 12F W: 126M, 53F				W	W	W	W						W
Sutker et al. (1980b)	Men arrested for drunk driving	B: 110M W: 390M	No differences found												
Patterson et al. (1981)															
Sample 1	VA inpatient alcoholics	B: 56M W: 272M						WM						BM	
Sample 2	Subsample: age, education, SES controlled	B: 52M W: 248M						WM							
Penk et al. (1981a)	VA heroin addicts and polydrug abusers: average IQ	B: 319M W: 458M					WM	WM	WM	WM	WM				WM
Penk et al. (1982)	VA polydrug abusers: age, education, SES, IQ controlled	B: 159M W: 494M	BM				WM	WM	WM			WM			

terms of profile deviation, the mean scores of white men and women are consistently more elevated than those of black men and women. Although the patterning of their scores is usually quite similar, if either group is more deviant it is more likely to be the white substance abuser than the black. Two important selective effects seem to be operating to produce this pattern. First, several investigators have suggested that the involvement with and abuse of alcohol or other drugs in these ways are less acceptable in the dominant white urban culture than they are in the black urban ghettos from which the black substance abuser is most likely to come. That is, the white man or woman who becomes involved with these substances is probably manifesting more severe emotional disorders than is a corresponding black man or woman with an equal degree of involvement with alcohol or drugs. This conjecture is likely to hold, however, only for black families of low socioeconomic status; middle-class standards in the black community may be even stronger in moral condemnation of the drinking of alcohol, the use of drugs, or any other addicting practice than in the white community (see Clark, 1965). For a middle-class black man or woman, therefore, involvement with or abuse of these substances would indicate an even greater degree of deviance from the standards and expectations of the supporting community than would be true of a white middle-class individual engaged in such activities.

The operation of a second biasing factor may be more important than differential acceptance of substance abuse in generating the findings reported in the MMPI research literature on black and white drug users—namely, the likelihood that white substance abusers will be seen in some agency of the mental health system while the black abuser ends up in the criminal justice system (see Goldsmith, Capel, Waddell, & Stewart, 1972; Lowe & Hodges, 1972). That is, the abuse pattern is dealt with in quite different ways if the individual is white, middle-class, and well educated than if he or she is black, lower-class, and both undereducated and underemployed. The shift in extent and pattern of deviation on MMPI scores found in the substance abuse literature serves to highlight the concerns first raised by Miller and her colleagues (1961) in regard to the importance of understanding the ways in which members of differing ethnic groups gain access to care and treatment in various institutional settings. If these kinds of selective processes are working to reduce the comparability of white and black individuals in terms of factors other than their ethnic status, then conclusions about the relationship between ethnicity and personality can be seriously faulted. The same caution must also be kept in mind in drawing conclusions about the suitability of a given test instrument for use with members of various ethnic minorities merely from the finding of group differences in patterns of scores derived from that test.

Community-based Samples

Access to subjects from various ethnic backgrounds for MMPI-based research has generally been most convenient in institutional settings where these men and women are both available for an examination lasting two to three hours and motivated to participate in the often tedious process involved in obtaining valid and complete records. As noted in earlier sections, the information available on ethnic differences has typically come from groups of individuals who are tested in some agency of the mental health or criminal justice systems. The powerful selective forces that are operating in such locations may, however, lead to quite biased and unrepresentative samples from American minorities. It would be highly desirable to evaluate individuals who are neither involved in criminal activities nor manifesting severe emotional disorders to gain a better insight into the nature of differences in personality of members of these ethnic groups and to assess the potential bias that may be operating in the MMPI or any other contemporary psychological test instruments. Community-based samples have accordingly been studied to provide this much needed evidence. Unfortunately, most of these samples have also come from another institutional setting: various components of the American educational system.

One of the earliest ethnic comparisons in which the subjects were students was published by Ball in 1960 (table 2.5). Pupils in the ninth grade of two recently integrated high schools in Lexington, Kentucky, were examined in a total class survey. (Twenty-four records had to be discarded because of elevated validity indicators, leaving 200 valid records.) Mean MMPI profiles from the two groups of black and white boys differed from each other less than did the mean scores of the two groups of girls, but the scores from all four groups closely resembled the results obtained by Hathaway and Monachesi (1963) in their survey of Minnesota ninth-grade students. That is, these mean profiles showed elevations of about one standard deviation on scales F, 4, 8, and 9.

Although the students in Ball's study all came from the same residential school districts, he found that over a third of the black ninth-graders came from homes in which the family had been disrupted by separation of the parents; in a majority of these families, the head of household worked at a job that fell within the lowest two of the seven levels on the Minnesota Occupational Scale (Goodenough & Anderson, 1931). The white boys and girls, however, came predominantly from intact families that fell in the middle levels of parental occupation. Ball suggested that the MMPI differences between black and white students could be explained by the differences in family background between the two ethnic groups.

Table 2.5. MMPI Studies of Normal Black and White Samples

Source	Subjects	*N*	MMPI Scales												
			L	F	K	Hs	D	Hy	Pd	Mf	Pa	Pt	Sc	Ma	Si
Ball (1960)	9th graders	B: 14M, 17F W: 81M, 88F		BF	WF	BM		WF					BF		BF
McDonald & Gynther (1962)	High school seniors	B: 158M,196F W: 131M,132F	BFM	BFM	BM	BFM	BFM	WF	WF	BF	WF	WF		BFM	BF
McDonald & Gynther (1963)	Subsample: high school seniors, SES contr.	B: 90M, 90F W: 90M, 90F	B	B			B			B			B	B	
Butcher et al. (1964) Sample 1	College students	B: 50M, 50F W: 50M, 50F	BFM							WF	WFM			BM	
Sample 2	Subsample: college students, SES controlled	B: 26M, 16F W: 26M, 16F	BFM		BM					WFM	WFM	WM		BM	WM
Harrison & Kass (1967)	Indigent pregnant women	B: 383F W: 389F		BF		BF							BF	BF	
Harrison & Kass (1968)	Subsample: indigent pregnant women, validity, literacy controlled	B: 179F W: 147F		BF										BF	BF
Baughman & Dahlstrom (1968)	Rural 8th graders	B: 59M, 81F W: 52M, 66F		BFM			BFM				BFM		BFM	BFM	
Erdberg (1969)	Community residents (rural and urban)	B: 30M, 30F W: 30M, 30F	W	B	W			W	B	W	B		B	B	
White (1974)	College students	B: 114M,228F W: 104M,184F		B					B				B	B	
Bull (1976)	Technical institute students	B: 20M, 32F W: 25M, 36F		BM	WM			WM					BFM	BM	
King et al. (1977)	Employees of chemical company matched for mental ability, education	B: 56M W: 56M									WM			BM	
McGill (1980)	Welfare recipients: low average education	B: 50F W: 78F							No differences found						
Moore & Handal (1980)	High school students: similar age, SES	B: 19M, 19F W: 19M, 19F	B	B											

McDonald and Gynther (1963) tried to confirm this formulation from data obtained in testing graduating seniors in racially segregated high schools in Columbia, South Carolina. Using a somewhat cruder index of occupational level than that employed by Ball, these investigators formed equivalent groups of black and white boys and girls at three levels of fathers' employment. These classifications were based primarily on level of skill required and extent of supervisory responsibilities of the head of household. The authors could not find any systematic differences in MMPI scores related to this index of status of the family of origin of the students who were tested. Similarly, Butcher, Ball, and Ray (1964) found that the pattern of differences that they identified between black and white college students was relatively unchanged when they matched their students as closely as possible on the level of socioeconomic status of their family of origin. The pattern of significant differences that they found between black and white students was quite different from that reported by McDonald and Gynther, however, and they proposed that the selection of those students going on to college among black high school graduates was not at all equivalent to that for white graduates. (The proportion of black students entering high school who drop out prior to graduation from twelfth grade is also considerably higher than among white students; this differential survival was particularly marked in the early 1960s when these studies were carried out.)

Baughman and Dahlstrom (1968) attempted to offset the effects of differential dropout rates between black and white students by sampling pupils from the eighth grade (prior to the large high-school level exodus) and by additional testing at the seventh-grade level to assure inclusion of age peers of the eighth-grade students who had been held back on the basis of academic failures. As an additional step to minimize invalid MMPI records resulting from marginal reading ability, they used a tape-recorded version of the inventory in their survey of the pupils in the four segregated rural schools in central North Carolina in which they carried out this research, also in the early 1960s. The mean profiles from these four groups of students were all more deviant than the Minnesota and Kentucky adolescents; the black boys and girls were more deviant than the corresponding profiles from the white boys and girls, particularly on scales F, 2, 6, 8, and 9. In supplementary analyses based on the larger clusters of items identified by Harrison and Kass (1967) in their study of MMPI items showing the largest differences between their black and white women (see discussion below), Baughman and Dahlstrom found that the black eighth-grade students scored higher on groups of items reflecting estrangement from and cynicism about the society around them. At the same time, these minority students were denying minor personal faults, acknowledging fewer deviant beliefs and behaviors, and expressing greater interest in intellectual and cultural activities. Thus, while avoiding a general set to give socially unfavorable answers or to yield to a temptation to answer the MMPI items in a deviant way, the black boys and girls seemed to be describing some personally distressing experiences in their racially segregated schools and community and expressing considerable pessimism about the future they faced in that kind of world.

In some ways it was surprising to find the pattern of alienation and cynicism that Harrison and Kass had noted in their analyses, based on the MMPI responses of black lower-class women in an obstetrical clinic in Boston, appearing so clearly in young boys and girls in the rural South. However, in a supplementary report to their 1967 study, Harrison and Kass (1968) noted that those black women who had been born somewhere in the South and who had subsequently moved north were somewhat more deviant in their responses to the MMPI than were the black women who had been born and raised in or around the Boston area. This finding suggested that aspects of life in the racially segregated South of the 1940s and 1950s may have been important in determining the views of themselves and the world that black individuals were reporting on the MMPI. Harrison and Kass also reported in this second publication that when they imposed more stringent limits on the reading level of their subjects and on the range of scores that they obtained on the validity indicators, the number and extent of differences between the black and white indigent women were also considerably reduced. (See the summaries of their 1967 and 1968 analyses in table 2.5.) The item-level analyses carried out by Harrison and Kass are summarized in the next section.

Two more recent studies based on samples of southern black and white groups have also been included in table 2.5. The data from Bull (1976), reported in Appendix G of this volume, were based on a survey of students in a technical institute in southeastern North Carolina. Three ethnic groups (white, black, and native American) were compared; all three deviated markedly from the norms but not greatly from each other.

The other study was carried out in Alabama by Erdberg (1969). His subjects were recruited by community leaders from among those individuals free of any history of contact with the mental health or criminal justice systems, who were over 18 years of age, who had schooling of at least the ninth grade, and who were making less than $9,000 per year in cash income. Equal numbers of black and white men and women from rural and urban communities of central Alabama were tested by means of a tape-recorded version of the MMPI. (The means and standard deviations on the basic MMPI scales from his eight groups of subjects were summarized in tables 6.8 and 6.9 of Dahlstrom, et al., 1975.) The black and white groups differed significantly on a number of component scales of the MMPI (table 2.5): white men and women were more elevated on scales L, K, 3, and 5, whereas black adults were significantly higher on scales F, 4, 6, 8, and 9. (The results of the item-level analyses that Erdberg also carried out are summarized in the next section.)

In some contrast to the results reported on various samples of teenagers and adults from the South, McGill (1980) found no systematic differences between black and white indigent women tested at the time they were applying for aid for dependent children in two cities in north Texas. The data from McGill's study also included results from Mexican-American women; the three groups of women showed similar deviations from the norms but their scores were not statistically different from each other. That is, the three groups involved in this investigation all manifested evidence of emotional problems and difficulties that could be attributable to the financial, marital, and social stresses in which these women found themselves at the time of the testing. This set of circumstances in which women of all three ethnic groups are caught can perhaps be seen as an explanation underlying the personality deviations shown on the basic scales of the MMPI that McGill reported. If so, these different life circumstances may offer an alternative to basic differences in ethnic personality characteristics as explanations in those earlier studies in which black subjects scored more deviantly than white subjects. These alternatives will be explored more fully in the data to be reported in later chapters of this volume.

Item Analyses

Scale-score comparisons are by far the most common type of analysis, but several investigators have also examined the responses of blacks and whites at the item level (table 2.6). The first such study was published by Harrison and Kass (1967), who analyzed the MMPIs of 383 black and 389 white females who were successive admissions to a city hospital prenatal clinic. Comparisons of item endorsements of these subjects revealed that 213 of the MMPI statements differentiated the two ethnic groups. (Most analyses of two groups contrasted on some factor result in from 25 to 75 differentiating items.) Harrison and Kass factor-analyzed the 150 most discriminating items. Twenty clusters were identified by these authors; the content areas of the item sets with the largest number of items are listed in table 2.6. In addition, they carried out a discriminant function between black and white groups using these cluster scales. The most differentiating scales in this analysis were estrangement and impulse-ridden fantasy, both higher for the black women, and self-consciousness and dislike of school, both higher for the white women.

Table 2.6. MMPI Studies of Differences in Item Endorsements between Black and White Subjects

Samples Studied	Number of Item Differences	Principal Differentiating Content
Normal women during pregnancy (Harrison & Kass, 1967)	213	Estrangement, cynicism, intellectual and cultural interests, religiousness, impulse-ridden fantasy, self-consciousness, denial of deviant behavior
Male psychiatric patients (Miller et al., 1968)	190	Incorporation of conventional standards, denial of interpersonal anxiety, physical symptoms, mistrust of society
Urban and rural southern community adults (Erdberg, 1969)	177	Distantiation, unusual thought patterns, aspiration-reality conflict, admission of fears, absence of optimism
Psychiatric patients		Aspiration-reality conflict, feelings of separation and resentment, pessimistic attitudes about the future
Male	65	
Female	58	
(Costello, 1973)		
Midwestern university undergraduates (White, 1974)	208	Discontent, estrangement, cynicism
Psychiatric patients		. . .
Ages 12-17	1	
18-30	19	
31-46	5	
(Bertelson et al., 1982)		

The next item analysis was carried out by Miller, Knapp, and Daniels (1968), who compared the responses of 100 black and 100 white male mental hygiene clinic patients. The approximately 190 differentiating items were grouped subjectively into rationally meaningful clusters, which are enumerated in table 2.6. Blacks scored higher on every cluster.

Erdberg (1969), whose sample consisted of 60 black and 60 white rural and urban community residents, also factor analyzed his 177 race-sensitive items. The most important factor was labeled *distantiation* which was defined as feelings of cynicism about the motives of others. Blacks were significantly higher than whites. The other factors are given in the table. Blacks were higher on all these factors.

Costello (1973) studied item endorsements of 54 black and 54 white female psychiatric patients matched on age and socioeconomic status and 37 black and 37 white male prisoners matched on age, educational level, test estimate of IQ, and rate of recidivism. He found 58 items that discriminated between the female samples and 65 items that discriminated between the male samples. Factor analysis revealed that blacks of both groups more often reported the conflicts, feelings, and attitudes indicated in table 2.6.

White (1974) evaluated the item responses of 342 black and 288 white college students. White divided these 630 subjects into construction and validation samples. His analyses revealed 208 significantly differentiating items in the construction sample; 126 of these items were confirmed as differentiators in the validation sample. White factor-analyzed his 27 most discriminating items and found one factor that accounted for 54% of the common variance in both the construction and validation samples. He concluded that "the factor appears to be related to the discontent characteristic of the acculturation process with high emphasis on estrangement and cynicism" (White, 1974, p. 106). Blacks were higher on this factor.

Bertelson, Marks, and May (1982) performed chi-square analyses on the first 400 MMPI items of 232 black and 232 white psychiatric patients who were matched for education, marital status, employment, socioeconomic status, residence, and hospital status. Alpha level was set at .01. Differentiating items totaled one for the teenagers ($N=146$), 19 for the young adults ($N=222$), and five for their older adults ($N=96$). No further analyses were carried out because the differences were only about what one would expect by chance.

Jones (1978) gave junior college students Haan's (1965) coping and defense scales, which were derived from both MMPI and CPI (California Psychological Inventory) items. Although this study is not directly comparable to those using the full MMPI item pool, it is interesting to note that 288 or 79.8% of the 361 items, nearly half of which were from the MMPI, discriminated between blacks and whites, 175 at the .01 level or better.

The data presented in table 2.6 may be summarized as follows: many items, about 200 out of the 550 MMPI statements, are answered differently by normal members of these two ethnic groups; smaller numbers of items, varying from chance to approximately 190, differentiated blacks and whites who are psychiatric patients or prisoners; meaningful factors emerged from analysis of the differentiating items; the most distinctive factor associated with blacks, especially normals, has been labeled *distantiation, estrangement,* or *discontent*; and other factors seem to be a function of the sample studied. The major source of variance at the item level reflects the content of both scales F and 8 that have frequently distinguished black and white subjects.

Alternative Views of MMPI Ethnic Differences

Since the results of the comparisons of black and white personality characteristics as revealed by the MMPI have been quite contradictory, it is understandable that the interpretations that have been offered to account for these findings have also been diverse and often mutually exclusive as well. The general design of the MMPI called for a technique to provide objective assessment of the kind and degree of psychopathology. Accordingly, some investigators have concluded that the two ethnic groups do in fact differ in rates of various forms of emotional disorder and in the severity of these disturbances when they appear (e.g., Caldwell, 1954; Hokanson & Calden, 1960). Since these conclusions have often been in accord with epidemiological data of various kinds from different institutional settings (Dreger & Miller, 1968; Fischer, 1969; Draguns & Phillips, 1972; See & Miller, 1973; See, 1976; Kramer, 1977; Milazzo-Sayre, 1977; Steinberg, Pardes, Bjork, & Sporty, 1977; Goldberg & Huxley, 1980), many investigators have concluded that the MMPI was working appropriately to assess the emotional problems of prisoners, patients, or clients in these various agencies.

According to a variation on this line of reasoning, the data support the conclusion that some psychopathological rates are higher for black Americans than for white but only because the forms of psychopathology that are identified with this ethnic group are manifested more in lower socioeconomic status individuals of *any* ethnic membership. The fact that black adults, like members of several other ethnic groups in this country, fall disproportionately into lower status levels than is true for white adults provides a basis for some of the ethnic differences reported in the MMPI literature. If so, then more appropriate matching or statistical controls for differential socioeconomic levels among subjects from the various ethnic populations under study should serve to reduce or eliminate the trends in test data based on findings from groups that are lacking this kind of balance in representation of educational, occupational, or income levels (see Cowan, Watkins, & Davis, 1975; Warheit, Holzer, & Arey, 1975).

A study that embodies many of these desirable features was carried out by Fillenbaum and Pfeiffer (1976) on aged community residents in Durham, North Carolina. Unfortunately, they were unable to use the full-scale MMPI in their door-to-door survey but had space in their battery of questions for only the Kincannon (1968) 71-item Mini-Mult version. Their procedures included both the administration of this inventory and the gathering of considerable data as the basis for ratings of the social, physical, economic, and health adjustment of these elderly men and women of both races. The Mini-Mult profiles showed that the black men and women scored higher to a statistically significant degree on scales F, 4, 8, and 9. In subsequent analyses (Fillenbaum, personal communication), it was found that these elderly black residents were also rated as showing significantly more maladjustment in several interrelated aspects of their lives in this southern community. If their financial, health, and social problems were more severe and if they were less effective in dealing with them than their elderly white counterparts, then the trends on the Mini-Mult may be less a matter of bias in even this small subset of MMPI-like items and more a useful index of the extent to which these men and women are in need of additional financial and psychological support.

Quite a different line of interpretation is based on the same point of origin, namely, the derivation of the MMPI in a psychiatric nosology. The assumption is made that the MMPI contains an inherent pathology bias in its items and its scale construction that intrudes into any application of the test in surveys of the sort under discussion here. However, since the test also contains ranges of scores that are generally interpreted as indicating relative freedom from various forms of emotional disorder, it is difficult to accept this formulation as a simple explanation of the nature of the *differences* that may be found in the studies of ethnic groups. That is, if both groups are equally disturbed, or equally free of disturbance, there is no basis in the psychiatric origins or derivational history of the MMPI that would lead to the expectation of a difference arising merely from a psychopathology focus per se. Simply because the MMPI focuses on emotional disorders, this emphasis itself should not generate differences between groups.

The psychopathology framework of the MMPI does have relevance, however, when explanations are sought for any differences that are found in the component scores of the inventory: any such difference is likely to be interpreted as a difference in kind or degree of psychopathology (see Powell & Johnson, 1976; Adebimpe, Gigandet, & Harris, 1979; Gray-Little, 1983). Since there is ample evidence in the literature of the MMPI (Dahlstrom, Welsh, & Dahlstrom, 1972, 1975) that elevations on the component scales of the test have often served to indicate personological assets rather than liabilities in particular score ranges and in some settings or endeavors, this conclusion is not always justified. (For example, moderate elevations on scales 4 and 9 are probably positive aspects of a personality likely to be successful in face-to-face selling situations.) Nevertheless, there is a strong temptation to conclude from any particular set of differences that the group that scores higher is in fact more disturbed, less adaptive, more pathologically impaired, or under greater stress.

The issue, then, is the fundamental one of the transsituational validity of the test and its component scores. (See Porterfield, 1967; Elion &

Megargee, 1975; Shore, 1976; Gearing, 1979; Kirk & Zucker, 1979, 1980; Newmark, Gentry, Warren, & Finch, 1981.) Can answers to the MMPI that have been found to reflect some particular form of psychopathology in a given setting with some specific range of clients or patients be trusted to reflect the same pathological process in other kinds of clients, in different settings, under very different circumstances? If individuals with vastly different backgrounds and experiences tend to interpret sets of items on the MMPI in some special way that happens to coincide with the basis for discriminating a pathological criterion group from the normal group, then that set of answers is likely to be misinterpreted as valid resemblance to the criterion group when it should be ascribed to some special set of experiences, stresses, or self-views deriving from those backgrounds or histories. As Pritchard and Rosenblatt (1980a, 1980b) have aptly pointed out, the finding of ethnic differences cannot in itself be used as evidence that such a process is operating to produce spurious differences between the groups under study. Instead, investigations must be designed in ways that can detect a *differential* validity for each ethnic group. The question that is fundamental in evaluating the possibility of test bias, as noted by Gulliksen and Wilks (1950), is whether the errors of estimate can be considered the same or not in the various populations from which the samples under study were drawn. (See Jensen [1980] for several examples.) Similar issues have been raised by Thorndike (1971) and Linn (1978).

Unfortunately, the design and execution of studies with the needed characteristics are extremely difficult (see Kline, Lachar, & Sprague, 1985). Dependable data on nontest characteristics relevant to the test constructs under scrutiny must be available. Since the test instruments themselves are designed to minimize known sources of bias (ethnic, sexist, or whatever) in the human judgments usually utilized in constructing and validating psychological tests, there is an inevitable circularity in trying to document the nature and extent of possible ethnic bias in the scores from tests against external criteria that may also be subject to unknown degrees of similar ethnic bias (see Luepnitz, Randolph, & Gutsch, 1982; Vernon & Roberts, 1982). In addition, care must be taken in the administration and scoring of the test itself to minimize the spoiling of test records because of poor reading ability, inadequate comprehension of the language and idioms of the component items, inattention or confusion in marking answers and conforming to the basic task of the test, and the numerous sources of clerical error in processing the test responses and generating the raw scores and T-score values. Furthermore, since the findings in the present research literature suggest that the men in the various ethnic groups differ from the women in important ways and that there may be age differences as well that could affect test validity, the numbers of subjects in research samples must be both substantial and diverse.

In the light of the stringency of the requirements for adequate appraisal of the question of ethnic bias in a test like the MMPI, the studies to be reported later in the present volume must be considered as only a start on the kind of research that will be needed to evaluate these issues of MMPI bias, not only for black American subjects but for numerous other minorities, some of which are discussed in chapter 3. Nevertheless, the several questions that have been raised about the suitability of the MMPI and similar tests for the assessment of American minorities and the challenges that have been made to the existing items, scales, and norms of the test make it imperative that a start be made on this set of problems. The test is now so widely used in such diverse settings, and the results have been incorporated into so many interpretive systems—clinical, semiautomated, or computer based—that the answers to these questions must be assiduously pursued.

CHAPTER 3

MMPI Findings on Other American Minority Groups

Leona E. Dahlstrom

Although not as extensively investigated as the black American population, other minority groups in the United States have frequently been studied with the MMPI. New waves of immigrants have entered this country, some desiring only temporary residence but many hoping for permanent American citizenship. Increasing problems associated with their assimilation have demanded attention. Similarly, the culture of native Americans has long been in conflict with that of the dominant European-derived majority. Often these problems have directly concerned psychologists, whether they work with mental health programs, criminal justice systems, welfare agencies, or educational institutions. The need for an efficient means of evaluating personality, especially in terms of the stresses that are put upon the new immigrant (or the native American) in the existing society, has led to the increasing use of well-established tests like the MMPI. Usually the test has been administered in its routine English-language format; occasionally a translation has been used with the minority group.

When large differences between the new group and the majority population appear, however, they have often led to a reaction of dismay and distress from the investigators themselves. How can a "normal" group of minority Americans look so different on the MMPI from "normal" white Americans of long residence in this country? As a matter of fact, though, very few "normal" groups of minority Americans have actually been surveyed, although the call for such appropriate comparisons is often heard. There are many reasons that are not difficult to understand for the lack of such data—for example, the need for the examiner to be not only well trained but a trusted member of the group in question, and the desirability of collecting as much background information as possible to make interpretation of the results more meaningful. A means of rating the degree of assimilation or acculturation, which might also be desirable, would require the collection of large numbers of subjects to permit such analyses. These and many other considerations need to be taken into account in the collection of minority normative data.

As in the case of blacks, it is often seen as the fault of the test when minority groups show large differences from the majority results, especially in the case of presumed normals. As a corrective measure, it is occasionally suggested that new conversions from raw to T scores should be developed for each subgroup so that an individual might be judged in relation to his or her own peers and not subjected to invidious comparison with members of the dominant white culture. Although such a procedure has its uses (as does the dual profile method sometimes used with adolescents, comparing the individuals both to their contemporaries and to the adult population), there is a danger that important sources of conflict with the dominant culture may be minimized. If all deviations are thus "explained away" as only typical reactions of his or her cultural group, the stresses that the individual's coping strategies put upon the respondent may be obscured. By analogy, should the observation that black Americans tend to have more frequent incidence of high blood pressure lead us to set new norms for the instrument for the black group and dismiss the result of a test because it is "only typical" of their group? Of course, it is necessary to examine the predictive use to which such procedures are put as the determiner of their usefulness; that is, if blacks are, in fact, more likely to have circulatory disorders and related illnesses, as predicted by the higher blood pressure measurements (as seems to be the case), then attaching importance to their blood pressure readings is a valid medical prediction and it is appropriate to use these results in this way. However, if it could be shown that high blood pressure readings among black subjects did not have such negative consequences, but instead were benign and nonpredictive of serious complications, then a modified interpretation would be called for. In the case of elevated MMPI profiles in normal minority subjects, there may well be environmental situations that require a change of interpretation of, say, high scores on scale 6 (Pa) from members of the groups; but it would seem advisable to be aware of other possible meanings of such score elevations, rather than to introduce a priori statistical suppression of the differences. In other words, it seems more reasonable to expect the psychologist to investigate why the minority group members react in this way, rather than to dismiss the findings as simply "typical of group *X*."

Regional Differences

Minority or ethnic status has been defined in many ways; some of these definitions are implicit in the work reported in other sections of this volume. Aside from identifiers such as racial characteristics, country of origin, cultural background, language, and religious differences, there has been some attention given in the MMPI literature to regional differences in the United States. Some of the data reported in chapters 4 and 5 permit comparisons of normal black subjects from the large northern city of Detroit, midsized cities in the Middle South of North Carolina, and small Alabama towns and rural areas in the Deep South. In chapter 2, two studies were discussed (Harrison & Kass, 1968; Erdberg, 1969) in which regional differences were examined as part of larger investigations.

A survey more directly addressed to the question of whether regional differences exist that may affect MMPI results was conducted by Webb (1971), who analyzed the data from 2,000 psychiatric patients; the 1,200 professionals who submitted the data had their test protocols scored and interpreted by computer methods by the Roche Psychiatric Service Institute. Proportions of high-point occurrences did not differ significantly across five regions of the United States; these results confirmed earlier studies of college students (Goodstein, 1954; Black, 1956) and of prisoners (Smith, 1955). Although Webb's data did show significant sex differences in high-point codes (scales 3 [Hy] and 6 [Pa] more frequently the high scores for women, whereas scales 1 [Hs] and 7 [Pt] were most often highest for men) and these findings were consistent with an earlier study by Aaronson (1958), there were no systematic regional effects for men or women.

Although women are sometimes seen as a minority group in such matters as hiring decisions or professional advancement, this would seem to be a special meaning of the term *minority*, unlike the various distinctions under present consideration. This is, of course, one instance in which special norms (for some of the scales) have been built into the test in the form of different T scores for the two sexes. Clinicians have also learned to take note of different profile patterns for men and women and thus, in this sense, have adjusted their interpretations to fit the different situations of the two sexes.

Religious Differences

From the earliest days of the application of the MMPI to normal groups, there was interest in the possibility that differing religious backgrounds and systems of belief would result in different patterns of response. In

between religious groups may be accounted for by various tenets of belief that lead to differential responses to the items involving religious content; larger differences require other kinds of interpretation, with implications involving pervasive attitudes affecting more than those items having religious content.

In an unusual study reported in 1969, Tellegen, Gerrard, Gerrard, and Butcher contrasted two groups of normal subjects in a rural coal-mining area of southern West Virginia. One group of subjects was made up of members of a conventional Protestant denomination (Methodist); a matched sample, most of whose members belonged to a Holiness church, was from a sect that practiced snake-handling in their worship services. Both sexes were represented, and a wide range of ages was included. Although other concerns were addressed by this study (e.g., attempts by skilled clinicians to predict church membership from the MMPI profiles), interesting differences were revealed by the mean profiles when they were divided into subgroups of male-female, young-old, conventional-unconventional church. The codes for these categories are given in table G-2 in the appendix (unfortunately, scores on scale 5 [Mf] were not reported). The snake-handling group in general was highest on scales 4 (Pd) and 9 (Ma); the conventional group's highest scores were on K and scale 3 (Hy). Older subjects had higher scores on scales 1 (Hs), 2 (D), 3 (Hy), 0 (Si), and L; however, scale 2 (D) was less likely to be high among the older snake-handling church members. The authors characterized the snake-handling group as being more frank, less defensive, more impulsive and extraverted and as showing a "psychological youthfulness" in their test responses.

Comparison may be made to similar subgroups among prisoners in a nearby state. As part of a large-scale survey of felons in the North Carolina state prisons, Panton (1980) provided mean profiles for various religious groups (see table G-3 in the appendix for the codes of these profiles). Although these men had all run afoul of the law and had been sentenced to varying terms of confinement, there are some similarities in the codes between the conventional Protestant groups in this North Carolina sample and those in the Tellegen et al. group from West Virginia, particularly among the older subjects in the West Virginia study. The prison group of Holiness church members shows some similarities to the older, male snake-handling groups from West Virginia as well.

Two studies of religious differences among VA neuropsychiatric patients are available. In a survey made by Devries (1966) in a Los Angeles VA hospital, MMPIs were administered to 600 Caucasian males. Various demographic variables were tabulated and comparisons made between groups on the basis of diagnosis, religion, educational level, type of occupation, marital status, age level, and number of VA hospital admissions. Of these, only religious differences (Protestant, Catholic, and Hebrew categories) did not show significant differences in item endorsement rates.

Groesch and Davis (1977) studied four groups of 18 patients each in an Indiana VA neuropsychiatric hospital; they used the MMPI to determine whether people raised as Roman Catholics might have differing attitudes toward other people and concerning authority, sin, and guilt from the attitudes of those raised as Protestants. The patients were divided into two diagnostic groups (thought disordered [or schizophrenic] and drug dependent) as well as by religious upbringing. The codes for the mean profiles are given in table G-4 in the appendix. Using canonical correlational techniques, the authors concluded that religious background was a variable of great influence, interacting with age and diagnosis in relation to several of the MMPI scales to differing degrees; scales 2 (D), 3 (Hy), 5 (Mf), 6 (Pa), and 8 (Sc) together with the L scale were those most clearly affected in this complex relationship. However, the small size of the subgroups makes generalization difficult.

From this range of investigations dealing with differences in response based upon religious background, it is possible to conclude that there may well be systematic differences but that they are likely to be small and must be considered in the larger view of the individual being tested. That is, other aspects such as age and social background may interact to produce differences from one religious group to the next. It seems unlikely that only the items with religious content are involved; differences between religious groups appear to manifest themselves in more generalized and pervasive aspects of personality. The clinician should keep the possibility of such influences in mind.

Ethnic Differences: Asian-Americans

A rapidly growing minority in the United States is the group called Asian-Americans (sometimes including the Pacific Islander immigrants). Earlier migrations of Japanese, Chinese, Koreans, and Filipinos have been augmented recently by Vietnamese, Cambodians, Hmong, and Samoans, among others. These groups form a heterogeneous body, coming as they do from diverse countries of origin, speaking many languages, often having different religious beliefs, and with widely differing periods of assimilation into the American culture. An entirely uniform set of attitudes and values is unlikely to prevail throughout this diverse group, but some characteristic ways of behaving have been noted. Acosta, Yamamoto, and Evans (1982), in a manual directed primarily toward choosing effective psychotherapeutic techniques with minority groups, call attention to a common Confucian-based set of values among Asian peoples (even in those who are of the Catholic faith, such as most of the Filipino group) that emphasizes loyalty toward superiors (such as employers), close emotional ties between parents and children, propriety between husbands and wives, order between elders and juniors, and trust between friends. They conclude that such a basic foundation of values will result in the Asian-American appearing to Western eyes to be "passive-aggressive" or "nonassertive" or "overly submissive to authority." Also, the high value placed by many Orientals on the virtues of a tranquil state of mind has led, they feel, to the notion that Asians are "inscrutable," in the sense of reduced affective tone. This has its foundation in the unwillingness of the Asians to reveal and discuss their emotions in public and with strangers. In addition, they point out that mental illness may often be viewed as a manifestation of sins committed by ancestors and that admission of such problems could result in "losing face," thereby reflecting on the family and affecting other members as well. Hence, physical illness may be more personally acceptable and may be unconsciously substituted for more distressing mental illness in clinical populations.

Although the MMPI literature on this group is not extensive, there are some findings available that may illuminate these speculations. Table 3.1 briefly summarizes the research studies concerning Asian-Americans; these are discussed in more detail below, and in some cases tabular material is presented in Appendix G.

Normal Subjects

Before examining the results of the studies done with Asian-Americans who were ill at the time of testing, it would be of interest to consider what is known of normal groups. An early study of normal adult Asian-Americans (Abe, 1958) was done with a group of nisei (second-generation Japanese-Americans) from cities in Utah, Idaho, and southern California, using both the Edwards Personal Preference Schedule (Edwards, 1959) and the MMPI. The latter test was completed by 102 men and 100 women. Their ages ranged from 21 to 48, with means for both sexes falling in the early thirties; educational level for the two subgroups averaged between one and two years of college.

Abe was particularly interested in the nisei because of their intermediate position between, and their need to adjust to, two disparate standards of behavior. On the one hand, they were expected to compete in the less structured American middle-class world with its emphasis on individual freedom and assertiveness. On the other hand, they had come from homes where the parents, who were issei (first-generation immigrants), had been brought up in pre-World War II Japan in an atmosphere of

Table 3. 1. MMPI Studies of Asian-Americans

Source	Subjects	*N*	Scales Used	Comments
		Normal Subjects		
Abe (1958)[a]	Normal adult nisei (Japanese)	J: 102M, 100F	Basic + A, R	Comparison to normal college composites. M: lower K, higher 2; F: lower K and 3, higher 2. No comparable W sample.
Marsella et al. (1975)	Normal college students (Chinese, Japanese, white)	C: 36M, 37F J: 50M, 50F W: 39M, 37F	Scale 2 only	Five measures of depression, including MMPI. M: J highest, C next, W lowest; F: C highest, J next, W lowest.
Garside (1966)	Normal college students (Polynesian, Asian, white)	P: 50M&F A: 55M&F W: 41M&F	Basic	Data reported for mixed-sex groups. P and A mean profiles: many scales in 60-70 range; W: all scales below 60.
		Medical-Neurological Groups		
Tsushima & Onorato (1982)[a]	Medical and neurological patients (Japanese, white)	J: 38M, 29F W: 54M, 43F	Basic	WM higher on scale 5, M higher than F on nine clinical scales; no significant ethnic differences.
		Mental Health Groups		
Sue & Sue (1974)	Mental health clinic cases, college students (Asian, white)	A: 18M, 28F W: 60M, 60F	Basic	Student body 8% A, only 4% of clinic population A. AM: higher on L, F, 1, 2, 4, 6, 7, 8, 0; AF: higher on L, F, 0.
Finney (1963)	Mental health clinic patients (Asian, white, other Hawaiians)	A: 69M&F W: 100M&F O: 46M&F	Scales 4, 7, A, R only	Data reported for mixed-sex groups; Portuguese highest on all scales used.
RPSI survey (1978)[a]	Psychiatric patients (white, black, Hispanic, Asian)	W: 36,539M, 38,998F B: 3,350M, 2,819F H: 1,182M, 768F A: 137M, 145F	Basic	Very large *N*'s: all differences statistically significant; mean profiles of AM and AF lowest of four groups.

[a]More complete data may be found in Appendix G.

traditional class structure with a rigid social code and formal obligations to family and society. Parental discipline was administered by the family's rejecting and placing shame on the one who misbehaved. Unacceptable behavior was treated as reflecting on the family as a whole. Japanese boys were favored and accorded more status; girls were expected to be submissive and compliant. The position of the nisei, then, would seem to lead to many potentially anxiety-producing situations as they confronted the new cultural expectations. Many of these individuals had also undergone geographical displacement during the federal internment program during World War II.

The MMPI results shown in table G-5 in the appendix throw some light on these emotional characteristics but are not entirely consistent with this picture. In comparisons made between the male nisei and the Minnesota normative sample, there were significant differences on nearly all scales of the MMPI. Except for lower scores on L and R (and no difference appearing on the K scale), the nisei males scored higher on all other scales. The largest difference occurred on scale 5 (Mf), with the nisei men scoring one standard deviation higher; scales 7 (Pt) and 9 (Ma) were almost as deviant. Fewer significant differences were noted in comparisons of the nisei women with the normative sample. As with the men, lower scores on L and R were obtained, with higher than normal scores on several other scales. The largest differences fell on scale 0 (Si), with smaller but significant differences on scales 6 (Pa), 7 (Pt), 8 (Sc), and 9 (Ma).

Although Abe concluded that special norms were needed for this group, he noted that their mean profiles closely resembled those reported in earlier studies with college student normals by Goodstein (1954) for males and by Black (1956) for females. Since the nisei subjects were of a similar educational level, although older, such a comparison was seen as appropriate. For men, only scale 2 (D) was appreciably higher in the nisei, whereas K was lower when compared with Goodstein's composite profile for male students. For women, scale 2 was also significantly higher than Black's female composite sample; scales 3 (Hy) and K were lower.

It was Abe's interpretation that the scale 2 and K scale scores reflected the tendency of these men and women to "overadmit" problems and to be more depressed in their attempts to adjust to the two cultures. In addition, Abe believed that the low L and R scores reflected more than average denial of problems, as did the lower score on scale 3 (Hy) for the women. In fact, the mean profiles seem to suggest more a tendency toward self-criticism and high personal standards, rather than simple repression and denial. In his conclusions, Abe stated:

> That such characteristics are related to a culture conflict seems substantiated by the results of this investigation wherein it was found

> that Nisei are in the paradoxical position of having to fulfill more stringent requirements than their American counterparts, but at the same time, seem most ill-prepared for the task. Psychodynamically, it appears that they have little choice but to internalize the hostility they feel primarily toward their parents and to adjust through self-depreciation and depression. (1958, p. 65)

Two other studies involving normal Asian-Americans add information. Both were done in Hawaii on multiethnic groups. As part of a larger report on measures of depression in college students of Chinese, Japanese, and Caucasian ancestry, Marsella, Sanborn, Kameoka, Shizuru, and Brennan (1975) administered the Depression scale from the MMPI, together with four other self-report measures of depression. Among the males, the Japanese were highest (with a mean T score of 63.2), then the Chinese (58.0), followed by the Caucasians (54.8). Among the women, the Chinese had the highest scores on scale 2 (T score of 61.4), followed by the Japanese (59.8) and the Caucasians (54.2). These college students reported higher levels of depression than Abe's adults and even higher levels than the earlier college surveys done by Goodstein and by Black.

Garside (1966) compared students of differing ethnic backgrounds attending a church-related college in Hawaii. An ambitious plan to include many ethnic subgroups resulted in three broad categories of subjects: 50 Polynesians (including Tongan, Samoan, Tahitian, Maori, and Hawaiian); 55 Orientals (Japanese, Chinese, and Korean); and 41 Caucasians (from both the mainland and Hawaii). The codes for the three mean profiles were as follows:

Polynesians	'98 764-2301/	-F/K
Orientals	'879624-031/	-F/K
Caucasians	-748936 210/	-FK/

T-score means were reported for mixed-sex groups, making comparison with other college student scores difficult (and scale 5 [Mf] results meaningless); hence, scale 5 has been omitted from the codes. The L-scale results were not reported. Although the profile for the Caucasian students is less deviant than those for the other two groups, both the Polynesians and the Orientals were more likely to admit problems, as reflected in the low K scores.

Medical-Neurological Groups

Although not much is yet known of responses of normal Asian-Americans on the MMPI, some data have begun to accumulate on samples showing various forms of illness. In a careful study done in Hawaii with Caucasian and Japanese-American medical patients, Tsushima and Onorato (1982) matched the two groups by differences in pathology to determine whether what is often called racial bias in the test was actually accurate measurement of important criterion differences. MMPI records from 164 patients from the psychiatry and psychology departments of a private Hawaiian medical center were obtained. Of these, 67 were nisei (38 male, 29 female); the comparison group of Caucasians included 54 males and 43 females. One hundred of the total group had been diagnosed as having a psychophysiological, or somatization, disorder, with varying complaints of pain, fatigue, and other symptoms; the remaining 64 showed symptoms of organic brain syndrome.

Table G-6 in the appendix gives the T-score means and standard deviations for the groups divided by race, sex, and diagnostic grouping. Profile codes for the eight subgroups are also given. The scores were subjected to a hierarchical multivariate analysis that revealed significant effects for sex and diagnostic group, as well as a sex × race interaction. Males were higher than females on scales 1 (Hs), 2 (D), 3 (Hy), 4 (Pd), 5 (Mf), 7 (Pt), 8 (Sc), and 9 (Ma), and they were lower on 0 (Si). The neurological groups were higher than the somatization cases on scales 7 (Pt) and 8 (Sc) and, to some extent, scale 3 (Hy), and they were lower on scale 4 (Pd). The only race-linked difference was the higher scores on scale 5 (Mf) attained by white males, in contrast to the white females and the Japanese-Americans of both sexes. Tsushima and Onorato recognized the limitation of their select sample, with its narrow range of problems, but they suggested that careful matching of pathology is crucial to decisions of whether the test is biased and inappropriate for use with minority subjects. (For an interesting discussion of these issues, see Pritchard & Rosenblatt, 1980a, 1980b.)

Mental Health Groups

Another study of Asian college students, this time of self-referred clients in a university mental health clinic in the Pacific Northwest, was done by Sue and Sue (1974). An examination of the clinic files revealed that only 4% of the clinic population was of Asian ancestry (Chinese, Japanese, or Korean), whereas 8% of the total student body could be so classified. To test whether this represented better adjustment among these Asian groups or simply greater reluctance to use mental health resources, the authors compared MMPI scores of their subjects with those from a randomly sampled comparison group of non-Asians from the same clinic. A critical item list of somatic and family discord items was also used. Significantly higher scores were obtained from the Asian male group on scales L, F, 1 (Hs), 2 (D), 4 (Pd), 6 (Pa), 7 (Pt), 8 (Sc), and 0 (Si). Female Asians were higher than the comparison group on L, F, and scale 0 (Si). (Those Asian women who had requested abortions were higher than their non-Asian counterparts on scales L, F, 6 [Pa], 7 [Pt], 8 [Sc], and 0 [Si].) Asians also reported more somatic complaints and family problems. The authors concluded that Asians only appeared to be better adjusted and that severity was greater in the Asian students who seemed to have held back longer before seeking help. They attributed this tendency to cultural traditions of not expressing negative impulses and failures, and the emphasis on physical complaints to the greater acceptability of such problems.

In another Hawaiian study, Finney (1963) contrasted several of the many ethnic groups living there in an effort to understand real personality differences as distinct from expectations based on popular stereotypes. The first part of his report dealt with differences in diagnostic rates among the various ethnic groups represented in a general medical hospital; the second involved an analysis of symptoms exhibited by some of these ethnic groups as patients in a mental hospital; and, finally, an analysis was made of some test data (including part of the MMPI) from patients at outpatient mental health clinics. Groups that were included were Japanese, Chinese, Hawaiian, Filipino, Portuguese, and other Caucasians; 88 men and 215 women were studied in the total sample. As in the case of the Garside study cited above, means were reported for mixed-sex groups, making interpretation difficult. Also, of the basic scales, only scales 4 (Pd) and 7 (Pt) were included in Finney's battery, together with the A and R scales. On scale 4, the highest scores were noted for Portuguese and Filipino groups, whereas the Portuguese and Japanese were highest on scale 7. Portuguese were also highest on A (with Hawaiians next) and on R (with the Japanese next). Although several interesting leads are suggested by Finney's results, a careful equating of subgroups, as was done by Tsushima and Onorato, would have provided a more complete picture.

Finally, a large-scale tabulation of records accumulated by the Roche Psychiatric Service Institute in 1978 gives a set of T-score means and standard deviations for a subgroup of Asians (see table G-7 in the appendix). For comparative purposes, the means and standard deviations of the much larger majority group, as well as those of other minorities, are given. The sample comprised patients seen by psychiatrists and psychologists around the United States who subscribed to the MMPI scoring and interpretation service offered by Roche. Differences between Asians and Caucasians are not large for any of the basic scales.

Ethnic Differences: Native Americans

As with Asian-Americans, the native American minority in this country includes a wide-ranging set of subgroups, differing not only in region of residence and linguistic background but in degree of acceptance of and by the majority culture. However, some values common to Indian tribal cultures can perhaps be discerned. LaDue (1982) described a group of highly traditional native Americans as "more likely to be involved with others, to have stronger support systems, have less undirected activity, . . . and to be more involved in spiritual activities." An interesting discussion by Highwater (1981) of what he terms the *primal mind* emphasizes the close identification of the Indian individual with his or her tribe and its tribal religion, with much less ego orientation and social narcissism than that of the dominant culture. A pervasive sense of interrelatedness, not only to other tribal members but to all living beings, is often coupled with an openness to alternative identities and a tolerance of deviant behavior. Although many native Americans have moved away from their traditional values, their position in the dominant culture continues to be an ambiguous one and a possible source of stress when emotional problems arise, especially if community support is no longer readily available to them.

Table 3.2 presents in brief summary form the studies discussed below that involve native American subjects. For some of the entries in the table, additional data are provided in Appendix G.

Normal Subjects

As in the case of the Asian-Americans, few MMPI results are available at present on normal Indian subjects. One recent study by LaDue (1982) partly fills this gap. She administered the MMPI to a large sample of normal adult Indians living on or near a reservation in the northwestern section of the United States. (Data were also collected on the Holmes-Rahe Social Readjustment Rating Scale [1967] and a biographical questionnaire devised by LaDue to assess degree of identification with traditional Indian culture.) Mean profiles and codes are given in table G-8 in the appendix for the 63 men and 71 women of her sample.

LaDue had expected to find significantly higher scores (i.e., one standard deviation or more above the mean of 50) for her subjects on scales F, 2 (D), 4 (Pd), 6 (Pa), and 8 (Sc) as well as on the MacAndrew Alcoholism scale, based on an earlier study done on an Indian clinical population by Pollack and Shore (1980) (see discussion below). For both sexes, these expectations were fulfilled, with the exception of scale 2. In addition, males scored higher than the norms on scales 5 (Mf) and 7 (Pt), and both sexes did so on scale 9 (Ma) and on the MacAndrew scale. (However, the black and white contemporary samples reported at length in chapters 4 and 5 also score somewhat higher than the original Minnesota normative sample did.)

Age-related relationships were demonstrated with scale 1 (Hs) (*r* of .20)

Table 3.2. MMPI Studies of Native Americans

Source	Subjects	*N*	Scales Used	Comments
		Normal Subjects		
LaDue (1982)[a]	Normal adults (Indian)	I: 63M, 71F	Basic + MacAndrew	M: higher on F, 4, 5, 6, 7, 8, 9; F: higher on F, 4, 6, 8, 9. Assessed identification with traditional culture. No comparison sample.
Arthur (1944)	Normal 12th-grade students (Indian)	I: 29M,51F	Scale 2 + early 1, 3, 4	Scales used not generally comparable; unknown selection factors for enrollment.
Bryde (1966)[a]	Normal students in 8th, 9th, 12th grade (Indian, white)	I: 226M, 189F W: 114M, 109F	Basic + A, R, Es	Comparisons of I and W (total groups) similar in pattern, I higher. Highest elevation: dropouts.
Herreid & Herreid (1966)[a]	Normal college students (native, white)	N: 51M, 40F W: 50M, 50F	Basic	Natives (Aleuts, Eskimos, Indians) compared with nonnative Alaskans and college composites; natives higher on most scales.
Bull (1976)[a]	Normal technical institute students (white, black, Indian)	W: 25M, 36F B: 20M, 32F I: 24M, 29F	Basic	M: several scales over 60 (B: scales 8, 9 over 70); F: several over 60 for B, I.
Hoffman et al. (1985)	Normal adults (Indian)	I: 37M, 32F	MMPI-168	Short form: elevations on 4, F. Related to educ/occup. scale of acculturation measure.
		Alcoholic Treatment Groups		
Kline et al. (1973)	Alcoholic program inpatients (Indian)	I: 45M	Basic	Variety of profile patterns found (esp. elevations of F and 4, often 8).
Uecker et al. (1980)[a]	Alcoholic program inpatients (white, Indian)	W: 40M I: 40M	Basic + MacAndrew	W: higher on 4 and 5. No significant results on measure of degree of cultural identification.
Page & Bozlee (1982)[a]	Alcoholic program inpatients (white, Indian, Hispanic)	W: 11M I: 11M H: 11M	Basic + MacAndrew	No significant differences between I and W. Small *N*'s; considerable variety of patterns.
Westermeyer (1972)	Alcoholic program inpatients (Indian, non-Indian)	I: 30M&F N: 200M&F	Basic	No means or significant differences reported; no significant ethnic differences.

		Prisoner Groups		
Panton (1980, 1983)[a]	Felons in general prison population (total, Indian)	T: 2,551M I: 153M	Basic	Total prison sample higher on 4, 5; I sample higher on L.
Wormith et al. (1984)[a]	Felons in general prison population (total, Indian) Felons in psychiatric prison (total, Indian)	T: 1,460M I: 298M T: 325M I: 58M	Basic	General prison: I higher on F, 8; total group on 5. Psychiatric prison: I higher on F, 8; total group on 5.
Mandelzys (1979) and Mandelzys & Lane (1980)[a]	Psychiatric prison center (total, Indian)	T: 497M I: 95M	Basic	Total group higher on K, 5; I higher on F, 1, 6, 7, 8, 9.
		Mental Health Groups		
Pollack & Shore (1980)[a]	Mental health center patients (Indian)	I: 68M, 74F	Basic	M: scale 8 over 70; F: scales 4, 6, 8, F over 70.
Peniston (1978)	Outpatient suicide attempters	I: 13M, 17F	Scale 2 + Es	High scale 2, but unrelated to number of attempts; low Es correlated with more attempts and associated alcohol consumption.
Butcher et al. (1983)[a]	Psychiatric inpatients (white, black, Indian)	W: 60M, 37F B: 60M, 37F W: 17M, 19F I: 17M, 19F	Basic	Statistically significant differences on F, 6, 8, 9; when F criterion applied, only difference was on 9 (B higher than W). Ethnic differences in presenting symptoms noted.

[a]More complete data may be found in Appendix G.

and scale 9 (Ma) (r of $-.21$); in addition, the measure of Indian traditionalism was significantly related to lower scores on scales 9 (Ma) and 0 (Si) and to higher scores on the MacAndrew scale. In light of these findings, LaDue explored whether these more traditional subjects were, in fact, more likely to be alcohol abusers. Data from her biographical questionnaire, however, indicated that her subgroup of tradition-oriented native Americans showed, instead, less likelihood of being alcoholic. Her suggested explanation for elevations on the MacAndrew scale lay with the possibility that a religious or spiritual orientation may have led to endorsement of some items included in this scale (such as "My soul sometimes leaves my body" or "Evil spirits possess me at times"). Although only three items on the 51-item MacAndrew scale are what are usually classed as (conventional) religious items (e.g., "I pray several times a week"), an additional three might be seen as having content that could be interpreted as having spiritual meaning by some subjects (e.g., "I have had blank spells in which my activities were interrupted and I did not know what was going on around me"). Perhaps a critical item list of such statements might be considered for use with individuals who are thought to be particularly sensitive to their native traditions and attuned to spiritualistic beliefs.

Although LaDue's study was unusual in being directed toward a sample of normal adult men and women, several groups of Indian students have been studied with the MMPI. A very early investigation by Arthur (1944) of twelfth-grade Indian students at a federal school in Minnesota was done during the period when the MMPI scales were still being developed. The Indian students were reported to score higher on early forms of scales 4 (Pd) and 2 (D) and lower on the predecessor of scale 1 (Hs) than did Minnesota college students. However, aside from the lack of comparability to present versions of these scales, selection factors affecting the composition of the school population were unknown and make these results difficult to interpret.

A more extensive study of Indian school children was conducted by Bryde (1966). To test the observation that Indian students were likely to show a drop in school achievement at about the seventh-grade level after performance in the earlier grades that was equal to or better than whites, Bryde administered the California Achievement Test and the MMPI to a sample of Oglala Sioux Indian students in federal, private, and mission schools on a reservation in South Dakota. There were 164 eighth-graders and 126 ninth-graders in his Indian sample; they were compared with 76 eighth-grade and 126 ninth-grade white students from public schools near the reservation. In addition, 92 Sioux twelfth-graders were tested for comparison with the younger Indian students, as well as with a group of

59 early dropouts from the school system. Table G-9 in the appendix presents the means and standard deviations for all male and all female Indian and all male and all female white students. As can be seen from the profile codes, the pattern of response for each sex is similar for Indians and whites; the overall elevation of the profiles, however, is significantly higher for the Indian groups.

Bryde made some further comparisons of these students over the range from eighth grade to twelfth grade. Unfortunately, in these analyses the data from the sexes were combined, making the results for scale 5 (Mf) unusable. With this caution in mind, it is interesting to note that profile codes for the three grades (in each case, containing some individuals who were soon-to-be dropouts) reflect a progressive reduction in elevation as follows:

Eighth-graders	'4698 210-37/	F'-L/K
Ninth-graders	'964208-137/	F'-L/K
Twelfth-graders	'94-602138/7	'F-L/K
Dropouts	'6984 201-37/	F'-L/K

Dropouts from all grades were combined; their profile code is also shown above. Scales F, 6 (Pa), and 8 (Sc) show a marked shift, especially in comparison with the twelfth-graders. Although many adolescents have MMPI profiles with elevations like those of the dropout group, it is likely to be those who feel most rejected, alienated, and withdrawn who do so. (See the work of Hathaway and Monachesi [1963] for further discussion of MMPI characteristics of adolescent dropouts.) As Bryde noted, at the time he was studying these Indian adolescents, only 40% of the group finished high school. The pattern of personality test results, as well as lower achievement scores, do indeed suggest a picture of frustration and withdrawal from an unsatisfying school environment.

Bryde also examined the relation between MMPI scores and degree of Indian ancestry ("full-blooded," 3/4, 1/2, and 1/4): here again, the more deviant patterns and the lowest achievement scores were found among those with the greatest degree of Indian ancestry. These full-blooded Indian adolescents showed somewhat more feelings of rejection and alienation with depression and anxiety present and had less ego strength than their mixed-blood contemporaries. Some similarity to LaDue's findings discussed above is suggested by these results.

Herreid and Herreid (1966) evaluated entering freshmen at the University of Alaska in the early 1960s. The authors compared groups of students from three native Alaskan groups (Aleuts, Eskimos, and Indians) to nonnative students (i.e., Caucasians) and also to earlier published composite surveys of large numbers of male college students by Goodstein (1954) and of female college students by Black (1956). Table G-10 in the appendix gives the profile codes for these groups.

In comparing the native and nonnative groups, higher scores were obtained by native Alaskans on almost all scales except scales 3 (Hy) and 5 (Mf) for males and scales 3 (Hy), 6 (Pa), and 9 (Ma) for females. Even the nonnative Caucasian Alaskan students responded somewhat more deviantly than did the large U.S. student survey groups, although the native Alaskans exceeded both. Mean profiles were reported for the subgroups as well, but some of the samples were quite small and hence single individuals with deviant scores were perhaps given undue weight. However, Herreid and Herreid pointed out that for both sexes the Aleut group seemed to be most deviant; their suggested explanation for these and other differences was that they stem from relative degree of acculturation into mainstream American society.

Bull (1976) administered the MMPI to male and female students of three racial groups at a technical institute in a rural area of North Carolina. Most of these students were in their twenties, and the composition of the student body closely reflected the distribution in the area of whites, blacks, and Indians (Lumbees). Codes for the mean profiles are given in table G-11 in the appendix. Although these profiles are not as deviant as those found in another study of individuals living in an isolated community (Gynther, Fowler, & Erdberg, 1971; see the discussion in chapter 2), they do represent considerable departure from the norm, especially in subjects who were nearly all high school graduates and who were students at a technical institute. Bull attributed this divergence at least in part to the local cultural norms that had developed in an area where isolation had led to deprivation and insulation from the usual standards of modern life. He believed that a combination of frontier mentality with a strong mystical and superstitious orientation had led to a tendency for these subjects to respond very differently from other young adults.

A recent study of normal Indian adults in South Dakota was reported by Hoffmann, Dana, and Bolton (1985). The authors tested a group of 69 Sioux (37 men and 32 women) from the Rosebud Indian Reservation; unfortunately, only a short form of the test was used, together with a measure of acculturation. The education/occupation dimension of their scale of acculturation was most highly correlated with elevations on the clinical scales, which they attributed to socioeconomic differences.

Alcoholic Treatment Groups

Several studies of alcohol misuse have compared Indian samples with other ethnic groups. The results of three of these reports are presented in table G-12 in the appendix. Kline, Rozynko, Flint, and Roberts (1973) presented MMPI results from a sample of male Indians in an inpatient treatment program for alcohol abusers in California. The authors found a variety of profile patterns among their subjects' records (in contrast to the uniformity of response noted by Pollack and Shore in the study discussed below), with scales 4 (Pd) and F usually elevated plus a large number of cases with scale 8 (Sc) elevations as well. They concluded that further research was needed to understand both the personality dynamics of native Americans and the role that alcohol plays within the context of their culture. Although no direct comparisons were made in their study to other ethnic groups, the authors cited earlier work by Mogar, Wilson, and Helm (1970) with white alcoholic patients as a point of reference.

Uecker, Boutilier, and Richardson reported in 1980 a study based on 40 white and 40 Indian alcoholics, all of whom had been admitted to an alcoholism treatment program at a VA hospital in South Dakota. The men in these groups were matched on age, education, and duration and severity of problem drinking; the Indian subjects were all of the Northern Plains culture, mostly Sioux, and most had grown up on reservations. Testing occurred after the patients had been in the hospital at least two weeks, thus assuring a preliminary period of sobriety and minimizing the acute effects of alcohol.

Mean profiles for the two racial groups were quite similar (see table G-12). Only the whites' higher scores on scales 4 (Pd) and 5 (Mf) reached statistical significance at the .05 level, and the MacAndrew Alcoholism scale scores for each group were almost equivalent. The large standard deviations for some scales, however, probably reflect the grouping together of many different types of alcoholics, all of whom had drinking problems but who showed various MMPI configurations.

Uecker et al. also administered a somewhat controversial questionnaire that was devised by one of the authors to measure strength of Indian cultural identification. Correlations between this questionnaire and the MMPI scales were not high enough to suggest that cultural conflict alone underlay the psychopathology measured by the MMPI. (For further comments on this measure of identification with the Sioux culture, see Walker, Cohen, & Walker [1981] and Uecker, Boutilier, & Richardson [1981].)

The third set of data presented in table G-12 consists of means and standard deviations from a study by Page and Bozlee (1982) of three small groups of VA patients in an alcohol treatment program in the state of Washington. Whites, Indians, and Hispanics were tested after at least one week in the hospital. Educational levels were roughly equivalent; although the mean age for the Hispanic sample was somewhat higher than the others, the range of ages for all groups was wide. Unique characteristics of the

Hispanic group will be reported in the next section below. Comparison of the Indian and white groups resulted in no significant differences between the two, including scores on the MacAndrew Alcoholism scale. A tabulation of high-point elevations was reported to reveal considerable variability, with the whites showing more scale 4 (Pd) spike and 49/94 configurations, the Indian group more often having scales 1 (Hs), 6 (Pa), or 9 (Ma) as the high point. The authors concluded that the ethnic groups were more similar than dissimilar in their responses to the test, as well as in secondary clinical diagnoses, and that the results did not indicate the need for separate norms for these groups.

One further study of Indian and white alcoholics has been reported by Westermeyer (1972); it attempted to answer the question of whether Indian drinking patterns were of a different sort from those of other alcoholics. Thirty Chippewa (Ojibwa or Anishinabe) alcoholic patients were tested in hospitals in Minneapolis and St. Paul and compared with a group of 200 non-Indian alcoholics; all were residents of the Twin Cities metropolitan area. No means or standard deviations were reported from Westermeyer's combined-sex groups; however, the author indicated that no signficant ethnic differences emerged in the scale analyses. Although psychiatric evaluation did not disclose frequent occurrence of psychosis in either group, demographic variables (such as unemployment or absence of a spouse) and differences in the course of the alcoholic disorder did appear to be important differentiators. Westermeyer concluded that sociocultural variables, rather than intrinsic differences in the alcoholism syndrome, accounted for those variations that did appear.

Prisoner Groups

MMPI data from prison populations that included Indian subgroups are available from several sources. From North Carolina Central Prison, Panton (personal communication, 1983) has made available the means and standard deviations from a group of 153 Indian felons (140 of whom were Lumbees from the same area described by Bull [1976]); for comparison, the results from the total prison population of felons for the year 1976-77 (Panton, 1980) are also given in table G-13 in the appendix. (This group included members of various minorities, primarily black; however, data from some of the felons in the smaller Indian sample are included in the larger baseline sample.) Differences between the two samples are not large, and, except for somewhat higher scale 4 (Pd) and scale 5 (Mf) means for the total group, the profile codes are quite similar.

Three surveys conducted in Canada that deal with Indians from tribal cultures common to the two countries are also presented in table G-13. MMPI records have been compiled by Wormith, Borzecki, and Black

(1984) from prisoners in Canadian penitentiaries in the Prairie region; table G-13 also gives these data for the total and Indian groups confined in general prisons. In addition, the table shows data from two regional psychiatric centers (Pacific and Prairie regions) of the Canadian maximum-security prison system, again contrasting the whole prison population with the native groups (Wormith et al., 1984; Mandelzys, 1979; Mandelzys & Lane, 1980). The profile codes reveal close similarities between the heterogeneous groups of prisoners and the Indian groups, with relative elevation being the most striking difference between the general prison populations and the psychiatric groups. In both sorts of surveys, it is again the F scale and scale 8 (Sc) that seem to be more prominent in the native profiles. Mandelzys and Lane (1980) also used measures of offense severity and recidivism prediction in their studies of native and total prison groups. Although the 1979 Mandelzys report on the larger group of prisoners revealed relationships between MMPI elevations and both offense severity and the recidivism predictor, none of the scales showed a significant relationship with the measure of offense severity in the Indian group; only scales 4 (Pd) and 9 (Ma) showed modest correlations with the recidivism measure. The authors believed that use of the test with minority subjects was much less useful and, in fact, suspect because of the failure to include Indians in the Minnesota normative sample.

Mental Health Groups

Three recent studies have dealt with mental health problems in Indians. In the Pollack and Shore study (1980) referred to by LaDue, the intent was to determine the validity of the MMPI as used with native Americans. A group of 68 male and 74 female Indian patients from the Pacific Northwest (including individuals from Northwest Coastal, Plateau, and Plains cultures) was tested as part of the evaluations conducted at a regional mental health center in Oregon. Table G-14 in the appendix provides, separately for men and women, the scale means and standard deviations.

Of this group, 53 were independently diagnosed by one of three senior personnel using DSM-II criteria. The authors were concerned that diagnosed groups of Indian clients were not distinguishable from one another by means of their MMPI profile patterns and hence that the test was not to be considered a valid measure of psychopathology for these patients. Inspection of the codes given in table G-15 does indeed reveal similarities between the schizophrenic and depressive cases; the situational reaction and alcoholic groups are also quite similar to each other with respect to profile shape. However, the sample sizes are small, the sexes are combined for this analysis, and, except for the statement that the antisocial alcoholics were imprisoned, there is little nontest information provided on which to base a judgment as to the adequacy of the MMPI patterns in describing the psychopathology in these individuals. Although, as the authors note, 48/84 profile codes are often associated with unusual and deviant behavior, the degree of deviation may be exaggerated by the difficult situation in which members of minorities find themselves: that is, resentment and distrust of the dominant culture may influence test performance.

Pollack and Shore concluded that a generalized response pattern prevailed across these Indian groups; very small differences were found between men and women, older and younger individuals, and members of the three different tribal cultures represented (although some differences were suggested in the results from the small subgroup of Plains Indians). They advised that the use of the MMPI in a cross-cultural setting was likely to lead to false perceptions of the degree of psychopathology present. Certainly much additional work in such contexts was felt to be essential before valid interpretation could be assured.

A study published in 1978 by Peniston focused on a group of 30 Ute Indian suicide attempters who were seen in an outpatient clinic. Although scale 2 (D) was elevated in these patients, scores on this scale were unrelated to number of suicide attempts. However, low scores on Es (ego strength) were related both to number of attempts and to associated alcohol consumption.

Another survey, this time of all psychiatric inpatients for a five-year period who were tested on admission to two metropolitan hospitals in Minneapolis and St. Paul, has been reported by Butcher, Braswell, and Raney (1983). The authors surveyed records in the two hospitals and located all available MMPIs on minorities and on a large heterogeneous sample of white patients. In addition to reporting the means and standard deviations on these individuals, the authors formed matched groups, separately by sex, of blacks and whites and of Indians and whites, taking social class criteria into account. Table G-16 in the appendix shows the means and standard deviations, together with the profile codes, for these smaller matched groups. One-way ANOVA procedures showed statistically significant results on scales F, 6 (Pa), 8 (Sc), and 9 (Ma) among these groups. The small number of subjects available for the matchings, however, did not permit a conservative cutoff point on F-scale elevations. (The authors attributed these high scores on F to possible limitations in reading comprehension.) When a more stringent F criterion was applied, 48 of the 143 matched pairs had to be eliminated, and the only remaining significant difference was on scale 9 (Ma) between blacks and whites.

Butcher et al. also examined the hospital records and grouped the patients by presenting problems. The subjects in the matched subgroups differed significantly on symptoms related to depression (whites and Indians exceeding blacks), aggression, and paranoid reaction (in both of the latter, blacks exceeded whites and Indians). No systematic differences were noted on symptoms related to anxiety, alcohol abuse, or confusional states.

The authors stressed the value of inclusion of more than one minority group in investigations of this kind. The nontest data they collected on their subjects documented some of the reasons for the MMPI differences they obtained. Their results suggest that some of the differences reported for minority subjects may be racial only in the sense that social class differences exist between the groups compared and that matching of demographic characteristics throws light on these differences.

Ethnic Differences: Hispanic-Americans

The Hispanic minority in this country is a large one, second only to black Americans in numbers. Although the term is used to denote people from several different areas (including Cuba, Puerto Rico, other parts of the Caribbean, as well as Central and South America), it has been the Mexican-Americans, mostly of the southwestern United States, who have been the almost exclusive focus of study with the MMPI. Except for a large national survey that included Hispanic patients from many countries of origin (Roche Psychiatric Service Institute, 1978) and one recent dissertation (Nugueras, 1983) based on Puerto Ricans, only Mexican-Americans have been reported in the research literature. Certainly not all Hispanics can be thought to be alike, but, until further investigations are reported, what can be gleaned from the following discussion can only be applied to this one subgroup.

Historically, Mexican-American culture is a blend of Indian and Spanish antecedents strongly influenced by a Catholic heritage and with Spanish as the mother tongue. Acosta, Yamamoto, and Evans (1982), in their suggestions for effective therapy with this group, point out that:

> the family has traditionally been one of the most valued and proud aspects of life among Hispanic-Americans. A great deal of importance has typically been placed on preserving family unity, respect, and loyalty, and the family tends to be a source of strength for Hispanic-Americans. The family structure is usually hierarchical with special respect and much authority given to the husband and father. The wife and mother is often obedient to her husband and also receives respect and much emotional reward from the children. Sex-role identification for the Hispanic-American is thus much

stricter than that of the general population of the United States. (1982, p. 55)

However, this picture is disputed as being stereotypical by Ruiz (1981) in another therapy manual; in his view, studies of lower socioeconomic status individuals of Anglo, black, and Mexican-American background reveal no differences in traditional sex roles, and some of the underutilization of mental health services often commented upon may well be related to difficulties in reaching such services and in finding Spanish-language help when arriving there.

There does seem to be agreement that the family (and often the church) is a source of strength for the Hispanic individual, but the same motivational forces may lead to an unwillingness to seek outside help from mental health professionals. Some of the discussion that follows shows how this defensiveness may manifest itself in patterns of MMPI responses. Since this group is partially defined by linguistic characteristics, it is encouraging to note that substantial work has been done on the development of an alternative Spanish-language version of the test for use with Hispanics. Recent reports by García (1983), Ledwin (1983), and Morris (1983) concerning the adequacy of this alternative version suggest that this is a very promising line of investigation; García and Azán (1984) have recently prepared a new translation for use with Hispanic-Americans.

Table 3.3 presents in summary form the studies that have had Hispanic-Americans as their subjects. These will be discussed below; in some cases, additional data are provided in the appendix.

Normal Subjects

Most of the work that has been done with the MMPI on normal Mexican-American individuals has focused upon high school and college students. Fitch (1972) investigated whether de facto minority status resulted in personality differences. That is, were the effects of being a member of a cultural minority, such as an Hispanic-American, different from those of being a member of a statistical minority in a school where the Hispanic culture dominated? Two groups (one Anglo, one Hispanic) of adolescent girls (15 in each group) were studied from each of two high schools in a county in northwestern Colorado. In one of the high schools the Anglo-Americans were in the majority; in the other, the Hispanic-Americans were more numerous. Fitch used only four scales from the MMPI (scales 1 [Hs], 2 [D], 3 [Hy], and 0 [Si]) but he first checked the test records to see that all validity scores were within normal limits and he added an appropriate K-correction to all of the scale-1 scores. He also compared the data with adolescent data from Minnesota (Hathaway & Monachesi, 1963).

His results seem to indicate that, in both situations, the groups that were the de facto minorities were closer to the Minnesota adolescent survey findings. The majority in each school was more deviant than the comparison minority. In the case of the Anglo majority, much higher scores on scale 1 and somewhat lower scores on scale 0 were found, whereas the majority Hispanic-American girls showed the largest differences on scale 0 (higher) and had modest elevations on scales 1 and 3. As Fitch concluded, there seemed to be no typical minority profile (at least in these small samples and with this reduced set of scales); members of a majority culture may indeed exhibit personality characteristics of a minority group when they are placed in that situation. Certainly further investigation would be of interest with larger groups and more complete testing.

Francis (1964) tested the validity of stereotyped descriptions of Mexican-American males as authoritarian, irresponsible, rebellious, and "macho" and of Mexican-American females as submissive, self-sacrificing, overly restrained, and self-belittling. Testing was conducted in a Tucson high school; his group of sophomores included 101 Mexican-Americans and 131 Anglo-Americans. Table G-17 in the appendix gives the codes for the mean profiles of these groups, separately by sex. Analyses of variance, testing effects of age, culture, sex, and serial birth order upon MMPI scores, showed few significant differences. Only when all males were compared to all females were differences found on scales 2 (D), 7 (Pt), and 9 (Ma). Although he commented that his subjects were young and perhaps were unusually well integrated into the majority culture, Francis found little support for the differences assumed by the stereotypical descriptions of Mexican-American men and women.

In a study of Puerto Rican adolescents, Nugueras (1983) contrasted three groups of subjects aged 15 to 18 on a Spanish-language version of the MMPI. A group of returned migrants and a group of island residents showed significant differences on scales F, K, 1 (Hs), 5 (Mf), and 0 (Si), and the test differentiated a group of adolescents with mental health needs from the normal group.

In a study of college students, Reilley and Knight (1970) contrasted subgroups of Anglo- and Mexican-American freshmen at a southwestern university. Table G-18 in the appendix gives the means and standard deviations for these groups, separately for sex and ethnic group. Significant differences between men and women were noted for scales 2 (D) and 0 (Si); in each case, the women scored higher. The Mexican-Americans were somewhat higher on L, as were the Anglo-Americans on scale 6 (Pa). Interaction effects were noted for scales 7 (Pt) and 8 (Sc), and especially for scale 0 (Si), with male Mexican-Americans and female Anglo-Americans scoring highest on these scales. Although differences were

Table 3. 3. MMPI Studies of Hispanic-Americans

Source	Subjects	*N*	Scales Used	Comments
		Normal Subjects		
Fitch (1972)	High school students (white, Hispanic)	W: 30F H: 30F	Scales 1, 2, 3, 0 only	De facto minority status considered; majority in each case more deviant (most W higher on 1, lower on 0; most H higher on 0).
Francis (1964)[a]	High school students (white, Hispanic)	W: 63M, 68F H: 41M, 60F	Basic	Few significant differences except gender (M: higher on 2, 7, 9).
Nugueras (1983)	Adolescents: Puerto Rican islanders, returned migrants	H: 785M&F	Basic	Significant differences between returned migrants and islanders on F, K, 1, 5, 0. Significant differences between normals and those with mental health problems.
Reilley & Knight (1970)[a]	College students (white, Hispanic)	W: 36M, 32F H: 36M, 32F	Basic	F higher on 2, 0; H higher on L, W on 6. MH and FW highest on 7, 8, 0.
Murphy (1978)[a]	College students (white, Hispanic)	W: 22M, 17F H: 22M, 17F	Basic	In larger groups, differences on L, 1, 4, 8, 0. In matched groups differences only on L, 1 (H higher).
Padilla et al. (1982)	College students (white, Hispanic)	W: 46M, 52F H: 94M, 80F	Basic	Measures of acculturation: less acculturated showed differences on L, K, 1, 4, 5.
Montgomery & Orozco (1985)	College students (white, Hispanic)	W: 21M, 65F H: 99M, 180F	Basic	H: higher on L, F, 1, 2, 7, 8, 9, 0; W: higher on K. When acculturation scale used, only differences on L for both sexes, 5 for F.
Guzmán (1970)	College students (white, Hispanic)	W: 30M H: 30M	Basic	Profile code for H only: no elevations over 69T.
McGill (1980)	Mothers on welfare (white, black, Hispanic)	W: 78F B: 50F H: 51F	Basic	Education variable related to differences on 5, 0; H higher than W on L, K, lower on 9. No significant W-B differences.
Goldberg (1980)	Worker compensation cases (Hispanic)	H: 20M	Scale 4 only	Weighting of ethnic and disability factors recommended to avoid misinterpretation.
		Alcoholic and Drug Treatment Groups		
Page & Bozlee (1982)[a]	Alcoholic program inpatients (white, Indian, Hispanic)	W: 11M I: 11M H: 11M	Basic + MacAndrew	H highest, esp. on scale 2. Small *N*'s; considerable variety of profile patterns.
Herl (1976)	Heroin addicts (white, Hispanic)	W: 24M H: 31M W&H: 15F	Basic	WM had more elevations over T69. Both M groups more diagnostic groupings of "emotional disturb."; F, "character disturb."
Penk et al. (1981b)[a]	Heroin addicts (white, black, Hispanic)	W: 161M B: 268M H: 41M	Basic	H: lower on 5, 9, higher on L. Differences accounted for by significance of drug addiction in minority culture.
Dolan et al. (1983)	Heroin addicts (white, black, Hispanic)	W: 154M B: 229M H: 40M	Wiggins scales	H lower than W on SOC, HOS; H lower than B on FEM.

		Prisoner Groups		
Fisher (1967)	Corrections reception center (white, black, Hispanic)	W: 492M B: 182M H: 108M	Basic	B and H more defensive than W prisoners; comparisons to Marlowe-Crowne test.
Holland (1979)[a]	Short-term felony offenders: probation hearings (white, black, Hispanic)	W: 396M B: 208M H: 114M	Basic	W higher than H on 3, 5, 6; B higher than H on 4, 5, 7, 8, 9; B higher than W on F, 8, 9. Need for replicable profile correlates.
McCreary & Padilla (1977)[a]	Misdemeanor offenders: presentencing evaluation (white, black, Hispanic)	W: 36M B: 36M W: 32M H: 32M	Basic + special scales	Minority groups matched with W on SES. W higher than B on K, 3, lower on 9; H higher than W on L, K, and OH.
		Medical-Psychiatric Groups		
Ojeda (1980)	Abusive mothers (white, Hispanic)	W: ?F H: 40F	Basic	Abusive mothers higher than H controls. No data for W.
Selters (1973)[a]	VA medical patients: psychiatric referrals (white, black, Hispanic)	W: 173M B: 99M H: 118M	Basic	H higher than W on L, F; H higher than B on 2. B higher than W on L, 5, 9; B higher than H or 5.
	VA psychiatric patients (white, black, Hispanic)	W: 55M B: 39M H: 34M	Basic	Differences on L only (H higher than W).
Plemons (1977)[a]	Mental health center outpatients (white, Hispanic)	W: 44M, 65F H: 18M, 22F	Basic	With K-correction, only L, K higher for total and scale 5 higher for WM; uncorrected recommended.
Plemons (1980)	Psychiatric outpatients (white, Hispanic)	W: 29M, 48F H: 26M, 46F	Basic + special scales	Only scale 5 higher for FH. H higher on R, Pr; lower on Do, Cn, St. Small *N* subgroups divided by levels of acculturation (medium M least deviant).
Quiroga (1972)	Psychiatric patients (Hispanic)	H: 192M, 208F	Basic	Psychotic H higher on L, 4, lower on 0; nonpsychotic H lower on 5, 0. Linear discriminant function developed.
Lawson et al. (1982).	Community mental health patients (white, Hispanic)	W: 60M&F H: 25M&F	Basic	H higher on L; W higher on 0. Comparison on scale measuring attitudes toward psychopathology and hospitalization.
Frye (1973)	County psychiatric inpatients (white, Hispanic)	W: 162M&F H: 113M&F	Basic	Same data base as Hibbs et al. study.
Hibbs et al. (1979)[a]	County psychiatric inpatients (white, Hispanic)	W: 51M, 94F H: 38M, 57F	Basic	Very deviant scores for all groups, highest for youngest. Interaction of ethnicity with age, sex variables.
RPSI survey (1978)[a]	Psychiatric patients (white, black, Hispanic, Asian)	W: 36,539M 38,998F B: 3,350M, 2,819F H: 1,182M, 768F A: 137M, 145F	Basic	Very large *N*'s: all differences statistically significant. H higher than W on L, F, 1, 8 + 5 for F.

[a]More complete data may be found in Appendix G.

small, the authors suggested that the scale elevations in the Mexican-American men and the Anglo-American women reflected somewhat greater tendencies toward worry and anxiety, greater social alienation, and increased shyness and introversion.

Murphy (1978) also studied Mexican- and Anglo-American college students. Although significant differences on scales L, 1 (Hs), 4 (Pd), 8 (Sc), and 0 (Si) seemed to be present in the analyses conducted first on the total group of 71 Mexican- and 184 Anglo-Americans, a much smaller set of subgroups matched for age, education, and parental socioeconomic status left only differences on L and scale 1, with the Mexican-American group somewhat higher on these scales. Table G-19 in the appendix presents the results for the matched groups. Murphy also examined the items endorsed differentially by the two ethnic groups (in the larger unmatched samples) for both men and women. Applications of profile classification systems were described as well, with significantly higher numbers of the Mexican-Americans classified as having pathological patterns of response. Recommendations were made concerning possible modifications of the test in the form of interpretive adjustments when used with this group.

Similar elevations on the L scale and scale 1 (Hs) (together with lower scale 5 [Mf] scores as well) were found with a subgroup of less acculturated subjects in a study of Mexican- and Anglo-American college students by Padilla, Olmedo, and Loya (1982). Another component of acculturation status, socioeconomic status (as well as attitudes toward masculinity), was negatively related to scale 4 (Pd) and positively to the L and K scales.

Further consideration of the relationship of level of acculturation was made in a study by Montgomery and Orozco (1985). A large sample of college freshmen attending a university in south Texas was studied, including 279 Mexican-Americans (99 males, 180 females) and 86 Anglo-Americans (21 males, 65 females). Most of the MMPI scales showed significant differences between the two ethnic groups (with sexes combined); Mexican-Americans were higher on L, F, 1 (Hs), 2 (D), 7 (Pt), 8 (Sc), 9 (Ma), and 0 (Si), whereas Anglo-Americans were higher on K. However, when a scale devised by Cuellar, Harris, and Jasso (1980) was used to control for level of acculturation in the Mexican-American sample, only differences on the L scale (for both sexes) and on scale 5 (Mf) (for females) remained. The authors concluded that the L-scale differences, which have appeared in many studies, represented a genuine characteristic of the Mexican-American group and probably reflected a tendency toward conventionality and concern for making a good impression. The stereotype of more macho Mexican-American males was not upheld; only the Mexican-American female subjects were more masculine in their interest patterns than were the Anglo-American women.

A study of college students cited by Velásquez (1984) was conducted by Guzmán (1970), who reported MMPI results for a sample of 30 Mexican-American males. The profile code for this group was as follows: '48 7902-1365/ 'F-LK/. A comparison group of 30 male Anglo-American students was also tested; results from this group were not available in the summary provided.

McGill (1980) tested women receiving Aid to Families with Dependent Children in two Texas cities; the group included 78 Anglo-Americans, 50 blacks, and 51 Mexican-Americans. It was his hypothesis that all of these individuals would be seeking help because of similar social and economic pressures and that racial differences, if significant, would be related to some other factor such as education, social environment, or degree of assimilation into the dominant culture. Profile codes for the three groups were as follows:

Anglo-Americans	'869-723015/	-FL/K
Blacks	'86-9702 135/	'F-/LK
Mexican-Americans	'28-67053 19/	-FLK/

An analysis of covariance by race with education as the covariate revealed that the educational variable was related to scales 5 (Mf) and 0 (Si). After covarying on education, Anglo-Mexican differences were noted on four scales (Mexicans were higher on L, K, and scale 5 and lower on scale 9). No Anglo-black differences were obtained. It was the author's conviction that the differences found in the incidence of mental disorders in racial minorities might well be a function of the proportion of members of those groups who share economic and social stress. Further research, with special attention given to the specific environmental factors involved, would be needed to clarify the source of these differences.

A similar concern for the importance of social and cultural factors underlying deviant responses on the MMPI by Mexican-Americans was noted by Goldberg (1980). Using only scale 4 (Pd) with a group of 20 injured Mexican-American men applying for worker compensation, he recommended the weighting of these factors as a way of arriving at a less biased scoring and interpretation, on the assumption that both ethnicity and the sequelae of disability led to misinterpretation of the scale's results.

Alcoholic and Drug Treatment Groups

Several studies of groups of alcohol and drug abusers include Hispanic-Americans in their reports. In the study by Page and Bozlee (1982) that was discussed earlier (see table G-12), the small group of Hispanic-American VA alcoholic patients from the state of Washington showed the most deviant profile of the three ethnic groups, with much higher elevation on scale 2 (D). The profile, in fact, suggests a different type of alcoholic pattern than that of the whites or of the Indians.

Herl (1976) tested a group of heroin addicts applying to a methadone maintenance program in Phoenix, Arizona. Two male groups were studied, one composed of 31 Mexican-Americans and the other of 24 Anglo-Americans, as well as a small mixed group of 15 females. Scale score data are not available, but MMPI scale elevations greater than a T score of 69 were more common among the Anglo-American men. In terms of presenting psychopathology, both male groups revealed "emotional disturbance" in about one-half of the cases, whereas the women more frequently reported symptoms typical of "characterological disorder." Mexican-American men were also less well educated, more likely to be married, and more likely to have spent time in prison than the male Anglo-Americans in the study.

At the Dallas VA Medical Center, Penk, Robinowitz, Roberts, Dolan, and Atkins (1981b) reported on a large group of first-admission male heroin addicts, the subjects in each group averaging four years of heavy drug use. The authors conjectured that the Mexican-American addicts, as well as the blacks, would appear comparatively better adjusted than the whites. They based this hypothesis on the notion that the cultural disparity for minority groups led to a different type of individual being subject to addiction: better adjusted, better educated, and from a higher socioeconomic level. They also predicted from earlier studies done with Mexican-Americans who were prisoners or psychiatric patients (some of these studies are reviewed below) that differences on some specific MMPI scales would be found: higher scores on L and K because of a reluctance to admit symptoms and a defensive attitude, and lower scale 5 (Mf) scores consistent with a "macho" image. Table G-20 in the appendix gives the means and standard deviations for the 161 whites, 268 blacks, and 41 Hispanics. Although the profile patterns were not markedly different, the Hispanics did score significantly lower than the whites and the blacks on scales 5 (Mf) and 9 (Ma) (and on scale 4 [Pd] in comparison with the whites) and higher on the L scale. Even though group differences on K were not found (perhaps partly as the result of using an upper cutting score on K as one of the validity measures), the other expectations were fulfilled. The different meaning of such deviant behavior as drug addiction in a minority culture and its relationship to the needs of its members were discussed.

Additional analyses of the Wiggins content scales for the MMPI were carried out by Dolan, Roberts, Penk, Robinowitz, and Atkins (1983), with results generally supportive of the hypothesis that minority addicts showed somewhat better adjustment than the majority group. The Hispanic-American subjects in their study scored significantly lower than whites on scales measuring social maladjustment and manifest hostility and lower than blacks on the scale for feminine interests. Thus, the complex interrelationships of socioeconomic status, education, and intragroup attitudes toward addiction with ethnic background must be considered in test interpretation with these groups.

Prisoner Groups

Three studies including Hispanic prisoners have been located. The first of these by Fisher (1967) included 108 Mexican-American, 182 black, and 492 white prisoners at a corrections reception center in southern California. Although the main focus of the Fisher study was on the Marlowe-Crowne Social Desirability Scale (Crowne & Marlowe, 1960) and MMPI means and standard deviations for the subgroups were not reported, the author concluded from the intercorrelations of the results from the two tests that both the blacks and the Mexican-Americans were significantly more defensive than were the white criminals.

Holland (1979) studied a group of male short-term felony offenders who were referred for assessment of suitability for probation. Data were presented for 396 whites and 114 Mexican-Americans; comparison was also made to a group of 208 black prisoners (see table G-21 in the appendix). The scores for the whites on scales 3 (Hy), 5 (Mf), and 6 (Pa) were significantly higher than those of the Mexican-Americans (and blacks were higher than the Mexican-American group on scales 4 [Pd], 5 [Mf], 7 [Pt], 8 [Sc], and 9[Ma]). Holland suggested that replicable profile correlates be identified for the major ethnic groups across different clinical populations before any consideration be given to a differential weighting procedure for minority profiles.

McCreary and Padilla (1977) also studied three ethnic groups of prisoners, all male misdemeanor offenders who were referred for presentencing psychiatric evaluations. Although some scale differences were found when the total groups were compared, a set of comparisons using smaller groups more carefully matched for educational and occupational level showed statistically significant differences only on the L and K scales (and the Over-controlled Hostility scale). These data (for the smaller matched groups of whites and blacks and of whites and Mexican-Americans) are to be found in table G-22 in the appendix.

Medical-Psychiatric Groups

Some research has been done with medical and psychiatric patients who were of Hispanic background. Ojeda (1980), in a study cited by Velásquez (1984), contrasted two groups of Mexican-American women (20 in each group). For those women who were abusive mothers, the mean profile code was as follows: 4826'317 90-5/ 'F-LK/. The comparison group of nonabusive mothers yielded a coded mean profile of '428 3670-195/ 'F-LK/. Anglo-American mothers were also included in this study, but these data were not available in the summary provided.

In a study of male VA patients in two hospitals in Texas, Selters (1973) first contrasted white, black, and Mexican-American psychiatric referrals who had been tested while in a general medical hospital. He later obtained MMPIs from another sample in a neuropsychiatric hospital. His results for the two sets of MMPI scores are presented in table G-23 in the appendix. In the first phase of the study, with differences in level of intelligence controlled statistically, significant differences between the whites and the Mexican-Americans were found only on the L and F scales (whites lower); whites were also lower than blacks on L, 5 (Mf), and 9 (Ma). Blacks also scored higher than Mexican-Americans on scale 5 and lower on scale 2 (D). In the second phase involving the groups in a psychiatric hospital, only the difference on L between whites and Mexican-Americans was significant when educational and occupational levels were controlled. The author noted a greater number of items that might be viewed as objectionable by minority members and therefore urged caution in the application of the test to such groups.

Plemons (1977) also directed his attention to Mexican- and Anglo-American psychiatric patients. He collected MMPIs, background information, and ratings of occupational levels from a sample drawn from a community mental health center in California. Table G-24 in the appendix provides, separately by sex, the means, both with and without K-corrections, for the two groups. When the K-corrected profiles are considered, only L and K showed statistically significant differences for the total groups, and Anglo-American males were higher on scale 5 (Mf) than the Mexican-American men. When the uncorrected scores are considered, however, Mexican-Americans were lower on scales 4 (Pd), 7 (Pt), and 9 (Ma). Plemons therefore recommended using uncorrected scores because he believed that K and L were inappropriate suppressor measures for this group. Inspection of the table, however, reveals that it is only the males among the Mexican-American group who were higher on K and on some of the clinical scales; using the uncorrected scale scores has the effect of reducing the elevation of these profiles (which are from psychiatric patients) to close to normal levels, whereas those from the Mexican-American women (and the two Anglo-American groups) remain about the same.

Plemons (1980) also reported on a large group of Mexican- and Anglo-American psychiatric outpatients (partially overlapping the cases in his 1977 study) in an effort to examine differences between these groups on the basic scales, with and without K, and some special scales as well. To try to assess the influence of level of acculturation of the Hispanic group and any possible relationship to MMPI scores, he divided his Mexican-American group into low, medium, and high levels of acculturation—that is, the extent to which they were judged by three clinicians to be adapted to the dominant culture. All MMPIs were administered in English. Although the basic profile scales did not show consistent relationship to level of acculturation (except for higher scale 5 [Mf] scores among the Mexican-American females), the groups did differ on some special MMPI scales: Mexican-Americans scored higher on scales measuring repression and prejudice and lower on scales measuring dominance, control, and social status. The author believed that the role of educational deprivation was perhaps more important than that of cultural background.

Quiroga (1972), surveying studies in the research literature in which Mexican-American and Anglo-American psychiatric groups were the subjects of investigation, found a consistent picture of psychotic Mexican-Americans scoring higher than Anglo-American psychotics on the L scale and scale 4 (Pd) and lower on scale 0 (Si) and nonpsychotic Hispanics scoring lower on scales 5 (Mf) and 0 (Si). He also developed a linear discriminant function to classify psychotic and nonpsychotic Hispanic groups, using a sample of psychiatric referrals at the University of Texas Medical Center. The initial classification rate of 84% dropped in cross-validation to 69%. He concluded that development of special norms would be a more fruitful approach than the use of the discriminant function.

In a study of low-income community mental health center patients, Lawson, Kahn, and Heiman (1982) reported MMPI results on a group of 60 European-Americans with a mean profile of 8″2476′3190-/ F′-L/K and a group of 25 Mexican-Americans with a mean profile of 8″64721′93-0/ F′-LK/. (Results were reported for combined-sex groups, hence scale 5 is not included in the codes.) Only two scales showed significant differences: Mexican-Americans scored higher on L and European-Americans were higher on scale 0 (Si). The two groups were also compared on a scale measuring attitudes toward hospitalization and psychopathology. The

Mexican-American group was more antagonistic on this measure, and the authors attributed their low rate of usage of this mental health facility to the greater prevalence of these negative attitudes.

A study by Frye (1973), cited by Velásquez (1984), was based on a sample of 275 psychiatric inpatients (113 of whom were Mexican-Americans). This same sample, slightly reduced, was reported by Hibbs, Kobos, and González (1979). These individuals were patients in a county hospital psychiatric unit in Texas that served medically indigent clients (see table G-25 in the appendix). The authors also analyzed scores across five age ranges and showed that the most deviant scores were usually those obtained from the youngest subjects. The interaction of ethnicity with sex was also noted, for example, in low scores on scale 1 (Hs) for Anglo-American women and in higher scores on scale 6 (Pa) for Mexican-American women.

The same large survey of records accumulated by the Roche Psychiatric Service Institute in 1978 that was previously noted in the discussion on Asian-Americans also provides some data on Hispanic psychiatric outpatients. In this case, "Hispanic" probably includes more than Mexican-Americans; that is, it is likely that at least Cubans and Puerto Ricans made up part of the group because it was a nationwide sample. These means and standard deviations can be found in table G-7 in the appendix, together with the large white comparison group and the scores of other minorities. The largest differences between the white and Hispanic groups occur on the L and F scales and on scales 1 (Hs) and 8 (Sc), with the addition of scale 5 (Mf) in the case of the women.

Summary

The preceding survey of research on the MMPI with various minority groups is not an exhaustive review of all that is available. New reports continue to appear in the journals and in the lists of theses and dissertations. Even with those available to us now, the picture is far from complete and resembles a jigsaw puzzle with only the first few pieces in place. Much more work will be required before the adequacy of the MMPI for use with minority individuals can be fairly judged. A valuable resource has recently become available in the form of a survey of work done on the test with various groups of Mexican-Americans, including most of the studies cited above. In his catalog, Velásquez (1984) has acknowledged that certain assumptions made by clinicians and researchers dealing with these individuals may go unquestioned and may result in misinterpretations of test results. Although he is primarily concerned with test-based judgments as applied to Hispanic groups, his concerns have broader implications for use of the MMPI with other minority groups discussed in the present chapter and in the previous discussion of black Americans as well. As Veláasquez sees it, the following assumptions are untested, and possibly unwarranted:

1. Differences in MMPI performance can be attributed solely to the factor of cultural or ethnic group membership.
2. Even when interactions are present, researchers continue to give greater importance to cultural group membership, based on past clinical stereotypes.
3. The Chicano as an ethnic group is homogeneous in its general make-up (i.e., socioeconomic status, education, etc.).
4. Acculturation level is not an important variable in MMPI performance.
5. MMPI cookbooks can be easily applied to all Chicano samples.
6. The etiology and distribution (i.e., base rate) of disorders for Chicanos is similar or equivalent to the general population. (1984, pp. 10-11)

The call for special norms for any given minority group (and the complaint that the standardization group did not include members of that minority) presents a special challenge in a country like the United States, which has an ethnically diverse population that is constantly growing and being assimilated at varying rates. Even a large-scale, new American sampling for the purpose of constructing new norms could only be expected to include a relatively small number of individuals from any particular ethnic background, and current complaints would not be adequately answered. If such special norms for minority groups are to be used, it would seem desirable for those psychologists most interested in the group in question to begin systematic collection of such data. Then it might become feasible to compare two profiles for each individual, one plotted on the usual norms (perhaps as a reflection of how the individual is viewed by the dominant culture) and another against the new minority-based standards (comparing him or her with the peer group). Even more valuable would be the collection of nontest correlates of MMPI scores, such as the code book correlates available for profile high points that are now widely used with the cultural majority. These compilations of information would greatly aid in the interpretation of high-scoring profiles.

There are many suggestions in the studies that have been cited in this chapter that adverse circumstances accompanying minority status in this country at the present time (primarily lower educational and economic levels) result in considerable stress and strain being put upon even "normal" minority individuals. This interpretation is supported by the fact that when clinical populations are considered, and majority and minority groups are more closely matched, many of these differences disappear. It seems plausible, then, that the MMPI is reflecting among normal minority individuals the increased difficulties they face in their daily lives. Rather than suppressing these differences statistically, it is to be hoped that continued study will throw some light on the nature of these stresses and the methods used to cope with them.

CHAPTER 4

Community Samples of Black and White Adults

W. Grant Dahlstrom, David Lachar, Malcolm D. Gynther, and James T. Webb

Two sizable groups of normal adult men and women were examined during the 1970s through surveys made in various locations in the eastern United States. Each subject in these two samples completed the MMPI and provided additional data on his or her background and recent history that provided a basis for evaluating the relationship between factors in the lives of these subjects and the ways in which the MMPI was answered. The primary concern is test differences between individuals who identified themselves as either black or white, but the additional data permit a more systematic analysis of other factors affecting racial or ethnic differences in MMPI responses. Although the methods of collecting the data in the two surveys were not identical, their general designs were sufficiently similar to make the kinds of comparisons envisioned here possible.

The Tri-State Sample of Black Adults

As part of a federally supported investigation of the relationship between personality characteristics and various patterns of abuse of prescription drugs (Wesson, Carlin, Adams, & Beschner, 1978; Keegan & Lachar, 1979), the MMPI was administered to both black and white polydrug abusers. Preliminary analyses of these data revealed MMPI differences between the samples of black and white adults that were generally consistent with the findings from other studies based upon selected samples of black and white subjects but unlike the findings from abusers of illicit drugs (see the summaries in chapter 2). In an effort to provide a more adequate basis for evaluating the role of ethnic membership in such analyses, a special project was initiated in which D. Lachar, M. D. Gynther, and W. G. Dahlstrom gathered data during 1976 on black adult men and women in three localities: metropolitan Detroit, Michigan; central North Carolina; and east central Alabama. Although the background data on these subjects (see table 4.1) indicated some geographic mobility, the men and women tested in these areas had spent their lives in close proximity to the places where they were tested.

Table 4.1. Description of the Tri-State Black Sample

	Male		Female	
Background	***N***	**%**	***N***	**%**
Age				
18-24	61	20.8	120	24.0
25-34	81	27.6	170	33.9
35-49	98	33.4	133	26.5
≧ 50	53	18.1	78	15.6
	293		501	
Education				
≦ 12	117	40.5	213	43.3
13-15	86	29.8	122	24.8
≧ 16	86	29.8	157	31.9
	289		492	
Type of Classes Attended				
Integrated	97	33.2	148	29.4
Segregated	195	66.8	355	70.6
	292		503	
Occupational Level (SES)				
I	80	27.3	120	23.9
II	79	27.0	134	26.6
III	107	36.5	156	31.0
IV	22	7.5	86	17.1
V	5	1.7	7	1.4
	293		503	
Region of Origin (Where Educated)				
Deep South	115	39.2	173	34.5
Mid South	98	33.4	215	42.8
North	80	27.3	114	22.7
	293		502	

	Male		Female	
Background	***N***	**%**	***N***	**%**
Region of Predominant Residence				
Deep South	108	36.9	164	32.6
Mid South	84	28.7	215	42.7
North	101	34.5	124	24.7
	293		503	
Community Size				
Rural	39	13.5	39	7.8
Town	40	13.9	65	13.1
Small city	85	29.5	208	41.9
Large city	40	13.9	81	16.3
Metropolitan	84	29.2	104	20.9
	288		497	
Marital Status				
Single	82	28.0	147	29.2
Married	182	62.1	255	50.7
Separated	3	1.0	21	4.2
Divorced	15	5.1	50	9.9
Widowed	11	3.8	30	6.0
	293		503	
Medical Problems Present				
No	256	87.4	434	86.3
Yes	37	12.6	69	13.7
	293		503	
Emotional Problems Present				
No	283	96.6	469	93.2
Yes	10	3.4	34	6.8
	293		503	

In each location, black examiners and supervisors were recruited to make the contacts, conduct the examinations, and gather the background information needed from each subject. Examiners were paid a standard amount ($2.50) for each subject who produced a valid MMPI protocol and completed questionnaire. Since no individual subject was asked to give his or her name, it was not possible to check back to obtain missing information; accordingly, the examiners were careful to have each subject provide a full MMPI answer sheet and completely fill out a background questionnaire (see Appendix A for the items included in the questionnaire).

The survey team members contacted a variety of church congregations, alumni groups, social and civic clubs, and other organizations made up of black adults. To each organization an appeal was made for volunteers to take part in the survey by completing the personality inventory and by providing the background data called for in the questionnaire. For each member of the organization who completed both instruments, the investigators were authorized to offer the organization treasury a standard sum of money ($5.00).

Almost all of the organizations contacted by the survey teams saw this offer as an opportunity to gain additional funds for their various needs and projects. Appeals to the membership usually brought out enthusiastic support for the survey and somewhat overly optimistic projections of attendance on the evenings when the testing was to be carried out. That is, the examiners would come prepared to test several dozen subjects and find far fewer in attendance than had been promised. The subjects who were examined, therefore, would seem to be those who were more closely identified with the particular organization (church, club, or union) than those who had originally indicated willingness to participate but who did not appear for the actual testing session. The precise effect of this kind of selection bias is difficult to assess, but it suggests that the subjects in this survey may be more responsible and altruistic than people in general. The members of the survey team, after encountering several disappointing showings at their test sessions, began to incorporate competitive elements into their appeal for more complete participation on the part of the membership of organizations that they contacted later (e.g., "The last church we approached had 35 members of the congregation show up, and we know you can do even better."). This kind of appeal seemed to be more effective in assuring a good turnout. All their appeals seemed to work better in contacts with college-educated subjects (alumnae of nursing schools, members of medical societies or civic booster organizations) than they did with men and women with less than a high school education. Accordingly, as will be shown below (see table 4.3), when the men and women in this survey are compared with the distribution of black adults in the U.S. census of 1970 on the basis of socioeconomic status, the sample shows a marked excess in the higher levels (professional and managerial) and a severe underrepresentation in the lower levels (semiskilled and unskilled or unemployed). The same bias appears in both the male and female samples.

The MMPI was administered by means of the standard group form test booklet with a separate answer sheet. Most subjects in the survey did not appear to have any difficulty in completing this form of the inventory, but in the test sessions carried out in North Carolina the occasional subject who had difficulty reading the items was taken aside and given a tape-administered form (the standard tape version developed by the Psychological Corporation). The use of the oral administration may have led to somewhat lower scores on the F (infrequency) scale of the MMPI from men and women examined in this locale.

Table 4.1 provides additional information about the men and women who constitute the samples of black adults in this study. More subjects, proportionately, came from North Carolina than from the other two locales, and a disproportionate number of them were women. The modal age of these subjects fell in the mid-thirties, with the men ranging a little older than the women. More of the North Carolina subjects were married, and married to each other, than was true of the volunteers from Michigan and Alabama. Although most subjects were native to the region where they were tested, the small amount of migration noted was from the Deep and Middle South to the North. Only about a fourth of these men and women were living in rural areas or small towns, the rest were in medium-sized cities or metropolitan areas. Those in the North also tended to earn larger cash incomes, although the levels of earnings in all three locales were substantially below the average annual incomes for the nation as a whole at that time. Fewer subjects from North Carolina were currently under the care of a physician than those from Michigan or Alabama, but more reported some period of time in jail or prison.

The Two-State Sample of White Adults

In a project unrelated to the survey described above, James Webb and his students at Ohio University in Athens carried out a survey of adults in southeastern Ohio and west central West Virginia during 1973. Data from this survey were summarized by Diehl (1977). Three communities were included: two small towns in Ohio and a midsized city in West Virginia. These places were chosen for the survey on the basis of their convenient proximity to the university in Athens and their typicality in respect to the majority of midwestern communities. Each locality had a range of businesses and industries, and all were generally prosperous and thriving at the time of the survey. No large metropolitan area was included, but some of the people working in these communities lived in distinctly rural circumstances. Because these localities did not provide the investigators with enough numbers of racial minorities, the sample of adults obtained through this survey is restricted to Caucasian men and women.

Volunteers for the survey were recruited through contacts with various church congregations, city departments (police, fire, and jail personnel), civic groups, National Guard units, and community organizations. Each subject completed, in order, a demographic questionnaire (see Appendix A), the Shipley-Hartford (Institute of Living) Intelligence Scale (1940), the Holmes and Rahe Social Readjustment Rating Scale (1967) (entitled the "Life Events Checklist"; see Appendix A), and the MMPI. The SRRS was completed on the basis of events in the individual's life during the previous six months. No monetary incentive was offered either to the individual subject or to the organization. No one was asked to give his or her name, and confidentiality was assured for any information provided to the survey team. The standard group form booklet and answer sheets of the MMPI were used. The background characteristics of this sample of men and women are summarized in table 4.2.

Table 4.2. Description of the Two-State White Sample

	Male		Female	
Background	***N***	**%**	***N***	**%**
Age				
18-24	47	25.0	35	15.4
25-34	58	31.0	53	23.2
35-49	50	26.6	70	30.7
≧ 50	33	17.6	70	30.7
	188		228	
Education				
≦ 12	92	48.9	132	57.9
13-15	38	20.2	41	18.0
≧ 16	58	31.0	55	24.1
	188		228	
IQ Level				
≦ 100	28	15.7	10	5.0
101-109	48	27.0	31	15.3
110-118	60	33.7	87	43.1
≧ 119	42	23.6	74	36.6
	178		202	
Occupational Level				
I	12	6.4	12	5.3
II	49	26.1	56	24.6
III	73	38.8	114	50.0
IV	49	26.1	39	17.1
V	5	2.7	7	3.1
	188		228	
Marital Status				
Single	34	18.1	29	12.7
Married	150	80.0	169	74.1
Separated	0	0.0	1	0.4
Divorced	2	1.1	12	5.3
Widowed	2	1.1	17	7.5
	188		228	
SRRS Levels				
≦ 99	87	47.5	121	57.9
100-199	67	36.6	59	28.2
≧ 200	29	15.8	29	13.9
	183		209	
Medical Problems Present				
No	175	95.6	200	95.7
Yes	8	4.4	9	4.3
	183		209	
Emotional Problems Present				
No	151	82.5	170	81.3
Yes	32	17.5	39	18.7
	183		209	

As was true in the survey of black adults, more women volunteered to participate than men. The numbers of subjects in both the highest and lowest occupational levels were underrepresented in these samples in comparison with the data from the 1970 U.S. census (table 4.3). The ages of the volunteeers ranged from 16 to 84 years, with the modal age for both men and women in the late thirties. More of the subjects in this survey were married than was true of the volunteers in the black adult survey.

The number of years of schooling ranged from six grades completed to four years of postcollege work, with the average level nearly two years beyond high school graduation. The performance of these subjects on the Shipley scale also showed a wide range, from 80 to 130 IQ points, with the mean falling about a standard deviation above the national average. Both of these indicators suggest that the men and women in this survey were distinctly above average in intellective and academic performance but somewhat lower than the tri-state black sample.

Table 4.3. Percentage Distribution of Socioeconomic Status of Research Samples Compared with U.S. Census Figures

	White			Black		
	1970	Two-State (1973)		1970	Tri-State (1976)	
Occupation	Census	Male	Female	Census	Male	Female
I (Professional, technical)	14%	6%	5%	6%	27%	24%
II (Managerial, administrative)	11	26	25	3	27	27
III (Clerical, sales)	35	39	50	26	36	31
IV (Semiskilled)	22	26	17	30	8	17
V (Unskilled, unemployed)	18	3	3	35	2	1
	100	100	100	100	100	100

MMPI Comparisons of Black and White Community Samples

The MMPI answer sheets were carefully screened for excessive numbers of item omissions, double answers, or other evidence of failure to comply with the general instructions given to participants in these testing surveys. The protocols were then scored on the standard scales of the MMPI plus a number of special content and research measures. Any MMPI protocol that had a score beyond 25 raw score points on the F scale, a raw score difference on F minus K greater than 16, or 30 or more unanswered items was excluded from further analysis.

The raw scores were converted into T-score values from the appropriate sex norms based on the original means and standard deviations obtained from the Minnesota adults who participated in the development and standardization of the MMPI during the early 1940s. Varying amounts of the appropriate K-scale weights were added to the raw scores of scales 1 (Hs), 4 (Pd), 7 (Pt), 8 (Sc), and 9 (Ma) before the T-score values were determined. For some special analyses, the profile pattern of each subject was coded by means of the total (Welsh) coding method (see Appendix B). In addition, a number of item analyses were carried out on these test protocols.

Table 4.4. Effects of Sex and Race on MMPI Basic and Special Scales Compared by Multivariate Analyses of Variance

Variable	No. of Levels	df	*F*	*p*
	Standard Scales, A, R, and Es			
Sex	2	16,1193	41.81	.0001
Race	2	16,1193	19.91	.0001
Sex X race		16,1193	4.05	.0001
	Wiggins Content Scales			
Sex	2	13,1196	11.92	.0001
Race	2	13,1196	42.27	.0001
Sex X race		13,1196	8.66	.0001
	Race-Related Scales			
Sex	2	2,1206	2.30	.1004
Race	2	2,1206	426.23	.0001
Sex X race		2,1206	7.91	.0004

The standard scores from the MMPI for the white and black men and women were compared by means of two separate multivariate analyses of variance (MANOVAs) in which the relationship of the scores to race and sex were examined. In one MANOVA, the dependent variables were the 13 basic scales (validity and clinical) of the standard MMPI profile plus Welsh's (1956) factor scales A (Anxiety) and R (Repression) and Barron's (1953) Es (Ego strength) scale; the second set comprised all 13 of Wiggins's (1966) content scales. The results of these overall MANOVAs are shown in table 4.4. Both sex and race membership are significant factors in the patterns of scores on both sets of MMPI scales. Interestingly, in spite of the separate conversion tables for the T-score values for men and women, sex membership is still a significant contributor to scale score differences, especially for the analyses involving the basic MMPI scales. A third MANOVA was carried out on two additional scales developed on the basis of items that showed the largest differences between black and white subjects: Costello's Black-White (B-W) scale (1977) and White's Race-sensitive (Rs) scale (1974) (see the discussion of these two lines of research in chapter 2). In the present samples, racial membership was highly significant but gender was not a reliable basis for differentiation on these two research scales. Since these MANOVAs generated overall *F* values that were highly significant, the specific findings on the various component scales merit closer examination.

Table 4.5. Means, Standard Deviations, and *F* Ratios of MMPI Basic and Special Scales for White and Black Males and Females

	White Males (N = 188)		Black Males (N = 293)		White Females (N = 228)		Black Females (N = 503)		Sex Effect		Race Effect		Sex × Race Effect	
Scale	Mean	S.D.	Mean	S.D.	Mean	S.D.	Mean	S.D.	*F*	*p*	*F*	*p*	*F*	*p*
L	48.1	7.5	51.7	7.9	48.9	6.3	49.9	7.7	4.41	.05	16.40	.001	2.98	
F	54.9	10.7	58.9	11.9	52.2	7.5	58.3	12.0	6.07	.05	55.34	.001	2.31	
K	54.2	8.8	53.8	8.8	55.9	9.4	51.5	9.2	0.29		18.27	.001	12.92	.001
Hs	55.0	10.3	58.0	11.4	52.1	9.0	53.5	9.5	35.48	.001	13.08	.001	1.58	
D	57.0	11.8	57.7	10.1	51.9	10.2	54.2	9.4	46.17	.001	5.77	.05	1.65	
Hy	57.4	8.5	57.3	9.3	56.6	8.4	54.3	9.3	11.15	.001	5.04	.05	3.76	
Pd	58.2	11.3	61.5	10.5	57.4	10.1	60.1	10.2	2.82		21.76	.001	0.22	
Mf	59.4	10.1	62.2	9.4	46.0	9.1	51.7	8.8	450.27	.001	56.74	.001	6.60	.01
Pa	56.5	12.5	55.9	11.4	55.4	8.5	57.1	12.5	0.02		0.64		2.42	
Pt	56.8	11.7	57.4	10.1	53.8	9.0	54.3	9.5	23.54	.001	0.81		0.01	
Sc	56.2	13.4	62.7	14.1	55.2	9.5	60.3	13.4	4.61	.05	52.04	.001	0.71	
Ma	56.9	11.1	63.7	11.1	55.9	9.6	60.3	11.4	10.51	.001	68.57	.001	2.88	
Si	52.3	10.5	52.0	7.8	51.7	9.6	54.7	8.4	3.84	.05	5.68	.05	9.27	.01
A	49.2	9.4	50.2	9.3	45.9	9.9	50.0	10.2	9.09	.01	16.75	.001	6.22	.05
R	51.5	9.1	50.7	9.6	49.2	9.6	48.3	9.9	16.01	.001	2.14		0.01	
Es	55.7	9.8	50.0	10.0	55.6	10.9	51.7	9.5	1.89		62.57	.001	2.24	
ORG	50.1	9.5	53.7	10.9	47.2	10.1	51.8	11.0	13.82	.001	38.76	.001	0.54	
HEA	50.7	9.4	54.7	9.9	47.5	9.6	52.7	10.0	18.75	.001	56.93	.001	1.05	
DEP	49.8	10.0	51.1	9.3	46.5	9.8	51.0	10.9	7.51	.01	20.77	.001	6.60	.01
MOR	48.2	9.7	48.1	9.0	45.1	10.4	48.3	10.2	5.73	.05	6.52	.01	7.52	.01
SOC	52.3	11.8	51.2	8.3	47.2	10.4	49.6	8.4	34.09	.001	1.36		9.14	.01
HOS	48.7	8.8	49.4	9.0	47.4	8.9	51.5	10.3	0.54		17.35	.001	8.43	.01
FAM	51.3	11.5	57.0	11.1	51.2	10.9	58.1	10.7	0.58		88.83	.001	0.80	
AUT	48.6	10.5	53.6	9.4	46.5	9.5	56.1	9.2	0.06		155.57	.001	15.38	.001
FEM	50.7	10.2	59.5	9.6	51.5	9.1	50.4	8.5	54.64	.001	46.54	.001	75.61	.001
PHO	52.4	10.8	56.9	10.4	48.2	9.7	55.7	9.4	19.68	.001	98.28	.001	6.34	.01
PSY	49.2	8.8	56.9	11.1	49.5	9.1	58.8	14.5	2.14		132.06	.001	1.13	
HYP	51.6	8.1	53.1	9.3	50.0	8.9	51.9	10.0	6.17	.05	8.20	.001	0.13	
REL	51.3	10.0	54.5	9.5	51.0	9.7	53.6	9.0	1.00		25.14	.001	0.33	

As was expected, the comparisons involving individual scales showed numerous significant differences; see the results in table 4.5, where the means and standard deviations of the white and black men and women on these various scales are listed, together with the corresponding *F* values obtained from the contrasts involving race and sex as well as their interaction in these MANOVAs. In figures 4.1 through 4.4 are plotted the mean MMPI profiles of the white men, black men, white women, and black women, respectively. With the single exception of the mean on scale 5 (Mf) for white women, these four groups of subjects score higher than the Minnesota normal men and women on every clinical scale in the basic MMPI profile. These elevations range from a few T-score points on scale 0 (Si) to nearly one-and-one-half standard deviations for black men on scale 8 (Sc). When the four groups are compared with each other, however, the average differences among black and white men and women in these surveys are less salient than their respective deviations from the MMPI test norms.

The most deviant mean profile ('9854-127360/ -FKL/) was obtained from the black men. These subjects departed by over one standard deviation from the norms for males on scales 4 (Pd), 5 (Mf), 8 (Sc), and 9 (Ma). In general, this pattern of deviations is consistent with the findings in previous studies involving samples of black males as summarized in chapter 2. The size of the elevation of scale 5 (Mf), however, is surprising because this scale is not usually prominent in the mean profiles of normal black male subjects. The pattern of scores in the mean profile for black women is similar ('894-6037215/-FKL/); the deviations from the norms for females also exceed one standard deviation on scales 4 (Pd), 8 (Sc), and 9 (Ma). In this pattern of scores, too, the elevation on scale 5 (Mf) (although not prominent in the code for the mean profile) is rather high. (The level of scale 5 in figure 4.3 for white women is more typical for such samples, falling substantially below the Minnesota-based norms.)

The mean profile for white males (-5432976810/ -FK/L) contains no elevation over one standard deviation from the norms for males, but it shows generally upward deviations on all scales (except the L scale). The highest score is on scale 5 (Mf), which is also unusual in samples of normal American men. The mean profile for white women (-439687 120/5-KF/L) is the least deviant of the four groups, but it shows relatively small upward deviations on all scales except the L scale and scale 5.

The results of these preliminary analyses, both in respect to the mean MMPI profiles of the four groups and the specific differences related to sex and race membership, reflect the general characteristics of these samples that were noted earlier. Since the two racial groups are not closely

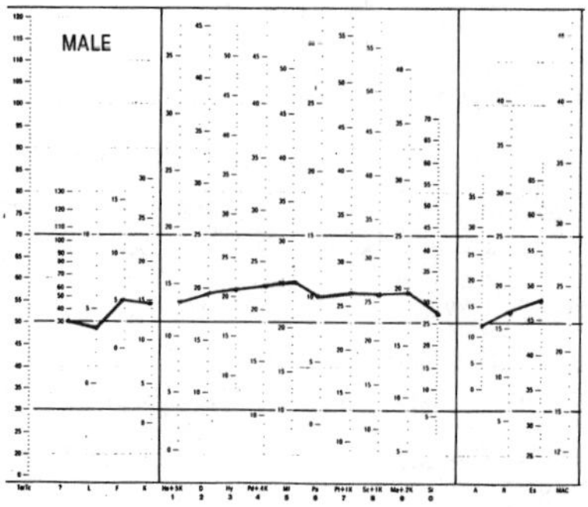

Figure 4.1. Mean profile of two-state white male cases ($N = 188$).
Code: -5432976810/ -FK/L.

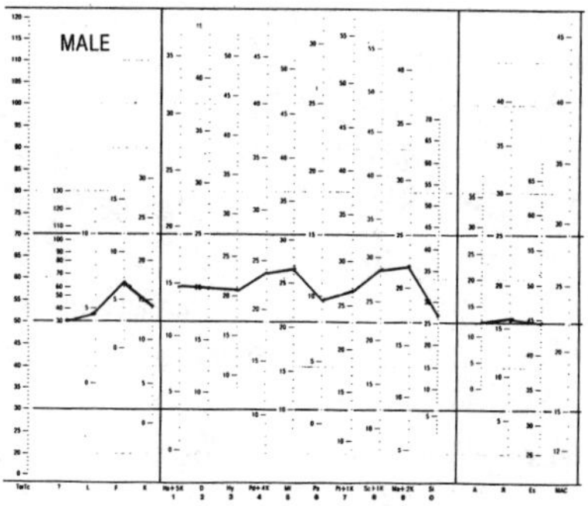

Figure 4.2. Mean profile of tri-state black male cases ($N = 293$).
Code: '9854-127360/ -FKL/.

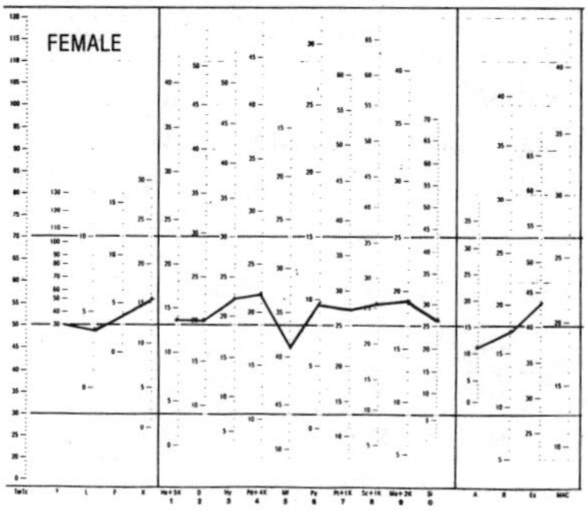

Figure 4.3. Mean profile of two-state white females cases ($N = 228$).
Code: -439687 120/5 -KF/L.

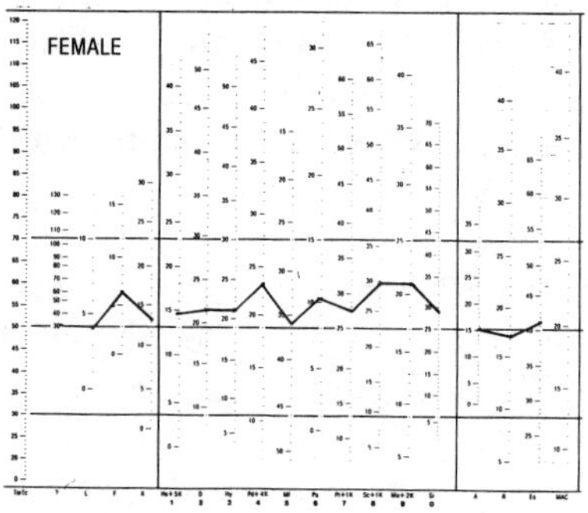

Figure 4.4. Mean profile of tri-state black female cases ($N = 503$).
Code: '894 6037215/ -FK/L.

comparable in regard to many important background features, more careful and detailed analyses of the data are needed to clarify the nature and extent of these and other differences in test performance that may be reflected in the behavior of the research subjects. These analyses will be reported in the next three chapters.

Application of Race-Related MMPI Scales

Research on ethnic differences on the MMPI has led to the publication of at least two special scales based on item analyses of the differences in endorsements by black and white adults (see chapter 2). White (1974) gathered data from black and white undergraduates at the University of Missouri in Columbia to develop the Rs scale, by means of which he proposed to identify black subjects whose response patterns were sufficiently different from the MMPI standardization norms to require corrections applied to selected clinical scales. (See the presentation in chapter 6 of the present volume.) The item composition of this 27-item scale is shown in Appendix C. Costello (1973, 1977) based his analyses on the item-endorsement differences between black and white psychiatric patients. His B-W scale is made up of 32 items (see Appendix C). In spite of the similarity in scale construction, only six items of the B-W scale overlap with White's Rs scale. (See the discussion in chapter 7 of these item differences.)

The MMPI protocols from the white and black men and women in the two-state and tri-state surveys were scored on each of these scales. (The overall results of the MANOVA that was carried out on these data were reported in table 4.4.) The means and standard deviations for these four groups on the B-W and Rs scales are listed in table 4.6. The white men and women endorsed on the average about one-fourth of the items on the B-W scale. Their means were a little lower than the scores of the white male police cadets reported by Costello (1977) in his normal comparison group (mean of 9.7 with a standard deviation of 3.0). The black men and women, however, ranged five to seven points higher than the white men and women with somewhat larger dispersions as well. Their means and standard deviations were quite similar to the scores earned by the black police cadets reported by Costello (mean of 13.4 with a standard deviation of 3.9).

The results of the analyses of the Rs scale were comparable to the pattern of findings on the B-W scale. That is, whereas the white men and women on the average answered about one-third of the items in the significant direction, both the black men and the black women endorsed over one-half of them. The black men and women were also more variable

Table 4.6. Means, Standard Deviations, and *F* Ratios on Two MMPI Race-Related Scales for White and Black Males and Females

	White Males (*N* = 188)		Black Males (*N* = 293)		White Females (*N* = 228)		Black Females (*N* = 503)		Sex Effect		Race Effect		Sex × Race Effect	
Scale	Mean	S.D.	Mean	S.D.	Mean	S.D.	Mean	S.D.	*F*	*p*	*F*	*p*	*F*	*p*
B-W	9.1	3.0	15.7	3.8	8.6	3.2	15.3	4.3	4.43	.05	802.50	.001	0.09	
Rs	8.5	4.0	13.2	4.4	7.1	3.7	13.7	4.6	2.24		456.77	.001	12.22	.001

Note. The B-W scale (Costello, 1977) contains 32 items; the Rs scale (White, 1974) contains 27 items.

on the Rs scale than were their white counterparts. The white undergraduate subjects in White's original study scored on the average a little lower than the two-state white adults (with means of 8.1 for males and 7.3 for females and with standard deviations of 3.8 and 3.5, respectively). The black students in White's study also scored a little lower than the black men and women in the tri-state sample, earning means of 13.0 for men and 12.3 for women and with standard deviations of 4.1 and 4.3 on Rs, respectively.

Table 4.7. Accuracy of Identification of Racial Membership of Normal Adult Subjects by Use of the Special Race-Related Scales of the MMPI

Scale	Male Samples (Actual)		Female Samples (Actual)	
	B-W Scale			
Predicted	Black	White	Black	White
White	36.6%	64.1%	36.3%	59.5%
Black	63.4	35.9	63.7	40.5
	Rs Scale			
Predicted	Black	White	Black	White
White	37.3	67.5	41.5	70.6
Black	62.7	32.5	58.5	29.4
	B-W and Rs Combined			
Predicted	Black	White	Black	White
White	20.5	86.6	21.5	85.5
Black	79.5	13.4	78.5	14.5

With differences on both special scales as large and consistent as these data reveal and with so little item overlap between the two measures, it was important to evaluate the extent to which these scores, separately and in combination, could correctly classify the test subjects by ethnic membership. Accordingly, three discriminant functions were computed (for each sex separately) in an attempt to classify black and white adults using B-W, Rs, and a combination of B-W and Rs. Table 4.7 summarizes the results of these analyses. Each scale separately identified the actual racial membership of the men and women in samples with an accuracy well beyond chance. Although the differences in relative accuracy for each race between the two race-related measures were not large, the B-W scale was slightly more accurate in identifying black adults and the Rs scale was more accurate in categorizing white subjects. This differential accuracy, together with the increased reliability afforded by the use of twice as many items, no doubt accounts for the finding that the multiple discriminant functions for the two sex groups based on scores from both scales classified these subjects into ethnic subgroups with an accuracy of over 80 percent. The accuracy of the combined functions was a little higher for classifying white subjects than for identifying black subjects, again because of the differential accuracy noted above. The potential usefulness of scales of this sort in other than normal populations is discussed in chapter 6.

Configural Patterns among the Basic Scales

Since usage of the information provided by the MMPI has traditionally relied not only on the T-score elevation of individual scales but also on the patterning among the basic scales on the test profile, several additional analyses were carried out on the codes obtained from these same research groups. As noted previously, each subject's profile was summarized in coded form. The frequency of the various combinations of the two highest scores (without regard to elevation) in these profiles was tabulated; the percentage of each high-point pair was calculated and summarized in tables B-1 through B-4 in the appendix.

A few general trends can be seen in those tabulations. For example, scale 4 (Pd) occupies the first or second highest position most frequently in profiles from white women, but scale 5 (Mf) is the most frequent scale in these positions among the profiles from the white men. In the profiles from the black adults, scale 9 (Ma) is most frequent in the first or second position in profiles from the men, but scales 4 (Pd) and 9 (Ma) are equally prominent in profiles from the women. As is clear from an inspection of the data presented in Appendix B, however, the incidence of particular high-point pairs is generally so low as to make any direct group comparisons of this sort too variable and imprecise. One solution to this limitation is to group the various codes into code types or, even more broadly, into code-type categories.

One standard approach to the definition of both code types and broad categories of code types has been developed by Lachar (1974), based upon the psychiatric diagnoses most often assigned to cases with particular code patterns. Using the total code (but omitting scale 5), this method is based both on levels of elevation of the clinical scales and on combinations of the two most highly elevated clinical scales (codes with entries to the left of the prime). The Lachar method divides the profiles into those that are *invalid* (profiles with F-scale elevations greater than a raw score of 25, or F minus K raw score greater than 16); *normal* (no clinical scale at a primed level); pathological (*neurotic*, *characterological*, or *psychotic*, depending upon the scale or scale pair greater than a T score of 69); or *other* (indeterminate). Some of the pathological types are formed by single scales (the so-called spikes) that exceed a score of 69; most are defined by scale pairs (without regard to order), both of which are at the primed level or beyond. (See the entries in table B-5 in the appendix for the specific combinations in the code that fall into the various code-type categorics.) Additional applications of this category system have been made by Lachar, Klinge, and Grisell (1976); Lachar, Schooff, Keegan, and Gdowski (1978); and Lachar and Sharp (1979).

Table 4.8. Percentages of Code-Type Categories in Three Normal Adult Samples

Code-Type Category	Minnesota White	Two-State White	Tri-State Black	*p* 1 vs. 2	*p* 1 vs. 3	*p* 2 vs. 3
		Males				
	($N = 199$)	($N = 190$)	($N = 306$)			
Invalid						
(F − K > 16 and F > 25)	0.5	1.1	4.2	...	.01	.05
Normal limits	78.4	53.7	40.5	.01	.01	.05
Neurotic	11.1	14.7	11.8	...	...	...
Characterological	5.0	20.5	22.5	.01	.01	...
Psychotic	4.0	6.3	18.3	...	.01	.01
Other	1.0	3.7	2.6	.05	...	...
		Females				
	($N = 277$)	($N = 231$)	($N = 526$)			
Invalid						
(F − K > 16 and F > 25)	0.0	1.3	4.4	...	.01	.05
Normal limits	78.3	66.7	53.0	...	.01	.05
Neurotic	9.4	6.5	4.9	...	.05	...
Characterological	4.0	15.6	16.0	.01	.01	...
Psychotic	4.3	6.9	17.9	...	.01	.01
Other	4.0	3.0	3.8	...	...	...

Note. Percentages are based on reduced *N* values after protocols with 30 or more unanswered items were removed from further analysis.

Table B-5 in the appendix reports the code-type classification of the profiles that constitute the Minnesota normative and the two contemporary normal adult samples described earlier. Table 4.8 presents the chi-square (goodness of fit) analyses of the relative frequencies of code-type categories across same-sex samples. These analyses were conducted in a pairwise fashion to suggest the primary source of the sample differences obtained. When both contemporary samples differed in the same direction from the Minnesota normative sample, but did not differ from each other, these results could be interpreted to reflect the results of cultural and societal changes from the late 1930s to the 1970s (change in cohort). When both white samples differed from the contemporary black sample, but did not differ from each other, these results could be interpreted to reflect cultural, experiential, and/or linguistic differences that are subsumed under the classification of race.

The code-type data summarized in table 4.8 are based upon records with fewer than 30 items omitted. The numbers of records that were found to be invalid based upon rather generous limits on the F score (a raw score higher than 25) alone or in combination with the K score (a raw score difference on F minus K larger than 16) were quite small, but both contemporary groups had more than did the original groups of Minnesota men and women (especially was this true of the black adults). More than three-quarters of the original Minnesota adults (both men and women) showed no elevation on the clinical scales as high as a T score of 70, falling into the category of a normal-limits profile in the Lachar typology. Only two-thirds of the contemporary white women had profiles in this range, and barely more than half of the white men and black women showed this level of profile patterning. A majority of the records from the black men fell outside the normal limits in the Lachar schema.

Analysis of the frequency of profile patterns associated with neurotic, characterological, and psychotic diagnoses in these three samples yielded statistical patterns that were more easily interpreted. Although there appear to be no appreciable differences in frequency for neurotic codes, both contemporary samples obtained a significantly greater number of characterological code-type profiles than the Minnesota normative sample, suggesting a cohort effect. The contemporary black normative sample obtained a significantly greater number of psychotic code-type profiles than either of the white samples, reflecting a possible race effect. The analysis of individual code types indicated a greater number of profiles with an isolated elevation on scale 4 (Pd) or on scale 9 (Ma) (both characterological types) in both contemporary samples and a greater frequency of psychotic code types (6-8/8-6 and 8-9/9-8) in the contemporary black sample. (See table B-5 in the appendix.)

The reasons for the increase in characterological profiles within contemporary samples are far from clear. For example, they may be accounted for by a gradual change in meaning or interpretation and hence validity of certain items in the Pd and Ma scales. (See the discussion in chapter 7.) Or they may reflect an actual increase in traits traditionally associated with Pd and Ma scale elevations. Similarly, the differences in frequency of profile patterns associated with a psychotic diagnosis require further exploration. As Pritchard and Rosenblatt (1980a) have noted, it is possible that the base rate of actual pathology in the general population is higher for American black adults, but it seems unlikely that nearly 20% of this contemporary black sample actually functioned at a psychotic level, since the process of sample collection seemed to assure community acceptance and participation of our survey subjects. Also, the sample demographics demonstrated that this contemporary black group was characterized by a greater educational and vocational attainment than that characteristic of the national black census population.

Summary

During the mid-1970s, two community-based samples of American adults were tested by means of the MMPI, one made up of black men and women, the other of white men and women. Although the surveys were not carried out in identical ways, the general designs were sufficiently similar to permit some direct comparisons with one another and with data from a sample of men and women who served as the standardization group for the MMPI just before World War II. The contemporary white adults were drawn from Ohio and West Virginia and the black men and women were tested in Michigan, North Carolina, and Alabama. Both samples ranged widely over age amd educational and occupational levels.

Preliminary analyses, on both the basic profile measures and on several research scales, of the MMPI scores that were obtained from the white and black men and women indicate that these subjects show many of the features that have been reported in the large research literature on black and white differences as summarized in chapter 2. Statistically significant differences between these four groups appeared on several scales. Combinations of special MMPI measures, proposed by White and by Costello as race-related scales, assigned these research subjects on the basis of race membership with a high degree of accuracy. Thus, it seemed clear that the test data from these samples amply demonstrate the kinds of variations between the races of both sexes that have been the subject of MMPI research for the last 40 years. It remains to be examined in these samples, however, whether these differences appear over all ages, at all educational or occupational levels, and without regard to geographic location, urban-rural residence, or medical and psychiatric status. These issues will be explored more extensively and in greater detail in the next three chapters.

CHAPTER 5

MMPI Correlates of the Demographic Characteristics of Black and White Normal Adults

W. Grant Dahlstrom, Luther A. Diehl, and David Lachar

The samples of black and white men and women available for study were gathered for somewhat different purposes (see chapter 4). Nevertheless, the timing of these surveys and their methods of subject selection were sufficiently similar to justify a few direct comparisons between them. Most pertinent to the present discussion, they may be compared in terms of major demographic characteristics and the ways in which each of these factors relates to component MMPI scales. In the following analyses and discussions, however, it should be kept in mind that these findings were not derived from a single, carefully planned sampling design. Accordingly, the results must be considered quite tentative; they may nevertheless be indicative of what could be gained by a properly designed national sample of adults from these two (and perhaps additional) ethnic groups. That is, the present set of comparisons may serve as a kind of pilot study for a more extensive investigation.

Methodological Issues

The authors of the MMPI took pains to avoid including any items in the basic scales of the test that would distinguish between criterion and normal subjects for one sex but not the other. In spite of their efforts, a number of the clinical scales revealed persistent differences in the way that normal men and women in the standardization group described themselves on the test. Accordingly, Hathaway and McKinley decided to use separate profile forms for each sex, using different raw score means and standard deviations to compute the T-score values for scales 1 (Hs), 2 (D), 3 (Hy), 5 (Mf), 7 (Pt), and 8 (Sc). In all subsequent assessments, then, men have been compared with men-in-general and women with women-in-general. Although this statistical technique rendered the T-score scaling more directly comparable across sex groups, it by no means eliminated sex differences on the MMPI, particularly in the patterns of profiles from each sex group. (See the tabulations of relative frequency of two-point high-point codes for each sex from various test populations listed in Appendix M of Dahlstrom, Welsh, & Dahlstrom, 1972.)

Although the age range of the subjects in the original standardization sample of Minnesota residents was 16 to 65 years, only a few subjects were younger than 20 or older than 60. The test authors found little need for separate T-score tables for the decades between 20 and 60 and hence provided only one set of T scores over this age range for each sex group. As usage of the test was extended downward into the adolescent range and upward into the older ages, some investigators urged the adoption of special T-score values for ages 14 through 17 and for adults aged 70 and over. In addition, many test users have used special T-score tables for males and females attending college. (See the T-score conversion tables for all of these groups on the basic scales in Appendix H of Dahlstrom, Welsh, & Dahlstrom, 1972.) In the case of college or university undergraduates, however, it is not clear whether these subjects are simply being compared with others who fall intermediate in age between the adolescent groups and adults-in-general or whether some additional socioeconomic and intellective considerations enter into such special profile scaling. That is, are college students merely late adolescents or are they manifesting some special status because of their educational achievements, occupational potential, or social class advantage?

Thus, in most applications the scores in the MMPI profile are based upon a standard sex-specific T-score format, with only occasional exceptions for age or educational placement. In most other countries in which the MMPI has been introduced, linguistic translation has been the only change; the scoring templates, T-score tables, and profile formats used in the United States have been retained. However, a few translations of the MMPI into foreign languages have also included the use of new T-score values that are based upon the administration of the test to samples of adult subjects in those countries (Butcher & Pancheri, 1976). In most instances, the traditional Minnesota-based profile has been used along with the new local T-score values; the practice is often to plot two parallel profiles on each test subject.

As indicated in chapters 2 and 3, there have been extended debates about the need for, or desirability of, additional norms as bases for computing T-score values for the MMPI profile. In addition to calls for more refined age breakdowns (Colligan, Osborne, Swenson, & Offord, 1983), there have been discussions about the significance of regional differences, marital status, religious affiliation, as well as cultural and ethnic backgrounds. As was suggested above in regard to college student T scores, the need for special norms for subjects from different socioeconomic levels has also been debated. The most persistent difficulty involved in resolving such issues is determining whether such special T-score procedures enhance or detract from the interpretive validity of the scales and the profile patterns for subjects from such groups. (Some of these problems will be further discussed in chapter 6 of this volume.) It should be borne in mind, however, that every change in T-score reference value introduces additional barriers to direct communication among test users about their findings.

In addition to the often emotional issues surrounding the question of special norms for different test applications, any investigation of the relation of MMPI findings to various background characteristics encounters methodological problems. For example, in a recent review of the relation of the MMPI results to age differences, Gynther (1979a) summed up the findings in the research literature as follows:

> Younger patients and normals obtain more peaks and higher scores on scales measuring nonconformity, rebelliousness, alienation, and energy level. Older patients and normals obtain more peaks and higher scores on scales measuring concern with health, introversion, and to a lesser extent scales involving depression and immaturity. Item analyses indicate that youthful subjects are sensation-seeking, restless, anxious for the approval of others, and have problems with impulse control. Older subjects appear to have more sedentary interests and to be more cautious and dutiful, while displaying less hostility and fewer family conflicts. The major personality dimension that differentiates the young from the elderly may be impulsivity-intellectual control rather than the traditional introversion-extraversion. . . . When one enlarges the scope of the task at hand and looks at data from other sources, one finds systematic increases and decreases, as well as rises and falls in various personality traits with age. Self-acceptance, self-control, socialization, dominance, and well-being all appear to increase from youth to middle age, then decline. Enthusiasm declines over the entire age range, while sensitiveness and control increase after the mid-30s. Needs for deference and affiliation increase with age, while needs for power and social activities decline. . . . All these results need to be qualified, however, owing to complex interactions with gender, health, status, ethnicity, and a host of other as yet uninvestigated change-variables (e.g., marriage, parenthood, etc.). That is, certain values may change with age for men, but not women. Early middle age may represent something different to blue-collar workers than it

> does to white-collar workers. Certain kinds of personalities, as yet largely unidentified, may respond favorably and successfully to retirement, while others of the same age despair and withdraw. (p. 64)

Gynther went on to note that the data that he was summarizing were almost exclusively from cross-sectional studies in which samples of individuals from each age level were being compared. In such research there is no assurance that younger individuals in these investigations will be just like the older persons when they reach the same age. In one of the rare exceptions to the cross-sectional design, Leon, Gillum, Gillum, and Gouze (1979) reported data on the same individuals retested at various intervals over a 30-year period. The subjects were college-level men in their mid-forties when first examined by means of the MMPI, so the course of any personality changes in their earlier years was not plotted in these data nor did these authors have any data bearing upon lower-status men or the comparable shifts in test findings on women. Nevertheless, it is reassuring to find not only considerable rank-order stability in the standing of the 77 men in this group (especially on scale 0 [Si]) but statistically significant shifts in the overall level of scores on the basic scales of the MMPI (especially on scale 2 [D]). That is, the findings from Leon et al. demonstrate both stability in the intragroup analysis and temporal changes in the group as a whole when compared with the basic test norms. The analyses of age effects to be reported below are based upon cross-sectional samples only; any differences will be confounded with any cohort effects that may be operating as well.

Data Analytic Procedures

For each of the MMPI scales previously examined for the effects of gender and race (see chapter 4), a stepwise multiple regression analysis was performed with age, education, and socioeconomic level as independent variables in addition to gender and racial membership. In this procedure, each independent variable (age, gender, education, race, and socioeconomic status) enters the analysis in the order of the magnitude of its contribution to the variance of the particular dependent variable (L, F, K, etc.) under investigation. For each dependent variable, the separate contribution of each of the independent variables is summarized as an R^2 value, together with a significance level indicating the probability that an R^2 value that large or larger would occur by chance given the number of degrees of freedom in the particular sample under study. The statistical

Table 5.1. R^2 **Values from a Stepwise Regression Analysis on Samples of Black and White Normal Adults (N = 1,196)**

Scale	Steps 1	2	3	4	5	R^2 Total
L	$.010_A^{***}$	$.014_R^{***}$	$.008_E^{***}$	$.006_G^{**}$	. . .	.038
F	$.071_E^{***}$	$.056_R^{***}$	$.025_A^{***}$	$.011_S^{***}$	$.005_G^{**}$	.168
K	$.052_E^{***}$	$.028_R^{***}$	$.006_S^{**}$	$.001_G$	. . .	.087
Hs	$.031_G^{***}$	$.013_E^{*}$	$.011_R^{***}$	$.011_A^{***}$	$.005_S^{*}$	.071
D	$.032_G^{***}$	$.020_E^{**}$	$.008_R^{***}$	$.005_S^{**}$	$.006_A^{**}$	.071
Hy	$.014_G^{***}$	$.005_R^{*}$	$.004_A^{*}$	$.001_E$	. . .	.024
Pd	$.042_A^{***}$	$.012_E^{*}$	$.013_R^{***}$	$.003_G$	$.002_S$	.072
Mf	$.256_G^{***}$	$.036_R^{***}$	$.004_E$	$.001_A$	. . .	.297
Pa	$.030_E^{***}$	$.014_A^{***}$	$.002_R$	$.001_S$	. . .	.047
Pt	$.021_S^{**}$	$.020_G^{***}$	$.008_A^{**}$	$.004_E^{*}$	$.001_R$	.054
Sc	$.039_R^{***}$	$.045_E^{***}$	$.027_A^{***}$	$.006_G^{**}$	$.005_S^{**}$	.122
Ma	$.056_A^{***}$	$.036_R^{***}$	$.012_G^{***}$	$.009_E^{**}$	. . .	.113
Si	$.057_E^{***}$	$.012_R^{***}$	$.016_S^{***}$	$.004_G^{*}$	$.003_A$	.092
A	$.057_E^{***}$	$.021_R^{***}$	$.012_S^{***}$	$.007_G^{**}$	. . .	.097
R	$.015_G^{***}$	$.004_A^{*}$	$.002_R$	$.001_S$	. . .	.022
Es	$.082_E^{***}$	$.058_R^{***}$	$.018_A^{***}$	$.019_S^{***}$	$.004_G^{*}$	.181
ORG	$.069_E^{***}$	$.038_R^{***}$	$.013_G^{***}$	$.013_A^{***}$	$.011_S^{***}$	.144
HEA	$.044_R^{***}$	$.040_E^{***}$	$.015_G^{***}$	$.009_S^{***}$	$.002_A$	.110
DEP	$.068_E^{***}$	$.026_R^{***}$	$.010_S^{***}$	$.005_G^{**}$	$.001_A$	.110
MOR	$.064_E^{***}$	$.011_R^{***}$	$.012_S^{***}$	$.004_G^{*}$	. . .	.091
SOC	$.036_E^{***}$	$.023_G^{***}$	$.009_S^{***}$	$.007_R^{**}$	$.001_A$	.076
HOS	$.037_E^{***}$	$.024_R^{***}$	$.008_A^{**}$	$.004_S^{*}$	$.001_G$	.074
FAM	$.076_R^{***}$	$.059_E^{***}$	$.014_A^{***}$	$.003_S^{*}$	. . .	.152
AUT	$.127_R^{***}$	$.045_S^{***}$	$.011_A^{***}$	$.009_E^{***}$	$.001_G$	.193
FEM	$.068_G^{***}$	$.024_A^{***}$	$.030_R^{***}$	$.002_S$	$.001_E$	.125
PHO	$.078_R^{***}$	$.046_E^{***}$	$.013_G^{***}$	$.008_S^{***}$	$.004_A^{*}$	.149
PSY	$.106_R^{***}$	$.072_E^{***}$	$.014_S^{***}$	$.008_A^{***}$	$.001_G$	.201
HYP	$.021_E^{***}$	$.009_R^{***}$	$.006_G^{**}$	$.004_A^{*}$	$.004_S^{*}$	.044
REL	$.052_A^{***}$	$.028_R^{***}$	$.006_S^{**}$	$.002_G$	. . .	.088
Rs	$.288_R^{***}$	$.061_E^{***}$	$.013_A^{***}$	$.010_S^{***}$	$.001_G$	.373
B-W	$.404_R^{***}$	$.019_E^{**}$	$.005_S^{***}$	$.003_A^{**}$	$.003_G^{*}$	.434

Note: Variables are identified as follows: A = age, G = gender, E = education, R = race, and S = socioeconomic status; * = $p < .05$, ** = $p < .01$, and *** = $p < .001$.

program also generates a multiple R^2 value that serves as an estimate of the total percentage of the variance in that dependent measure that is accounted for by the cumulative contributions of the separate independent variables. The results of this stepwise regression analysis are summarized in table 5.1 for all of the basic MMPI scales and for several special research scales.

Two sets of findings emerged rather dramatically in these stepwise regression analyses: the contribution of gender to the two MMPI scales developed to reflect sex-role patterns and the contribution of racial membership to the two scales developed on the basis of prior racial differences in item endorsement. That is, the size of the multiple R^2 values for scale 5 (Mf) and FEM reflects the different ways that men and women responded to these MMPI measures. (The FEM scale is essentially a subset of the items in the Mf scale that involve preferences for and interests in various kinds of activities, hobbies, and occupations.) Similarly, the Rs and B-W scales both showed very sizable multiple R^2 values primarily attributable to racial membership. Values of the R^2 statistic for the other basic and research scales of the MMPI are generally lower than those for scale 5, Rs, and B-W, indicating that relatively little can be predicted about how an individual will score on these scales from knowledge of that person's age, gender, race, schooling, or occupation either alone or even in some combination. Within these broad groupings, people still vary widely. Even for the scale with the largest R^2 value—the B-W scale with .434, in which each of these independent variables reached at least the .05 level of significance—less than half of the score variation (43%) is attributable to these general factors. The consistency with which both gender and racial membership contribute to the variance in these MMPI scales, however, made it desirable to carry out the further examination of the relationships between background factors and MMPI scale scores separately for each sex and for each race.

For this purpose, the data from the black and white men and women were treated separately in multivariate analyses of variance (MANOVAs) in which the relationships between various background characteristics and scores on the basic scales, as well as several selected special scales of the MMPI, were explored. The component scores of the basic clinical profile of the test, together with the scores from Welsh's (1956) factor scales A (Anxiety) and R (Repression) as well as Barron's (1953) Es (Ego strength) scale, were the dependent variables in the first of these MANOVAs. The second MANOVA was performed on the total set of content scales developed by Wiggins (1966). Since somewhat different information was known about the subjects in the white and black adult samples (see chapter 4), the independent variables differ to some extent in the

Table 5.2. Effects of Demographic Variables on MMPI Basic and Special Scales for the Two-State White Male Sample Compared by Multivariate Analyses of Variance

Variable	No. of Levels	*N*	df	*F*	*p*
Standard Scales, A, R, and Es by Demographic Variables					
Age	4	188	48,513	2.78	.0001
Education	3	188	32,342	2.77	.0001
IQ (Shipley)	4	178	48,483	2.20	.0001
Occupational level (SES)	3	188	32,342	3.25	.0001
Marital status	2	184	16,167	2.99	.0002
Social Readjustment Rating Scale (SRRS)	3	183	32,332	1.59	.0251
*Medical problems present	2	183	16,166	1.23	.2488
*Emotional problems present	2	183	16,166	1.57	.0812
Wiggins Content Scales by Demographic Variables					
Age	4	188	39,522	2.39	.0001
Education	3	188	26,348	2.63	.0001
IQ (Shipley)	4	178	39,492	1.85	.0017
Occupational level (SES)	3	188	26,348	3.02	.0001
Marital status	2	184	13,170	3.67	.0001
Social Readjustment Rating Scale (SRRS)	3	183	26,338	1.61	.0325
*Medical problems present	2	183	13,169	1.39	.1688
*Emotional problems present	2	183	13,169	1.58	.0940

*Scored from the SRRS.

Table 5.3. Effects of Demographic Variables on MMPI Basic and Special Scales for the Two-State White Female Sample Compared by Multivariate Analyses of Variance

Variable	No. of Levels	*N*	df	*F*	*p*
Standard Scales, A, R, and Es by Demographic Variables					
Age	4	228	48,633	2.25	.0001
Education	3	228	32,422	1.65	.0158
IQ (Shipley)	4	202	48,555	2.01	.0001
Occupational level (SES)	3	228	32,422	2.14	.0004
Marital status	2	198	16,181	1.21	.2650
Social Readjustment Rating Scale (SRRS)	3	209	32,384	1.65	.0162
*Medical problems present	2	209	16,192	1.07	.3833
*Emotional problems present	2	209	16,192	1.38	.1560
Wiggins Content Scales by Demographic Variables					
Age	4	228	39,642	2.46	.0001
Education	3	228	26,428	1.95	.0038
IQ (Shipley)	4	202	39,564	2.47	.0001
Occupational level (SES)	3	228	26,428	1.80	.0098
Marital status	2	198	13,184	1.29	.2221
Social Readjustment Rating Scale (SRRS)	3	209	26,390	2.42	.0002
*Medical problems present	2	209	13,195	1.04	.4184
*Emotional problems present	2	209	13,195	1.54	.1072

*Scored from the SRRS.

Table 5.4. Effects of Demographic Variables on MMPI Basic and Special Scales for the Tri-State Black Male Sample Compared by Multivariate Analyses of Variance

Variable	No. of Levels	*N*	df	*F*	*p*
Standard Scales, A, R, and Es by Demographic Variables					
Age	4	293	48,828	2.46	.0001
Education	3	289	32,544	2.84	.0001
Type of classes attended	2	292	16,275	2.59	.0009
Occupational level (SES)	3	293	32,552	2.15	.0003
Region of origin (where educated)	3	288	32,542	1.75	.0074
Region of predominant residence	3	290	32,546	1.64	.0162
Community size	4	288	48,813	1.44	.0288
Marital status	4	293	48,828	1.74	.0018
Medical problems present	2	293	16,276	2.53	.0012
Emotional problems present	2	293	16,276	3.23	.0001
Wiggins Content Scales by Demographic Variables					
Age	4	293	39,837	1.67	.0072
Education	3	289	26,550	2.26	.0004
Type of classes attended	2	292	13,278	2.19	.0101
Occupational level (SES)	3	293	26,558	1.93	.0040
Region of origin (where educated)	3	288	26,548	2.50	.0001
Region of predominant residence	3	290	26,552	2.32	.0003
Community size	4	288	39,822	1.73	.0041
Marital status	4	293	39,837	1.54	.0197
Medical problems present	2	293	13,279	1.93	.0271
Emotional problems present	2	293	13,279	3.53	.0001

Table 5.5. Effects of Demographic Variables on MMPI Basic and Special Scales for the Tri-State Black Female Sample Compared by Multivariate Analyses of Variance

Variable	No. of Levels	*N*	df	*F*	*p*
Standard Scales, A, R, and Es by Demographic Variables					
Age	4	501	48,1452	3.21	.0001
Education	3	492	32,950	6.14	.0001
Type of classes attended	2	503	16,486	2.73	.0003
Occupational level (SES)	3	503	32,972	2.83	.0001
Region of origin (where educated)	3	500	32,966	2.09	.0004
Region of predominant residence	3	501	32,968	1.83	.0034
Community size	4	497	48,1440	1.37	.0473
Marital status	4	503	48,1458	2.08	.0001
Medical problems present	2	503	16,486	3.71	.0001
Emotional problems present	2	503	16,486	3.76	.0001
Wiggins Content Scales by Demographic Variables					
Age	4	501	39,1461	3.22	.0001
Education	3	492	26,956	5.06	.0001
Type of classes attended	2	503	13,489	4.04	.0001
Occupational level (SES)	3	503	26,978	3.20	.0001
Region of origin (where educated)	3	500	26,972	3.54	.0001
Region of predominant residence	3	501	26,974	3.04	.0001
Community size	4	497	39,1449	1.78	.0023
Marital status	4	503	39,1467	2.72	.0001
Medical problems present	2	503	13,489	3.21	.0001
Emotional problems present	2	503	13,489	4.81	.0001

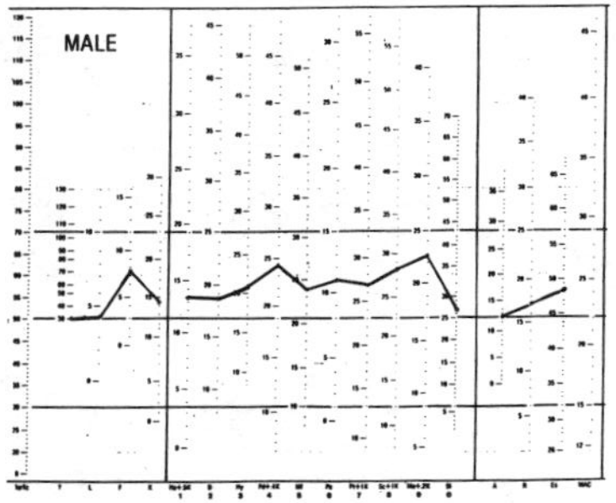

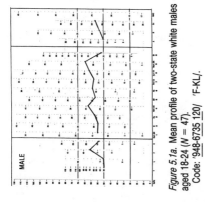

Figure 5.1a. Mean profile of two-state white males aged 18-24 (*N* = 47).
Code: '948-6735 120/ 'F-KL/.

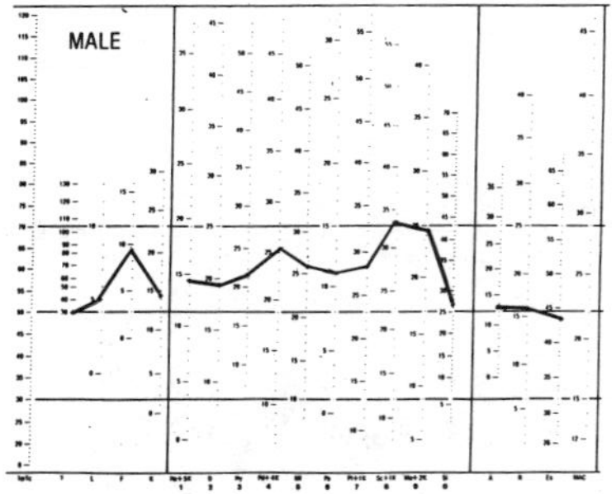

Figure 5.2a. Mean profile of tri-state black males aged 18-24 (*N* = 61).
Code: 8'9457-36120/ 'F-K/L.

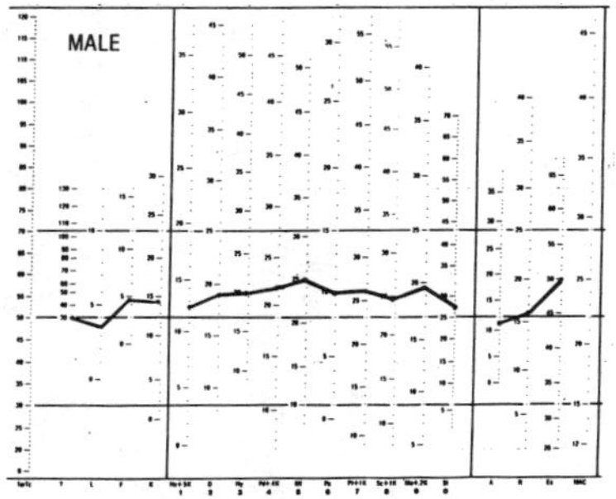

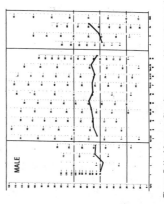

Figure 5.1b. Mean profile of two-state white males aged 25-34 (*N* = 58).
Code: -54932768 10/ -FK/L.

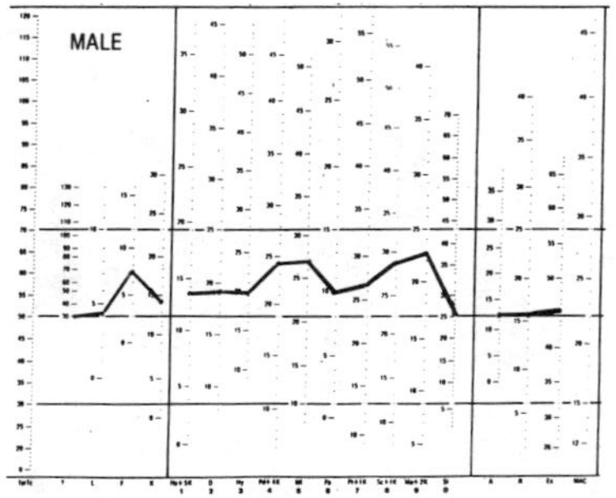

Figure 5.2b. Mean profile of tri-state black males aged 25-34 (*N* = 81).
Code: '9548-271360/ 'F-KL/.

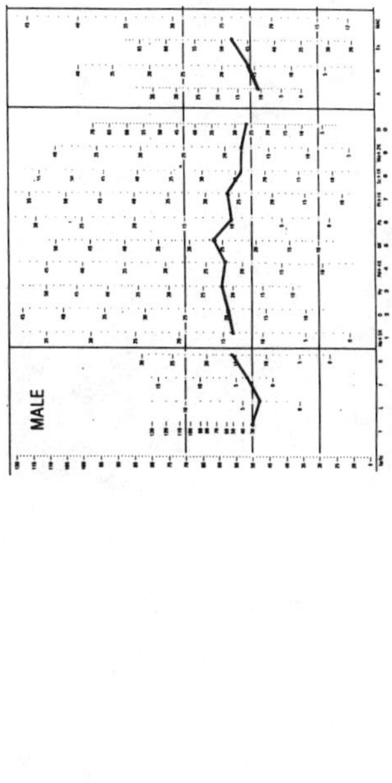

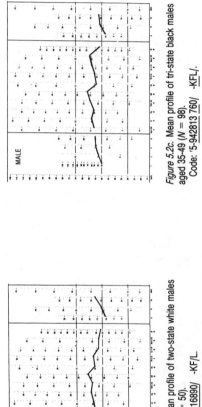

Figure 5.1c. Mean profile of two-state white males aged 35-49 (N = 50).
Code: '5-347216890/ -KF/L.

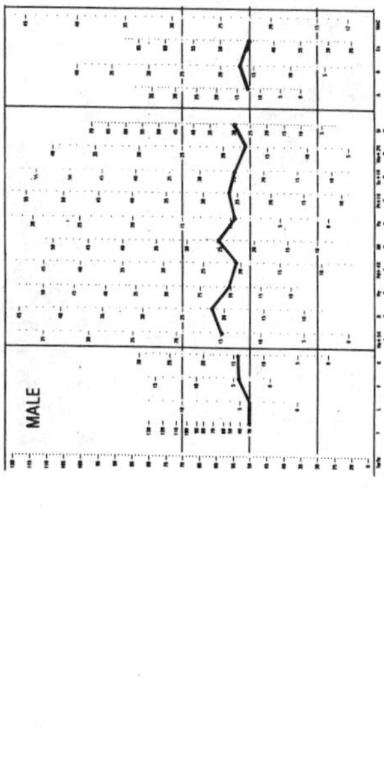

Figure 5.1d. Mean profile of two-state white males aged 50 or older (N = 33).
Code: '25-1 37 60489/ -KFL/.

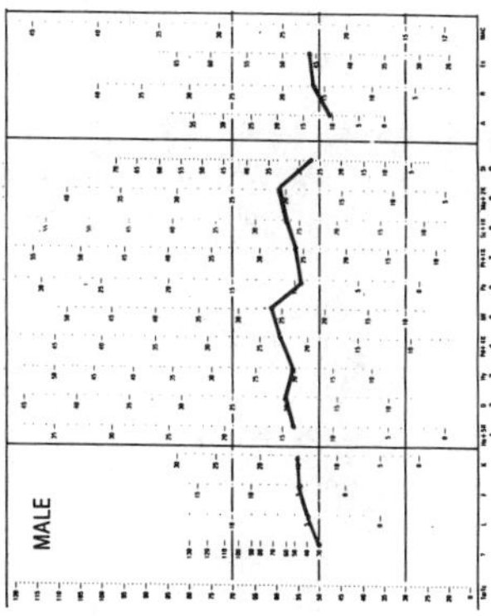

Figure 5.2c. Mean profile of tri-state black males aged 35-49 (N = 98).
Code: '5-942813 760/ -KFL/.

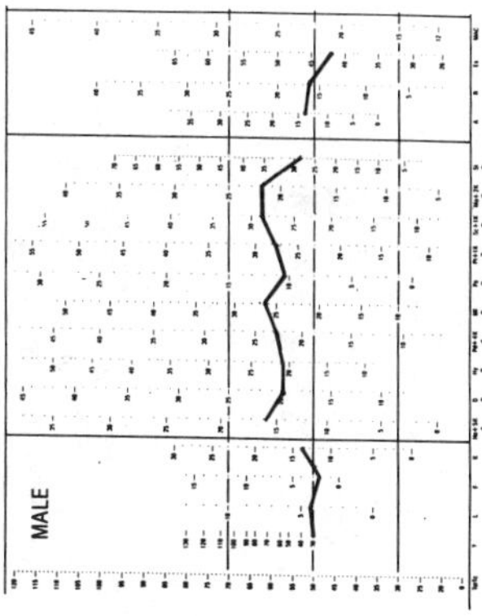

Figure 5.2d. Mean profile of tri-state black males aged 50 or older (N = 53).
Code: '9851-473260/ -KL/F.

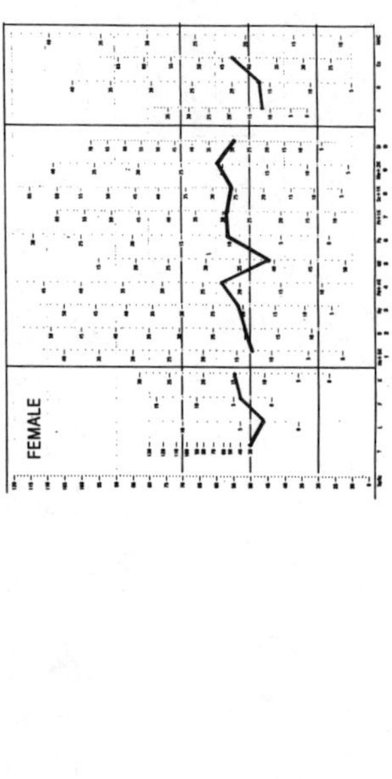

Figure 5.3a. Mean profile of two-state white females aged 18-24 (*N* = 35).
Code: -947680 32/15 -KF/L.

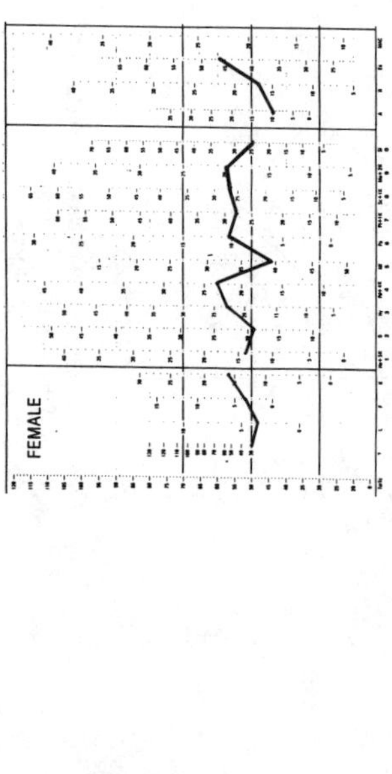

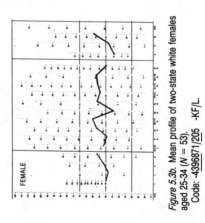

Figure 5.3b. Mean profile of two-state white females aged 25-34 (*N* = 53).
Code: -4396871/205 -KF/L.

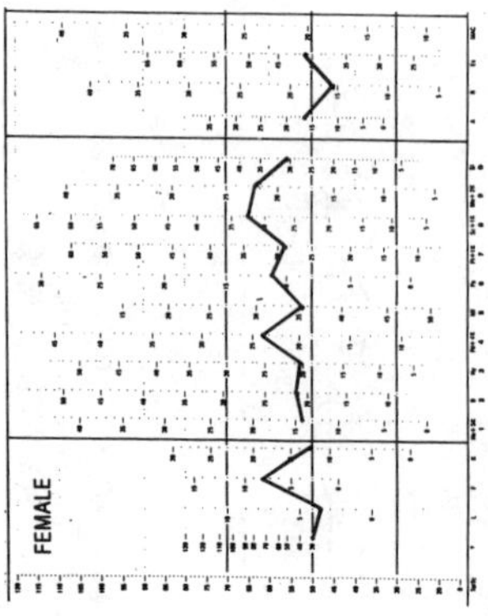

Figure 5.4a. Mean profile of tri-state black females aged 18-24 (*N* = 120).
Code: '894-6702 315/ 'F-K/L.

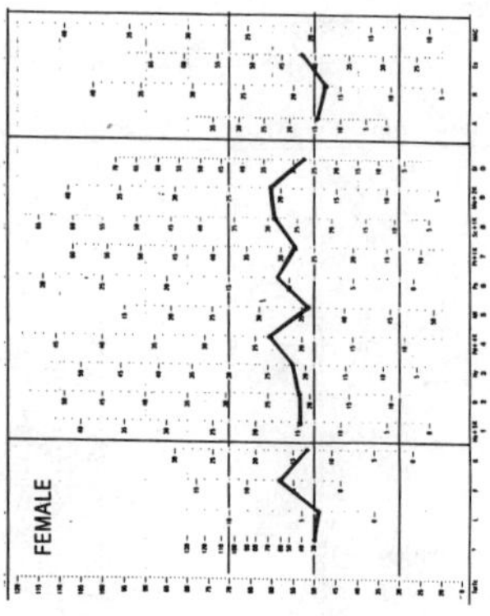

Figure 5.4b. Mean profile of tri-state black females aged 25-34 (*N* = 170).
Code: '49-86372105/ -FK/L.

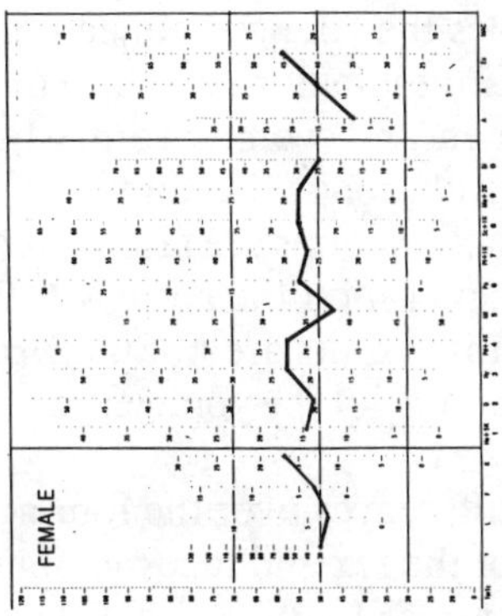

Figure 5.3c. Mean profile of two-state white females aged 35-49 (*N* = 70).
Code: -34 869 17 2/05 -KF/L.

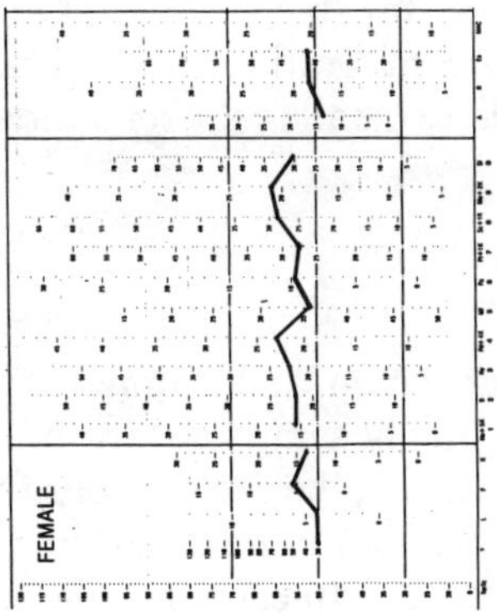

Figure 5.4c. Mean profile of tri-state black females aged 35-49 (*N* = 133).
Code: -498 0632175/ -FKL/.

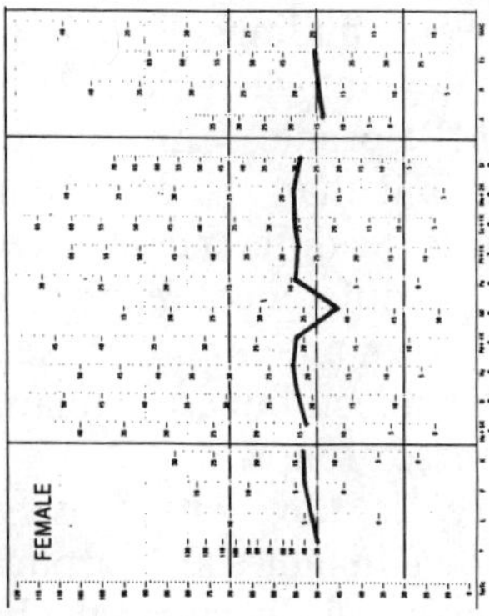

Figure 5.3d. Mean profile of two-state white females aged 50 or older (*N* = 70).
Code: -346928071/5 -KFL/.

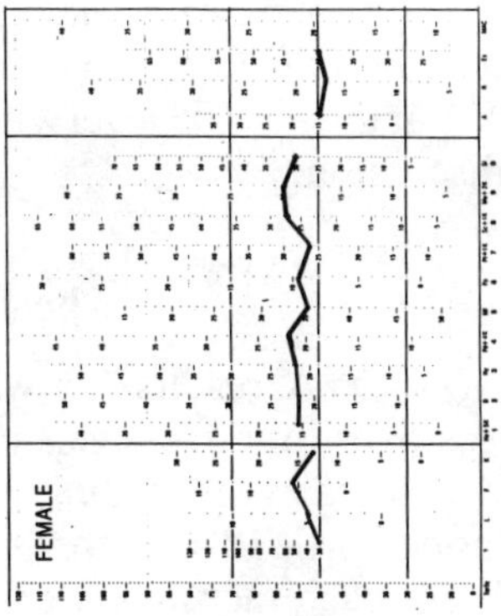

Figure 5.4d. Mean profile of tri-state black females aged 50 or older (*N* = 78).
Code: -984 0132657/ -FLK/.

MANOVAs being reported for these two groups. Tables 5.2 through 5.5 list the background variables that were investigated, the numbers of subjects of each race and sex on whom the requisite information was available for each analysis, the numbers of groups formed on each background characteristic, the degrees of freedom involved in the comparisons among these groups, as well as the overall level of statistical significance reached by the MANOVA on each independent variable for that scale set. Only those background factors that obtained a significant *F* ratio on the overall MANOVA at the $p < .05$ level will be examined in detail in the remainder of this discussion.

Age Differences

In the MANOVA results for white and black men and women, the differences over four age levels proved to be highly significant for both sets of MMPI scales. Accordingly, the means and standard deviations for the component MMPI scales are reported in tables D-1 through D-4 in the appendix for each race and sex subgroup separately. In each of these tables, the level of significance obtained on each MMPI scale for the *F* ratio across age levels is also reported. In addition, the mean profiles on the basic MMPI scales for each age level for the four race and sex membership groups are presented in figures 5.1 through 5.4.

The results of contrasting these men and women of each racial group across the four levels on age yield two very general trends as well as a number of specific findings. First, in all four samples the younger subjects are the most deviant when plotted on the basic Minnesota norms in the standard MMPI profile, with the young black men and women somewhat more deviant than the corresponding white subgroups. Second, at the older levels the differences between the two racial groups are attenuated. That is, the differences reported earlier in chapter 4 on the basic MMPI scales between and among these black and white adults are not uniform across all subjects but are primarily in the responses of the younger members of these groups.

Four scales show consistently significant differences over the four age levels shown in tables D-1 through D-4 in all of the sex and race membership groups: scale 9 (Ma) in the basic profile and REL, PSY, and AUT in the Wiggins set. The youngest subgroup of each of these samples is elevated on the hypomania scale in comparison with the older men and women, whereas they are generally the lowest in "religious fundamentalism" and highest in "feelings of being misunderstood and wronged" and "conflict with authority." Thus, the most consistent differences emerging in the relationship between age level and MMPI scores characterize the young adults from all four samples as more sociable, outgoing, impulsive, and at times overly energetic individuals who espouse fewer fundamental religious convictions than their older counterparts but who express greater mistrust of those in authority and seem convinced that others are unscrupulous, dishonest, and hypocritical.

In the results from the black adults, the younger subjects are also characterized by elevated scores on the F scale and on scales 4 (Pd), 7 (Pt), and 8 (Sc) (the younger white males show comparable differences on F, 4, and 8). These scales generally reflect atypical self-descriptions, rebellious and impulsive relationships both with other family members and with authority figures, and alienation from self and society. Among the Wiggins measures, the younger black men and women score higher on the HOS scale in addition to the differences already noted above. These trends suggest that the younger adults report more retaliatory, competitive, and angry reactions in their interpersonal relationships.

Among the white adults, the differences over the age levels sampled show higher scores on Wiggins' ORG and PHO scales for the older subjects and a somewhat more complex pattern of difference on Barron's Ego strength scale, with these scores being somewhat lower for both the youngest and oldest subjects in the survey. Thus, insecurities and physical disabilities are more prevalent in the older subjects and self-confidence and relative freedom from disturbing emotional symptoms are more characteristic of the middle-year levels.

The meaning of the age differences revealed in this set of analyses is not easy to discern. That is, age per se may be less important than other aspects of the subjects who were examined at these various age levels. Therefore, any further discussion of the obtained differences should be delayed until the relation of MMPI scores to these other characteristics of the samples can be examined.

Educational Background

The black and white adults in these surveys reported widely diverse backgrounds in schooling. For purposes of analysis, the men and women in these samples were grouped over three levels of education: completion of 12 years of schooling or less, some college-level education but less than a full college degree, and completion of a college degree or beyond. Separate MANOVAs were performed on the same sets of MMPI variables as those used in analyzing the age differences reported above for each of the four groups of black and white men and women. The results indicated that level of education is strongly related to a number of MMPI scores. The means and standard deviations on these various dependent measures for

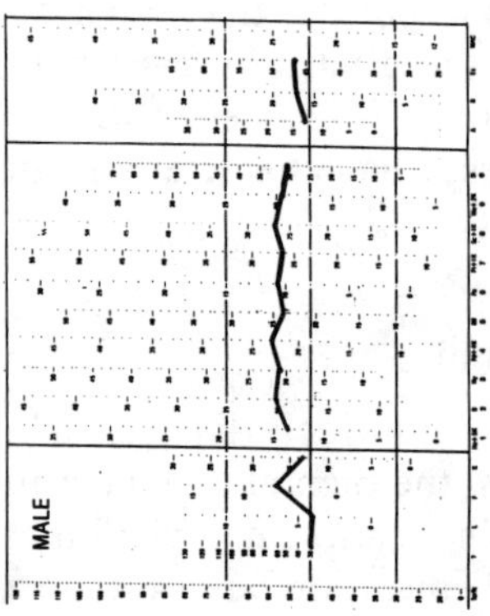

Figure 5.5a. Mean profile of two-state white males with 12 years or less of education (N = 92).
Code: -4826357910/ -FK/L

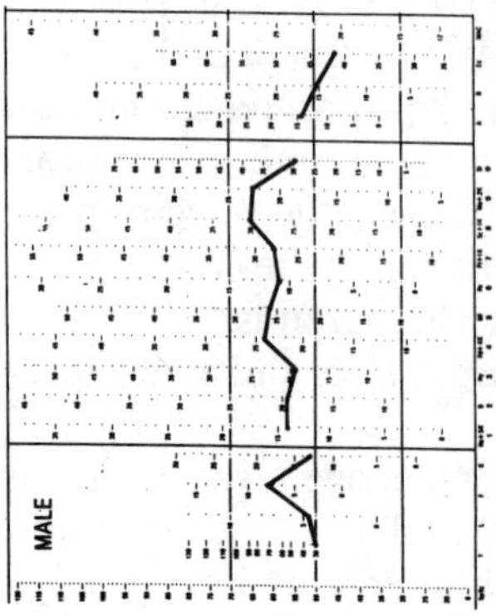

Figure 5.6a. Mean profile of tri-state black males with 12 years or less of education (N = 117).
Code: '89 45-721630/ 'F-LK/.

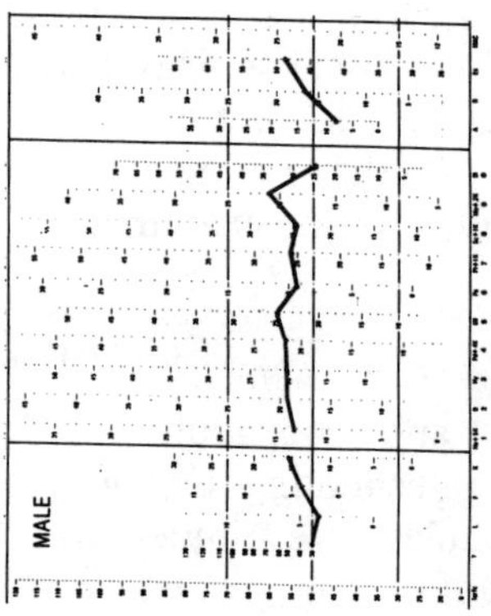

Figure 5.5b. Mean profile of two-state white males with 13-15 years of education (N = 38).
Code:P '9-54327168/0 -KF/L.

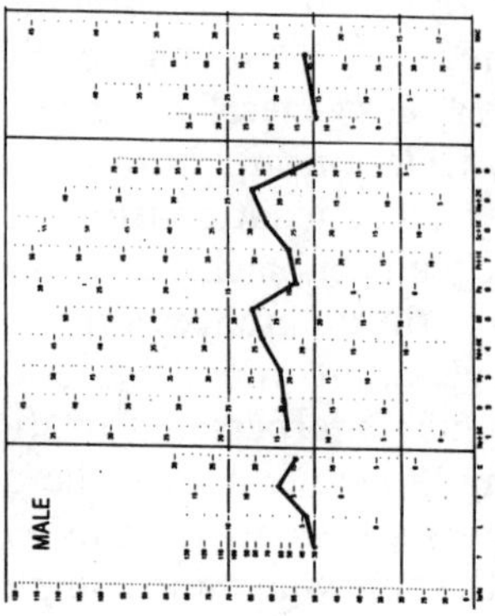

Figure 5.6b. Mean profile of tri-state black males with 13-15 years of education (N = 86).
Code: '9548-321760/ -FKL/.

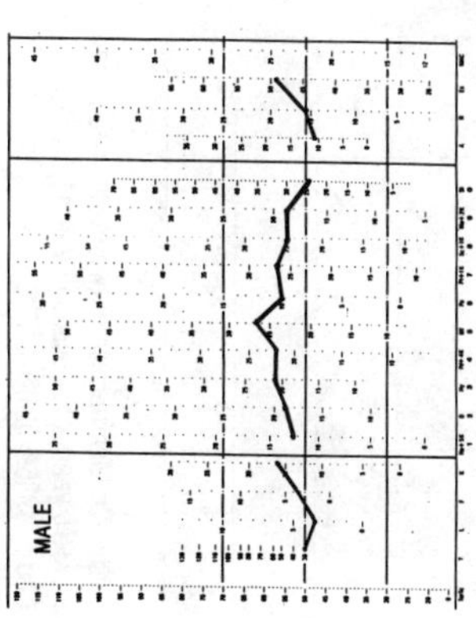

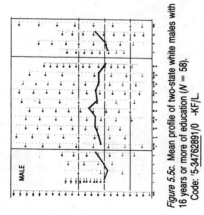

Figure 5.5c. Mean profile of two-state white males with 16 years or more of education (N = 58).
Code: '5-34762891/0 -KF/L.

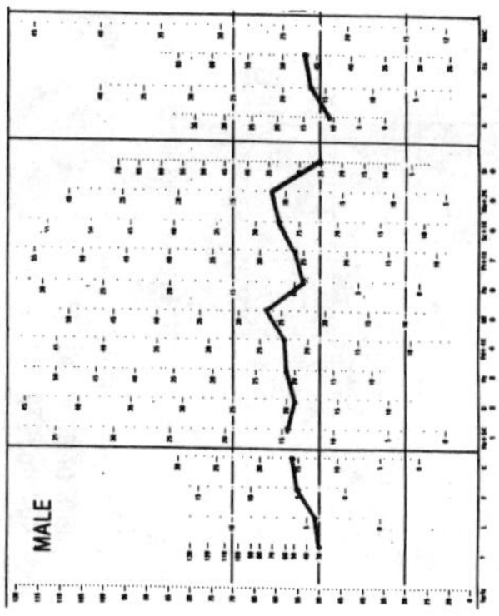

Figure 5.6c. Mean profile of tri-state black males with 16 years or more of education (N = 86).
Code: '59-8413 7260/ -KFL/.

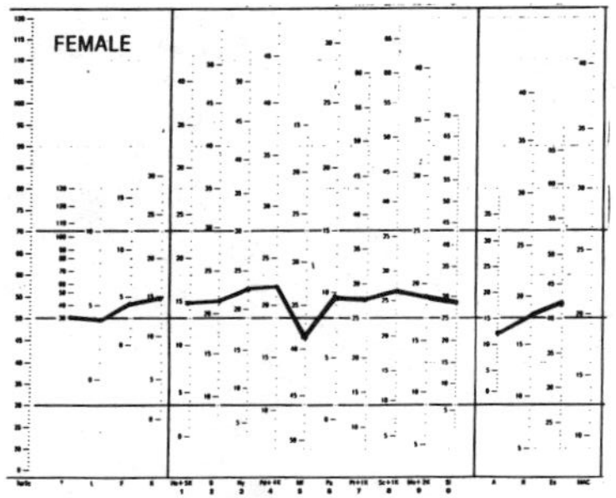

Figure 5.7a. Mean profile of two-state white females with 12 years or less of education (N = 132).
Code: -438697210/5 -KF/L.

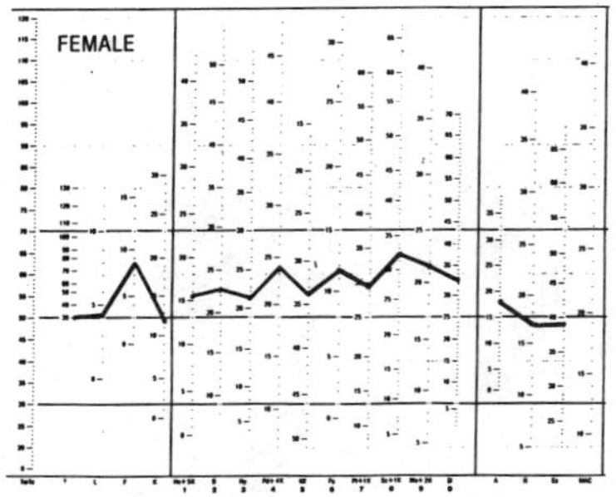

Figure 5.8a. Mean profile of tri-state black females with 12 years or less of education (N = 213).
Code: '8496-072513/ 'F-L/K.

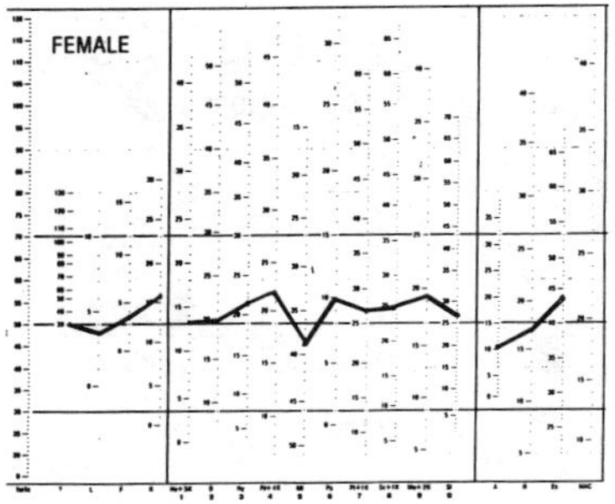

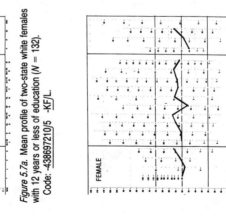

Figure 5.7b. Mean profile of two-state white females with 13-15 years of education (N = 41).
Code: -493687021/5 -KF/L.

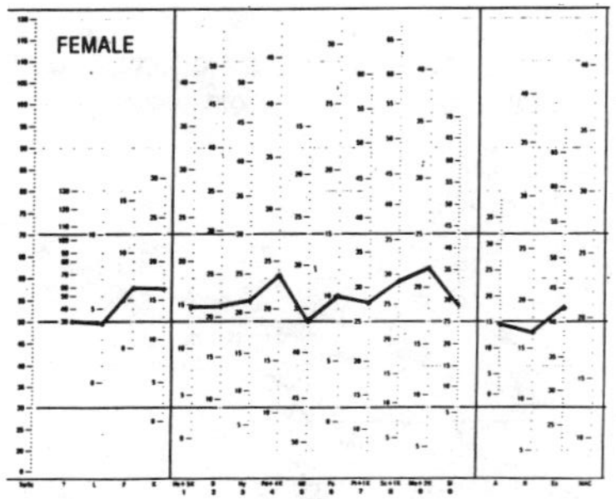

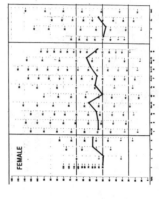

Figure 5.8b. Mean profile of tri-state black females with 13-15 years of education (N = 122).
Code: '94-86307215/ -FK/L.

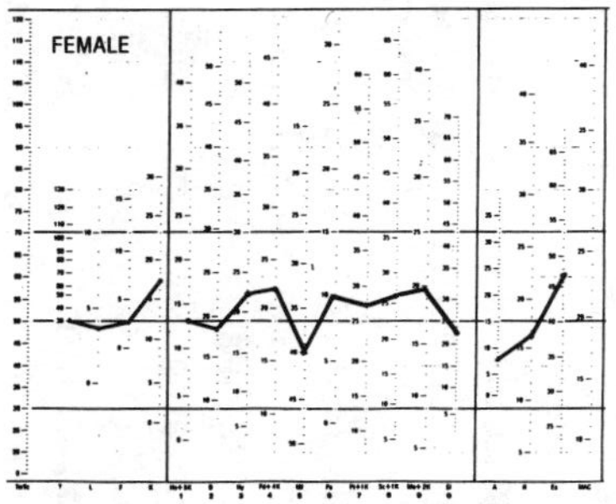

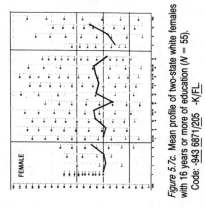

Figure 5.7c. Mean profile of two-state white females with 16 years or more of education ($N = 55$).
Code: -943 6871/205 -K/FL.

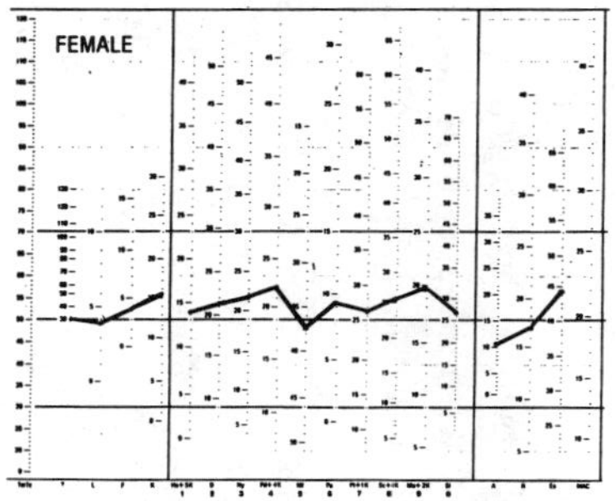

Figure 5.8c. Mean profile of tri-state black females with 16 years or more of education ($N = 157$).
Code: -49 83 62701/5 -KF/L.

each of the educational levels are listed in tables D-5 through D-8 in the appendix, together with the *F* ratios and levels of significance obtained for each MMPI scale.

The mean MMPI profiles at three different educational levels for the white men and white women are plotted in figures 5.5 and 5.7. The corresponding mean profiles at these three educational levels for black men and black women are shown in figures 5.6 and 5.8. These score patterns show an overall trend similar to that noted above in relation to age: at the higher levels of education, black and white subjects differ less than do subjects at the lower levels. Although many subjects with lower education are also young, there is a wide range of ages at all educational levels in all four of these groups of subjects.

Two of the three validity scales, K and F but not L, show highly consistent relationships to educational level in all four groups of subjects. The deviant responses reflected in the F scores are lower and the rather subtle test defensiveness and expressions of self-confidence and self-maintenance shown in typical answers to the K scale are higher in black and white men and women with higher levels of schooling. Similar trends are evident in the scores on Barron's Ego strength scale, the MMPI measure with the strongest and most consistent relationship to education in all four groups of subjects. In all these groups, subjects with higher education report fewer signs of anxiety on Welsh's A scale and indicate less social shyness and more social participation on scale 0 (Si). These general trends are consistent with previous research on the relationship of various MMPI measures to socioeconomic status (Dahlstrom, Welsh, & Dahlstrom, 1975).

Most of the scores on the Wiggins content scales also showed systematic differences over these ranges of schooling. Subjects with less education earned significantly higher scores on ORG, HEA, DEP, MOR, SOC, FAM, and PHO. Thus, those individuals with less education were reporting a larger number of health problems, lower morale, more social maladjustment, and greater numbers of family and emotional problems. Life is seen by the individuals who are less well educated, whether black or white, male or female, as much more problematic and difficult. Lacking self-confidence, with feelings of insecurity and threat, viewing the future as less hopeful or promising, and experiencing a variety of physical discomforts and miseries, such individuals seem to experience more despair and anxiety.

Previous studies of the relationship between level of education and MMPI measures (Dahlstrom, Welsh, & Dahlstrom, 1975) had shown quite consistent patterns with scale 5 (Mf), with higher education being related to fairly strong elevations for men and somewhat submerged scores for women. This same pattern was also present in the samples of both black and white men and women. In the sample of black men, however, elevated mean scores on scale 5 were found at all levels of education with some statistically significant variations from one educational level to another. Interestingly, the same pattern of relationship within these four groups of subjects between level of schooling and scores on the FEM scale was not found. Thus, the scale 5 scores do not appear to be primarily interests or preferences. For the white men and both groups of women, the subjects with higher levels of education showed fewer conflicts with authority on the Wiggins AUT scale; they reported less cynicism and mistrust of powerful others and less tendency to see life as a struggle. Although not extremely deviant, black men at all levels of education were prone to view their relationships with people in authority as problematic.

Black men and women with lower levels of schooling earned significantly higher scores on three of the standard clinical scales (6 [Pa], 7 [Pt], and 8 [Sc]) than black adults with more education. The range of mean scores on these scales (particularly on scale 8) over these educational levels is large and meaningful. Strong trends in such areas as interpersonal mistrust, insecurity, moral rigidity, and self-alienation are indicated by these elevated scores. At higher levels of education, however, neither black men nor black women deviate as markedly, either from the test norms or particularly from the mean scores of subjects at a similar educational level in the white samples.

In general, then, all subjects who report some education beyond the level of high school graduation are more likely to answer the MMPI in less deviant ways. Their scores are consistent with greater personal effectiveness, fewer interpersonal and emotional difficulties, and better morale. It seems quite consistent with these findings, therefore, to note that proportionately more black Americans are undereducated and therefore have lower socioeconomic status as well. It can be expected on this basis alone, then, that unselected samples of black adults will show more deviant MMPI patterns than unselected white adults.

Although no corresponding data were available on the black subjects, the administration of the Shipley-Institute of Living Intelligence Scale to most of the white men and women provided an opportunity to explore further the various possible implications of the pattern of relationships between educational level and MMPI scores by evaluating the contribution of academic aptitude. Do the same relationships between MMPI scores and level of schooling appear in analyses based upon test performance on this intelligence scale? That is, is a person's educational level primarily an index of intellective competence and general ability, or does the attainment of educational level reflect something more in the way of self-discipline, emotional maturity, or social effectiveness? It can be assumed that many individuals, for one reason or another, do not manage to complete as much education as they are capable of completing; the opposite situation (achieving more education than they seemed capable of) can also occur, although with considerably lower frequency. For each sex separately, the Shipley Scale IQ level, years of education completed, and level of occupation (to be discussed in the next section) were intercorrelated for subjects in this sample of white adults. The results are shown in table 5.6; the correlations for the male subjects are shown above the diagonal, those for the female subjects below. Since occupational level is scaled from I as the highest to V as the lowest, the correlations between this variable and the other two are negative. Thus, the two major indicators of socioeconomic level—years of education and level of occupation—are strongly correlated to the same degree in both men and women. The correlation between total years of education and IQ score on the Shipley Scale is statistically significant only for the men and is only of modest magnitude (0.33), whereas the relationship between these two variables for the women does not exceed a chance level. It is likely that the lack of correlation between Shipley scores and years of education for women reflects the possibility that they were capable of completing more schooling.

Table 5.6. Correlations between Occupational Levels, Shipley IQ Scores, and Years of Education for White Men (N =178) and White Women (N = 202)

	Occupation	IQ	Education
Occupational levels	. . .	-.22**	-.72***
Shipley IQ scores	-.14*	. . .	.33***
Years of education	-.71***	.10	. . .

Note: Values for men appear above the diagonal, those for women below. Ungrouped data on IQ and education were used for these correlations; * = $p < .05$, ** = $p < .01$, *** = $p < .001$.

As indicated in chapter 4, the Shipley Scale IQ values earned by these men and women ranged from 80 to 130. The subjects in each gender group were placed in one of four levels: a score of 100 or below; between 101 and 109; between 110 and 118; and 119 or higher. MANOVAs on the usual sets of dependent variables from the MMPI were carried out separately for each sex. The overall level of significance was high for both sexes (see tables 5.2 and 5.3). The means and standard deviations of the various MMPI scales for subjects at these four IQ levels, together with the various F ratios for the differences across ability levels, are shown in tables D-9 and D-10 in the appendix.

In spite of the fact that IQ level and years of education are only modestly correlated for the men, essentially the same pattern of relationships emerged between MMPI variables and level of intelligence as was found in regard to level of education. A similar pattern was also found in the relationships between level of Shipley scores and MMPI variables for women. For the women, not only was the pattern of relationships similar to that found for the men, but it was quite similar as well to the pattern found in women for educational level in spite of the lack of appreciable correlation between education and Shipley scores in this group. Thus, scores on the K scale among the validity scales, scales 5 (Mf) and 0 (Si) in the clinical profile, and Barron's Ego strength scale are related to IQ level in the same way that they are related to years of education. The same is also true of the various content scales in the Wiggins set. In the data for the women, two additional clinical scales (1 [Hs] and 2 [D]) show consistent patterns of lower scores for women with higher Shipley scores. (Scale 8 [Sc] shows statistically significant differences between IQ levels in the female group, but the pattern is not as consistent over these levels.)

Since the MMPI scores show similar relationships to both education and intelligence test performance, the possibility must be considered that some of the personality score elevations may be attributable to a lack of reading ability and the resulting comprehension difficulties in responding to some of the MMPI items. These individuals may also be subject to more stress and possess fewer coping skills and social supports. It is regrettable that similar measures of intellective ability were not available on the black men and women in these samples, because the variations in MMPI scores in relation to educational level were even more wide-ranging among these subjects. (Some of these issues will be taken up later in chapter 7 in discussions of the item analytic data.)

Since the black men and women reported in the biographical questionnaire whether they had attended racially integrated classes in their school years, it was feasible to examine the potential relationship between MMPI patterns and a history of school segregation or integration. One view of factors contributing to some MMPI differences between black and white subjects has been that those black students who had experienced only segregated schooling would show more deviant self-views on tests like the MMPI. For example, McDonald and Gynther (1963) noted in their study of black high school students attending segregated schools in Columbia, South Carolina, in the early 1960s that some of the answers to MMPI items might reflect a kind of ego assault resulting from the racial prejudice reflected in educational segregation. They concluded: "The prediction would be that the greater the integration between the races, the smaller the differences on MMPI scales" (p. 116). Although classroom segregation is likely to be only one part of a pattern of social exclusion and ostracism (see chapter 1), it is likely to be an important component in the formation of self-concept and ethnic identity. Accordingly, it was of interest to examine differences between the men and women in our black adult samples who differed in the nature of their educational experience in regard to racial segregation.

As the MANOVA results reported in tables 5.4 and 5.5 indicated, the overall differences were statistically significant for this contrast. The means and standard deviations for the two kinds of school experience for men and women in our black samples are given in tables D-11 and D-12 in the appendix. The pattern of differences is similar for both the men and the women in this set of contrasts between integrated and segregated school background, but there are relatively few statistically significant differences in the findings from the men. In both sexes, however, the direction of deviation is quite consistent: those subjects who report only segregated schooling score less deviantly on the validity and clinical scales of the MMPI. In this instance, at least, the prediction quoted above is not borne out; the subjects reporting exposure to racially integrated schools score more deviantly and hence show greater difference from both the (white) test norms of the MMPI and from test scores of contemporary white samples. One other possible explanation for the present findings is that these results reflect increased tensions and pressures resulting from what was perceived to be a more demanding and possibly threatening milieu.

Occupational Level

The subjects in both surveys reported their current employment or, in the case of a nonworking subject, the occupation of the head of household. Using a five-step hierarchy of occupations that is adapted from the Hollingshead and Redlich (1958) Index of Social Position, subjects in these samples were grouped on the basis of their occupation or the occupation of the head of household. Adults in the black and white surveys reported in chapter 4 differed from each other and, to an important degree, from the 1970 U.S. census breakdown for white and black adults-in-general (see table 4.3). Adequate numbers of these men and women were available at only three different levels: the subjects in levels I and II and those in IV and V had to be combined, leaving only three occupational levels in the MANOVAs carried out on the MMPI data from these four groups.

Since occupational level was a highly significant factor in the overall

MANOVAs reported in tables 5.2 through 5.5, the results for the component scales of the MMPI are summarized in tables D-13 through D-16 in the appendix, with the means and standard deviations for each of the levels used in these analyses, together with the *F* ratios found for each scale. The mean profiles for these occupational levels are shown in figures 5.9 through 5.12. The mean profiles show the operation of the same general trend noted earlier in regard to both age level and educational level: namely, the higher the occupational level, the smaller the differences in either elevation or pattern on the standard MMPI scales between and among the black and white men and women. Conversely, the largest and most significant differences between the racial and sex membership groups appear here among the lowest occupational levels. It is also apparent, from examination of the scale-by-scale *F* ratios, that a great many of the MMPI scales reflect these differences in occupational level.

All four groups—black and white men and women—show significant differences over these occupational levels on the F and K scales in the validity set and scale 0 (Si) in the clinical set of the basic profile. These findings are consistent with those found for educational level differences (as reported above), and they also fit in well with the literature on the relationship of MMPI variables to socioeconomic level (Dahlstrom, Welsh, & Dahlstrom, 1975). (It was also reported above that occupational level and educational level in the white samples are correlated –.72 for men and –.71 for women.) In addition, the Ego strength scale also showed a strong and consistent relationship to occupational level in all four groups of adults. Men and women occupying the highest levels of occupational status show greater self-confidence, manifest more freedom from shyness, worries, and concerns, and are more conventional in their replies to deviant items on the MMPI. Their answers, as shown on the Wiggins scales, reveal lower depression, fewer health or morale problems, and less social maladjustment or difficulties in interpersonal relationships (see ORG, HEA, DEP, MOR, and SOC scales).

Both male and female white adults, and black female subjects as well, showed systematic differences on scale 5 (Mf), with higher scores for males and lower scores for females at the upper occupational levels. These higher occupation subjects are endorsing a wide variety of content in scale 5, since those items in the Mf scale that reflect a broad range of interest and preferences for more cultural activities making up the FEM scale did not show this same pattern. Interestingly, the black men at these three different occupational levels did not show the expected variation on scale 5 or on FEM; these men had elevated mean values on both scales at *all* occupational status levels without statistically significant variations.

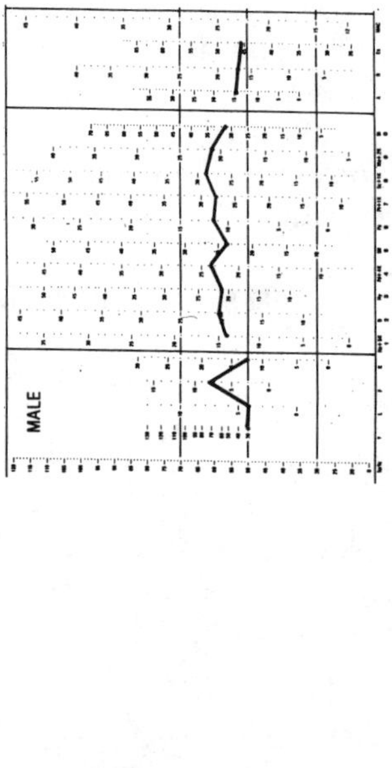

Figure 5.9a. Mean profile of two-state white males at SES levels IV & V (N = 54).
Code: '846-7923150/ 'F-K/L.

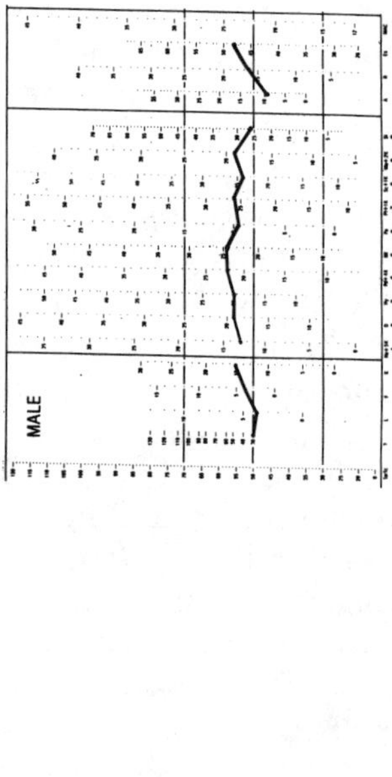

Figure 5.9b. Mean profile of two-state white males at SES level III (N = 73).
Code: -542937 6180/ -KF/L.

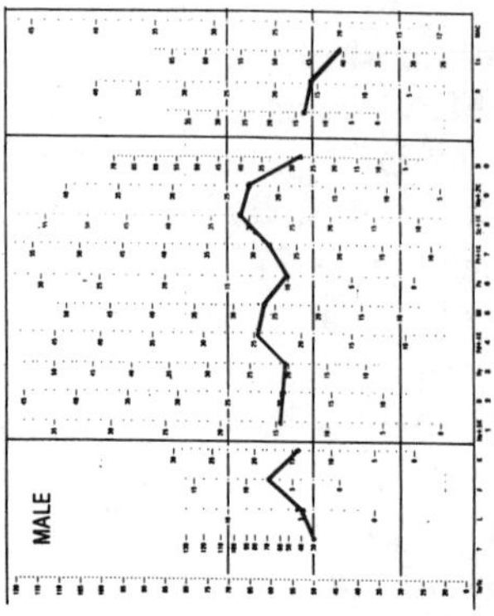

Figure 5.10a. Mean profile of tri-state black males at SES levels IV & V (N = 27).
Code: '89475-12360/ 'F-KL/.

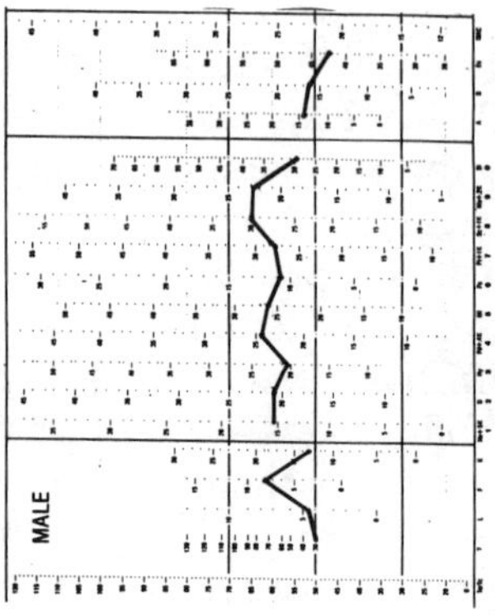

Figure 5.10b. Mean profile of tri-state black males at SES level III (N = 107).
Code: '8945-217630/ 'F-LK/.

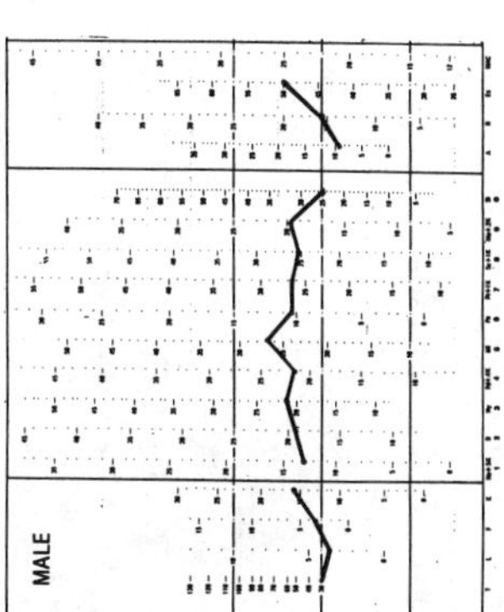

Figure 5.9c. Mean profile of two-state white males at SES levels I & II (N = 61).
Code: '5-34 296781/0 -KF/L.

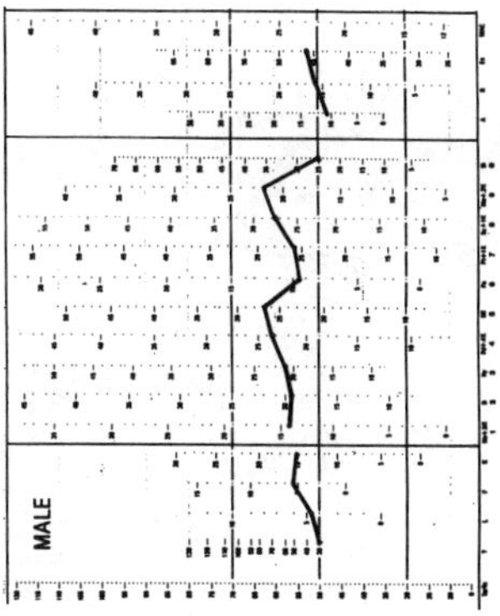

Figure 5.10c. Mean profile of tri-state black males at SES levels I & II (N = 159).
Code: '95 48-312760/ -FKL/.

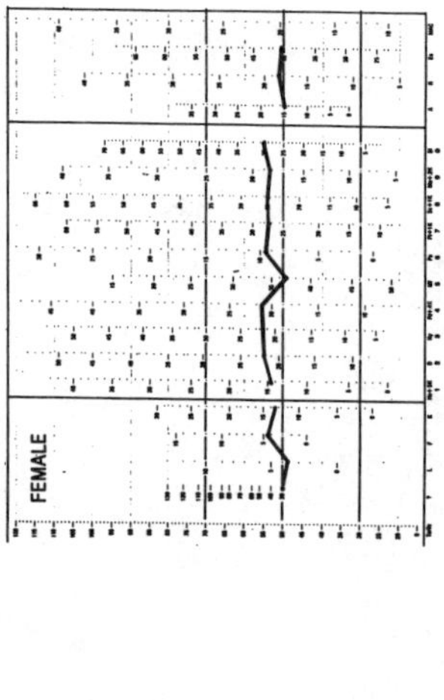

Figure 5.11a. Mean profile of two-state white females at SES levels IV & V (*N* = 46).
Code: -432068791/5 -FK/L.

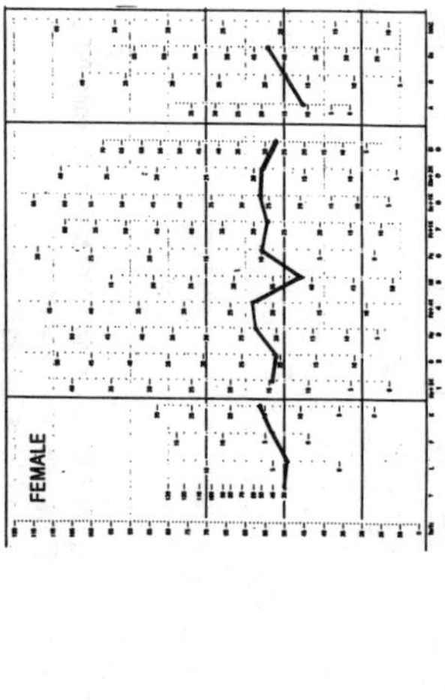

Figure 5.11b. Mean profile of two-state white females at SES level III (*N* = 114).
Code: -438697 120/5 -KF/L.

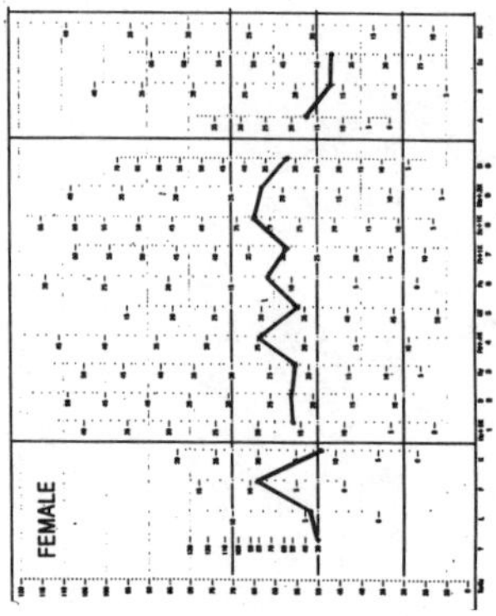

Figure 5.12a. Mean profile of tri-state black females at SES levels IV & V (*N* = 93).
Code: '8946-702135/ 'F-L/K.

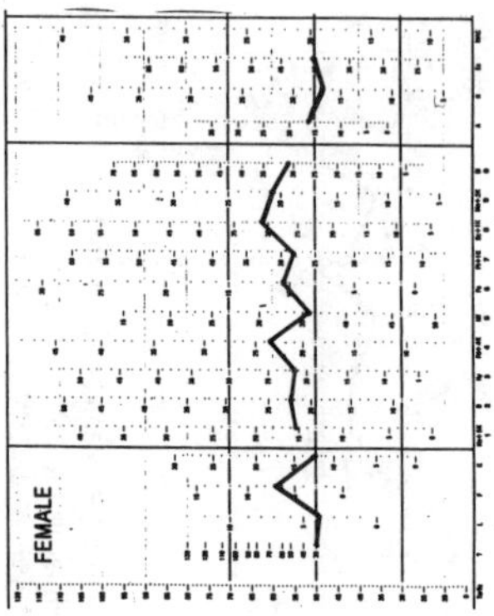

Figure 5.12b. Mean profile of tri-state black females at SES level III (*N* = 156).
Code: '84-9 6072315/ -FK/L.

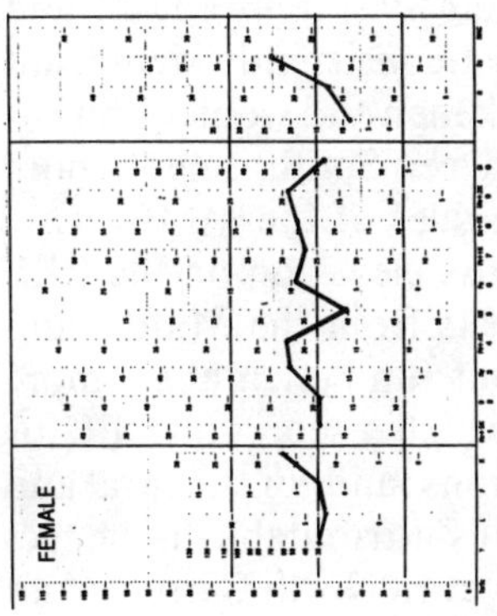

Figure 5.11c. Mean profile of two-state white females at SES levels I & II (N = 68).
Code: -943 687/1205 -K/FL.

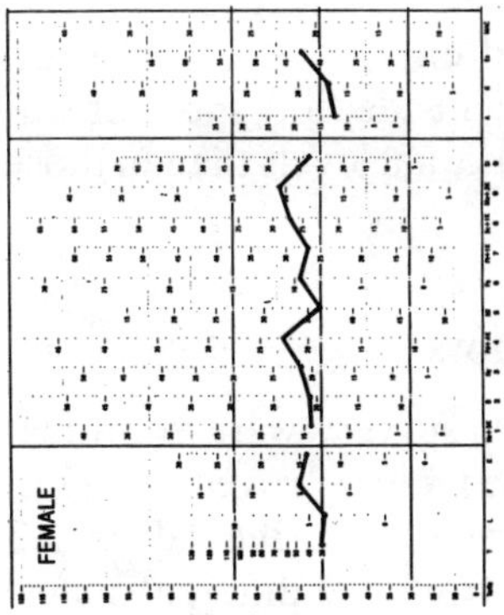

Figure 5.12c. Mean profile of tri-state black females at SES levels I & II (N = 254).
Code: -94863 20715/ -FK/L.

The black men and women showed significant variation over these levels of occupation on several additional scales: scale 9 (Ma) in the basic set, along with the Welsh A scale, and FAM, PHO, and PSY in the content set. These differences reflect increasing levels of psychopathology in subjects at lower occupational levels, with problems involving family disagreements and other patterns of interpersonal difficulty, mistrust and anger at the ways that society treats them, as well as worries, insecurities, and fears that haunt them with disturbing thoughts and emotional experiences. Mental health concerns, therefore, seem to be considerably more prevalent in the black subjects from the lowest occupational levels than in those at higher levels.

Other Background Factors

Several other aspects of the subjects in these two surveys were examined by means of MANOVAs, but only a few of these factors proved to be important in explaining variations in MMPI responses (see tables 5.2 through 5.5). Although the white subjects came from two different states, the region of residence of these men and women was geographically quite narrow. The black men and women, however, were drawn from three localities that were widely separated. Accordingly, several different ways of grouping these subjects were explored: area in which they lived while getting their basic education (tables D-17 and D-18 in the appendix); area where they lived for most of their lives (tables D-19 and D-20); and size of community in which they lived for most of their lives (tables D-21 and D-22). The classification that revealed the most consistently significant differences was the region where educated. Black men and women educated in the North (and, to a lesser extent, in the Deep South) scored more deviantly on several of the basic and special scales of the MMPI. One clear exception to this pattern, however, was the elevation on the REL scale in the Wiggins set, suggesting that subjects from the Middle and Deep South tended to endorse items of religious fundamentalism more than did subjects from the North. However, the higher scores on REL for the men and women from the two southern regions (and for the rural and smaller community dwellers as well) are probably attributable to the fact that the subjects who were recruited for the survey in North Carolina and Alabama were more frequently (57% and 62%, respectively) drawn from church congregations than were subjects from Detroit (only 23%). Answers to this content scale reflect a pattern of endorsement of fundamental Christian beliefs that sample religiousness or conventionality.

The results of the MANOVAs were rather inconsistent on the two scale sets in relation to the marital status of these subjects when they were examined (tables 5.2 through 5.5). In part, this inconsistency may be attributable to the circumstance that only two marital conditions (single and married) could be used in the analyses for the white men and women. That is, there were too few formerly married subjects in the white survey to provide stable results in these analyses. For the black men and women, the subjects who reported being either divorced or separated were combined for the MANOVAs to provide more dependable sample sizes.

Considerably more statistically significant differences were found in the data on marital status from the white men and from the black women. (See tables D-23 through D-26 in the appendix.) Single men, white or black, scored more deviantly on MMPI measures reflecting emotional difficulties, intrafamily tensions, authority problems, and alienation. Black men who had been widowed revealed similar personality characteristics. Although the widowed men earned the highest score of the four groups on scale 2, this level of depression is not significantly different from that of the other groups of black men.

Among the four groups of black women, those who were married at the time of testing proved to be the least deviant on both sets of MMPI scales. The group of single women, as in the case of black men, was the most deviant, with elevated scores on the MMPI measures reflecting primarily interpersonal rather than intrapersonal problems. Poor relationships with their own families, alienation from society, and poor control of anger and hostility—all characterize this group and suggest that these single women are only a little better off psychologically than the group of women who were widowed.

The white adults in the two-state survey also completed the Holmes and Rahe (1967) Social Readjustment Rating Scale. When the items that each subject had checked as being true in their lives during the previous six-month period were weighted by the appropriate values (see Appendix A), a wide range of scores was obtained on the total score of this Life Events Checklist. The men and women on whom these scores were available were grouped into those with low social stress scores (99 or less), moderate stress (between 100 and 199), and high stress scores (200 or more). The scores were somewhat more positively skewed for the women than the men. (The means and standard deviations on the selected MMPI scales, together with the *F* ratios across these levels of reported social stress, are shown in tables D-27 and D-28 in the appendix.) A somewhat dissimilar pattern of differences was obtained for the two sexes, although about the same number of scales showed significant differences at the .05 level or beyond.

For both men and women, scales F, 8 (Sc), and 9 (Ma) in the basic profile and DEP, FAM, PSY, and HYP in the Wiggins set showed reliable differences. Although these variations are not extensive, subjects with high reported social stress scored more pathologically on scales reflecting social and self-alienation, intrapsychic distress and pessimism, and difficulties with members of their own families. Although it is tempting to infer some causal link between the circumstances in the lives of the high-stress subjects and the MMPI differences that they manifest, some recent research on the Holmes and Rahe instrument suggests that individuals who are currently in some state of psychiatric disturbance tend to report prior events in ways that are systematically more adverse than they would if they were not in that emotional condition (Neugebauer, 1981). Thus, it is more likely that the SRRS data and the MMPI responses are drawing upon somewhat comparable conditions; both modes of self-report may be reflecting the prevalence of some forms of emotional disturbance (see Hendrie, Lachar, & Lennox, 1975).

This latter interpretation is strengthened by examining two special supplementary tallies from the Life Events Checklist: reports of some physical illness and reports of changes consistent with some form of psychiatric disturbance. For the former contrast, the overall results of the MANOVAs for the white men and women were not statistically significant. For the reports of more emotional problems (eating, sleeping, and problems in their social life), the MANOVA results on three of the four contrasts were statistically significant (see tables 5.2 and 5.3) for both sets of scores for the men and for the basic scale set for the women. (See also tables D-29 through D-32 in the appendix.)

For comparative purposes, the biographical questionnaires for the black adults were examined for any current medical problems or reports of prior emotional difficulties serious enough to cause them to seek psychiatric help. The corresponding analyses for the black men and women are shown in tables 5.4 and 5.5 (and the means, standard deviations, and *F* ratios for these groups are shown in tables D-33 through D-36 in the appendix). Unlike the analyses of the data from the white men and women, the report of current medical problems turned out to be related to several MMPI variables in the scores from the black sample. Generally, the adults who indicated that they had some medical problem were higher on scales with somatic content and, in addition, on scales reflecting more anxiety (for the men) and emotional distress (for the women).

Even clearer relationships were found between MMPI variables and reported emotional disturbance than were obtained in relation to medical difficulties. A wide variety of significant differences in both the basic scale set and in the Wiggins set appeared in these analyses. Judging from a report of a history of psychiatric care (in the backgrounds of the black adults) or from reports of disturbances in various key aspects of their emotional lives on the SRRS (for white adults), the MMPI responses reflect important differences within these community-based samples of variations in their emotional health and personal effectiveness.

In the analyses reported above, such factors in a subject's background as age grouping, educational level, or occupational level clearly made a difference in how he or she answered the MMPI. In separate analyses each of these broad characteristics was found to be related to scores on many of the component scales of the inventory. Two general concerns remain: To what extent are these factors contributing largely the same variance in each of these parallel analyses? Do these factors play a significant role in the differences found between members of the two racial groups under consideration here? If they do, then black and white adults who are similar in age and education or occupational level should resemble each other closely. To gain some insight into both of these questions, the data from these black and white individuals were subjected to an additional analysis to compare racial differences within more homogeneous subgroups. For this comparison, the few subjects with histories of medical or emotional problems were excluded and two broad age groups were formed (those 34 and younger and a second group 35 and older). Three of the basic scales from the MMPI that have been most consistently the focus of discussion in studies of black and white differences on the test (see chapter 2) were selected for special scrutiny: scales F, 8 (Sc), and 9 (Ma). Within each gender, black and white adults aged 35 years and older were systematically compared within the same educational levels. The results are shown in table 5.7 for men and women within three educational levels: 16 or more years of education; between 13 and 15 years; and 12 or fewer years. (Note that one of these cells contains only a few subjects, which may make some of the values relatively untrustworthy.)

At the ages reported in these comparisons, most men and women have completed their schooling and settled into occupational roles that will characterize them for the remainder of their careers, although there are certainly dramatic exceptions to this pattern, particularly for some women today. Accordingly, it is interesting to note that statistically significant differences for these individuals at the upper and middle educational levels are absent on all three of these scales in comparisons of black and white men and black and white women. At the lowest level of education, significant differences on all three scales appear between black and white adults of both sexes. Adults of each racial group who are close in age, and at levels of education beyond high school, are thus indistinguishable on MMPI scales that have most frequently reflected differences between groups of black and white subjects. That is, many of the kinds of differences that have previously been attributed to all members of these

Table 5.7. Means, Standard Deviations, and *F* Ratios of Differences between Racial Groups on Selected MMPI Scales for Men and Women Aged 35 or More at Three Educational Levels

Educational Level	Scales	Males						Females					
		White		Black				White		Black			
		Mean	S.D.	Mean	S.D.	*F*	*p*	Mean	S.D.	Mean	S.D.	*F*	*p*
16 or more years		(*N* = 36)		(*N* = 47)				(*N* = 28)		(*N* = 67)			
	F	51.5	5.7	54.0	9.6	0.43		49.7	5.1	52.0	7.4	1.38	
	8 (Sc)	54.9	10.2	58.7	13.3	1.37		56.4	7.6	54.7	9.1	3.43	
	9 (Ma)	54.4	8.9	59.5	10.2	3.62		56.6	8.2	57.2	10.9	0.65	
13-15 years		(*N* = 10)		(*N* = 33)				(*N* = 26)		(*N* = 29)			
	F	50.6	3.2	53.7	7.6	0.33		51.0	7.3	54.2	5.7	1.01	
	8 (Sc)	51.3	9.6	56.5	11.8	0.01		52.4	9.8	53.0	8.3	0.00	
	9 (Ma)	56.6	11.2	61.4	9.9	1.61		53.5	11.1	58.0	11.0	2.03	
12 or fewer years		(*N* = 37)		(*N* = 67)				(*N* = 86)		(*N* = 105)			
	F	53.0	10.8	58.6	11.0	6.12	.05	53.5	8.3	59.7	11.5	17.29	.001
	8 (Sc)	53.6	12.1	61.1	12.7	7.08	.01	54.9	9.9	61.8	13.6	14.59	.001
	9 (Ma)	49.8	10.1	61.1	10.6	18.31	.001	54.4	8.6	59.1	11.1	6.93	.01

racial groups are probably characteristic of only part of the ranges of these major demographic features. (The results on the other basic scales of the MMPI for both age groups may be found in tables D-37 through D-42 in the appendix.)

Summary

The analyses reported in this chapter offer ample evidence that the men and women in the two research surveys, both the two-state white sample and the tri-state black sample, are by no means homogeneous in the ways that they answer the MMPI. Both samples show differences within each sex group in relation to age, education, occupational level, health, and marital status that are often as large or larger than the differences in relation to racial membership. Many of the contrasts tend to show that white and black men and women are very much more similar at older age levels, higher educational and occupational levels, and when free of medical and emotional problems. The characteristics that were apparent in the mean profiles on the MMPI representing the total groups of white and black men and women (see chapter 4) by no means occur in any homogeneous way for all members of a particular racial or gender group. Rather, the salient differences between white and black adults tend to characterize the younger, less well-educated, lower-status subjects of both racial groups. Several of the supplementary analyses tended to support the view that the differences on the MMPI that have been attributed to racial membership may not actually reflect racial characteristics per se, but may emerge from black and white comparisons whenever the subjects in the two samples under consideration differ in regard to any or all of the complex set of factors that enter into social class membership.

Stricker (1982) has documented the complexity of socioeconomic indicators in contemporary American society. In particular, he has pointed out the basic difference that occupational level plays in the status hierarchy of black adults. Citing the prior work of Glenn (1963), Stricker notes that his own findings are consistent with Glenn's conclusions that occupational level "is a less important determinant of social status for blacks than whites. One obvious possibility is that the variation in functioning of occupation may be due to the long-run impact on blacks of discrimination and segregation" (p. 164). On the other hand, educational level seems to be a factor that plays a more comparable role in determining status in both white and black respondents, even though it too seems to be a more powerful determiner in white than in black groups (perhaps for the same reasons). The range of MMPI differences for these two facets of socioeconomic status is quite similar: that is, scores on MMPI scales vary over different levels of each factor in much the same way.

Although it is not possible to document that the differences that were obtained among each of these samples in regard to MMPI scores are valid ones reflecting bona fide and important differences in level of psychopathology, the findings to be reported in the next chapter indicate that MMPI scores on both black and white psychiatric patients carry equivalent valid variances against several real-world criteria of emotional disorder. Thus, the present findings tend to support the meaningfulness and dependability of previous research that shows that those men and women who are undereducated, occupy lower occupational status levels, earn lower incomes, have various medical problems, or have limited intellective abilities with which to cope with the stresses of contemporary American life also have a greater prevalence of various forms of emotional disorder. These circumstances, singly or in pernicious combination, are likely to be more prevalent and extreme in the lives of black men and women than is true for white adults, particularly if these black adults live in ghettos in a large metropolitan area or in isolated rural areas in the Deep South.

CHAPTER 6

Relationship of Ethnic Background and Other Demographic Characteristics to MMPI Patterns in Psychiatric Samples

David Lachar, W. Grant Dahlstrom, and Kevin L. Moreland

As indicated in chapters 2 and 3, many investigators, after identifying statistically significant differences on the MMPI between various samples of whites and blacks or other ethnic group members, have raised questions about the suitability of the MMPI norms (or even the use of the instrument itself) for assessing emotionally disturbed members of these minorities. This important research issue obviously demands careful examination and analysis. Unfortunately, most of the discussions in the research literature have been carried out in the absence of dependable criterion information on the emotional well-being of the men and women under consideration in these controversies. That is, the differences that have been noted may be valid reflections of important variations in emotional status or predispositions to psychopathology. The validity of these differences has to be evaluated. In addition, it is vital to know whether the sources of variance found to operate within groups of adults-in-general also contribute important variations in the scores from the MMPI when used with individuals who are manifesting various mental health problems.

Assessment of the Emotional Status of Minority Psychiatric Patients

To explore these possible difficulties in assessing the current mental status of black adult psychiatric patients by means of the MMPI and its largely white normative groups, a sample of 400 adult psychiatric patients who were seen at Lafayette Clinic in Detroit between 1973 and 1977 was surveyed. They were evenly drawn from the eight possible combinations of sex, race (white, black), and status (inpatient, outpatient) to balance these characteristics. Each patient had voluntarily participated in one or more diagnostic interviews and had completed the standard form of the MMPI presented on computer cards; only valid protocols (F scores less than 26, fewer than 30 Cannot Say responses) were included. The subjects ranged in age from 18 to 71 years (mean of 30.2, standard deviation of 10.0), with 50% of the subjects falling between 21 and 39 years old (see table 6.1). Educational levels ranged from 3 to 18 years (mean of 12.3, standard deviation of 2.1), with 60% of the subjects completing between 11 and 13 years of schooling. The medical records documenting the psychiatric evaluation of these patients were abstracted to cover those substantive areas that reflect patient motivation to seek assistance, as well as additional content foci that guide the inquiry of mental health professionals. A subsample of 50 records was studied to assess the reliability of the method of abstracting material in the content areas that were to serve as criteria to document the external validity of the MMPI. Two raters read the medical records independently and recorded the presence or absence of symptoms representing the criteria. The interrater reliability of the resulting ratings was estimated by calculating the percentage of agreement between the two raters, producing an agreement rate of 91% (Lachar & Wrobel, 1979).

Table 6.1. Means and Standard Deviations of Demographic Characteristics in Lafayette Clinic Psychiatric Sample by Race and Sex

	White Males (N = 100)		Black Males (N = 101)			White Females (N = 100)		Black Females (N = 99)		
Variable	Mean	S.D.	Mean	S.D.	p	Mean	S.D.	Mean	S.D.	p
Age	28.6	8.9	28.8	8.5	n.s.	33.0	12.5	30.5	9.2	n.s.
Education	12.3	2.0	11.8	2.3	n.s.	12.5	2.1	12.5	2.0	n.s.

This review of their hospital charts showed that these men and women presented a variety of problems on admission to the Lafayette Clinic. Two kinds of analyses were performed on the tabulations of presenting symptoms; table 6.2 lists the percentage of each race and sex group showing each separate psychiatric feature. The data for each gender were tested for the significance of differences between the racial groups by means of chi-square analyses. The probability levels of the significant differences are also given in table 6.2. Although the male and female groups differ in various characteristic ways in the prevalence of these problems, the patient groups differ less when compared by racial groups within each sex. That is, statistically significant values of chi-square in contrasts between black and white men emerged on only two presenting problems: more black men showed strong antisocial attitudes and more white men manifested sexual concerns. The differences in anxiety and depression on which the white men were higher did not reach statistical significance. Also, the black and white women were very similar in the problems that they presented on admission, differing significantly only on somatic concerns, with black women reporting more of these problems.

Table 6.2. Percentage of Occurrence of 14 Presenting Symptoms in Lafayette Clinic Psychiatric Samples by Race and Sex

Presenting Symptom	White Males ($N = 100$)	Black Males ($N = 101$)	p	White Females ($N = 100$)	Black Females ($N = 99$)	p
Anxiety	31.0	26.7		40.0	36.4	
Depression	52.0	39.6		72.0	68.7	
Sleep disturbance	20.0	21.8		32.0	44.4	
Deviant beliefs	26.0	26.7		20.0	19.2	
Deviant thinking	24.0	22.8		22.0	20.2	
Deviant behavior	17.0	21.8		15.0	14.1	
Drug/alcohol use	22.0	29.7		12.0	14.1	
Antisocial attitude	11.0	23.8	.05	6.0	6.1	
Family problems	22.0	19.8		25.0	19.2	
Problematic anger	23.0	20.8		11.0	14.1	
Sexual deviation	13.0	10.9		2.0	4.0	
Sexual concern	18.0	7.9	.05	11.0	7.1	
Somatic concern	17.0	16.8		19.0	44.4	.001
Neurological screening	4.0	6.9		6.0	12.1	

In addition, the presence or absence of these presenting problems was correlated with the presence or absence of each of the other problems, and the resulting intercorrelations were factor-analyzed (Wrobel & Lachar, 1982). Four major factors were derived: Reality Distortion (deviant beliefs, deviant thinking and experience, and deviant behavior); Sociopathy (drug/alcohol abuse, antisocial attitude, family trouble, and problematic anger); Emotional Discomfort (anxiety and worry, depression and/or suicidal ideation, and sleep disturbance); and Somatization (somatic concern and neurological screening). Scores for each patient on each factor dimension were computed and transformed into z-score format. The means and standard deviations for each of the four groups of patients on each of these factor scores are presented in table 6.3. The men in each racial group did not differ significantly on any of these summary scores; the women differed significantly only on the Somatization factor score, with the black women scoring higher (a finding that is consistent with the data in table 6.2).

The MMPI protocols from the 400 patients were scored on the basic scales and on the Wiggins content scales. The means and standard deviations on these measures are presented in table 6.4, together with statistical tests of significance between the means for each racial group, separately for each gender. Figures 6.1 through 6.4 show the mean profiles of these four patient groups on the basic scales using standard norms of the MMPI.

Table 6.3. Means and Standard Deviations of Factor-based z-scores for Lafayette Clinic Psychiatric Samples by Race and Sex

	White Males (*N* = 100)		Black Males (*N* = 101)			White Females (*N* = 100)		Black Females (*N* = 99)		
Factor	Mean	S.D.	Mean	S.D.	*p*	Mean	S.D.	Mean	S.D.	*p*
I: Reality distortion	0.05	0.78	0.06	0.87	n.s.	−0.02	0.82	−0.09	0.79	n.s.
II: Sociopathy	0.06	0.84	0.09	0.80	n.s.	−0.10	0.61	−0.05	0.70	n.s.
III: Emotional discomfort	−0.14	0.62	−0.24	0.64	n.s.	0.15	0.64	0.24	0.71	n.s.
IV: Somatization	−0.10	0.59	−0.22	0.64	n.s.	0.05	0.52	0.27	0.64	.01

Table 6.4. Means and Standard Deviations of MMPI Basic and Special Scales for Lafayette Clinic Psychiatric Samples by Race and Sex

	White Males (*N* = 100)		Black Males (*N* = 101)			White Females (*N* = 100)		Black Females (*N* = 99)		
Scale	Mean	S.D.	Mean	S.D.	*p*	Mean	S.D.	Mean	S.D.	*p*
L	49.7	9.6	51.6	9.7		49.1	8.9	50.0	9.9	
F	66.1	12.3	69.2	16.1		70.9	13.8	69.8	15.2	
K	49.8	8.8	48.1	8.2		50.3	8.8	50.4	9.5	
Hs	65.5	16.5	66.1	14.9		61.9	12.2	65.8	13.5	.05
D	80.3	19.5	74.6	16.5	.05	74.7	15.6	74.6	13.8	
Hy	69.5	11.7	65.5	12.3	.05	68.0	11.3	70.0	13.5	
Pd	75.7	12.3	73.0	12.3		72.7	13.4	74.4	11.2	
Mf	67.5	11.1	65.1	9.7		47.5	9.2	49.8	7.9	
Pa	67.1	12.9	67.4	13.7		70.1	13.8	69.9	13.2	
Pt	76.6	17.3	69.5	14.8	.01	69.9	13.1	67.1	12.8	
Sc	80.2	18.6	79.2	20.3		75.6	13.4	74.4	14.6	
Ma	60.2	13.4	68.2	12.2	.001	61.4	10.5	63.4	9.2	
Si	59.2	12.1	55.3	10.1	.05	61.1	11.3	59.0	9.8	
ORG	63.5	15.6	64.7	14.1		61.0	12.9	66.2	13.7	.01
HEA	61.5	12.5	63.4	11.8		62.1	12.2	64.5	11.8	
DEP	64.1	14.9	61.4	11.9		65.1	12.8	63.9	13.5	
MOR	60.2	13.2	56.4	10.8	.05	60.5	10.3	58.6	11.8	
SOC	59.0	14.5	54.2	12.5	.01	55.4	12.1	52.9	11.1	
HOS	52.9	10.1	54.4	10.4		53.7	9.3	54.5	9.3	
FAM	66.2	14.5	65.0	14.2		66.2	11.6	67.5	13.5	
AUT	51.6	10.6	56.5	9.8	.001	52.2	10.6	56.2	9.8	.01
FEM	55.2	11.3	58.6	10.9	.05	46.3	9.5	47.5	8.0	
PHO	58.6	12.0	58.6	11.1		54.3	11.3	55.9	9.1	
PSY	59.4	13.8	64.2	12.1	.01	62.8	12.7	63.8	14.0	
HYP	52.8	8.9	54.7	9.5		52.8	9.8	53.5	9.8	
REL	45.7	10.2	47.5	9.6		43.9	10.5	47.8	9.4	.01

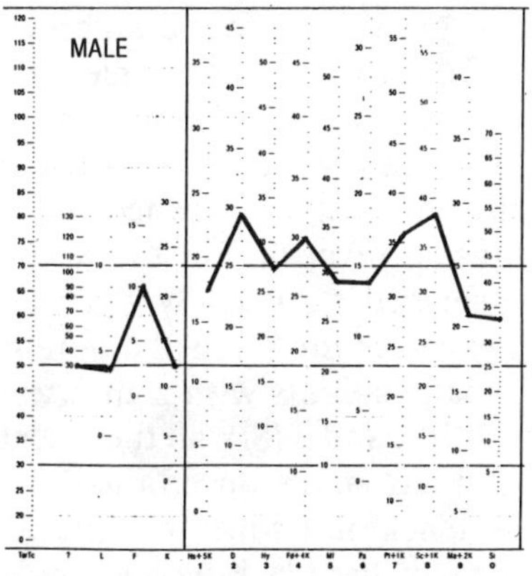

Figure 6.1. Mean profile of Lafayette Clinic white male sample (N = 100).
Code: 28″743561 9-0/ ′F-/KL.

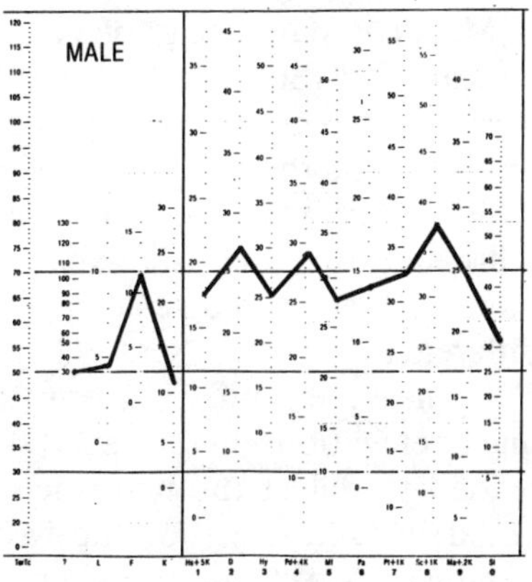

Figure 6.2. Mean profile of Lafayette Clinic black male sample (N = 101).
Code: 824′796135-0/ ′F-L/K.

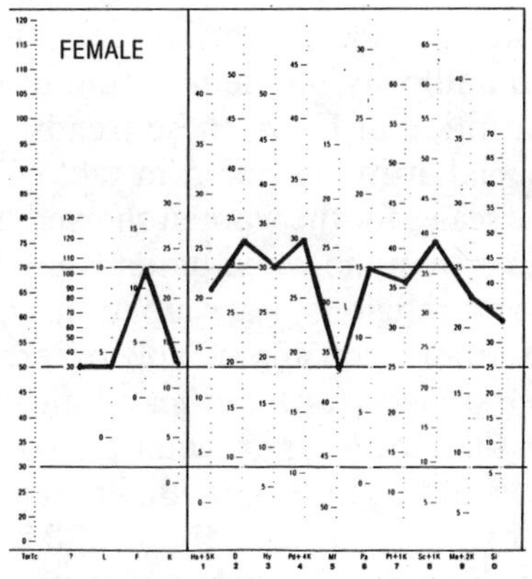

Figure 6.3. Mean profile of Lafayette Clinic white female sample (N = 100).
Code: 8246′73190-/5 F′-K/L.

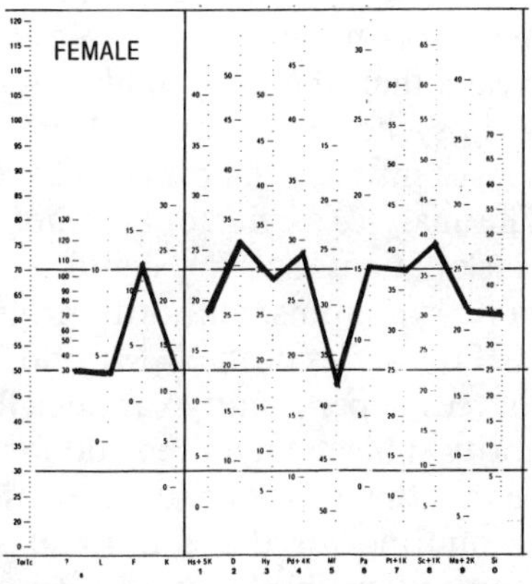

Figure 6.4. Mean profile of Lafayette Clinic black female sample (N = 99).
Code: 248 3′6 719-0/5 ′F-KL/.

Most comparisons of black and white subjects have found differences on scales F, 8 (Sc), and 9 (Ma) (see chapter 2). In the present samples, however, the two groups of male patients differed to a significant extent on only one of these three MMPI scales—namely, scale 9—with the difference on the F scale failing to reach statistical significance and the difference on scale 8 showing a nonsignificant reversal. For the women, none of these three scales (F, 8, or 9) showed statistically significant differences, with only scale 9 being in the expected direction of difference. The white men differed from the black male patients with significantly higher elevations on scales 2 (D), 3 (Hy), 7 (Pt), and 0 (Si); all these scales tended to reflect the neurotic aspects of their status on admission, as noted in table 6.2. For the women, the black and white patients differed even less; only the somatic concerns of the black women, as expressed on scale 1 (Hs), showed statistical significance. This same difference was noted in the presenting symptoms and the Somatization factor as well.

In the corresponding analyses that were carried out on the Wiggins content scale scores (table 6.4), the white men showed significantly higher means on measures of morale and problems in social relations and lower means than the black male patients on authority problems, femininity, and psychotic mentation. With the exception of FEM, these trends are consistent with the difference in antisocial attitudes noted in table 6.2. The analyses carried out on the Wiggins scales for the women showed the black patients scoring significantly higher than the white patients on organic symptoms, authority problems, and religious preoccupations.

If the scales of the MMPI do, in fact, draw upon appreciably different sources of personality variance for black subjects (or for other ethnic minority subjects) than they do for white, then the clear expectation would be that these various scores on the test would operate quite differently in accounting for the emotional status of patients from these different sociocultural backgrounds. To explore these possibilities, two different kinds of analyses were carried out comparing the MMPI scores from each of the four samples of patients and the presenting symptoms that were observed on admission. Each of the 14 symptoms was used as a separate dependent variable in two independent linear regression analyses: first, the set of 10 clinical scales in the basic profile was used as predictors, then the set of 13 Wiggins content scales. The results are listed in tables 6.5 and 6.6, respectively, for each predictor set. For each presenting symptom, the value of R^2 (which is equivalent to the percentage of variance accounted for in the four samples separately) is given, based first on the 10 basic clinical scales and then on the 13 content scales. Because there are three additional predictor scales in the Wiggins set, it was expected (and verified)

Table 6.5. R^2 Values from Linear Regression Analyses of 14 Presenting Symptoms Accounted for by MMPI Basic Clinical Scales for Lafayette Clinic Psychiatric Samples

	Males			Females		
Presenting Symptom	White (N = 100) (1)	Black (N = 101) (2)	t ratio (1 vs. 2)	White (N = 100) (3)	Black (N = 99) (4)	t ratio (3 vs. 4)
Anxiety	.180*	.153	0.513	.140	.141	0.020
Depression	.222**	.167	0.985	.226**	.230**	0.067
Sleep disturbance	.138	.118	0.423	.125	.117	0.173
Deviant beliefs	.145	.132	0.266	.198*	.072	2.653*
Deviant thinking	.113	.161	0.990	.146	.056	2.136*
Deviant behavior	.118	.144	0.545	.094	.183*	1.837
Drug/alcohol use	.221**	.099	2.386*	.089	.160	1.530
Antisocial attitude	.064	.156	2.102*	.090	.074	0.413
Family problems	.132	.091	0.923	.046	.109	1.678
Problematic anger	.079	.098	0.473	.123	.083	0.933
Sexual deviation	.056	.066	0.296	.124	.140	0.334
Sexual concern	.092	.124	0.730	.151	.063	2.034*
Somatic concern	.112	.158	0.954	.187*	.246**	1.016
Neurological screening	.132	.155	0.464	.107	.073	0.842

Note: * = $p < .05$; ** = $p < .01$; *** = $p < .001$.

Table 6.6. R^2 Values from Linear Regression Analysis of 14 Presenting Symptoms Accounted for by MMPI Wiggins Content Scales for Lafayette Clinic Psychiatric Samples

	Males			Females		
Presenting Symptom	White (N = 100) (1)	Black (N = 101) (2)	t ratio (1 vs. 2)	White (N = 100) (3)	Black (N = 99) (4)	t ratio (3 vs. 4)
Anxiety	.131	.150	0.387	.116	.145	0.609
Depression	.340**	.072	4.966***	.168	.275**	1.837
Sleep disturbance	.092	.127	0.793	.120	.171	1.025
Deviant beliefs	.226*	.174	0.921	.324**	.145	3.056**
Deviant thinking	.239*	.313**	1.175	.256*	.199	0.964
Deviant behavior	.189	.200	0.197	.165	.219*	0.972
Drug/alcohol use	.249*	.106	2.694**	.200	.108	1.817
Antisocial attitude	.111	.215	2.011*	.162	.160	0.038
Family problems	.219*	.216*	0.051	.131	.100	0.687
Problematic anger	.180	.147	0.632	.151	.209	1.071
Sexual deviation	.196	.086	2.263*	.134	.158	0.481
Sexual concern	.113	.181	1.364	.179	.064	2.528*
Somatic concern	.137	.291**	2.703**	.238*	.301**	1.007
Neurological screening	.184	.148	0.685	.187	.099	1.792

Note: * = $p < .05$; ** = $p < .01$; *** = $p < .001$.

that these percentages would run somewhat higher for the analyses using the Wiggins scales than for those based on the clinical scales.

Although the amount of variance accounted for in these symptoms varied widely (from over one-third of the variance to well under 10%), the general ranges of variance accounted for by these linear weights are not appreciably different for the two sexes nor for the two racial groups. There is some evidence, however, that the clinical symptoms manifested by white men or women are accounted for a little more accurately than are similar features shown by black patients. Some exceptions to this general pattern do appear, however, and it is difficult to be certain whether these departures reflect limitations in the component test scales or in the ranges of variation presented in these particular samples of psychiatric patients (see Bernstein, Schoenfeld, & Costello, 1982). For example, the regression weights assigned to the 10 basic clinical scales in the standard profile predict the presence and extent of symptomatic depression (from between one-fifth to one-fourth of this variance) in white male and female patients in this hospital and in the black female patients as well; but they predict less than one-fifth of the variance in rated depression seen in the presenting symptomatology of the black male patients. The percentage of black men showing depressive features, however, was appreciably lower than for the three other groups (i.e., under 40%, as compared with more than 50% for white men and nearly 70% for both groups of women; see table 6.2). Comparing the relative effectiveness of the clinical scale set and the Wiggins content scale set against the criterion of depression, the differences in percentage of variance accounted for by the content scales do not appear to be based on racial membership either, since these scores work well for white men and black women but not as well for the other two groups of patients.

The four factor scores derived from the ratings on the presenting symptoms (Wrobel & Lachar, 1982) show less variation in either means or standard deviations from one sex or racial group to another; accordingly, they should be more satisfactory than the individual symptoms as dependent variables. Two additional regression analyses using these factor scores and both the basic clinical scale set and the Wiggins content scale set were performed (tables 6.7 and 6.8). There were some important differences in the extent to which the two sets of scales were able to account for statistically significant proportions of variance in these factor scores. The Wiggins scales did considerably better than the basic profile scales for all four groups in predicting the Reality Distortion factor and a little better in predicting Somatic Concern in the black patient groups. The basic scale set did somewhat better in reflecting the degree of Emotional Discomfort, but neither of these two sets of MMPI scores was very accurate in reflecting variations in the Sociopathy dimension. There is little evidence in either of the analyses, however, to indicate that the basic or content scales from the MMPI fail to work as well in assessing emotional status for black patients as they do in assessing white patients. Against these factor-score criteria, the comparisons within each of the sex groups

Table 6.7. R^2 Values from Linear Regression Analyses of the Factor Score Dimensions of Presenting Symptoms Accounted for by MMPI Basic Clinical Scales (Lafayette Clinic Samples)

	Males			Females		
Factor Dimension	White (*N* = 100) (1)	Black (*N* = 101) (2)	*t* ratio (1 vs. 2)	White (*N* = 100) (3)	Black (*N* = 99) (4)	*t* ratio (3 vs. 4)
Reality distortion	.132	.148	0.326	.177	.084	1.971
Sociopathy	.139	.116	0.488	.095	.073	0.561
Emotional discomfort	.256**	.156	1.762	.204*	.224**	0.345
Somatization	.173	.225**	0.923	.105	.228**	2.367*

Note: * = $p < .05$; ** = $p < .01$; *** = $p < .001$.

Table 6.8. R^2 Values from Linear Regression Analyses of the Factor Score Dimensions of Presenting Symptoms Accounted for by MMPI Wiggins Content Scales (Lafayette Clinic Samples)

	Males			Females		
Factor Dimension	White (*N* = 100) (1)	Black (*N* = 101) (2)	*t* ratio (1 vs. 2)	White (*N* = 100) (3)	Black (*N* = 99) (4)	*t* ratio (3 vs. 4)
Reality distortion	.338**	.304**	0.515	.306**	.262**	0.691
Sociopathy	.212	.165	0.851	.124	.183	1.161
Emotional discomfort	.233*	.056	3.678***	.208	.219*	0.190
Somatization	.205	.274**	1.147	.154	.274**	2.091*

Note: * = $p < .05$; ** = $p < .01$; *** = $p < .001$.

that contrast data from the black and white patients seem to balance one another.

To determine the extent to which the test correlates among these presenting problems were comparable for black and white psychiatric patients, a series of additional analyses was performed separately for each racial group on the scores from the MMPI and from ratings of presence or absence of each presenting problem. For the purpose of these analyses, data from the men and women in each racial group were combined to lend greater stability to the findings. In addition to the basic scales and Wiggins content scales, three supplementary scales were included in the analyses: Welsh's factor scales, A (Anxiety) and R (Repression), and Barron's Ego strength scale, Es. Groups were formed on each scale of high and low scorers (usually a T score of 70 or above, and one of 69 or below). Both a chi-square and a phi coefficient were computed on the relationship of high or low scores and presence or absence of each presenting problem. The results of these analyses are summarized in Appendix E with the correlates that showed a statistically significant relationship with each of the basic scales, plus A, R, and Es listed in table E-1 and those for the Wiggins content scales in table E-2. These findings are not cross-validated, however, and there is likely to be some shrinkage in these values and changes in the particular correlates that were identified (especially those scale correlates that are more stable or consistent within one gender or the other in these data from the mixed-sex groups).

Examination of the patterns of scale correlates within each racial group shows a large variability in the extent to which particular scales of the MMPI are significantly related to the presenting problems identified in the admission notes of these psychiatric patients. There is also considerable variation in what is correlated with any one scale of the MMPI in comparisons across the two racial groups. That is, scales 1 (Hs) and 6 (Pa) are related to several presenting problems in the data from the white men and women but to only one or two problems in material from the black patients; the opposite seems to hold for scales 2 (D) and 3 (Hy), with several correlates appearing at a significant level for the black patients but with only a few for the white men and women. Nevertheless, when comparable correlates do appear for particular scales in both racial groups, there is no instance in which the direction of the relationship is reversed. The total numbers of scale correlates in each of these groups are also comparable. Little support was found in this set of findings for the conclusion that the MMPI does not work as well for black as for white patients.

Application of Black Norms to MMPI Records from Psychiatric Patients at Lafayette Clinic

To evaluate the effect on elevation and patterning of MMPI profiles from the use of a set of special T-score values based on the tri-state sample of normal black adults, test records from new and larger samples of both white and black patients examined in the psychiatric services of Lafayette Clinic were used. These records were drawn from the register of all patients to whom the MMPI had been given during a five-year interval. Patients from each racial group were selected to be as comparable as possible in gender, inpatient or outpatient status, age, and educational level. The average age and education of the men and women in each of these groups are presented in table 6.9.

The raw scores on the basic MMPI scales obtained by the white patients were corrected where necessary by the usual K weights and converted to T-score values on the Minnesota-based MMPI norms appropriate for each sex. In contrast, the raw scores on these same scales obtained by the black patients were converted after K correction to T-score values in two different ways: first, as with the white patients, using the Minnesota-based norms; second, using T-score conversion values derived from the means and standard deviations of the men and women in the tri-state sample of black adults (see Appendix H). The resulting T-score patterns on each patient were coded using the Welsh system (see Appendix B for these procedures and symbols). To evaluate the comparability of the profile patterns resulting from the two sets of T-score values on the records from the black men and women, all of the codes were categorized both by code type and by code-type category in the Lachar system (see chapter 4).

Table 6.9. Means and Standard Deviations of Demographic Characteristics by Race and Sex in Another Lafayette Clinic Psychiatric Sample

	White Males (*N* = 192)		Black Males (*N* = 197)			White Females (*N* = 286)		Black Females (*N* = 280)		
Variable	Mean	S.D.	Mean	S.D.	*p*	Mean	S.D.	Mean	S.D.	*p*
Age	28.8	9.3	29.0	9.0	n.s.	31.3	10.7	31.2	10.5	n.s.
Education	12.0	2.1	11.9	2.2	n.s.	12.3	2.0	12.3	2.0	n.s.

Table 6.10. Percentages of White and Black Lafayette Clinic Psychiatric Patients by MMPI Code-Type Categories

	Males		Females	
Category	White	Black	White	Black
Invalid	10.9	12.7	8.0	10.7
Normal	12.5	5.6	11.9	8.9
Neurotic	24.0	15.7	13.6	17.1
Characterological	19.3	35.0	31.1	30.4
Psychotic	32.3	29.4	29.4	28.6
Other	1.0	1.6	6.0	4.3
	100.0	100.0	100.0	100.0

Note: More detailed tabulation of code types appears in Appendix E.

The first comparison performed on the codes involved the patterns of basic scales based on the Minnesota norms used in the standard profile of the MMPI. When placed into code-type categories, the profile patterns from each group of patients fell into the categories shown in table 6.10. Invalid records were separated out on any one of three criteria: excessive numbers of Cannot Say responses (30 or more omitted items); F scale values in the random response range (26 raw score points or higher); or large differences between the raw scores on the F and K scales (F minus K greater than +16). Somewhat larger numbers of records from black patients were eliminated on these bases than were records from white patients. Profiles with no clinical scale (except scale 5) elevated at or beyond a T score of 70 on the Minnesota norms were classified as within normal limits. More of these "test misses" were found among the profiles from the white patients than were found in the test records from the black patients. In the remaining records, about 30% of the profiles from all four groups were classified as psychotic patterns based upon the elevation and configuration of the nine clinical scales (again omitting scores on scale 5); another one-third were called characterological disorders; and the remainder were called neurotic or were left unclassified. Black patients obtained significantly more records with the following code types: 13/31, 48/84, 89/98, and 9 spike. They obtained significantly fewer records within normal limits and 27/72 and 78/87 code types than did the white patients when both sets of records were scaled on the Minnesota-based T-score values.

Table 6.11. Percentage of Code-Type Categories in Profiles of Black Lafayette Clinic Psychiatric Patients Based on Standard and Tri-State Norms

Classification on Standard Norms	*N*	%	Classification on Tri-State Norms: Invalid (*N* = 7; 1.5%)	Normal (*N* = 146; 30.7%)	Neurotic (*N* = 176; 37.0%)	Characterological (*N* = 80; 16.8%)	Psychotic (*N* = 34; 7.1%)	Other (*N* = 33; 6.9%)
Invalid	42	8.8	16.7%	4.8%	19.0%	11.9%	31.0%	16.7%
Normal	36	7.6	0.0	100.0	0.0	0.0	0.0	0.0
Neurotic	84	17.6	0.0	17.9	81.0	0.0	0.0	1.1
Characterological	157	33.0	0.0	35.7	19.7	40.8	0.6	3.2
Psychotic	142	29.8	0.0	33.2	44.4	7.0	14.1	11.3
Other	15	3.0	0.0	26.7	40.0	6.6	0.0	26.7

In a second comparison, the profiles from the black patients were reclassified on the basis of T-score values derived from the tri-state sample. Based on these codes, the MMPI records from the black men and women were again assigned to a category in the Lachar profile typology. The extent of the shifts in type classification is shown in table E-3 in the appendix and is summarized in table 6.11. The data from both male and female samples were combined for these comparisons. Of the 42 profiles called invalid in the original classification based upon the standard norms, only 7 were still called invalid. All the records originally classified as within normal limits remained in this category and an additional 110 records were called normal (over 30% of this sample of psychiatric patients!). Thus, the number of test records from these psychiatric patients that were misidentified as within normal limits rose to a very unacceptable level on the basis of the use of these special black norms. In addition, the number of neurotic profile types more than doubled and the profiles in the psychotic and characterological categories were reduced by 76% and 49%, respectively. Only 27.5% of the 476 records from these black psychiatric patients maintained the same code pattern, while 40.3% of the profiles stayed within the same broad code-type category.

In an effort to determine whether the higher number of profiles from black patients that were categorized by code type into the psychotic group when they were plotted on the standard norms reflected less accurate placement for these patients than for the white patients, a sample of 41 black patients and 27 white patients with either 68/86 or 89/98 codes was selected for a special review of the hospital charts. Examination of these materials generated clear and conclusive bases for a psychotic diagnosis in 44% of the patients in the black group and 37% of the patients in the white group. Thus, there was little indication that the code category was any less accurate for the black psychiatric patients than it was for the white patients with the same MMPI profile patterns.

Effect of Plotting Psychiatric Patient Profiles on Tri-State Norms

The way in which a change in normative values can affect the accuracy of the resulting MMPI profile patterns is illustrated by examining the changes in test scores from two patients who were treated at the Lafayette Clinic. Patient A was a 21-year-old, single, black female who had earned a tenth-grade education in the Deep South. She had first experienced auditory hallucinations at the age of 16 and had been placed on medication at that time. The MMPI was completed as part of a routine admission assessment. She was hospitalized because she was unable to adjust to a boarding home placement that had followed a jail term of several months. This imprisonment occurred because she had murdered her brother with a kitchen knife during an argument. At this boarding home she had displayed symptoms of autism, self-preoccupation, withdrawal, and depression. On admission she was autistic, withdrawn, and confused; displayed inappropriate affect; and responded to visual hallucinations. During hospitalization she confided that she thought she was a witch because every time she left her house a German shepherd dog would die. She also noted that she had the ability to predict the death of various people, particularly those with whom she was angry. A review of the chart indicated that she was unable to be maintained as an outpatient and required subsequent hospitalizations for recurrent episodes of psychotic symptoms and threatening behavior. Patient A's MMPI profile is shown in figure 6.5.

Standard T-score elevations of scales F, 4 (Pd), 6 (Pa), 8 (Sc), and 9 (Ma) accurately reflect this patient's disorganized and aggressive behavior. The 68/86 high-point code type and the secondary elevations of scales 4 and 9 correspond to the seriousness and chronicity of her adjustment, as does the T score of 78 on the F scale. In comparison, the profile generated by the contemporary tri-state norms is essentially within normal limits. The elevation on scale 6 (Pa) would not provide even the most experienced MMPI clinician an indication of the magnitude of this patient's problems.

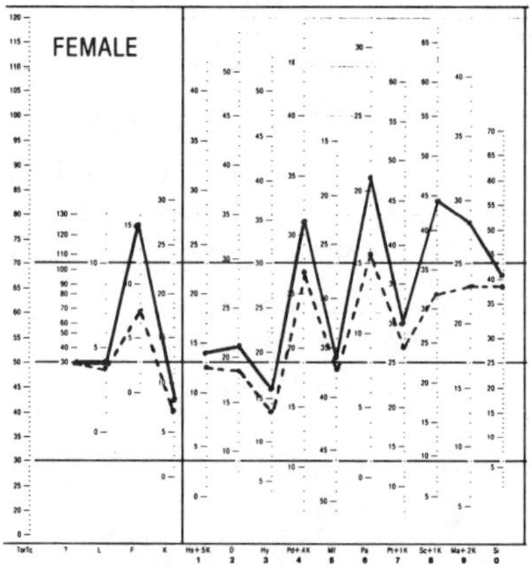

Figure 6.5. Patient A—single black woman; 21 years old.
Solid line: standard norms. Code: 68″49′0-7215/3 F′-/LK.
Dashed line: tri-state norms. Code: 6′4908-7/1523 F-/LK.

Patient B was a 38-year-old, divorced, black male with a tenth-grade education. This MMPI was obtained as part of an outpatient reevaluation following discharge from the hospital. In this interview, the patient complained that he was under a great deal of tension and having difficulty sleeping because he was the president of the United States, chief executive of the United Nations, and in charge of the city's police department. Because of the extensiveness of his delusions and the grandiose nature of his self-presentation, it was impossible to obtain information about his current situation. He claimed that he had killed his parents because they had committed treason and that his marriage had been annulled by Congress because he had been married at the age of seven. At this current evaluation he refused the recommendation of rehospitalization and eventually refused to continue his antipsychotic medication. During one subsequent interview he demanded methadone to treat a heroin addiction that he claimed had been previously supported by the Treasury Department. A review of his medical records indicated a 15-year history of psychosis manifested primarily by a variety of delusional systems that had led to at least three previous hospitalizations. His MMPI profile is shown in figure 6.6.

The T-score elevations based on the standard norms of scales F, 6 (Pa), 8 (Sc), and 9 (Ma) accurately reflect this patient's delusions, grandiose beliefs, and disorganization. Secondary elevations on scales 1 (Hs) and 5 (Mf) signal somatic and sexual concerns. In fact, concerns about his body image and sexual identification had been the focus of a previous delusional system that had led to this patient's first contact with mental health services. Blind analysis of the profile generated by contemporary tri-state norms, in contrast, would suggest some suspiciousness and oversensitivity, indirect expression of anger, and perhaps somatic concern in an otherwise energetic individual—a description far from accurate.

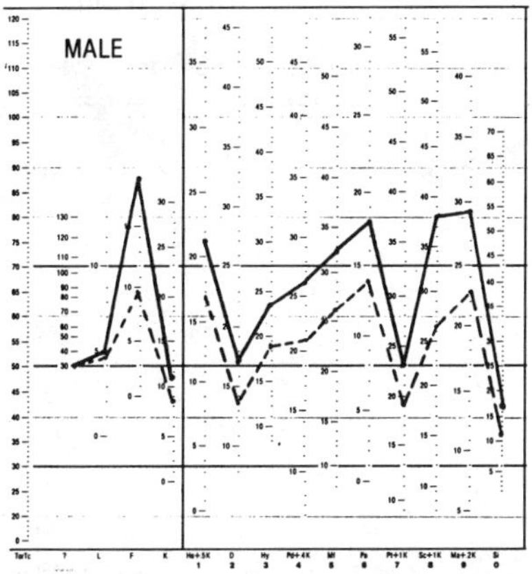

Figure 6.6. Patient B—divorced black man; 38 years old.
Solid line: standard norms. Code: 98″615′43-27/0 F″′-L/K.
Dashed line: tri-state norms. Code: ′6915-843/27:0 F-L/K.

Effect of Using Tri-State Norms on Screening for Emotional Disorder in a Personnel Setting

An additional comparison of changes in profile patterns resulting from the use of a different normative reference group was performed on a set of MMPI records from male applicants to the police academy in the city of Detroit. MMPI records from 200 black and 200 white applicants were used; the two groups were matched on age (mean of 26 years) and educational level (mean of 13 years). When the scores on the basic scales were plotted on the standard norms, there were 29 profiles from the white applicants that were both valid and had some elevation over a T score of 70 on at least one of the clinical scales (omitting scale 5); in the valid records from the black applicants, however, there were 55 with elevations over 70 (see table 6.12). Although the numbers of neurotic and psychotic patterns were comparable (each around 2% of the group), the number of characterological patterns found in the black applicants was over twice as large as that found in the profiles from the white applicants (46 vs. 21). The most frequent patterns in the characterological category were single elevations (spikes) on either scale 9 (Ma) or scale 4 (Pd), with the numbers of the former twice as prevalent as the latter. The results were altered considerably, however, when the MMPI profiles for the black police applicants were plotted on the tri-state T-score values (see Appendix H). The number of elevated profiles from the black applicants was markedly reduced (from 55 to 6). Only two of these profiles had a spike on scale 9 and one showed a spike on scale 4. In this set of data as well, it seems apparent that the use of the tri-state sample as a normative reference group overcorrects for the differences between the white and black applicants.

Table 6.12. Effect of Tri-State Norms on Code-Type Categorizations for Police Applicants

	White Applicants (*N* = 200)		Black Applicants (*N* = 200)			
	Minnesota Norms		Minnesota Norms		Black Norms	
Code-Type Category	*N*	%	*N*	%	*N*	%
Normal limits	171	85.5	145	72.5	194	97.0
Neurotic	4	2.0	4	2.0	0	0.0
Psychotic	4	2.0	5	2.5	0	0.0
Characterological	21	10.5	46	23.0	6	3.0
4′	(6)	(3.0)	(12)	(6.0)	(1)	(0.5)
9′	(9)	(4.5)	(24)	(12.0)	(2)	(1.0)

Background Characteristics and MMPI Scores from Cleveland Psychiatric Institute Patients

Because the samples of psychiatric patients from the Lafayette Clinic were drawn in such a way as to minimize differences between black and white men and women in age and education and were somewhat limited in total numbers as well, it was decided to add samples of psychiatric patients from the Cleveland Psychiatric Institute first reported by Graham, Allon, Friedman, and Lilly (1971). The information available on these patients made it possible to explore the relationships between MMPI scores and various other background factors in addition to ethnic membership. The patients were evaluated during the late 1960s as part of a large-scale, federally funded research investigation covering intake assessment, ward behavior, differential response to therapy, and need for continuing inpatient care. On admission, the MMPI was administered routinely and the intake clinician completed a set of descriptive ratings on the Overall and Gorham (1962) *Brief Psychiatric Rating Scales* (BPRS). During the first week, the nursing personnel also rated these patients in a ward setting using the Honigfeld, Gillis, and Klett (1966) *Nurses' Observation Scales for Inpatient Evaluation* (NOSIE-30). For each of these rating instruments, the original authors had also intercorrelated the variables generated by these various ratings and had factor-analyzed them. Based on those studies, there are four factor scores that can be computed for each subject from the 16 variables in the BPRS and six factor scores that can be derived from the 30 variables in the NOSIE. In the following analyses, only these factor scores were used in the exploration of background characteristics and MMPI variables.

Table 6.13. Background Characteristics of the Cleveland Psychiatric Institute Sample

	Males						Females					
	White			Black			White			Black		
	N	Mean	S.D.	*N*	Mean	S.D.	*N*	Mean	S.D.	*N*	Mean	S.D.
Age	262	39.3	12.0	103	36.0	11.0	409	39.7	13.1	163	33.5	11.4
Education	255	10.6	2.9	102	9.5	2.5	405	10.7	2.4	157	9.9	2.2
Socioeconomic status	255	11.6	4.3	102	10.2	3.6	406	11.8	3.9	160	9.7	3.0

Table 6.14. Means and Standard Deviations of BPRS and NOSIE Factor Scores for the Cleveland Psychiatric Institute Sample

	Males				Females			
	White (*N* = 262)		Black (*N* = 103)		White (*N* = 409)		Black (*N* = 163)	
Factor Dimension	Mean	S.D.	Mean	S.D.	Mean	S.D.	Mean	S.D.
BPRS[a]								
Thinking disturbance	6.7	4.2	8.2	5.0	7.6	4.3	9.7	4.6
Psychomotor retardation	8.9	3.5	9.2	4.3	10.8	4.2	12.3	4.3
Suspiciousness	4.4	2.9	4.5	2.7	5.6	3.1	6.8	3.3
Anxiety/depression	13.8	5.1	11.4	4.3	17.0	5.4	16.4	5.5
NOSIE[b]								
Social competence	33.1	8.0	31.4	9.0	32.6	8.7	29.1	10.5
Social interest	14.0	8.9	13.1	9.9	12.5	9.4	10.8	9.3
Personal neatness	24.2	6.7	22.5	7.3	23.5	7.7	20.9	8.5
Irritability	7.4	9.1	7.7	9.8	7.4	9.2	8.9	10.2
Manifest psychosis	3.6	6.4	5.1	7.5	3.1	5.7	5.3	7.2
Psychomotor retardation	5.9	4.9	6.5	5.0	6.5	5.7	7.9	6.0

[a]Brief Psychiatric Rating Scales (Overall & Gorham, 1962).
[b]Nurses' Observation Scales for Inpatient Evaluation (Honigfeld, Gillis, & Klett, 1966).

A summary of the age, education, and socioeconomic background of the black and white men and women included in this sample is provided in table 6.13. The patients averaged about 10 years older than those in the Lafayette Clinic sample (in their late thirties or early forties); they had an average educational level somewhat below that of the Lafayette Clinic patients (only about 10 years of schooling) and came from a lower class or lower-middle class family background. Table 6.14 lists the means and standard deviations on the factor scores for the same four groups on the BPRS and NOSIE ratings. These men and women displayed anxiety and depression most prominently, as rated by the treatment staff, with psychomotor retardation and social withdrawal as additional features. In their dealings with these patients on their wards, the nurses noted a lack of social interest and irritability as their main problems.

Table 6.15. Means and Standard Deviations on MMPI Basic and Special Scales for the Cleveland Psychiatric Institute Sample

	Males				Females			
	White (*N* = 262)		Black (*N* = 103)		White (*N* = 409)		Black (*N* = 163)	
Scale	Mean	S.D.	Mean	S.D.	Mean	S.D.	Mean	S.D.
L	51.8	8.3	51.5	8.5	54.2	8.7	52.9	8.0
F	62.8	12.8	70.8	13.8	63.3	12.9	66.5	13.9
K	52.5	9.9	49.5	9.3	52.3	9.5	49.9	9.5
Hs	62.0	14.9	62.1	14.1	59.5	12.9	57.9	11.0
D	69.5	17.5	65.7	13.0	64.6	14.9	61.3	12.2
Hy	61.9	11.1	59.6	11.5	61.7	12.1	58.1	11.6
Pd	69.3	12.2	71.1	12.2	67.8	12.3	67.5	12.4
Mf	58.5	10.3	59.6	9.6	51.9	10.2	54.5	9.5
Pa	61.2	11.9	67.3	14.3	64.3	12.6	64.4	15.1
Pt	65.5	14.2	67.0	13.5	62.9	12.5	60.3	11.7
Sc	68.2	17.2	76.0	17.9	67.5	15.2	68.4	15.7
Ma	62.9	11.9	69.5	11.1	62.0	12.7	64.2	12.4
Si	55.0	11.0	54.8	8.5	58.4	10.6	57.1	9.0
A	55.3	11.6	58.5	11.0	54.1	10.8	54.7	11.5
R	51.0	11.3	48.3	11.4	50.9	12.2	48.0	11.1
Es	42.3	11.4	37.9	11.4	43.6	11.1	41.8	12.6
ORG	57.8	14.4	62.0	13.5	57.2	14.2	59.4	14.2
HEA	56.5	12.4	58.2	10.5	55.7	11.8	57.0	10.5
DEP	58.8	12.9	61.7	12.1	58.2	13.4	58.1	12.8
MOR	54.6	11.5	56.1	10.5	53.9	11.1	53.7	11.3
SOC	53.6	11.9	52.9	9.5	52.5	10.9	50.9	8.7
HOS	50.5	9.2	54.2	9.8	51.1	10.2	54.3	9.7
FAM	59.2	14.4	63.9	14.3	59.5	13.6	61.2	12.6
AUT	54.3	9.9	57.8	9.3	53.2	11.4	57.4	10.3
FEM	44.6	10.2	41.6	9.3	47.8	9.2	48.4	8.4
PHO	57.0	12.3	62.7	13.3	54.2	11.1	57.1	10.2
PSY	56.0	12.0	65.6	14.6	58.9	15.0	64.5	16.5
HYP	53.9	10.0	56.6	9.7	52.7	10.3	54.5	11.0
REL	50.9	8.7	53.4	8.0	49.7	9.4	52.8	8.0

Table 6.15 lists the means and standard deviations that these four groups of patients earned on the basic and special scales upon admission to the hospital. Figures 6.7 through 6.10 show the mean profiles from the four patient groups. Only the black male patients showed appreciable departure from the average score levels presented on the various scales by

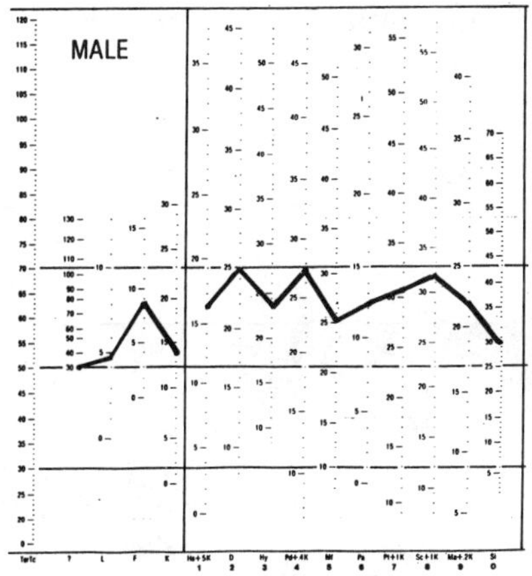

Figure 6.7. Mean profile of Cleveland white male sample (N = 262).
Code: '24879136-50/ 'F-KL/.

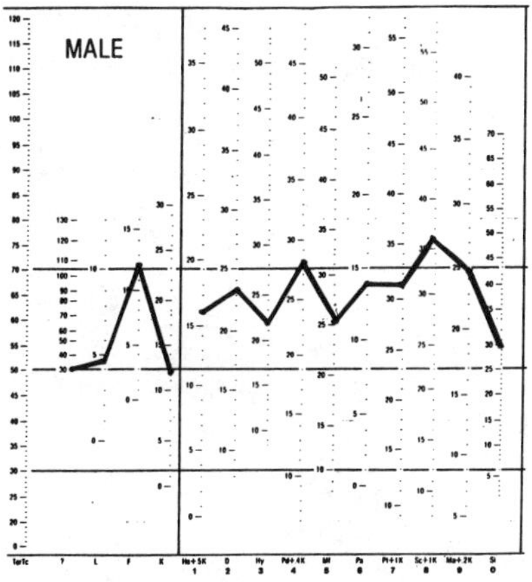

Figure 6.8. Mean profile of Cleveland black male sample (N = 103).
Code: 84'9 6721-350/ F'-L/K.

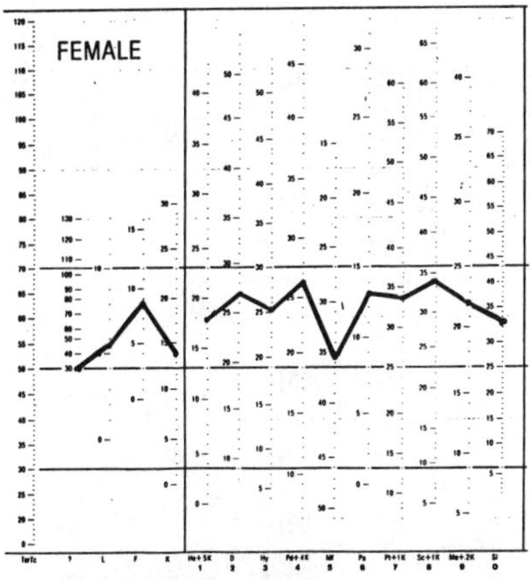

Figure 6.9. Mean profile of Cleveland white female sample (N = 409).
Code: '48 26793-105/ 'F-LK/.

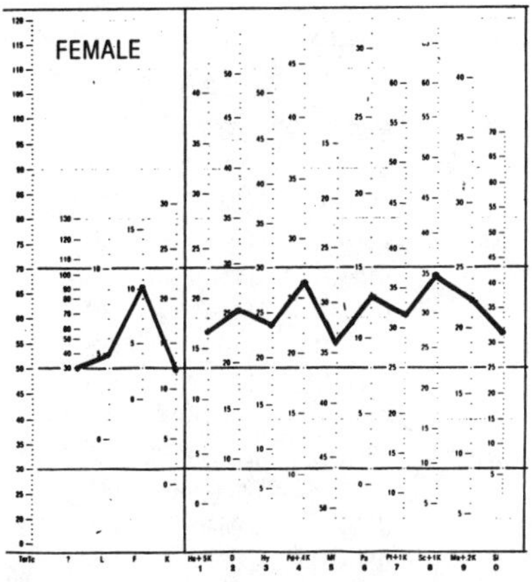

Figure 6.10. Mean profile of Cleveland black female sample (N = 163).
Code: '84 69 27-3105/ 'F-L/K.

the other three groups, ranging well above 70 on scale 8 (Sc) particularly. Generally, however, the means earned by these subjects are not as deviant as those found in the Lafayette Clinic samples.

Table 6.16. R^2 Values from a Stepwise Regression Analysis on Samples of Black and White Psychiatric Patients (N = 1,106)

	Steps							R^2
Scale	1	2	3	4	5	6	7	Total
L	$.023_{A}^{***}$	$.018_{G}^{***}$	$.004_{P}^{*}$	$.002_{R}$	$.002_{E}$	$.001_{O}$	...	.050
F	$.038_{S}^{*}$	$.015_{P}^{***}$	$.012_{A}^{**}$	$.008_{E}^{**}$	$.007_{G}^{**}$	$.008_{R}^{**}$	...	.088
K	$.034_{E}^{**}$	$.009_{R}^{*}$	$.002_{S}$	$.001_{O}$	$.001_{P}$	...	...	.047
Hs	$.020_{G}^{***}$	$.019_{S}^{*}$	$.009_{A}^{*}$	$.003_{P}$	$.002_{R}$	$.002_{E}$	...	.055
D	$.030_{G}^{***}$	$.008_{R}^{**}$	$.011_{S}^{*}$	$.002_{A}$	$.001_{O}$	...	...	.052
Hy	$.011_{R}^{**}$	$.002_{P}$	$.002_{G}$	$.001_{A}$	$.001_{E}$	...	...	.017
Pd	$.049_{A}^{***}$	$.003_{G}$	$.003_{S}$	$.001_{O}$	$.001_{P}$	$.001_{E}$	...	.058
Mf	$.057_{G}^{***}$	$.013_{E}^{*}$	$.003_{R}$	$.003_{A}$	$.003_{P}$	$.001_{O}$	...	.080
Pa	$.017_{P}^{***}$	$.017_{E}^{*}$	$.004_{R}$	$.003_{A}$	$.001_{S}$	...	...	.042
Pt	$.031_{G}$	$.004_{A}$	$.003_{S}$	$.002_{P}$	$.001_{R}$	$.001_{O}$	...	.042
Sc	$.020_{S}$	$.014_{G}^{***}$	$.014_{A}^{***}$	$.014_{P}^{***}$	$.004_{R}$	$.003_{E}$	...	.069
Ma	$.026_{R}^{***}$	$.014_{A}^{***}$	$.011_{G}^{***}$	$.009_{P}^{**}$	$.001_{E}$	$.001_{O}$	$.001_{S}$	.063
Si	$.021_{G}^{***}$	$.021_{S}^{**}$	$.004_{R}^{*}$	$.002_{O}$	$.001_{A}$	$.001_{P}$	$.001_{E}$	.051
A	$.020_{S}$	$.009_{G}$	$.003_{R}$	$.003_{E}$	$.002_{P}$	$.001_{A}$	$.001_{O}$	.039
R	$.015_{R}^{***}$	$.008_{A}^{**}$	$.001_{S}^{*}$	$.004_{E}$	$.002_{P}$	...	...	.030
Es	$.079_{S}^{**}$	$.015_{G}^{***}$	$.008_{A}^{**}$	$.008_{P}^{**}$	$.010_{E}^{**}$	$.005_{O}^{*}$	$.002_{R}$	.127
ORG	$.052_{S}^{*}$	$.008_{P}^{***}$	$.009_{G}^{**}$	$.008_{E}^{*}$	$.005_{O}^{*}$	$.002_{A}$	$.001_{S}$	.085
HEA	$.043_{S}^{*}$	$.009_{P}^{***}$	$.008_{E}^{**}$	$.005_{G}^{*}$	$.001_{O}$	...	...	.066
DEP	$.025_{E}^{*}$	$.005_{G}^{*}$	$.004_{S}$	$.005_{A}^{*}$	$.002_{O}$	$.001_{P}$	...	.042
MOR	$.021_{S}$	$.004_{G}^{*}$	$.001_{E}$	$.001_{P}$	$.001_{A}$	...	...	.028
SOC	$.015_{S}^{*}$	$.005_{R}^{*}$	$.003_{G}$	$.001_{P}$	$.001_{O}$	...	...	.025
HOS	$.024_{R}^{***}$	$.011_{E}^{*}$	$.007_{A}^{**}$	$.005_{P}^{*}$	...	...	...	.047
FAM	$.034_{A}^{***}$	$.010_{S}$	$.005_{R}^{*}$	$.001_{G}$	$.001_{P}$	...	...	.051
AUT	$.037_{E}^{**}$	$.021_{R}^{***}$	$.003_{A}$	$.002_{O}$	$.001_{S}$	$.001_{G}$	...	.065
FEM	$.042_{G}^{***}$	$.007_{S}$	$.004_{A}^{*}$	$.002_{P}$	$.001_{R}$	$.001_{O}$	$.001_{E}$	.058
PHO	$.064_{E}^{***}$	$.028_{G}^{***}$	$.012_{S}^{*}$	$.008_{P}^{**}$	$.006_{R}^{**}$	$.004_{A}$	$.001_{O}$	.123
PSY	$.063_{P}^{***}$	$.004_{G}$	$.002_{O}$	$.001_{S}$	$.001_{E}$	...	...	.071
HYP	$.012_{R}^{*}$	$.006_{E}^{*}$	$.005_{G}^{*}$	$.002_{A}$	$.001_{P}$	$.001_{S}$	...	.027
REL	$.011_{R}^{**}$	$.007_{A}^{*}$	$.004_{G}^{*}$	$.003_{E}$	$.002_{P}$	$.001_{O}$	...	.028
Rs	$.078_{R}^{***}$	$.035_{E}^{**}$	$.004_{O}$	$.003_{A}^{*}$	$.003_{G}^{*}$	$.004_{P}$	$.002_{S}$	.129
B-W	$.100_{R}^{***}$	$.026_{E}^{***}$	$.008_{P}^{**}$	$.001_{G}$	$.001_{A}$	...	...	.136

Note: Variables are identified as follows: A = age, E = education, G = gender, O = socioeconomic status of origin, P = BPRS pathology measure, R = race, and S = socioeconomic status; * = $p < .05$, ** = $p < .01$, *** = $p < .001$.

To determine the overall relative contribution to the variation found in each of the component scales of the MMPI from various general background characteristics and extent of psychopathology, a stepwise multiple regression analysis was performed with scores from each of the scales serving as a dependent variable. The approach was identical to that carried out on the MMPI scores from the combined two-state and tri-state samples (see table 5.1), but in the present analysis data on the socioeconomic status of the families of origin of these patients were included as well as on the status earned by each patient himself or herself. In addition, a general index of level of severity of psychopathology was included as an independent variable based on a simple composite of the ratings from the BPRS. Table 6.16 lists the R^2 values obtained for each independent variable on each of the component scales of the MMPI together with the cumulative multiple R^2 values for each scale resulting from the total set of independent variables.

Most noteworthy, perhaps, in the results of the stepwise multiple regression analyses was the relatively small amount of total variance in the MMPI scores that was accounted for by general background characteristics. Sizable components of variance in the two special race-related scales (Rs and B-W) are accounted for by racial membership and, similarly, in the two gender-related scales (Mf and FEM) by sex membership. The BPRS composite index was most clearly related to PSY, ORG, and HEA in the content scale set and to the F, 6 (Pa), 8 (Sc), 9 (Ma), and Es scales among the basic set. Age level was most strongly associated with scale 4 (Pd) and FAM scores. The level of socioeconomic status of the family of origin of these patients did not seem to add very much to the information provided by the patient's own earned social class level. Nevertheless, in this general analysis there was support for the decision to study the sex and racial groups separately in the explorations to be taken up next. Thus, two multivariate analyses of variance were performed within each of the racial and gender groups: one using the basic MMPI scales, plus A, R, and Es; the other based on the Wiggins content scales as the dependent variables.

The overall levels of significance of these MANOVAs are summarized in tables 6.17 to 6.20. Each of the independent variables involved in the analyses will be discussed separately below, but it should be noted here that the demographic background characteristics seem to be more clearly related to MMPI scores in the data from the white male and white female patients than they are in scores obtained from either of the black patient groups. This general lack of relationship may be attributable in part to the smaller sample sizes of black patients, but it may also arise from the different meanings that these background features have in determining the socioeconomic level of black men and women in this country, as noted by Stricker (1982). (See the discussion in chapters 1 and 5 of the present volume.)

Table 6.17. Effects of Demographic Variables on MMPI Basic and Special Scales for the White Male Cleveland Psychiatric Institute Sample Compared by Multivariate Analyses of Variance

Variable	No. of Levels	*N*	*F*	df	*p*
	Standard Scales, A, R, and Es by Demographic Variables				
Age	4	262	1.67	48,735	.0035
Education	3	255	3.47	32,476	.0001
Marital status	3	262	1.97	32,490	.0014
Socioeconomic status (SES)	3	262	1.70	32,490	.0110
SES of parents	2	262	0.84	16,245	.6409
SES mobility[a]	2	262	1.96	16,245	.0164
	Wiggins Content Scales by Demographic Variables				
Age	4	262	1.76	39,734	.0033
Education	3	255	2.74	26,482	.0001
Marital status	3	262	2.06	26,496	.0018
Socioeconomic status (SES)	3	262	2.13	26,496	.0011
SES of parents	2	262	0.34	13,248	.9842
SES mobility[a]	2	262	0.81	13,248	.6483

[a]Socioeconomic status of individual minus socioeconomic status of parents.

Table 6.18. Effects of Demographic Variables on MMPI Basic and Special Scales for the White Female Cleveland Psychiatric Institute Sample Compared by Multivariate Analyses of Variance

Variable	No. of Levels	*N*	*F*	df	*p*
	Standard Scales, A, R, and Es by Demographic Variables				
Age	4	409	2.27	48,1176	.0001
Education	3	405	4.83	32,776	.0001
Marital status	3	409	1.90	32,784	.0021
Socioeconomic status (SES)	3	409	3.18	32,784	.0001
SES of parents	2	409	2.27	16,392	.0036
SES mobility[a]	2	409	0.68	16,392	.8109
	Wiggins Content Scales by Demographic Variables				
Age	4	409	1.99	39,1185	.0003
Education	3	405	3.50	26,782	.0001
Marital status	3	409	1.53	26,790	.0441
Socioeconomic status (SES)	3	409	2.59	26,790	.0001
SES of parents	2	409	1.76	13,395	.0473
SES mobility[a]	2	409	1.29	13,395	.2162

[a]Socioeconomic status of individual minus socioeconomic status of parents.

Table 6.19. Effects of Demographic Variables on MMPI Basic and Special Scales for the Black Male Cleveland Psychiatric Institute Sample Compared by Multivariate Analyses of Variance

Variable	No. of Levels	*N*	*F*	df	*p*
	Standard Scales, A, R, and Es by Demographic Variables				
Age	4	103	0.97	48,258	.5369
Education	3	102	1.71	32,170	.0165
Marital status	3	102	1.08	32,170	.3582
Socioeconomic status (SES)	3	103	1.70	32,172	.0172
SES of parents	2	103	0.93	16,86	.5346
SES mobility[a]	2	103	0.56	16,86	.9039
	Wiggins Content Scales by Demographic Variables				
Age	4	103	1.62	39,267	.0157
Education	3	102	1.00	26,176	.4655
Marital status	3	102	1.45	26,176	.0841
Socioeconomic status (SES)	3	103	2.36	26,178	.0005
SES of parents	2	103	2.29	13,89	.0118
SES mobility[a]	2	103	0.90	13,89	.5595

[a]Socioeconomic status of individual minus socioeconomic status of parents.

Table 6.20. Effects of Demographic Variables on MMPI Basic and Special Scales for the Black Female Cleveland Psychiatric Institute Sample Compared by Multivariate Analyses of Variance

Variable	No. of Levels	*N*	*F*	df	*p*
	Standard Scales, A, R, and Es by Demographic Variables				
Age	4	163	1.42	48,438	.0397
Education	3	157	1.43	32,280	.0688
Marital status	3	163	1.66	32,292	.0168
Socioeconomic status (SES)	3	163	1.10	32,292	.3317
SES of parents	2	163	0.54	16,146	.9213
SES mobility[a]	2	163	1.40	16,146	.1509
	Wiggins Content Scales by Demographic Variables				
Age	4	163	1.77	39,447	.0037
Education	3	157	1.46	26,286	.0741
Marital status	3	163	0.81	26,298	.7373
Socioeconomic status (SES)	3	163	1.46	26,298	.0743
SES of parents	2	163	0.68	13,149	.7850
SES mobility[a]	2	163	0.53	13,149	.9014

[a]Socioeconomic status of individual minus socioeconomic status of parents.

Age

In the results reported above on the various MANOVAs that were run on these data, age differences proved to be the most consistently related to MMPI scale levels in all four groups of psychiatric patients, with only the standard scale set in the black male group (the group with the smallest number of subjects) failing to reach at least the .05 level of statistical significance. Tables E-4 through E-7 in the appendix list the means and standard deviations on the standard and special scales of the MMPI earned by the white and black patients at four different age levels among the patient groups in the Cleveland Psychiatric Institute. There are only a few specific scales, however, on which these age trends emerge. On Barron's Ego strength scale, the means are consistently lower in the upper age levels among all four patient groups, although this trend failed to reach statistical significance in the sample of black males. A weaker trend is also apparent in the scores on FEM (but not on scale 5 in the basic MMPI set), with higher scores associated with older age; this trend reached statistical significance in the groups of black women and white men but not in the other two groups. Greater concern for health appeared in all four groups at the upper age levels, but it was significant only on scale 1 (Hs) (for white women) and ORG (for black women).

One marked difference between the black and white groups was an increased religious concern of older black men and women that did not appear to any appreciable degree in the scores from white patients. Older white men and women showed fewer elevations on scale 4 (Pd) and on the related endorsements of family problems on the Wiggins FAM scale than the younger white patients. The older white patients also reported increased fears and anxieties on the PHO scale. Although these trends were present to some extent for the black patients as well, none of the differences reached statistically significant levels.

Thus, in these patients in a midwestern psychiatric hospital, the younger ones seemed to be beset with interpersonal difficulties but were bothered by fewer internalized miseries, whereas the older patients seemed less able to cope with the world and were more preoccupied with somatic concerns, fears, and insecurities. Older men and women alike showed more feminine trends, and the older black patients were endorsing more conventional religious practices and beliefs as well. By and large, however, age did not appear to be important in determining answers to the MMPI for these patients in their early twenties to late thirties.

Years of Education

In the MANOVAs (and in subsequent scale-level analyses) of the MMPI scores from these four groups in relation to their level of schooling, the results proved to be remarkably different for the two racial groups: there were many MMPI scales that proved to be systematically related to educational level in the answers from the white male and female patients, but very few in the data from the black samples (see tables E-8 through E-11 in the appendix). One reason for the distinct contrast with this same kind of analysis carried out on data from the normal samples reported in chapter 5 is the rather narrow range of educational levels reached by the men and women of either race represented in these patient groups. That is, among the black and white adults in the normal samples, the number of years of schooling ranged so widely that it was possible to partition the groups into three levels, from 12 years or less to postcollege levels. By contrast, the range of education among these patients was so narrow that the upper two groups here correspond to the subjects reported in the lowest level among the normal samples. In these patient samples the "below high school group" has been divided into two levels: no more than a junior high school education versus some schoolwork beyond that level but short of high school graduation. Some differences when the results from the normal samples are compared with the present findings may reflect this shift to a distinctly lower range of educational achievement.

The MANOVA results (see tables 6.19 and 6.20) indicate that variations among these MMPI scales related to schooling for the black patients are statistically significant only for scores from the men on the basic scale set; the results of the scale-by-scale analysis for this group show significant differences only on scale 6 (Pa). The general trend on the other scales in this set (and for the special scales for both black men and black women) is that subjects who had at least completed high school tend to obtain lower scores.

The MANOVA results on the white patient groups, however (see tables 6.17 and 6.18), indicate that scores in both sets of scales vary significantly over these levels of schooling for both the men and the women. In fact, the pattern of results is quite similar, with both men and women with at least a high school education reporting fewer somatic concerns (on scale 1, HEA, and ORG), more feminine interests and preferences (on scale 5 and FEM), better self-management (on Es), fewer difficulties with authority figures (on AUT), and fewer fears and bizarre experiences (on PHO and PSY). In addition, the white female patients with better education are more defensive (lower F and higher K scores), less conventional in religious beliefs and practices (on REL), and more comfortable in interpersonal relationships (on scale 0 and SOC).

Thus, for the white patients in the Cleveland Psychiatric Institute sample, the more education that they completed, the less gross psychopathology they seem to be manifesting on the MMPI. They seem better able to manage their lives, experience better interpersonal relationships, and have fewer deleterious problems with authority figures. The few trends in the MMPI scores from the black patients indicate some differences in the same direction, but the role of schooling in their lives does not seem to lead to the coping capabilities or reduction of stresses that it does in the lives of the white men and women.

Marital Status

The pattern of results of the MANOVAs (see tables 6.17 through 6.20) that contrast single, married, and other marital status (widowed, divorced, or separated) of the men and women patients from the Cleveland Psychiatric Institute turns out to be similar to the pattern yielded in the MANOVAs for educational level; that is, the data from the white men and women are statistically significant for both sets of MMPI measures, but only one of the four MANOVAs for the black groups reaches a statistically significant level (the basic set of scales for black women). In this set of data (see tables E-12 through E-15 in the appendix), the scale-by-scale analysis proved to be relatively uninformative, with only the scores on scale 5 (Mf) showing systematic variation among the three marital status groups. (A similar trend, not statistically significant, also appeared in the scores on scale 5 for the black males.)

The differences appearing on the various scales of the MMPI from the white patients with these different marital status characteristics are generally consistent with the well-established finding that married adults manifest fewer emotional difficulties. On each of the scales on which statistically significant differences appear, the married men and women proved to be less deviant than those who had never been married or who had undergone some disruption in their previous marriages. Thus, white married men scored lower on femininity (on scale 5 and FEM) and on schizoid features (on scale 8). White married women also scored lower on scale 8 and expressed fewer interpersonal difficulties (on scale 4 and FAM) with members of their families. It is not possible to determine from these results, however, whether it is the psychologically healthier individuals who can effectively develop and maintain an ongoing marital relationship better than those with more deviant personalities, or whether an intact marriage serves to buffer individuals sufficiently to lessen their emotional difficulties. Perhaps the individual's marital status and related MMPI score patterns reflect both processes in the lives of these psychiatric patients. It is even less clear why these relationships are so attenuated in the test scores from black men and women.

Socioeconomic Status (SES)

The complex weighting schema used by Srole, Langner, Michael, Opler, and Rennie (1962) to characterize the social class membership of the men and women whom they interviewed in their community survey of the mental health status of the residents of midtown Manhattan was used by Graham et al. (1971) to summarize the socioeconomic status of the patients in the Cleveland Psychiatric Institute who served as subjects in the present analyses. The primary weight in this index of SES goes to an individual's occupational level, but additional weights are given for level of education and for level of annual income as well, if that information is known. Accordingly, higher scores indicate higher SES, unlike the schema of Hollingshead and Redlich (1958) used in the analyses reported earlier on the normal samples (in chapter 5), in which ranges from level I to level V indicate SES from high to low. The range of SES levels on the Srole et al. index for these four patient groups was quite narrow; accordingly, only three levels were partitioned for the MANOVAs on these four samples. These levels correspond roughly to lower-lower class, upper-lower class, and lower-middle class, respectively. The general caution sounded by Stricker (1982) about the difference in meaning of these traditional SES indicators for black and white adults should be borne in mind here and in the next two sets of analyses on socioeconomic level of the family of origin and the related characterization of extent of upward socioeconomic mobility of these patients.

The MANOVAs reported on SES differences for these four groups (tables 6.17 through 6.20) indicate that for both sets of MMPI measures there are statistically significant differences in the data from white men and women and from black men but not from black women. Since the data used to determine the Srole et al. index of SES are based upon head of household, it is possible that this index yields quite different information among black women, so many of whom are serving as heads of their households compared with the role of the white women in their families. For whatever reason, however, the general trends observed in the data from the black female patients on the MMPI are similar to those in the other three groups in which the statistical results are more clear-cut.

There is a consistent tendency among the white men and women and the black men for higher SES subjects to demonstrate greater ability at self-management, as shown on the Es scale (see tables E-16 through E-19 in the appendix). Similarly, the higher status subjects manifest fewer somatic concerns (either on scale 1 or on ORG and HEA), and the men of both racial groups experience fewer fears and anxieties (on the A and PHO scales). The white men and women show increased endorsement of feminine interests and orientations (on scale 5) at the higher SES levels, but the black men show lower feminine orientation (on FEM) at the upper SES level. The MMPI literature documents a consistent positive relationship between various SES indices and K-scale scores (Dahlstrom, Welsh, & Dahlstrom, 1975). The present findings support this relationship even within the narrow range of SES differences obtained in these samples; the only result that reaches a statistically significant level, however, is for the white female patients. Overall, then, the evidence from these analyses of the MMPI data indicates that those patients with higher education, better-paying jobs (and perhaps more satisfying occupations), and greater financial resources are psychologically more integrated and less distressed.

Socioeconomic Level of Family of Origin

The socioeconomic status of parents did not prove to be very differentiating in regard to the MMPI results of these psychiatric patients (tables 6.17 through 6.20). There are strong, consistent trends at a statistically significant level only for the white women, but some additional findings appear in the Wiggins content scales from the black men. The directions of the resulting differences are quite consistent with the relationship of MMPI scores to the patients' SES levels that were reported in the section above (see tables E-20 through E-23 in the appendix). That is, women from higher-status homes, as judged by their fathers' education and occupation, are more effective in coping with their problems (as reflected by higher Es scores), show fewer somatic concerns (on scale 1, ORG, and HEA), are more feminine in interests and values (on scale 5), and have fewer fears and depressive concerns (on PHO and DEP) than women from lower-status homes. Other sets of findings reveal similar trends in less severe psychopathology and greater self-management but the range of variation in family background is too narrow in these patient groups to provide very sharp contrast in such analyses.

Socioeconomic Mobility

Because the patients did not differ appreciably in either the social class of their families of origin or the socioeconomic status established for themselves and their own families, there is only a narrow range of class variation over which these men and women could be noted to rise or fall. Instances in which the patient had drifted down from the social class level of the home from which he or she came are so few and the shift so small that they are included in the group who show no upward shift. Thus, the MANOVAs reported in tables 6.17 through 6.20 are based on a contrast of the presence or absence of upward social mobility. The results are generally nonsignificant, with only the set of differences on the basic scale set from the white men reaching a significant level (see tables E-24 through E-27 in the appendix). The evidence is slim, then, of any appreciable relationship between MMPI characteristics and upward social mobility; the trends are in the direction of less psychotic involvement (on scales F, 8, and 9) and fewer somatic concerns (on scale 1, ORG, and HEA). More adequate tests of such relationships, however, obviously await samples of patients showing more clear-cut evidence of social mobility, upward or downward.

Racial Differences in the Factor Structure of the MMPI

To gain additional understanding of the nature of the variance that is reflected in the scores of the standard scales of the MMPI from these patients from the Cleveland Psychiatric Institute, their T scores on the basic scales were intercorrelated separately for each sex and racial group. The resulting four correlational matrices were each subjected to a principal-components factor analysis, with each analysis carried out until the eigenvalues dropped below one. Thus, these solutions were judged complete with varying numbers of factors extracted from each data set. The factors that were identified accounted for more than 90% of the common variance in each of these sets of intercorrelations. Within each racial group, the scores from the female patients required one more dimension to account adequately for these relationships. Within each sex group, the pattern of scale relationship from the MMPI scores of the white patients required one more dimension than was needed for the black data set. The reasons for these differences in factor complexity seem to be diverse; the sample sizes may have played some part in determining the stability of the factor weights, but the ranges of psychopathology manifested by the patients and the ways that their reactions are reflected in the component scores of the MMPI are also relevant to this issue.

After orthogonal rotation to the Varimax criteria (Kaiser, 1958), the factor loadings for each scale on these dimensions were obtained for each sample as shown in table 6.21. The patterns of loadings on these various factors reveal a common neuroticism dimension in each set (factor I in the white male and black female data and factor II in the remaining two samples). There is a little less consistency in regard to a psychoticism dimension (fairly clearly represented in factor I in the white female and black male samples and in factor III in the other two data sets). For those samples in which more than two dimensions were isolated (factor II in the white male and black female data and factor III in the white female data), the pattern of loadings seems to reflect a dimension of anxiety and distress. The remaining dimension in the data from the white female patients (factor IV) appears to be a femininity dimension that is relatively independent of other components in the MMPI profile. (In the data from the black female patients this dimension seems to be collapsed into the third factor—that is, to be merged with the dimension of psychoticism.)

Table 6.21. Factor Loadings for Varimax Rotation on Cleveland Psychiatric Institute Sample by Race and Sex

	Males								
	White (N = 262)					Black (N = 103)			
Scale	I	II	III	IV	h^2	I	II	III	h^2
L	.05	-.68	-.17		.49	-.69	.21		.52
F	.39	.29	.68		.71	.70	.46		.71
K	-.02	-.86	-.31		.85	-.88	.08		.78
Hs	.74	.22	.32		.70	.23	.77		.65
D	.89	.28	-.14		.88	.07	.86		.74
Hy	.83	-.29	.08		.78	-.23	.86		.79
Pd	.49	.33	.38		.49	.47	.50		.48
Mf	.32	.07	.23		.16	.04	.61		.37
Pa	.53	.08	.62		.67	.60	.51		.62
Pt	.54	.70	.35		.91	.82	.41		.84
Sc	.50	.56	.57		.89	.83	.46		.90
Ma	-.18	.20	.86		.81	.82	-.14		.69
Si	.57	.69	-.10		.81	.51	.42		.43
% Var.	37.0	29.5	25.0			47.4	37.8		
	Females								
	White (N = 409)					Black (N = 163)			
Scale	I	II	III	IV	h^2	I	II	III	h^2
L	-.21	.02	-.78	-.30	.74	.00	-.78	.29	.70
F	.81	.26	.16	-.29	.82	.51	.39	.65	.83
K	-.25	-.30	-.81	.20	.84	-.17	-.89	-.02	.82
Hs	.43	.69	-.03	.10	.67	.79	.30	.09	.72
D	.13	.89	-.01	.22	.85	.87	.04	-.05	.77
Hy	.29	.61	-.41	.45	.83	.83	-.23	-.09	.75
Pd	.65	.32	.24	.25	.64	.61	.31	.06	.47
Mf	-.11	.12	.08	.86	.78	.24	.18	-.72	.61
Pa	.79	.25	.01	.04	.69	.59	.26	.55	.71
Pt	.46	.67	.48	.03	.89	.62	.70	.14	.90
Sc	.73	.47	.40	-.10	.92	.61	.62	.41	.92
Ma	.69	-.31	.44	-.07	.77	.04	.73	.31	.63
Si	.08	.84	.30	-.10	.81	.51	.44	.01	.46
% Var.	33.2	34.3	21.9	13.1		41.6	34.9	16.4	

From the communality (h^2) values, it can be seen that the amount of variance that is accounted for in particular scales by these factor loadings shows a rather similar pattern across the four groups (table 6.21). Thus, scales L, 4, 5, and 0 are consistently the lowest in common factor loadings across sex and race groups, whereas scales F, K, 2, 7, and 8 share consistently larger amounts. The basic scales, then, seem to be showing similar but by no means identical psychometric properties in black and white patients' scores in this kind of analysis; the differences found are no larger between the race groups than they are between the two sexes.

Relationships between MMPI Scores and Rated Characteristics of Black and White Psychiatric Patients

The men and women in the Cleveland Psychiatric Institute study were interviewed on admission and rated on the BPRS dimensions by the psychiatrist or psychologist serving as their supervising clinician close in time to the administration of the MMPI. The patients were also observed for a week and then rated on the NOSIE-30 by the ward nurses. The BPRS ratings were summarized in four independent factor scores derived from the weights assigned the 16 separate ratings, and six factor scores were generated to summarize the information from the 30 NOSIE tallies. The BPRS scores summarize *degree* of deviation noted by the clinician, whereas the NOSIE scores reflect relative *frequency* of occurrence of deviant behaviors. Important evidence bearing on the relative accuracy of the MMPI measures

Table 6.22. R^2 Values from Linear Regression Analyses of Rated Characteristics Accounted for by MMPI Basic Clinical Scales (Cleveland Psychiatric Institute Samples)

	Males			Females		
Factor Dimension	White (*N* = 262) (1)	Black (*N* = 103) (2)	*t* ratio (1 vs. 2)	White (*N* = 409) (3)	Black (*N* = 163) (4)	*t* ratio (3 vs. 4)
BPRS[a]						
Thinking disturbance	.158****	.191	0.736	.247****	.196***	1.353
Psychomotor retardation	.086*	.107	0.599	.126****	.134*	0.255
Suspiciousness	.122**	.121	0.026	.117****	.102	0.526
Anxiety/depression	.097*	.132	0.920	.149****	.115	1.112
NOSIE[b]						
Social competence	.114**	.228*	2.491*	.132****	.129	0.096
Social interest	.121**	.164	1.032	.080**	.114	0.202
Personal neatness	.069	.137	1.822	.150****	.113	1.215
Irritability	.054	.165	2.835**	.064	.111	1.714
Manifest psychosis	.079	.181	2.462*	.079*	.171**	2.842**
Psychomotor retardation	.075	.120	1.253	.059	.070	0.476

Note: * = $p < .05$; ** = $p < .01$; *** = $p < .001$; **** = $p < .0001$.
[a]Brief Psychiatric Rating Scales (Overall & Gorham, 1962).
[b]Nurses' Observation Scales for Inpatient Evaluation (Honigfeld, Gillis, & Klett, 1966).

applied to white and to black patients can be gained by examining the relationships between various test-based scores and these clinical ratings.

With each of the 10 different factor scores serving as a dependent variable, linear regression analyses were run to determine the amount of variance of each factor that could be accounted for by the 13 scales in the basic MMPI profile and by the 13 content scales in the Wiggins set. The results of these regression analyses on the four sex and racial groups are shown in tables 6.22 and 6.23. The levels of statistical significance achieved for these particular samples depended heavily upon the numbers of cases available in each group. Appreciably fewer valid profiles and completed sets of ratings were available on the black men and women; accordingly, the significance levels reported for these groups are lower, especially for the men. The amounts of variance that are accounted for, however, can usefully be compared across groups. These analyses also involve linear regression weights that have not been cross-validated; some shrinkage is to be expected in the values for all four groups (see Bernstein, Schoenfeld, & Costello, 1982). Many investigators use various nonlinear methods, such as code types or patterning rules, with greater accuracy than the linear approach used with these data; the present methods have the advantage of direct comparability across clinical samples.

Table 6.23. R^2 Values from Linear Regression Analyses of Rated Characteristics Accounted for by MMPI Wiggins Content Scales (Cleveland Psychiatric Institute Samples)

	Males			Females		
Factor Dimension	White (N = 262) (1)	Black (N = 103) (2)	t ratio (1 vs. 2)	White (N = 409) (3)	Black (N = 163) (4)	t ratio (3 vs. 4)
BPRS[a]						
Thinking disturbance	.151***	.155	0.095	.224****	.203***	0.558
Psychomotor retardation	.102*	.145	1.091	.105***	.129	0.792
Suspiciousness	.119**	.157	0.926	.084**	.065	0.802
Anxiety/depression	.120**	.209	1.986	.125****	.123	0.066
NOSIE[b]						
Social competence	.093*	.138	1.171	.079**	.092	0.495
Social interest	.118**	.074	1.350	.139****	.065	2.869**
Personal neatness	.077	.130	1.432	.095**	.074	0.836
Irritability	.026	.131	3.029**	.057	.088	1.241
Manifest psychosis	.102*	.158	1.382	.096**	.109	0.457
Psychomotor retardation	.061	.125	1.788	.086**	.033	2.691**

Note: * = $p < .05$; ** = $p < .01$; *** = $p < .001$; **** = $p < .0001$.

[a]Brief Psychiatric Rating Scales (Overall & Gorham, 1962).

[b]Nurses' Observation Scales for Inpatient Evaluation (Honigfeld, Gillis, & Klett, 1966).

There is little support in the results of these regression analyses for the assumption that the MMPI scores, either in the basic clinical profile or in the content set, are any less valid for black men and women than they are for the white patients. When the amount of variance accounted for on 10 different dependent variables on the four groups of patients is examined, significantly more variance was accounted for by the basic MMPI scales in three instances for the black male patients and on one variable for the black female patients. Although the results for the Wiggins content scales were even more clearly in favor of the ratings from the black male patients, a statistically significant difference between white and black men appeared on only one dependent variable. Two ratings showed the white female patients with the largest amount of variance accounted for; in no instance were the highest values on these analyses found for either the white male or the black female patient groups.

The actual amount of variance in these various factor scores on the criterion ratings that was accounted for by the MMPI variables ranged extremely widely in these patient groups, from less than 3% to nearly 25%. This variability stems in part from the differences in pathology of the various kinds manifested in these patients during the period of observation by the clinicians and the nursing staff. Most of the distributions of these attributes were markedly skewed. The differences, of course, also reflect variations in the extent to which MMPI scores, basic or content, are sensitive to these forms of pathology.

Relationship of Special Race-Related Scales of the MMPI to Racial Membership of Psychiatric Patients

The MMPI records from the patients in the Cleveland Psychiatric Institute study were scored on two scales derived by comparing black and white groups of subjects: White's (1974) Race-sensitive (Rs) scale of 27 items derived on midwestern university undergraduates and Costello's (1977) Black-White (B-W) scale of 32 items developed on psychiatric patients. The means and standard deviations on each of these scales obtained on the four groups of psychiatric patients are shown in table 6.24. The results of the MANOVAs carried out on these data indicate that the race difference in both of the means was highly significant and that the sex difference on the Rs scale was also significant. This pattern of results is similar, but not identical, to that found in the normal groups of white and black men and women reported in chapter 4.

The scores earned by the white men and women in this sample of

Table 6.24. Means, Standard Deviations, and *F* Ratios on Two MMPI Race-Related Scales for White and Black Men and Women from the Cleveland Psychiatric Institute

Scale	White Males ($N = 262$)		Black Males ($N = 103$)		White Females ($N = 409$)		Black Females ($N = 163$)		Sex Effect		Race Effect		Sex × Race Effect	
	Mean	S.D.	Mean	S.D.	Mean	S.D.	Mean	S.D.	*F*	*p*	*F*	*p*	*F*	*p*
B-W	13.1	4.3	16.5	4.5	12.8	4.5	16.4	4.7	120.7	.001	0.5		0.1	
Rs	12.2	4.5	15.6	4.8	11.7	4.8	14.4	4.6	75.2	.001	4.7	.05	0.9	

Note: The Black-White scale (B-W) (Costello, 1977) contains 32 items; the Race-sensitive scale (Rs) (White, 1974) contains 27 items.

psychiatric patients, particularly on the B-W scale, were almost as elevated as the scores from the normal black men and women in the tri-state sample that were reported in chapter 4. However, the black psychiatric patients, both men and women, earned even higher means on these scales than the white patients did. The magnitude of these differences between white and black psychiatric groups was not as large as found between white and black normal adults. That is, the differences between the racial groups, both men and women, are in the same direction and nearly of the same magnitude as the differences found between normal and psychiatric subjects *within* each racial group. Thus, both these scales appear to be reflecting important aspects of emotional disturbance in addition to racial differences. This pattern emerged on both the Rs scale and the B-W scale even though the research population used in the first instance was normal college undergraduates with very different demographic backgrounds from the subjects in Costello's psychiatric samples (see the discussion in chapter 2).

Table 6.25. Percentage of Correct Assignment to Racial Membership by Means of MMPI Race-Related Scales on the Cleveland Psychiatric Institute Sample

Scale		Males			Females	
		Black	White		Black	White
B-W	White	36.6%	64.1%	White	36.3%	59.5%
	Black	63.4	35.9	Black	63.7	40.5
	Total	100.0	100.0	Total	100.0	100.0
		Hits = 64%			Hits = 61%	
		Black	White		Black	White
Rs	White	37.3	67.5	White	41.5	70.6
	Black	62.7	32.5	Black	58.5	29.4
	Total	100.0	100.0	Total	100.0	100.0
		Hits = 66%			Hits = 67%	
		Black	White		Black	White
B-W and Rs combined	White	32.0	72.2	White	33.7	72.1
	Black	68.0	27.8	Black	66.3	27.9
	Total	100.0	100.0	Total	100.0	100.0
		Hits = 70%			Hits = 70%	

Note: The Black-White scale (B-W) (Costello, 1977) contains 32 items; the Race-Sensitive scale (Rs) (White, 1974) contains 27 items.

Using an optimal cutting score separately for each sex, the extent to which each of these special scales served to identify correctly the racial membership of each patient was determined (table 6.25). Overall, the two scales identified membership in the two races at statistically significant levels, with the Rs scale resulting in a little less overlap than the B-W scale.

The white patients were correctly classified at a slightly higher rate of accuracy than the black patients of each sex. Since the two scales are largely made up of different items and show only a low correlation, the two scores were entered into a linear discriminant function to determine how well the combined scores could separate these two groups of black and white patients. The overall accuracy of classification using both scales was 70% for both males and females. Obviously, these analyses are of psychometric interest only; there would be little reason to apply the scales to this kind of task. Rather, the results provide support for the use advanced by White for his Rs scale—namely, the identification and correction of MMPI records to reduce racial bias. If such a correction is found to enhance MMPI accuracy, the data in these discriminant analyses, along with the similar results reported in chapter 4, suggest that a combination of the two measures might work even better.

Use of White's Rs Scale as a Basis for Correcting MMPI Profiles for Racial Bias

White (1974) proposed the use of the Rs scale as a means of identifying those MMPI records from black subjects that are most likely to have been artificially elevated by a style of responding that is markedly different from that of the population on whom the MMPI was originally derived (see chapter 2). For any record with a raw score of 12 or higher on the Rs scale, White proposed reducing the raw scores by 0.2 of the Rs raw score for the F scale, 0.3 Rs for scales 4 (Pd) and 9 (Ma), and 0.6 Rs for scale 8 (Sc). (The same corrections apply for male and female records, and the appropriate K-scale weights are added to scales 4, 8, and 9 in the usual way before converting these raw scores to T-score values.) White found that these statistical corrections reduced the mean T-score values of his black college student samples to a level at which they no longer differed significantly from the means of the white students obtained in the same study.

The white and black men and women from the Cleveland Psychiatric Institute were divided for the present purposes into two approximately equal halves to serve as derivation and cross-validation samples for a series of discriminant functions to be used to evaluate the impact of the Rs scale corrections on the MMPI profiles from the black patients. Using the basic MMPI scores from each half (A and B) of the white men, a multiple linear discriminant function was separately derived on each against eight different external criteria: a three-way diagnostic categorization (neurotic, psychotic, character-disordered); and dichotomized ratings (presence/absence) of somatic concern, anxiety, conceptual disorganization, depressed mood, hostility, suspiciousness, and unusual thought content. The accuracy of categorization by each set of discriminant function weights was then calculated for the alternate halves (B or A) of the white males and black males separately. These weights were then applied to the records from the black male patients after application of White's corrections. A parallel set of multiple linear discriminant functions was calculated on each half of the records from the white and black female patients and cross-validated in the same way on the MMPIs from the alternate half of the white women and the black women, with and without the Rs scale corrections. The results of the series of cross-validational hit-rate determinations are presented in table E-28 in the appendix.

In table E-28, the chance level for each of the rates of correct identification of the clinical characteristic is 50% for all dependent variables except the diagnostic categories, where the chance level is 33.3%. A few of the hit rates based upon profiles drawn on the standard norms approach a chance level, but most of them show some improvement over a random assignment. Only one of the comparisons between white and black samples exceeds a chance level of difference, however, when both sets of records are drawn on standard MMPI norms; for one sample of males, the accuracy for black patients' ratings of suspiciousness was significantly better than the accuracy for white patients. However, application of the Rs scale corrections to profiles from black patients resulted in six instances in which the accuracy was significantly lower as opposed to only two in which the improvement was better than chance (table E-28).

If the total set of comparisons between white hit rates and the corresponding discriminations on these dependent variables for black patients, with and without the Rs corrections, is examined and any hit rate within 5% of the other is called equivalent, then the use of a standard profile shows no systematic difference in black or white accuracy; however, the application of the Rs correction shifts the hit rates to a more accurate discrimination for the white patients (table 6.26).

Table 6.26. Frequency of Hit-Rate Comparisons Showing Relative Accuracy for Black Patients on Discriminant Weights Using Standard Norms and Two Types of Profile Corrections

Comparison	Standard Norms	White's Rs Corrections	Tri-State Norms
White > black[a]	7	10	15
White = black[b]	16	17	11
White < black[a]	9	5	6

[a]Differences greater than 5%.
[b]Differences within 5%.

In 16 (or half) of these 32 cross-validational comparisons, there was no effective difference in accuracy of classification for either racial group when the test was scored in the usual manner. In the other half of the comparisons, 9 indicated that the accuracy was higher for black men or women and 7 reflected higher hit rates for the white group. The accuracy for black males in these comparisons was a little more frequent than for white males, but the reverse was true in comparisons involving the white and black women. In only one of these comparisons, however, was the difference large enough to reach statistical significance.

When the profiles from the black patients whose Rs raw scores reached or exceeded a cutting score of 12 were corrected by means of the weights recommended by White, the instances in which the accuracy dropped were twice as numerous as the comparisons in which the accuracy improved. That is, for 17 of the 32 applications of White's correction, there was no appreciable gain or loss in accuracy of classification by means of the discriminant function; in 5 comparisons there was an increase in accuracy, and in 10 there was an appreciable drop. In 8 of these shifts in accuracy, the difference was greater than would be expected by chance alone. Thus, the usefulness of the selective corrections proposed by White based on levels of his Rs scale is not supported by these applications to a sample of white and black male and female patients from a midwestern psychiatric institution. The scores without the Rs correction seem to be a better foundation on which to base discriminations of this kind for black patients of either sex.

Use of the Tri-State Norms to Correct Profiles of Psychiatric Patients for Racial Bias

A second method of modifying the profile patterns of black patients from the Cleveland Psychiatric Institute was also explored. Using the means and standard deviations from the men and women in the tri-state black sample, T scores for the basic scales of the MMPI were calculated (see Appendix H). The profiles from the black men and women in the Cleveland sample were redrawn on the basis of these T-score values. Within the sample of white men, the group was randomly divided into approximately equal halves for derivation and cross-validation purposes; similarly, the sample of white women was redivided at random into equal halves. (These divisions were not the same as the split for the Rs scale study reported above.)

Parallel discriminant analyses were carried out to determine whether application of the tri-state black norms to the records of the black Cleveland Psychiatric Institute patients would improve validity of MMPI scores (see table E-29 in the appendix). The summary of these results (presented in table 6.26) indicates that this method of correction for racial bias reduces the predictive accuracy of the MMPI even more than does White's procedure. Accuracy is reduced in almost three times as many comparisons as it is increased. This is especially noteworthy because the application of the tri-state norms, which changes the entire basic profile pattern, represents a more radical attempt at adjustment than does the use of White's corrections, which are applied to only four scales. Thus, both attempts to reduce "racial bias" not only failed to achieve that end, they actually introduced racial bias.

Summary

To evaluate the way in which scores from the MMPI derived from test records of patients in a psychiatric service related to various background characteristics and presenting problems in men and women from different ethnic groups, two different samples of patients seen in midwestern psychiatric installations were subjected to a variety of analyses. Even though the range of education, occupation, and status of family of origin was quite restricted, important variations were found in the ways that these background factors were related to the basic MMPI scales and to various special measures on the test as well. Within each sex group, variations in socioeconomic level seemed to be more important than racial membership in accounting for MMPI score variance. Men and women of either racial group who had more years of schooling, who held better jobs, and who earned more money were found to manifest less severe psychopathology on component measures in the MMPI. There was also evidence within these groups that age was another important determiner of test scores and patterns. The two racial groups represented in these samples of psychiatric patients did not differ so much from each other on MMPI scores as did the white and black men and women in the two-state and tri-state community-based surveys.

The component scores from the MMPIs administered to these two sets of patients were also evaluated as independent variables in an effort to predict several different kinds of external criteria. Both linear weighting and coding methods of summarizing the MMPI findings were used in these clinical applications. In general, against both diagnostic and descriptive summaries, the MMPI-based discriminations for the white and black groups were found to be comparable in relative accuracy. Also, as judged against these external criteria, neither the total score transformations for the MMPI scales provided by the special black norms nor the special selective corrections of some records from black patients that were based on the Rs scale proved to be helpful. Either the benefits were equivocal or the results were clearly detrimental to the MMPI-based discriminations. Similarly, use of the black norms for determining the T-score values for MMPI profiles obtained in a personnel selection situation (black applicants to a police academy) resulted in the black applicants appearing to be unusually well adjusted in comparison with white applicants scored on the standard norms. Against a variety of nontest standards, then, there was little evidence that the standard MMPI profile scales contain serious biases or systematic error.

CHAPTER 7

Patterns of Item Endorsement on the MMPI

David Lachar, W. Grant Dahlstrom, and Kevin L. Moreland

The general effectiveness of an empirically keyed scale is the result of small but cumulative relationships between scale items and external criteria. Valid scales result when these cumulative relationships far outweigh the effects of other variables, which for the most part are random and have no additive effect. However, a scale with highly skewed items and limited variability in a normative sample could be significantly influenced if only a few items were to be consistently answered as a reflection of racial membership rather than the personality dimension (or dimensions) being predicted (see Gynther, Lachar, & Dahlstrom, 1978). Interest in item content is most relevant in the study of minority test performance. Because many empirically keyed profile scales are heterogeneous in content, it would be reasonable to assume that the influence of racial membership might be demonstrable on only a limited number of dimensions represented by a given scale. In its most direct sense, investigation at the item level seems to provide substantive support for hypotheses generated at the scale or profile level (see Costello, 1973; Jones, 1978).

Items sensitive to racial membership have been identified and scales constructed to predict racial membership, or more precisely, the effect of a potentially confounding influence that is race-related (see chapter 2) (White, 1974; Costello, 1977). Although item composition has varied with population studied and item selection methodology, there does appear to be a consistent racial effect at the item level. Efforts described in chapter 6 were not successful in demonstrating that taking this variance into account improved the predictive power of the MMPI profile scales.

What do these item differences reflect? In samples matched for level and type of psychopathology, age, sex, ability, and socioeconomic status, such differences, if obtained, may in part or whole reflect differences in interpretation of content and desirability of this content quite independent of the presence of the predicted criteria (see Witt & Gynther, 1975). In most studies, however, such controls have not been applied. In addition, because small differences in response are statistically significant when obtained in large samples, replication is essential to provide some evidence of the stability or reliability of these differences. A first impulse would be to compare men and women separately on item response rates in the tri-state black sample and the original normative sample, a comparison that would directly assess the basis for the deviations obtained using the standard profile form. The difficulty with this approach, previously demonstrated in table 4.8, is that comparison of responses collected more than 35 years apart is just as likely to identify changes *over time* of item interpretation—in other words, cohort effects. These changes may be related to shifts in the meaning of words and phrases, the acceptability of various wordings and complaints, as well as changes in the manner in which the MMPI is administered. For example, the use of the Cannot Say option in contemporary application is often discouraged or even forbidden (see Marks, Seeman, & Haller, 1974), causing the response to certain items found to be objectionable or inappropriate to be higher than the original normative response rates, which were collected at a time when the Cannot Say option was more liberally used. Because the present authors had access to three separate samples of normal subjects, the influence of cohort change could not only be statistically controlled but its effects could be identified and evaluated. Items were classified as race-related for one sex only when the response rate significantly ($p < .01$) separated both the original and two-state white contemporary samples from the tri-state contemporary black sample in two individual 2×2 chi-square analyses. Items classified as race-related for both sexes were identified through two of these triangulation procedures. Because four separate significant chi-square analyses were required to achieve such a classification, only the .05 level of significance was required of each analysis.

Items were classified as cohort-related when the two same-sex contemporary samples consistently differed from the original normative sample. Items significant for both sexes or for only one sex were identified using the same guidelines established for classification of race-related items. Table F-1 in the appendix presents the True and Cannot Say response rates by sex for the three normative samples studied and the results of the six 2×2 chi-square analyses for each inventory item. The table shows that significant, consistent differences for both "1 vs. 2" and "2 vs.3" classify an item as race-related for a given sex, whereas consistent differences in "1 vs.2" and "1vs.3" classify an item as cohort-related for a given sex. A given item can, in this fashion, be classified as both race- and cohort-related. For example, #73: "I am an important person" was answered True by 17% of the male and 9% of the female Minnesota normative sample, by 49% of the male and 69% of the female two-state contemporary white sample, and by 80% of the male and 78% of the female tri-state contemporary black sample. That is, not only was a significant response shift demonstrated with change of cohort, but significant differences were also obtained between contemporary white and black samples.

Table 7.1. Summary of Race-Related and Cohort-Related Items by Gender in Normative Samples

	Race-Related			Cohort-Related[a]		
Samples	Total	Basic	Content	Total	Basic	Content
Male and female	59	59%	68%	50	52%	28%
Male only	6	50%	67%	18	72%	44%
Female only	57	65%	56%	28	36%	14%
Total	122	61%	62%	96	51%	27%

[a]Only 495 items were available for these analyses.

Item Analyses Applied to Three Normative Samples

In the manner detailed above, differences in endorsement of 122 MMPI items (22%) were classified as race-related and 96 (17%) were classified as cohort-related. Table 7.1 documents that 59 item differences were race-related for both men and women, whereas 6 were race-related for men only and 57 were race-related for women only. This disparity between gender-specific items was far less noticeable in the classification of cohort-related items. Fifty item differences were generalizable to both sexes, whereas 18 were classified as cohort-related in the analysis of the male samples and 28 were similarly classified in the analysis of the female samples. The predominant response direction of black subjects to the race-related items was True (75%), whereas the predominant response direction of contemporary subjects to cohort-related items was False (70%) (χ^2 [1] = 42.77, $p < .001$). Table F-2 in the appendix presents each of these items, the sample involved, and item membership on various scales together with the results of previous analyses of race effect.

An examination of these two item sets identified those item responses more characteristic of black or contemporary subjects that are scored in the same direction on any of the basic scales or Wiggins content scales. Table 7.1 documents that 50 to 60% of both race- and cohort-related items appear on one or more basic scales. In comparison, approximately

Table 7.2. Classification of Basic Scale Items as Race-Related and/or Cohort-Related

		Race-Related		Cohort-Related		Combined[a]	
	No. of	Male	Female	Male	Female	Male	Female
Scale	Items	*N* (%)	*N* (%)	*N* (%)	*N* (%)	*N* (%)	*N* (%)
L	15	2 (13)	2 (13)	0 (0)	0 (0)	2 (13)	2 (13)
F	64	3 (5)	16 (25)	3 (5)	4 (6)	6 (9)	20 (31)
K	30	0 (0)	0 (0)	4 (13)	8 (27)	4 (13)	8 (27)
1 (Hs)	33	2 (6)	1 (3)	3 (9)	1 (3)	4 (12)	1 (3)
2 (D)	60	5 (8)	6 (10)	3 (5)	2 (3)	7 (12)	7 (12)
3 (Hy)	60	1 (2)	3 (5)	10 (17)	8 (13)	11 (18)	11 (18)
4 (Pd)	50	6 (12)	15 (30)	9 (18)	8 (16)	13 (26)	20 (40)
5 (Mf)[b]	60	4 (7)	4 (7)	13 (22)	7 (12)	14 (23)	8 (13)
6 (Pa)	40	6 (15)	13 (33)	3 (8)	2 (5)	9 (23)	15 (38)
7 (Pt)	48	3 (6)	10 (21)	3 (6)	2 (4)	5 (10)	11 (23)
8 (Sc)	78	12 (15)	25 (32)	5 (6)	6 (8)	16 (21)	30 (38)
9 (Ma)	46	11 (24)	12 (26)	8 (17)	8 (17)	17 (37)	18 (39)
0 (Si)[c]	70	6 (9)	8 (11)	2 (3)	1 (1)	7 (10)	8 (11)

Note: Reported race and cohort effects are limited to items in scored direction.
[a]Corrected for race/cohort item overlap.
[b]Only 36 Mf items were available for the cohort analyses.
[c]Only 66 Si items were available for the cohort analyses.

half as many cohort-related items (27%) appear on a content scale. Table 7.2 presents the number of race- and cohort-related items that appear on each basic scale and the total number of race- and/or cohort-related items per scale. The data presented in the last two columns of table 7.2 provide an estimate based on differences at the item level of the cumulative deviation from the standard norms for a contemporary black normal sample. Neither race- nor cohort-related items are evenly distributed across basic scales, although cohort-related items do not have the influence upon these scales that is demonstrated for race-related items. The largest number of cohort-related items found on one scale is on scale 5 (Mf), in which 13 items for men and 7 items for women obtained significant response shifts over the 35-year interval. The number of cohort-related items on scale 5 may actually be higher; 24 Mf items were added to the MMPI after the Minnesota normals took the test and, hence, could not be investigated for cohort effects. Most of the items on scale 5 that were not administered to the Minnesota normals deal with occupations and interests, items whose endorsement rates seem likely to have changed over the elapsed 35 years. It is interesting to observe that, of the cohort-related items, only two deal directly with sex content: #179: "I am worried about sex matters" (T) for both men and women, and #133: "I have never indulged in any unusual sex practices" (F) for men only. Classification by the Pepper and Strong

(1958) factors of race- and cohort-related scale 5 items revealed that all race-related and the majority of cohort-related items were classified by the factor labeled Personal and Emotional Sensitivity, fewer falling on the Sexual Identification and Altruism factors.

Although only two basic scales had at least 20% of their items classified as cohort-related for at least one sex, six of these 13 profile scales had at least 20% of their items classified as race-related for one sex or the other: F, 4 (Pd), 6 (Pa), 7 (Pt), 8 (Sc), and 9 (Ma). Scale 9 met this criterion for both the male and female samples. The two scales with the largest combined classification of race-related items across male and female samples are scales 8 and 9.

The Harris-Lingoes (1955, 1968) clusters of items within scales 4, 6, 8, and 9 were applied to highlight the presence of any dominant content dimensions that may be related to race or cohort. For scale 4, race-related items clustered in subscales labeled Familial Discord (struggle against familial control), Social Alienation (feelings of isolation from other people; lack of belongingness; externalization of blame for difficulties; lack of gratification in social relations), and Self-Alienation (lack of self-integration; avowal of guilt, exhibitionistically stated; despondency); cohort-related items, however, were evenly distributed over five possible categories. The race-related items of scale 6 fell predominantly into the category of Ideas of External Influence (externalization of blame for one's problems, frustrations, failures; in the extreme degree, persecutory ideas; projection of responsibility for negative feelings). It is noteworthy that 10 out of the 17 items in this cluster were classified as race-related. Race-related items on scale 8 were found in all six Harris-Lingoes clusters, although dimensions labeled Social Alienation (a feeling of lack of rapport with other people; withdrawal from meaningful relationships with others) and Sensorimotor Dissociation (a feeling of change in the perception of the self and the body image; feelings of depersonalization and estrangement) classified all but one of the 12 items as significant for both male and female subjects. Of the 10 scale 9 items found to be race-related for both sexes, four items fell in the cluster labeled Ego Inflation (feelings of self-importance to the point of unrealistic grandiosity).

Table 7.3 further clarifies the content manifested by race- and cohort-related items. Although none of the Wiggins content scales had as many as 20% cohort-sensitive items, five of these 13 nonoverlapping scales contained at least 20% race-related items for at least one sex: DEP (Depression), FAM (Family Problems), AUT (Authority Conflict), PHO (Phobias), and PSY (Psychoticism). Only three FEM items were available for the cohort analyses; thus, cohort effects on that scale cannot even be crudely estimated, although it is likely to be large.

Table 7.3. Classification of Content Scale Items as Race-Related and/or Cohort-Related

		Race-Related				Cohort-Related				Combined[a]			
		Male		Female		Male		Female		Male		Female	
Scale	No. of Items	*N*	(%)	*N*	(%)	*N*	(%)	*N*	(%)	*N*	(%)	*N*	(%)
ORG	36	3	(8)	4	(11)	2	(6)	0	(0)	5	(14)	4	(11)
HEA	28	3	(11)	2	(7)	3	(11)	3	(11)	5	(18)	4	(14)
DEP	33	2	(6)	7	(21)	0	(0)	1	(3)	2	(6)	8	(24)
MOR	23	0	(0)	2	(9)	1	(4)	0	(0)	1	(4)	2	(9)
SOC	27	2	(7)	2	(7)	1	(4)	1	(4)	3	(11)	3	(11)
HOS	27	1	(4)	5	(19)	0	(0)	1	(4)	1	(4)	6	(22)
FAM	16	5	(31)	8	(50)	3	(19)	2	(13)	6	(38)	8	(50)
AUT	20	6	(31)	8	(40)	2	(10)	1	(5)	8	(40)	9	(45)
FEM[b]	30	0	(0)	0	(0)	0	(0)	0	(0)	0	(0)	0	(0)
PHO	27	8	(30)	9	(33)	4	(15)	2	(7)	10	(37)	10	(37)
PSY	48	11	(23)	22	(46)	2	(4)	3	(6)	12	(25)	24	(50)
HYP	25	1	(4)	3	(12)	2	(8)	2	(8)	2	(8)	4	(16)
REL	12	2	(16)	0	(0)	2	(16)	2	(16)	4	(33)	2	(16)

Note: Reported race and cohort effects are limited to items in scored direction.
[a]Corrected for race/cohort item overlap.
[b]Only three FEM items were available for the cohort analyses.

The general influence of race- and cohort-related items was also explored in other ways. Wiener (1948) identified items on scales 2 (D), 3 (Hy), 4 (Pd), 6 (Pa), and 9 (Ma) that were relatively easy to detect as indicating emotional disturbance (called Obvious subscales), as well as items that were relatively difficult to detect as indicating emotional disturbance (Subtle subscales). Wrobel and Lachar (1982) presented data to support the conclusion that the obvious items are clearly related to external criteria of psychopathology, whereas the subtle items are not. In the current analyses, 52 of the race-related items and 36 of the cohort-related items had been included in the Wiener classification. Twice as many race-related items (73%) in comparison with cohort-related items (39%) were classified as obvious (χ^2 [1] = 10.28, $p < .01$).

Christian, Burkhart, and Gynther (1978) presented mean obvious/subtle ratings for responses of True and False to each MMPI item (listed by Form R item numbers). Raters were instructed to read each item carefully and to judge how clearly a response to each item was indicative of a psychological problem. Very obvious items were assigned a rating of 5; obvious, a rating of 4; neither obvious nor subtle, a rating of 3; subtle, a rating of 2; and very subtle, a rating of 1. Classification of the discriminating direction of each race- and cohort-related item indicated that the response direction judged by Christian et al. to be the least indicative of psychopathology was obtained for only 17% of race-related items in comparison with 55% of cohort-related items (χ^2 [1] = 34.59, $p < .001$). In addition, comparison of the distribution of obvious-subtle ratings for race-related items ($N = 122$, mean = 3.15, S.D. = .78) and cohort-related items ($N = 96$, mean = 2.42, S.D. = .60) demonstrated the race-related items to be significantly more obvious (t [216] = 7.52, $p < .001$).

Recent studies of the effectiveness of individual inventory items to predict clinical criteria have produced two empirically validated critical item sets (Koss, Butcher, & Hoffman, 1976; Lachar & Wrobel, 1979). Application of the Lachar-Wrobel system to race- and cohort-related items identified 29 critical items within the race-related set and 11 critical items within the cohort-related set. Most of the race-related critical items were classified within categories of Deviant Beliefs, Deviant Thinking and Experience, Antisocial Attitude, and Family Conflict, whereas only Sexual Concern and Deviation, of 11 possible categories, included more than 2 cohort-related items.

Tabulation of inventory items not appearing in the scored direction on either a basic or a content scale revealed that 22 of 122, or 18%, of race-related items did not enter into the scoring of at least 1 of these 26 scales, whereas 39 of the 96, or 41%, of cohort-related items were so classified.

How many of these items had been previously identified as being related to race? Tabulation of the items identified by Costello (1977) in his composite B-W scale, by White (1974) as replicated or placed on the Rs scale, or by Erdberg (1969) resulted in a classification rate of 64% (78 of the 122 race-related items). A similar classification of the cohort-related items provided an estimate of possible cohort effect contamination within previous black-white item analyses. Only 12 of the 96 cohort-related items (12.5%) had been previously identified as race-related by at least one of these three investigators. When the 7 items that were also classified as race-related in the present study were removed, this rate was reduced to only 6% (5 of 89 cohort-related items), supporting the conclusion that the race-related item differences obtained in these analyses are meaningful and relatively stable across samples.

Item Analyses Applied to Two Contemporary Psychiatric Samples

Differences between black and white psychiatric test performance were explored at the item level using both the Lafayette Clinic and Cleveland Psychiatric Institute samples previously described in chapter 6. Inventory items were selected only if consistent differences for a given sex were obtained in both populations—that is, if all reported differences were replicated. In comparison with the finding of 59 race-related items in the normal samples generalizable to both males and females, only 17 such items were found in the analysis of psychiatric samples. All but 4 of these items, or 76%, were also obtained in the analysis of normal samples. Many sex-specific items were also identified: 27 for males and 50 for females. Seven of the male-only and 25 of the female-only items had previously been identified as race-related within the analysis of normal samples, for a replication rate of 48% for these 94 race-related items.

Applying the same selection criteria used above, 65 of these 94 items had been previously found to be related to racial membership of the respondent, or 69% (compared with 64% in normal samples). Tabulation of the number of items not keyed in the scored direction on any of the basic or content scales resulted in 26 items, or 28% versus 18% in the normal sample analysis. Of those race-related items scored for any of scales 2 (D), 3 (Hy), 4 (Pd), 6 (Pa), or 9 (Ma), 14 were classified as obvious and 7 as subtle. The proportion of obvious items within these two sets of race-related items was quite similar (normal, 73%; psychiatric, 67%). Seventeen of these items appear on the Lachar-Wrobel critical item set, with 2 or more items appearing in categories labeled Deviant Beliefs, Deviant Thinking and Experience, and Somatic Symptoms.

Forty percent of these items are scored in the response direction more characteristic of blacks for one or more basic scales, as are 56% of these items for the content scales. Classification of these 94 race-related items by specific basic and content scale membership and direction of response, however, revealed a significantly reduced influence at the scale level in comparison with that obtained for the normal sample analyses (tables 7.2 and 7.3). Within basic scales, male patients obtained a maximum race effect on scale 5 (Mf), in which 4 of 60 possible items were classified as race-related. For female patients, maximum numbers of race-related items were obtained for scales F (7 vs. 16 in normal samples), 4 (Pd) (5 vs. 15 in normal samples), 6 (Pa) (6 vs. 13 in normal samples), and 8 (Sc) (8 vs. 25 in normal samples). For the content scales, the impact of race-related variance remained fairly comparable in these hospital samples to that demonstrated in previous analyses of normal groups for only Authority Conflict (females) and Psychoticism (males and females).

Summary

Race effects on inventory items were found to parallel those obtained for scales and profile configurations. Items identified as race-related within normal samples reflected feelings of alienation from self and others, with conflict especially noted within the family and with authority figures. Fears, beliefs of external control, and deviant experiences were also found to be race-related. These results are even more notable given the character of the black normative samples collected. The tri-state sample was of significantly higher socioeconomic status than census estimates and was collected through church, social, and professional organizations, which probably made it more likely that each participant would demonstrate adequate social and personal adjustment. The proportion of race-related items present in frequently used MMPI scales appears to have significant implications for the application of the test to normal black samples, such as in psychiatric screening within a personnel selection process.

The question remains as to the meaning of the differences obtained between samples of normal whites and normal blacks. In spite of the selection process used to collect the normal black protocols, was this group less well adjusted in their personal and social life than the contemporary white sample? Assuming equivalence of samples, the only conclusion is that the item endorsements reflect differences in the interpretive process. If, on the other hand, elevated scale scores obtained from nonreferred black community members are found to be associated with poorer personal and social adjustment when compared with low-scoring black community members, these scale elevations reflect variances that can be clearly interpreted. The possible reasons for such disproportionate responses have been discussed at the beginning of this volume.

The proportion of race-related items obtained in analysis of the protocols of psychiatric patients was considerably smaller than that obtained within samples of normal community residents. Taking into consideration the distribution of these fewer items across scales also suggested that the race differences evidenced at the item level would have little if any effect on the application of the MMPI to black psychiatric patients.

The evaluation of items associated with differences in response rates between cohorts supports a quite unexpected conclusion: even the increased "openness" of the 1970s and decreased use of the Cannot Say response option have not increased the frequency of pathological responses to inventory items. Forty percent of cohort-related items did not appear to be on any of the basic or content scales, and more than half (55%) of these items were associated with greater response of the contemporary samples in the item direction judged to be the least deviant! Such results, as well as the performance obtained in the application of contemporary black norms detailed in the previous chapter, suggest that considerable thought and consideration will be necessary before the popular inclination to update test norms is acted upon. Investigators supporting the need for such norms need to demonstrate that their application will result in actual increased test validity.

CHAPTER 8

Overview and Conclusions

W. Grant Dahlstrom, David Lachar, and Leona E. Dahlstrom

In an effort to disentangle some of the complex questions involving the use of the MMPI with various ethnic and subcultural groups in the United States, data from community-based samples of white and black men and women were analyzed from a number of different points of view. Some of the major questions under consideration were the following: To what extent are the systematic differences that have been reported on recent samples of black Americans on the MMPI a function of general changes in the American community, white and black alike, since the original (white) normative sample was tested in 1940? Do the reported characteristics manifested by virtually all black subjects reflect pervasive features of some common cultural origin in individuals identified as members of an ethnic subgroup? Are these features, instead, more circumscribed within this ethnic group and hence more reasonably attributed to the selective effects of the obvious inequities to which most black Americans have been exposed? Are the origins of the differences that appear in MMPI scores, alternatively, features of the test stimuli or other aspects of the assessment process per se, rather than identifiable characteristics of the men and women completing the inventory? Do the differences between white and black test patterns reflect some serious forms of test score error that may attenuate the usefulness of MMPI-based personality assessments of black subjects, or are these components of variance valid and relevant to such appraisals? These issues and related questions were explored at the item level, at the scale level, and at the level of profile patterning. In addition, the existing MMPI literature on other minorities in the United States was combed to locate the available empirical data on these subjects in order to examine the extent to which these other groups show comparable patterns in their answers to the MMPI. This information was used to document the similarities and differences between the other groups and the black and white adults in this present investigation and to determine how and in what direction further research should be focused.

Methodological Problems

In the traditions of social and behavioral research, the personality and emotional variables that the MMPI was intended to assess have an anomalous role because they serve both as dependent variables (e.g., as outcomes of various processes in personality development) and independent variables (e.g., as predictors of some later social or behavioral outcome). For example, an individual may have become depressed because he or she was immature and formed an overly dependent relationship upon someone who has now departed. This depressed state, then, would be the focus of an assessment by means of the MMPI and be appraised in terms of its severity and duration. Once the individual has sought help for this abnormal state, an accurate evaluation of the depression by means of the MMPI could in turn be used to estimate need for hospitalization or to decide between treatment alternatives. Most of the comparative research on ethnic differences has conceptualized the personological assessments in the former, or dependent variable, framework. The research in the present volume has tried to appraise the findings from the MMPI in both contexts: as attributes of current status and as potentially important determiners of subsequent behavior patterns and outcomes.

This distinction between independent and dependent variables in this kind of research is by no means an easy one to maintain. For example, is there any evidence in the MMPI research literature to support the common view that Scandinavian-Americans are particularly susceptible to alcohol abuse? Are personological features associated with alcoholism any more prevalent in their descendants in this country? When members of this ethnic minority are identified as problem drinkers, does their status as churchgoing or nonchurchgoing (or anything else associated with such ethnic status) interfere with the use of the MMPI in psychological assessment? Precise answers to questions of this sort are very difficult to extract.

Studies in the MMPI research literature dating from the early years in which the test was still under development at the University of Minnesota and up to the present have demonstrated the existence of differences in component scores between various ethnic groups in the United States. Although the definition of ethnic status has often shifted from one investigation to another, most of these studies have focused on racial membership. Religious, linguistic, nationalistic, and subcultural groups have received some attention in this context, but the largest body of research involves racial characteristics as the basis for ethnic membership. Native American,

Hispanic (of Caribbean and Mexican origin), Asian-American, and Pacific Islander groups have all received some attention in this burgeoning research literature. However, by far the most frequent publications have dealt with the differences between white and black groups. In all of these investigations, racial group membership has been defined on the basis of self-assignment to one or another group.

Earlier chapters in this volume have served to highlight the difficulties inherent in the definition and conceptualization of ethnic identity and the interaction of biological, cultural, and individual life experiences in the formation of these self-views. The transmission of these patterns down through the succeeding generations is also complex and poorly understood (e.g., the discussion by Onoda [1976] of the fate of traditional Japanese valuation of scholarly achievement in the third, or sansei, generation of Japanese-Americans). Various kinds of evidence of some greater lack of self-esteem in black adolescents and adults have been advanced, together with the interpretation that a lack or defect exists in the ethnic culture in which these individuals have developed and that this deficiency has produced such an end result in the members of the subculture. More recent studies (see Gray-Little & Appelbaum, 1979; Gray-Little, 1983) have raised serious doubts about the findings themselves and the implication that these individuals were brought up in a deficient subculture. They have offered as an alternative explanation for the low self-esteem of some minority members the victimizing effects of racial barriers and social inequities in the dominant white culture within which all Americans must live and grow.

Unfortunately, many of the published studies contrasting these various ethnic groups obtained their subjects in ways that resulted in the comparison groups being quite different, not only in ethnic background but also in other important characteristics that are known to be related to MMPI responses and scores. At times, differences on these other factors have been obvious, as when the subjects under study have been obtained from populations in which it is well known that American ethnic group members are not equitably represented; all too often, however, the operation of such selective effects and biases has not been recognized. That is, studies of groups of institutionalized delinquents or prisoners, medical or psychiatric patients, drug or alcohol abusers have been published in which little attention has been paid to the ways in which the research subjects have entered the particular setting and have thus become available for testing. If the criminal justice system in this country works more favorably for white than for nonwhite individuals (which appears to be the case), and if, as a result, a nonwhite defendant is more likely to get an active prison sentence or be placed in a training school than is a comparable white defendant, then comparisons of test performances from only incarcerated members of various ethnic groups are likely to show differences quite unrelated to ethnic status per se but more related to the financial status of the individual (ability to hire competent lawyers), social supports (willingness of others to testify on behalf of the defendant), or even social skills (in reacting "properly" to a police officer and thus avoiding arrest in the first place). More subtle selective effects may also generate inappropriate and highly selective representation of various ethnic groups in such research settings. For example, if members of some ethnic minority group have a pervasive mistrust of authority figures, and if mental health professionals are included in such mistrust, then members of this group may delay treatment longer before seeking help and thus, as a group, appear to be sicker than members of contrasting ethnic groups when they do appear at the agency (see Sue & Sue, 1974).

The results of numerous studies of the differential rates of admission of patients showing various forms of psychopathology to public and private psychiatric hospitals (e.g., Keeler & Vitols, 1963; Vitols, Waters, & Keeler, 1963; Fischer, 1969; See & Miller, 1973; See, 1976; and Steinberg et al., 1977) have been used, perhaps erroneously, to try to document the likelihood that American ethnic groups differ in both the basic prevalence, as well as the kinds, of emotional disorder. The findings that have been reported in such studies, however—that ethnic minorities who are studied while patients in federal, state, or private psychiatric facilities are likely to show disproportionate frequencies of particular forms of psychopathology—are consistent with results showing corresponding personality test patterns in line with these differences. That is, if black adults in a schizophreniform psychotic episode are more likely than white adult patients to manifest paranoid features (Steinberg et al., 1977) or auditory or visual hallucinations (Vitols et al., 1963), then it would be expected that MMPI patterns from black and white schizophrenic patients would differ in ways that are consistent with these results, regardless of basic prevalence rates in the general population. In this regard, the study of Peteroy and Pirrello (1982), in which only patients on a voluntary admission were included, is significant because the white psychiatric patients scored higher on two MMPI scales (F and 8 [Sc]) that most studies have found more elevated in black patients (although scale 9 [Ma] still showed a larger value for blacks).

Only a few investigations have selected subjects for ethnic comparisons in ways that were intended to reduce the operation of these more obvious kinds of sampling bias. Community-based samples are presumed to be freer of the operation of these physical, mental, and emotional factors that by definition enter into the process whereby a person is imprisoned, hospitalized, or otherwise institutionalized. The community-based approach, however, by no means assures complete equality in or freedom from emotional disorders. It should be obvious that the people who enter prison, seek psychological treatment, or fall ill are all, at one time or another, members of the general community. During that time they are subject to stresses, suffer losses, gain or lose jobs, marry or divorce spouses. (See tables D-27 and D-28 in the appendix on SRRS relationships to MMPI scores in the two-state sample.) Consequently, they may be community members (and available for study as such) one day but manifest some overt problem the next, and in so doing leave the community and become members of a special group. Thus, with regard to various emotional disorders, differential rates of these problems may be found in community-based samples as well (cf. Pritchard & Rosenblatt, 1980a). Such individuals may also show evidence on test patterns of these imminent breakdowns (e.g., the findings of Loper, Kammeier, & Hoffmann [1973] on college students with subsequent histories of alcohol abuse). If so, then deviations on scores of the MMPI in such samples of individuals cannot be summarily dismissed as test misses (false positives). Similarly, upon their return to the community, individuals may still show some residual evidence of the disturbance or disorder that led to their arrest, hospitalization, or treatment (see data in the appendix in tables D-29 through D-36). Careful attention to such complications in research on even "normal" subjects may help to explain various kinds of apparent contradictions in the research literature on this complex issue of ethnic bias in psychological testing.

A considerable research literature is now available that deals more directly with the question of systematic differences in rates of mental or emotional disorder among various ethnic groups in the United States, but few of them have used MMPI-based procedures in the case-finding process. As noted in chapter 2, Fillenbaum and Pfeiffer (1976) used the 71 items in Kincannon's Mini-Mult (1968) along with a detailed interview schedule in a community-based survey covering the emotional, health, social, and economic adjustment of elderly, urban, black and white men and women. The adequacy of general adjustment to daily life was also judged good or poor based on a composite of the other interview data. These authors found a disproportionate number of black men and women making a poor general adjustment (76 to 241 or 24% for black adults, 118 to 481 or 20% for white adults) and an even greater disproportion in the rate of poor emotional adjustment (94 to 220 or 29% for the elderly black, 133 to 465 or 22% for the white men and women). Even though the Mini-Mult version (as compared with the full MMPI) is limited in its coverage and dependability, the men and women of both racial groups with less adequate adjustment in these various aspects of urban life were found to score significantly higher than their better adjusted counterparts on all of the Mini-Mult scales except K. Black individuals with poor adjustment scored significantly higher than poorly adjusted white adults on scales F and 4 (Pd).

Many other community-based surveys have documented the higher base rate of different emotional disorders in members of American minority groups (Warheit, Holzer, & Schwab, 1973; Warheit et al., 1975; Warheit, Holzer, Bell, & Arey, 1976; Schwab, Bell, Warheit, & Schwab, 1979; Roberts, 1980, Vernon & Roberts, 1982; Warheit, Bell, Schwab, & Buhl, 1984). The results of Fillenbaum and Pfeiffer and of these other studies serve to highlight the caution sounded by Pritchard and Rosenblatt (1980a) that the use of community-based sampling procedures does not automatically assure an investigator that the survey subjects are equal in regard to proportions of emotionally disordered subjects in racial or ethnic samples obtained in this way.

Such factors as years of education, kind of occupation, and level of income (that is, various aspects of socioeconomic status)—in addition to age, marital status, and urban/rural and geographic region of residence—were also found to be related to such differences in prevalence in important ways. In several of the studies cited above, when samples of black and white adults were equated for the socioeconomic and other background factors, the differences between the ethnic groups in rate and severity of mental disorder were no longer detectable. That is, the overall differences between black adults (or those of other ethnic minorities) and white comparison groups appeared to reflect systematic differences in the proportion of socially disadvantaged individuals represented in each ethnic group. Some of these same trends were found in the results of the present investigation as well.

Background Factors in Normal Subjects

The ways in which each of the contemporary community-based samples of white and black men and women were collected for the present investigation differed in several respects that affected the final composition of these research groups. It would have been desirable if each of these surveys had provided reasonably representative cross sections of the white and black populations of the United States as summarized in the 1970 census. Unfortunately, this was not the case. The men and women in the white sample were seriously underrepresented in both the highest and lowest socioeconomic levels. The men and women in the survey of black adults were heavily overrepresented at the upper socioeconomic levels and even more underrepresented in the lower ones than the white sample. The subjects who were included in each survey, however, turned out to be sufficiently diverse with regard to various background characteristics to provide an adequate basis for a number of important analyses. If the sampling had been better, the trends would probably have been strengthened, not weakened. That is, in spite of these sampling deficiencies, it was gratifying to note that the overall results of statistical analyses on the MMPI scales demonstrated most of the general findings reported in previous investigations. Thus, it was possible to explore several hypotheses about the ways in which known differences between white and black Americans in education, income, occupation, and regional background might have contributed to the findings of previous studies. In addition, the availability of two sets of black and white men and women who were tested in urban psychiatric settings provided further opportunities to examine the usefulness of the MMPI in several traditional clinical applications.

Instrument-related Factors

Some aspects of the MMPI protocols that were obtained from the research subjects should be noted first because there appeared to be some subtle but pervasive effects stemming from the assessment process and the instrument itself that are important in making sense of the general findings from this study. One of the more subtle influences in this investigation (and in many other recent studies as well) was the low rate of item omissions. This greater willingness to answer MMPI items definitively True or False rather than deciding to leave some unanswered had a general effect on the resulting test profile of raising the raw scores of the various component scales and thus elevating the mean T scores (but *lowering* the Mf-scale T scores for women) to some unknown extent, at least a few T-score points. Because both community-based samples demonstrated mean profiles that generally were several T-score points higher than the like-sex reference group from the 1940 Minnesota survey (again, with the exception of lower Mf scale values for females), this difference probably constitutes one of the sources of variation between contemporary samples—normal or pathological, ethnic majority or ethnic minority—and the 1940 test norms of the MMPI.

Another general consequence of this change in endorsement rate would be to shift the whole score distribution upward on each of the component scales and thereby to increase the number of scores above the 70 T-score point (the common reference value for abnormal profiles). For example, such profiles would then meet the Lachar typology definition of pathology with correspondingly greater frequency. Since both the white and black men and women in our contemporary samples had higher percentages of "pathological" profiles in this typology (see table 4.8) than did the Minnesota reference group, this variance, which stems from cohort differences, may be an important but extraneous factor entering into the ongoing discussions about possible test biases in data from various American minority groups. That is, investigators who have discovered what appears to be ethnically related evidence of elevated MMPI profiles in their samples of various cultural minorities in the United States may in fact be mistakenly interpreting variance more accurately attributable either to differences in test instructions or to alterations in the normative behavior of contemporary American men and women that are systematically different from the scale values on pre-World War II norms.

Test-taking Attitudes and Competencies

Findings reported in chapter 5 on differences related to level of schooling in both black and white samples (and to level of IQ as determined by the Shipley-Institute of Living Scale for the white sample) suggested that some of the variation in MMPI performance between American minorities may arise from deficiencies in reading comprehension. That is, subjects at the lower educational levels (as indicated by years of schooling completed), among both normals and patients, tended to earn higher scores on both the basic and special scales of the test. In addition, among those subjects in the white sample for whom intelligence test scores were available, the same pattern of elevations of MMPI scores that was found for educational level appeared in relation to differences in intellective level as well. Some of these educational limitations may result in poor reading comprehension, difficulties in complying with test instructions, and general frustrations in dealing once more with rather schoollike tasks such as using a pencil, marking answer spaces, tracking item numbers, and the like. More important, certainly, are the social and occupational limitations imposed on such individuals by their low educational level; but there is a clear possibility that intellective and literacy handicaps may interfere with adequate and appropriate compliance with the test instructions, comprehension of item content, and accuracy in recording test answers.

In addition to general tendencies to answer or omit test items and variations in competence to understand and comply with test procedures, several previous investigations designed to clarify the sources of ethnic differences on the MMPI have explored various ways of assessing the perceived desirability of answering test items one way or another. The basic assumption in such research (Gynther, 1972; Witt & Gynther, 1975) is that if the members of one or another minority group perceive the implications of endorsing a given item as true of themselves as more favorable or less undesirable than do the members of another group, then they will be more willing to endorse such an attribute without regard to the veridicality of such an admission. However, research on this aspect of item endorsement behavior (see the summary of the literature on MMPI item desirability characteristics in Dahlstrom, Welsh, & Dahlstrom, 1975) has demonstrated that individuals for whom a given characteristic is in fact true are more likely to rate the admission of such a characteristic as more desirable (or less undesirable) than are those individuals for whom the attribute is absent. Thus, hypochondriacal patients rate physical complaint items (like those in scale 1 or in the ORG or HEA content scales of the MMPI) as considerably less undesirable in their personological implications than do subjects not manifesting such neurotic traits. Because of the inherent circularity in this approach, then, the utility of social desirability ratings as a way of accounting for the higher scores on scales for psychopathology found in studies of various minority groups has proven to be disappointing. It is by no means easy to disentangle a person's willingness to endorse such features from his or her self-conceptions and perceptions that are the bases for valid test inference (see Taylor, Carithers, & Coyne, 1976). The differences found at both the item and scale level on the MMPI between black and white adults do not show the across-the-board increases on all measures of psychopathology or across all items with adverse personological implications that the social desirability explanation would require (see the discussion below). Instead, the differences are quite delimited both in the content of items and in the sorts of individuals who manifest these patterns.

As was noted in the item analytic findings reported in chapter 7, none of the items in the K scale were found to show race-related differences in endorsement frequency. The K scale is a bipolar measure of the tendency to slant answers in terms of the desirability of a given direction of endorsement (high scores indicating socially favorable slanting, low indicating unfavorable responding). The lack of race-related differences on the items making up this scale is further evidence against any simple explanation of the differences between black and white subjects on the basis of differences in perceived desirability of answers to MMPI items.

Ethnic Differences

The findings on endorsement differences summarized in chapter 7 also serve to highlight the relative paucity of items that show consistent race-related differences across both sexes and in all three previous item analytic investigations. Only two items emerged as demonstrating such consistent and stable separations between white and black subjects: #11—"A person should try to understand his dreams and be guided by or take warning from them" (T); and #364—"People say insulting and vulgar things about me" (T). An additional 24 items demonstrated robust differences across both sexes in the present samples of white and black adults and were also reported in at least *two* of the three other studies. Considerably more items emerged from these comparisons, but they were significant in data from only one or the other sex. Such analyses appear to be uncovering differential kinds of experiences and various forms of emotional response to adverse social conditions rather than revealing pervasive aspects of ethnic identity per se.

Age Differences

Systematic differences between younger and older subjects in both community-based samples were found on a number of the basic and special scales of the MMPI (see figures 5.1 through 5.4 in the text and tables D-1 through D-4 in the appendix). On these scales the younger subjects were characterized as more sociable, outgoing, impulsive, at times overly energetic, and less conventionally religious; they were generally more cynical about the motives and intentions of others and mistrustful of those in authority. Older subjects seemed to have found their place in society and to have accepted the world much as it is; they did not describe themselves as nearly so rebellious, competitive, or alienated as did the young men and women of both racial groups. In the tri-state sample of black adults, it was primarily the younger men and women who showed the differences that have been ascribed to blacks in general in the earlier studies in the MMPI literature (see chapter 2), with elevations on scales F, 4 (Pd), 7 (Pt), 8 (Sc), and 9 (Ma). Younger white men also showed this pattern, although scale 7 was not as prominent. Since these features do not apply with equal accuracy to all members of the ethnic minority and since they do appear with appreciable frequency in individuals not members of that ethnic subgroup, the finding of this kind of age-cohort effect within our community samples raises doubts about the appropriateness of attributing these differences solely or primarily to *ethnicity*. Similar reservations about this tendency to generalize such differences to a whole minority group are raised by the findings in respect to socioeconomic status as well.

Socioeconomic Status Differences

Two different aspects of socioeconomic status (educational level and occupational level) were examined in relation to the basic and special scales of the MMPI in the two community-based samples reported in chapter 5. MMPI scores of individuals completing different levels of schooling in these two samples were reported in figures 5.5 through 5.8 in the chapter and in tables D-5 through D-8 in the appendix; comparable data on these same subjects classified by occupational level (or occupational level of spouse) are presented in figures 5.9 through 5.12 and tables D-13 through D-16. Both of these kinds of analyses showed similar trends: white and black men and women with more education and higher status occupations differed far less from each other than did the individuals in these two ethnic groups with no more than a high school education or with the lowest levels of occupations. In these analyses, the same scales previously reported in the MMPI literature on black and white differences (primarily scales F, 8, and 9 but also K, 5 [Mf], and 0 [Si] in some contrasts) were found to reflect differences in SES.

Results comparable to those found in the present investigation on the role of background factors in the kind and extent of racial differences were also discernible in the research summaries provided in tables 2.1 through 2.5 of the text. That is, when the samples of black and white subjects included in the investigation were generally from a uniform level of schooling completed (Fry, 1949; Flanagan & Lewis, 1969; Cooke et al., 1974; Davis & Jones, 1974; Penk & Robinowitz, 1974; Davis, 1975; King et al., 1977; McCreary & Padilla, 1977; Sutker et al., 1978; McGill, 1980; Moore & Handal, 1980) or when special subsamples were identified and compared that are more equivalent on number of years of education (Davis et al., 1973; Penk et al., 1978; Patterson et al., 1981), then the MMPI profile differences tend to be reduced or eliminated. Similar results are evident in those studies using intelligence tests to form comparable groups (Holcomb & Adams, 1982; Penk et al., 1982; Holcomb et al., 1984) or to form subgroups matched for intelligence test performance (Costello, 1973; Rosenblatt & Pritchard, 1978). Special selection for a test protocol with acceptable validity indicators before a subject is included in a study (e.g., Costello et al., 1972; Butcher et al., 1983) may be an effort to control the same kind of variance as that reflected in years of education or level of intellective competence. Bertelson, Marks, and May (1982) did not impose any selection on the validity indicator values in the protocols from their psychiatric patients but instead used an elaborate matching procedure including sex, age, rural or urban residence, working or nonworking status, level of occupation for those working, education completed, marital status, as well as inpatient or outpatient status. (In their analyses, an additional control was the comparison of adolescents directly on age-appropriate non-K-corrected T-score values; the adult scores were plotted on the usual K-corrected norms.) It is rare to have samples large enough to be in a position to carry out such an elaborate matching procedure. With black and white samples as similar as possible on these various background characteristics, the authors found that the usual differences that others had reported on black and white groups were not in evidence at either scale or patterning level. The number of differences at the item analytic level were no more than those to be expected by chance (table 2.6).

This general pattern of findings strongly supports the important role of socioeconomic status in the way the adults in the present investigation presented themselves on the test. Although there were still small differences between their means on some scales, the convergence of MMPI scores at the upper socioeconomic levels for like-sex groups of white and black adults was quite striking. The obvious lack of homogeneity within the black sample and the common trends within each racial and sex group over these educational and occupational levels do not support an explanation that assumes that racial differences on MMPI scores of blacks merely reflect some common cultural heritage. Although there may well be a common heritage that includes identity formation, intrafamily attitudes, and interpersonal or social patterns unique to the black experience in the United States, there appears to be little support in these analyses at the scale level (nor any consistent evidence in the item endorsement analyses) for any common cultural factor operating among the black men and women in the tri-state survey leading them to answer the items on this test (which measures psychopathology) in some homogeneous fashion. Data presented in table 5.7 (and in tables D-37 through D-42 in the appendix), in which findings on the selected scales for groups homogeneous for race, sex, age level, and educational level, highlight the special significance of low socioeconomic status in these black subjects.

Alienation and the Black Experience

Among the alternative formulations offered in chapter 1 for the possible presence and nature of psychological differences between the majority white population and various ethnic minority groups in the United States today—genetic, cultural, labeled deviance, caste structure, socioeconomic, or characteristics of coping with systematic exclusion and frustrations—the first four seem to require that pervasive if not universal features be manifested in members of any given ethnic group, whereas the latter two seem to permit much greater heterogeneity within such groups. So long as there is an excess in the prevalence of some attributes that could generate the differences that are reported, variation in socioeconomic status or in coping skills could appear within ethnic minorities with sufficient frequency to bring about the heterogeneity found in the present samples. Various comparisons of the two-state and tri-state samples, and of the Ohio and Michigan samples of black and white psychiatric patients as well, that were reported in earlier chapters document the greater prevalence of certain personality features and attributes in these minority groups. Nevertheless, the various characteristics did not prove to be sufficiently universal in the samples of black men and women, normal or psychiatric, to be deemed ethnic or "black." Instead, the present findings, as well as those of others who have been able to introduce adequate controls for differential socioeconomic success, highlight the special adaptational difficulties of individuals who live under the multiple disadvantages of limited education, low income, lack of occupational skills or training, and the barriers and exclusions associated with minority ethnic status as well. Members of this same ethnic minority, however, who have managed to reach higher educational levels, gain better occupational skills, and earn more equitable incomes, do not differ in the ways they answer the MMPI from members of the white comparison groups of the same sex and similar age level.

Middleton (1963) epitomized the syndrome of alienation from the dominant cultural group as powerlessness, or inability to do anything about one's predicament; meaninglessness, or inability to make sense of a world too complex to be understood; normlessness, or being forced to do things that one knows are wrong; social estrangement, or loneliness; and work estrangement, or lack of satisfaction from one's job. Most of these features fit well the pattern of characterological consequences that Chestang (1972) envisioned as developing in those ethnic minority members who are forced to defer their personal dreams and to experience repeated frustrations of their ambitions in trying to overcome a social order that may degrade them but to which they had been consigned by the accidents of birth and circumstance.

Chestang points out that the circumstances that confront a minority member in America are characterized by societal inconsistency, social injustice, and personal impotence. As a consequence, many individuals in the face of such a world develop recognizable patterns or styles of coping that come to be termed the *black experience* or what others have called a *culture of poverty* (Steinberg, 1981). This latter formulation has often been interpreted to mean that there exists a general cultural or ethnic tradition that is transmitted or reproduced down through successive generations of American minorities that leads to (nearly) universal deficiencies of character, personality, and values in members of such groups. In some contrast to this view, Chestang's explanation applies to each separate individual and the ways in which he or she may succeed or fail to meet these special challenges to adaptation or adjustment. For members of these subgroups, that is, the experiences they face may have many features in common, but the ways in which individual men and women cope differ widely.

Many individuals, then, may come out of such experiences showing deep social and personal alienation. These men and women may show pervasive discontent, cynicism, estrangement, or distantiation (see chapters 2 and 7). The same sorts of attitudes emerged from analyses of the differences between black and white psychiatric patients, with black subjects expressing more mistrust of society, resentment, and feelings of separation from others. (See also Kirk & Zucker, 1979, 1980.)

In terms of the various background factors that have been found in this investigation (as well as in other studies) to be related to the tendency to obtain elevated scores on particular MMPI scales, it is interesting to note how many of them appear to have been operating in the sample of black subjects reported by Gynther et al. (1971) drawn from the small community of Riverbend. Although they ranged over several decades in age, the modal ages were in the lower twenties, the education completed was typically at the grade school level, the location was both rural and geographically isolated, the religious outlook was fundamentalist, and the residents were at the bottom of the socioeconomic scale in occupation and cash income. That is, every factor reported in previous studies and examined in the normal and psychiatric samples summarized here can be identified as present in the Riverbend sample, all working in the direction of elevated scores. In addition, with average values as high as those reported for the F scale, a significant number of the test records probably would not have met the present standards for validity indicators. Exclusion of those questionable records, however, would not have reduced the mean profile for these men and women very much. Rather, the anomie, powerlessness, and sense of alienation that they experienced may reflect their distance from the circumstances of mainstream contemporary American society and may provide the basis for the self-descriptions that they report on the MMPI. These same features were also reflected in the scores from rural adults, black and white, who were studied by Erdberg (1969). They were also shared, at least to some degree, by all three ethnic samples (black, white, and Indian) of young adults studied by Bull (1976) in rural North Carolina and by both black and white adolescents in another rural area of the same state by Baughman and Dahlstrom (1968). They were not present in sufficient degree, however, in the well-educated, highly trained, upper socioeconomic, black men and women in the tri-state sample to justify calling these characteristics part of a "black personality."

Although the differences between white and black adults on the MMPI do not seem to be consistent with an explanation based on some common ethnic subculture, a more economical explanation for the findings from this series of statistical analyses appears to encompass a range of perceptions and views that mirror the adaptive and coping efforts of individuals who have encountered varying amounts and kinds of social, economic, and physical stress or deprivation (Jones, 1978). In this perspective, individuals who have been most successful in overcoming educational and occupational barriers, who have achieved some status and recognition in spite of the special difficulties facing minority group members—those who can now be described as middle- or upper-middle-class black Americans—show the least deviations from the way that white Americans of comparable socioeconomic level present themselves on this test. Low-income, underemployed or unemployed, poorly educated, physically ill, or socially isolated individuals, particularly if they are also members of a minority group that lacks respect and full acceptance by the dominant group, show in their test responses the effects of such deprivations. They are cynical about the leaders of society, disdainful of authority figures, mistrustful in their dealings with their neighbors, and often in turmoil in their relationships with members of their own families. Although such attitudes and expectations are quite understandable, and to some extent necessary in their daily encounters with a hostile and unsupportive society, these same defenses may also limit their adaptive flexibility under altered circumstances and increase the risk of their losing emotional control under the pressure of new stressors, thereby raising the likelihood of their manifesting some psychiatric disorder and requiring special support and treatment.

It should be clear from this formulation that by no means all deviations (as reflected in elevated MMPI scores or in similar measures) are evidence for disorder. Individuals who lack the kinds of adaptations and defenses sketched above are themselves likely to be particularly vulnerable to the sustained stressors and frustrations of modern-day urban ghettos, isolated federal reservations, or poverty-stricken farms and towns. Information about just which adaptations work well under various stressful circumstances and which ones constitute special vulnerabilities is urgently needed. The evidence in the present investigation, however, indicates that the MMPI may be useful in the task of characterizing the various coping and defense mechanisms to which minority individuals may resort in their efforts to deal with the special circumstances that they all too often encounter in America today.

Recommendations

When all the background factors introduced in these analyses are considered, it is apparent that they do not account for the major portion of the variance in the component scales of the MMPI. The procedures that were used were selected to show whether these potential sources of variance play a large or small role in how individual adults answer the inventory. Since the test is intended as a measure of psychopathology or personality disturbance—and since age, gender, socioeconomic status, and ethnic membership are not to be measured but rather to be appraised as possible sources of test-score distortion—the small (although often statistically significant) contribution that these factors make to the scores is quite reassuring. The primary sources of variation should be (and apparently are) the various specific kinds of personality patterns and various degrees of emotional disturbance that separate one subject from another. Measurement error when identified must be dealt with in some way; but if these contributions are in fact not very large, then greater trust can be placed in the variations of interest in these MMPI scores.

In the course of the various analyses that were carried out as part of the present investigation, it was also possible to examine the implications of a number of proposals that have been made in the MMPI literature about how to deal with the differences emerging from comparisons of ethnic groups. The most frequent recommendation has been a call for special subgroup norms. The results of applying such a special set of T-score conversions to generate new profiles for black men and women were not encouraging. A very large number of bona fide psychiatric patients whose MMPI profiles on the standard test norms reflected serious emotional problems ended with test patterns, when these new T scores were used, that failed to indicate that they were in need of care and treatment. The use of such norms for black adults overcorrected deviations and eliminated valid test-score variance.

A variation on the application of special black norms was proposed by White (1974) in which only selected protocols from black men and women would be corrected, based upon their performance on a special race-sensitive scale for the MMPI. Using his cutting scores and corrective weights, a set of records from black adults was used to predict broad diagnostic category assignments, psychological and nursing ratings, and selected symptoms. Although the accuracy of these predictions turned out to be comparable for black and white patient groups when the standard MMPI T scores were used for both, the application of the White corrections based upon Rs-scale scores more often reduced the hit-rate accuracy than improved it against these several external criteria. Other cutting scores and differential weighting formulas might be derived and applied, but the need for such a special set of adjustments was not supported since the data from the black patients was equally dependable using the standard profile methods in these comparisons with white patients.

A previously published, special F scale for black adults developed from a set of early analyses of the findings from the tri-state survey (Gynther,

Lachar, & Dahlstrom, 1978) seems to have been premature; comparisons with the set of MMPI data from the two-state white sample that became available later indicated that the items on this black F scale were also infrequently endorsed by contemporary white subjects. The elevated scores on the standard F scale, then, appear to be merely part of the pattern of self-presentation by those black adults who are also describing themselves in similarly deviant ways on items in a number of the other scales in the test. Current evidence suggests that these responses may be the result of the operation of either poor test compliance in general or of adaptive coping styles in the face of social discrimination and stressful living conditions.

The way in which the various race-related scales of the MMPI, particularly White's Rs scale and Costello's B-W scale, differed between normal and psychiatric groups of white and black men and women suggested that these research measures reflect to an important degree differences in emotional disorder. If this is the case, then it is reasonable to expect that subtracting variance reflected in race-related scales from test scores of some psychiatric cases could result in the loss of discriminatory power in the profiles that have been so altered.

At this stage in the development of the knowledge of how to use the MMPI in personnel and psychiatric assessment with various minority subjects or clients, the best procedure would seem to be to accept the pattern of results generated by the standard scales on the basic MMPI profile, male or female, and, when the pattern is markedly deviant, to take special pains to explore in detail the life circumstances of that individual in order to understand as fully as possible the nature and degree of his or her problems and demands. In this regard, the development of critical item lists specific to the characteristics of the group under consideration might prove more valuable than the application of special subgroup norms or T-score corrections. In addition, careful consideration should be given to the assessment of the adequacy of the individual's efforts to deal with what are all too often extremely difficult and intransigent life circumstances, a full knowledge of which may make the test results both understandable and relevant as well. The possibility of test invalidity, of course, must also be constantly borne in mind, since the distortions that may arise from poor or careless reading of the items, impulsive answering after only partial reading of the longer statements, wandering attention and lack of care in marking the answer sheet, or loss of interest toward the end of a long and fatiguing task may enter into any test administration and attenuate or destroy the meaningfulness of otherwise important scores and patterns.

The results of the present series of investigations are both reassuring and sobering. The evidence presented here documents the lack of serious bias or distortion in the use of the MMPI in mental health settings for the assessment of the emotional status of black clients, since the relative accuracy of these scores was as good or better for this ethnic minority as it was for white clients. The overall level of accuracy for neither group, however, was very high against the available external criteria; it would be desirable to have both better criterion data and more satisfactory test-based indices for use in future research, for the black minority and other American minorities as well.

In addition, the information that was available on the subjects making up the two community-based samples provided many insights into the nature of the differences between black and white adults in the United States and served to highlight the many ways in which middle-class adults in both ethnic groups resemble, rather than differ from, each other, as suggested by previous research reports. At the same time, it was disheartening to find how cynical and alienated many lower-status black citizens, especially the young men, appear to be with both the dominant white society and themselves. The MMPI scores obtained from these subgroups of black adults reflect coping strategies that may be ineffective or even disadvantageous. However necessary such defenses may be in the stressful world in which they find themselves, the trends noted in these analyses seem ominous and disturbing for the future mental health of these young people. It is also clear from the available literature on other minorities that similar processes may well be operating there. Research on the relationship of these personological indicators to future emotional breakdown or need for treatment is an urgent priority. Knowledge is now lacking on the possible linkages between such test-based indicators of potential disturbance and later appearances in mental health or criminal justice settings. Both the retrospective findings reported here and the relationships between MMPI indicators and future outcomes (so far found in studies based primarily on white subjects) lend strong support to such an empirical outcome, but it remains to be documented in appropriately designed research in the future.

APPENDIX A
Research Forms

Tri-State Survey

Please do not put your name on this form or the questionnaire answer sheet. All of your answers are to be both anonymous and confidential. Please complete all items.

FACE SHEET

MMPI Black Standardization Study

IDENTIFICATION

______( ) AGE:___( ) SEX: (1) Male ( ) MARITAL STATUS: ( )
years (2) Female ( )

(1) Single
(2) Married
(3) Widowed
(4) Divorced
(5) Separated

HEALTH INFORMATION

Are you currently receiving treatment for any illness? YES NO ( )

If YES, what type of illness is it and how long have you had it?________________________

____

Have you ever been treated for an emotional problem or a nervous condition?: YES NO ( )

If YES, have you received this treatment within the last year? YES NO ( )

EDUCATION

Circle one: ( )
(7) Less than 7 years of school
(6) Junior High School
(5) Partial High School
(4) High School Graduate (or GED)
(3) Partial College Training
(2) College Graduate (4 years)
(1) Graduate Professional Training

Most of my childhood education was obtained in:

____
city county state

____
( )

My public school eduation was obtained at schools that were mainly:

( ) (1) Part of a city school system
(2) Part of a country, rural school system

These schools were mainly: (1) Integrated (2) Segregated ( )

HISTORICAL INFORMATION

I have lived most of my life in: ______________________________
city county state

____
( )

This area is: (1) a rural, farm area
(2) a town (under 100,000)
(3) a small city (100,000-250,000)
(4) a large city (over 250,000)

Last year's income (husband and wife if both employed): ______________________
( )

Last year the head of the household (single or divorced man or woman, husband if woman married) was mainly: (1) employed (2) unemployed ( )

Description of job of head of household: ______________________________

____

______________________________________ (code: __________)
( )

Two-State Survey

I.D. ______________________________

SEX: Male Female

AGE: __________

RACE: White Non-White

LAST YEAR OF SCHOOL COMPLETED: _______________

MARITAL STATUS: Single, Married, Separated, Divorced, Widowed

HUSBAND'S OCCUPATION:____

HUSBAND'S INCOME: $__________________________________ per year

WIFE'S OCCUPATION:____

WIFE'S INCOME: $__________________________________ per year

OCCUPATION OF FATHER:____

INCOME OF FATHER: $__________________________________ per year

OCCUPATION OF MOTHER:____

INCOME OF MOTHER: $__________________________________ per year

Do you live in town, or outside of town?____________________________________

Social Readjustment Rating Scale (Life Events Checklist)

Holmes and Rahe, 1967

LIFE EVENTS CHECKLIST

Listed below are Life Events which happen to a great many people. Please circle each event listed below if it has happened to you in the last six months.

	Item weights*
1. Being fired from work.	47
2. Beginning or ending school or college.	26
3. Death of a close friend.	37
4. Son or daughter leaving home (marriage, attending college, etc.).	29
5. Put in jail or other institution.	63
6. Had a vacation.	13
7. Husband or wife beginning or ending work outside the home.	26
8. Pregnancy of wife.	40
9. Changing to a different line of work.	36
10. Taking on a mortgage or loan greater than $10,000 (purchasing a home, business, etc.).	31
11. Taking on a mortgage or loan less than $10,000 (purchasing a car, TV, freezer, etc.).	17
12. Minor violations of the law (traffic tickets, jaywalking, disturbing the peace, etc.).	11
13. Changing to a new school or college.	20
14. Marriage.	50
15. Troubles with the boss.	23
16. Change in day-to-day habits (dress, manners, friends, etc.).	24
17. Death of close family member.	63
18. Marital separation from husband or wife.	65

*Item weights added for research analyses.

19. Marital reconciliation with husband or wife.	45
20. Outstanding personal achievement.	28
21. Change in residence (moving to a new address).	20
22. Gaining a new family member (through birth, adoption, older relative or friend moving in).	39
23. Sexual problems or difficulties.	39
24. Major change in church activities (a lot more or a lot less than usual).	19
25. Foreclosure on a mortgage or loan.	30
26. Death of husband or wife.	100
27. Major change in number of family get-togethers (a lot more or a lot less than usual).	15
28. Retirement from work.	45
29. Major change in salary, income, or money you have (a lot worse off or a lot better off than usual).	38
30. Major personal injury or illness.	53
31. Major change in your business or work (bankruptcy, merger, reorganization, etc.).	39
32. Major change in the number of arguments or fights with husband or wife (either a lot more or a lot less than usual).	35
33. Major change in social activities (clubs, dancing, movies, visiting, etc.).	18
34. Troubles with in-laws (arguments, disagreements, etc.).	29
35. Divorce.	73
36. Major change in sleeping habits (a lot more or a lot less sleep, or change in part of day when you sleep).	16
37. Major change in the place where you live (building a new home, adding a room or apartment, home or neighborhood getting run-down).	25
38. Major change in eating habits (eating a lot more or a lot less food, different meal hours or surroundings, etc.).	15
39. Major change in the health or activities of a family member.	44
40. Major change in duties at work (promotion, demotion, transfer).	29
41. Major change in usual kind or amount of recreation.	19
42. Major change in working hours or conditions (new shift, new place, new boss, etc.).	20

APPENDIX B
Scale Designations and Profile Coding

Brief Descriptions of Correlates Associated with Elevations on Various MMPI Scales

Scale Designations		Correlates
		Validity Indicators
?	Cannot Say score	The total number of items left unanswered or double answered; high scores may reflect confusion, evasiveness, obsessive doubts, reading deficiencies.
L	Lie scale	Composed of items dealing with common personal faults usually freely acknowledged; high scores may reflect attempt to present oneself as highly virtuous or in an overly favorable way.
F	(In)frequency scale	Composed of items rarely endorsed; high scores may reflect carelessness, confusion, poor cooperation, malingering, symptom exaggeration, or random responding.
K	Correction scale	Developed as a suppressor variable for test-taking attitude; high scores may reflect a more subtle defensiveness; low scores suggest unusual openness in self-revelation.
		Basic Clinical Scales
1 Hs	Hypochondriasis	High scores may indicate somatic preoccupations and concern over bodily functions, cynicism, defeatist attitudes, and narcissistic complaining.
2 D	Depression	High scores may indicate depressive affect, despondency, pessimism, moodiness, or dysphoria.

3 Hy	Hysteria	High scores may reflect one or more physical complaints with a psychological component, excessive repression, dependency, naiveté, and demonstrativeness.
4 Pd	Psychopathic Deviate	High scores reflect tendency to be at odds with social standards, rebellious, impulsive, hedonistic, with history of difficulties in family life and problems with authority.
5 Mf	Masculinity-Femininity	High scores for males reflect sensitivity, passivity, and aesthetic or "feminine" interests. Low scores for males reflect narrow "masculine" interests and pursuits. High scores for females show rebelliousness, aggressiveness, and assertiveness; low scores for females show more passivity and acceptance of traditional role.
6 Pa	Paranoia	High scores reflect mistrust of others' motivations, guardedness, and suspiciousness, as well as unwillingness to accept personal criticism or blame.
7 Pt	Psychasthenia	High scores indicate anxiety and fears, ruminative preoccupations, obsessions or phobias, rigid personal standards, and extreme self-condemning tendencies.
8 Sc	Schizophrenia	High scores reflect strange and unusual thoughts or beliefs, social withdrawal and self-alienation; in severe cases, bizarre delusions and hallucinations may be present.
9 Ma	Hypomania	High scores indicate outgoing, sociable, and overly energetic patterns; tendencies to act impulsively and with poor judgment; and tendency to take on too much.
0 Si	Social Introversion	High scores suggest social shyness, inhibition, and tendency to be self-effacing; low scores reflect outgoing, sociable, and self-confident patterns.

Supplementary Scales

A	Anxiety (Welsh)	High scores reveal a lack of poise, tendency to become rattled and upset, overconcern with evaluations, tendency to rationalize, excuse, and avoid criticism.
R	Repression (Welsh)	High scores show submissiveness and conventionality, phlegmatic style, and inability to face unpleasant or disagreeable situations.
Es	Ego Strength (Barron)	High scores reflect independence, persistence, and initiative, self-confidence and poise.

Content Scales (Wiggins)

ORG	Organic Symptoms	High scorers admit to symptoms that are often indicative of organic involvement, ranging widely over various body systems.
HEA	Poor Health	High scorers are concerned about their health and have admitted to a variety of gastrointestinal complaints.
DEP	Depression	High scorers experience guilt, regret, worry, unhappiness, and a feeling that life has lost its zest.
MOR	Poor Morale	High scorers are lacking in self-confidence, feel that they have failed in life, and are given to despair and a tendency to give up hope; they are overly sensitive to criticism.
SOC	Social Maladjustment	High scorers are socially bashful, shy, embarrassed, reticent, self-conscious, and extremely reserved.
HOS	Manifest Hostility	High scorers admit tendencies to be cross, grouchy, argumentative, and uncooperative, and may also be competitive, aggressive, and retaliatory in interpersonal relationships.
FAM	Family Problems	High scorers feel that they have had unpleasant home lives characterized by a lack of love in the family and parents who were unnecessarily critical, nervous, quarrelsome, and quick-tempered.

AUT	Authority Conflict	High scorers have little respect for authority and are convinced that others are unscrupulous, dishonest, hypocritical, and motivated only by personal profit.
FEM	Feminine Interests	High scorers admit to preferences and liking for games, hobbies, and vocations that are considered "feminine."
PHO	Phobias	High scorers have admitted to a number of fears, many of them of the classically phobic variety, such as heights, darkness, closed spaces, etc.
PSY	Psychoticism	High scorers admit to a number of classic psychotic symptoms of a primarily paranoid nature (strange and peculiar experiences, hallucinations, loss of control, feelings of unreality, etc.).
HYP	Hypomania	High scorers are characterized by feelings of excitement, well-being, restlessness, and tension; they show many enthusiams and interests, constantly seeking change.
REL	Religious Fundamentalism	High scorers see themselves as religious, churchgoing people who accept as true a number of fundamentalist religious convictions.

Source: Adapted from Butcher, J. N. *Objective personality assessment*. New York: General Learning Press, 1971; and Wiggins, J. S. Substantive dimensions of self-report in the MMPI item pool. *Psychological Monographs*, 1966, 80, 22 (whole no. 630).

Profile Coding Procedures

The coding scheme for MMPI profiles that is used throughout this volume is that devised by Welsh (1948). In this method, each scale in the clinical profile is listed serially by numerical designation in order from highest T-score value to lowest. Next, the elevation symbols given below are inserted into this series at the appropriate points in the sequence. The validity indicators are then listed and the elevations indicated in the same way by inserting the appropriate symbols. In the case of identical elevations, the lower value numeral is listed first. Tied scores or values within one T-score point are indicated by underlining the code designations.

Elevation	*Symbol*
Over 100	**
99-90	*
89-80	"
79-70	'
69-60	-
59-50	/
49-40	:
39-30	#

Table B-1. Percentage of Codes from Two-State White Male Adults (N = 188) in Which Each Pair of High Points Occurs

Second Point	High Point 1	2	3	4	5	6	7	8	9	0	Second Point Total
1		1.6	2.7	0.5		0.5	0.5	0.5	1.1	1.6	9.1
2	2.1		2.1	0.5	3.2		1.1	1.1		1.6	11.8
3	1.1			1.1	3.2		1.1	0.5	2.1		9.1
4	1.1	1.6	1.6		3.2	1.6	1.1	1.6	4.8		16.6
5		2.1	0.5	2.1		0.5	0.5	0.5	5.3	1.6	13.4
6		0.5	1.6	0.5	3.7		0.5		2.1		9.1
7		2.1	1.1	1.6	1.6	1.6			1.6		9.6
8	0.5	1.1		1.6	1.1	0.5	1.1		1.6	0.5	8.0
9		0.5	0.5	2.7	2.1	1.1		0.5			7.5
0	1.1	1.6	0.5		1.1	1.1			0.5		5.9
High point total	5.9	11.2	10.7	10.7	19.3	7.0	5.9	4.8	19.3	5.3	100.1

Table B-2. Percentage of Codes from Two-State White Female Adults (N = 228) in Which Each Pair of High Points Occurs

Second Point	High Point 1	2	3	4	5	6	7	8	9	0	Second Point Total
1		0.4	4.4	0.4					0.4	0.4	6.1
2	1.3		0.4	0.4	0.9	0.9	0.9	0.4	0.4	2.6	8.3
3	2.2	1.7		4.8		2.6		0.9	4.4	0.4	17.0
4	0.4	1.7	5.7		1.3	1.7	0.9	1.3	5.7	1.3	20.1
5				0.4		0.4			1.3		2.2
6			0.9	2.2	0.9		0.4	0.9	2.6	1.7	9.6
7		0.4	0.9	0.4		0.4		1.7	1.3	1.7	7.0
8	0.4		1.7	3.5		0.9	0.4				7.0
9			2.2	5.7	1.7	2.2	0.4	0.4		0.9	13.5
0		1.3	0.9			1.3	0.4	1.7	3.5		9.2
High point total	4.4	5.6	17.0	17.9	4.8	10.5	3.5	7.4	19.7	9.2	100.0

Table B-3. Percentage of Codes from Tri-State Black Male Adults (N = 293) in Which Each Pair of High Points Occurs

Second Point	High Point 1	2	3	4	5	6	7	8	9	0	Second Point Total
1		1.4	1.0		3.4		0.3	1.4	2.7	0.3	10.6
2	1.4			1.0	1.7	1.7	0.3	1.0	1.4	0.3	8.9
3	2.0	1.0		1.0	3.4	0.7	0.7		0.7		9.6
4	0.7	1.7	1.4		3.8	0.3		2.7	4.8		15.4
5	1.0	0.7	1.4	1.0			0.3	0.7	5.8	0.7	11.6
6				0.3	0.7			1.7	2.7		5.5
7		0.7		1.4	1.0	0.3		2.7			6.1
8	0.3	0.3		3.1	1.4	1.4	0.3		4.8		11.6
9	0.3	2.4	0.3	2.0	6.1	1.0	0.3	5.1		0.7	18.3
0		0.7	0.3		0.7				0.7		2.4
High point total	5.8	8.9	4.4	9.9	22.2	5.5	2.4	15.4	23.5	2.0	100.0

Table B-4. Percentage of Codes from Tri-State Black Female Adults (N = 503) in Which Each Pair of High Points Occurs

Second Point	High Point 1	2	3	4	5	6	7	8	9	0	Second Point Total
1		0.4	1.0	1.0	0.2	0.2		0.8	1.2	0.8	5.6
2	1.2		0.6	2.4	0.6	0.4	0.2	0.8	1.0	2.8	9.9
3	1.0	0.6		2.4	0.6	1.0	0.4		1.6	0.6	8.2
4	0.4	1.4	3.2		1.4	1.8	0.2	2.8	7.0	1.2	19.3
5	0.2		0.6	1.2		0.4		0.8	2.8	0.4	6.4
6	0.4	0.2	1.2	1.6	0.6		0.2	3.0	4.0	1.0	12.1
7	0.2	0.4		0.8		0.2		1.2		0.4	3.2
8	0.4	1.2	0.4	3.6	0.2	3.0	0.4		3.6	0.6	13.3
9	0.8	0.2	0.6	3.2	1.8	1.8	0.4	5.0		1.0	14.7
0	0.2	0.6	0.4	2.0	0.4	0.8	0.2	1.2	1.6		7.4
High Point Total	4.8	5.0	8.0	18.1	5.8	9.5	2.0	15.5	22.7	8.7	100.1

Table B-5. Code-Type Distribution of Male and Female Normal Adult Samples

Profile Classification	Male: Minnesota White Sample (*N* = 225)	Male: Two-State White Sample (*N* = 190)	Male: Tri-State Black Sample (*N* = 321)	Female: Minnesota White Sample (*N* = 315)	Female: Two-State White Sample (*N* = 231)	Female: Tri-State Black Sample (*N* = 561)
? ≥ 30 (removed from analysis)	26	0	15	38	0	35
Remaining cases	199	190	306	277	231	526
Invalid (F − K > 16 and F > 25)	1	2	13	0	3	23
%	0.5	1.1	4.2	0.0	1.3	4.4
Normal limits profiles	156	102	124	217	154	279
%	78.4	53.7	40.5	78.3	66.7	53.0
Neurotic:						
1 spike	3	3	12	0	1	8
2 spike	4	5	4	4	0	2
3 spike	0	0	1	4	4	6
7 spike	3	5	3	1	0	1
12/21	4	2	4	3	2	4
13/31	2	4	7	5	4	3
17/71	2	0	0	0	1	0
23/32	1	4	1	1	1	1
27/72	3	3	2	4	2	1
20/02	0	1	1	3	0	0
37/73	0	1	1	1	0	0
Total neurotic	22	28	36	26	15	26
%	11.1	14.7	11.8	9.4	6.5	4.9
Characterological:						
4 spike	3	3	8	2	10	17
9 spike	6	15	33	4	13	32
14/41	1	2	1	1	0	0
24/42	0	3	3	0	3	5
34/43	0	2	0	1	1	5
46/64	0	3	4	1	2	4
47/74	0	4	4	1	2	0
48/84	0	4	12	1	0	14
49/94	0	3	4	0	5	7
Total characterological	10	39	69	11	36	84
%	5.0	20.5	22.5	4.0	15.6	16.0
Psychotic:						
6 spike	0	3	3	3	4	9
8 spike	2	0	6	0	6	10
18/81	0	1	4	1	1	5
28/82	0	2	1	0	1	5
38/83	0	0	1	0	1	0
68/86	2	1	9	4	0	24
69/96	0	1	4	0	2	12
78/87	2	3	6	2	1	6
89/98	2	1	22	2	0	23
Total psychotic	8	12	56	12	16	94
%	4.0	6.3	18.3	4.3	6.9	17.9

Other:						
0 spike	1	3	1	8	6	11
16/61	0	1	0	2	0	1
19/91	0	0	2	0	1	1
10/01	0	1	0	0	0	0
26/62	1	0	1	0	0	0
29/92	0	0	2	0	0	1
36/63	0	0	1	0	0	0
39/93	0	0	1	1	0	0
40/04	0	0	0	0	0	1
67/76	0	1	0	0	0	1
60/06	0	1	0	0	0	2
70/07	0	0	0	0	0	1
80/08	0	0	0	0	0	1
Total other	2	7	8	11	7	20
%	1.0	3.7	2.6	4.0	3.0	3.8

APPENDIX C
Special Race-Related Scales

Table C-1. Composition of the Black-White (B-W) Scale (32 items) (Costello, 1977)

Group Form Booklet No.	Item	Scoring Direction	Also on Scales
4	I think I would like the work of a librarian.	T	t5
* 11	A person should try to understand his dreams and be guided by or take warning from them.	T	t9
30	At times I feel like swearing.	F	fLK23
* 73	I am an important person.	T	t9, PSY
78	I like poetry.	T	t5, FEM
* 81	I think I would like the kind of work a forest ranger does.	F	f(5), R, FEM
*124	Most people will use somewhat unfair means to gain profit or an advantage rather than to lose it.	T	t0, AUT f(K36)
165	I like to know some important people because it makes me feel important.	T	fL
167	It wouldn't make me nervous if any members of my family got into trouble with the law.	T	t9
170	What others think of me does not bother me.	T	fK34
184	I commonly hear voices without knowing where they come from.	T	tF, PSY
206	I am very religious (more than most people).	T	tF, REL
213	In walking I am very careful to step over sidewalk cracks.	T	f(35)
221	I like science.	T	tEs f5, R, FEM
*264	I am entirely self-confident.	T	f5, MOR
280	Most people make friends because friends are likely to be useful to them.	T	tAUT f(5)
304	In school I found it very hard to talk before the class.	F	t70, SOC
349	I have strange and peculiar thoughts.	T	t78, PSY fEs
*364	People say insulting and vulgar things about me.	T	t68, PSY
386	I like to keep people guessing what I am going to do next.	T	tHYP
400	If given the chance, I could do some things that would be of great benefit to the world.	T	tPSY f(0)
415	If given the chance, I would make a good leader of people.	T	f0, R
420	I have had some very unusual religious experiences.	T	tPSY fEs
429	I like to attend lectures on serious subjects.	T	fR
433	I used to have imaginary companions.	T	tPSY
446	I enjoy gambling for small stakes.	F	tAUT f(0)
456	A person shouldn't be punished for breaking a law that he thinks is unreasonable.	T	. . .
457	I believe that a person should never taste an alcoholic drink.	T	. . .
490	I read in the Bible several times a week.	T	tREL
498	It is always a good thing to be frank.	T	. . .
513	I think Lincoln was greater than Washington.	T	tEs
527	The members of my family and my close relatives get along quite well.	T	fFAM

*Also on Race-sensitive (Rs) scale (White, 1974)

Table C-2. Composition of the Race-Sensitive (Rs) Scale (27 items) (White, 1974)

Group Form Booklet No.	Item	Scoring Direction	Also on Scales
* 11	A person should try to understand his dreams and be guided by or take warning from them.	T	t9
16	I am sure I get a raw deal from life.	T	t468, PSY
59	I have often had to take orders from someone who did not know as much as I did.	T	t9, AUT
67	I wish I could be as happy as others seem to be.	T	t2470, A, DEP
* 73	I am an important person.	T	t9, PSY
* 81	I think I would like the kind of work a forest ranger does.	F	f(5), R, FEM
84	These days I find it hard not to give up hope of amounting to something.	T	t4, MOR
93	I think most people would lie to get ahead.	T	tAUT f(36)
117	Most people are honest chiefly through fear of being caught.	T	t0, AUT f(56)
*124	Most people will use somewhat unfair means to gain profit or an advantage rather than to lose it.	T	t0, AUT f(K36)
135	If I could get into a movie without paying and be sure I was not seen I would probably do it.	T	fL
147	I have often lost out on things because I couldn't make up my mind soon enough.	T	t0, A f(3)
157	I feel that I have often been punished without cause.	T	t689
222	It is not hard for me to ask help from my friends even though I cannot return the favor.	T	t9
226	Some of my family have habits that bother and annoy me very much.	T	t59, FAM
229	I should like to belong to several clubs or lodges.	T	f50
239	I have been disappointed in love.	T	t45, FAM
241	I dream frequently about things that are best kept to myself.	T	t8 f(2), Es
*264	I am entirely self-confident.	T	f5, MOR
275	Someone has control over my mind.	T	tF6, PSY
284	I am sure I am being talked about.	T	t46, PSY
298	If several people find themselves in trouble, the best thing for them to do is to agree upon a story and stick to it.	T	t9, AUT
316	I think nearly anyone would tell a lie to keep out of trouble.	T	t0, AUT f(K6)
319	Most people inwardly dislike putting themselves out to help other people.	T	tAUT f(6)
343	I usually have to stop and think before I act even in trifling matters.	T	t7, A
347	I have no enemies who really wish to harm me.	F	f6, PSY
*364	People say insulting and vulgar things about me.	T	t68, PSY

*Also on Black-White (B-W) scale (Costello, 1977).

Table C-3. Composition of a Proposed F Scale for Blacks (33 items) (Gynther, Lachar, & Dahlstrom, 1978)

Group Form Booklet No.	Item	Scoring Directions	Also on Scales
2	I have a good appetite.	F	tEs f123, HEA
10	There seems to be a lump in my throat much of the time.	T	t37, HEA
* 14	I have diarrhea once a month or more.	T	tF, HEA fEs
* 23	I am troubled by attacks of nausea and vomiting.	T	tF123, ORG
* 48	When I am with people I am bothered by hearing very queer things.	T	tF, PSY fEs
* 49	It would be better if almost all laws were thrown away.	T	tF
* 75	I get angry sometimes.	F	fLF
* 85	Sometimes I am strongly attracted by the personal articles of others such as shoes, gloves, etc., so that I want to handle or steal them though I have no use for them.	T	tF
88	I usually feel that life is worthwhile.	F	f2, DEP
90	Once in a while I put off until tomorrow what I ought to do today.	F	fL
104	I don't seem to care what happens to me.	T	t28, DEP
*113	I believe in law enforcement.	F	fF
*123	I believe I am being followed.	T	tF6, PSY
*151	Someone has been trying to poison me.	T	tF6, PSY
*177	My mother was a good woman.	F	fF8
*196	I like to visit places where I have never been before.	F	tHYP fF8
*197	Someone has been trying to rob me.	T	tF, PSY
*210	Everything tastes the same.	T	tF8, DEP
*211	I can sleep during the day but not at night.	T	tF
*220	I loved my mother.	F	fF8, FAM
*227	I have been told that I walk during sleep.	T	tF
*246	My neck spots with red often.	T	tF
*257	I usually expect to succeed in things I do.	F	fF
*258	I believe there is a God.	F	tREL fF
*272	At times I am full of energy.	F	tHYP fFK2, R
*276	I enjoy children.	F	fF8
285	Once in a while I laugh at a dirty joke.	F	fL2
*291	At one or more times in my life I feel that someone was making me do things by hypnotizing me.	T	tF68, PSY
324	I have never been in love with anyone.	T	t8
339	Most of the time I wish I were dead.	T	t8, DEP
365	I feel uneasy indoors.	T	t6, PHO
393	Horses that don't pull should be beaten or kicked.	T	...
565	I feel like jumping off when I am on a high place.	T	...

*Also on standard F scale.

APPENDIX D
Analyses of Relationships between MMPI Scores and Background Factors in Normal Samples

Table D-1. Means and Standard Deviations of MMPI Basic and Special Scales for White Males at Four Age Levels

	18-24 (*N* = 47)		25-34 (*N* = 58)		35-49 (*N* = 50)		≥ 50 (*N* = 33)			
Scale	**Mean**	**S.D.**	**Mean**	**S.D.**	**Mean**	**S.D.**	**Mean**	**S.D.**	*F*	*p*
L	50.2	8.0	48.3	7.9	48.2	5.3	50.0	8.8	0.93	
F	60.8	15.3	54.2	7.0	51.3	5.5	53.3	11.1	7.72	.001
K	53.9	9.4	53.6	9.8	55.8	6.9	53.5	8.7	0.77	
Hs	54.9	10.3	52.3	10.5	55.7	10.4	58.8	8.5	3.03	.05
D	54.8	12.0	56.3	12.6	56.3	11.4	62.2	9.3	2.84	.05
Hy	57.6	10.0	56.5	8.9	58.5	7.1	57.0	7.6	0.52	
Pd	62.8	11.3	57.3	12.2	57.3	10.0	54.6	9.7	4.12	.01
Mf	56.7	9.9	59.3	10.3	61.5	10.0	60.3	9.6	1.91	
Pa	59.6	16.3	55.7	11.7	55.3	10.0	55.0	10.5	1.40	
Pt	58.1	13.1	55.8	11.7	56.5	11.4	56.8	10.4	0.34	
Sc	62.3	15.6	54.7	13.4	53.5	10.2	54.5	12.1	4.58	.01
Ma	64.4	10.1	57.1	10.1	53.3	9.2	51.6	11.2	13.89	.001
Si	51.6	10.6	52.0	10.5	51.6	11.0	54.9	9.8	0.83	
A	50.0	9.3	48.7	10.8	48.1	8.1	50.8	8.9	0.73	
R	52.3	8.5	50.8	10.1	50.7	8.6	52.8	9.1	0.61	
Es	55.4	10.4	58.9	8.3	56.0	8.9	50.0	10.5	6.37	.001
ORG	51.2	10.3	47.9	8.7	48.4	7.7	55.2	10.4	5.18	.01
HEA	51.2	9.4	49.3	9.4	50.6	9.0	52.8	10.0	1.06	
DEP	51.3	11.1	48.4	10.3	49.0	9.2	51.7	8.4	1.25	
MOR	50.6	10.6	47.7	10.0	46.6	8.9	48.4	8.7	1.49	
SOC	51.7	11.8	50.8	11.5	52.5	12.5	55.4	11.0	1.13	
HOS	51.1	9.1	48.8	10.4	46.5	6.3	48.4	7.8	2.36	
FAM	57.3	12.0	50.4	11.8	48.5	9.7	48.4	10.3	6.47	.001
AUT	52.7	10.3	49.3	11.5	45.3	8.8	46.6	9.3	4.76	.01
FEM	48.1	10.4	48.8	9.9	52.7	10.4	54.7	8.9	4.22	.01
PHO	52.8	11.2	49.3	9.6	53.3	10.5	55.9	11.6	2.96	.05
PSY	53.1	11.5	48.6	8.1	46.9	5.8	48.5	7.7	4.75	.01
HYP	54.6	8.2	51.7	8.6	49.8	7.2	50.2	7.7	3.42	.05
REL	47.0	9.8	49.8	9.0	54.1	9.5	55.5	9.8	7.34	.001

Table D-2. Means and Standard Deviations of MMPI Basic and Special Scales for White Females at Four Age Levels

	18-24 (*N* = 35)		25-34 (*N* = 53)		35-49 (*N* = 70)		≥ 50 (*N* = 70)			
Scale	Mean	S.D.	Mean	S.D.	Mean	S.D.	Mean	S.D.	*F*	*p*
L	46.5	5.4	48.1	6.8	48.3	6.1	51.3	6.0	5.82	.001
F	52.9	7.8	51.6	7.0	51.5	6.7	53.0	8.5	0.71	
K	54.6	9.5	57.4	10.6	58.2	7.7	53.2	9.2	4.27	.01
Hs	49.6	6.2	51.5	8.7	53.0	9.6	52.9	9.8	1.40	
D	51.5	10.6	49.8	9.4	51.3	10.7	54.4	10.0	2.27	
Hy	52.8	8.4	56.8	7.6	58.4	8.3	56.7	8.6	3.53	.05
Pd	57.6	10.7	59.8	9.8	57.9	9.8	55.1	10.1	2.34	
Mf	45.3	9.9	44.8	8.1	47.0	9.0	46.1	9.6	0.66	
Pa	56.1	9.1	56.3	6.8	55.0	9.3	54.9	8.8	0.41	
Pt	56.7	8.2	53.7	7.9	52.7	9.3	53.7	9.9	1.55	
Sc	55.9	10.1	56.0	9.0	55.1	9.3	54.3	9.8	0.41	
Ma	59.6	10.1	56.7	10.1	54.8	8.3	54.6	9.8	2.65	.05
Si	54.5	11.4	49.6	9.1	49.8	8.2	53.9	9.6	4.29	.01
A	47.2	10.4	44.5	10.9	43.3	8.0	48.9	9.7	4.62	.01
R	47.7	8.5	48.4	8.7	50.2	11.2	49.7	8.9	0.74	
Es	54.8	11.5	59.2	9.5	58.6	11.0	50.5	9.6	9.80	.001
ORG	43.9	6.5	44.4	10.1	46.8	9.2	51.6	11.0	7.77	.001
HEA	46.4	8.6	47.0	10.2	46.2	9.2	49.8	9.9	1.97	
DEP	48.0	10.7	45.4	10.2	44.5	9.0	48.7	9.4	2.71	.05
MOR	46.7	11.3	43.4	10.4	42.1	8.7	48.7	10.3	5.81	.001
SOC	50.8	12.3	46.2	9.9	44.7	9.0	48.6	10.6	3.45	.05
HOS	47.7	8.0	46.2	9.9	46.1	8.4	49.5	8.6	2.13	
FAM	52.4	9.1	51.6	13.7	49.8	9.9	51.6	10.6	0.59	
AUT	48.5	9.1	44.3	9.8	44.5	7.9	49.0	10.3	4.15	.01
FEM	50.1	10.7	50.0	8.0	51.3	10.5	53.4	7.3	1.78	
PHO	46.5	9.7	46.9	10.8	45.9	8.7	52.1	8.9	6.08	.001
PSY	52.3	9.3	50.0	10.4	46.5	6.8	50.8	9.2	4.34	.01
HYP	51.0	8.4	48.7	10.3	48.4	8.5	52.1	8.2	2.51	
REL	49.0	11.7	49.5	9.8	49.7	8.9	54.5	8.6	4.62	.01

Table D-3. Means and Standard Deviations of MMPI Basic and Special Scales for Black Males at Four Age Levels

	18-24 (*N* = 61)		25-34 (*N* = 81)		35-49 (*N* = 98)		≥ 50 (*N* = 53)			
Scale	Mean	S.D.	Mean	S.D.	Mean	S.D.	Mean	S.D.	*F*	*p*
L	52.9	8.2	50.5	7.2	52.7	8.2	50.5	7.9	2.07	
F	64.3	13.4	60.0	12.3	55.0	8.8	48.5	12.2	8.45	.001
K	53.8	9.3	53.3	8.2	55.1	8.9	52.6	8.8	1.12	
Hs	58.1	13.3	56.5	10.4	57.4	9.7	61.2	13.1	1.96	
D	57.1	11.8	56.9	9.0	58.6	10.1	57.7	9.4	0.47	
Hy	58.5	10.4	56.2	8.6	57.1	8.5	57.8	10.5	0.74	
Pd	65.7	11.3	62.2	10.0	59.7	9.5	59.0	10.6	5.47	.001
Mf	61.3	9.1	62.7	9.3	62.8	10.2	61.5	8.1	0.48	
Pa	58.4	13.3	56.1	10.7	54.2	10.4	56.1	11.6	1.74	
Pt	60.4	11.2	56.9	9.3	55.2	9.0	58.5	10.9	3.74	.01
Sc	71.0	15.1	62.0	13.4	58.4	12.0	62.0	14.0	11.18	.001
Ma	68.9	11.9	65.3	10.4	59.8	9.9	62.1	10.8	10.11	.001
Si	51.6	8.8	50.9	7.1	52.1	7.9	53.8	7.2	1.54	
A	51.2	9.8	50.1	9.6	48.4	8.5	52.5	9.2	2.54	
R	50.6	10.5	50.0	8.2	51.3	9.6	51.0	10.8	0.27	
Es	48.3	9.2	51.0	10.1	52.2	9.0	46.2	11.1	5.23	.01
ORG	55.0	12.3	53.1	10.3	51.6	10.2	57.0	10.6	3.31	.05
HEA	55.5	9.8	53.9	10.1	53.4	9.3	57.2	10.1	2.06	
DEP	52.7	10.2	50.5	8.9	49.5	9.0	53.0	9.3	2.35	
MOR	48.6	9.0	47.6	8.9	47.1	8.6	50.3	9.7	1.58	
SOC	50.9	9.1	51.0	7.5	51.0	9.4	52.4	6.4	0.41	
HOS	51.2	9.6	50.0	8.8	47.3	8.1	50.1	9.4	3.18	.05
FAM	59.4	12.4	57.1	11.1	55.2	10.4	57.4	10.2	1.88	
AUT	56.2	9.8	54.4	9.6	51.8	9.5	52.3	8.1	3.14	.05
FEM	57.5	9.5	59.1	10.4	60.1	9.7	61.1	8.0	1.54	
PHO	58.5	11.9	56.0	9.6	55.1	10.0	59.8	10.0	3.05	.05
PSY	60.9	11.4	56.4	10.4	53.7	8.9	59.4	13.4	6.73	.001
HYP	54.6	10.0	53.5	8.7	51.1	8.8	54.4	9.7	2.41	
REL	53.8	8.1	51.1	10.2	55.2	9.5	59.3	7.6	9.07	.001

Table D-4. Means and Standard Deviations of MMPI Basic and Special Scales for Black Females at Four Age Levels

	18-24 (N = 120)		25-34 (N = 170)		35-49 (N = 133)		≥ 50 (N = 78)			
Scale	Mean	S.D.	Mean	S.D.	Mean	S.D.	Mean	S.D.	F	p
L	48.8	8.0	49.1	7.1	50.4	7.7	52.9	7.8	5.55	.001
F	61.7	14.0	58.3	12.3	56.2	10.6	56.7	9.3	5.14	.01
K	50.3	9.6	51.7	8.4	52.7	9.9	51.6	8.5	1.56	
Hs	52.3	8.6	53.6	9.8	54.1	9.5	54.9	9.8	1.34	
D	54.6	9.7	53.9	9.5	54.2	9.6	54.5	8.5	0.16	
Hy	52.6	9.8	54.8	8.4	55.2	9.3	54.9	10.0	2.07	
Pd	61.6	9.9	61.7	10.5	59.1	10.0	56.5	9.4	6.12	.001
Mf	52.1	8.6	51.2	8.5	51.5	8.7	52.5	9.9	0.45	
Pa	59.2	14.0	58.3	13.2	55.5	11.3	54.4	9.2	3.60	.05
Pt	56.4	10.2	54.4	9.7	54.0	9.1	51.9	8.0	3.64	.05
Sc	65.4	14.8	59.6	13.0	58.8	12.7	57.0	10.6	8.47	.001
Ma	63.6	11.2	60.6	11.6	58.9	11.6	57.4	9.3	6.04	.001
Si	55.7	8.8	53.2	8.4	55.6	8.3	55.0	7.6	2.92	.05
A	52.1	11.3	49.4	10.2	48.4	9.8	50.0	8.6	2.96	.05
R	45.8	8.9	47.8	9.6	51.2	11.1	48.3	8.7	6.56	.001
Es	51.6	10.1	52.7	9.6	51.7	9.6	49.9	8.2	1.60	
ORG	51.8	11.3	50.8	11.3	52.0	10.7	53.8	10.1	1.35	
HEA	52.8	9.5	53.0	10.6	53.0	10.5	51.4	8.3	0.51	
DEP	53.3	12.4	50.9	11.1	49.6	9.9	49.9	8.9	2.82	.05
MOR	49.3	10.5	47.8	10.2	47.3	10.2	49.6	10.0	1.36	
SOC	50.7	8.4	47.8	8.5	50.4	8.8	50.2	7.3	3.82	.01
HOS	54.4	11.0	51.4	10.2	49.4	10.1	50.9	8.7	5.34	.001
FAM	60.7	11.1	58.5	10.8	56.2	10.5	56.8	9.7	4.31	.01
AUT	58.9	9.4	55.7	8.6	54.7	9.9	54.9	8.3	5.38	.001
FEM	49.3	9.8	50.2	7.9	50.9	8.6	51.7	7.2	1.54	
PHO	55.6	9.9	55.5	9.7	55.8	9.1	56.2	8.7	0.11	
PSY	63.1	16.2	58.5	14.6	55.6	13.3	58.6	11.9	5.81	.001
HYP	53.6	10.0	52.5	10.1	49.5	10.0	51.8	9.1	3.92	.01
REL	50.8	10.0	53.1	8.7	54.4	7.8	57.7	8.6	10.46	.001

Table D-5. Means and Standard Deviations of MMPI Basic and Special Scales for White Males for Three Levels of Education

	≤ 12 years (*N* = 92)		13-15 years (*N* = 38)		≥ 16 years (*N* = 58)			
Scale	Mean	S.D.	Mean	S.D.	Mean	S.D.	*F*	*p*
L	49.9	7.8	48.9	8.9	47.8	5.9	1.34	
F	57.9	13.4	52.6	6.6	51.7	5.3	7.78	.001
K	52.1	8.6	55.5	10.0	56.8	7.5	5.84	.01
Hs	56.4	11.9	53.9	7.7	53.4	8.7	1.72	
D	58.1	12.3	56.1	10.9	55.8	11.5	0.80	
Hy	57.6	9.6	56.2	7.3	57.9	7.5	0.48	
Pd	59.3	12.3	56.7	9.7	57.5	10.6	0.94	
Mf	57.4	9.3	58.9	10.6	62.9	10.2	5.63	.01
Pa	58.0	15.0	53.4	9.0	56.0	9.3	1.85	
Pt	57.4	13.1	54.8	10.2	57.0	10.2	0.71	
Sc	58.3	15.3	53.2	12.3	54.9	10.0	2.44	
Ma	56.8	12.2	60.5	10.6	54.8	8.8	3.16	.05
Si	55.4	10.2	49.3	10.0	49.5	10.2	8.06	.001
A	51.0	9.0	46.8	9.2	48.0	9.8	3.42	.05
R	52.4	9.4	51.8	8.1	50.0	9.3	1.23	
Es	53.1	9.7	57.8	9.8	58.5	9.1	6.75	.01
ORG	53.3	10.5	47.5	7.2	46.8	7.3	11.41	.001
HEA	53.3	9.2	49.4	9.3	47.5	8.7	7.89	.001
DEP	52.3	10.1	46.5	8.6	48.2	9.8	6.02	.01
MOR	50.4	9.6	46.6	9.1	45.9	9.6	4.75	.01
SOC	55.1	11.7	48.4	11.1	50.3	11.3	5.87	.01
HOS	50.7	8.5	47.6	9.2	46.3	8.4	5.06	.01
FAM	51.2	11.0	50.3	11.3	47.2	11.4	7.09	.001
AUT	51.2	10.4	48.9	10.7	44.4	9.1	8.11	.001
FEM	48.9	9.6	52.3	11.1	52.6	10.2	2.95	
PHO	55.5	10.9	49.8	10.0	49.2	9.7	8.20	.001
PSY	51.8	10.5	46.1	6.0	47.3	5.7	8.32	.001
HYP	52.5	8.8	51.5	8.2	50.4	7.0	1.25	
REL	50.9	9.8	50.3	10.0	52.6	10.1	0.79	

Table D-6. Means and Standard Deviations of MMPI Basic and Special Scales for White Females for Three Levels of Education

	≤ 12 years (*N* = 132)		13-15 years (*N* = 41)		≥ 16 years (*N* = 55)			
Scale	Mean	S.D.	Mean	S.D.	Mean	S.D.	*F*	*p*
L	49.5	6.2	48.6	7.5	47.6	5.5	1.90	
F	53.6	7.8	51.4	8.5	49.4	4.6	6.52	.01
K	54.6	9.4	56.1	9.8	59.1	8.3	4.63	.01
Hs	53.5	9.4	50.2	7.9	50.0	8.2	4.18	.05
D	53.9	10.7	50.9	10.5	48.1	7.5	6.69	.01
Hy	57.0	8.9	55.6	7.1	56.5	8.0	0.48	
Pd	57.6	10.6	57.4	10.7	57.1	8.6	0.05	
Mf	46.7	8.6	46.3	7.9	44.1	10.8	1.62	
Pa	55.6	8.9	55.4	8.5	55.1	7.6	0.08	
Pt	54.5	9.9	53.0	9.0	53.1	6.4	0.66	
Sc	56.0	10.1	53.7	10.2	54.5	7.0	1.10	
Ma	55.0	9.2	56.5	11.4	57.6	8.8	1.52	
Si	53.4	9.9	52.0	9.9	47.7	7.0	7.36	.001
A	47.6	10.5	45.4	9.9	42.1	6.9	6.47	.01
R	50.4	9.4	48.2	8.7	47.2	10.2	2.56	
Es	53.3	10.8	56.5	10.2	60.5	10.1	9.23	.001
ORG	49.3	11.5	44.8	7.0	44.1	6.6	6.81	.001
HEA	49.2	10.2	45.4	8.7	45.1	8.0	4.78	.01
DEP	48.4	10.0	46.3	11.2	42.1	6.2	8.65	.001
MOR	46.7	10.4	43.8	11.1	42.3	8.9	4.14	.05
SOC	48.9	10.5	47.2	11.9	42.9	7.7	6.76	.001
HOS	48.0	8.6	47.5	10.3	46.0	8.4	1.00	
FAM	52.5	11.2	51.3	12.3	48.0	8.4	3.52	.05
AUT	47.7	10.0	46.8	8.4	43.1	8.4	4.63	.01
FEM	51.6	8.3	51.8	7.5	50.8	11.8	0.20	
PHO	49.8	9.9	46.9	9.3	45.1	9.0	5.30	.01
PSY	50.4	9.5	49.8	10.1	47.3	6.7	2.36	
HYP	50.7	9.1	50.0	8.0	48.3	9.1	1.38	
REL	51.1	10.0	54.0	6.7	48.6	10.6	3.83	.05

Table D-7. Means and Standard Deviations of MMPI Basic and Special Scales for Black Males for Three Levels of Education

	≤ 12 years (*N* = 117)		13-15 years (*N* = 86)		≥ 16 years (*N* = 86)			
Scale	**Mean**	**S.D.**	**Mean**	**S.D.**	**Mean**	**S.D.**	***F***	***p***
L	52.0	7.6	51.7	7.7	51.0	8.6	0.41	
F	61.8	12.9	58.3	11.4	55.4	10.0	7.62	.001
K	51.5	8.3	54.3	8.4	56.3	9.0	8.33	.001
Hs	58.5	12.4	57.3	12.0	57.7	9.5	0.31	
D	58.6	11.5	58.0	8.4	55.6	9.2	2.36	
Hy	56.0	10.5	58.4	8.7	57.6	8.0	1.82	
Pd	62.4	11.0	62.6	10.9	58.9	8.9	3.66	.05
Mf	60.5	8.0	64.4	10.6	62.2	9.6	4.27	.05
Pa	58.3	12.7	54.3	10.9	54.0	9.2	4.79	.01
Pt	59.1	10.7	56.2	9.9	55.9	9.1	3.32	.05
Sc	65.6	14.9	61.5	14.1	59.3	12.2	5.55	.01
Ma	64.5	11.7	65.0	10.9	61.4	10.3	2.70	
Si	54.1	7.7	50.9	7.4	50.1	7.8	8.09	.001
A	52.7	9.0	49.3	8.7	47.8	9.5	8.04	.001
R	49.4	10.0	50.7	8.6	52.0	9.7	1.78	
Es	46.1	9.7	51.9	9.2	53.3	9.6	16.63	.001
ORG	57.3	11.6	51.2	9.8	51.1	9.4	11.92	.001
HEA	56.9	9.6	53.1	10.0	53.0	9.4	5.55	.01
DEP	54.4	8.5	49.7	9.2	48.0	9.2	14.31	.001
MOR	50.8	9.1	47.0	8.3	45.6	8.6	9.67	.001
SOC	53.1	8.0	50.5	8.5	49.3	8.3	5.71	.01
HOS	50.9	8.5	49.6	8.8	47.6	9.3	3.54	.05
FAM	59.6	10.4	57.9	12.0	52.8	9.7	10.39	.001
AUT	54.6	9.1	54.0	9.3	52.0	10.0	2.06	
FEM	59.5	8.8	59.5	10.1	59.5	10.3	0.00	
PHO	59.9	9.6	55.7	10.4	54.1	10.8	8.68	.001
PSY	60.5	11.2	55.6	10.8	53.4	9.7	11.89	.001
HYP	55.0	9.0	52.8	9.2	51.0	9.3	4.75	.01
REL	56.6	9.0	52.0	9.3	54.0	9.7	6.12	.01

Table D-8. Means and Standard Deviations of MMPI Basic and Special Scales for Black Females at Three Levels of Education

	≤ 12 years (*N* = 213)		13-15 years (*N* = 122)		≥ 16 years (*N* = 157)			
Scale	Mean	S.D.	Mean	S.D.	Mean	S.D.	*F*	*p*
L	50.8	7.6	49.5	7.9	49.0	7.3	2.77	
F	62.9	13.5	57.9	10.4	52.3	8.0	40.48	.001
K	49.0	8.8	57.2	8.8	55.3	8.8	22.86	.001
Hs	55.1	10.1	53.4	8.9	51.6	8.6	6.43	.01
D	56.1	9.4	53.6	9.8	52.4	9.0	7.55	.001
Hy	54.2	10.2	54.4	8.4	54.7	8.8	0.14	
Pd	61.7	10.7	60.7	10.1	57.9	9.4	6.69	.01
Mf	54.6	8.5	50.0	8.5	48.7	7.9	25.70	.001
Pa	60.9	14.3	56.1	11.4	53.1	9.1	19.65	.001
Pt	56.5	10.2	53.8	9.4	51.9	8.0	11.44	.001
Sc	64.9	15.1	59.3	12.5	54.9	9.1	28.34	.001
Ma	61.7	12.8	61.9	10.3	57.2	9.8	8.91	.001
Si	57.1	7.9	53.9	8.5	51.8	8.2	19.90	.001
A	53.4	10.0	49.3	10.3	45.6	8.7	29.59	.001
R	48.1	10.5	48.0	9.2	48.6	9.6	0.14	
Es	48.0	9.1	52.4	8.7	56.2	8.8	38.74	.001
ORG	55.6	10.8	50.9	11.7	47.0	8.5	30.85	.001
HEA	55.0	10.2	52.2	9.6	49.8	9.5	12.71	.001
DEP	54.5	11.0	50.8	10.9	46.4	8.9	27.66	.001
MOR	52.0	9.8	47.5	10.0	44.0	9.3	31.61	.001
SOC	51.3	7.8	49.4	8.5	47.2	8.6	11.35	.001
HOS	54.3	10.3	52.0	10.0	47.6	9.2	21.07	.001
FAM	61.1	10.0	59.3	10.5	53.6	10.5	24.54	.001
AUT	58.0	8.8	57.1	9.0	52.4	9.1	18.76	.001
FEM	49.5	8.5	50.8	8.3	51.4	8.5	2.35	
PHO	58.5	8.8	54.0	9.2	53.5	9.6	16.02	.001
PSY	64.2	16.0	57.8	13.0	52.3	10.2	34.61	.001
HYP	53.4	10.6	52.8	9.1	49.0	9.4	9.53	.001
REL	54.0	8.7	53.7	8.8	52.9	9.8	0.62	

Table D-9. Means and Standard Deviations of MMPI Basic and Special Scales for White Males at Four Shipley IQ Levels

	≤ 100 (N = 28)		101-109 (N = 48)		110-118 (N = 60)		≥ 119 (N = 42)			
Scale	Mean	S.D.	Mean	S.D.	Mean	S.D.	Mean	S.D.	F	p
L	52.0	8.6	48.8	6.4	49.5	8.3	46.8	6.0	3.00	.05
F	58.3	12.4	55.4	10.7	53.8	10.4	52.3	5.5	2.30	
K	50.2	8.6	52.5	7.9	55.5	9.0	57.3	7.9	5.20	.01
Hs	54.9	9.9	57.3	10.8	55.1	11.3	53.0	7.7	1.31	
D	58.9	12.1	57.8	12.2	55.7	11.2	56.3	12.0	0.60	
Hy	56.8	8.3	58.2	10.1	57.2	8.8	57.9	6.7	0.21	
Pd	59.0	11.7	58.9	10.8	57.4	11.6	57.6	10.2	0.26	
Mf	55.4	9.3	56.4	8.6	60.1	10.3	64.0	10.6	6.26	.001
Pa	59.2	16.0	54.9	12.7	56.0	9.7	55.0	9.3	0.98	
Pt	57.4	13.8	57.8	12.0	55.3	11.4	57.2	10.6	0.46	
Sc	56.2	12.7	57.7	13.0	54.9	16.0	55.9	10.2	0.38	
Ma	54.5	9.7	59.0	12.8	56.2	11.0	56.2	10.1	1.14	
Si	58.0	10.0	53.8	9.5	50.4	10.7	50.1	11.0	4.53	.01
A	52.1	10.0	50.8	8.5	47.9	9.4	47.5	10.1	2.15	
R	52.1	6.5	51.6	7.9	51.9	9.9	50.2	10.9	0.36	
Es	49.8	9.8	53.4	9.2	57.3	9.3	59.8	7.7	8.55	.001
ORG	54.0	10.2	53.4	9.0	48.8	9.5	45.7	6.3	7.96	.001
HEA	52.8	7.6	52.5	8.7	48.8	9.4	49.4	9.7	2.33	
DEP	54.1	10.1	50.7	9.7	48.7	9.9	47.0	9.4	3.32	.05
MOR	51.6	11.6	50.5	8.8	46.8	9.1	45.0	9.6	4.10	.01
SOC	56.1	11.1	53.7	12.4	50.1	11.5	51.7	12.2	1.87	
HOS	50.1	8.0	50.8	8.6	47.7	8.7	46.0	9.1	2.73	.05
FAM	54.1	10.9	55.0	11.3	48.2	11.4	49.5	11.1	4.21	.01
AUT	52.7	10.9	51.1	9.4	47.5	10.2	44.9	9.6	4.84	.01
FEM	49.0	9.3	48.4	8.2	52.4	11.4	52.3	10.4	2.01	
PHO	58.3	13.5	54.0	9.3	51.3	11.0	49.0	9.1	4.83	.01
PSY	52.2	10.0	50.8	10.2	48.4	7.9	46.5	6.5	3.22	.05
HYP	53.1	8.1	53.9	8.3	50.4	7.9	49.6	7.7	2.98	.05
REL	55.7	7.5	51.1	8.9	51.4	11.2	50.4	9.7	1.89	

Table D-10. Means and Standard Deviations of MMPI Basic and Special Scales for White Females at Four Shipley IQ Levels

	≤ 100 (N = 10)		101-109 (N = 31)		110-118 (N = 87)		≥ 119 (N = 74)			
Scale	Mean	S.D.	Mean	S.D.	Mean	S.D.	Mean	S.D.	F	p
L	49.6	5.7	50.5	6.5	48.4	6.1	49.0	6.7	0.87	
F	57.4	12.0	56.2	9.7	51.6	5.3	50.8	7.7	5.78	.001
K	46.6	10.2	53.8	7.8	54.7	7.9	58.7	9.6	7.47	.001
Hs	58.3	11.0	56.2	11.3	51.1	7.9	50.7	8.0	5.04	.01
D	55.6	8.7	56.5	11.6	52.1	9.6	50.3	10.8	3.08	.05
Hy	57.8	7.5	58.4	9.8	55.4	7.8	57.3	7.8	1.34	
Pd	50.2	10.4	58.5	8.3	56.7	10.5	58.2	9.2	2.26	
Mf	52.8	12.5	49.5	7.4	44.8	7.8	44.4	10.6	4.56	.01
Pa	56.7	11.5	55.5	8.5	55.7	8.7	55.0	8.7	0.16	
Pt	54.6	10.6	55.7	10.5	53.4	9.4	53.6	8.1	0.55	
Sc	55.1	11.2	58.9	10.9	53.8	8.8	55.8	9.3	2.35	
Ma	56.6	8.2	55.6	11.9	56.0	9.3	56.3	9.0	0.04	
Si	55.7	6.2	54.9	8.3	52.9	10.0	49.6	9.4	3.44	.05
A	53.4	10.8	49.5	9.3	46.6	9.4	43.2	10.0	5.40	.01
R	49.9	9.0	50.1	12.0	49.5	8.6	48.4	9.2	0.33	
Es	42.5	14.5	51.5	9.2	54.8	9.7	59.3	10.9	10.13	.001
ORG	62.2	18.0	51.5	8.1	46.9	8.2	44.5	9.4	12.76	.001
HEA	56.1	9.9	51.5	9.8	47.4	9.4	45.3	8.7	6.22	.001
DEP	54.9	10.3	50.3	9.5	47.2	8.8	43.7	10.4	6.32	.001
MOR	53.0	11.7	47.3	9.1	46.0	10.0	42.4	10.4	4.52	.01
SOC	48.0	7.1	49.9	10.4	49.3	11.0	44.1	9.9	4.12	.01
HOS	53.9	9.8	49.8	9.4	47.8	7.7	46.0	9.2	3.28	.05
FAM	53.8	13.1	52.6	8.6	52.3	10.9	49.5	11.5	1.25	
AUT	58.7	10.3	47.9	8.0	46.9	8.6	43.7	8.9	9.42	.001
FEM	56.0	8.8	49.5	8.4	52.2	8.1	51.3	11.0	1.40	
PHO	57.9	11.8	51.5	9.4	48.8	8.7	45.4	9.8	7.08	.001
PSY	54.7	11.0	52.5	12.3	49.1	7.3	48.1	8.9	2.77	.05
HYP	57.8	12.8	51.4	9.4	51.6	7.1	47.5	8.3	6.44	.001
REL	50.3	7.9	50.7	9.0	51.5	10.0	49.7	10.3	0.41	

Table D-11. Means and Standard Deviations of MMPI Basic and Special Scales for Black Males by Type of Classes Attended

	Segregated (N = 195)		Integrated (N = 97)			
Scale	Mean	S.D.	Mean	S.D.	F	p
L	52.1	7.9	50.9	8.0	1.44	
F	57.9	11.3	61.2	12.9	5.22	.05
K	54.3	8.6	53.1	9.2	1.11	
Hs	58.7	11.1	56.8	11.9	1.77	
D	58.2	10.1	56.9	9.8	1.09	
Hy	56.8	9.0	58.3	9.7	1.57	
Pd	60.6	10.3	63.6	10.5	5.63	.05
Mf	61.8	9.5	63.1	9.1	1.43	
Pa	55.5	11.3	56.8	11.7	0.80	
Pt	56.9	9.9	58.5	10.3	1.70	
Sc	61.5	13.5	65.2	15.1	4.61	.05
Ma	62.1	10.4	66.7	12.0	11.20	.001
Si	52.4	7.7	51.2	7.9	1.51	
A	49.8	9.0	51.0	9.9	1.02	
R	51.1	9.5	50.1	9.8	0.64	
Es	50.1	9.8	49.6	10.4	0.20	
ORG	54.2	10.7	52.8	11.3	1.19	
HEA	54.9	9.8	54.3	10.1	0.23	
DEP	50.9	9.1	51.6	9.9	0.39	
MOR	48.1	9.0	48.2	9.0	0.00	
SOC	51.5	8.3	50.6	8.5	0.83	
HOS	48.7	8.4	50.8	9.8	3.81	
FAM	56.5	10.8	58.0	11.6	1.25	
AUT	52.4	9.4	55.8	9.2	8.63	.01
FEM	59.8	9.9	58.7	8.9	0.82	
PHO	57.3	10.2	56.2	11.0	0.67	
PSY	56.4	10.8	58.1	11.7	1.42	
HYP	52.6	8.7	54.1	10.3	1.70	
REL	56.0	9.0	51.4	9.7	16.55	.001

Table D-12. Means and Standard Deviations of MMPI Basic and Special Scales for Black Females by Type of Classes Attended

	Segregated (N = 355)		Integrated (N = 148)			
Scale	Mean	S.D.	Mean	S.D.	F	p
L	49.9	7.5	50.1	8.2	0.04	
F	57.1	11.2	61.1	13.4	11.64	.001
K	52.2	9.2	50.1	8.8	5.58	.05
Hs	53.8	9.4	53.0	9.7	0.73	
D	53.8	9.6	55.2	9.0	2.24	
Hy	54.6	9.2	53.0	9.5	0.91	
Pd	59.3	10.3	62.2	9.8	8.39	.01
Mf	51.8	8.9	51.3	8.6	0.34	
Pa	56.1	11.7	59.5	13.9	7.95	.01
Pt	53.6	9.0	56.1	10.5	7.57	.01
Sc	58.9	12.5	63.6	14.9	13.56	.001
Ma	59.4	11.0	62.5	12.0	7.80	.01
Si	54.1	8.3	56.1	8.5	6.24	.05
A	49.2	9.7	57.4	11.1	4.57	.05
R	48.6	10.2	47.6	9.1	0.93	
Es	52.3	9.5	50.4	9.6	4.37	.05
ORG	51.3	10.7	52.9	11.7	2.28	
HEA	52.7	10.1	52.5	9.7	0.05	
DEP	50.1	10.3	53.1	11.8	7.88	.01
MOR	48.0	10.2	49.1	10.5	1.05	
SOC	49.3	8.3	50.3	8.6	1.63	
HOS	50.6	10.0	53.7	10.7	9.84	.01
FAM	57.4	10.5	56.0	11.0	6.28	.05
AUT	55.3	9.4	57.9	8.6	8.21	.01
FEM	50.9	8.2	49.3	9.0	3.70	
PHO	55.9	9.2	55.3	9.9	0.39	
PSY	57.6	13.6	61.6	16.1	7.90	.01
HYP	51.6	9.7	52.6	10.6	1.01	
REL	54.6	8.4	51.2	10.0	14.81	.001

Table D-13. Means and Standard Deviations of MMPI Basic and Special Scales for White Males at Three Occupational Levels

	IV and V (*N* = 54)		III (*N* = 73)		I and II (*N* = 61)			
Scale	**Mean**	**S.D.**	**Mean**	**S.D.**	**Mean**	**S.D.**	***F***	***p***
L	49.9	7.9	49.1	8.4	48.3	5.9	0.63	
F	61.6	15.8	52.8	6.2	51.4	5.6	18.06	.001
K	50.1	9.0	55.2	9.0	56.6	7.2	9.35	.001
Hs	57.5	13.3	53.8	8.5	54.2	8.7	2.40	
D	58.8	12.8	56.4	11.0	56.0	11.8	0.92	
Hy	58.5	10.7	56.1	8.0	58.1	6.8	1.55	
Pd	61.3	13.5	57.3	10.0	56.5	10.3	3.04	.05
Mf	57.5	9.8	57.6	9.7	63.3	9.8	7.18	.001
Pa	60.0	16.0	54.3	11.6	55.9	8.9	3.40	.05
Pt	59.3	13.8	55.6	11.2	55.9	10.1	1.85	
Sc	62.0	17.8	53.0	10.8	55.0	9.7	7.97	.001
Ma	59.1	12.6	56.2	10.4	56.0	10.3	1.47	
Si	57.0	10.4	51.0	9.9	49.8	10.1	8.40	.001
A	53.6	9.4	47.4	8.6	47.5	9.2	9.12	.001
R	52.8	9.0	51.6	8.8	50.2	9.6	1.14	
Es	51.3	10.1	56.4	9.2	58.8	9.0	9.48	.001
ORG	56.1	11.5	48.2	6.9	47.2	7.9	17.55	.001
HEA	54.8	9.3	49.6	9.3	48.4	8.6	7.99	.001
DEP	55.1	10.8	47.6	8.2	47.8	9.6	12.00	.001
MOR	53.6	10.6	46.4	8.0	45.7	9.0	13.12	.001
SOC	55.9	11.9	50.8	11.0	50.8	12.1	3.77	.05
HOS	52.8	8.9	47.4	8.3	46.5	8.0	9.46	.001
FAM	58.1	10.8	49.2	10.0	47.7	11.4	15.68	.001
AUT	53.0	10.0	49.0	10.7	44.2	8.9	11.31	.001
FEM	48.7	9.6	51.0	10.6	52.1	10.2	1.61	
PHO	57.5	12.1	51.8	9.3	48.6	9.5	10.91	.001
PSY	54.8	12.0	47.1	5.9	46.9	5.7	17.60	.001
HYP	54.5	8.7	50.8	8.0	50.1	7.3	5.12	.01
REL	51.2	9.5	50.3	10.4	52.7	9.8	0.93	

Table D-14. Means and Standard Deviations of MMPI Basic and Special Scales for White Females at Three Occupational Levels

	IV and V (*N* = 46)		III (*N* = 114)		I and II (*N* = 68)			
Scale	Mean	S.D.	Mean	S.D.	Mean	S.D.	*F*	*p*
L	48.9	6.0	49.2	6.8	48.3	5.7	0.52	
F	53.8	6.9	53.0	8.2	49.8	6.2	5.56	.01
K	52.0	10.6	56.2	9.1	58.2	8.2	6.18	.01
Hs	53.0	10.0	53.2	9.1	49.6	7.8	3.65	.05
D	55.3	11.6	52.2	10.5	49.1	8.0	5.26	.01
Hy	55.5	10.0	57.2	8.5	56.5	7.0	0.68	
Pd	55.6	11.8	58.4	10.4	57.1	8.2	1.26	
Mf	49.3	8.9	46.0	8.0	43.7	10.3	5.39	.01
Pa	54.5	9.2	56.1	8.8	55.0	7.6	0.69	
Pt	53.7	9.8	54.5	9.8	52.8	6.9	0.79	
Sc	54.0	10.6	56.3	10.1	54.3	7.3	1.46	
Ma	53.7	8.7	56.0	10.0	57.2	9.3	1.90	
Si	55.0	10.2	52.2	9.6	48.7	8.2	6.51	.01
A	49.6	10.3	46.1	10.4	43.0	7.7	6.43	.01
R	51.0	12.1	49.7	8.2	47.2	9.6	2.44	
Es	50.8	10.1	54.9	10.8	60.1	10.0	11.52	.001
ORG	50.0	10.3	47.8	11.4	44.4	6.2	4.85	.01
HEA	50.6	9.8	47.9	10.4	44.8	7.3	7.27	.01
DEP	50.5	9.9	46.8	10.5	43.4	7.1	7.80	.001
MOR	48.8	9.8	45.1	10.7	42.6	9.4	5.04	.01
SOC	50.5	10.5	47.7	10.4	44.0	9.8	5.89	.01
HOS	49.4	9.5	47.0	8.6	46.7	8.9	1.47	
FAM	51.2	9.4	52.1	12.1	49.5	9.8	1.21	
AUT	49.7	10.7	46.8	9.3	43.7	8.3	5.89	.01
FEM	50.9	9.1	51.7	8.3	51.5	10.5	0.13	
PHO	50.4	9.1	48.3	10.3	46.4	9.0	2.27	
PSY	51.2	9.2	50.1	9.7	47.5	7.4	2.79	
HYP	51.1	9.9	50.3	8.7	48.9	8.6	0.91	
REL	51.7	9.5	52.1	9.4	48.7	10.2	2.81	

Table D-15. Means and Standard Deviations of MMPI Basic and Special Scales for Black Males at Three Occupational Levels

	IV and V (*N* = 27)		III (*N* = 107)		I and II (*N* = 159)			
Scale	Mean	S.D.	Mean	S.D.	Mean	S.D.	*F*	*p*
L	52.4	7.2	51.7	8.1	51.6	8.0	0.13	
F	60.3	9.7	61.9	12.8	56.8	11.3	6.20	.01
K	53.8	10.1	51.7	8.4	55.3	8.5	5.65	.01
Hs	58.5	10.3	59.3	13.5	57.1	9.9	1.20	
D	57.7	7.6	59.7	11.6	56.3	9.1	3.80	.05
Hy	56.7	8.7	56.6	10.9	57.8	8.2	0.63	
Pd	63.1	9.9	63.0	12.6	60.2	8.8	2.64	
Mf	61.2	9.4	61.5	8.3	62.9	10.0	0.85	
Pa	56.2	13.7	57.8	12.7	54.6	9.9	2.68	
Pt	61.7	7.2	58.8	10.7	55.6	9.7	6.30	.01
Sc	67.3	12.0	65.4	15.6	60.0	12.8	6.48	.01
Ma	65.1	11.7	64.3	11.9	63.0	10.5	0.70	
Si	52.9	7.2	54.7	7.6	50.0	7.4	13.26	.001
A	52.2	9.4	52.6	9.2	48.2	9.0	8.00	.001
R	50.0	9.6	51.3	10.7	50.5	8.9	0.31	
Es	44.5	10.3	47.5	9.9	52.5	9.2	13.52	.001
ORG	55.6	10.5	56.7	12.3	51.4	9.4	8.50	.001
HEA	54.9	7.5	57.6	11.2	52.7	8.8	8.29	.001
DEP	52.6	9.9	53.8	9.1	49.0	8.9	9.15	.001
MOR	49.8	10.4	50.7	9.0	46.1	8.3	9.39	.001
SOC	52.8	7.0	53.5	8.1	49.4	8.3	8.39	.001
HOS	49.7	8.3	50.4	9.1	48.7	9.0	1.24	
FAM	59.0	10.9	59.2	11.9	55.2	10.2	4.87	.01
AUT	54.3	8.2	55.2	9.1	52.4	9.7	2.98	
FEM	58.2	8.8	59.8	9.6	59.4	9.8	0.28	
PHO	59.4	9.0	59.4	10.3	54.8	10.3	7.36	.001
PSY	60.6	13.1	60.0	11.4	54.4	9.8	9.99	.001
HYP	54.7	9.1	54.2	9.4	52.1	9.2	2.08	
REL	57.1	9.4	55.1	9.2	53.7	9.6	1.80	

Table D-16. Means and Standard Deviations of MMPI Basic and Special Scales for Black Females at Three Occupational Levels

	IV and V ($N = 93$)		III ($N = 156$)		I and II ($N = 254$)			
Scale	Mean	S.D.	Mean	S.D.	Mean	S.D.	F	p
L	51.5	8.3	49.5	7.8	49.7	7.3	2.22	
F	64.7	14.3	59.6	11.6	55.2	10.2	24.87	.001
K	49.3	8.6	50.2	9.4	53.2	8.9	9.13	.001
Hs	56.1	11.0	54.0	9.6	52.3	8.6	5.77	.01
D	56.6	9.0	55.1	9.3	52.8	9.5	6.62	.01
Hy	55.2	11.1	54.4	9.6	54.0	8.3	0.59	
Pd	62.7	12.0	60.9	9.7	58.7	9.7	5.97	.01
Mf	54.6	8.8	52.0	8.7	50.4	8.5	8.07	.001
Pa	61.4	14.9	57.7	13.2	55.2	10.6	8.82	.001
Pt	57.2	11.3	55.5	9.7	52.6	8.4	9.93	.001
Sc	65.8	16.3	61.9	13.4	57.2	11.4	16.64	.001
Ma	63.7	12.2	59.9	12.1	59.4	10.3	5.29	.01
Si	57.1	7.4	56.6	8.2	52.7	8.4	15.72	.001
A	53.3	10.2	51.7	10.2	47.5	9.6	15.74	.001
R	47.5	10.7	48.4	10.1	48.5	9.5	0.34	
Es	47.4	9.0	50.2	9.5	54.2	9.0	22.24	.001
ORG	55.9	12.3	53.4	10.8	49.2	10.0	16.20	.001
HEA	55.0	10.4	54.2	10.2	50.9	9.4	8.63	.001
DEP	54.2	11.0	53.2	11.3	48.4	9.9	15.63	.001
MOR	51.8	9.8	50.2	10.3	45.9	9.8	15.97	.001
SOC	51.7	7.2	51.3	8.1	47.8	8.6	12.47	.001
HOS	55.0	10.0	52.6	10.3	49.6	9.9	10.93	.001
FAM	60.6	9.4	60.1	10.6	56.0	10.9	10.71	.001
AUT	59.9	8.0	57.0	8.9	54.1	9.3	15.63	.001
FEM	49.1	8.1	50.6	8.5	50.7	8.6	1.29	
PHO	57.8	9.8	57.5	8.5	53.9	9.4	9.95	.001
PSY	65.9	16.3	60.6	15.1	55.1	12.1	22.15	.001
HYP	54.4	10.4	52.7	10.2	50.4	9.5	6.18	.01
REL	54.2	9.3	54.8	8.2	52.6	9.3	3.06	.05

Table D-17. Means and Standard Deviations of MMPI Basic and Special Scales for Black Males for Three Regions of Origin (Where Educated)

	Deep South (N = 115)		Mid South (N = 98)		North (N = 75)			
Scale	Mean	S.D.	Mean	S.D.	Mean	S.D.	F	p
L	52.4	8.7	51.9	7.4	50.6	7.4	1.22	
F	59.6	13.4	57.5	10.0	59.7	12.1	1.04	
K	54.8	9.1	53.8	8.2	52.6	8.9	1.53	
Hs	59.6	13.0	57.7	9.6	56.1	10.6	2.13	
D	58.3	11.2	57.2	9.8	57.1	8.7	0.47	
Hy	57.3	9.9	56.5	8.4	58.2	9.6	0.64	
Pd	61.5	10.7	59.5	9.8	63.9	10.9	3.79	.05
Mf	61.2	9.7	60.7	8.3	65.3	8.6	6.20	.01
Pa	55.8	12.2	54.8	10.5	56.7	10.9	0.58	
Pt	57.2	10.5	57.6	9.5	56.9	10.0	0.10	
Sc	53.6	15.5	60.8	11.5	63.4	14.7	1.23	
Ma	62.1	10.7	62.8	10.5	67.1	12.0	5.08	.01
Si	52.4	8.0	52.4	7.9	50.8	7.3	1.15	
A	49.5	10.0	50.3	8.1	50.6	9.7	0.34	
R	51.9	10.1	50.5	8.5	49.6	10.2	1.38	
Es	49.7	10.5	50.0	9.1	50.5	10.6	0.14	
ORG	53.9	11.9	54.1	9.8	52.9	11.0	0.29	
HEA	55.9	10.9	54.1	8.5	53.8	9.8	1.28	
DEP	51.1	10.1	51.2	8.2	50.8	9.5	0.05	
MOR	47.8	9.2	48.6	8.9	47.8	9.1	0.21	
SOC	50.9	8.5	52.1	8.6	50.5	7.7	0.96	
HOS	49.1	9.1	48.4	8.4	50.9	9.3	1.73	
FAM	56.2	11.2	57.0	9.7	57.9	12.2	0.56	
AUT	52.7	9.7	53.0	9.3	55.9	9.1	2.92	
FEM	60.1	10.1	58.0	9.2	60.2	9.3	1.52	
PHO	57.3	10.2	58.0	10.7	55.4	10.5	1.35	
PSY	56.9	11.6	56.6	10.7	57.2	10.8	0.07	
HYP	51.8	9.1	53.0	8.6	54.6	10.0	2.08	
REL	56.3	8.0	56.7	8.5	49.0	10.8	19.28	.001

Table D-18. Means and Standard Deviations of MMPI Basic and Special Scales for Black Females for Three Regions of Origin (Where Educated)

	Deep South (*N* = 173)		Mid South (*N* = 215)		North (*N* = 112)			
Scale	Mean	S.D.	Mean	S.D.	Mean	S.D.	*F*	*p*
L	50.7	7.6	49.3	7.7	50.0	7.6	1.73	
F	58.1	12.4	57.8	11.3	59.3	12.9	0.57	
K	51.6	10.3	51.7	8.8	51.1	8.2	0.15	
Hs	53.1	8.8	54.5	10.2	52.0	8.5	2.74	
D	54.6	9.5	54.0	9.5	53.8	9.1	0.34	
Hy	53.8	9.3	55.3	9.6	53.0	8.5	2.49	
Pd	60.0	9.7	59.6	10.2	61.3	11.2	1.10	
Mf	52.0	8.8	52.2	8.8	50.3	8.8	1.79	
Pa	57.8	13.8	56.4	11.1	57.4	13.0	0.66	
Pt	54.5	9.5	54.2	9.2	54.0	10.1	0.09	
Sc	60.6	13.1	59.5	12.7	61.0	15.2	0.54	
Ma	58.8	11.2	60.4	11.1	62.6	12.0	3.86	.05
Si	55.3	8.6	54.0	8.2	54.8	8.3	1.02	
A	50.4	10.9	49.7	9.8	49.3	9.8	0.44	
R	48.2	10.0	48.2	10.2	48.2	9.0	0.00	
Es	51.4	9.8	51.4	9.3	53.0	9.6	1.25	
ORG	51.3	10.2	52.6	11.8	50.5	10.3	1.57	
HEA	52.5	9.8	53.4	10.8	51.1	8.3	2.05	
DEP	51.6	11.6	51.0	10.6	49.9	10.3	0.74	
MOR	49.2	11.0	48.4	10.2	46.9	9.2	1.70	
SOC	49.7	8.4	49.4	8.5	49.5	8.1	0.04	
HOS	51.6	10.6	51.1	10.0	52.6	10.2	0.84	
FAM	57.3	10.7	58.3	10.7	59.2	11.0	1.18	
AUT	55.4	9.8	55.7	8.6	57.9	9.4	2.94	
FEM	50.4	8.4	51.5	8.3	48.5	8.5	4.61	.01
PHO	56.8	9.5	56.1	9.1	53.5	9.6	4.55	.01
PSY	59.6	16.0	57.8	12.9	59.5	15.1	0.87	
HYP	51.5	10.8	52.2	9.3	51.6	10.2	0.29	
REL	54.6	8.3	54.8	8.1	49.4	10.5	16.11	.001

Table D-19. Means and Standard Deviations of MMPI Basic and Special Scales for Black Males for Three Regions of Residence

	Deep South (*N* = 108)		Mid South (*N* = 84)		North (*N* = 98)			
Scale	Mean	S.D.	Mean	S.D.	Mean	S.D.	*F*	*p*
L	52.6	8.8	51.2	7.1	51.2	7.6	1.07	
F	59.8	13.8	58.1	10.4	58.6	11.2	0.49	
K	54.9	9.1	53.6	8.3	53.0	8.6	1.37	
Hs	60.0	13.0	57.4	9.6	56.7	10.8	2.21	
D	57.9	11.6	57.6	10.1	57.5	8.2	0.05	
Hy	57.5	9.9	56.3	8.8	58.0	9.1	0.73	
Pd	61.4	10.8	59.9	9.5	62.9	11.0	1.84	
Mf	60.5	9.4	60.5	8.5	65.4	9.3	9.57	.001
Pa	55.6	12.3	54.7	10.3	56.9	11.2	0.94	
Pt	57.0	10.8	57.7	9.0	57.4	10.1	0.10	
Sc	63.5	16.0	60.9	11.4	63.2	14.2	0.92	
Ma	62.4	10.7	63.1	10.5	65.5	12.1	2.08	
Si	51.8	8.1	52.7	7.9	51.4	7.4	0.58	
A	49.6	10.1	50.4	8.0	50.5	9.5	0.29	
R	51.4	10.3	50.8	8.8	50.2	9.6	0.43	
Es	49.9	10.6	49.6	8.9	50.4	10.3	0.15	
ORG	54.0	12.1	53.9	9.8	53.2	10.7	0.17	
HEA	56.1	11.0	54.2	8.7	53.7	9.3	1.73	
DEP	50.7	10.2	51.7	8.2	50.9	9.3	0.31	
MOR	47.9	9.2	49.0	8.9	47.5	9.0	0.70	
SOC	50.4	8.4	52.7	8.6	50.8	7.8	2.06	
HOS	49.3	9.4	48.6	8.6	50.1	8.8	0.61	
FAM	56.4	11.4	57.4	10.1	57.4	11.4	0.26	
AUT	52.9	9.9	53.7	9.1	54.4	9.3	0.63	
FEM	59.3	10.1	57.7	9.3	61.0	9.2	2.76	
PHO	57.1	10.2	58.5	10.7	55.5	10.3	1.91	
PSY	56.5	12.0	56.6	10.7	57.4	10.3	0.20	
HYP	51.9	9.1	53.0	8.7	54.2	9.7	1.61	
REL	56.4	7.9	56.7	8.6	50.6	10.7	13.58	.001

Table D-20. Means and Standard Deviations of MMPI Basic and Special Scales for Black Females for Three Regions of Residence

	Deep South (N = 164)		Mid South (N = 215)		North (N = 122)			
Scale	Mean	S.D.	Mean	S.D.	Mean	S.D.	F	p
L	50.7	7.4	49.3	7.8	50.1	7.8	1.43	
F	58.4	12.6	57.7	11.3	59.1	12.5	0.52	
K	51.3	10.1	51.9	8.7	51.2	8.7	0.25	
Hs	53.2	8.9	54.5	10.1	52.0	8.6	3.01	.05
D	55.0	9.6	54.1	9.5	53.4	9.1	1.02	
Hy	53.9	9.2	55.3	9.5	52.9	8.7	2.84	
Pd	60.2	9.7	59.5	10.1	61.1	11.3	0.90	
Mf	52.0	8.9	52.1	8.7	50.6	8.8	1.23	
Pa	58.3	13.9	56.3	11.1	57.0	12.8	1.25	
Pt	54.7	9.6	54.1	9.2	54.0	10.1	0.26	
Sc	60.9	13.1	59.6	12.7	60.5	14.9	0.49	
Ma	59.1	11.0	60.4	11.2	61.8	12.1	1.96	
Si	55.7	8.8	54.0	8.1	54.4	8.2	1.83	
A	50.8	11.0	49.5	9.8	49.2	10.0	1.03	
R	48.2	10.0	48.3	10.2	48.2	9.3	0.01	
Es	51.2	9.8	51.6	9.3	52.9	9.6	1.23	
ORG	51.4	10.3	52.7	11.8	50.4	10.3	1.77	
HEA	52.7	9.8	53.3	10.8	51.2	8.5	1.83	
DEP	52.0	11.6	50.7	10.6	49.9	10.4	1.38	
MOR	49.5	10.9	48.3	10.1	46.9	9.5	2.27	
SOC	50.1	8.7	49.3	8.5	49.2	7.8	0.46	
HOS	51.6	10.6	50.9	10.0	52.7	10.2	1.13	
FAM	57.7	10.4	58.1	10.7	58.8	11.3	0.41	
AUT	55.6	9.7	55.7	8.6	57.4	9.7	1.66	
FEM	50.4	8.6	51.4	8.3	48.8	8.3	3.82	.05
PHO	57.2	9.3	56.1	9.1	53.3	9.8	6.35	.01
PSY	60.0	16.1	57.7	12.9	59.0	14.9	1.18	
HYP	51.8	10.6	52.1	9.2	51.6	10.6	0.10	
REL	54.5	8.4	54.8	8.0	50.2	10.6	11.97	.001

Table D-21. Means and Standard Deviations of MMPI Basic and Special Scales for Black Males at Four Levels of Community Size

	Rural/Town (N = 79)		Small City (N = 85)		Large City (N = 40)		Metropolitan (N = 84)			
Scale	Mean	S.D.	Mean	S.D.	Mean	S.D.	Mean	S.D.	F	p
L	52.0	7.7	51.7	8.2	52.1	8.0	51.0	7.5	0.31	
F	59.3	11.2	59.6	13.1	56.0	9.3	58.9	12.0	0.95	
K	53.5	8.6	54.3	8.6	56.7	10.5	52.6	8.2	2.15	
Hs	57.5	10.0	59.6	12.4	58.2	10.1	56.6	11.2	1.03	
D	57.7	9.6	57.7	11.2	57.7	9.2	57.3	9.1	0.03	
Hy	56.2	8.2	57.4	10.1	58.2	8.5	57.8	9.1	0.63	
Pd	59.6	10.2	61.1	10.7	62.8	9.4	62.8	10.8	1.56	
Mf	59.4	9.2	60.8	9.1	62.3	7.7	66.1	9.5	8.21	.001
Pa	55.6	12.2	55.4	11.4	55.3	10.9	56.5	10.9	0.16	
Pt	55.9	8.8	57.3	11.1	59.5	9.0	57.3	10.3	1.12	
Sc	61.4	13.4	63.1	15.0	62.1	11.0	63.2	14.5	0.31	
Ma	61.2	10.4	63.6	10.9	65.2	11.2	65.5	12.0	2.24	
Si	52.6	8.2	52.1	7.7	51.6	7.8	51.2	7.5	0.48	
A	50.2	9.3	50.1	9.1	48.5	9.9	50.8	9.4	0.53	
R	51.3	9.1	50.9	8.9	52.2	9.4	49.0	10.1	1.37	
Es	49.3	9.6	50.1	10.1	50.6	10.9	50.4	9.9	0.24	
ORG	54.1	9.9	54.0	11.4	51.9	9.6	53.4	11.4	0.43	
HEA	55.7	8.7	55.8	10.6	53.6	9.5	53.8	9.8	0.76	
DEP	50.8	9.0	51.5	9.6	50.1	10.7	50.9	8.8	0.23	
MOR	48.0	8.8	48.7	8.8	47.0	9.8	47.9	9.0	0.32	
SOC	51.9	8.7	50.8	8.3	51.1	8.8	50.7	7.9	0.34	
HOS	48.6	8.7	49.5	8.8	48.7	10.3	50.5	8.6	0.69	
FAM	56.6	10.4	57.5	11.8	53.7	11.2	58.1	10.9	1.57	
AUT	54.4	8.6	53.0	9.2	51.6	11.3	54.6	9.5	1.27	
FEM	57.8	8.9	59.0	10.7	59.4	8.2	61.5	9.6	2.15	
PHO	57.0	9.5	57.9	10.6	57.6	11.0	55.3	10.9	1.00	
PSY	57.8	12.4	55.9	11.1	55.2	10.1	57.6	10.3	0.85	
HYP	53.1	9.0	52.1	8.8	53.5	9.1	54.0	10.1	0.62	
REL	57.5	8.5	55.4	8.2	54.6	9.7	50.4	10.4	8.68	.001

Table D-22. Means and Standard Deviations of MMPI Basic and Special Scales for Black Females at Four Levels of Community Size

	Rural/Town (N = 104)		Small City (N = 208)		Large City (N = 81)		Metropolitan (N = 104)			
Scale	Mean	S.D.	Mean	S.D.	Mean	S.D.	Mean	S.D.	F	p
L	49.3	7.3	50.1	7.6	50.4	8.3	50.0	7.8	0.35	
F	58.0	12.0	57.9	12.1	57.3	10.3	60.2	13.0	1.19	
K	50.6	9.9	52.2	9.4	52.5	7.8	50.4	8.8	1.58	
Hs	54.5	10.1	53.5	9.7	54.1	9.2	52.3	8.8	1.05	
D	55.5	10.2	54.1	9.7	53.5	7.8	53.6	9.1	0.96	
Hy	54.9	10.1	54.7	8.9	54.6	9.7	52.9	8.7	1.09	
Pd	59.8	10.3	59.9	9.9	60.3	9.6	60.6	11.4	0.14	
Mf	52.7	9.1	51.3	8.3	53.6	8.7	50.1	9.2	3.03	.05
Pa	56.4	13.2	57.6	12.2	56.4	10.9	57.4	13.6	0.32	
Pt	54.8	9.9	54.4	9.4	54.0	8.9	54.0	10.0	0.19	
Sc	59.5	13.6	60.2	13.0	60.2	12.0	61.1	15.2	0.22	
Ma	59.9	12.6	59.0	10.5	61.2	9.9	62.5	12.5	2.50	
Si	56.0	8.6	54.5	8.8	53.4	7.2	54.8	8.3	1.54	
A	51.1	10.7	49.4	10.0	48.9	9.9	50.0	10.1	0.91	
R	49.2	11.0	48.7	10.1	48.3	8.6	46.6	9.3	1.39	
Es	49.9	9.5	52.4	9.3	52.2	9.9	52.1	9.6	1.65	
ORG	52.7	10.8	51.5	10.9	51.6	11.4	51.3	11.3	0.36	
HEA	53.5	11.2	52.9	10.0	51.9	10.1	52.1	8.8	0.57	
DEP	52.2	11.6	50.6	10.7	50.6	10.3	50.7	10.8	0.53	
MOR	49.4	11.0	48.4	10.3	47.2	10.0	48.2	9.8	0.71	
SOC	50.9	8.6	49.2	9.0	49.1	7.6	49.6	7.6	1.16	
HOS	51.8	10.2	50.5	9.8	50.5	10.5	53.7	10.7	2.55	.05
FAM	58.7	10.6	57.3	10.9	57.9	10.3	59.1	11.0	0.80	
AUT	56.3	9.5	55.9	9.1	56.5	8.9	57.6	9.2	2.20	
FEM	50.2	8.0	50.9	8.9	50.2	8.0	49.6	8.4	0.56	
PHO	56.9	9.8	56.6	9.1	54.6	9.2	53.7	9.4	3.16	.05
PSY	59.3	14.7	58.0	14.1	58.3	13.9	60.0	15.3	0.49	
HYP	52.0	9.9	51.8	10.0	51.5	9.7	52.2	10.4	0.10	
REL	54.0	8.1	54.7	8.4	55.4	7.7	49.5	10.8	9.77	.001

Table D-23. Means and Standard Deviations of MMPI Basic and Special Scales for White Males by Marital Status

	Single (N = 34)		Married (N = 150)			
Scale	Mean	S.D.	Mean	S.D.	F	p
L	49.2	7.4	49.0	7.7	0.01	
F	61.5	15.4	53.4	8.8	17.00	.001
K	53.1	9.3	54.5	8.7	0.63	
Hs	53.9	10.1	55.1	10.4	0.38	
D	54.3	10.1	57.6	12.2	2.13	
Hy	57.1	11.2	57.5	7.9	0.07	
Pd	62.2	10.5	57.4	11.3	5.11	.05
Mf	59.7	10.9	59.4	10.0	0.02	
Pa	60.2	15.0	55.7	11.8	3.59	
Pt	60.1	13.2	56.2	11.3	3.10	
Sc	62.1	16.4	55.1	12.5	7.74	.01
Ma	63.8	11.8	55.3	10.3	17.57	.001
Si	52.8	9.3	52.3	10.9	0.04	
A	50.9	10.6	48.9	9.1	1.32	
R	51.6	8.3	51.5	9.3	0.00	
Es	55.1	10.9	56.2	9.3	0.37	
ORG	50.2	11.2	50.0	9.2	0.01	
HEA	50.9	9.0	50.7	9.6	0.01	
DEP	52.3	12.7	49.3	9.3	2.47	
MOR	50.6	10.5	47.8	9.5	2.26	
SOC	52.3	10.4	52.3	12.2	0.00	
HOS	50.8	9.7	48.3	8.5	2.31	
FAM	56.1	13.0	50.2	11.0	7.61	.01
AUT	53.6	10.4	47.3	10.1	10.86	.001
FEM	49.2	11.1	50.9	10.1	0.70	
PHO	50.3	10.7	52.9	10.9	1.62	
PSY	55.2	11.4	47.9	7.5	20.98	.001
HYP	55.1	9.1	51.0	7.8	7.18	.01
REL	48.9	11.2	51.8	9.6	2.43	

Table D-24. Means and Standard Deviations of MMPI Basic and Special Scales for White Females by Marital Status

	Single (*N* = 29)		Married (*N* = 169)			
Scale	**Mean**	**S.D.**	**Mean**	**S.D.**	***F***	***p***
L	47.7	6.0	48.9	6.3	0.87	
F	50.8	6.0	51.9	7.3	0.68	
K	58.7	10.1	56.0	9.3	2.04	
Hs	51.7	6.4	52.2	9.2	0.07	
D	49.7	10.7	51.9	10.2	1.17	
Hy	56.2	6.5	56.8	8.4	0.17	
Pd	59.8	8.5	56.7	9.9	2.43	
Mf	43.2	8.8	46.6	9.2	3.25	
Pa	57.1	7.4	54.8	8.5	1.92	
Pt	56.6	6.2	53.6	9.4	2.74	
Sc	57.5	5.9	54.6	9.6	2.40	
Ma	57.7	9.7	55.0	9.3	2.03	
Si	51.4	12.7	51.6	9.2	0.00	
A	45.2	10.2	45.4	10.0	0.01	
R	48.9	8.6	49.3	9.8	0.05	
Es	57.8	9.4	56.0	11.4	0.67	
ORG	43.8	7.6	47.6	10.8	3.31	
HEA	46.3	9.6	47.5	9.9	0.37	
DEP	45.8	10.2	46.1	9.7	0.03	
MOR	44.6	12.2	44.6	10.4	0.00	
SOC	48.0	13.2	46.8	10.2	0.34	
HOS	46.9	8.4	47.2	8.9	0.02	
FAM	52.1	11.3	50.8	11.1	0.33	
AUT	46.2	9.0	46.0	9.6	0.02	
FEM	52.0	8.8	51.3	9.6	0.14	
PHO	45.5	10.0	48.2	9.8	1.86	
PSY	51.1	8.2	48.8	9.2	1.53	
HYP	48.6	9.9	49.9	9.1	0.55	
REL	52.6	10.4	50.7	9.7	0.92	

Table D-25. Means and Standard Deviations of MMPI Basic and Special Scales for Black Males by Marital Status

	Single (N = 82)		Married (N = 182)		Divorced or Separated (N = 18)		Widowed (N = 11)			
Scale	Mean	S.D.	Mean	S.D.	Mean	S.D.	Mean	S.D.	F	p
L	52.1	8.0	51.8	7.9	50.6	6.3	48.6	9.3	0.74	
F	62.3	13.2	57.4	11.1	58.3	10.2	60.5	13.6	3.37	.05
K	54.2	9.8	54.1	8.5	52.3	7.7	50.0	6.9	0.97	
Hs	56.5	11.4	58.9	11.7	54.7	8.2	59.6	11.0	1.39	
D	56.6	10.1	58.2	10.0	56.2	10.2	59.4	11.2	0.68	
Hy	57.1	10.1	57.7	9.2	53.3	6.6	57.9	8.8	1.21	
Pd	63.6	10.5	60.5	10.4	59.8	8.6	65.3	13.0	2.27	
Mf	63.0	9.8	61.3	8.8	65.2	12.7	66.4	6.1	2.09	
Pa	57.0	13.0	55.4	10.8	56.4	10.1	55.5	11.8	0.37	
Pt	59.3	10.4	56.7	10.0	54.2	7.2	58.2	11.0	1.90	
Sc	67.8	14.5	60.6	13.3	58.7	10.9	65.0	19.6	5.70	.001
Ma	67.5	11.4	62.0	10.5	60.1	12.3	68.0	10.6	6.09	.001
Si	51.4	8.5	51.9	7.1	54.4	9.3	54.2	9.5	1.07	
A	50.9	10.0	49.5	8.9	50.0	9.7	56.1	8.6	1.92	
R	49.9	10.2	51.2	9.5	50.2	10.4	50.5	4.8	0.34	
Es	49.6	10.0	50.3	9.9	48.4	12.1	49.8	8.6	0.26	
ORG	53.0	10.6	53.8	11.1	53.0	9.1	57.8	12.4	0.66	
HEA	53.6	9.9	55.0	10.0	54.6	8.4	56.6	10.0	0.53	
DEP	51.5	10.3	50.6	8.8	50.2	9.7	57.1	8.5	1.77	
MOR	48.0	9.4	47.7	8.8	50.0	9.6	53.6	7.4	1.79	
SOC	50.9	8.7	51.0	7.7	53.0	10.1	53.5	11.7	0.63	
HOS	50.9	9.9	48.6	8.6	50.3	7.5	49.9	8.7	1.26	
FAM	58.1	12.0	56.1	10.4	57.4	10.3	63.8	14.0	2.13	
AUT	55.0	10.1	52.3	9.2	55.5	6.8	54.7	9.3	3.30	.05
FEM	58.9	10.1	59.1	9.3	65.8	10.7	59.1	6.0	2.90	.05
PHO	56.1	11.3	56.9	9.9	59.8	10.4	58.5	12.8	0.70	
PSY	59.5	12.1	55.5	10.5	57.8	10.1	59.9	11.0	2.81	.05
HYP	54.4	9.9	52.6	9.0	52.1	9.6	52.9	8.7	0.74	
REL	52.0	10.0	55.5	9.0	55.7	10.9	54.6	8.9	2.74	.05

Table D-26. Means and Standard Deviations of MMPI Basic and Special Scales for Black Females by Marital Status

	Single (*N* = 147)		Married (*N* = 255)		Divorced or Separated (*N* = 71)		Widowed (*N* = 30)			
Scale	Mean	S.D.	Mean	S.D.	Mean	S.D.	Mean	S.D.	*F*	*p*
L	49.4	7.9	50.2	7.7	49.7	6.8	50.9	8.1	0.45	
F	61.6	13.8	55.9	10.7	58.6	10.5	62.2	12.3	8.61	.001
K	50.2	9.3	53.0	9.0	49.6	8.7	50.4	9.4	4.48	.01
Hs	52.4	9.7	53.7	8.8	53.0	10.2	59.0	11.3	4.09	.01
D	53.8	10.0	54.2	9.6	54.0	7.8	57.2	9.2	1.12	
Hy	52.3	10.0	55.1	8.1	54.5	10.2	57.6	11.3	4.33	.01
Pd	62.0	10.3	58.8	9.4	60.2	11.4	62.0	12.4	3.51	.05
Mf	52.6	8.9	51.2	8.5	50.5	8.5	53.9	10.4	1.88	
Pa	59.9	13.8	54.9	11.4	58.8	12.6	58.7	11.8	5.85	.001
Pt	55.6	9.8	53.6	9.1	53.6	9.8	56.2	11.2	1.88	
Sc	64.4	14.0	57.9	11.8	58.9	14.0	63.2	17.0	8.42	.001
Ma	63.4	11.5	58.4	11.0	61.3	12.3	59.7	7.9	6.33	.001
Si	55.1	8.5	54.5	8.6	54.3	8.0	55.2	7.6	0.25	
A	51.3	10.8	48.3	9.8	51.4	10.0	52.3	9.4	4.12	.01
R	46.3	9.8	49.5	10.0	47.7	9.8	49.0	8.3	3.45	.05
Es	51.6	9.7	52.4	9.6	50.4	9.0	49.4	9.6	1.50	
ORG	51.6	11.1	51.2	10.6	52.3	11.2	56.2	12.6	1.95	
HEA	52.4	10.0	52.4	9.4	52.2	10.1	57.0	13.0	1.99	
DEP	52.7	11.6	49.4	10.4	52.3	11.0	53.0	8.7	3.78	.01
MOR	48.7	10.3	47.3	10.4	49.7	9.5	51.8	9.7	2.53	
SOC	50.4	8.3	49.2	8.5	49.2	8.6	49.3	8.0	0.72	
HOS	54.2	10.9	49.5	9.8	52.5	10.0	53.1	8.2	7.25	.001
FAM	60.7	10.9	55.9	10.5	59.9	9.8	60.7	10.5	8.08	.001
AUT	58.4	8.5	54.7	9.5	55.3	9.2	57.6	8.2	5.50	.001
FEM	48.9	9.3	50.9	8.1	52.1	7.2	49.2	9.4	3.09	.05
PHO	55.5	9.8	55.4	9.4	55.9	8.4	59.5	9.6	1.79	
PSY	63.1	16.2	56.1	12.9	58.7	14.7	60.7	13.0	7.65	.001
HYP	52.9	10.0	50.6	9.8	54.2	10.4	51.9	9.3	3.13	.05
REL	52.0	9.3	54.0	8.5	54.7	9.2	55.0	10.4	2.29	

Table D-27. Means and Standard Deviations of MMPI Basic and Special Scales for White Males at Three Social Readjustment Rating Scale (SRRS) Levels

	≤ 99 (*N* = 87)		100-199 (*N* = 67)		≥ 200 (*N* = 29)			
Scale	**Mean**	**S.D.**	**Mean**	**S.D.**	**Mean**	**S.D.**	***F***	***p***
L	49.4	7.9	49.0	7.3	48.3	6.9	0.20	
F	52.2	7.1	56.5	11.0	59.1	15.9	6.19	.01
K	55.3	9.2	53.4	7.6	51.7	10.0	2.17	
Hs	54.0	8.4	56.6	12.0	54.8	10.7	1.23	
D	55.8	10.5	58.3	12.2	58.0	14.2	1.03	
Hy	56.6	7.0	58.3	9.7	58.6	9.7	1.03	
Pd	55.0	9.3	59.1	12.0	65.4	12.1	10.65	.001
Mf	58.5	8.7	60.1	11.5	61.2	10.6	0.97	
Pa	55.0	10.1	56.4	12.5	61.6	17.7	3.04	.05
Pt	54.3	8.5	58.1	13.3	60.2	14.7	3.71	.05
Sc	53.6	9.9	56.8	14.7	62.0	17.0	4.68	.01
Ma	55.0	10.3	56.1	11.4	63.6	9.8	7.23	.001
Si	51.5	10.6	53.4	10.5	53.4	10.6	0.79	
A	47.0	8.4	50.9	9.1	52.6	11.6	5.51	.01
R	52.5	10.1	51.1	8.1	49.5	8.5	1.30	
Es	57.4	9.6	53.9	9.3	53.8	10.3	3.14	.05
ORG	47.9	8.6	52.1	9.4	53.0	10.8	5.42	.01
HEA	49.4	8.1	51.2	9.9	53.8	11.2	2.52	
DEP	47.2	8.4	51.8	9.7	53.8	12.9	7.02	.001
MOR	45.8	8.4	50.1	10.0	51.9	11.0	6.14	.01
SOC	51.7	12.2	53.1	12.0	53.1	10.4	0.29	
HOS	47.8	8.8	48.5	8.0	51.8	9.8	2.32	
FAM	48.9	9.6	51.1	11.3	58.8	13.6	8.86	.001
AUT	47.5	10.4	48.8	10.0	51.5	11.2	1.66	
FEM	51.2	9.2	50.9	11.5	49.7	10.1	0.24	
PHO	51.5	10.5	54.0	11.7	52.3	9.2	1.06	
PSY	47.3	7.1	50.4	9.1	53.0	11.3	5.75	.01
HYP	50.0	8.8	52.3	6.8	55.0	8.0	4.55	.01
REL	51.2	9.8	53.5	9.9	47.2	9.2	4.26	.05

Table D-28. Means and Standard Deviations of MMPI Basic and Special Scales for White Females at Three Social Readjustment Rating Scale (SRRS) Levels

	≤ 99 (*N* = 121)		100-199 (*N* = 59)		≥ 200 (*N* = 29)			
Scale	Mean	S.D.	Mean	S.D.	Mean	S.D.	*F*	*p*
L	49.7	6.2	48.7	6.0	47.5	7.6	1.50	
F	50.8	6.7	53.3	7.5	56.2	10.5	6.86	.001
K	57.5	8.4	53.8	9.0	51.6	9.6	7.08	.001
Hs	51.4	7.9	53.3	9.5	52.4	11.8	0.84	
D	51.6	9.4	53.1	11.8	53.7	11.7	0.67	
Hy	56.2	7.1	57.3	9.4	57.2	9.7	0.47	
Pd	56.6	9.3	57.1	9.7	60.1	12.6	1.47	
Mf	46.7	9.7	44.8	8.7	43.6	7.7	1.82	
Pa	54.3	8.0	56.2	9.7	58.9	9.1	3.70	.05
Pt	53.2	8.9	53.6	8.7	56.8	10.1	1.90	
Sc	54.6	8.4	54.6	11.0	59.1	10.1	2.89	
Ma	55.0	8.9	54.2	9.3	62.4	9.6	9.04	.001
Si	51.7	9.4	52.8	10.4	52.7	8.0	0.32	
A	44.3	9.1	47.5	10.6	51.0	10.3	6.29	.01
R	50.7	9.3	48.4	9.0	44.9	9.3	5.02	.01
Es	56.7	11.0	55.4	10.8	50.5	10.8	3.74	.05
ORG	46.4	9.5	48.9	10.7	48.5	11.2	1.36	
HEA	46.2	9.4	49.4	9.5	50.5	9.9	3.73	.05
DEP	45.2	9.1	47.5	10.4	51.4	10.7	4.96	.01
MOR	43.9	10.1	46.4	10.6	48.5	10.0	2.89	
SOC	47.3	11.1	48.2	10.3	46.8	8.2	0.21	
HOS	46.3	8.4	48.5	9.1	51.9	8.4	5.23	.01
FAM	48.8	10.0	52.7	12.0	58.4	9.4	10.74	.001
AUT	46.1	9.4	45.8	8.6	49.8	9.5	2.10	
FEM	50.9	9.4	51.9	9.4	53.9	8.3	1.32	
PHO	48.1	9.8	47.5	9.3	51.8	9.6	2.10	
PSY	47.6	7.9	50.7	9.2	56.2	10.5	12.02	.001
HYP	48.5	8.2	50.6	8.2	56.3	8.5	10.77	.001
REL	50.4	9.6	51.8	10.1	50.9	10.3	0.40	

Table D-29. Means and Standard Deviations of MMPI Basic and Special Scales for White Males by Medical Problems

	Absent ($N = 175$)		Present ($N = 8$)			
Scale	**Mean**	**S.D.**	**Mean**	**S.D.**	***F***	***p***
L	48.9	7.5	52.6	7.7	1.87	
F	54.6	10.0	63.1	21.6	4.88	.05
K	54.1	8.7	53.3	12.7	0.07	
Hs	55.0	10.0	55.3	15.7	0.00	
D	57.1	11.8	57.1	11.7	0.00	
Hy	57.4	8.2	59.3	15.7	0.36	
Pd	58.0	11.3	61.4	13.6	0.67	
Mf	59.7	10.1	52.5	8.7	3.96	.05
Pa	56.3	11.9	61.6	23.6	1.36	
Pt	56.6	11.4	60.6	17.8	0.91	
Sc	55.8	12.7	66.1	25.6	4.51	.05
Ma	56.5	10.8	66.0	13.5	5.79	.05
Si	52.5	10.6	53.0	10.4	0.02	
A	49.2	9.2	53.0	13.3	1.23	
R	51.5	9.2	52.8	7.0	0.15	
Es	55.6	9.6	53.6	12.8	0.33	
ORG	50.1	9.1	53.0	16.4	0.71	
HEA	50.8	9.3	49.6	11.4	0.12	
DEP	49.8	9.6	54.1	16.8	1.45	
MOR	48.2	9.5	53.0	13.6	1.90	
SOC	52.5	11.8	52.1	12.1	0.01	
HOS	48.6	8.5	52.3	12.9	1.36	
FAM	51.0	11.2	59.9	15.6	4.65	.05
AUT	48.5	10.4	52.5	10.1	1.12	
FEM	51.1	10.2	42.4	7.2	5.76	.05
PHO	52.6	10.8	53.1	11.1	0.02	
PSY	49.2	8.1	53.9	19.5	2.19	
HYP	51.6	8.0	52.6	12.1	0.11	
REL	51.4	9.9	48.1	12.4	0.84	

Table D-30. Means and Standard Deviations of MMPI Basic and Special Scales for White Females by Medical Problems

	Absent (*N* = 200)		Present (*N* = 9)			
Scale	**Mean**	**S.D.**	**Mean**	**S.D.**	***F***	***p***
L	49.1	6.3	50.1	7.4	0.24	
F	52.2	7.7	52.7	7.8	0.03	
K	55.5	9.1	57.2	8.5	0.31	
Hs	51.9	8.9	56.7	9.4	2.50	
D	52.3	10.4	52.7	9.9	0.01	
Hy	56.6	8.1	55.7	10.9	0.12	
Pd	57.1	10.0	58.2	9.2	0.10	
Mf	45.9	9.4	43.4	5.3	0.61	
Pa	55.5	8.7	55.8	10.6	0.01	
Pt	53.8	9.1	53.0	7.5	0.07	
Sc	55.2	9.6	54.9	5.0	0.01	
Ma	55.7	9.3	58.7	12.7	0.84	
Si	52.2	9.6	52.2	7.2	0.00	
A	46.4	10.1	42.7	6.7	1.18	
R	49.0	9.4	52.1	8.5	0.92	
Es	55.4	11.2	54.7	7.3	0.04	
ORG	47.5	10.2	47.4	7.8	0.00	
HEA	47.6	9.6	50.0	8.5	0.53	
DEP	46.9	9.9	44.8	8.8	0.39	
MOR	45.5	10.4	41.8	6.9	1.10	
SOC	47.5	10.5	48.8	10.1	0.14	
HOS	47.7	8.7	48.4	9.9	0.06	
FAM	51.4	11.0	47.3	9.6	1.18	
AUT	46.6	9.3	46.3	9.0	0.01	
FEM	51.5	9.4	52.2	7.4	0.05	
PHO	48.7	9.8	43.6	5.7	2.43	
PSY	49.7	9.0	50.4	12.0	0.06	
HYP	50.2	8.5	48.8	10.3	0.25	
REL	50.9	9.9	50.8	9.1	0.00	

Table D-31. Means and Standard Deviations of MMPI Basic and Special Scales for White Males by Emotional Problems

	Absent (*N* = 151)		Present (*N* = 32)			
Scale	Mean	S.D.	Mean	S.D.	*F*	*p*
L	49.4	7.6	47.8	6.9	1.20	
F	54.3	9.9	58.3	13.8	3.62	
K	54.3	9.1	53.2	7.6	0.42	
Hs	54.4	9.8	57.9	11.9	3.11	
D	56.4	11.1	60.5	14.1	3.37	
Hy	57.1	8.4	59.4	9.0	2.07	
Pd	57.0	10.8	63.7	12.2	9.64	.01
Mf	59.2	9.8	60.6	11.5	0.54	
Pa	56.1	11.4	58.9	17.2	1.38	
Pt	55.8	10.7	61.1	15.4	5.43	.05
Sc	55.6	13.3	59.6	14.4	2.35	
Ma	56.8	11.0	57.6	11.7	0.13	
Si	52.0	10.5	54.8	10.6	1.91	
A	48.6	9.2	53.0	9.7	5.75	.05
R	51.3	9.7	52.6	6.2	0.49	
Es	55.9	9.5	54.0	10.7	1.03	
ORG	49.4	9.1	54.3	10.2	7.31	.01
HEA	50.1	9.3	53.8	9.2	4.27	.05
DEP	48.9	9.4	55.2	11.4	11.25	.001
MOR	47.8	9.3	51.4	11.1	3.73	
SOC	51.8	11.9	55.8	10.7	3.06	
HOS	48.3	9.0	50.8	7.2	2.23	
FAM	51.2	11.3	52.2	12.4	0.17	
AUT	48.5	10.5	49.6	10.3	0.27	
FEM	50.8	10.3	50.6	10.1	0.01	
PHO	51.7	10.4	57.0	11.9	6.69	.01
PSY	49.0	8.8	50.9	8.8	1.17	
HYP	51.5	8.5	52.3	6.1	0.26	
REL	51.7	9.8	49.5	10.8	1.29	

Table D-32. Means and Standard Deviations of MMPI Basic and Special Scales for White Females by Emotional Problems

	Absent (N = 170)		Present (N = 39)			
Scale	Mean	S.D.	Mean	S.D.	F	p
L	49.0	6.2	49.5	7.1	0.18	
F	52.0	7.4	53.4	9.0	1.12	
K	56.1	9.1	53.2	8.8	3.21	
Hs	51.9	8.5	52.7	10.8	0.22	
D	52.2	10.5	52.6	10.2	0.04	
Hy	56.5	7.6	57.1	10.5	0.17	
Pd	57.7	9.7	55.0	10.7	2.36	
Mf	46.2	9.5	43.9	8.0	1.94	
Pa	55.5	8.9	55.3	8.0	0.03	
Pt	53.8	9.4	53.7	7.3	0.01	
Sc	55.3	9.6	55.0	8.8	0.03	
Ma	55.6	8.9	56.9	11.7	0.58	
Si	52.1	9.7	52.7	8.4	0.11	
A	45.6	10.1	48.9	9.1	3.71	
R	49.7	9.5	46.9	8.3	2.74	
Es	56.0	11.1	52.8	10.7	2.52	
ORG	47.1	9.7	48.9	11.6	0.95	
HEA	47.3	9.5	49.4	9.9	1.45	
DEP	46.5	10.1	48.2	8.2	1.04	
MOR	44.9	10.6	47.2	9.0	1.58	
SOC	47.3	10.9	48.3	8.7	0.28	
HOS	47.5	8.9	48.9	8.3	0.89	
FAM	50.9	11.3	52.7	9.0	0.85	
AUT	46.4	9.3	47.5	9.2	0.44	
FEM	51.0	9.4	53.8	8.5	2.94	
PHO	48.2	9.8	49.4	9.4	0.48	
PSY	48.9	8.8	53.2	9.6	7.25	.01
HYP	49.4	8.5	53.8	8.3	8.67	.01
REL	50.4	9.4	53.3	11.4	2.75	

Table D-33. Means and Standard Deviations of MMPI Basic and Special Scales for Black Males by Medical Problems

	Absent (N = 256)		Present (N = 37)			
Scale	Mean	S.D.	Mean	S.D.	F	p
L	52.0	8.0	50.0	6.8	1.97	
F	58.6	12.2	61.3	9.8	1.65	
K	54.3	9.0	50.5	5.7	6.33	.05
Hs	57.1	10.7	64.2	14.3	12.97	.001
D	57.1	9.6	61.7	12.0	6.98	.01
Hy	56.8	8.9	60.4	11.5	4.74	.05
Pd	61.3	10.2	63.3	12.6	1.25	
Mf	62.0	9.1	63.9	11.1	1.31	
Pa	55.9	11.4	55.9	11.3	0.00	
Pt	57.1	9.8	59.1	11.9	1.29	
Sc	62.5	13.9	63.6	15.6	0.20	
Ma	63.5	11.0	64.5	12.2	0.24	
Si	51.7	7.8	54.0	7.6	2.81	
A	49.5	9.3	54.6	8.6	9.69	.01
R	50.7	9.7	50.9	9.6	0.01	
Es	50.6	9.8	45.2	10.3	9.77	.01
ORG	52.9	10.5	59.0	12.2	10.44	.01
HEA	53.8	9.1	60.4	12.7	14.81	.001
DEP	50.5	9.3	55.4	8.5	9.06	.01
MOR	47.7	9.0	51.4	8.1	5.53	.05
SOC	51.0	8.4	52.9	7.8	1.79	
HOS	48.9	8.9	53.0	8.6	6.92	.01
FAM	56.4	11.0	61.5	10.7	7.07	.01
AUT	53.3	9.7	55.8	7.4	2.24	
FEM	59.2	9.5	61.5	10.1	1.92	
PHO	56.7	10.5	58.7	10.0	1.24	
PSY	56.6	11.2	59.5	9.6	2.34	
HYP	52.6	9.3	56.2	8.3	4.97	.05
REL	54.3	9.6	55.9	8.7	0.96	

Table D-34. Means and Standard Deviations of MMPI Basic and Special Scales for Black Females by Medical Problems

	Absent (N = 434)		Present (N = 69)			
Scale	Mean	S.D.	Mean	S.D.	F	p
L	49.8	7.7	51.1	7.5	1.67	
F	58.5	12.4	57.1	9.1	0.79	
K	51.8	9.2	50.0	8.7	2.21	
Hs	53.0	9.3	56.8	10.0	9.46	.01
D	54.1	9.3	55.2	10.4	0.85	
Hy	53.9	9.1	57.2	10.2	7.57	.01
Pd	60.4	10.4	58.3	9.2	2.44	
Mf	51.8	8.7	51.2	9.5	0.21	
Pa	57.3	12.8	56.2	10.4	0.42	
Pt	54.4	9.6	54.1	9.3	0.07	
Sc	60.5	13.8	58.8	10.8	1.01	
Ma	60.2	11.5	61.0	10.3	0.32	
Si	54.6	8.5	55.6	7.3	0.83	
A	49.5	10.3	51.9	9.2	3.10	
R	48.1	9.6	49.2	11.8	0.74	
Es	52.4	9.4	47.7	9.6	14.64	.001
ORG	51.0	10.8	56.2	11.3	13.56	.001
HEA	52.2	9.8	55.6	10.6	6.86	.01
DEP	50.7	11.0	52.6	9.7	1.83	
MOR	48.0	10.3	50.7	9.5	4.25	.05
SOC	49.5	8.4	50.0	8.2	0.18	
HOS	51.5	10.4	51.7	9.5	0.02	
FAM	58.1	10.8	58.5	10.2	0.11	
AUT	55.9	9.2	56.8	9.1	0.55	
FEM	50.2	8.4	51.8	8.6	2.28	
PHO	55.5	9.7	57.0	7.2	1.48	
PSY	58.7	14.6	59.6	13.6	0.24	
HYP	51.4	9.9	54.5	10.4	5.57	.05
REL	53.1	9.1	56.7	7.7	9.46	.01

Table D-35. Means and Standard Deviations of MMPI and Special Scales for Black Males by Emotional Problems

	Absent (N = 283)		Present (N = 10)			
Scale	Mean	S.D.	Mean	S.D.	F	p
L	51.8	7.9	49.8	7.1	0.60	
F	58.6	11.9	69.1	9.5	7.66	.01
K	54.0	8.8	49.7	7.1	2.32	
Hs	57.5	11.0	70.6	15.0	13.14	.001
D	57.4	10.0	63.8	10.3	3.90	.05
Hy	56.9	9.1	67.6	10.6	13.32	.001
Pd	61.0	10.1	76.9	10.5	23.95	.001
Mf	61.9	9.2	72.0	8.5	11.72	.001
Pa	55.7	11.4	62.8	10.2	3.81	
Pt	57.0	9.9	66.2	12.2	8.20	.01
Sc	62.2	13.8	74.7	19.1	7.72	.01
Ma	63.3	11.1	73.5	8.6	8.30	.01
Si	51.9	7.7	55.0	8.3	1.57	
A	50.0	9.2	56.0	10.1	4.09	.05
R	50.7	9.7	52.3	6.9	0.28	
Es	50.2	10.0	43.6	8.4	4.26	.05
ORG	53.3	10.5	66.1	14.7	13.99	.001
HEA	54.3	9.7	65.2	9.8	12.31	.001
DEP	50.8	9.3	59.1	6.9	7.79	.01
MOR	47.9	8.9	54.8	7.7	5.80	.05
SOC	51.1	8.3	55.6	7.2	2.90	
HOS	49.3	6.8	54.0	11.6	2.73	
FAM	56.4	10.5	76.3	12.2	31.20	.001
AUT	53.5	9.5	55.6	7.4	0.46	
FEM	59.4	9.5	59.9	11.3	0.02	
PHO	56.8	10.3	59.4	13.3	0.59	
PSY	56.8	11.1	62.0	9.6	2.17	
HYP	52.9	9.4	57.9	4.5	2.80	
REL	54.5	9.4	54.1	13.0	0.02	

Table D-36. Means and Standard Deviations of MMPI Basic and Special Scales for Black Females by Emotional Problems

	Absent (*N* = 469)		Present (*N* = 34)			
Scale	Mean	S.D.	Mean	S.D.	*F*	*p*
L	50.1	7.7	48.1	6.6	2.22	
F	52.9	11.9	63.9	11.9	7.97	.01
K	51.8	9.3	47.6	6.7	6.89	.01
Hs	53.0	9.3	60.5	9.7	20.51	.001
D	54.0	9.3	57.9	10.0	5.70	.05
Hy	53.9	9.2	60.1	8.7	14.49	.001
Pd	60.0	10.2	63.7	10.5	4.46	.05
Mf	51.7	8.7	51.2	10.0	0.10	
Pa	56.7	12.5	62.7	11.2	7.29	.01
Pt	53.8	9.3	61.7	10.1	22.69	.001
Sc	59.6	13.1	69.8	14.5	19.17	.001
Ma	60.8	11.2	67.9	11.0	16.62	.001
Si	54.5	8.4	56.9	7.5	2.55	
A	49.3	10.0	57.5	9.6	21.31	.001
R	48.4	10.0	46.2	7.4	1.56	
Es	52.3	9.3	43.5	9.8	28.57	.001
ORG	51.0	10.4	62.6	13.0	37.97	.001
HEA	52.2	9.7	59.0	11.2	15.19	.001
DEP	50.5	10.8	58.0	9.3	15.66	.001
MOR	47.8	10.2	55.7	8.6	19.52	.001
SOC	49.5	8.5	50.8	7.7	0.71	
HOS	51.1	10.2	58.0	8.7	14.74	.001
FAM	57.7	10.7	64.2	9.3	12.10	.001
AUT	56.0	9.2	57.2	9.3	0.59	
FEM	50.3	8.5	51.1	8.6	0.24	
PHO	55.3	9.4	61.4	7.7	13.57	.001
PSY	58.1	14.3	68.3	14.3	16.10	.001
HYP	51.4	9.9	58.7	8.4	17.63	.001
REL	53.4	9.0	56.8	8.1	4.68	.05

Table D-37. Means, Standard Deviations, and *F*-Ratios of Differences between Racial Groups on Basic MMPI Scales for Men and Women Aged 34 Years or Younger with 12 or Fewer Years of Education

	Males						Females					
	White (*N* = 55)		Black (*N* = 50)				White (*N* = 46)		Black (*N* = 106)			
Scales	Mean	S.D.	Mean	S.D.	*F*	*p*	Mean	S.D.	Mean	S.D.	*F*	*p*
L	50.2	8.1	52.8	7.1	2.95		46.9	6.1	50.2	7.6	3.44	
F	61.2	14.1	66.2	14.1	4.60	.05	53.8	7.0	66.3	14.5	82.86	.001
K	51.2	9.2	52.0	8.7	0.32		55.1	10.8	48.2	8.2	34.71	.001
Hs	55.4	12.5	58.6	13.0	2.26		52.0	8.7	55.3	8.8	2.51	
D	57.0	13.4	58.3	12.5	0.26		54.2	11.3	56.3	9.2	1.94	
Hy	58.0	10.3	56.0	11.1	1.40		56.6	9.4	54.2	10.1	4.12	.05
Pd	61.9	13.0	66.8	10.4	4.98	.05	61.4	10.2	63.9	10.2	8.78	.01
Mf	57.1	10.1	60.5	7.9	2.83		45.8	8.0	54.5	8.2	14.37	.001
Pa	60.6	17.2	60.4	13.4	0.06		57.5	7.7	64.9	15.2	38.88	.001
Pt	58.2	13.9	61.7	11.5	2.66		56.5	9.1	58.3	10.8	4.47	.05
Sc	61.5	16.5	71.7	15.5	15.80	.001	58.0	10.2	68.5	15.4	48.38	.001
Ma	61.5	11.2	69.0	11.8	11.19	.001	56.1	10.3	64.6	13.7	27.93	.001
Si	54.4	10.1	53.3	7.7	0.44		53.7	11.3	56.9	8.1	13.11	.001
A	51.9	9.6	53.5	9.6	0.40		47.5	12.1	54.8	10.5	34.34	.001
R	52.2	10.3	49.6	9.8	2.07		49.3	9.6	46.3	10.9	8.00	.01
Es	53.5	10.1	46.1	9.9	15.40	.001	54.5	10.7	47.8	9.3	27.68	.001

Table D-38. Means, Standard Deviations, and *F*-Ratios of Differences between Racial Groups on Basic MMPI Scales for Men and Women Aged 34 Years or Younger with 13 to 15 Years of Education

	Males						Females					
	White (*N* = 28)		Black (*N* = 53)				White (*N* = 15)		Black (*N* = 93)			
Scales	Mean	S.D.	Mean	S.D.	*F*	*p*	Mean	S.D.	Mean	S.D.	*F*	*p*
L	49.6	9.4	51.7	8.2	2.37		49.2	8.9	48.7	7.5	1.90	
F	53.8	7.4	61.2	12.5	12.78	.001	52.1	10.6	59.1	11.3	9.15	.01
K	56.1	10.7	53.5	8.9	0.79		54.7	11.2	50.4	8.8	12.15	.001
Hs	52.8	7.9	57.3	13.1	4.61	.05	48.7	7.1	53.0	8.8	0.25	
D	54.3	11.1	58.3	8.3	4.78	.05	47.8	5.3	54.0	10.1	0.03	
Hy	55.6	7.8	58.6	9.4	3.33		54.3	5.5	53.7	8.1	4.45	.05
Pd	57.0	9.5	63.7	11.5	9.99	.01	59.5	11.1	61.6	10.5	3.50	
Mf	57.7	9.5	64.3	9.9	28.23	.001	47.4	7.7	50.0	8.2	10.15	.001
Pa	52.7	8.9	55.3	12.1	0.19		56.6	7.0	57.3	11.6	0.82	
Pt	54.2	11.3	57.2	10.1	2.28		54.8	6.9	54.9	9.6	0.06	
Sc	53.9	13.2	64.6	14.7	15.60	.001	55.8	10.8	61.3	12.9	4.49	.05
Ma	61.9	10.3	67.2	11.0	12.41	.001	61.9	10.3	63.2	9.8	7.96	.01
Si	49.1	10.5	50.8	7.4	0.01		52.4	10.7	54.3	8.5	2.36	
A	46.0	9.5	50.0	9.6	2.44		47.6	11.0	50.7	10.5	3.74	
R	51.6	8.4	50.7	9.1	0.00		46.9	8.9	46.9	8.0	4.66	.05
Es	60.4	6.5	50.5	9.3	15.50	.001	55.9	11.4	52.3	9.2	1.07	

Table D-39. Means, Standard Deviations, and *F*-Ratios of Differences between Racial Groups on Basic MMPI Scales for Men and Women Aged 34 Years or Younger with 16 or More Years of Education

	Males						Females					
	White (*N* – 22)		Black (*N* = 39)				White (*N* = 27)		Black (*N* = 90)			
Scales	Mean	S.D.	Mean	S.D.	*F*	*p*	Mean	S.D.	Mean	S.D.	*F*	*p*
L	45.9	4.3	49.5	7.5	1.59		47.3	4.9	47.7	6.9	3.05	
F	51.9	4.8	57.1	10.2	2.32		49.1	4.1	52.5	8.5	1.57	
K	56.9	7.6	55.4	8.1	0.00		59.2	8.5	55.3	8.4	0.02	
Hs	49.3	5.8	55.4	7.2	3.65		49.7	6.2	50.6	8.7	4.43	.05
D	54.0	11.0	53.6	8.9	0.18		45.6	6.1	51.9	9.0	0.04	
Hy	56.4	9.1	56.8	6.8	0.14		53.4	6.7	53.8	8.7	2.21	
Pd	57.9	12.1	59.5	8.7	0.20		54.4	8.1	59.0	9.6	0.83	
Mf	61.2	11.0	61.2	9.4	2.84		42.4	10.2	49.9	8.3	1.05	
Pa	55.7	7.1	55.2	8.5	0.15		53.9	7.8	52.6	9.9	4.53	.05
Pt	56.9	8.9	55.6	7.4	0.10		52.1	6.0	52.0	8.2	3.92	.05
Sc	54.9	9.9	59.9	10.8	1.68		52.7	5.9	55.0	9.2	1.77	
Ma	55.4	8.8	63.7	10.0	9.20	.01	58.6	9.4	57.2	9.0	2.40	
Si	49.0	10.5	49.1	8.1	0.95		47.5	6.7	50.7	8.1	0.30	
A	46.6	10.6	47.6	9.1	0.00		41.1	6.3	45.2	8.8	1.22	
R	49.5	8.3	50.4	9.0	0.23		46.7	6.3	47.8	8.8	0.84	
Es	63.0	5.9	53.9	8.7	6.20	.05	63.3	7.0	57.4	8.6	1.59	

Table D-40. Means, Standard Deviations, and *F*-Ratios of Differences between Racial Groups on Basic MMPI Scales for Men and Women Aged 35 Years and Older with 12 or Fewer Years of Education

	Males						Females					
	White (*N* = 37)		Black (*N* = 67)				White (*N* = 86)		Black (*N* = 105)			
Scales	Mean	S.D.	Mean	S.D.	*F*	*p*	Mean	S.D.	Mean	S.D.	*F*	*p*
L	49.4	7.4	51.3	8.0	2.24		50.9	5.9	51.5	7.7	0.62	
F	53.0	10.8	58.6	11.0	6.12	.05	53.5	8.3	59.7	11.5	17.29	.001
K	53.4	7.7	51.0	8.0	3.08		54.3	8.7	50.1	9.3	12.11	.001
Hs	57.8	11.1	58.5	12.1	2.03		54.4	9.8	55.3	10.2	0.47	
D	59.6	10.6	58.8	10.9	0.67		53.7	10.4	56.0	9.5	2.62	
Hy	57.1	8.6	55.9	10.2	0.24		57.3	8.7	54.4	10.1	4.84	.05
Pd	55.5	10.1	59.2	10.5	1.36		55.5	10.2	59.7	10.7	6.59	.01
Mf	57.9	8.2	60.6	8.1	9.99	.01	47.1	8.9	54.4	8.8	29.05	.001
Pa	54.1	10.0	56.7	12.0	0.87		54.6	9.4	57.1	12.0	2.22	
Pt	56.3	11.9	57.2	9.7	0.73		53.5	10.2	55.1	9.3	1.21	
Sc	53.6	12.1	61.1	12.7	7.08	.01	54.9	9.9	61.8	13.6	14.59	.001
Ma	49.8	10.1	61.1	10.6	18.31	.001	54.4	8.6	59.1	11.1	6.93	.01
Si	56.8	10.3	54.7	7.7	0.11		53.2	9.2	57.3	7.7	13.37	.001
A	49.5	7.8	52.2	8.6	3.92	.05	47.7	9.6	52.0	9.5	10.56	.001
R	52.6	8.0	49.3	10.3	1.86		51.0	9.3	50.0	9.9	0.30	
Es	52.5	9.0	46.2	9.6	20.14	.001	52.7	10.9	48.2	9.0	13.28	.001

Table D-41. Means, Standard Deviations, and *F*-Ratios of Differences between Racial Groups on Basic MMPI Scales for Men and Women Aged 35 Years and Older with 13 to 15 Years of Education

	Males						Females					
	White (*N* = 10)		Black (*N* = 33)				White (*N* = 26)		Black (*N* = 29)			
Scales	Mean	S.D.	Mean	S.D.	*F*	*p*	Mean	S.D.	Mean	S.D.	*F*	*p*
L	46.8	7.0	51.7	6.8	3.47		48.3	6.7	51.9	8.7	3.27	
F	50.6	3.2	53.7	7.6	0.33		51.0	7.3	54.2	5.7	1.01	
K	53.9	7.7	55.7	7.4	1.56		56.9	9.1	53.6	8.6	1.67	
Hs	57.1	6.5	57.4	10.1	1.15		51.1	8.4	54.4	9.4	1.31	
D	61.3	9.1	57.6	8.7	0.11		52.6	12.4	52.1	8.8	0.10	
Hy	58.0	5.6	58.1	7.5	0.70		56.3	7.8	56.6	9.2	0.01	
Pd	55.7	10.8	60.7	9.9	1.26		56.3	10.6	57.8	8.1	0.20	
Mf	61.9	13.2	64.6	11.7	20.48	.001	45.7	8.1	50.0	9.6	2.18	
Pa	55.4	9.5	52.7	8.6	2.34		54.7	9.3	52.1	9.8	0.94	
Pt	56.4	6.7	54.4	9.4	0.43		52.0	10.0	50.0	7.8	0.88	
Sc	51.3	9.6	56.5	11.8	0.01		52.4	9.8	53.0	8.3	0.00	
Ma	56.6	11.2	61.4	9.9	1.61		53.5	11.1	58.0	11.0	2.03	
Si	49.7	8.8	51.0	7.5	0.39		51.7	9.6	52.6	8.4	0.11	
A	49.0	8.4	48.1	7.2	0.25		44.1	9.2	44.8	8.2	0.01	
R	52.2	7.5	50.8	8.0	0.06		48.9	8.7	51.4	11.8	1.01	
Es	50.3	13.4	54.3	8.7	1.45		56.8	9.6	52.7	7.3	2.44	

Table D-42. Means, Standard Deviations, and *F*-Ratios of Differences between Racial Groups on Basic MMPI Scales for Men and Women Aged 35 Years and Older with 16 or More Years of Education

	Males						Females					
	White (*N* = 36)		Black (*N* = 47)				White (*N* = 28)		Black (*N* = 67)			
Scales	Mean	S.D.	Mean	S.D.	*F*	*p*	Mean	S.D.	Mean	S.D.	*F*	*p*
L	49.0	6.5	52.2	9.2	4.20	.05	47.8	6.0	50.6	7.5	2.71	
F	51.5	5.7	54.0	9.6	0.43		49.7	5.1	52.0	7.4	1.38	
K	56.8	7.6	57.1	9.7	0.45		59.0	8.3	55.3	9.4	0.11	
Hs	56.0	9.2	59.6	10.7	4.11	.05	50.3	9.9	52.9	8.5	0.00	
D	56.9	11.8	57.3	9.1	0.19		50.6	8.1	53.0	9.0	0.01	
Hy	58.8	6.3	58.2	8.9	0.00		59.5	8.2	55.9	8.8	1.49	
Pd	57.2	9.8	58.3	9.1	0.07		59.7	8.3	56.3	9.0	5.18	.05
Mf	64.0	9.6	63.1	9.6	0.71		45.7	11.3	47.3	7.1	6.74	.01
Pa	56.2	10.5	53.0	9.8	2.32		56.2	7.4	53.7	7.9	2.75	
Pt	57.0	11.1	56.1	10.3	0.07		54.0	6.8	51.7	7.9	4.80	.05
Sc	54.9	10.2	58.7	13.3	1.37		56.4	7.6	54.7	9.1	3.43	
Ma	54.4	8.9	59.5	10.2	3.62		56.6	8.2	57.2	10.9	0.65	
Si	49.9	10.2	51.0	7.5	0.04		47.8	7.4	53.4	8.1	4.19	.05
A	48.8	9.4	47.9	9.9	0.27		43.1	7.4	46.1	8.6	0.12	
R	50.3	9.9	53.2	10.2	2.80		47.8	13.0	49.6	10.6	0.38	
ES	55.7	9.6	52.8	10.3	1.51		57.9	11.9	54.5	9.0	0.08	

APPENDIX E
Analyses of Relationships between MMPI Scores and Background Factors in Psychiatric Samples

Table E-1. Correlates (Presenting Symptoms) Associated with MMPI Basic and Special Scales for White and Black Psychiatric Patients (Lafayette Clinic Samples)

	Cutting	White Males and Females (N = 200)			Black Males and Females (N = 200)		
Scale	Score	Correlate	$p(\chi^2)$	Φ	Correlate	$p(\chi^2)$	Φ
L	> 59 T	Deviant beliefs	.0001	.27	Deviant thinking	.05	.14
		Deviant thinking	.05	.17			
F	> 69 T	Anxiety	.05	.17	. . .		
K	> 59 T	Deviant behavior	.05	.15	*Anxiety	.05	.17
		*Drug/alcohol use	.05	.14	*Depression	.05	.16
		*Problematic anger	.05	.14	Deviant beliefs	.05	.16
					Deviant behavior	.0001	.34
Hs	> 69 T	Anxiety	.05	.15	Somatic concern	.0001	.29
		Depression	.01	.19			
		Drug/alcohol use	.05	.14			
		Somatic concern	.01	.20			
D	> 69 T	Depression	.0001	.31	Anxiety	.05	.16
		Sleep disturbance	.05	.15	Depression	.01	.21
					Sleep disturbance	.05	.14
					Somatic concern	.01	.21
Hy	> 69 T	Depression	.01	.21	Anxiety	.05	.16
		Somatic concern	.01	.18	Depression	.01	.18
					Sleep disturbance	.05	.17
					*Antisocial attitude	.01	.19
					Somatic concern	.001	.27
Pd	> 69 T	*Deviant behavior	.05	.14	Depression	.01	.20
Mf (males)	> 69 T	*Problematic anger	.05	.21	Sleep disturbance	.05	.22
					*Problematic anger	.05	.24
Mf (females)	< 46 T	. . .			. . .		
Pa	> 69 T	Anxiety	.05	.16	Sleep disturbance	.05	.15
		Depression	.05	.16			
		Sleep disturbance	.05	.14			
		Deviant beliefs	.05	.14			
Pt	> 69 T	Depression	.001	.23	Sleep disturbance	.05	.14
		*Deviant behavior	.05	.14			
Sc	> 69 T	Depression	.001	.23	. . .		
Ma	> 69 T	Drug/alcohol use	.01	.22	Antisocial attitude	.01	.19
Si	> 69 T	Depression	.05	.16	Anxiety	.01	.19
		*Deviant behavior	.05	.17	*Antisocial attitude	.05	.14
A	> 69 T	Depression	.001	.24	Depression	.01	.22
		*Deviant behavior	.05	.15			
R	> 59 T	Deviant thinking	.05	.16	Deviant behavior	.05	.16
					*Drug/alcohol use	.01	.22
					*Antisocial attitude	.05	.16
Es	> 49 T	*Depression	.0001	.27	*Anxiety	.01	.19
		*Sleep disturbance	.05	.17	*Depression	.01	.18
		*Deviant beliefs	.01	.18	Deviant behavior	.01	.18
		Antisocial attitude	.05	.17			

Note: Asterisk indicates that increased scale elevation is associated with decreased incidence of correlate.

Table E-2. Frequency of Code Types and Categories in Profiles of Black

Standard Norms	Code Type	N	Invalid	Normal	1 spike	2 spike	3 spike	7 spike	12/21	13/31	17/71	23/32	27/72	20/02	37/73	4 spike	9 spike	14/41	24/42	34/43	46/64
Tri-State Norms					Neurotic										Characterological						
	Invalid (8.8%)	42	7	2					2		2		3	1			1		2	1	
	Normal (7.6%)	36		36																	
Neurotic (*N* = 84; 17.6%)	1 spike	2		2	—																
	2 spike	8		5		3															
	3 spike	1		1			—														
	7 spike	0						—													
	12/21	14		2	2	1			7			2									
	13/31	21		1	3		3		3	11											
	17/71	0									—										
	23/32	17		3		1	2					10		1							
	27/72	13		1		3							8	1							
	20/02	7												6							
	37/73	1													1						
Characterological (*N* = 157; 33.0%)	4 spike	14		13												1					
	9 spike	20		16													4				
	14/41	2		1														1			
	24/42	37		7		7	1					3	1	3		1			11	1	
	34/43	14		3						2		3								6	
	46/64	10		2								1				4			1		—
	47/74	4						1												1	
	48/84	44		10					1	2		3			1	8		2	5	1	1
	49/94	12		4						1		1					3		1		1
Psychotic (*N* = 142; 29.8%)	6 spike	5		5																	
	8 spike	2		2																	
	18/81	4			1				1	1	1										
	28/82	51		8		7			1			3	12	14					3		
	38/83	8					2			3		1									
	68/86	33		4				1			1		5	2		1					2
	69/96	2		1																	
	78/87	17					1	1					4		1		1				
	89/98	20		13													1				
	80/08	0																			
Other (*N* = 15; 3.0%)	0 spike	1																			
	16/61	1							1												
	19/91	1																			
	26/62	7		1		2							2						1		
	36/63	0																			
	39/93	3		2						1											
	67/76	0																			
	70/07	0																			
	79/97	2		1																	
		476	7	146	6	24	9	3	16	21	4	27	35	28	3	15	10	3	24	10	4
			Invalid (1.5%)	Normal (30.7%)	Neurotic (*N* = 176; 37.0%)										Characterological (*N* = 80; 16.8%)						

Lafayette Clinic Psychiatric Patients Based on Standard and Tri-State Norms

			Psychotic										Other									
47/74	48/84	49/94	6 spike	8 spike	18/81	28/82	38/83	68/86	69/96	78/87	89/98	80/08	0 spike	16/61	19/91	26/62	36/63	39/93	67/76	70/07	79/97	
		1				3		3	1	4	1	1				1	2		3	1		Invalid
																						Normal
																						1 spike
																						2 spike
																						3 spike
																						7 spike
																						12/21
																						13/31
																						17/71
																						23/32
																						27/72
													1									20/02
																						37/73
																						4 spike
																						9 spike
																						14/41
													2									24/42
																						34/43
		1											1									46/64
1													1									47/74
6	2				1								1									48/84
		1																				49/94
			—																			6 spike
				—																		8 spike
					—																	18/81
				1		1										1						28/82
							2															38/83
			3			1		1		3			1	1		5			2			68/86
			1						—													69/96
										5						2			1		1	78/87
		2									2		1								1	89/98
												—										80/08
													1									0 spike
														—								16/61
															1							19/91
																1						26/62
																	—					36/63
																		—				39/93
																			—			67/76
																				—		70/07
																					1	79/97
7	2	5	4	1	1	5	2	4	1	12	3	1	9	1	1	10	2	0	6	1	3	Same code 131/476 (27.5%)
			Psychotic (*N* = 34; 7.1%)										Other (*N* = 33; 6.9%)									

Table E-3. Correlates (Presenting Symptoms) Associated with MMPI Wiggins Content Scales for White and Black Psychiatric Patients (Lafayette Clinic Samples)

	Cutting	White Males and Females (N = 200)			Black Males and Females (N = 200)		
Scale	Score	Correlate	$p(\chi^2)$	Φ	Correlate	$p(\chi^2)$	Φ
ORG	> 69 T	Anxiety	.05	.14	Depression	.05	.14
		Depression	.001	.24	Somatic concern	.01	.22
		Somatic concern	.05	.17	Neurological screening	.01	.18
HEA	> 69 T	Depression	.001	.24	Somatic concern	.0001	.29
		Somatic concern	.01	.21	Neurological screening	.05	.16
DEP	> 69 T	Depression	.0001	.35	Depression	.0001	.28
		Sleep disturbance	.05	.15	Sleep disturbance	.05	.17
		*Deviant thinking	.01	.20	*Deviant thinking	.05	.14
		*Deviant behavior	.01	.20	*Deviant behavior	.05	.17
		*Drug/alcohol use	.001	.23			
MOR	> 69 T	Depression	.0001	.29	Anxiety	.01	.22
					Sleep disturbance	.01	.18
SOC	> 69 T	. . .			Anxiety	.05	.15
					*Antisocial attitude	.05	.14
HOS	> 59 T	Problematic anger	.05	.17	Antisocial attitude	.05	.14
FAM	> 69 T	Deviant behavior	.01	.21	Depression	.01	.20
					Deviant behavior	.05	.15
					Sexual concern	.05	.15
AUT	> 59 T	. . .			Drug/alcohol use	.05	.15
					*Family problems	.01	.17
FEM	> 59 T	Sexual deviation	.001	.26	*Depression	.01	.21
					Deviant behavior	.01	.18
					*Family problems	.05	.14
					*Problematic anger	.01	.17
					Sexual deviation	.05	.14
					*Somatic concern	.01	.18
PHO	> 69 T	Anxiety	.01	.21	. . .		
PSY	> 69 T	Anxiety	.05	.14	Deviant thinking	.05	.15
		Deviant beliefs	.001	.23			
		*Sexual concern	.05	.14			
HYP	> 59 T	Anxiety	.05	.16	. . .		
REL	> 59 T	*Drug/alcohol use	.05	.14	Deviant thinking	.05	.15
		Neurological screening	.01	.18	Neurological screening	.01	.20

Note: Asterisk indicates that increased scale elevation is associated with decreased incidence of correlate.

Table E-4. Means and Standard Deviations of MMPI Basic and Special Scales for the White Male Cleveland Psychiatric Institute Sample at Four Age Levels

	18-24 ($N = 31$)		25-34 ($N = 68$)		35-44 ($N = 76$)		> 45 ($N = 87$)			
Scale	Mean	S.D.	Mean	S.D.	Mean	S.D.	Mean	S.D.	*F*	*p*
L	49.2	6.3	51.5	8.7	52.5	8.6	52.4	8.4	1.37	
F	66.1	14.7	63.8	12.6	60.1	12.7	63.2	12.1	1.97	
K	51.6	7.0	52.7	10.4	53.6	10.1	51.7	10.4	0.57	
Hs	58.5	13.5	61.2	13.4	60.5	15.0	65.3	15.9	2.39	
D	67.1	18.6	68.8	16.7	68.0	18.9	72.3	16.4	1.17	
Hy	59.5	10.8	62.2	11.1	61.7	10.2	62.6	12.0	0.61	
Pd	72.3	11.8	72.3	13.4	68.4	11.8	66.5	11.1	3.74	.01
Mf	56.7	10.8	56.7	10.2	60.5	10.6	58.9	9.9	2.05	
Pa	62.2	11.9	62.2	12.5	60.0	11.7	61.5	11.7	0.60	
Pt	65.7	13.4	66.9	13.8	63.3	14.1	66.4	14.9	0.94	
Sc	71.8	18.3	69.1	16.8	65.8	17.0	68.4	17.1	1.04	
Ma	65.8	13.5	63.1	12.0	62.4	11.7	62.1	11.4	0.81	
Si	55.0	11.3	54.0	9.8	54.1	11.9	56.6	11.0	1.00	
A	56.2	10.2	55.1	11.8	53.3	11.5	56.9	12.1	1.40	
R	49.8	11.5	49.8	12.0	50.8	10.6	52.6	11.2	0.97	
Es	44.3	11.2	44.5	9.5	43.3	12.1	39.1	11.8	3.78	.01
ORG	56.8	14.2	56.6	13.8	55.5	15.3	61.1	13.6	2.42	
HEA	56.6	12.4	56.4	12.1	55.9	14.5	59.5	12.2	1.26	
DEP	59.1	12.6	59.0	13.3	56.4	11.8	60.7	13.5	1.54	
MOR	55.5	10.2	55.1	11.4	52.3	11.7	56.1	11.8	1.57	
SOC	54.2	12.3	52.9	10.2	51.6	12.5	55.7	12.4	1.69	
HOS	53.5	7.7	50.2	10.3	48.9	9.3	51.2	8.5	2.07	
FAM	64.4	14.5	62.8	15.0	56.6	13.4	56.9	13.8	4.56	.01
AUT	55.9	7.0	53.3	10.3	54.6	9.9	54.3	10.6	0.52	
FEM	51.7	11.4	52.1	9.3	57.5	10.4	57.4	9.3	6.34	.001
PHO	57.5	10.6	54.5	11.2	55.8	12.5	59.9	13.0	2.92	.05
PSY	51.9	11.5	55.9	11.9	54.3	11.8	57.0	12.4	0.94	
HYP	54.7	7.6	54.4	10.7	52.7	9.4	54.3	10.6	0.56	
REL	51.6	8.0	51.3	8.7	50.5	8.7	50.6	8.9	0.20	

Table E-5. Means and Standard Deviations of MMPI Basic and Special Scales for the White Female Cleveland Psychiatric Institute Sample at Four Age Levels

	18-24 (N = 51)		25-34 (N = 105)		35-44 (N = 110)		> 45 (N = 143)			
Scale	Mean	S.D.	Mean	S.D.	Mean	S.D.	Mean	S.D.	F	p
L	54.1	8.7	53.2	8.7	53.2	8.0	55.7	9.2	2.26	
F	67.0	15.1	63.7	12.7	61.5	12.0	63.1	12.9	2.14	
K	53.5	10.0	51.6	9.3	51.8	9.6	52.7	9.5	0.65	
Hs	58.9	12.7	58.7	12.5	57.5	12.2	61.9	13.6	2.69	.05
D	63.9	14.9	65.1	14.9	63.5	15.3	65.2	14.6	0.35	
Hy	62.2	11.7	62.4	12.1	60.3	12.8	62.1	11.9	0.67	
Pd	72.5	12.6	69.9	12.6	67.5	11.8	64.9	11.6	6.30	.001
Mf	50.2	9.8	52.5	11.2	51.2	9.7	52.5	10.0	0.92	
Pa	65.9	14.3	65.0	11.5	62.6	12.0	64.5	13.1	1.03	
Pt	64.7	12.5	63.5	13.7	61.4	12.0	63.0	11.9	0.93	
Sc	70.7	16.5	68.8	16.1	65.2	14.1	67.2	14.8	1.87	
Ma	62.7	13.0	64.6	14.1	60.9	12.2	60.7	11.7	2.30	
Si	58.8	11.4	57.6	11.3	59.1	10.8	58.4	9.6	0.35	
A	53.9	12.3	54.5	11.0	53.7	10.3	54.1	10.6	0.11	
R	50.9	11.4	49.8	12.9	50.7	12.3	51.8	12.0	0.55	
Es	47.4	12.3	44.2	11.7	43.3	11.2	42.0	9.9	3.03	.05
ORG	55.4	14.8	57.5	15.4	55.4	12.9	59.0	14.0	1.69	
HEA	55.5	12.4	56.3	12.0	55.8	12.1	57.4	12.7	0.48	
DEP	60.4	15.1	59.3	13.9	56.8	12.4	57.7	13.1	1.14	
MOR	53.1	12.2	53.9	11.2	54.2	11.3	53.9	10.7	0.11	
SOC	54.5	13.0	50.9	11.6	53.1	11.4	52.5	9.0	1.38	
HOS	49.5	10.7	52.0	11.2	51.1	9.1	50.9	10.2	0.70	
FAM	62.9	13.8	61.6	14.5	60.1	12.8	56.3	13.0	4.57	.01
AUT	52.1	11.2	53.5	12.6	53.1	11.4	53.4	10.7	0.19	
FEM	46.8	9.9	46.8	10.8	48.2	8.5	48.6	8.1	1.03	
PHO	50.5	10.9	53.0	11.3	54.5	11.5	56.1	10.3	3.83	.01
PSY	59.1	14.5	59.1	14.4	57.5	15.0	59.9	15.6	0.51	
HYP	52.1	11.4	53.3	10.1	53.1	10.4	52.1	9.9	0.44	
REL	48.7	9.5	49.8	9.9	49.1	8.2	50.3	9.9	0.49	

Table E-6. Means and Standard Deviations of MMPI Basic and Special Scales for the Black Male Cleveland Psychiatric Institute Sample at Four Age Levels

	18-24 (*N* = 20)		25-34 (*N* = 26)		35-44 (*N* = 37)		> 45 (*N* = 20)			
Scale	Mean	S.D.	Mean	S.D.	Mean	S.D.	Mean	S.D.	*F*	*p*
L	52.9	7.5	52.9	9.8	50.4	7.6	50.4	9.3	0.70	
F	75.8	13.8	68.6	14.9	70.6	13.6	69.2	12.6	1.19	
K	50.3	9.0	51.6	11.3	48.2	8.3	48.6	8.2	0.79	
Hs	61.1	17.4	58.8	13.9	63.4	13.6	64.9	11.8	0.86	
D	63.4	14.2	62.8	13.1	67.4	13.2	68.7	10.6	1.22	
Hy	58.0	12.9	59.8	8.0	59.3	13.5	61.6	10.0	0.34	
Pd	74.3	12.4	71.5	13.1	68.3	12.1	72.6	10.6	1.22	
Mf	59.8	11.2	59.7	9.5	60.4	9.0	58.0	9.9	0.28	
Pa	68.4	14.3	64.2	12.8	68.4	13.8	68.4	17.5	0.55	
Pt	68.4	15.7	66.0	11.8	66.2	13.3	68.5	14.1	0.24	
Sc	79.0	21.5	73.6	14.6	76.3	17.8	75.4	18.9	0.35	
Ma	72.3	12.4	68.2	10.9	69.0	11.3	69.4	10.2	0.56	
Si	56.6	8.5	55.6	8.3	54.0	7.5	53.5	10.3	0.63	
A	58.1	10.5	55.9	12.3	59.9	9.7	59.6	12.2	0.74	
R	50.0	10.0	50.1	12.3	46.7	10.6	47.1	13.1	0.67	
Es	41.3	9.6	41.3	12.3	35.8	10.9	34.1	11.6	2.63	
ORG	60.5	14.7	57.4	13.0	64.1	11.9	65.5	14.8	1.87	
HEA	56.7	11.8	56.3	11.4	60.9	11.0	61.1	9.4	1.40	
DEP	61.4	11.8	59.4	13.8	62.8	10.5	63.3	13.1	0.52	
MOR	55.1	10.1	53.9	11.4	56.8	9.8	58.5	11.1	0.83	
SOC	55.2	10.0	54.2	9.1	51.6	8.2	51.4	11.5	0.94	
HOS	56.6	10.5	51.2	10.5	54.9	9.6	54.5	7.9	1.33	
FAM	68.0	13.0	66.5	14.6	60.1	13.0	63.7	16.3	1.77	
AUT	58.4	10.1	57.0	10.8	57.7	9.3	58.3	6.9	0.10	
FEM	55.8	8.4	56.4	10.3	60.4	8.5	60.0	9.5	1.72	
PHO	57.5	11.1	60.9	12.3	65.9	12.5	64.6	16.7	2.06	
PSY	66.5	13.0	62.0	15.6	67.8	14.8	65.5	14.1	0.83	
HYP	55.3	9.5	55.7	10.2	58.0	9.6	56.3	9.7	0.45	
REL	49.8	7.7	52.3	8.5	54.5	7.1	56.5	8.3	2.84	.05

Table E-7. Means and Standard Deviations of MMPI Basic and Special Scales for the Black Female Cleveland Psychiatric Institute Sample at Four Age Levels

	18-24 (*N* = 45)		25-34 (*N* = 49)		35-44 (*N* = 43)		> 45 (*N* = 26)			
Scale	**Mean**	**S.D.**	**Mean**	**S.D.**	**Mean**	**S.D.**	**Mean**	**S.D.**	***F***	***p***
L	52.2	7.8	53.0	8.9	53.6	7.9	52.6	6.8	0.22	
F	66.1	12.6	64.8	14.5	66.4	14.6	70.7	13.4	1.04	
K	49.5	9.6	50.6	10.1	50.6	9.2	48.3	9.3	0.42	
Hs	56.6	10.9	57.6	10.0	56.3	9.3	63.2	14.3	2.60	
D	59.5	12.1	61.5	12.1	60.4	10.5	65.5	14.5	1.44	
Hy	56.4	11.2	60.2	11.3	56.2	9.6	60.2	14.8	1.59	
Pd	69.6	12.2	68.5	12.6	65.6	12.5	65.5	12.2	1.09	
Mf	55.8	7.3	52.0	8.7	56.0	11.2	54.5	10.7	1.77	
Pa	60.7	14.8	63.7	13.4	66.3	17.0	68.8	14.9	1.93	
Pt	59.7	10.9	60.3	12.1	59.3	11.1	63.0	13.4	0.62	
Sc	66.2	14.5	67.2	17.1	68.2	14.0	74.7	16.6	1.80	
Ma	66.4	11.4	63.2	11.8	62.2	13.8	65.1	12.5	1.01	
Si	56.1	9.5	56.3	8.7	58.0	8.9	58.8	8.9	0.76	
A	54.6	10.6	53.9	11.3	53.8	12.7	58.0	11.6	0.88	
R	46.5	11.4	50.1	10.4	48.9	13.1	45.3	7.4	1.48	
Es	45.7	11.5	41.8	12.3	40.9	12.9	36.8	13.0	2.97	.05
ORG	57.3	13.1	58.6	15.3	57.3	10.9	67.6	16.4	3.70	.05
HEA	56.7	10.5	58.3	10.0	55.8	8.4	61.1	15.5	1.46	
DEP	58.4	11.9	57.4	13.0	57.2	13.2	60.7	13.8	0.47	
MOR	53.6	11.6	53.3	11.0	52.6	11.8	56.5	10.4	0.71	
SOC	49.7	8.9	49.8	9.3	52.5	7.8	52.7	8.6	1.30	
HOS	55.3	9.7	54.0	9.7	52.3	9.7	56.6	9.8	1.23	
FAM	61.0	12.5	60.9	12.7	60.7	12.5	63.1	13.3	0.23	
AUT	59.8	10.5	55.3	10.2	55.9	10.3	59.5	9.4	2.26	
FEM	47.8	8.4	48.9	8.3	46.2	8.2	52.3	7.6	3.17	.05
PHO	56.0	10.0	55.9	10.3	57.8	11.0	60.0	8.9	1.17	
PSY	63.4	15.3	62.1	15.9	65.4	18.0	69.4	16.9	1.25	
HYP	55.8	9.6	53.6	11.9	53.7	11.9	55.2	10.6	0.41	
REL	50.3	7.7	52.2	7.8	52.0	7.8	59.3	6.3	8.33	.001

Table E-8. Means and Standard Deviations of MMPI Basic and Special Scales for the White Male Cleveland Psychiatric Institute Sample at Three Educational Levels

	≤ 8 years (N = 58)		9-11 years (N = 85)		≥ 12 years (N = 112)			
Scale	Mean	S.D.	Mean	S.D.	Mean	S.D.	F	p
L	53.7	9.0	51.0	8.1	51.2	7.9	2.23	
F	65.4	13.3	62.3	13.0	61.9	12.3	1.58	
K	51.1	11.0	52.4	9.6	53.2	9.3	0.89	
Hs	66.5	17.0	62.1	14.7	59.7	13.4	4.06	.05
D	70.8	16.6	67.8	16.1	70.2	18.9	0.68	
Hy	61.5	12.8	61.9	11.4	62.2	10.0	0.07	
Pd	67.5	12.3	71.6	12.6	68.0	11.5	2.84	
Mf	55.8	9.4	55.5	10.3	62.0	10.0	12.80	.001
Pa	62.8	14.1	60.4	11.6	61.3	10.9	0.71	
Pt	67.2	14.8	62.0	13.3	67.2	14.1	3.94	.05
Sc	72.1	17.4	64.7	16.5	68.5	16.4	3.49	.05
Ma	62.3	11.8	63.5	12.5	62.6	11.4	0.22	
Si	57.3	10.7	53.1	9.8	55.2	11.3	2.67	
A	57.2	11.8	54.1	10.6	55.2	12.0	1.20	
R	50.8	11.2	50.3	9.2	51.6	12.7	0.30	
Es	36.9	11.8	43.0	10.2	44.8	11.0	10.34	.001
ORG	64.1	15.2	56.9	14.0	55.3	13.2	7.83	.001
HEA	60.5	12.7	57.8	13.1	55.1	11.9	3.65	.05
DEP	60.4	12.8	58.4	12.1	58.3	13.2	0.58	
MOR	56.5	11.1	53.4	10.7	54.7	12.1	1.28	
SOC	55.7	12.1	51.3	10.6	54.3	12.3	2.72	
HOS	51.0	8.8	50.8	9.1	50.1	9.4	0.22	
FAM	57.8	12.9	59.7	14.1	59.3	15.3	0.33	
AUT	55.4	9.5	56.2	9.8	52.2	9.7	4.71	.01
FEM	57.9	8.6	52.9	10.2	55.9	10.7	4.60	.01
PHO	62.6	13.0	55.4	11.7	55.4	11.4	8.20	.001
PSY	60.2	13.9	54.1	11.1	55.2	11.2	4.91	.01
HYP	54.1	10.7	54.6	10.1	53.2	9.5	0.54	
REL	52.0	8.5	50.5	7.9	50.8	9.3	0.53	

Table E-9. Means and Standard Deviations of MMPI Basic and Special Scales for the White Female Cleveland Psychiatric Institute Sample at Three Educational Levels

	≤ 8 years (N = 77)		9-11 years (N = 152)		≥ 12 years (N = 176)			
Scale	**Mean**	**S.D.**	**Mean**	**S.D.**	**Mean**	**S.D.**	F	p
L	55.8	7.4	53.8	9.5	53.6	9.3	1.88	
F	65.3	13.9	64.9	12.9	61.0	12.2	4.93	.01
K	49.4	9.0	51.1	9.0	54.6	9.6	10.50	.001
Hs	61.8	12.8	60.9	13.2	57.4	12.4	4.43	.05
D	66.3	13.5	64.8	14.0	63.7	16.3	0.82	
Hy	60.3	12.9	62.3	12.5	62.0	11.5	0.72	
Pd	65.6	12.9	69.4	11.8	67.5	12.4	2.53	
Mf	57.5	9.9	53.7	10.1	47.8	8.8	32.55	.001
Pa	65.0	15.3	64.8	11.9	63.7	11.6	0.43	
Pt	63.3	13.0	62.7	11.7	63.0	13.0	0.06	
Sc	67.5	16.7	68.1	14.7	67.1	15.1	0.20	
Ma	60.2	12.4	62.6	13.5	62.1	12.0	0.95	
Si	61.6	8.8	59.0	10.2	56.6	11.4	6.57	.01
A	55.8	10.1	54.8	10.2	52.8	11.4	2.57	
R	52.3	12.5	50.3	12.7	50.8	11.8	0.72	
Es	38.9	10.5	43.1	11.2	46.1	10.7	11.94	.001
ORG	61.8	13.7	58.6	14.0	54.0	14.0	9.65	.001
HEA	60.9	12.3	58.1	12.2	53.1	11.6	13.57	.001
DEP	60.8	12.5	59.2	12.2	56.2	14.5	3.90	.05
MOR	55.8	10.4	54.6	10.2	52.5	12.1	2.99	
SOC	55.2	9.8	52.7	10.4	51.2	11.7	3.63	.05
HOS	51.5	9.9	52.3	9.9	49.8	10.4	2.66	
FAM	57.7	13.3	61.8	12.9	58.4	14.0	3.46	.05
AUT	55.4	10.6	55.4	11.0	50.3	11.5	10.38	.001
FEM	47.2	8.5	46.5	10.0	49.2	8.6	3.61	.05
PHO	59.1	10.3	53.9	11.4	52.3	10.6	10.82	.001
PSY	62.2	16.8	59.6	15.2	56.9	13.4	3.74	.05
HYP	54.2	10.3	53.0	10.1	51.8	10.3	1.68	
REL	52.0	8.2	48.8	9.6	49.2	9.6	3.31	.05

Table E-10. Means and Standard Deviations of MMPI Basic and Special Scales for the Black Male Cleveland Psychiatric Institute Sample at Three Educational Levels

	≤ 8 years (*N* = 31)		9-11 years (*N* = 47)		≥ 12 years (*N* = 24)			
Scale	Mean	S.D.	Mean	S.D.	Mean	S.D.	*F*	*p*
L	53.7	9.2	50.6	8.4	50.5	7.5	1.55	
F	73.3	12.0	70.6	14.3	68.8	14.9	0.74	
K	49.4	9.8	49.1	9.1	50.0	9.0	0.08	
Hs	66.0	13.9	61.3	13.8	58.1	14.5	2.24	
D	66.0	12.1	67.5	13.4	61.5	12.9	1.77	
Hy	59.3	11.0	59.5	12.4	59.5	10.0	0.00	
Pd	71.4	10.4	71.4	12.0	70.0	15.0	0.12	
Mf	59.8	8.7	59.0	10.1	59.9	10.0	0.10	
Pa	68.6	12.1	70.0	15.7	60.5	12.7	3.80	.05
Pt	65.4	11.3	68.6	14.9	66.3	13.4	0.58	
Sc	78.1	14.8	77.4	20.3	71.4	15.6	1.15	
Ma	69.7	11.9	69.5	11.2	69.8	10.4	0.01	
Si	55.7	6.6	55.2	8.9	53.2	9.6	0.66	
A	58.2	11.3	59.5	11.1	57.5	10.5	0.30	
R	50.3	13.2	47.2	11.2	47.5	9.5	0.74	
Es	35.5	10.9	38.1	12.1	39.8	10.2	1.00	
ORG	66.7	14.4	61.4	12.8	57.0	12.3	3.76	.05
HEA	62.6	11.2	58.0	9.8	56.2	12.5	2.68	
DEP	62.1	10.8	62.3	12.0	60.7	14.0	0.15	
MOR	56.0	9.3	56.9	10.2	55.4	12.4	0.16	
SOC	53.6	7.2	54.3	10.4	49.7	9.6	2.03	
HOS	53.5	10.1	54.7	9.5	54.6	10.2	0.15	
FAM	64.5	14.3	64.1	14.6	63.5	13.8	0.03	
AUT	56.6	9.7	58.0	9.5	59.7	7.5	0.75	
FEM	61.3	8.3	56.8	9.2	58.2	10.3	2.26	
PHO	66.9	10.5	63.3	15.4	56.9	10.0	4.10	.05
PSY	66.6	14.9	66.3	15.0	63.8	13.2	0.30	
HYP	54.9	10.8	57.4	9.5	57.4	8.6	0.74	
REL	54.8	7.7	52.1	8.1	55.0	7.7	1.61	

Table E-11. Means and Standard Deviations of MMPI Basic and Special Scales for the Black Female Cleveland Psychiatric Institute Sample at Three Educational Levels

	≤ 8 years (*N* = 35)		9-11 years (*N* = 83)		≥ 12 years (*N* = 39)			
Scale	**Mean**	**S.D.**	**Mean**	**S.D.**	**Mean**	**S.D.**	***F***	***p***
L	52.1	6.8	53.0	8.7	53.3	7.8	0.22	
F	70.3	13.9	65.8	13.5	64.3	13.6	2.05	
K	47.3	8.4	50.1	9.8	52.6	9.5	2.82	
Hs	57.5	10.4	58.6	11.2	56.9	11.6	0.33	
D	61.6	11.6	61.8	12.5	60.3	12.7	0.21	
Hy	55.3	11.0	59.0	12.0	59.8	10.5	1.68	
Pd	65.6	11.5	69.1	12.2	67.1	13.4	1.06	
Mf	59.3	10.0	54.1	9.3	50.4	7.8	8.73	.001
Pa	66.4	15.4	63.6	15.6	62.8	12.7	0.59	
Pt	60.8	12.0	61.0	11.9	58.6	10.9	0.61	
Sc	72.2	14.5	67.4	16.5	66.7	14.3	1.43	
Ma	64.6	14.6	63.7	10.7	63.7	13.9	0.08	
Si	58.2	9.0	57.2	8.4	55.6	9.8	0.84	
A	57.0	12.2	54.5	11.4	52.2	10.9	1.61	
R	46.2	12.8	49.0	10.8	48.1	10.4	0.81	
Es	38.7	12.0	42.2	12.9	44.5	11.9	2.03	
ORG	63.6	12.8	58.9	15.0	56.3	13.6	2.52	
HEA	56.9	10.9	59.3	10.9	54.4	11.0	2.66	
DEP	60.4	12.5	58.2	12.8	54.5	12.4	2.10	
MOR	56.1	11.5	53.6	11.1	51.5	11.3	1.53	
SOC	53.2	8.8	50.7	8.1	49.4	9.8	1.80	
HOS	56.8	9.8	54.3	10.2	51.5	8.1	2.75	
FAM	63.6	10.0	61.1	13.6	59.6	13.2	0.90	
AUT	60.0	8.7	58.0	10.2	53.7	11.3	3.86	.05
FEM	46.9	8.6	48.2	8.4	50.5	7.8	1.88	
PHO	59.3	12.2	57.6	9.8	53.7	8.7	3.16	.05
PSY	69.3	17.8	63.8	16.3	60.6	14.8	2.74	
HYP	55.9	13.5	54.6	10.3	52.9	10.0	0.71	
REL	54.8	8.8	51.6	7.3	53.1	8.6	2.09	

Table E-12. Means and Standard Deviations of MMPI Basic and Special Scales for the White Male Cleveland Psychiatric Institute Sample by Marital Status

	Single (N = 87)		Married (N = 98)		Other[a] (N = 77)			
Scale	Mean	S.D.	Mean	S.D.	Mean	S.D.	F	p
L	52.6	8.8	50.9	8.1	52.0	8.0	1.06	
F	66.0	14.1	59.9	11.6	62.8	11.9	5.44	.01
K	54.0	9.5	51.6	10.8	52.1	9.2	1.44	
Hs	63.8	16.2	60.5	13.5	62.0	15.0	1.09	
D	71.0	18.1	68.4	16.9	69.3	17.8	0.48	
Hy	62.5	12.1	61.5	10.1	61.7	11.3	0.17	
Pd	70.2	12.2	65.5	12.0	69.1	12.4	0.50	
Mf	59.7	9.8	56.0	9.7	60.5	11.1	5.13	.01
Pa	63.6	12.6	59.9	11.9	60.3	10.9	2.53	
Pt	67.4	14.6	64.6	14.2	64.7	13.8	1.07	
Sc	73.3	17.8	63.5	16.3	68.5	16.0	7.90	.001
Ma	63.4	12.6	62.5	12.6	62.8	10.2	0.15	
Si	56.3	10.7	54.5	11.1	54.2	11.1	0.96	
A	54.8	10.8	55.0	12.4	56.1	11.7	0.30	
R	53.4	12.5	49.8	11.0	49.9	9.7	2.87	
Es	41.5	11.5	43.6	11.0	41.6	11.9	0.99	
ORG	59.2	14.9	55.8	13.1	58.7	15.2	1.52	
HEA	58.6	13.3	56.1	12.1	57.4	13.5	0.84	
DEP	58.5	12.4	58.2	12.6	60.0	13.9	0.46	
MOR	54.3	11.1	54.9	11.6	54.8	12.1	0.07	
SOC	55.0	10.8	53.2	12.9	52.5	11.9	0.99	
HOS	49.9	9.4	51.0	9.3	50.6	9.0	0.29	
FAM	60.0	14.4	57.3	11.6	60.9	13.9	1.53	
AUT	53.1	9.6	54.2	10.0	56.0	10.0	1.80	
FEM	56.8	10.1	52.7	10.6	57.2	9.1	5.60	.01
PHO	59.0	12.5	56.1	12.7	56.0	11.2	1.70	
PSY	57.8	12.6	54.4	12.0	56.1	11.2	1.87	
HYP	52.0	9.5	54.9	10.4	54.7	9.7	2.40	
REL	52.0	8.9	49.9	8.3	50.9	8.8	1.31	

[a]Includes those not currently living with spouse (divorced, separated, widowed).

Table E-13. Means and Standard Deviations of MMPI Basic and Special Scales for the White Female Cleveland Psychiatric Institute Sample by Marital Status

	Single (N = 85)		Married (N = 172)		Other[a] (N = 152)			
Scale	Mean	S.D.	Mean	S.D.	Mean	S.D.	F	p
L	54.8	9.5	54.2	8.3	53.8	8.8	0.39	
F	65.1	12.8	62.0	13.2	63.8	12.7	1.90	
K	54.4	10.1	52.4	9.4	51.0	9.2	3.46	.05
Hs	59.1	13.5	60.1	12.2	59.1	13.4	0.31	
D	64.4	15.4	63.8	15.5	65.5	13.9	0.51	
Hy	61.9	12.1	62.8	12.5	60.4	11.7	1.68	
Pd	71.2	13.5	66.1	12.0	67.8	11.5	5.08	.01
Mf	51.4	9.4	52.1	10.5	51.8	10.3	0.16	
Pa	66.2	12.8	63.4	12.4	64.2	12.6	1.39	
Pt	64.8	13.6	62.6	12.7	62.7	11.6	1.30	
Sc	72.1	16.1	66.3	15.5	66.3	14.0	4.87	.01
Ma	63.2	12.7	61.7	12.8	61.6	12.6	0.48	
Si	58.9	10.9	57.8	10.8	58.9	10.2	0.54	
A	54.3	11.5	53.4	10.9	54.7	10.3	0.66	
R	51.0	12.5	50.6	11.7	51.1	12.8	0.06	
Es	44.6	11.4	43.7	11.5	42.9	10.6	0.67	
ORG	56.2	14.5	58.2	14.6	56.6	13.6	0.74	
HEA	55.4	11.8	56.9	12.3	56.5	12.6	0.43	
DEP	58.2	14.7	57.6	13.4	58.8	12.7	0.34	
MOR	53.5	11.3	53.3	11.6	54.7	10.6	0.69	
SOC	53.6	11.4	51.4	10.8	53.1	10.8	1.51	
HOS	50.9	10.6	50.4	9.7	51.9	10.6	0.90	
FAM	62.0	14.5	57.2	12.6	60.8	13.9	4.77	.01
AUT	52.0	11.1	52.5	11.1	54.6	12.0	1.90	
FEM	47.0	8.4	48.6	8.8	47.4	10.1	1.08	
PHO	52.7	10.7	54.3	11.3	54.9	11.0	1.13	
PSY	60.0	14.7	58.4	14.6	59.0	15.6	0.35	
HYP	51.1	11.2	53.2	9.2	53.0	10.9	1.31	
REL	50.1	9.5	50.6	8.9	48.4	9.9	2.29	

[a]Includes those not currently living with spouse (divorced, separated, widowed).

Table E-14. Means and Standard Deviations of MMPI Basic and Special Scales for the Black Male Cleveland Psychiatric Institute Sample by Marital Status

	Single (*N* = 29)		Married (*N* = 26)		Other[a] (*N* = 47)			
Scale	Mean	S.D.	Mean	S.D.	Mean	S.D.	*F*	*p*
L	53.6	9.4	51.3	8.5	50.3	7.9	1.32	
F	72.7	14.5	72.3	13.2	69.2	13.7	0.74	
K	51.9	10.4	48.5	7.6	48.4	9.2	1.47	
Hs	63.7	17.7	61.4	12.6	61.3	12.7	0.28	
D	64.5	13.8	64.3	13.0	67.1	12.6	0.52	
Hy	59.2	13.0	59.2	8.6	59.6	11.8	0.02	
Pd	69.6	12.7	72.9	13.0	70.9	11.6	0.49	
Mf	60.0	10.9	57.8	9.9	60.1	8.6	0.53	
Pa	64.8	13.7	69.3	14.0	67.9	15.1	0.71	
Pt	64.6	13.5	67.0	14.5	68.7	12.9	0.84	
Sc	78.2	19.6	74.5	16.3	75.9	17.6	0.29	
Ma	68.8	11.9	70.0	8.9	69.9	11.9	0.11	
Si	55.4	7.3	56.0	9.7	54.0	8.4	0.54	
A	56.4	11.2	59.3	10.0	59.6	11.3	0.84	
R	51.4	12.2	46.7	9.1	47.0	11.9	1.65	
Es	39.7	11.7	39.7	9.8	35.4	11.7	1.82	
ORG	61.4	15.4	61.8	12.2	62.5	13.3	0.05	
HEA	60.1	14.0	57.7	10.0	59.0	9.7	0.34	
DEP	58.9	11.7	63.9	12.1	62.6	12.1	1.35	
MOR	53.3	9.5	58.0	10.5	57.1	10.8	1.70	
SOC	55.4	8.6	54.3	10.9	50.8	8.8	2.51	
HOS	53.0	11.3	55.7	7.2	54.4	10.1	0.52	
FAM	65.7	13.8	62.3	14.9	64.2	14.2	0.39	
AUT	55.4	11.3	58.8	7.8	59.1	8.2	1.58	
FEM	57.8	9.2	55.0	9.7	60.8	8.6	3.46	.05
PHO	60.6	13.3	61.5	14.0	65.1	12.8	1.23	
PSY	62.7	13.8	67.0	13.0	67.0	15.6	0.91	
HYP	53.4	10.1	57.3	8.8	58.3	15.6	2.40	
REL	51.0	9.5	52.3	8.2	55.9	6.0	3.99	.05

[a]Includes those not currently living with spouse (divorced, separated, widowed).

Table E-15. Means and Standard Deviations of MMPI Basic and Special Scales for the Black Female Cleveland Psychiatric Institute Sample by Marital Status

	Single (*N* = 39)		Married (*N* = 43)		Other[a] (*N* = 81)			
Scale	Mean	S.D.	Mean	S.D.	Mean	S.D.	*F*	*p*
L	51.6	7.5	53.8	6.5	52.9	8.9	0.80	
F	66.4	12.2	64.6	14.9	67.6	14.1	0.66	
K	48.4	8.9	52.0	8.1	49.6	10.4	1.59	
Hs	56.4	9.8	57.6	9.7	58.7	12.2	0.61	
D	60.2	11.2	58.5	12.2	63.3	12.4	2.45	
Hy	58.5	11.9	56.2	9.6	58.9	12.3	0.81	
Pd	71.3	13.5	64.6	11.5	67.3	12.0	3.02	
Mf	56.6	8.1	56.1	9.4	52.7	10.0	3.10	.05
Pa	64.4	12.8	62.7	16.7	65.2	15.4	0.37	
Pt	60.6	11.2	58.6	12.7	61.1	11.4	0.66	
Sc	68.5	15.0	67.7	16.3	68.7	15.8	0.06	
Ma	66.5	13.1	65.7	12.4	62.2	11.8	2.02	
Si	55.8	9.1	56.6	8.7	58.0	9.1	0.85	
A	55.4	11.3	52.0	10.1	55.8	12.2	1.67	
R	46.3	10.6	46.7	11.3	49.6	11.2	1.60	
Es	43.6	10.5	43.8	11.6	39.9	13.7	1.83	
ORG	58.8	14.0	59.0	13.5	59.9	14.8	0.09	
HEA	57.4	10.8	56.1	10.7	58.6	11.1	0.74	
DEP	59.0	12.4	54.9	11.5	59.4	13.6	1.92	
MOR	55.4	11.9	51.0	9.6	54.4	11.6	1.85	
SOC	49.2	8.3	51.0	7.9	51.6	9.3	1.01	
HOS	55.4	10.2	53.9	7.9	54.0	10.4	0.33	
FAM	62.6	14.4	58.9	10.8	61.8	12.6	1.02	
AUT	60.1	10.1	56.6	9.7	56.5	10.7	1.74	
FEM	47.9	8.3	48.1	7.6	48.9	8.8	0.24	
PHO	57.3	10.2	56.1	10.0	57.5	10.4	0.28	
PSY	65.9	15.5	62.7	15.7	64.7	17.5	0.40	
HYP	55.9	10.5	52.8	10.1	54.8	11.8	0.84	
REL	52.5	6.8	52.5	8.5	53.0	8.4	0.07	

[a]Includes those not currently living with spouse (divorced, separated, widowed).

Table E-16. Means and Standard Deviations of MMPI Basic and Special Scales for the White Male Cleveland Psychiatric Institute Sample at Three Socioeconomic Levels

	Lower-Lower (N = 70)		Upper-Lower (N = 48)		Lower-Middle (N = 144)			
Scale	Mean	S.D.	Mean	S.D.	Mean	S.D.	F	p
L	53.8	9.2	50.5	8.3	51.3	7.7	3.05	.05
F	64.5	13.0	62.1	11.0	62.2	13.2	0.87	
K	52.6	11.3	51.2	8.1	53.0	9.8	0.57	
Hs	62.8	16.4	59.5	15.1	60.6	13.5	5.24	.01
D	72.0	15.4	66.6	18.7	69.3	18.0	1.35	
Hy	62.4	12.3	60.5	11.9	62.1	10.3	0.49	
Pd	69.0	11.1	68.4	12.8	69.7	12.5	0.21	
Mf	56.1	10.0	58.2	8.3	59.8	10.9	3.17	.05
Pa	61.7	12.4	59.0	12.4	61.8	11.5	1.01	
Pt	67.0	13.5	61.5	14.0	66.2	14.5	2.53	
Sc	70.8	16.2	65.2	17.2	68.0	17.5	1.56	
Ma	61.7	11.9	62.8	10.4	63.5	12.3	0.58	
Si	57.2	10.4	54.3	10.9	54.2	11.3	1.84	
A	56.3	11.8	54.4	9.5	55.1	12.3	0.42	
R	52.4	11.4	49.8	10.3	50.7	11.5	0.79	
Es	38.3	12.0	43.6	11.5	43.9	10.8	6.26	.01
ORG	62.2	15.4	55.6	12.8	56.4	14.0	4.69	.01
HEA	60.1	11.8	56.0	13.6	56.4	13.1	2.28	
DEP	59.6	12.7	57.9	11.7	58.8	13.4	0.25	
MOR	55.6	11.3	54.8	10.1	54.2	12.1	0.37	
SOC	55.1	11.8	53.4	11.7	53.0	12.1	0.74	
HOS	50.5	9.3	49.2	7.7	51.0	9.6	0.65	
FAM	57.6	13.5	62.4	13.1	59.0	15.1	1.66	
AUT	54.8	10.0	56.7	8.4	53.3	10.3	2.24	
FEM	57.5	8.8	53.4	9.8	55.0	10.8	2.54	
PHO	61.4	12.9	54.5	10.4	55.8	12.1	6.36	.01
PSY	57.7	13.4	54.1	10.3	55.8	11.8	1.30	
HYP	52.7	11.2	55.0	7.9	54.1	9.9	0.79	
REL	51.7	9.0	51.0	9.1	50.5	8.4	0.51	

Table E-17. Means and Standard Deviations of MMPI Basic and Special Scales for the White Female Cleveland Psychiatric Institute Sample at Three Socioeconomic Levels

	Lower-Lower (N = 90)		Upper-Lower (N = 103)		Lower-Middle (N = 216)			
Scale	Mean	S.D.	Mean	S.D.	Mean	S.D.	F	p
L	55.8	8.9	52.9	8.4	54.1	8.7	2.62	
F	65.3	12.4	64.2	12.8	62.1	13.1	2.24	
K	51.1	9.3	50.7	9.9	53.6	9.3	4.07	.05
Hs	62.7	14.2	60.5	12.5	57.8	12.3	4.94	.01
D	65.9	12.7	65.6	13.6	63.5	16.2	1.13	
Hy	61.9	13.5	61.1	12.6	61.9	11.4	0.17	
Pd	68.4	11.5	67.4	12.3	67.8	12.6	0.18	
Mf	55.2	9.9	53.7	10.5	50.0	9.7	12.65	.001
Pa	64.4	14.4	66.2	11.9	63.4	12.0	1.70	
Pt	62.7	12.8	63.3	11.4	62.7	12.9	0.09	
Sc	67.4	15.7	68.4	13.4	67.1	15.9	0.26	
Ma	61.3	13.1	62.3	11.3	62.1	13.2	0.16	
Si	60.7	9.4	58.7	9.4	57.3	11.4	3.25	.05
A	55.1	10.4	55.2	10.5	53.1	11.1	1.81	
R	52.6	12.7	50.0	12.0	50.6	12.1	1.25	
Es	40.0	11.3	41.3	10.5	46.2	10.7	13.52	.001
ORG	59.4	14.5	60.4	13.5	54.8	14.1	7.04	.001
HEA	60.5	12.9	57.6	11.8	54.3	11.9	8.94	.001
DEP	59.1	12.4	59.5	12.3	57.2	14.3	1.28	
MOR	54.8	10.0	55.7	10.7	52.6	11.7	3.12	.05
SOC	54.4	10.6	52.5	9.8	51.7	11.5	1.97	
HOS	51.3	10.5	51.9	10.0	50.6	10.2	0.60	
FAM	60.5	12.9	58.5	12.9	59.6	14.3	0.54	
AUT	55.8	11.8	54.1	11.5	51.7	11.1	4.56	.05
FEM	47.1	9.6	47.2	10.3	48.4	8.5	1.02	
PHO	57.2	11.0	54.5	11.2	52.8	10.9	5.14	.01
PSY	60.4	16.4	60.9	14.2	57.4	14.6	2.42	
HYP	52.8	11.3	52.8	10.6	52.6	9.7	0.03	
REL	50.9	8.7	49.2	9.6	49.3	9.6	1.05	

Table E-18. Means and Standard Deviations of MMPI Basic and Special Scales for the Black Male Cleveland Psychiatric Institute Sample at Three Socioeconomic Levels

	Lower-Lower (*N* = 33)		Upper-Lower (*N* = 28)		Lower-Middle (*N* = 42)			
Scale	Mean	S.D.	Mean	S.D.	Mean	S.D.	*F*	*p*
L	52.0	9.1	50.1	8.5	52.1	8.1	0.55	
F	74.0	12.2	71.6	10.9	67.8	16.2	1.99	
K	47.3	9.9	48.6	7.7	51.9	9.4	2.54	
Hs	64.5	13.8	59.9	13.7	61.7	14.7	0.82	
D	67.0	11.8	67.8	14.2	63.3	12.9	1.24	
Hy	58.4	10.9	59.3	13.2	60.8	10.8	0.42	
Pd	70.5	10.6	70.0	12.6	72.3	13.2	0.34	
Mf	61.2	8.9	57.8	7.8	59.6	11.2	0.98	
Pa	70.0	12.0	67.9	16.9	65.2	14.2	0.89	
Pt	68.0	11.2	68.1	13.1	65.5	15.4	0.46	
Sc	80.8	13.9	76.7	16.3	71.6	20.8	2.54	
Ma	70.1	12.0	69.7	9.8	69.0	11.5	0.09	
Si	57.4	6.5	56.0	8.5	52.0	9.1	4.46	.05
A	60.9	11.3	60.4	10.1	55.2	10.8	3.22	.05
R	48.3	13.7	48.4	11.2	48.2	9.6	0.00	
Es	32.3	10.3	36.0	11.1	43.6	10.0	11.51	.001
ORG	67.4	13.1	62.8	11.1	57.2	13.8	5.82	.01
HEA	63.1	11.0	57.8	9.4	56.5	11.4	3.74	.05
DEP	63.8	10.6	64.0	10.7	58.7	13.5	2.34	
MOR	58.9	9.8	56.5	10.4	53.6	10.8	2.48	
SOC	54.7	6.2	55.2	11.5	49.9	9.5	3.66	.05
HOS	55.0	10.2	55.0	9.2	53.1	9.9	0.47	
FAM	67.2	12.8	61.3	14.3	63.1	15.2	1.45	
AUT	57.6	8.9	58.4	9.1	57.5	10.0	0.10	
FEM	61.6	8.3	59.6	8.7	55.2	9.5	5.09	.01
PHO	68.6	10.5	66.4	13.6	55.7	12.1	12.32	.001
PSY	69.3	14.6	66.5	13.0	62.0	15.0	2.46	
HYP	56.9	10.8	56.8	8.3	56.1	9.8	0.07	
REL	56.4	7.3	55.3	6.6	49.9	8.2	8.21	.001

Table E-19. Means and Standard Deviations of MMPI Basic and Special Scales for the Black Female Cleveland Psychiatric Institute Sample at Three Socioeconomic Levels

	Lower-Lower (*N* = 68)		Upper-Lower (*N* = 44)		Lower-Middle (*N* = 51)			
Scale	Mean	S.D.	Mean	S.D.	Mean	S.D.	*F*	*p*
L	52.3	7.9	53.7	7.9	52.9	8.2	0.43	
F	69.4	14.4	66.9	12.0	62.4	13.8	3.84	.05
K	48.1	9.6	50.8	8.7	51.6	9.9	2.18	
Hs	59.1	11.9	59.3	10.7	55.0	9.7	2.56	
D	63.0	11.9	64.0	12.3	56.7	11.4	5.68	.01
Hy	58.4	11.8	60.9	12.0	55.4	10.4	2.82	
Pd	67.3	11.9	70.5	12.9	65.3	12.3	2.16	
Mf	56.3	10.2	53.2	10.2	53.2	7.6	2.05	
Pa	66.6	14.9	65.8	13.6	60.1	16.1	2.98	
Pt	61.7	12.3	62.2	10.2	56.8	11.5	3.50	.05
Sc	71.7	16.1	69.2	12.9	63.2	16.1	4.61	.05
Ma	64.4	13.6	63.2	12.5	64.7	10.6	0.20	
Si	58.6	8.3	57.0	9.1	55.1	9.5	2.37	
A	56.5	11.9	55.7	10.4	51.3	11.3	3.29	.05
R	47.7	11.9	48.7	9.6	47.8	11.5	0.12	
Es	39.8	12.3	41.9	12.1	44.5	13.0	2.14	
ORG	63.4	14.4	59.0	12.2	54.4	14.2	6.32	.01
HEA	59.8	11.7	58.0	8.8	54.4	10.8	3.67	.05
DEP	60.4	12.8	59.7	12.2	53.9	12.5	4.30	.05
MOR	55.8	11.5	54.2	10.1	50.5	11.4	3.30	.05
SOC	52.9	7.9	50.7	8.8	48.5	9.3	3.88	.05
HOS	56.2	10.0	53.9	9.2	52.2	9.6	2.50	
FAM	61.9	11.8	63.1	14.2	58.7	12.1	1.60	
AUT	58.8	9.8	55.1	10.4	57.4	10.8	1.73	
FEM	47.1	8.8	48.5	8.0	50.2	7.9	2.06	
PHO	58.3	11.0	56.2	9.4	56.2	9.8	0.88	
PSY	67.6	17.1	64.7	15.4	60.2	16.0	2.96	
HYP	54.9	13.1	55.1	9.1	53.5	9.5	0.32	
REL	53.4	8.0	50.9	8.6	53.5	7.4	1.63	

Table E-20. Means and Standard Deviations of MMPI Basic and Special Scales for the White Male Cleveland Psychiatric Institute Sample at Two Socioeconomic Levels of Parents

	Lower (N = 105)		Lower-Middle (N = 157)			
Scale	Mean	S.D.	Mean	S.D.	F	p
L	52.2	8.8	51.5	8.0	0.45	
F	61.6	11.6	63.6	13.5	1.56	
K	52.1	10.8	52.8	9.3	0.37	
Hs	62.4	15.1	61.8	14.8	0.13	
D	69.8	17.7	69.3	17.5	0.04	
Hy	62.1	11.3	61.8	11.1	0.04	
Pd	69.2	12.4	69.3	12.0	0.01	
Mf	57.2	11.0	59.4	9.8	3.04	
Pa	60.7	12.8	61.6	11.3	0.36	
Pt	65.0	14.2	65.9	14.2	0.26	
Sc	66.6	15.9	69.3	17.9	1.67	
Ma	61.4	11.6	63.9	12.0	2.76	
Si	55.6	10.5	54.6	11.3	0.47	
A	55.6	11.8	55.1	11.6	0.13	
R	51.1	10.9	51.0	11.5	0.01	
Es	41.8	12.1	42.7	11.0	0.37	
ORG	57.6	15.0	57.9	14.0	0.03	
HEA	57.4	11.8	57.3	13.6	0.00	
DEP	59.2	12.7	58.6	13.1	0.14	
MOR	55.3	11.9	54.2	11.3	0.62	
SOC	53.9	11.9	53.4	12.0	0.09	
HOS	50.8	9.5	50.3	9.1	0.15	
FAM	58.6	14.4	59.6	14.4	0.28	
AUT	54.8	9.6	54.0	10.1	0.33	
FEM	55.2	10.1	55.5	10.3	0.05	
PHO	56.9	12.0	57.1	12.5	0.02	
PSY	55.9	12.5	56.1	11.7	0.01	
HYP	53.6	10.2	54.1	9.8	0.14	
REL	51.0	9.0	50.8	8.4	0.03	

Table E-21. Means and Standard Deviations of MMPI Basic and Special Scales for the White Female Cleveland Psychiatric Institute Sample at Two Socioeconomic Levels of Parents

	Lower (N = 175)		Lower-Middle (N = 234)			
Scale	Mean	S.D.	Mean	S.D.	F	p
L	54.5	9.2	54.0	8.4	0.29	
F	63.9	13.2	62.8	12.8	0.75	
K	51.7	9.8	52.8	9.3	1.41	
Hs	61.2	12.7	58.3	13.0	4.86	.05
D	66.2	14.8	63.4	14.9	3.63	
Hy	62.4	12.3	61.3	12.0	0.86	
Pd	68.6	12.5	67.2	12.1	1.29	
Mf	53.2	9.2	50.9	10.8	5.26	.05
Pa	64.9	13.1	63.9	12.2	0.66	
Pt	64.3	12.2	61.9	12.7	3.68	
Sc	69.0	16.0	66.4	14.6	2.85	
Ma	62.2	13.3	61.8	12.3	0.09	
Si	59.1	10.2	58.0	10.8	1.05	
A	55.0	10.7	53.4	10.9	2.20	
R	51.8	12.7	50.2	11.9	1.72	
Es	41.2	10.7	45.4	11.1	14.60	.001
ORG	60.0	13.8	55.1	14.2	11.80	.001
HEA	58.1	12.4	55.3	12.1	5.36	.05
DEP	59.7	13.2	57.0	13.5	4.09	.05
MOR	54.8	11.3	53.2	11.0	2.29	
SOC	52.9	10.5	52.1	11.3	0.55	
HOS	51.9	10.2	51.1	10.2	0.00	
FAM	59.4	14.0	59.6	13.4	0.03	
AUT	54.3	11.3	52.3	11.5	3.16	
FEM	48.0	8.3	47.7	9.9	0.13	
PHO	55.4	11.4	53.3	10.8	3.87	.05
PSY	60.3	15.3	58.0	14.7	2.33	
HYP	53.1	10.8	52.3	9.9	0.60	
REL	50.4	8.7	49.1	9.9	1.68	

Table E-22. Means and Standard Deviations of MMPI Basic and Special Scales for the Black Male Cleveland Psychiatric Institute Sample at Two Socioeconomic Levels of Parents

	Lower (*N* = 59)		Lower-Middle (*N* = 44)			
Scale	Mean	S.D.	Mean	S.D.	*F*	*p*
L	51.1	8.5	52.1	8.5	0.35	
F	71.3	12.3	70.2	15.8	0.18	
K	48.2	9.1	51.4	9.3	3.03	
Hs	61.5	14.3	62.9	14.1	0.27	
D	65.9	12.9	65.5	13.2	0.03	
Hy	58.5	11.3	61.1	11.6	1.27	
Pd	69.8	12.0	72.8	12.3	1.52	
Mf	59.7	9.4	59.5	10.0	0.02	
Pa	67.0	14.4	67.7	14.4	0.06	
Pt	67.0	13.1	67.0	14.1	0.00	
Sc	77.7	17.1	73.7	18.8	1.27	
Ma	70.1	10.1	68.8	12.5	0.32	
Si	55.3	7.0	54.1	10.1	0.52	
A	59.9	10.6	56.6	11.3	2.23	
R	47.2	11.0	49.8	11.9	1.33	
Es	36.0	11.1	40.5	11.5	4.01	.05
ORG	64.3	12.9	58.9	13.8	4.10	.05
HEA	58.7	10.7	59.3	11.6	0.07	
DEP	62.1	11.2	61.3	13.3	0.09	
MOR	57.4	10.3	54.3	10.6	2.29	
SOC	53.5	8.8	52.1	10.3	0.49	
HOS	55.3	9.5	52.8	10.1	1.60	
FAM	64.9	13.7	62.6	15.0	0.63	
AUT	58.9	8.3	56.3	10.5	2.05	
FEM	59.4	9.5	57.0	8.9	1.69	
PHO	65.0	13.4	59.8	12.8	3.94	.05
PSY	67.7	14.3	62.8	14.6	2.99	
HYP	57.4	9.4	55.5	10.1	0.96	
REL	54.4	7.9	52.2	8.2	1.89	

Table E-23. Means and Standard Deviations of MMPI Basic and Special Scales for the Black Female Cleveland Psychiatric Institute Sample at Two Socioeconomic Levels of Parents

	Lower (N = 86)		Lower-Middle (N = 77)			
Scale	Mean	S.D.	Mean	S.D.	F	p
L	52.7	8.2	53.0	7.8	0.08	
F	67.9	14.0	65.0	13.6	1.84	
K	49.2	9.7	50.7	9.4	0.97	
Hs	59.1	12.1	56.5	9.5	2.15	
D	62.8	11.7	59.6	12.6	2.78	
Hy	59.3	12.3	56.8	10.6	2.03	
Pd	67.7	11.9	67.3	13.0	0.04	
Mf	54.4	9.7	54.6	9.4	0.03	
Pa	66.2	13.9	62.3	16.2	2.83	
Pt	62.2	11.7	58.3	11.4	4.59	.05
Sc	70.8	15.1	65.6	15.9	4.53	.05
Ma	65.5	13.0	62.7	11.6	2.04	
Si	58.2	8.6	55.8	9.3	2.91	
A	56.5	11.6	52.7	11.2	4.40	.05
R	47.7	9.7	48.3	12.6	0.12	
Es	40.1	13.0	43.8	11.8	3.50	
ORG	61.1	14.9	57.5	13.3	2.61	
HEA	58.8	12.2	56.4	9.2	2.01	
DEP	59.6	12.1	56.5	13.4	2.39	
MOR	55.1	11.1	52.2	11.3	2.84	
SOC	52.0	9.1	49.6	8.2	3.07	
HOS	54.8	9.8	53.8	9.7	0.46	
FAM	62.9	13.4	59.3	11.4	3.41	
AUT	57.9	10.5	56.8	10.2	0.52	
FEM	48.8	8.0	48.0	8.8	0.37	
PHO	57.9	10.6	56.2	9.7	1.16	
PSY	66.6	15.9	62.1	17.0	3.12	
HYP	55.7	11.1	53.2	10.9	3.02	
REL	53.7	7.7	51.7	8.3	2.41	

Table E-24. Means and Standard Deviations of MMPI Basic and Special Scales for the White Male Cleveland Psychiatric Institute Sample with Respect to Upward Mobility in Socioeconomic Status

	Absent (N = 122)		Present (N = 140)			
Scale	Mean	S.D.	Mean	S.D.	F	p
L	51.2	8.2	52.3	8.4	1.01	
F	64.9	13.5	60.9	11.9	6.44	.05
K	52.6	10.1	52.5	9.8	0.01	
Hs	64.7	15.8	59.7	13.6	7.50	.01
D	71.1	17.6	68.1	17.4	1.89	
Hy	62.9	11.4	61.0	10.8	1.75	
Pd	69.8	12.4	68.7	12.0	0.54	
Mf	58.1	9.0	58.9	11.4	0.44	
Pa	61.9	12.5	60.7	11.4	0.72	
Pt	67.0	14.8	64.3	13.6	2.28	
Sc	71.2	17.9	65.7	16.1	6.89	.01
Ma	64.8	12.1	61.2	11.4	6.05	.05
Si	55.1	10.6	54.9	11.4	0.02	
A	55.8	11.9	54.9	11.5	0.41	
R	51.6	12.3	50.5	10.3	0.70	
Es	41.3	11.7	43.2	11.2	1.68	
ORG	60.0	15.0	56.0	13.6	5.11	.05
HEA	59.2	12.8	55.7	12.8	4.97	.05
DEP	59.3	13.7	58.4	12.2	0.29	
MOR	55.1	11.5	54.2	11.6	0.37	
SOC	53.9	11.7	53.3	12.2	0.20	
HOS	50.8	9.3	50.3	9.2	0.19	
FAM	60.1	14.2	58.5	14.5	0.83	
AUT	55.1	9.8	53.7	10.0	1.28	
FEM	55.1	9.8	55.6	10.5	0.20	
PHO	57.6	12.2	56.5	12.4	0.51	
PSY	57.2	13.0	55.0	11.0	2.17	
HYP	54.2	10.6	53.6	9.4	0.26	
REL	50.9	9.3	50.9	8.1	0.01	

Table E-25. Means and Standard Deviations of MMPI Basic and Special Scales for the White Female Cleveland Psychiatric Institute Sample with Respect to Upward Mobility in Socioeconomic Status

	Absent (N = 206)		Present (N = 203)			
Scale	Mean	S.D.	Mean	S.D.	F	p
L	54.0	8.7	54.4	8.8	0.16	
F	63.1	11.7	63.5	14.1	0.09	
K	52.3	9.4	52.3	9.7	0.00	
Hs	59.0	12.7	60.1	13.2	0.62	
D	64.0	13.2	65.1	16.4	0.55	
Hy	61.2	11.9	62.2	12.4	0.69	
Pd	67.7	11.5	67.9	13.0	0.03	
Mf	51.5	10.4	52.3	10.0	0.67	
Pa	64.9	12.0	63.7	13.1	0.83	
Pt	62.7	11.7	63.1	13.3	0.13	
Sc	67.3	14.5	67.7	16.0	0.06	
Ma	62.0	12.2	62.0	13.2	0.00	
Si	58.8	9.9	58.0	11.2	0.59	
A	53.9	10.8	54.2	10.9	0.06	
R	51.3	12.6	50.5	11.9	0.37	
Es	43.8	11.1	43.4	11.2	0.18	
ORG	56.8	13.9	57.6	14.6	0.27	
HEA	56.6	12.3	56.3	12.3	0.06	
DEP	57.6	13.0	58.8	13.8	0.75	
MOR	53.9	10.9	53.8	11.4	0.01	
SOC	53.2	10.6	51.7	11.2	1.99	
HOS	50.9	10.5	51.3	9.9	0.14	
FAM	59.6	12.9	59.4	14.4	0.03	
AUT	52.2	11.7	54.2	11.1	3.16	
FEM	47.4	10.1	48.3	8.2	0.87	
PHO	54.6	11.2	53.8	11.1	0.44	
PSY	58.9	14.4	59.0	15.6	0.01	
HYP	52.1	10.4	53.2	10.2	1.10	
REL	50.1	9.7	49.2	9.1	0.77	

Table E-26. Means and Standard Deviations of MMPI Basic and Special Scales for the Black Male Cleveland Psychiatric Institute Sample with Respect to Upward Mobility in Socioeconomic Status

	Absent (N = 48)		Present (N = 55)			
Scale	Mean	S.D.	Mean	S.D.	F	p
L	51.2	8.9	51.8	8.2	0.13	
F	72.3	13.9	69.5	13.8	1.07	
K	49.0	9.0	50.0	9.5	0.31	
Hs	63.0	13.8	61.3	14.5	0.36	
D	67.4	13.4	64.2	12.5	1.57	
Hy	59.4	11.5	59.8	11.5	0.03	
Pd	72.8	11.6	69.6	12.6	1.69	
Mf	60.4	10.0	58.9	9.3	0.58	
Pa	68.8	14.2	66.1	14.5	0.91	
Pt	68.8	12.7	65.4	14.0	1.68	
Sc	78.5	16.3	73.7	19.0	1.84	
Ma	70.6	11.4	68.5	10.9	0.89	
Si	55.9	8.4	53.8	8.5	1.61	
A	59.9	10.8	57.2	11.1	1.51	
R	48.6	12.8	47.9	10.1	0.10	
Es	36.8	12.3	38.9	10.7	0.91	
ORG	64.7	13.8	59.6	12.9	3.65	
HEA	60.2	9.5	57.8	12.2	1.18	
DEP	63.3	10.7	60.4	13.1	1.44	
MOR	57.5	10.1	54.8	10.8	1.65	
SOC	53.6	9.6	52.3	9.5	0.53	
HOS	55.3	9.6	53.3	9.9	1.16	
FAM	64.8	13.7	63.2	14.8	0.32	
AUT	57.5	8.7	58.0	10.0	0.07	
FEM	60.4	9.1	56.7	9.2	4.31	.05
PHO	64.3	13.2	61.4	13.4	1.21	
PSY	67.0	13.8	64.3	15.2	0.87	
HYP	56.5	10.1	56.6	9.4	0.00	
REL	53.6	7.7	53.3	8.3	0.02	

Table E-27. Means and Standard Deviations of MMPI Basic and Special Scales for the Black Female Cleveland Psychiatric Institute Sample with Respect to Upward Mobility in Socioeconomic Status

	Absent ($N = 55$)		Present ($N = 108$)			
Scale	Mean	S.D.	Mean	S.D.	F	p
L	53.5	8.4	52.5	7.8	0.53	
F	67.9	12.9	65.8	14.4	0.81	
K	49.4	10.1	50.2	9.3	0.28	
Hs	57.3	11.4	58.1	10.9	0.21	
D	62.5	12.1	60.7	12.2	0.81	
Hy	57.8	10.9	58.3	11.9	0.07	
Pd	68.9	13.1	66.8	12.0	1.03	
Mf	55.6	9.4	53.9	9.6	1.20	
Pa	64.1	12.9	64.5	16.2	0.02	
Pt	60.5	11.0	60.2	12.1	0.02	
Sc	69.0	15.2	68.1	16.0	0.12	
Ma	62.1	13.5	65.2	11.7	2.34	
Si	56.7	8.6	57.3	9.2	0.17	
A	54.8	11.9	54.6	11.4	0.01	
R	47.0	10.9	48.6	11.3	0.73	
Es	41.9	11.4	41.8	13.1	0.00	
ORG	60.3	13.9	58.9	14.4	0.37	
HEA	56.8	10.7	58.1	11.0	0.50	
DEP	58.9	13.5	57.8	12.5	0.26	
MOR	54.4	11.4	53.4	11.2	0.30	
SOC	51.2	7.9	50.7	9.2	0.12	
HOS	55.5	9.6	53.7	9.8	1.33	
FAM	60.6	13.0	61.5	12.5	0.18	
AUT	58.2	10.6	56.9	10.2	0.57	
FEM	48.3	8.3	48.5	8.4	0.02	
PHO	57.1	10.3	57.1	10.2	0.00	
PSY	64.2	16.7	64.6	16.5	0.02	
HYP	55.0	11.8	54.2	10.7	0.19	
REL	53.3	8.0	52.5	8.1	0.40	

Table E-28. Relative Cross-Validational Accuracy of Discriminant Function Categorization of White and Black Psychiatric Patients, Using Standard and Rs-Corrected Profiles

Dependent Variable	Sex	Standard Profiles White (1)	Standard Profiles Black (2)	Rs-Corrected Black (3)	1 vs. 2	1 vs. 3	2 vs. 3
Diagnosis	M	48/108 (44%)	38/75 (51%)	26/75 (35%)			7.56**
	M	40/102 (39%)	28/75 (37%)	28/75 (37%)			
	F	93/186 (50%)	84/146 (58%)	70/146 (48%)			
	F	96/180 (53%)	81/146 (55%)	73/146 (50%)			
Somatic concern	M	72/120 (60%)	57/92 (62%)	56/92 (61%)			
	M	69/112 (62%)	52/92 (57%)	65/92 (71%)			6.86*
	F	110/188 (59%)	84/156 (54%)	91/156 (58%)			
	F	96/169 (57%)	80/156 (51%)	71/156 (46%)			
Anxiety	M	65/118 (55%)	49/92 (53%)	57/92 (62%)			
	M	66/112 (59%)	54/92 (59%)	49/92 (53%)			
	F	114/184 (62%)	99/155 (64%)	101/155 (65%)			
	F	102/168 (61%)	91/155 (59%)	98/155 (63%)			
Conceptual disorganization	M	66/118 (56%)	50/90 (55%)	45/90 (50%)			
	M	60/112 (54%)	46/90 (51%)	45/90 (50%)			
	F	114/186 (61%)	86/155 (55%)	66/155 (43%)			
	F	106/168 (63%)	101/155 (65%)	101/155 (65%)			
Depressive mood	M	69/120 (58%)	58/91 (64%)	55/91 (60%)			
	M	64/112 (57%)	51/91 (56%)	54/91 (59%)			
	F	124/184 (67%)	102/156 (65%)	121/156 (78%)			15.43***
	F	116/169 (69%)	93/156 (60%)	84/156 (54%)		6.89*	7.11*
Hostility	M	64/120 (53%)	54/92 (59%)	50/92 (54%)			
	M	61/110 (55%)	43/92 (47%)	53/92 (58%)			
	F	99/188 (53%)	94/157 (60%)	99/157 (63%)			
	F	91/169 (54%)	108/157 (69%)	64/157 (41%)			24.33***
Suspiciousness	M	60/120 (50%)	61/91 (67%)	57/91 (63%)	5.46*		
	M	61/110 (55%)	57/91 (63%)	53/91 (58%)			
	F	112/188 (60%)	89/155 (57%)	86/155 (55%)			
	F	102/169 (60%)	94/155 (61%)	53/155 (34%)		21.14***	27.12***
Unusual thought content	M	53/117 (45%)	49/91 (54%)	43/91 (47%)			
	M	55/110 (50%)	47/91 (52%)	42/91 (46%)			
	F	120/185 (65%)	95/153 (62%)	83/153 (54%)			5.50*
	F	112/168 (67%)	85/153 (56%)	69/153 (45%)		14.28***	7.03*

Note: Data are from the Cleveland Psychiatric Institute; * = $p < .05$, ** = $p < .01$, and *** = $p < .001$.

Table E-29. Relative Cross-Validational Accuracy of Discriminant Function Categorization of White and Black Psychiatric Patients, Using Minnesota and Tri-State Black Norms

Dependent Variable	Sex	Minnesota Norms White (1)	Minnesota Norms Black (2)	Tri-State Norms Black (3)	1 vs. 2	1 vs. 3	2 vs. 3
Diagnosis	M	52/108 (48%)	39/75 (52%)	28/75 (37%)			7.69*
	M	38/102 (37%)	37/75 (49%)	23/75 (31%)			
	F	89/186 (48%)	83/146 (57%)	68/146 (47%)			
	F	93/180 (52%)	79/146 (54%)	72/146 (49%)			
Somatic concern	M	78/121 (64%)	52/92 (57%)	62/92 (67%)			
	M	61/111 (55%)	53/92 (58%)	48/92 (52%)			
	F	99/179 (55%)	90/156 (58%)	87/156 (56%)			
	F	94/178 (53%)	92/156 (59%)	91/156 (58%)			
Anxiety	M	65/118 (55%)	49/92 (53%)	44/92 (48%)			
	M	74/112 (66%)	57/92 (62%)	53/92 (58%)			
	F	114/184 (62%)	95/155 (61%)	103/155 (66%)			
	F	95/168 (57%)	93/155 (60%)	127/155 (82%)		17.63***	23.01***
Conceptual disorganization	M	63/118 (53%)	48/90 (53%)	43/90 (48%)			
	M	64/112 (57%)	48/90 (53%)	45/90 (50%)			
	F	119/186 (64%)	87/155 (56%)	71/155 (46%)		10.59*	
	F	105/168 (63%)	102/155 (66%)	89/155 (57%)			8.47*
Depressive mood	M	67/120 (56%)	59/91 (65%)	46/91 (51%)			
	M	65/112 (58%)	50/91 (55%)	54/91 (59%)			
	F	127/184 (69%)	98/156 (63%)	125/156 (80%)			23.31***
	F	112/169 (66%)	83/156 (53%)	71/156 (46%)		13.38**	6.72*
Hostility	M	63/120 (53%)	53/92 (58%)	56/92 (61%)			
	M	68/110 (62%)	44/92 (48%)	50/92 (54%)			
	F	95/180 (53%)	91/157 (58%)	90/157 (57%)			
	F	92/177 (52%)	93/157 (59%)	100/157 (64%)			
Suspiciousness	M	63/120 (53%)	65/91 (71%)	55/91 (60%)	7.00*		
	M	63/110 (57%)	57/91 (63%)	49/91 (54%)			
	F	118/188 (63%)	94/155 (61%)	78/155 (50%)			8.65*
	F	104/169 (62%)	89/155 (57%)	72/155 (46%)			8.83*
Unusual thought content	M	54/117 (46%)	62/91 (57%)	47/91 (52%)			
	M	55/110 (50%)	50/91 (55%)	40/91 (44%)			
	F	112/185 (61%)	93/153 (61%)	81/153 (53%)			
	F	114/168 (68%)	87/153 (57%)	75/153 (49%)		10.97**	

Note: Data are from the Cleveland Psychiatric Institute; * = $p < .05$, ** = $p < .01$, and *** = $p < .001$.

APPENDIX F
Item Data on Normal and Psychiatric Samples

Table F-1. Percentage of True and Cannot Say Responses for Three Samples of Normal Adults

	1. Minnesota White Sample				2. Two-State White Sample				3. Tri-State Black Sample				Males			Females		
	Males (*N* = 225)		Females (*N* = 315)		Males (*N* = 188)		Females (*N* = 228)		Males (*N* = 293)		Females (*N* = 503)		1 vs. 2	1 vs. 3	2 vs. 3	1 vs. 2	1 vs. 3	2 vs. 3
Booklet No.	T	?	T	?	T	?	T	?	T	?	T	?	p^a	p	p	p	p	p
1	...		...		66	1	14	1	57	0	12	1	...	...		...	...	
2	95	0	95	0	97	0	95	0	95	0	95	0						
3	82	0	75	1	64	0	68	0	77	0	70	1	.01		.01			
4	...		...		11	1	30	1	22	1	42	1	...	...	.01	...	...	.01
5	32	1	59	0	41	0	53	0	63	0	68	1		.01	.01		.01	.01
6	49	3	30	1	43	1	33	0	51	0	44	2					.01	.01
7	88	0	74	0	87	0	69	0	86	0	73	1						
8 (318)	89	0	88	0	82	0	89	0	83	0	78	0	.05				.01	.01
9	88	0	85	1	90	1	84	1	84	0	83	0						
10	8	0	10	1	4	0	2	0	6	0	8	0				.01		.01
11	13	8	15	11	17	1	18	0	42	1	49	1		.01	.01		.01	.01
12	69	3	45	1	61	0	58	0	71	0	69	0			.05	.01	.01	.01
13 (290)	27	5	23	2	47	1	30	1	29	0	33	1	.01		.01		.01	
14	5	6	4	1	9	0	12	1	5	0	10	0				.01	.01	
15 (314)	51	1	32	1	38	0	38	0	42	1	51	0	.01	.05			.01	.01
16 (315)	5	4	4	3	7	0	3	1	15	0	15	1		.01	.01		.01	.01
17	93	2	94	2	93	0	90	0	87	2	83	2		.05		.05	.01	.05
18	79	1	69	1	85	0	80	0	74	1	66	1			.05	.01		.01
19	32	8	22	14	19	1	8	1	22	1	21	2	.01	.01		.01		.01
20 (310)	88	1	84	6	84	1	79	1	90	1	82	2				.01	.05	
21 (308)	24	1	30	1	27	1	35	0	39	0	53	1		.01	.05		.01	.01
22 (326)	4	0	13	0	6	0	17	0	8	0	17	0						
23 (288)	4	2	7	0	3	0	7	0	1	1	6	0						
24 (333)	7	3	6	2	7	1	8	0	14	0	19	1		.05	.05		.01	.01

Note: The Minnesota sample was collected by Hathaway and McKinley in 1940; the two-state sample by Webb in 1973; and the tri-state sample by Lachar, Gynther, and Dahlstrom in 1976.

[a]Probability values are based on chi-square test with Yates's correction for continuity.

Table F-1. Percentage of True and Cannot Say Responses for Three Samples of Normal Adults—continued

	1. Minnesota White Sample				2. Two-State White Sample				3. Tri-State Black Sample				Males			Females		
	Males (*N* = 225)		Females (*N* = 315)		Males (*N* = 188)		Females (*N* = 228)		Males (*N* = 293)		Females (*N* = 503)		1 vs. 2	1 vs. 3	2 vs. 3	1 vs. 2	1 vs. 3	2 vs. 3
Booklet No.	T	?	T	?	T	?	T	?	T	?	T	?	*p*[a]	*p*	*p*	*p*	*p*	*p*
25	...		...		34	0	40	0	50	2	48	1	...	...	.01	...	...	
26	68	4	78	4	36	0	34	0	43	2	42	1	.01	.01		.01	.01	.05
27	8	3	6	2	13	0	6	0	16	0	15	0		.05			.01	.01
28	28	1	12	1	20	0	10	0	20	0	19	0		.05			.05	.01
29	22	1	17	1	19	0	14	0	19	0	17	1						
30	81	0	69	0	82	0	86	0	61	0	68	0		.01	.01	.01		.01
31	5	1	7	1	11	0	4	1	7	0	10	0						.05
32 (328)	12	1	15	0	13	0	14	0	13	0	16	0						
33 (323)	35	2	22	0	23	0	22	0	39	0	33	1	.01		.01		.01	.01
34	12	0	6	1	11	0	8	0	10	1	9	0						
35 (331)	9	3	7	2	3	0	0	0	13	0	9	1	.01		.01	.01		.01
36	73	0	72	0	67	1	70	0	58	0	57	0		.01			.01	.01
37 (302)	93	0	84	1	80	0	80	0	78	0	75	1	.01	.01			.01	
38 (311)	24	3	9	1	48	0	23	0	47	1	26	1	.01	.01		.01	.01	
39	38	0	37	0	44	0	46	0	32	1	39	1			.05	.05		
40	8	1	10	0	11	0	8	0	16	0	22	0		.01			.01	.01
41	14	1	26	0	23	0	29	0	28	0	35	1	.05	.01			.01	
42	8	9	5	4	7	0	7	2	11	0	8	0						
43	7	1	16	1	9	0	14	1	12	0	14	0						
44	4	1	4	1	4	0	4	0	7	0	13	0					.01	.01
45	66	3	59	2	57	0	56	0	66	1	71	1	.05		.05		.01	.01
46	67	18	60	23	77	1	73	0	77	1	74	2						
47	5	1	14	2	9	0	12	0	9	0	20	0					.05	.05
48	5	0	3	0	4	0	3	0	7	0	7	0						.05
49	8	1	3	4	6	1	3	0	7	0	7	0					.05	.05
50	8	18	4	13	4	1	3	0	11	1	9	4			.01			.01

51	84	3	84	3	88	0	89	0	81	1	85	1			.05			
52	13	0	23	1	11	0	14	0	9	0	13	0				.05	.01	
53	4	9	5	11	9	2	9	0	13	1	14	2		.01			.01	.05
54	86	12	79	16	95	1	96	0	93	1	87	1					.01	.01
55	79	2	70	0	75	0	82	0	69	0	71	1		.01		.01		.01
56	10	1	4	0	11	0	2	0	22	0	12	0		.01	.01		.01	.01
57	67	13	62	8	70	0	75	0	79	1	77	2			.05		.01	
58	52	29	54	31	45	3	51	3	62	4	75	4	.01	.05	.01	.01		.01
59	51	4	39	4	53	0	39	0	73	0	68	0		.01	.01		.01	.01
60	88	0	85	0	90	0	95	0	88	0	91	0				.01	.05	
61	23	12	10	8	22	1	17	1	34	0	30	1			.01		.01	.01
62	26	1	35	1	23	0	28	0	28	0	41	1						.01
63	81	1	77	0	88	0	75	0	74	0	72	1			.01			
64	43	5	34	5	38	0	42	0	38	0	30	1						.01
65	95	1	95	1	91	0	93	0	86	2	89	1		.01			.01	
66	11	4	6	1	10	0	10	0	17	0	11	1			.05		.05	
67	49	1	49	3	34	0	37	0	45	1	50	2	.01		.05	.01		.01
68	82	0	73	0	77	0	79	0	78	1	74	1						
69	28	10	30	9	8	0	7	0	12	1	13	0	.01	.01		.01	.01	.05
70	...		...		30	2	71	2	22	5	44	3	...	...		...	...	.01
71	76	7	82	4	80	0	64	0	77	0	80	0				.01		.01
72	12	0	12	1	11	0	7	0	11	0	15	0						.01
73	17	11	9	9	49	1	69	0	80	1	78	1	.01	.01	.01	.01	.01	.05
74	...		...		7	0	81	0	6	1	70	1	...	...		...	...	.01
75	94	0	97	0	96	0	95	0	96	0	96	1						
76	5	0	10	1	9	0	7	0	10	0	19	0					.01	.01
77	44	3	71	2	28	1	76	0	39	0	79	0	.01		.05		.05	
78	...		...		47	1	79	0	70	1	83	0	...	...	.01	...	...	
79	65	0	44	2	57	1	44	0	66	0	51	0						
80	45	0	21	0	26	0	7	0	32	1	21	0	.01	.01		.01		.01
81	...		...		68	0	29	0	35	0	11	0	...	...	.01	...	...	.01
82	24	2	37	5	21	0	30	0	16	0	33	1		.05		.05		

Table F-1. Percentage of True and Cannot Say Responses for Three Samples of Normal Adults—continued

Booklet No.	1. Minnesota White Sample				2. Two-State White Sample				3. Tri-State Black Sample				Males			Females		
	Males (N = 225)		Females (N = 315)		Males (N = 188)		Females (N = 228)		Males (N = 293)		Females (N = 503)		1 vs. 2	1 vs. 3	2 vs. 3	1 vs. 2	1 vs. 3	2 vs. 3
	T	?	T	?	T	?	T	?	T	?	T	?	p[a]	p	p	p	p	p
83	90	1	90	1	94	0	94	0	85	1	90	0			.05			
84	49	3	44	3	37	1	30	0	51	2	57	1	.05		.01	.01	.01	.01
85	6	1	2	0	0	0	1	0	2	0	7	1	.01	.05			.01	.01
86	24	4	34	2	25	0	29	0	17	1	26	1					.05	
87	...		...		7	0	29	0	10	0	20	0	...	...		...	...	.05
88	97	0	95	0	97	0	98	0	95	0	94	0						.05
89	60	6	57	9	47	0	33	1	63	0	66	1	.01		.01	.01		.01
90	85	0	90	0	97	0	94	0	91	0	93	1	.01	.05	.05		.05	
91	53	1	31	1	42	1	29	0	45	1	37	0	.05					
92	...		...		5	1	38	0	12	0	39	0	...	...	.05	...	...	
93	48	6	41	9	50	0	36	0	72	0	73	0		.01	.01		.01	.01
94	31	6	43	3	35	1	26	0	34	0	38	1				.01		.01
95	43	2	55	1	45	0	62	0	55	0	65	0		.05	.05		.01	
96	91	0	86	1	79	1	84	0	76	0	74	0	.01	.01			.01	.01
97	13	1	14	1	20	1	16	0	19	0	26	0					.01	.01
98	57	18	68	12	69	0	81	1	78	2	85	2		.05	.01		.01	
99	58	1	38	0	53	1	42	0	47	0	46	1		.05			.05	
100	56	4	49	8	61	1	58	0	53	1	61	1					.05	
101	74	9	52	15	84	1	71	0	69	1	67	1		.01	.01	.05		
102	54	3	51	5	63	1	77	0	67	0	69	0		.05		.01	.01	.05
103	89	0	78	2	87	1	87	0	81	0	79	0		.05		.05		.05
104	11	1	5	0	4	1	5	0	6	0	6	0	.05					
105	76	1	90	0	84	0	93	0	64	1	76	1		.01	.01		.01	.01
106	12	0	10	1	11	1	10	0	13	1	19	0					.01	.01
107	91	0	88	1	92	0	93	0	89	0	87	0						.05
108	17	2	10	1	12	1	8	0	10	1	11	0		.05				

109	43	1	59	1	38	1	47	0	42	0	54	1				.01		
110	12	10	11	12	8	1	4	0	17	1	19	1			.01	.01	.05	.01
111	53	1	66	0	24	1	45	0	48	1	61	0	.01		.01	.01		.01
112	78	0	83	0	80	0	73	0	85	0	84	0				.01		.01
113	98	0	97	2	97	1	97	1	94	1	95	0		.05			.05	
114	6	0	10	1	5	1	9	0	11	1	15	0			.05			.05
115	77	11	87	6	81	0	91	1	76	2	82	2		.05			.01	
116	39	1	33	4	36	1	23	0	26	1	22	1		.01	.05	.05	.01	
117	40	6	35	10	50	1	32	0	64	0	61	0		.01	.01		.01	.01
118	36	1	15	1	35	1	13	0	34	1	17	0						
119	84	1	83	2	77	0	85	0	62	1	69	0		.01	.01		.01	.01
120	71	0	63	0	76	0	61	0	66	0	69	0			.05			
121	6	4	2	2	4	1	0	0	9	0	8	1					.01	.01
122	87	6	85	4	92	0	90	0	91	0	88	0						
123	3	2	2	1	3	0	1	0	7	0	4	0						.05
124	66	10	55	16	55	0	44	0	78	1	78	0	.01		.01	.01	.01	.01
125	14	0	11	0	7	0	8	0	12	0	13	1	.05					
126	...		...		44	0	76	0	70	1	83	0	...	...	.01	...	...	.05
127	28	9	27	9	54	1	74	1	64	1	66	1	.01	.01	.05	.01	.01	.05
128	84	0	62	1	70	0	61	0	70	0	55	0	.01	.01				
129	48	3	61	1	38	1	41	0	30	1	39	1	.05	.01		.01	.01	
130	84	1	77	0	80	0	85	0	67	0	74	1		.01	.01	.05		.01
131	75	1	67	0	70	0	81	0	59	0	56	0		.01	.05	.01	.01	.01
132	...		...		24	0	70	0	50	0	78	0	...	...	.01	...	...	.05
133	81	4	81	1	60	1	79	0	73	0	76	0	.01	.01	.01			
134	55	4	60	3	78	0	85	0	82	0	79	1	.01	.01		.01	.01	
135	26	2	18	3	37	0	15	0	39	1	38	0	.05	.01			.01	.01
136	49	5	48	2	41	0	22	0	58	0	50	0	.05		.01	.01		.01
137	92	1	95	0	91	0	90	0	86	0	84	0		.05		.05	.01	.05
138	52	1	75	0	38	0	47	0	39	0	51	1	.01	.01		.01	.01	
139	9	1	5	0	10	0	5	0	13	0	14	0					.01	.01
140	...		...		48	0	79	0	58	0	74	0	...	...	.05	...	...	

Table F-1. Percentage of True and Cannot Say Responses for Three Samples of Normal Adults—continued

Booklet No.	1. Minnesota White Sample				2. Two-State White Sample				3. Tri-State Black Sample				Males			Females		
	Males (*N* = 225)		Females (*N* = 315)		Males (*N* = 188)		Females (*N* = 228)		Males (*N* = 293)		Females (*N* = 503)		1 vs. 2	1 vs. 3	2 vs. 3	1 vs. 2	1 vs. 3	2 vs. 3
	T	?	T	?	T	?	T	?	T	?	T	?	*p*[a]	*p*	*p*	*p*	*p*	*p*
141	50	6	47	4	60	0	53	0	56	0	48	0						
142	44	0	51	1	54	0	49	0	39	0	47	0	.05		.01			
143	32	1	25	3	41	0	34	0	40	0	32	0						
144	...		...		20	1	2	0	23	0	7	0	...	...		...	...	.05
145	24	1	17	0	18	0	7	0	15	0	10	0		.05		.01	.01	
146	16	1	9	2	14	0	8	0	16	0	10	0						
147	43	2	36	3	42	0	29	0	49	0	48	1					.01	.01
148	48	1	49	2	35	0	33	0	42	0	42	1	.01			.01	.05	.05
149	...		...		12	0	59	0	16	0	47	0	...	...		...	...	.01
150	86	2	79	3	90	0	89	0	86	0	80	0				.05		.01
151	1	1	1	2	3	0	0	0	5	0	5	0		.05			.01	.01
152	74	0	73	1	70	0	75	0	70	0	66	0					.05	.05
153	88	0	84	0	94	0	90	0	89	0	86	1						
154	83	0	80	0	91	0	95	0	90	0	87	1	.05	.05		.01	.01	.01
155	83	0	71	2	64	0	60	0	48	1	43	0	.01	.01	.01	.01	.01	.01
156	11	1	7	3	6	0	8	0	14	0	12	0			.01		.05	
157	18	3	27	3	15	1	11	0	25	0	32	1			.05	.01		.01
158	16	0	54	1	11	0	39	0	17	0	54	0				.01		.01
159	6	1	12	1	19	0	17	0	17	0	23	0	.01	.01			.01	
160	52	3	49	6	47	0	49	0	44	0	43	0		.05			.05	
161	17	1	18	1	8	0	13	0	18	0	21	0	.01		.01			.05
162	43	4	46	4	47	1	57	0	40	1	44	1				.05		.01
163	80	1	62	0	64	0	60	0	68	0	58	0	.01	.01				
164	95	1	94	1	88	0	92	0	88	0	87	0	.01	.01			.01	
165	43	1	44	4	50	0	49	0	53	1	47	0		.05				

166	38	1	65	0	47	0	55	0	43	0	66	0				.05		.01
167	31	3	14	2	26	0	11	0	32	0	26	0					.01	.01
168	2	6	3	2	6	0	3	0	8	0	10	0	.05	.01			.01	.01
169	96	0	90	0	94	0	93	0	91	0	87	0						.05
170	60	1	46	1	35	0	23	0	49	1	49	1	.01	.05	.01	.01		.01
171	49	2	54	1	46	0	53	0	57	1	62	2			.05		.05	.05
172	35	1	38	1	47	1	39	0	40	0	43	1	.05					
173	81	2	89	0	76	0	85	0	84	0	86	0			.05			
174	66	0	46	0	75	1	48	0	74	1	62	0		.05			.01	.01
175	82	0	71	1	86	0	80	0	81	0	72	1				.05		.05
176	76	0	39	1	63	1	44	0	47	0	31	1	.01	.01	.01		.05	.01
177	95	1	100	0	97	0	96	0	95	1	94	1				.01	.01	
178	92	1	91	1	86	0	90	0	90	0	87	0					.05	
179	7	2	8	1	16	0	14	0	13	0	16	1	.01	.05		.05	.01	
180	41	0	46	1	48	0	33	0	35	0	38	0			.01	.01	.05	
181	50	1	44	2	51	0	51	0	51	0	50	0						
182	4	1	4	2	6	0	9	0	11	0	15	0		.05		.05	.01	.05
183	53	4	49	5	44	0	36	0	43	0	45	1	.05	.05		.01		.05
184	5	0	2	0	2	0	2	0	8	0	11	0			.05		.01	.01
185	89	1	87	0	84	0	91	0	85	0	88	0						
186	24	0	27	0	12	0	14	0	20	0	19	0	.01		.05	.01	.01	
187	86	1	80	1	90	0	91	0	85	0	80	1				.01		.01
188	66	0	51	1	56	0	67	0	56	0	56	1	.05	.05		.01		.01
189	8	0	11	0	5	0	6	0	12	0	11	1			.05			.05
190	81	0	74	0	81	0	73	0	84	1	72	0						
191	31	0	31	1	26	0	32	0	30	0	29	1						
192	93	0	88	0	93	1	89	0	86	0	84	0		.01	.05			
193	86	1	77	1	82	0	81	0	75	0	73	0		.01				.05
194	12	1	8	1	7	0	5	0	13	0	11	0						.05
195	78	1	85	1	86	0	90	0	70	1	74	0			.01		.01	.01
196	98	0	97	0	96	1	97	0	94	0	95	0						

Table F-1. Percentage of True and Cannot Say Responses for Three Samples of Normal Adults—continued

Booklet No.	1. Minnesota White Sample				2. Two-State White Sample				3. Tri-State Black Sample				Males			Females		
	Males (*N* = 225)		Females (*N* = 315)		Males (*N* = 188)		Females (*N* = 228)		Males (*N* = 293)		Females (*N* = 503)		1 vs. 2	1 vs. 3	2 vs. 3	1 vs. 2	1 vs. 3	2 vs. 3
	T	?	T	?	T	?	T	?	T	?	T	?	*p*[a]	*p*	*p*	*p*	*p*	*p*
197	4	1	2	2	1	0	2	0	6	0	4	0			.05			
198	73	0	65	1	63	0	71	0	64	0	64	0	.05	.05				
199	87	4	90	4	87	0	92	0	80	1	86	1		.01			.01	
200	8	7	3	4	3	0	3	0	15	0	10	0	.05	.05	.01		.01	.01
201	33	1	39	1	48	1	41	0	39	0	44	1	.01					
202	6	5	2	3	3	0	1	0	7	0	10	0					.01	.01
203	...		...		21	0	41	0	29	0	36	0	...	...	.01	...	...	
204	...		...		21	0	33	0	35	1	25	0	...	...	.01	...	...	.05
205	6	1	2	0	4	0	2	0	9	0	8	0					.01	.01
206	8	9	11	8	22	1	22	0	31	1	29	1	.01	.01		.01	.01	
207	91	0	84	1	82	1	86	0	90	0	88	1	.05		.05			
208	34	2	24	3	62	1	46	0	46	1	39	0	.01	.05	.01	.01	.01	
209	11	9	6	4	8	0	2	0	10	1	8	1				.05		.01
210	1	2	0	0	2	0	2	0	4	0	2	1					.05	
211	4	1	4	1	3	1	4	0	7	0	6	1						
212	8	1	9	1	7	1	8	0	16	1	20	0		.01	.01		.01	.01
213	28	3	25	1	4	0	6	0	22	0	26	1	.01		.01	.01		.01
214	78	1	71	0	57	0	53	0	52	0	46	0	.01	.01		.01	.01	
215	9	1	4	1	33	0	13	0	25	1	12	0	.01	.01		.01	.01	
216	12	1	9	1	11	0	7	0	12	1	17	1					.01	.01
217	49	0	69	0	52	0	57	0	46	0	57	0				.01	.01	
218	12	1	6	0	11	0	4	0	12	1	8	1						.05
219	...		...		56	0	14	0	41	2	13	1	...	...	.01	...	...	
220	96	1	98	0	95	0	93	0	91	2	95	1				.05		
221	...		...		81	0	51	0	80	1	64	1	...	...		...	...	.01
222	23	1	24	1	47	0	39	0	46	1	44	1	.01	.01		.01	.01	

223	...		...		48	0	6	0	34	1	9	1	...	...	.01	...	...	
224	28	1	27	1	21	0	17	0	31	1	32	1			.05	.01		.01
225	73	1	87	1	81	0	92	0	67	2	88	1			.01			
226	28	1	39	1	47	1	57	0	58	1	69	0	.01	.01	.05	.01	.01	.01
227	4	1	8	1	8	0	3	0	8	1	5	1				.05	.05	
228	72	3	78	3	71	0	80	0	84	1	81	1		.01	.01			
229	52	2	42	1	34	0	27	0	40	1	42	0	.01	.01		.01		.01
230	67	1	56	1	65	0	74	0	60	1	61	1				.01		.01
231	38	1	20	2	66	1	30	0	68	1	53	1	.01	.01		.05	.01	.01
232	42	14	50	15	36	1	30	1	48	1	40	1	.05		.01	.01	.01	.01
233	28	5	29	9	40	1	27	0	25	1	19	1	.05		.01		.01	.05
234	52	0	58	2	49	0	41	0	43	1	48	0				.01	.01	
235	70	0	63	3	54	0	61	0	61	1	54	1	.01				.01	
236	15	2	20	0	13	0	14	1	13	1	19	1						
237	46	19	55	18	47	1	53	2	39	2	38	1		.01		.01	.01	.01
238	38	0	33	1	38	0	29	0	29	1	25	1		.05	.05		.05	
239	24	2	23	1	38	1	39	0	51	1	61	1	.01	.01	.01	.01	.01	.01
240	52	1	42	1	28	0	14	0	39	1	30	1	.01	.01	.05	.01	.01	.01
241	25	2	26	2	27	0	24	0	42	1	47	0		.01	.01		.01	.01
242	79	3	71	3	82	0	81	0	77	1	76	0						
243	84	0	77	0	84	0	81	0	76	0	74	0						
244	54	5	52	7	35	0	30	0	51	1	49	0	.01		.01	.01	.05	.01
245	8	3	11	4	12	0	9	0	16	0	21	1		.05			.01	.01
246	4	2	11	2	4	0	7	0	5	0	4	0					.01	
247	8	1	7	1	7	0	7	0	10	0	14	0					.01	.05
248	39	3	43	4	39	0	37	0	51	1	49	0		.05	.05			.01
249	63	14	66	15	58	2	64	1	68	2	73	2			.05	.01		.01
250	34	5	31	8	35	0	26	0	45	1	50	0	.01	.05	.05		.01	.01
251	6	1	8	1	6	0	6	0	13	1	11	0		.01	.05			.05
252	12	4	9	2	9	0	6	0	15	0	19	1			.05		.01	.01
253	71	0	72	1	77	0	86	0	74	1	77	0				.01		.05
254	62	0	35	2	44	0	26	0	18	2	14	0	.01	.01	.01	.05	.01	.01

Table F-1. Percentage of True and Cannot Say Responses for Three Samples of Normal Adults—continued

	1. Minnesota White Sample				2. Two-State White Sample				3. Tri-State Black Sample				Males			Females		
	Males (*N* = 225)		Females (*N* = 315)		Males (*N* = 188)		Females (*N* = 228)		Males (*N* = 293)		Females (*N* = 503)		1 vs. 2	1 vs. 3	2 vs. 3	1 vs. 2	1 vs. 3	2 vs. 3
Booklet No.	T	?	T	?	T	?	T	?	T	?	T	?	*p*[a]	*p*	*p*	*p*	*p*	*p*
255	57	5	55	6	69	0	78	1	51	0	56	1		.05	.01	.01		.01
256	10	1	7	1	7	0	4	0	5	1	12	0		.05			.05	.01
257	95	0	93	1	93	0	92	0	92	0	92	0						
258	92	5	96	2	91	1	97	1	94	1	95	0	.05					
259	29	0	26	0	29	0	29	0	30	0	30	0						
260	26	2	16	2	27	0	11	0	23	0	16	0						
261	...		...		27	0	62	0	37	1	52	1	...	...	.05	...	...	.05
262	89	0	81	1	76	1	71	0	85	0	74	1	.01		.05	.01	.05	
263	38	1	23	1	33	0	17	0	35	0	26	0						.05
264	52	10	34	7	33	0	24	0	60	1	49	1	.01		.01	.01	.01	.01
265	46	6	40	6	16	0	11	0	22	1	27	1	.01	.01		.01	.01	.01
266	10	2	18	2	24	0	25	0	33	1	36	1	.01	.01	.05	.05	.01	.01
267	44	0	44	2	38	0	34	0	25	1	40	1		.01	.01	.05		
268	58	5	70	2	67	0	79	1	69	1	77	1		.05		.05		
269	15	2	3	1	9	0	4	0	15	1	12	0					.01	.01
270	58	2	46	1	52	1	50	0	26	1	22	0		.01	.01		.01	.01
271	27	6	24	10	14	0	11	0	28	0	25	1	.01		.01	.01		.01
272	89	0	91	1	89	0	91	0	91	0	80	1						
273	6	1	10	2	12	0	9	0	12	0	13	1	.05	.05				
274	72	1	56	2	57	0	56	0	54	0	50	1	.01	.01			.05	
275	5	1	3	1	3	0	3	0	8	0	10	1					.01	.01
276	95	1	94	0	96	0	94	0	92	0	92	1						
277	15	3	6	5	44	0	30	0	44	0	25	1	.01	.01		.01	.01	
278	32	2	40	2	33	0	31	0	36	0	40	1				.05		.05
279	36	1	29	2	15	0	9	0	27	1	19	1	.01	.05	.01	.01	.01	.01
280	50	4	38	10	26	1	19	0	52	1	46	1	.01		.01	.01		.01

281	84	0	76	1	77	1	86	0	71	0	70	1		.01		.01		.01
282	23	1	26	0	27	0	41	0	23	0	35	1				.01	.01	
283	...		...		59	0	17	0	69	1	28	1	...	...	.05	...	...	.01
284	21	9	22	10	31	0	18	0	44	0	47	1		.01	.01		.01	.01
285	90	0	78	1	93	0	93	0	90	1	91	1				.01	.01	
286	10	2	7	1	10	0	7	0	11	1	13	1					.05	.05
287	49	24	55	19	55	1	58	0	59	2	60	3						
288 (23)	4	2	7	0	5	0	5	0	6	1	8	0						
289	75	2	78	7	62	0	68	1	61	0	72	1	.01	.01		.01	.01	
290 (13)	27	5	23	2	46	0	27	0	29	0	32	1	.01		.01		.01	
291	5	2	3	1	4	1	3	0	6	0	6	1						
292	40	1	48	0	25	0	22	0	22	0	23	1	.01	.01		.01	.01	
293	12	5	8	1	3	0	4	0	15	0	14	0	.01		.01		.05	.01
294	80	0	92	0	64	0	88	0	68	1	85	1	.01	.01			.01	
295	...		...		54	1	73	1	45	3	66	2	...	...		...	...	
296	61	2	70	3	62	1	72	0	69	0	75	1						
297	22	7	11	8	15	2	13	1	21	1	22	2					.01	.01
298	40	11	37	12	20	1	18	0	39	1	33	1	.01		.01	.01	.05	.01
299	23	17	32	15	37	0	42	1	37	1	36	1		.05				
300	...		...		68	0	11	0	60	1	13	1	...	...		...	...	
301	15	2	18	1	19	0	13	0	19	0	22	0						.01
302 (37)	93	0	84	1	84	1	86	0	81	0	82	1	.01	.01				
303	18	1	26	1	14	0	18	0	28	1	32	0		.05	.01	.05		.01
304	45	1	53	1	54	1	47	0	36	0	46	0		.05	.01		.05	
305 (366)	15	0	16	0	14	0	15	0	15	0	20	0						
306	89	2	83	5	88	0	91	0	79	1	72	1		.01	.05		.01	.01
307	38	0	38	1	43	0	44	0	36	0	47	0					.05	
308 (21)	24	1	30	1	26	0	35	0	36	0	50	1		.01	.05		.01	.01
309	87	3	85	1	81	0	88	0	85	0	83	1	.05					
310 (20)	88	1	84	6	83	2	77	1	87	0	84	1				.01	.05	.05
311 (38)	24	3	9	1	51	0	22	1	44	0	24	0	.01	.01		.01	.01	
312	8	1	6	1	7	0	2	0	12	0	11	0					.05	.01

Table F-1. Percentage of True and Cannot Say Responses for Three Samples of Normal Adults—continued

	1. Minnesota White Sample				2. Two-State White Sample				3. Tri-State Black Sample				Males			Females		
	Males (N = 225)		Females (N = 315)		Males (N = 188)		Females (N = 228)		Males (N = 293)		Females (N = 503)		1 vs. 2	1 vs. 3	2 vs. 3	1 vs. 2	1 vs. 3	2 vs. 3
Booklet No.	T	?	T	?	T	?	T	?	T	?	T	?	p[a]	p	p	p	p	p
313	60	2	63	7	55	0	51	0	68	0	67	0			.01	.01		.01
314 (15)	51	1	32	1	31	0	29	0	41	0	43	0	.01	.05			.01	.01
315 (16)	5	4	4	3	5	0	2	0	12	0	15	0		.05	.05		.01	.01
316	52	4	50	9	43	0	38	0	69	0	70	0	.05	.01	.01	.01	.01	.01
317 (362)	22	9	32	8	29	0	37	1	33	0	37	1		.05				
318 (8)	89	0	88	0	78	0	89	1	82	0	80	0	.01	.05			.01	.01
319	49	6	47	8	38	0	28	0	56	0	56	1	.01		.01	.01		.01
320	17	1	7	1	26	1	8	0	13	0	13	0					.01	
321	36	0	52	2	41	0	37	0	24	0	39	0		.01	.01	.01	.01	
322	52	1	58	2	46	0	39	1	43	0	44	0		.05		.01	.01	
323 (33)	35	2	22	0	23	0	19	0	41	0	30	1	.01		.01		.05	.01
324	11	1	11	0	5	0	3	0	9	0	7	0	.05			.01		.05
325	13	1	25	2	22	0	32	0	41	0	49	1	.05	.01	.01		.01	.01
326 (22)	4	0	13	0	6	0	14	1	11	0	16	0		.01				
327	72	2	66	3	59	0	74	0	75	1	76	0	.01		.01		.05	
328 (32)	12	1	15	0	16	1	14	0	12	0	11	1						
329	54	0	36	1	46	1	41	0	31	1	26	2		.01	.01		.01	.01
330	80	0	77	0	88	0	83	1	73	1	76	1	.05		.01			
331 (35)	9	3	7	2	6	0	2	0	13	1	11	0			.05	.05		.01
332	10	1	11	1	11	0	1	0	28	0	31	0		.01	.01		.01	.01
333 (24)	7	3	6	2	6	1	6	0	11	0	15	0					.01	.01
334	18	2	17	2	12	1	14	0	23	0	26	1			.01		.01	.01
335	14	2	23	0	14	1	15	0	18	0	20	0				.05		
336	34	1	39	1	36	1	33	0	27	0	33	0			.05			
337	26	3	37	2	16	1	18	0	21	0	22	1	.05			.01	.01	
338	31	4	37	3	28	1	24	1	45	0	49	0		.01	.01	.01	.01	.01

339	3	1	3	0	5	1	4	0	5	0	6	0					.05	
340	38	0	60	0	50	1	52	0	52	0	52	1	.05	.01				
341	12	1	9	2	6	1	7	0	14	0	16	1			.05		.01	.01
342	12	1	12	1	14	1	11	0	14	0	15	1						
343	39	0	44	0	29	1	30	0	49	0	53	1	.05	.05	.01	.01	.05	.01
344	16	0	23	0	8	1	8	0	12	0	12	0	.05			.01	.01	
345	24	2	25	2	11	1	14	0	20	0	23	1	.01		.05	.01		.01
346	22	1	23	0	16	1	14	0	22	0	21	0				.05		.05
347	79	11	71	15	86	1	89	0	69	1	69	2		.01	.01		.01	.01
348	75	3	66	2	36	1	36	0	59	0	56	1	.01	.01	.01	.01	.01	.01
349	18	1	10	2	13	1	8	0	23	0	28	1			.05		.01	.01
350	6	0	11	0	5	1	4	0	13	0	17	0		.05	.01	.05	.05	.01
351	15	0	25	0	11	1	5	1	9	0	17	0				.01	.01	.01
352	17	1	22	2	20	1	20	0	21	1	31	1					.05	.01
353	76	1	66	1	69	1	61	0	66	1	58	1		.01			.05	
354	11	1	14	0	4	1	5	0	13	0	16	1	.05		.01	.01		.01
355	11	1	14	0	7	1	10	0	12	0	11	0						
356	20	5	23	5	22	1	19	0	16	0	22	1						
357	22	1	45	1	29	1	36	0	29	0	36	1				.05	.05	
358	16	1	13	0	12	1	10	0	16	0	22	1					.01	.01
359	28	0	43	0	29	1	32	0	35	1	42	0				.05		.05
360	4	1	7	0	3	1	6	0	7	0	9	1						
361	38	2	57	2	32	1	43	0	30	0	50	0		.05		.01	.05	
362 (317)	22	9	32	8	33	1	43	0	27	1	37	2						
363	27	3	17	2	6	1	6	0	15	1	13	1	.01	.01	.01	.01		.01
364	11	14	7	11	11	0	4	1	27	1	26	1		.01	.01		.01	.01
365	34	0	11	0	5	0	2	0	8	0	6	1	.01	.01		.01	.05	.05
366 (305)	15	0	16	0	13	0	14	0	15	1	17	1						
367	63	0	38	0	65	1	38	1	55	0	30	0			.05		.05	.05
368	42	0	49	0	39	0	47	1	48	0	53	0						
369	74	3	71	3	61	2	64	1	69	0	67	1	.01			.05		
370	68	0	81	0	71	0	76	1	78	0	86	0		.01				.01

Table F-1. Percentage of True and Cannot Say Responses for Three Samples of Normal Adults—continued

	1. Minnesota White Sample				2. Two-State White Sample				3. Tri-State Black Sample				Males			Females		
	Males (*N* = 225)		Females (*N* = 315)		Males (*N* = 188)		Females (*N* = 228)		Males (*N* = 293)		Females (*N* = 503)		1 vs. 2	1 vs. 3	2 vs. 3	1 vs. 2	1 vs. 3	2 vs. 3
Booklet No.	T	?	T	?	T	?	T	?	T	?	T	?	*p*[a]	*p*	*p*	*p*	*p*	*p*
371	68	3	64	1	67	0	77	0	67	1	64	1				.01		.01
372	58	5	65	3	64	1	69	1	65	0	60	1						.05
373	47	10	51	10	40	1	35	2	53	1	56	1	.05		.01	.01		.01
374	49	1	50	2	71	0	72	0	57	1	65	1	.01		.01	.01	.01	
375	34	3	43	3	18	0	23	1	29	1	36	1	.01		.01	.01	.05	.01
376	73	13	63	17	91	1	86	1	55	1	48	3	.05	.01	.01	.01	.01	.01
377	32	1	31	0	35	0	33	0	31	0	31	1						
378	77	1	70	2	54	0	48	1	47	0	32	1	.01	.01		.01	.01	.01
379	72	1	57	1	70	0	68	1	70	0	59	1				.05		.05
380	80	2	66	2	68	1	63	1	62	0	61	1	.01	.01				
381	32	1	32	2	23	0	22	1	30	1	29	3	.05			.01		.05
382	32	2	50	2	49	0	49	1	54	1	61	2	.01	.01			.01	.01
383	52	1	62	1	44	0	39	0	45	0	46	1				.01	.01	
384	41	4	46	1	40	0	39	1	47	0	53	1						.01
385	31	0	49	0	23	0	34	1	41	0	58	1		.05	.01	.01	.01	.01
386	45	2	30	1	21	0	20	1	45	0	41	2	.01		.01	.01	.01	.01
387	37	9	27	14	18	0	11	2	26	2	23	2	.01	.01		.01	.05	.01
388	5	1	23	0	9	1	9	1	11	1	24	1		.05		.01		.01
389	44	4	47	1	21	0	25	1	30	0	33	1	.01	.01		.01	.01	.05
390	60	3	64	3	51	1	48	1	61	0	65	1	.05		.05	.01		.01
391	48	1	60	1	41	1	63	0	56	0	63	1			.01			
392	30	1	53	0	10	0	28	1	25	0	52	1	.01		.01	.01		.01
393	6	2	5	1	6	0	3	1	9	0	4	1						
394	62	0	73	1	69	0	56	1	57	0	54	1			.05	.01	.01	
395	46	2	48	4	19	1	18	1	28	0	40	1	.01	.01	.05	.01	.05	.01

396	22	0	23	1	23	1	15	1	19	0	20	1				.05		
397	44	1	55	1	38	1	46	0	32	0	48	1		.01		.05	.05	
398	49	1	45	1	26	1	14	0	26	0	33	0	.01	.01		.01	.01	.01
399	70	1	67	1	63	1	75	1	71	0	65	1						.05
400	39	20	24	21	46	2	31	1	74	0	65	2		.01	.01		.01	.01
401	71	0	48	1	68	1	49	1	52	0	39	0		.01	.01		.01	.01
402	45	2	47	1	39	1	52	1	48	0	53	0						
403	90	4	82	6	87	1	91	1	83	0	77	1	.05	.01			.01	.01
404	60	8	58	6	47	1	38	1	60	0	63	1	.01		.05	.01		.01
405	92	0	92	0	93	0	93	1	89	0	88	1						
406	68	3	50	5	63	0	48	0	72	1	74	1			.05		.01	.01
407	86	1	64	1	79	0	78	1	88	0	75	1	.05		.01	.01	.01	
408	59	6	73	3	66	0	70	1	69	0	79	1						.05
409	56	2	74	0	70	0	83	1	67	0	79	0	.01	.05		.01		
410	56	4	39	11	53	0	24	1	57	0	48	1				.01		.01
411	34	1	35	1	20	1	17	0	20	0	24	1	.01	.01		.01	.01	.05
412	85	0	70	1	72	0	75	1	76	1	66	1	.01	.05				.05
413	40	13	30	18	25	0	15	1	28	1	26	1	.01	.01		.01	.01	.01
414	32	1	48	0	31	1	24	2	28	1	37	1				.01	.01	.01
415	36	28	21	17	58	1	33	1	75	1	58	2		.01	.01		.01	.01
416	42	1	54	1	37	1	48	1	45	0	59	0						.05
417	24	1	20	1	27	1	19	1	39	1	38	1		.01	.05		.01	.01
418	40	0	43	0	26	0	30	1	17	0	24	1	.01	.01	.05	.01	.01	
419	20	2	10	1	19	0	6	1	15	0	12	0						.01
420	21	4	13	2	13	0	17	2	31	1	22	1	.05	.05	.01		.01	
421	42	2	54	2	35	1	36	1	46	0	52	0			.05	.01		.01
422	13	0	15	1	9	1	7	2	18	0	17	0			.01	.01		.01
423	...		...		68	0	35	1	61	0	39	0	...	...		...	...	
424	19	0	13	1	14	1	15	1	16	0	20	0					.05	
425	47	0	66	1	31	1	52	1	48	0	50	0	.01		.01	.01	.01	
426	56	0	36	1	53	0	37	1	64	0	64	0			.05		.01	.01
427	39	2	66	2	18	0	43	0	25	0	38	0	.01	.01	.05	.01	.01	

Table F-1. Percentage of True and Cannot Say Responses for Three Samples of Normal Adults—continued

	1. Minnesota White Sample				2. Two-State White Sample				3. Tri-State Black Sample				Males			Females		
	Males (*N* = 225)		Females (*N* = 315)		Males (*N* = 188)		Females (*N* = 228)		Males (*N* = 293)		Females (*N* = 503)		1 vs. 2	1 vs. 3	2 vs. 3	1 vs. 2	1 vs. 3	2 vs. 3
Booklet No.	T	?	T	?	T	?	T	?	T	?	T	?	*p*[a]	*p*	*p*	*p*	*p*	*p*
428	72	1	75	1	67	1	61	1	69	0	53	0				.01	.01	
429	60	2	54	3	53	1	64	1	71	0	64	1		.05			.05	
430	59	5	48	8	87	1	80	1	85	0	85	1	.01	.01		.01	.01	
431	...		...		27	1	20	1	34	0	39	0	...	...		...	...	.01
432	37	4	28	4	46	1	32	1	52	0	36	0		.01				
433	...		...		10	1	15	1	22	1	20	0	...	...	.01	...	...	
434	...		...		40	1	13	1	24	0	11	0	...	...	.01	...	...	
435	...		...		23	0	30	1	40	1	28	1	...	...	.01	...	...	
436	81	3	78	9	69	1	65	0	80	0	85	0	.01		.05	.01		.01
437	38	6	29	9	37	1	32	2	59	0	58	1		.01	.01		.01	.01
438	31	2	29	3	43	1	28	1	31	0	33	1	.05		.05			
439	53	0	65	1	55	1	54	2	43	0	50	1		.05	.01	.05	.01	
440	80	0	77	0	80	0	75	0	82	0	84	0					.01	.01
441	...		...		59	1	62	2	57	1	35	4	...	...		...	...	.01
442	55	0	69	0	57	1	58	1	52	0	65	1				.05		
443	31	4	40	3	29	1	35	1	36	0	44	1						.05
444	48	4	57	1	37	1	39	2	38	1	41	1	.05	.05		.01	.01	
445	85	3	78	2	80	0	86	1	83	1	80	1				.05		
446	40	0	29	0	54	1	44	0	33	0	25	1	.01		.01	.01		.01
447	45	5	45	4	46	1	36	1	49	0	37	1				.05	.05	
448	12	0	13	1	11	1	14	1	10	1	19	1						
449	76	1	71	1	68	1	86	0	71	0	76	1				.01		.01
450	72	2	70	1	66	1	68	1	54	0	52	1		.01	.01		.01	.01
451	74	1	74	2	68	1	81	0	64	0	73	1		.05				.05
452	13	0	7	0	38	0	15	1	20	0	14	0	.01		.01	.01	.01	
453	31	2	34	1	32	1	36	1	54	0	59	0		.01	.01		.01	.01

454	21	4	14	3	27	0	14	1	20	1	19	1						
455	44	7	50	4	45	2	46	0	55	1	54	2			.05			.05
456	24	6	19	13	14	1	10	1	27	0	23	2	.01		.01	.01		.01
457	31	4	33	7	12	1	9	1	17	0	17	1	.01	.01		.01	.01	.05
458	...		...		36	1	41	1	47	0	47	1	...	...	.05	...	...	
459	24	1	11	3	18	1	14	1	24	0	22	0					.01	.05
460	89	1	79	1	81	1	90	1	77	0	73	1	.05	.01		.01		.01
461	65	2	64	1	46	1	40	0	52	0	47	1	.01	.01		.01	.01	
462	82	1	77	1	82	1	88	0	76	0	81	1				.01		.05
463	...		...		34	1	90	2	51	0	90	0	...	...	.01	...	...	
464	66	4	66	1	78	1	82	1	69	0	65	1	.05		.05	.01		.01
465	45	7	37	6	60	2	47	2	68	0	68	1	.05	.01			.01	.01
466	86	0	86	1	81	1	83	2	72	0	73	0		.01	.05		.01	.01
467	26	0	23	0	23	1	18	1	30	0	29	0						.01
468	50	2	72	1	51	2	61	1	35	0	51	0		.01	.01	.01	.01	.01
469	37	5	26	8	19	1	17	0	40	0	40	1	.01		.01	.01	.01	.01
470	31	9	43	5	7	1	11	1	8	0	13	1	.01	.01		.01	.01	
471	14	1	4	1	12	1	5	1	13	1	9	1					.05	
472	29	5	26	1	16	1	8	1	15	0	12	0	.01	.01		.01	.01	
473	25	1	26	0	28	1	17	0	35	0	33	0		.05		.05	.05	.01
474	73	7	69	6	76	1	73	2	70	0	68	1						
475	44	5	35	5	44	2	46	3	52	0	51	1				.05	.01	
476	14	12	16	20	10	3	17	3	38	1	33	4		.01	.01		.01	.01
477	36	13	32	19	45	1	44	2	34	1	26	1			.05		.01	.01
478	68	2	54	1	67	1	54	1	51	0	40	2		.01	.01		.01	.01
479	88	0	82	0	81	1	86	0	87	0	77	1						.05
480	...		...		10	1	13	2	12	0	24	1	...	...		...	...	.01
481	37	1	35	0	59	1	52	1	57	0	58	0	.01	.01		.01	.01	
482	74	1	57	0	63	1	73	1	62	0	57	1	.05	.01		.01		.01
483	69	16	77	15	78	2	88	3	78	3	81	4					.05	.05
484	29	7	25	8	32	2	32	2	36	0	36	1					.05	
485	32	8	23	19	43	1	24	2	45	1	41	2		.05			.01	.01
486	91	0	80	2	88	1	82	2	78	0	79	1		.01	.01			

Table F-1. Percentage of True and Cannot Say Responses for Three Samples of Normal Adults—continued

	1. Minnesota White Sample				2. Two-State White Sample				3. Tri-State Black Sample				Males			Females		
	Males (N = 225)		Females (N = 315)		Males (N = 188)		Females (N = 228)		Males (N = 293)		Females (N = 503)		1 vs. 2	1 vs. 3	2 vs. 3	1 vs. 2	1 vs. 3	2 vs. 3
Booklet No.	T	?	T	?	T	?	T	?	T	?	T	?	p[a]	p	p	p	p	p
487	17	0	30	0	19	1	21	0	19	0	27	1				.05		
488	51	2	74	1	41	1	69	2	65	0	72	2		.01	.01			
489	49	2	50	0	49	1	49	2	63	0	68	1		.01	.01		.01	.01
490	21	2	30	2	21	1	24	3	33	0	31	1		.01	.01			
491	40	4	43	10	22	1	31	2	22	1	24	2	.01	.01		.01	.01	
492	46	2	57	3	40	1	56	2	61	1	77	1		.01	.01		.01	.01
493	80	4	72	4	64	1	68	2	57	0	62	1	.01	.01			.01	
494	5	0	11	1	13	1	16	2	19	0	26	1	.05	.01			.01	.01
495	75	5	64	10	74	1	64	2	72	1	70	2						
496	82	2	73	3	78	1	82	2	72	1	69	1		.01		.05		.01
497	93	0	83	0	89	1	92	2	86	0	86	1		.05		.01		.05
498	81	2	68	3	56	1	43	1	73	1	73	0	.01	.05	.01	.01		.01
499	46	2	69	1	59	1	64	2	59	0	72	0	.05	.01				
500	47	3	43	4	48	1	47	2	47	0	49	1						
501	81	1	79	1	62	1	66	2	70	0	75	0	.01	.01		.01		.05
502	69	1	67	2	77	1	70	0	84	0	83	0		.01			.01	.01
503	52	8	53	4	47	1	50	1	48	0	52	0						
504	38	7	28	4	29	1	21	2	49	1	49	1	.05	.05	.01		.01	.01
505	38	1	29	1	19	1	13	0	32	0	24	1	.01		.01	.01		.01
506	18	4	31	5	26	1	28	1	34	1	33	1		.01				
507	47	5	38	9	34	0	25	1	67	0	58	0	.01	.01	.01	.01	.01	.01
508	90	3	94	1	88	0	90	1	87	0	89	0		.05			.05	
509	32	2	39	2	34	1	29	1	30	0	39	1				.05		.05
510	35	1	61	2	21	0	21	1	29	0	34	1	.01			.01	.01	.01
511	24	0	28	1	20	0	14	2	33	0	37	0		.05	.01	.01	.05	.01
512	...		...		7	0	6	1	13	0	6	0	...	...		...	...	

513	...		...		46	3	52	3	62	3	54	4	...	...	.01	...	...	
514	...		...		9	2	5	1	21	1	10	3	...	...	.01	...	...	.05
515	88	0	91	0	89	0	92	2	78	0	83	1		.01	.01		.01	.01
516	73	0	79	2	63	1	64	1	74	0	81	1	.05		.05	.01		.01
517	6	1	7	3	5	0	6	2	9	0	8	0						
518	22	1	35	2	24	0	23	1	31	0	36	0		.05		.01		.01
519	12	2	25	1	8	1	3	2	10	0	9	0				.01	.01	.05
520	83	3	78	2	72	0	68	1	73	0	73	0	.01	.01		.01	.05	
521	70	2	55	2	74	0	79	0	78	0	69	1				.01	.01	.05
522	79	1	56	1	57	0	37	2	51	0	29	1	.01	.01		.01	.01	.05
523	56	4	54	1	52	0	56	1	45	0	37	0		.01			.01	.01
524	73	1	66	1	85	0	88	1	70	0	70	1	.05		.01	.01		.01
525	14	0	29	0	40	0	43	1	55	1	72	1	.01	.01	.01	.01	.01	.01
526	12	0	9	2	5	1	4	1	9	0	9	1	.05			.05		.01
527	88	1	85	1	85	0	82	3	83	0	85	0						
528	81	3	80	2	77	0	77	1	78	1	79	0						
529	...		...		66	1	72	1	68	1	70	1	...	...		...	...	
530	20	0	28	1	18	0	17	1	20	0	26	1				.01		.05
531	24	1	32	2	24	0	25	1	19	0	28	0						
532	...		...		86	0	86	1	67	2	58	2	...	...	.01	...	...	.01
533	65	1	69	0	76	0	86	1	71	0	67	1	.05			.01		.01
534	75	4	62	3	61	0	60	2	70	0	61	0	.01	.05				
535	8	0	5	1	12	1	10	1	13	0	13	1					.01	
536	...		...		53	0	47	1	64	1	62	1	...	...	.05	...	...	.01
537	...		...		33	1	9	1	18	0	7	1	...	...	.01	...	...	
538	...		...		6	0	27	2	19	1	56	1	...	...	.01	...	...	.01
539	91	0	65	0	87	0	56	1	78	0	33	1		.01	.05	.05	.01	.01
540	88	0	84	1	91	0	93	1	90	0	88	1				.01		.05
541	26	3	25	3	13	0	17	1	23	0	19	0	.01		.01	.05	.01	
542	74	8	72	9	73	0	72	1	64	1	64	1		.01			.01	.05
543	5	1	10	1	8	0	7	1	17	0	17	0		.01	.01		.05	.01
544	...		...		26	0	27	1	29	0	38	0	...	...		...	...	.01
545	...		...		18	0	27	1	29	0	40	1	...	...	.01	...	...	.01

Table F-1. Percentage of True and Cannot Say Responses for Three Samples of Normal Adults—continued

	1. Minnesota White Sample				2. Two-State White Sample				3. Tri-State Black Sample				Males			Females		
	Males (*N* = 225)		Females (*N* = 315)		Males (*N* = 188)		Females (*N* = 228)		Males (*N* = 293)		Females (*N* = 503)		1 vs. 2	1 vs. 3	2 vs. 3	1 vs. 2	1 vs. 3	2 vs. 3
Booklet No.	T	?	T	?	T	?	T	?	T	?	T	?	*p*[a]	*p*	*p*	*p*	*p*	*p*
546	78	0	64	0	72	0	68	1	71	0	64	1						
547	...		...		71	0	82	1	73	0	78	0	...	...		...	...	
548	51	1	68	1	25	1	40	2	30	0	44	1	.01	.01		.01	.01	
549	...		...		23	0	23	1	21	1	33	0	...	...		...	...	.05
550	...		...		55	1	15	1	49	0	18	1	...	...		...	...	
551	27	0	33	3	34	0	49	1	39	0	44	1		.01		.01	.01	
552	70	4	60	3	71	0	44	1	72	0	58	0				.01		.01
553	6	1	18	2	7	0	7	1	14	0	25	1		.01	.05	.01	.05	.01
554	...		...		46	1	76	1	66	0	69	0	...	...	.01	...	...	
555	...		...		20	0	35	1	23	1	41	0	...	...		...	...	
556	...		...		54	0	68	2	82	1	86	1	...	...	.01	...	...	.01
557	...		...		7	0	33	2	11	1	37	2	...	...		...	...	
558	69	12	62	21	38	0	33	2	56	2	49	4	.01	.01	.01	.01	.01	.01
559	...		...		7	0	12	2	19	0	36	1	...	...	.01	...	...	.01
560	25	0	32	1	27	0	35	2	38	0	44	2		.01	.05		.01	.05
561	...		...		43	0	39	2	45	0	34	2	...	...		...	...	
562	...		...		48	1	64	2	71	1	77	3	...	...	.01	...	...	.01
563	...		...		87	1	37	3	70	1	32	2	...	...	.01	...	...	
564	39	3	48	3	39	0	43	1	34	0	39	1					.01	
565	...		...		10	0	7	2	8	0	7	1	...	...		...	...	
566	...		...		61	0	79	2	73	1	81	2	...	...	.01	...	...	

Table F-2. Content of Race-Related and Cohort-Related Items by Gender in Normative Samples

Item No. and Direction of Response[a]		Scored Same Way on[b]	Comparison with Other Groups[c]	Content
		Race-Related: Males and Females		
5	T	2-S, CI, W, E	Rpm	I am easily awakened by noise.
11	T	9-S, Rs, B-W, E	Rp	A person should try to understand his dreams and be guided by or take warning from them.
16	T	4-O, 6-O, 8, PSY, CI, Rs, E	Rpf	I am sure I get a raw deal from life.
21	T	4-S, 8, 9-S, FAM, CI, W		At times I have very much wanted to leave home.
24	T	4-O, 6-O, 8, PSY, W, E	Rpf	No one seems to understand me.
56	T	F, CI	Rp	As a youngster I was suspended from school one or more times for cutting up.
59	T	9-O, AUT, Rs, E	Rpf	I have often had to take orders from someone who did not know as much as I did.
73	T	9-O, PSY, B-W, E	C	I am an important person.
93	T	AUT, Rs, E	Rp	I think most people would lie to get ahead.
105	F	L, 9-S		Sometimes when I am not feeling well I am cross.
117	T	0, AUT, Rs, E		Most people are honest chiefly through fear of being caught.
119	F	8, 9-O, 0, ORG, W		My speech is the same as always (not faster or slower, or slurring; no hoarseness).
131	F	2-O, PHO, W		I do not worry about catching diseases.
155	F	1, 2-S, 4-S, HEA, E	C	I am neither gaining nor losing weight.
176	F	5, PHO	CmRpm	I do not have a great fear of snakes.
200	T	F, PSY, CI, W, E		There are persons who are trying to steal my thoughts and ideas.
212	T	8, 9-O, FAM, W		My people treat me more like a child than a grown-up.

[a]Indicates direction in which blacks exceeded whites for race-related items and in which both 1970s samples exceeded 1940 sample for cohort-related items.

[b]For designations of basic and content scales, see Appendix B. Others are as follows: O = obvious scale item, S = subtle scale item, m = male only, f = female only, CI = Lachar-Wrobel Critical Item, Rs = Race-sensitive scale (White, 1974), W = replicated race-sensitive item not on Rs scale, E = race-discriminating item in Erdberg analysis (1969), and B-W = Black-White scale (Costello, 1977).

[c]C = also cohort-related, R = also race-related, and Rp = also race-related in psychiatric sample analyses.

Table F-2. Content of Race-Related and Cohort-Related Items by Gender in Normative Samples—continued

Item No. and Direction of Response[a]		Scored Same Way on[b]	Comparison with Other Groups[c]	Content
		Race-Related: Males and Females		
226	T	5, 9-O, FAM, Rs, E	C	Some of my family have habits that bother and annoy me very much.
239	T	4-S, 5, FAM, Rs, E	CRpf	I have been disappointed in love.
241	T	8, Rs, E	Rpf	I dream frequently about things that are best kept to myself.
250	T	9-O, AUT, CI, W, E		I don't blame anyone for trying to grab everything he can get in this world.
254	F	5, 0	C	I like to be with a crowd who play jokes on one another.
266	T	7, 8, 9-O, HYP	C	Once a week or oftener I become very excited.
270	F	2-O, W	Rpm	When I leave home I do not worry about whether the door is locked and the windows closed.
284	T	4-O, 6-O, PSY, CI, Rs, E	Rp	I am sure I am being talked about.
306	F	8, W		I get all the sympathy I should.
316	T	0, AUT, Rs, E	Rp	I think nearly anyone would tell a lie to keep out of trouble.
325	T	8, FAM, W		The things that some of my family have done have frightened me.
329	F	7, E		I almost never dream.
332	T	8, 0, ORG, E	Rp	Sometimes my voice leaves me or changes even though I have no cold.
338	T	6-O, DEP, W, E		I have certainly had more than my share of things to worry about.
343	T	7, Rs, E		I usually have to stop and think before I act even in trifling matters.
347	F	6-O, PSY, CI, Rs, E	Rp	I have no enemies who really wish to harm me.
350	T	8, PSY, CI, E		I hear strange things when I am alone.
364	T	6-O, 8, PSY, CI, Rs, B-W, E	Rpf	People say insulting and vulgar things about me.
376	F	W, E	Rp	Policemen are usually honest.

		Race-Related: Males and Females		
385	T	PHO, W	Rpf	Lightning is one of my fears.
400	T	PSY, B-W, E	Rp	If given the chance I could do some things that would be of great benefit to the world.
401	F	PHO		I have no fear of water.
415	T	B-W, E	Rpm	If given the chance I would make a good leader of people.
417	T	HOS, E		I am often so annoyed when someone tries to get ahead of me in a line of people that I speak to him about it.
437	T	AUT, W, E	Rpf	It is all right to get around the law if you don't actually break it.
450	F	0, SOC		I enjoy the excitement of a crowd.
453	T	SOC	Rpf	When I was a child I didn't care to be a member of a crowd or gang.
466	F	CI, W		Except by a doctor's orders I never take drugs or sleeping powders.
468	F	. . .	Cf	I am often sorry because I am so cross and grouchy.
476	T	PSY	Rp	I am a special agent of God.
478	F	W		I have never been made especially nervous over trouble that any members of my family have gotten into.
489	T	. . .		I feel sympathetic towards people who tend to hang on to their griefs and troubles.
492	T	PHO, W		I dread the thought of an earthquake.
504	T	W		I do not try to cover up my poor opinion or pity of a person so that he won't know how I feel.
507	T	. . .	Rpf	I have frequently worked under people who seem to have things arranged so that they get credit for good work but are able to pass off mistakes onto those under them.
511	T	PSY, W, E	Rp	I have a daydream life about which I do not tell other people.
515	F	E	Rpm	In my home we have always had the ordinary necessities (such as enough food, clothing, etc.).
525	T	PHO, W	CRpm	I am made nervous by certain animals.

Table F-2. Content of Race-Related and Cohort-Related Items by Gender in Normative Samples—continued

Item No. and Direction of Response[a]		Scored Same Way on[b]	Comparison with Other Groups[c]	Content
		Race-Related: Males and Females		
539	F	PHO		I am not afraid of mice.
543	T	DEP, CI, W, E		Several times a week I feel as if something dreadful is about to happen.
553	T	PHO, W, E		I am afraid of being alone in a wide-open place.
560	T	ORG, W	Rpf	I am greatly bothered by forgetting where I put things.
		Race-Related: Males Only		
30	F	L, K, 2-S, 3-S, B-W		At times I feel like swearing.
101	F	9-S, W		I believe women ought to have as much sexual freedom as men.
130	F	1, HEA		I have never vomited blood or coughed up blood.
486	F	HEA	Rpf	I have never noticed any blood in my urine.
488	T	REL		I pray several times a week.
490	T	REL, B-W	Rpf	I read the Bible several times a week.
		Race-Related: Females Only		
6	T	W, E	Rp	I like to read newspaper articles on crime.
8	F	2-O, 3-O, 4-O, 7, 8, DEP		My daily life is full of things that keep me interested.
12	T	. . .	Cf	I enjoy detective or mystery stories.
15	T	6-S, 7, 8		Once in a while I think of things too bad to talk about.
27	T	F, 6-O, PSY	Rpf	Evil spirits possess me at times.
33	T	4-O, 8, PSY, CI, W		I have had very peculiar and strange experiences.
36	F	2-O, 7, HEA, CI		I seldom worry about my health.
40	T	F, 8, PSY, W, E		Most any time I would rather sit and daydream than to do anything else.
44	T	3-O, ORG, CI		Much of the time my head seems to hurt all over.
45	T	W, E		I do not always tell the truth.
61	T	4-O, DEP		I have not lived the right kind of life.

		Race-Related: Females Only		
76	T	3-O, 7, 8, DEP, CI, E		Most of the time I feel blue.
84	T	4-O, MOR, Rs, E	Rpf	These days I find it hard not to give up hope of amounting to something.
85	T	F		Sometimes I am strongly attracted by the personal articles of others such as shoes, gloves, etc., so that I want to handle or steal them though I have no use for them.
96	F	4-S, FAM, CI, E	Cm	I have very few quarrels with members of my family.
97	T	8, 9-O, CI, E		At times I have a strong urge to do something harmful or shocking.
106	T	4-O, 7, DEP, E		Much of the time I feel as if I have done something wrong or evil.
121	T	F, 6-O, 8, PSY, CI		I believe I am being plotted against.
124	T	0, AUT, Rs, B-W, E	Rpf	Most people will use somewhat unfair means to gain profit or an advantage rather than to lose it.
135	T	Rs, E	Rpf	If I could get into a movie without paying and be sure I was not seen I would probably do it.
139	T	F, HOS		Sometimes I feel as if I must injure either myself or someone else.
147	T	0, Rs, E	Rpf	I have often lost out on things because I couldn't make up my mind soon enough.
151	T	F, 6-O, PSY, CI		Someone has been trying to poison me.
167	T	9-O, B-W, E		It wouldn't make me nervous if any members of my family got into trouble with the law.
168	T	F, 8, PSY, CI		There is something wrong with my mind.
174	T	. . .		I have never had a fainting spell.
184	T	F, PSY, CI, B-W, E	Rpf	I commonly hear voices without knowing where they come from.
195	F	L		I do not like everyone I know.
202	T	F, 6-O, 8, DEP		I believe I am a condemned person.
205	T	F, CI		At times it has been impossible for me to keep from stealing or shoplifting something.

Table F-2. Content of Race-Related and Cohort-Related Items by Gender in Normative Samples—continued

Item No. and Direction of Response[a]		Scored Same Way on[b]	Comparison with Other Groups[c]	Content
		Race-Related: Females Only		
216	T	4-O, FAM		There is very little love and companionship in my family compared to other homes.
231	T	5m, E	Rpm	I like to talk about sex.
237	F	4-S	Cf	My relatives are nearly all in sympathy with me.
245	T	F, 4-O, FAM, CI, E		My parents and family find more fault with me than they should.
252	T	F, W, E		No one cares much what happens to you.
264	T	Rs, B-W, E	Rpf	I am entirely self-confident.
269	T	F, HOS, CI		I can easily make other people afraid of me, and sometimes do for the fun of it.
275	T	F, 6-O, PSY, CI, Rs, E		Someone has control over my mind.
297	T	5m, 8		I wish I were not bothered by thoughts about sex.
334	T	8, PSY, CI, W	Rpf	Peculiar odors come to me at times.
341	T	6-O, 8, PSY, CI		At times I hear so well it bothers me.
349	T	7, 8, PSY, CI, W, B-W, E	Rpf	I have strange and peculiar thoughts.
358	T	7, W, E	Rpf	Bad words, often terrible words, come into my mind and I cannot get rid of them.
378	F	W	C	I do not like to see women smoke.
382	T	MOR, W, E	Cm	I wish I could get over worrying about things I have said that may have injured other people's feelings.
386	T	HYP, W, B-W, E	Rpf	I like to keep people guessing what I'm going to do next.
403	F	. . .		It is great to be living in these times when so much is going on.
406	T	AUT		I have often met people who were supposed to be experts who were no better than I.
426	T	HOS, W	Rpf	I have at times had to be rough with people who were rude or annoying.

		Race-Related: Females Only		
440	T	. . .		I try to remember good stories to pass them on to other people.
465	T	HYP		I have several times had a change of heart about my life work.
469	T	HOS, W, E	Rp	I have often found people jealous of my good ideas, just because they had not thought of them first.
477	F	. . .		If I were in trouble with several friends who were equally to blame, I would rather take the whole blame than to give them away.
485	T	E		When a man is with a woman he is usually thinking about things related to her sex.
494	T	PHO, W, E		I am afraid of finding myself in a closet or small closed place.
502	T	. . .		I like to let people know where I stand on things.
523	F	. . .		I practically never blush.
		Cohort-Related: Males and Females		
26	F	3-S, 5		I feel that it is certainly best to keep my mouth shut when I'm in trouble.
38	T	4-O, 8, CI		During one period when I was a youngster I engaged in petty thievery.
69	F	CI		I am very strongly attracted by members of my own sex.
73	T	9-O, PSY, B-W, E	R	I am an important person.
127	T	4-S, 6-S, 9-S, PSY		I know who is responsible for most of my troubles.
129	F	K, 3-S		Often I can't understand why I have been so cross and grouchy.
134	T	5, 9-S, HYP, CI		At times my thoughts have raced ahead faster than I could speak them.
138	F	K		Criticism or scolding hurts me terribly.
154	T	CI		I have never had a fit or convulsion.
155	F	1, 2-S, 4-S, HEA, E	R	I am neither gaining nor losing weight.
179	T	3-O, 5m, 8, CI		I am worried about sex matters.

Table F-2. Content of Race-Related and Cohort-Related Items by Gender in Normative Samples—continued

Item No. and Direction of Response[a]		Scored Same Way on[b]	Comparison with Other Groups[c]	Content
		Cohort-Related: Males and Females		
206	T	F, REL, B-W, E		I am very religious (more than most people).
208	T	. . .		I like to flirt.
214	F	5, HEA		I have never had any breaking out on my skin that has worried me.
215	T	F, 4-O, CI		I have used alcohol excessively.
222	T	9-S, Rs, E		It is not hard for me to ask help from my friends even though I cannot return the favor.
226	T	5, 9-O, FAM, E	R	Some of my family have habits that bother and annoy me very much.
231	T	K, E		I like to talk about sex.
239	T	4-S, 5, FAM, Rs, E	R	I have been disappointed in love.
254	F	5, 0	R	I like to be with a crowd who play jokes on one another.
265	F	3-S		It is safer to trust nobody.
266	T	7, 8, 9-O, HYP	R	Once a week or oftener I become very excited.
277	T	9-O, Aut		At times I have been so entertained by the cleverness of a crook that I have hoped that he would get by with it.
279	F	3-S		I drink an unusually large amount of water every day.
289	F	3-S, 4-S, 9, E		I am always disgusted with the law when a criminal is freed through the arguments of a smart lawyer.
292	F	3-S		I am likely not to speak to people until they speak to me.
348	F	6-S		I tend to be on my guard with people who are somewhat more friendly than I had expected.
365	F	. . .		I feel uneasy indoors.
378	F	W	Rf	I do not like to see women smoke.
387	F	. . .		The only miracles I know of are simply tricks that people play on one another.

		Cohort-Related: Males and Females		
389	F	. . .		My plans have frequently seemed so full of difficulties that I have had to give them up.
395	F	. . .		The future is too uncertain for a person to make serious plans.
398	F	K		I often think, "I wish I were a child again."
411	F	. . .		It makes me feel like a failure when I hear of the success of someone I know well.
413	F	. . .		I deserve severe punishment for my sins.
418	F	. . .		At times I think that I am no good at all.
427	F	. . .		I am embarrassed by dirty stories.
430	T	. . .		I am attracted by members of the opposite sex.
444	F	. . .		I do not try to correct people who express an ignorant belief.
457	F	. . .		I believe that a person should never taste an alcoholic drink.
461	F	K		I find it hard to set aside a task that I have undertaken, even for a short time.
470	F	. . .		Sexual things disgust me.
472	F	. . .		I am fascinated by fire.
481	T	W		I can remember "playing sick" to get out of something.
491	F	REL		I have no patience with people who believe there is only one true religion.
520	F	SOC		I strongly defend my own opinions as a rule.
522	F	PHO		I have no fear of spiders.
525	T	PHO, W	R	I am made nervous by certain animals.
548	F	. . .		I never attend a sexy show if I can avoid it.
558	F	. . .		A large number of people are guilty of bad sexual conduct.
		Cohort-Related: Males Only		
19	F	5		When I take a new job, I like to be tipped off on who should be gotten next to.

Table F-2. Content of Race-Related and Cohort-Related Items by Gender in Normative Samples—continued

Item No. and Direction of Response[a]		Scored Same Way on[b]	Comparison with Other Groups[c]	Content
		Cohort-Related: Males Only		
37	F	4-O, 8, CI		I have never been in trouble because of my sex behavior.
80	F	2-S, 5		I sometimes tease animals.
96	F	4-S, FAM, CI	Rf	I have very few quarrels with members of my family.
128	F	3-O, PHO		The sight of blood neither frightens me nor makes me sick.
133	F	5m, CI		I have never indulged in any unusual sex practices.
159	T	2-O, 7, 8, ORG		I cannot understand what I read as well as I used to.
163	F	1, 3-O, HEA		I do not tire quickly.
164	F	F, 7		I like to study and read about things that I am working at.
176	F	5, PHO	R	I do not have a great fear of snakes.
229	F	5, 0		I should like to belong to several clubs or lodges.
274	F	1, 3-O, ORG		My eyesight is as good as it has been for years.
294	F	4-O, 6-O, AUT, CI		I have never been in trouble with the law.
363	F	. . .		At times I have enjoyed being hurt by someone I loved.
380	F	. . .		When someone says silly or ignorant things about something I know about, I try to set him right.
382	T	MOR, W, E	Rf	I wish I could get over worrying about things I have said that may have injured other people's feelings.
493	F	. . .		I prefer work which requires close attention, to work which allows me to be careless.
501	F	. . .		I usually work things out for myself rather than get someone to show me how.
		Cohort-Related: Females Only		
12	T	. . .	Rf	I enjoy detective or mystery stories.
14	T	F, HEA		I have diarrhea once a month or more.

		Cohort-Related: Females Only		
102	T	4-S, 7		My hardest battles are with myself.
145	F	2-S		At times I feel like picking a fist fight with someone.
177	F	F, 8, W		My mother was a good woman.
186	F	. . .		I frequently notice my hand shakes when I try to do something.
217	F	K		I frequently find myself worrying about something.
232	F	. . .		I have been inspired to a program of life based on duty which I have since carefully followed.
234	F	K, 3-S		I get mad easily and then get over it soon.
237	F	4-S	Rf	My relatives are nearly all in sympathy with me.
282	T	5, 8, HOS		Once in a while I feel hate toward members of my family whom I usually love.
285	T	. . .		Once in a while I laugh at a dirty joke.
321	F	. . .		I am easily embarrassed.
322	F	K, 8		I worry over money and business.
337	F	. . .		I feel anxiety about something or someone almost all the time.
344	F	. . .		Often I cross the street in order not to meet someone I see.
351	F	. . .		I get anxious and upset when I have to make a short trip away from home.
374	T	DEP		At periods my mind seems to work more slowly than usual.
383	F	K		People often disappoint me.
407	T	. . .		I am usually calm and not easily upset.
414	F	. . .		I am apt to take disappointments so keenly that I can't put them out of my mind.
425	F	. . .		I dream frequently.
428	F	. . .		I like to read newspaper editorials.
468	F	. . .	R	I am often sorry because I am so cross and grouchy.
510	F	. . .		Dirt frightens or disgusts me.

Table F-2. Content of Race-Related and Cohort-Related Items by Gender in Normative Samples—continued

Item No. and Direction of Response[a]		Scored Same Way on[b]	Comparison with Other Groups[c]	Content
		Cohort-Related: Females Only		
519	F	...		There is something wrong with my sex organs.
521	T	...		In a group of people I would not be embarrassed to be called upon to start a discussion or give an opinion about something I know well.
551	T	PSY, CI		Sometimes I am sure that other people can tell what I am thinking.

Table F-3. Percentage of True and Cannot Say Responses for Two Psychiatric Samples

	Michigan Sample[a]										Ohio Sample[a]									
	Males					Females					Males					Females				
	White (N = 192)		Black (N = 197)			White (N = 286)		Black (N = 281)			White (N = 310)		Black (N = 125)			White (N = 460)		Black (N = 211)		
Booklet No.	T	?	T	?	p[b]	T	?	T	?	p	T	?	T	?	p	T	?	T	?	p
1	51	0	46	1		12	1	11	1		66	3	62	6		23	1	22	4	
2	77	1	73	1		72	1	66	1		85	0	86	1		74	1	81	1	.05
3	36	0	45	1		34	1	33	1		64	0	64	1		55	1	66	1	.05
4	22	1	23	1		29	1	28	1		25	2	31	2		34	1	48	2	.01
5	42	1	62	1	.01	54	1	68	1	.01	61	0	74	1	.05	63	2	70	1	
6	43	1	53	0	.05	30	1	39	1	.05	44	0	54	2	.05	33	1	46	1	.01
7	79	0	79	0		51	1	48	1		87	1	80	1	.05	70	1	73	2	
8 (318)	39	1	49	1		37	1	33	1		67	1	71	2		61	1	64	1	
9	61	1	62	0		50	0	52	1		64	1	70	1		56	1	63	1	
10	21	0	19	0		24	1	33	1	.05	20	0	18	1		19	0	28	1	.01
11	38	3	57	1	.01	42	2	59	1	.01	39	1	61	2	.01	36	2	55	1	.01
12	60	1	70	1	.05	53	1	61	1		60	0	62	2		52	0	61	1	.05
13 (290)	61	1	56	0		57	0	59	1		50	1	40	3		47	1	36	2	.05
14	27	0	22	1		32	0	21	1	.01	23	2	18	2		16	1	16	3	
15 (314)	56	1	56	0		56	0	64	1		50	1	57	2		43	1	51	1	
16 (315)	34	0	35	1		29	1	38	2	.05	26	1	30	3		25	1	39	1	.01
17	78	1	78	1		74	1	61	1	.01	84	2	75	3		81	2	74	3	
18	68	0	58	1		58	0	59	1		68	1	62	2		64	1	61	2	
19	32	2	36	1		19	1	16	1		37	1	42	1		28	3	31	2	
20 (310)	43	1	61	1	.01	37	0	49	1	.01	70	2	82	1	.05	62	3	68	1	

[a]Michigan data are from the Lafayette Clinic; Ohio data are from the Cleveland Psychiatric Institute.
[b]Probability values are based on chi-square test with Yates's correction for continuity.

Table F-3. Percentage of True and Cannot Say Responses for Two Psychiatric Samples—continued

	Michigan Sample[a]										Ohio Sample[a]									
	Males					Females					Males					Females				
	White (N = 192)		Black (N = 197)			White (N = 286)		Black (N = 281)			White (N = 310)		Black (N = 125)			White (N = 460)		Black (N = 211)		
Booklet No.	T	?	T	?	p[b]	T	?	T	?	p	T	?	T	?	p	T	?	T	?	p
21 (308)	71	1	66	0		72	1	77	1		50	0	56	2		51	2	61	1	.05
22 (326)	24	0	26	0		50	0	52	1		26	1	22	0		30	1	37	2	
23 (288)	18	0	14	1		24	1	27	1		22	1	15	1		22	1	27	1	
24 (333)	41	1	46	1		49	1	58	1	.05	32	3	32	2		33	2	46	1	.01
25	41	1	47	0		38	1	39	1		37	1	42	2		33	1	48	3	.01
26	50	0	47	0		45	0	45	1		55	1	56	2		51	1	45	4	
27	21	1	24	1		12	1	25	2	.01	19	1	28	2	.05	17	3	28	3	.01
28	37	2	43	0		23	1	30	1		30	3	35	2		19	2	27	4	
29	31	1	32	0		32	1	36	1		32	1	23	1	.05	26	1	24	2	
30	86	1	79	1		88	0	83	1		72	1	73	2		68	1	65	0	
31	22	1	24	0		29	1	32	1		21	1	32	1	.05	22	1	27	2	
32 (328)	57	0	38	0	.01	57	0	56	1		32	2	28	0		32	2	25	1	
33 (323)	53	0	59	0		46	1	50	1		42	1	58	1	.01	41	1	56	0	.01
34	19	0	19	1		21	1	21	1		21	0	25	1		20	2	23	2	
35 (331)	24	1	27	0		13	1	20	1		27	0	38	0	.05	20	4	31	3	.01
36	51	0	50	0		41	1	41	1		57	0	56	1		56	1	52	0	
37 (302)	73	1	71	0		64	1	63	2		76	1	76	0		66	2	71	3	
38 (311)	63	0	62	0		44	1	39	1		50	1	53	1		28	2	33	1	
39	62	0	54	0		64	1	61	1		45	1	42	1		41	1	46	1	
40	40	1	30	0		37	0	41	1		23	1	29	1		26	1	30	1	
41	64	0	62	0		73	0	73	1		51	1	52	2		53	0	54	1	
42	21	3	22	1		17	1	13	1		26	3	18	2		18	4	26	5	.05
43	41	0	42	0		50	1	55	1		34	1	41	2		37	2	34	2	
44	20	0	20	0		31	1	40	1	.05	20	1	21	2		23	1	29	2	
45	69	0	74	0		65	1	68	1		61	1	74	1	.05	47	1	60	0	.01

46	45	2	52	1		38	2	35	1		53	4	57	1		51	2	58	1	
47	23	1	28	0		31	1	38	1		24	2	25	1		36	2	39	1	
48	18	0	21	1		14	1	18	1		22	2	26	1		13	1	25	1	.01
49	16	0	13	1		5	1	11	1	.05	11	1	12	0		9	0	8	1	
50	16	1	16	0		16	1	16	1		14	3	18	2		13	0	17	3	
51	61	0	62	1		66	1	56	1	.05	68	2	70	2		67	1	74	0	
52	43	0	28	0	.01	43	0	38	1		25	3	31	1		30	2	27	2	
53	12	1	15	0		8	1	18	1	.01	19	2	29	2	.05	18	2	29	4	.01
54	75	2	81	0		77	1	81	1		84	1	86	2		82	2	85	1	
55	59	1	58	1		55	0	45	1	.05	72	2	58	0	.01	65	0	64	1	
56	32	1	47	0	.01	12	1	24	1	.01	27	2	38	1	.05	16	1	35	1	.01
57	46	1	64	0	.01	52	1	56	1		62	2	79	1	.01	64	2	72	1	.05
58	36	3	52	3	.01	34	3	57	3	.01	52	8	73	4	.01	52	6	70	4	.01
59	55	1	64	0		47	0	62	1	.01	66	3	72	2		51	1	65	2	.01
60	88	0	85	0		88	1	81	1	.05	85	1	84	1		79	0	82	1	
61	53	1	58	0		48	1	47	2		57	2	67	2		45	1	55	2	.05
62	46	1	51	0		51	1	60	2	.05	40	1	46	1		41	2	53	1	.01
63	69	0	67	1		63	0	63	1		69	1	63	2		62	1	62	0	
64	52	1	46	0		51	1	47	1		55	1	54	0		48	2	44	1	
65	76	1	76	1		78	2	73	1		81	3	80	6		83	3	82	1	
66	18	0	16	1		15	1	17	1		19	1	20	0		15	1	25	1	.01
67	70	1	68	0		79	0	80	1		68	1	74	2		74	1	70	0	
68	69	0	61	1		50	0	52	1		75	2	71	2		69	1	67	1	
69	15	1	20	0		13	2	16	1		22	2	37	4	.01	22	1	27	1	
70	9	2	15	3		23	2	21	2		26	4	30	3		46	2	36	1	.01
71	63	1	71	1		61	1	64	1		73	1	74	0		71	2	76	0	
72	32	0	33	1		42	1	43	1		28	2	27	2		27	2	32	0	
73	50	1	67	1	.01	49	1	57	1		45	1	54	2		37	2	51	2	.01
74	13	1	11	1		58	0	53	1		11	2	6	3		63	2	63	3	
75	96	0	94	0		95	0	95	1		89	1	86	1		89	1	89	1	
76	57	0	46	0	.05	65	1	64	1		34	1	40	2		41	1	44	1	
77	28	0	38	0	.05	57	0	59	1		31	1	44	1	.01	59	1	72	0	.01
78	44	0	59	0	.01	65	0	65	2		56	1	65	3		72	1	72	2	

Table F-3. Percentage of True and Cannot Say Responses for Two Psychiatric Samples—continued

	Michigan Sample[a]										Ohio Sample[a]									
	Males					Females					Males					Females				
	White (N = 192)		Black (N = 197)			White (N = 286)		Black (N = 281)			White (N = 310)		Black (N = 125)			White (N = 460)		Black (N = 211)		
Booklet No.	T	?	T	?	p[b]	T	?	T	?	p	T	?	T	?	p	T	?	T	?	p
79	39	0	52	0	.01	16	1	27	1	.01	50	1	67	2	.01	38	1	45	0	
80	27	1	29	0		17	1	18	1		28	0	27	4		17	1	31	0	.01
81	57	1	37	1	.01	34	1	14	1	.01	51	0	38	2	.05	20	1	15	1	
82	42	1	31	1	.05	51	0	43	1		41	0	42	2		48	1	40	1	
83	85	1	84	0		80	1	83	1		90	0	92	2		90	1	92	0	
84	60	0	64	0		65	0	73	1	.05	62	2	69	2		58	1	70	1	.01
85	9	0	10	0		4	1	7	1		11	1	21	2	.05	9	1	18	0	.01
86	69	1	43	1	.01	75	1	67	2	.05	44	1	30	2	.01	51	0	47	1	
87	13	1	11	1		27	1	14	1	.01	22	1	22	3		28	1	29	1	
88	73	0	84	1	.01	64	1	71	1		87	0	88	2		79	1	84	1	
89	51	1	67	2	.01	49	1	60	1	.05	60	1	75	1	.01	54	1	73	3	.01
90	89	1	88	1		88	0	86	1		82	1	82	1		82	1	83	0	
91	28	0	41	2	.01	24	1	28	1		47	1	52	2		36	1	41	1	
92	15	0	9	2		41	1	36	1		17	1	17	2		45	1	49	0	
93	67	1	77	2	.05	63	0	75	1	.01	61	0	71	2	.05	51	1	68	1	.01
94	60	0	53	1		58	1	59	1		60	1	68	2		57	1	62	3	
95	18	0	15	1		26	1	23	1		32	0	28	1		40	1	36	1	
96	52	1	58	1		52	1	53	1		60	1	69	2		67	1	62	1	
97	43	1	37	2		43	1	49	1		25	0	29	1		26	0	29	2	
98	49	2	53	2		50	2	65	2	.01	63	3	71	2		61	3	82	1	.01
99	51	0	53	1		50	1	46	1		57	1	65	1		50	0	58	2	.05
100	66	1	66	0		73	1	75	1		65	1	76	1	.05	67	3	68	2	
101	79	1	72	1		76	0	58	1	.01	60	3	67	1		39	2	47	1	
102	82	0	75	0		86	0	78	1	.05	70	1	70	0		73	1	64	0	.05
103	65	0	56	0		58	0	54	1		73	1	65	1		69	0	67	0	

104	31	0	24	0		34	1	35	1		23	0	26	0		25	0	22	0	
105	85	1	66	0	.01	86	0	80	1		72	0	71	0		77	0	75	0	
106	41	0	29	1	.05	39	1	44	1		27	0	42	2	.01	32	0	39	1	
107	43	0	53	1		33	1	34	1		65	1	65	2		60	1	65	1	
108	28	0	25	0		24	1	31	1		31	0	28	2		29	1	34	1	
109	46	1	45	0		53	1	56	1		40	2	50	2		48	1	62	1	.01
110	23	1	22	1		18	1	23	2		24	2	34	0	.05	20	1	30	1	.01
111	40	0	40	0		43	0	49	1		54	1	53	0		58	1	66	1	.05
112	72	1	77	0		77	0	78	1		79	1	86	1		74	1	82	1	.05
113	88	1	85	1		93	0	89	1		94	0	87	1	.05	92	1	87	2	
114	26	0	25	0		31	1	41	1	.05	21	0	26	1		24	1	29	1	
115	58	1	54	1		66	1	65	2		76	2	78	1		72	3	73	0	
116	38	1	42	0		27	1	34	1		57	0	51	1		40	1	37	0	
117	52	1	62	1		48	1	55	1		58	0	68	1		48	1	62	1	.01
118	49	0	56	0		24	0	32	1		46	0	58	0	.01	23	1	44	1	.01
119	59	1	55	0		62	0	58	1		69	0	63	2		66	2	64	1	
120	55	0	50	0		53	1	60	1		56	1	54	2		47	1	59	2	.01
121	18	1	21	1		14	1	18	2		20	1	27	2		18	0	26	1	.05
122	75	1	80	1		72	1	77	1		81	2	78	1		73	1	78	2	
123	12	1	10	1		11	1	14	1		15	1	19	2		13	0	20	1	.05
124	66	1	72	1		63	1	72	2	.05	61	1	76	2	.01	54	1	74	2	.01
125	24	0	28	0		33	1	36	1		24	1	24	3		23	0	29	1	
126	54	1	58	1		59	1	65	1		61	1	62	1		65	0	64	2	
127	61	0	64	1		63	1	65	2		61	1	65	2		62	1	72	2	.05
128	65	0	69	1		56	1	56	1		64	1	61	0		54	1	57	1	
129	48	1	44	1		64	1	63	1		49	2	52	0		53	1	49	0	
130	65	0	52	0	.05	69	0	62	1		60	0	54	1		70	1	56	0	.01
131	55	1	40	0	.01	59	0	50	1		57	0	54	1		67	1	53	1	.01
132	26	0	28	0		63	0	51	1	.01	42	0	44	1		68	0	67	1	
133	58	1	52	1		69	1	60	1	.05	68	2	58	4		75	1	70	3	
134	72	0	73	0		74	1	77	1		64	1	68	1		65	1	70	2	
135	52	0	46	0		29	1	38	1	.05	36	0	39	2		23	1	34	4	.01

Table F-3. Percentage of True and Cannot Say Responses for Two Psychiatric Samples—continued

	Michigan Sample[a]										Ohio Sample[a]									
	Males					Females					Males					Females				
	White (N = 192)		Black (N = 197)			White (N = 286)		Black (N = 281)			White (N = 310)		Black (N = 125)			White (N = 460)		Black (N = 211)		
Booklet No.	T	?	T	?	p[b]	T	?	T	?	p	T	?	T	?	p	T	?	T	?	p
136	51	0	61	0	.05	50	0	53	2		54	0	67	0	.05	47	1	55	3	.05
137	45	0	56	1	.05	43	1	44	1		62	1	60	0		65	2	66	2	
138	52	0	37	1	.01	75	1	64	1	.01	48	1	52	1		61	1	67	2	
139	31	0	30	1		35	1	36	1		22	1	30	1		25	1	28	1	
140	56	1	55	0		64	0	68	1		58	0	61	2		82	0	80	2	
141	57	1	50	1		59	1	49	1	.05	58	1	58	3		55	1	55	2	
142	74	0	64	0	.05	79	1	74	1		59	0	58	2		63	0	62	1	
143	38	1	41	0		27	0	26	1		48	1	51	3		34	0	39	2	
144	18	0	20	0		5	1	6	1		41	0	50	2		14	1	11	2	
145	36	0	25	1	.05	28	1	21	1		26	1	24	1		22	0	19	1	
146	36	0	30	0		23	1	23	2		32	1	42	2		24	2	26	0	
147	55	0	60	0		53	1	62	1	.05	60	0	74	2	.01	53	0	63	2	.05
148	45	1	42	0		42	1	48	1		46	1	56	2		47	2	55	3	
149	19	0	19	1		59	1	44	1	.01	17	1	23	2		45	1	43	1	
150	86	1	80	0		75	0	77	1		84	1	78	5		72	2	73	1	
151	8	0	7	0		4	1	6	1		10	1	15	0		8	1	17	0	.01
152	35	0	47	1	.05	36	1	31	1		59	1	62	2		56	0	61	0	
153	61	0	64	1		60	0	55	1		63	0	78	0	.01	63	0	67	1	
154	66	0	62	0		73	1	63	1	.05	76	1	69	1		78	1	70	1	
155	57	1	39	0	.01	37	1	36	1		57	1	45	2	.05	42	2	37	2	
156	31	0	25	0		27	1	28	1		33	0	39	2		29	1	35	1	
157	39	0	30	0		43	1	49	1		34	1	54	0	.01	40	1	51	1	.01
158	36	1	29	0		67	0	69	1		28	0	35	0		48	1	59	1	.01
159	45	1	33	0	.05	43	0	46	1		32	1	40	0		34	0	43	1	.05
160	18	0	22	1		16	2	16	1		33	0	40	2		29	0	35	1	

161	24	1	24	0		21	1	27	1		20	0	35	2	.01	27	0	34	1	
162	57	1	42	0	.01	57	1	54	1		53	1	54	1		49	2	55	1	
163	48	1	52	0		54	1	63	1		60	1	67	2		48	1	54	1	
164	70	0	77	0		72	1	77	1		85	0	77	1		82	1	82	2	
165	43	0	53	0		50	1	46	2		61	0	64	1		54	0	61	1	
166	50	1	46	0		62	1	63	1		44	0	50	1		64	0	68	0	
167	34	0	39	1		25	1	24	1		41	1	45	1		29	2	40	2	.01
168	52	1	43	0		45	2	52	2		28	4	31	4		26	3	25	2	
169	79	0	87	0	.05	80	0	82	1		87	0	82	0		79	1	82	1	
170	33	0	43	0		23	1	35	1	.01	50	0	52	2		40	1	50	0	.05
171	53	1	48	1		63	0	59	1		51	1	55	2		60	1	56	1	
172	45	1	41	1		57	0	53	1		45	1	49	2		52	1	55	0	
173	49	1	71	1	.01	70	0	72	1		73	1	76	2		72	1	80	1	.05
174	60	0	63	0		44	1	44	1		61	1	62	1		46	0	50	0	
175	62	0	59	1		54	0	48	1		68	1	54	3	.05	59	1	55	1	
176	67	0	55	0	.05	45	1	33	1	.01	56	0	43	1	.05	42	0	37	1	
177	86	1	86	1		81	1	81	1		89	2	93	1		89	0	89	1	
178	65	0	73	0		63	1	59	1		81	0	78	1		79	1	78	1	
179	58	0	34	0	.01	53	1	41	1	.01	28	0	24	1		27	0	26	2	
180	54	0	39	0	.01	54	1	49	1		50	1	42	0		51	0	52	1	
181	48	1	52	0		40	1	37	1		43	0	46	1		37	0	47	0	.05
182	41	1	37	1		48	0	52	1		33	1	34	1		31	1	31	1	
183	36	0	30	1		34	1	35	1		31	0	34	1		35	0	33	0	
184	12	0	16	0		9	1	20	1	.01	17	0	40	0	.01	15	0	25	1	.01
185	78	0	86	0		80	0	79	1		79	1	82	0		85	0	82	3	
186	39	0	38	0		42	0	53	1	.01	49	0	41	1		42	0	46	1	
187	66	1	62	0		59	1	54	1		74	1	66	1		70	0	63	1	
188	40	0	43	1		45	1	40	1		49	0	51	1		56	1	57	1	
189	38	0	29	1		40	0	44	1		24	0	33	3	.05	37	0	32	1	
190	64	0	67	2		49	1	46	1		76	1	72	0		67	0	64	1	
191	45	0	35	2		42	0	40	1		38	2	49	0	.05	45	0	49	0	
192	74	0	74	2		72	1	65	1		81	1	71	1	.05	72	1	66	1	
193	71	0	70	1		68	0	57	1	.01	78	0	72	1		74	0	72	2	

Table F-3. Percentage of True and Cannot Say Responses for Two Psychiatric Samples—continued

	Michigan Sample[a]										Ohio Sample[a]									
	Males					Females					Males					Females				
	White (N = 192)		Black (N = 197)			White (N = 286)		Black (N = 281)			White (N = 310)		Black (N = 125)			White (N = 460)		Black (N = 211)		
Booklet No.	T	?	T	?	p[b]	T	?	T	?	p	T	?	T	?	p	T	?	T	?	p
194	26	0	26	1		22	1	28	1		25	2	39	1	.01	31	2	41	2	.05
195	83	1	73	2	.05	90	0	80	1	.01	78	0	65	0	.01	75	0	70	0	
196	93	0	90	2		87	1	90	1		87	0	90	0		87	0	87	1	
197	12	0	13	1		6	1	13	1	.01	15	1	27	0	.05	15	0	25	1	.01
198	41	1	52	2	.05	35	1	40	1		65	0	66	0		65	0	63	1	
199	84	0	72	2	.05	84	1	78	1		79	1	67	0	.01	74	1	82	0	
200	16	0	19	1		9	1	14	1		19	1	23	1		14	1	27	0	.01
201	56	1	45	1	.05	55	0	49	1		48	0	46	1		49	1	57	1	.05
202	20	1	24	0		19	1	23	1		18	1	35	2	.01	15	1	25	1	.01
203	39	0	37	0		40	1	35	1		41	1	45	0		50	1	48	0	
204	38	0	37	1		35	1	33	1		35	0	35	1		32	0	32	0	
205	17	0	19	0		9	1	11	1		15	2	25	2	.05	12	0	18	1	.05
206	20	1	34	0	.01	23	1	23	1		23	1	40	0	.01	31	0	40	0	.05
207	72	1	81	0		67	0	67	1		76	1	78	2		71	1	78	1	
208	49	1	60	0	.05	55	0	47	1		45	1	49	2		38	0	36	0	
209	22	1	19	1		14	1	16	1		22	1	27	1		20	0	23	1	
210	11	0	11	1		9	1	13	1		9	1	12	1		13	1	13	1	
211	16	0	26	0	.05	21	1	27	1		17	1	25	0		19	0	28	2	.01
212	33	0	30	0		40	1	51	1	.05	26	1	48	0	.01	37	0	41	0	
213	17	1	24	1		10	1	25	1	.01	29	1	36	0		27	0	43	0	.01
214	46	0	37	1		44	0	41	1		58	1	58	1		56	1	50	0	
215	47	0	35	0	.05	26	1	30	1		55	1	57	1		22	0	35	1	.01
216	44	1	33	0	.05	38	0	43	1		32	1	32	2		36	2	40	1	
217	80	0	73	0		83	1	81	2		63	0	60	0		71	0	67	0	
218	9	0	21	0	.01	7	1	13	1	.05	15	0	21	0		12	0	17	0	

219	39	1	46	1		12	1	11	1		56	0	60	1		17	0	15	1	
220	82	0	87	1		83	0	86	1		87	1	90	2		88	0	89	1	
221	77	1	73	1		50	1	53	2		80	1	73	0		60	1	65	1	
222	42	0	43	1		34	1	29	1		41	1	57	0	.01	40	1	51	1	.01
223	38	0	31	1		10	1	10	1		53	0	54	1		20	0	19	1	
224	50	0	49	1		45	1	48	1		44	1	65	1	.01	40	0	55	1	.01
225	69	0	67	0		80	0	84	1		73	0	75	1		74	0	80	0	
226	61	0	52	0		71	1	71	1		41	1	62	1	.01	55	1	68	1	.01
227	8	1	12	0		12	1	12	1		12	0	18	0		12	0	19	1	.05
228	61	1	76	1	.01	51	1	66	1	.01	76	0	78	1		75	0	75	2	
229	37	0	40	1		38	1	39	1		58	0	62	1		48	0	56	1	.05
230	46	0	45	1		34	1	40	1		60	0	57	0		55	0	54	0	
231	51	1	62	0	.05	41	0	43	1		39	1	57	2	.01	26	0	38	1	.01
232	26	2	37	1	.05	24	1	30	1		43	3	50	1		46	2	41	3	
233	39	1	32	0		27	1	17	1	.01	38	2	46	2		36	1	40	3	
234	47	0	50	1		50	1	53	1		55	0	64	1		58	0	62	0	
235	59	0	64	0		46	1	58	1	.01	65	1	68	0		62	0	67	1	
236	47	0	31	1	.01	58	1	54	1		34	1	40	2		40	0	45	2	
237	45	1	45	1		42	1	42	1		50	2	58	1		49	1	57	1	
238	57	1	59	0		59	0	58	1		53	1	50	2		59	0	57	0	
239	62	0	69	1		73	1	81	1	.05	58	1	63	1		56	0	69	0	.01
240	24	0	42	1	.01	15	1	20	1		41	0	50	0		26	0	37	0	.01
241	41	1	43	0		35	1	50	1	.01	43	1	58	0	.01	38	0	54	1	.01
242	42	0	48	1		35	1	34	1		59	1	61	1		57	0	63	2	
243	62	0	57	1		55	0	48	1		73	1	68	1		69	0	68	1	
244	63	1	59	1		60	1	68	1		61	0	65	1		61	0	64	1	
245	38	1	33	1		38	1	40	1		35	1	43	0		39	1	37	1	
246	8	0	7	1		12	1	8	1		13	1	15	2		12	0	13	2	
247	21	0	21	0		34	1	28	1		22	1	26	1		24	1	27	2	
248	33	0	47	0	.01	36	1	39	1		40	1	42	0		42	0	52	1	.05
249	47	1	44	2		48	1	57	1	.05	64	4	65	1		64	1	69	1	
250	46	1	59	0	.05	38	1	44	1		46	1	48	0		37	1	45	1	.05

Table F-3. Percentage of True and Cannot Say Responses for Two Psychiatric Samples—continued

	Michigan Sample[a]										Ohio Sample[a]									
	Males					Females					Males					Females				
	White (N = 192)		Black (N = 197)			White (N = 286)		Black (N = 281)			White (N = 310)		Black (N = 125)			White (N = 460)		Black (N = 211)		
Booklet No.	T	?	T	?	p[b]	T	?	T	?	p	T	?	T	?	p	T	?	T	?	p
251	30	0	25	0		28	1	32	1		31	1	38	0		30	1	35	0	
252	37	1	30	1		28	2	36	1		30	0	38	0		27	1	33	0	
253	67	1	66	2		66	1	67	1		65	0	77	1	.05	66	0	66	1	
254	28	1	18	1	.05	19	1	12	1	.05	33	0	35	0		27	0	27	1	
255	46	1	40	1		56	1	52	1		50	2	39	2		45	2	46	2	
256	17	1	13	1		10	2	13	1		15	0	27	0	.01	14	0	22	0	.05
257	69	0	83	0	.01	66	0	79	1	.01	83	1	89	0		83	0	81	1	
258	78	1	87	1	.05	88	1	91	1		90	1	90	2		92	1	88	1	
259	60	0	53	0		63	0	57	1		47	0	46	3		46	0	45	1	
260	42	0	34	0		30	1	26	1		44	1	51	0		34	0	36	1	
261	27	1	35	2		55	0	41	1	.01	42	0	40	2		60	0	58	1	
262	64	0	74	0	.05	44	1	58	1	.01	75	0	77	1		60	0	72	1	.01
263	37	1	49	1	.05	35	0	39	1		41	1	50	1		38	0	42	1	
264	26	0	43	2	.01	12	1	25	1	.01	52	2	56	1		41	1	50	0	.05
265	41	0	37	0		37	1	41	1		37	1	35	1		34	0	36	1	
266	42	1	41	1		41	1	40	1		36	1	38	2		40	0	47	0	
267	59	0	44	1	.01	57	1	53	1		45	2	53	2		46	1	51	3	
268	42	1	61	1	.01	53	0	58	1		63	2	74	2	.05	61	2	71	0	.05
269	16	0	17	0		9	1	12	1		19	1	26	0		13	0	22	0	.01
270	34	0	22	0	.01	33	1	21	1	.01	41	1	27	1	.05	37	1	30	1	
271	23	0	32	0		18	1	18	1		29	1	42	2	.05	34	2	37	0	
272	78	0	81	0		77	1	76	1		81	1	86	2		80	1	80	0	
273	18	0	23	0		23	1	30	1		27	0	30	1		27	1	32	0	
274	64	1	62	1		58	0	44	1	.01	50	0	50	0		51	0	50	1	
275	11	0	14	2		11	1	16	1		18	1	26	0		17	0	20	1	

276	81	0	90	0	.05	81	1	85	1		88	0	90	0		89	1	85	1	
277	56	1	52	0		41	1	40	1		40	1	51	1	.05	23	1	34	0	.01
278	56	0	52	0		61	1	55	1		40	1	59	0	.01	47	0	56	1	.05
279	22	0	31	1		20	1	21	1		36	0	45	0		33	0	40	0	
280	45	0	56	0	.05	32	1	51	1	.01	57	1	70	0	.05	46	0	58	1	.01
281	66	1	55	0	.05	60	1	49	1	.05	70	1	58	0	.05	68	1	63	0	
282	60	0	44	0	.01	67	1	55	1	.01	45	1	45	1		47	0	48	0	
283	45	0	48	2		20	1	18	1		61	1	68	2		31	0	39	0	.05
284	43	1	54	1	.05	43	1	59	1	.01	42	1	57	0	.01	37	1	54	0	.01
285	86	1	85	0		90	0	87	1		86	1	90	1		78	0	81	1	
286	23	1	22	0		15	1	24	1	.05	17	1	28	1	.05	18	1	32	0	.01
287	32	1	49	1	.01	28	2	37	1	.05	51	1	62	1	.05	46	0	50	1	
288 (23)	15	0	13	1		21	1	22	1		19	1	20	1		18	0	29	0	.01
289	58	1	40	2	.01	66	1	58	1	.05	57	0	44	1	.05	61	1	62	1	
290 (13)	56	1	52	2		57	0	57	1		51	0	51	2		50	1	44	1	
291	13	0	15	2		9	1	14	1		16	1	25	0		16	0	23	0	.05
292	54	0	42	1	.05	44	1	42	1		45	0	36	0		46	0	39	0	
293	26	1	25	2		19	1	27	1	.05	25	0	31	1		20	0	30	1	.01
294	39	0	39	1		67	0	58	1	.05	43	1	36	1		69	0	61	0	
295	48	2	38	2	.05	66	0	54	1	.01	49	4	52	2		76	1	68	0	.05
296	57	0	65	2		64	1	70	1		61	0	69	1		60	1	70	1	.05
297	41	0	30	1	.05	35	1	35	1		30	0	43	0	.05	31	1	39	1	.05
298	39	1	47	2		24	1	32	1		50	0	57	2		43	1	52	0	.05
299	58	2	57	2		67	2	62	1		53	1	46	2		57	1	51	0	
300	60	0	57	1		18	1	20	1		61	0	47	2	.01	20	1	25	2	
301	61	1	53	1		62	1	62	1		43	1	47	0		43	0	44	1	
302 (37)	72	0	68	0		63	0	69	1		80	0	74	2		75	1	76	0	
303	43	0	32	0	.05	52	1	50	1		41	1	46	2		50	0	53	1	
304	69	0	51	0	.01	66	1	56	1	.05	49	1	53	1		60	0	58	0	
305 (366)	55	0	45	0		65	1	61	1		40	0	41	1		43	0	48	0	
306	66	1	68	1		69	1	57	1	.01	80	0	62	0	.01	73	1	73	0	
307	43	0	41	0		46	1	49	1		59	0	61	0		56	0	51	0	
308 (21)	69	0	64	0		75	1	75	1		50	1	65	1	.01	53	1	59	2	

Table F-3. Percentage of True and Cannot Say Responses for Two Psychiatric Samples—continued

	Michigan Sample[a]										Ohio Sample[a]									
	Males					Females					Males					Females				
	White (N = 192)		Black (N = 197)			White (N = 286)		Black (N = 281)			White (N = 310)		Black (N = 125)			White (N = 460)		Black (N = 211)		
Booklet No.	T	?	T	?	p[b]	T	?	T	?	p	T	?	T	?	p	T	?	T	?	p
309	59	1	68	1		62	1	60	1		78	0	81	1		73	0	78	1	
310 (20)	42	0	65	1	.01	42	1	56	1	.01	73	1	81	1		66	3	77	2	.01
311 (38)	60	0	61	1		39	1	36	1		50	1	52	1		28	1	36	2	.05
312	20	1	23	1		16	1	19	1		18	0	22	0		17	0	25	0	.05
313	54	0	59	1		54	0	60	1		74	1	70	1		74	1	75	3	
314 (15)	46	0	47	0		48	1	52	1		45	2	56	3	.05	44	2	48	2	
315 (16)	25	0	26	1		27	0	32	1		26	0	30	1		24	0	36	0	.01
316	58	1	73	1	.01	62	1	71	1	.05	61	0	75	0	.01	54	0	65	0	.01
317 (362)..........	59	1	61	1		69	0	64	1		54	0	50	0		62	0	55	0	
318 (8)............	36	1	43	1		34	1	30	1		61	0	74	1	.05	57	0	60	0	
319	53	2	60	1		47	1	61	1	.01	60	1	66	1		53	0	66	0	.01
320	32	1	30	0		22	1	24	1		19	1	30	0	.05	16	0	20	1	
321	49	0	32	1	.01	63	0	58	1		46	0	47	1		63	0	62	0	
322	65	0	65	0		69	1	67	1		60	0	62	0		62	0	52	2	.05
323 (33)	43	0	55	0	.05	42	1	46	1		43	1	58	1	.01	43	0	58	0	.01
324	13	1	15	0		12	1	9	1		15	0	15	0		14	0	13	1	
325	38	0	36	0		50	1	43	1		32	0	44	0	.05	38	0	44	1	
326 (22)	20	0	24	0		43	0	42	1		19	0	26	0		28	0	34	1	
327	67	1	65	0		73	1	72	1		67	0	72	2		63	2	71	0	
328 (32)	52	0	37	1	.01	52	0	53	1		31	0	32	1		33	2	33	0	
329	30	0	33	1		24	1	29	1		45	1	26	0	.01	41	0	32	1	.05
330	67	1	55	0	.05	66	0	53	1	.01	73	1	72	0		69	0	60	1	.05
331 (35)	23	1	22	0		13	1	16	1		26	1	34	3		20	2	35	2	.01
332	28	0	39	0	.05	26	1	40	1	.01	27	1	46	1	.01	33	0	47	0	.01
333 (24)	35	1	38	1		40	1	53	1	.01	26	1	28	0		31	1	41	0	.05

334	20	0	28	0		20	1	28	1	.05	28	1	42	1	.01	28	1	44	1	.01
335	43	1	39	0		50	1	52	1		31	1	46	0	.01	31	0	35	1	
336	61	0	46	1	.01	61	1	53	1		40	1	50	1		40	0	44	0	
337	58	1	39	0	.01	63	1	54	1	.05	43	1	51	0		48	0	44	3	
338	60	1	63	0		62	0	72	1	.01	62	0	65	0		65	0	66	0	
339	26	0	20	1		28	1	31	1		17	1	21	1		22	1	22	0	
340	59	0	61	0		58	0	64	1		55	1	64	0		59	0	61	2	
341	21	0	22	1		23	1	26	1		26	0	41	0	.01	26	0	38	1	.01
342	36	0	28	0		38	1	31	1		21	0	29	0		24	0	34	0	.05
343	49	1	51	0		52	1	58	1		48	0	62	0	.05	52	0	62	0	.05
344	29	1	29	0		31	0	28	1		26	0	42	0	.01	26	0	35	1	.05
345	35	1	36	1		44	1	41	1		28	0	42	0	.01	33	0	39	0	
346	28	1	25	0		27	1	28	1		30	0	37	0		25	1	37	1	.01
347	70	1	56	1	.01	72	1	61	1	.05	74	1	58	1	.01	76	0	62	2	.01
348	59	0	63	0		57	1	62	2		67	1	67	1		55	0	63	1	
349	40	1	37	1		37	1	46	1	.05	29	1	51	2	.01	28	0	41	2	.01
350	16	1	19	1		17	1	22	1		17	0	30	1	.01	18	1	30	0	.01
351	19	1	16	0		27	0	25	1		24	0	34	0	.05	33	0	35	1	
352	31	1	27	0		42	1	35	1		26	0	42	0	.01	30	1	40	1	.01
353	56	0	56	1		43	1	50	1		61	1	62	2		61	1	61	1	
354	12	0	17	1		17	1	14	1		19	1	30	0	.05	18	0	27	1	.01
355	18	0	14	0		20	0	17	1		17	0	27	0	.05	18	1	18	1	
356	59	1	46	0	.05	57	1	49	1		36	0	42	0		38	0	45	2	
357	55	0	48	0		64	0	57	1		52	1	52	2		50	0	55	1	
358	26	1	30	0		24	1	34	1	.05	27	0	44	0	.01	25	0	42	0	.01
359	49	1	40	0		55	0	63	1	.05	41	1	57	0	.01	47	0	55	0	.05
360	28	0	15	1	.01	29	1	19	1	.01	18	1	26	2		22	1	25	2	
361	63	0	55	0		79	1	75	1		58	0	50	0		69	0	61	1	
362 (317)	61	1	55	1		72	1	67	1		54	0	50	0		66	0	54	1	.01
363	14	1	18	1		15	1	12	1		16	0	30	1	.01	19	0	27	1	.05
364	28	2	35	1		19	1	33	1	.01	29	1	54	1	.01	27	0	45	1	.01
365	27	0	29	0		17	1	19	1		28	0	42	1	.01	24	1	32	2	.05

Table F-3. Percentage of True and Cannot Say Responses for Two Psychiatric Samples—continued

	Michigan Sample[a]										Ohio Sample[a]									
	Males					Females					Males					Females				
	White (N = 192)		Black (N = 197)			White (N = 286)		Black (N = 281)			White (N = 310)		Black (N = 125)			White (N = 460)		Black (N = 211)		
Booklet No.	T	?	T	?	p[b]	T	?	T	?	p	T	?	T	?	p	T	?	T	?	p
366 (305)	46	1	38	0		65	1	58	1		34	1	42	0		43	0	43	0	
367	55	0	56	0		43	1	32	1	.01	54	1	54	1		41	1	42	2	
368	53	0	52	0		57	0	62	1		60	1	68	0		60	0	69	0	.05
369	65	1	60	0		60	0	58	1		67	0	73	0		64	1	69	1	
370	77	0	76	0		74	0	77	1		78	0	78	0		79	0	83	0	
371	51	0	58	1		39	1	41	1		62	0	56	0		57	0	52	1	
372	61	0	60	1		60	1	62	1		64	0	65	0		60	0	67	1	
373	34	2	36	2		34	1	37	1		48	3	58	1		46	1	55	1	.05
374	73	1	64	0		80	0	72	1	.05	56	0	65	0		54	0	64	0	.05
375	40	1	40	0		38	1	44	1		38	0	53	0	.01	40	0	53	1	.01
376	63	1	45	2	.01	73	2	43	1	.01	83	2	66	0	.01	85	0	70	1	.01
377	56	0	47	0		55	1	50	1		49	2	43	0		46	1	45	0	
378	30	1	27	0		25	1	16	1	.01	40	2	40	2		23	2	30	2	
379	39	0	45	1		22	1	28	1		54	1	54	3		45	1	57	0	.01
380	69	1	61	0		68	0	62	1		70	1	74	1		60	0	73	1	.01
381	39	1	41	0		37	1	46	1	.05	41	0	46	1		43	0	48	0	
382	58	0	54	0		66	0	65	1		57	0	63	2		61	1	68	2	
383	65	1	60	0		63	0	69	1		49	1	58	2		53	1	57	3	
384	53	1	49	0		50	1	67	1	.01	48	3	46	2		50	1	55	4	
385	19	0	23	1		28	1	44	1	.01	31	0	57	1	.01	47	0	64	1	.01
386	30	0	36	0		23	1	37	1	.01	34	1	53	0	.01	25	0	47	2	.01
387	33	2	29	1		20	1	22	1		42	2	52	0		39	1	46	1	
388	18	0	11	1		36	1	24	1	.01	17	0	25	1		31	0	35	0	
389	56	1	46	1		58	1	60	1		47	0	48	0		56	0	57	1	
390	57	2	65	1		65	1	70	1		68	1	70	1		67	1	77	0	.05

391	41	1	58	1	.01	57	1	62	1		59	0	72	0	.05	62	1	67	1	
392	16	0	15	2		23	1	33	1	.01	26	0	50	2	.01	42	1	55	1	.01
393	11	0	7	1		4	1	7	1		18	0	20	0		10	1	15	0	
394	54	0	56	2		63	1	53	1	.05	62	1	61	2		58	1	65	1	
395	38	0	36	2		40	2	46	1		43	0	61	1	.01	48	1	61	0	.01
396	39	0	37	2		55	1	47	1		37	1	36	2		40	0	40	1	
397	71	0	61	0		81	0	75	1		61	1	58	1		67	0	63	0	
398	49	0	43	1		41	1	49	1		39	1	38	1		35	0	45	0	.05
399	53	0	57	3		48	1	47	1		66	2	68	2		60	2	56	1	
400	53	0	74	0	.01	44	1	56	2	.01	58	1	70	1	.05	52	1	66	0	.01
401	65	0	71	1		57	0	51	1		70	0	57	1	.05	53	1	49	1	
402	41	1	38	1		47	0	49	1		50	0	56	0		52	1	61	1	.05
403	58	1	71	1	.05	52	2	56	1		78	1	80	2		72	0	78	1	
404	61	3	67	0		60	1	71	1	.01	72	1	75	1		63	1	81	2	.01
405	83	0	86	0		79	0	74	1		82	1	79	1		77	1	81	0	
406	61	0	69	1		57	1	67	1	.05	69	0	71	2		56	2	64	0	
407	54	0	68	1	.01	33	1	41	1	.05	62	0	72	0		58	0	64	2	
408	76	1	69	0		84	0	82	1		68	1	74	0		75	1	75	1	
409	60	1	70	0		76	1	74	1		73	0	73	0		77	0	78	1	
410	53	1	59	0		28	1	40	1	.01	53	0	58	2		38	0	56	0	.01
411	47	0	37	0		51	0	42	1	.05	37	0	46	2		34	2	45	1	.01
412	72	1	72	0		73	1	64	1	.05	75	1	74	1		70	0	72	1	
413	21	1	19	2		15	1	20	1		40	1	53	1	.05	33	1	37	2	
414	59	0	44	1	.01	64	1	64	1		50	0	59	1		53	1	55	0	
415	50	1	72	1	.01	37	1	43	2		54	3	65	3	.05	38	1	62	3	.01
416	69	0	47	0	.01	66	1	68	1		56	0	71	0	.01	66	1	73	1	
417	39	1	42	0		31	0	39	1		40	0	55	0	.01	33	0	48	1	.01
418	60	0	42	1	.01	69	1	60	1	.05	45	1	41	2		46	2	45	2	
419	35	0	37	0		24	1	26	1		38	0	46	0		22	1	28	1	
420	22	0	31	1	.05	17	1	24	1		29	0	50	1	.01	26	1	45	2	.01
421	59	0	53	0		71	1	67	1		43	1	47	1		56	0	58	1	
422	17	0	17	1		16	1	21	1		23	1	34	1	.05	22	1	27	2	
423	59	1	53	0		41	1	38	1		69	0	51	1	.01	48	0	52	2	

Table F-3. Percentage of True and Cannot Say Responses for Two Psychiatric Samples—continued

	Michigan Sample[a]										Ohio Sample[a]									
	Males					Females					Males					Females				
	White (N = 192)		Black (N = 197)			White (N = 286)		Black (N = 281)			White (N = 310)		Black (N = 125)			White (N = 460)		Black (N = 211)		
Booklet No.	T	?	T	?	p[b]	T	?	T	?	p	T	?	T	?	p	T	?	T	?	p
424	32	1	25	0		36	1	34	1		25	0	37	1	.05	24	1	34	0	.01
425	48	1	48	0		61	1	58	1		43	0	50	0		48	1	58	2	.05
426	54	0	66	1	.05	48	0	62	1	.01	59	0	63	0		50	0	70	0	.01
427	17	0	18	0		41	1	36	1		41	0	47	1		58	1	58	0	
428	49	0	56	2		48	1	46	1		71	1	68	2		67	2	63	3	
429	53	0	59	0		54	1	52	1		64	0	71	0		58	0	61	0	
430	86	1	78	1		87	1	80	1		74	0	73	1		67	1	65	3	
431	65	0	54	0	.05	67	1	67	1		54	0	59	2		57	0	57	0	
432	42	0	54	0	.05	29	1	30	1		48	0	54	1		33	1	45	1	.01
433	18	0	23	2		19	0	26	1		22	0	34	1	.05	16	0	36	1	.01
434	46	0	23	0	.01	16	1	12	1		33	0	34	0		14	0	14	0	
435	37	1	48	0	.05	26	1	24	1		31	0	52	1	.01	46	1	44	1	
436	77	1	76	1		74	0	79	1		74	0	71	2		72	2	78	1	
437	61	0	66	1		44	1	59	1	.01	54	2	70	1	.01	46	1	61	1	.01
438	50	0	48	1		48	1	43	1		37	2	43	0		34	1	39	1	
439	78	0	60	0	.01	77	0	68	1	.05	59	0	59	0		70	0	68	0	
440	70	1	71	0		70	0	68	1		80	0	79	2		76	1	84	0	.05
441	48	1	70	0	.01	41	1	28	2	.01	54	0	50	1		42	2	33	2	.05
442	76	0	70	0		84	0	81	1		72	0	69	0		75	0	75	0	
443	39	0	43	1		53	0	54	1		51	0	57	2		51	1	56	1	
444	39	0	39	0		36	1	42	1		47	2	49	2		57	1	54	4	
445	80	0	83	0		74	0	72	1		84	0	80	1		75	1	77	2	
446	56	0	51	0		44	1	42	1		58	0	50	3		42	1	31	1	
447	54	1	51	0		41	0	41	1		54	0	59	0		45	1	58	0	.01
448	34	1	24	0	.05	36	1	32	1		29	1	38	2		32	0	36	1	

449	58	1	62	0		67	1	69	1		69	0	73	2		71	1	78	1	
450	50	1	57	0		52	0	47	1		65	0	65	1		62	1	58	2	
451	59	0	58	1		58	1	60	1		74	0	81	0		70	1	73	1	
452	28	0	18	1	.05	13	0	14	1		20	1	37	0	.01	14	1	27	2	.01
453	42	0	41	1		38	1	50	1	.01	45	0	47	2		47	0	57	1	.05
454	40	1	32	0		27	1	28	1		37	1	30	1		25	1	27	2	
455	51	0	48	1		49	0	56	1		61	1	56	0		56	1	59	1	
456	32	0	36	2		25	2	25	1		31	1	36	3		30	2	42	1	.01
457	15	0	18	1		9	1	14	1		31	0	35	0		22	0	30	0	.05
458	41	0	39	1		44	1	42	1		47	0	58	0	.05	47	1	54	0	
459	30	1	30	1		31	1	29	1		35	0	42	2		30	0	39	1	.05
460	67	0	70	1		77	0	76	1		65	2	62	6		75	1	69	4	
461	40	0	46	1		35	1	41	1		57	1	66	2		55	2	62	3	
462	75	0	75	1		71	0	64	1		75	0	71	0		70	0	71	3	
463	40	1	44	1		86	0	87	1		46	1	51	1		87	0	86	1	
464	68	0	50	1	.01	70	0	53	1	.01	69	1	44	2	.01	71	0	59	1	.01
465	72	0	66	1		70	1	69	1		66	1	74	0		64	1	70	3	
466	60	0	53	1		60	0	63	1		78	0	62	1	.01	72	0	71	1	
467	19	0	28	1	.05	25	1	30	1		36	1	53	2	.01	33	0	45	0	.01
468	53	0	51	1		73	0	69	1		59	1	41	2	.01	67	1	61	2	
469	30	0	42	1	.05	26	0	37	1	.01	44	1	62	0	.01	31	0	50	1	.01
470	10	0	11	1		15	1	13	1		26	1	27	1		32	1	28	1	
471	31	1	26	1		16	2	16	1		27	1	37	2	.05	17	1	24	2	
472	26	0	20	1		20	1	14	1		21	0	30	0		12	0	26	0	.01
473	47	0	49	1		38	1	45	1		42	1	47	1		40	1	53	2	.01
474	68	1	65	1		60	0	63	1		72	1	62	0		70	1	64	2	
475	57	0	54	1		63	1	59	1		57	1	59	1		48	1	59	2	.05
476	14	0	23	2	.05	8	1	14	1	.05	19	1	34	1	.01	17	1	31	3	.01
477	50	1	48	1		38	1	32	1		49	1	50	2		52	0	45	2	
478	52	0	43	1		44	0	39	1		53	2	49	0		43	1	44	2	
479	67	0	78	1	.05	72	0	70	1		82	0	84	0		73	1	72	1	
480	19	0	12	1		35	1	26	1	.05	19	1	27	2		31	1	40	2	.05

Table F-3. Percentage of True and Cannot Say Responses for Two Psychiatric Samples—continued

	Michigan Sample[a]										Ohio Sample[a]									
	Males					Females					Males					Females				
	White (N = 192)		Black (N = 197)			White (N = 286)		Black (N = 281)			White (N = 310)		Black (N = 125)			White (N = 460)		Black (N = 211)		
Booklet No.	T	?	T	?	p[b]	T	?	T	?	p	T	?	T	?	p	T	?	T	?	p
481	68	0	61	1		64	1	55	1	.05	54	0	61	0		46	0	54	1	
482	40	0	51	1	.05	44	1	51	1		66	0	62	1		58	0	56	1	
483	61	1	54	3		62	1	67	2		73	3	75	4		78	3	77	4	
484	38	1	38	1		47	2	45	1		50	1	54	2		54	0	54	1	
485	53	0	53	2		49	2	50	1		46	1	54	0		48	1	53	1	
486	88	0	79	1		82	0	68	1	.01	82	0	73	2		78	0	69	1	.05
487	52	0	41	1	.05	60	1	51	1	.05	41	0	45	1		48	0	51	0	
488	39	0	44	2		45	1	55	1	.05	57	0	59	0		70	0	71	0	
489	53	1	57	2		54	1	62	1	.05	72	1	76	0		71	0	73	1	
490	15	1	20	2		12	1	25	1	.01	19	1	30	3	.05	27	1	50	3	.01
491	32	0	32	2		35	1	28	1		35	1	42	2		31	1	37	2	
492	42	0	50	2		55	1	60	1		55	0	60	1		62	0	67	0	
493	47	0	45	2		54	1	52	1		59	1	62	4		63	1	58	2	
494	22	0	22	2		36	1	31	1		25	1	38	3	.05	36	0	36	2	
495	65	1	74	2		63	0	66	1		75	0	79	1		65	0	72	1	
496	64	1	53	2		65	1	55	1	.05	67	1	62	2		65	2	57	2	
497	87	1	81	2		84	0	74	1	.01	86	0	80	1		80	1	75	1	
498	63	0	70	2		57	0	60	1		69	2	82	2	.01	72	2	77	1	
499	72	0	63	2		79	1	80	1		68	0	70	1		73	1	76	0	
500	46	1	57	1	.05	50	1	47	1		63	0	67	0		61	1	70	1	.05
501	61	0	72	1	.05	57	1	69	1	.01	65	1	67	2		66	1	73	1	
502	70	1	83	1	.01	73	0	76	1		80	0	86	1		71	0	82	1	.01
503	53	0	56	1		49	1	53	1		54	1	58	1		60	2	58	2	

504	39	1	49	1	.05	29	1	40	1	.05	43	1	50	2		48	2	46	1	
505	31	1	46	1	.01	28	1	33	1		44	0	59	1	.01	39	0	53	1	.01
506	61	1	46	1	.01	60	1	53	1		51	2	46	2		55	3	49	3	
507	49	1	57	1		35	1	50	1	.01	58	2	60	3		43	2	53	3	.05
508	80	0	83	0		85	0	84	1		84	0	88	2		89	1	84	2	
509	52	0	44	0		56	0	51	1		53	1	54	1		56	1	61	1	
510	27	0	36	1		33	1	40	1		38	1	50	2	.05	48	0	53	2	
511	29	0	42	0	.05	30	1	41	1	.01	28	1	48	0	.01	28	0	50	1	.01
512	14	1	11	0		10	1	9	1		15	2	16	0		8	2	11	1	
513	38	3	54	1	.01	45	3	38	2		40	3	51	3	.05	43	2	49	2	
514	11	1	21	1	.05	7	1	9	2		21	1	28	0		10	0	16	1	.05
515	84	0	70	0	.01	85	0	68	1	.01	76	0	65	0	.05	79	0	73	2	
516	77	0	69	0		83	1	83	1		67	1	78	0	.05	79	0	81	2	
517	24	0	16	1		26	1	21	1		18	1	22	2		20	0	24	0	
518	36	1	36	0		36	1	45	1	.05	43	2	57	0	.05	38	1	52	2	.01
519	14	0	17	1		13	1	19	1		16	1	17	2		14	2	19	3	
520	65	0	70	0		57	0	66	1	.05	73	1	68	2		62	1	69	1	
521	56	0	70	0	.01	59	1	60	1		66	0	67	2		57	2	62	1	
522	54	0	63	0		40	1	27	1	.01	61	0	54	2		40	1	39	0	
523	52	1	48	0		42	1	35	1		55	1	46	2		46	1	47	3	
524	78	0	69	1		77	0	67	1	.05	72	0	61	0	.05	72	1	64	3	
525	41	0	52	1	.05	59	0	64	1		45	0	58	1	.05	45	2	65	3	.01
526	35	0	23	1	.05	39	1	40	1		24	1	33	1		29	0	35	2	
527	56	0	62	0		56	1	54	1		69	1	76	0		70	1	76	2	
528	66	0	70	1		71	0	62	1	.05	71	1	70	2		69	1	72	3	
529	60	1	77	0	.01	71	0	75	1		69	0	75	2		68	1	71	2	
530	22	0	24	1		25	0	34	1	.05	28	0	35	2		32	0	38	1	
531	38	0	29	0		53	0	41	1	.01	39	1	35	1		44	0	40	2	
532	69	0	67	2		68	1	53	2	.01	75	1	56	2	.01	70	2	57	4	.01
533	61	0	56	0		64	1	51	1	.01	65	2	62	1		67	1	65	2	
534	62	0	64	0		54	1	60	1		71	1	74	1		63	1	70	1	
535	18	1	26	1		31	1	36	1		26	1	34	2		37	0	36	1	

Table F-3. Percentage of True and Cannot Say Responses for Two Psychiatric Samples—continued

	Michigan Sample[a]										Ohio Sample[a]									
	Males					Females					Males					Females				
	White (N = 192)		Black (N = 197)			White (N = 286)		Black (N = 281)			White (N = 310)		Black (N = 125)			White (N = 460)		Black (N = 211)		
Booklet No.	T	?	T	?	p[b]	T	?	T	?	p	T	?	T	?	p	T	?	T	?	p
536	70	1	65	0		65	0	68	1		61	0	66	2		59	2	67	3	.05
537	30	1	23	1		10	1	10	1		35	0	34	0		14	0	15	0	
538	11	1	18	1		27	1	36	1	.05	15	1	22	2		35	0	64	1	.01
539	73	0	73	0		46	1	30	1	.01	80	0	66	1	.01	51	0	44	0	
540	80	2	72	1		86	1	72	1	.01	86	1	70	2	.01	84	0	81	1	
541	22	0	26	0		20	1	34	1	.01	28	1	37	2		28	1	43	0	.01
542	63	0	57	1		60	0	54	1		63	1	65	0		65	1	52	1	.01
543	38	0	28	0		35	0	41	1		28	1	41	0		30	1	40	0	.01
544	61	0	52	0		72	0	68	1		44	1	47	1		55	1	53	0	
545	33	0	37	0		45	1	48	1		29	0	43	2	.01	35	1	43	0	
546	67	0	65	1		53	1	49	1		76	1	73	2		59	1	70	0	.01
547	63	0	72	0		69	0	71	1		73	2	75	3		72	1	79	3	.05
548	35	1	31	0		44	1	46	1		50	2	50	2		60	1	57	0	
549	49	0	30	0	.01	51	0	45	1		42	0	36	2		44	1	45	0	
550	42	1	45	1		20	1	19	1		56	0	59	2		24	1	30	1	
551	44	1	45	0		50	0	46	1		47	0	48	0		46	0	48	0	
552	70	0	64	0		44	1	46	1		75	0	72	1		56	1	61	1	
553	13	1	12	1		20	1	22	1		16	1	22	0		27	0	39	2	.01
554	47	0	51	1		60	1	52	1		55	1	63	2		68	1	72	2	
555	59	0	59	1		80	0	77	1		46	1	49	0		61	1	64	1	
556	53	0	74	0	.01	60	0	77	1	.01	75	1	75	2		78	1	84	2	.05
557	11	0	14	2		31	0	38	1		22	1	29	1		39	1	45	2	
558	34	1	41	1		33	0	41	2	.05	63	1	66	2		55	2	69	3	.01

559	24	1	25	0		44	1	51	1		27	1	52	0	.01	38	1	50	1	.01
560	43	0	42	0		51	1	60	1	.05	32	1	38	2		40	1	49	1	.05
561	53	1	58	1		49	0	46	1		60	1	62	5		51	1	41	5	
562	59	0	68	0		66	0	65	1		65	4	70	5		67	2	74	6	.01
563	74	1	64	1	.05	45	1	36	1	.05	82	1	70	1	.01	49	1	41	1	
564	48	0	45	0		52	0	52	1		47	1	50	2		48	2	55	0	
565	19	0	18	0		18	1	24	1		17	0	18	2		15	0	17	1	
566	59	3	67	3		71	1	73	2		54	2	55	4		67	2	79	2	.01

Table F-4. Content of Race-Related Items by Gender in Psychiatric Samples

Item No. and Direction of Response[a]		Scored Same Way on[b]	Comparison with Other Groups[c]	Content
		Race-Related: Males and Females		
6	T	W, E	Rnf	I like to read newspaper articles on crime.
11	T	9-S, Rs, B-W, E	Rn	A person should try to understand his dreams and be guided by or take warning from them.
56	T	F, CI	Rn	As a youngster I was suspended from school one or more times for cutting up.
58	T	REL		Everything is turning out just like the prophets of the Bible said it would.
89	T	HOS, W, E		It takes a lot of argument to convince most people of the truth.
93	T	AUT, Rs, E	Rn	I think that most people would lie to get ahead.
280	T	AUT, W, B-W, E		Most people make friends because friends are likely to be useful to them.
284	T	4-O, 6-O, PSY, CI, Rs, E	Rn	I am sure I am being talked about.
316	T	0, AUT, Rs, E	Rn	I think nearly anyone would tell a lie to keep out of trouble.
332	T	8, 0, ORG, E	Rn	Sometimes my voice leaves me or changes even though I have no cold.
347	F	PSY, CI, Rs, E	Rn	I have no enemies who really wish to harm me.
376	F	W, E	Rn	Policemen are usually honest.
400	T	PSY, B-W, E	Rn	If given the chance I could do some things that would be of great benefit to the world.
464	F	PSY, CI, W		I have never seen a vision.
469	T	HOS, W, E	Rnf	I have often found people jealous of my good ideas, just because they had not thought of them first.

[a]Indicates direction in which blacks exceeded whites for race-related items.

[b]For designations of basic and content scales, see Appendix B. Others are as follows: O = obvious scale item, S = subtle scale item, m = male only, f = female only, CI = Lachar-Wrobel Critical Item, Rs = Race-sensitive scale (White, 1974), W = replicated race-sensitive item not on Rs scale, E = race-discriminating item in Erdberg analysis (1969), and B-W = Black-White scale (Costello, 1977).

[c]Rn = also race-related in normative sample analysis.

		Race-Related: Males and Females		
476	T	PSY	Rn	I am a special agent of God.
511	T	PSY, W, E	Rn	I have a daydream life about which I do not tell other people.
		Race-Related: Males Only		
5	T	2-S, CI, W, E	Rn	I am easily awakened by noise.
20	T	CI		My sex life is satisfactory.
57	T	W, E		I am a good mixer.
77	T	5, FEM		I enjoy reading love stories.
79	T	. . .		My feelings are not easily hurt.
81	F	5, FEM, Rs, B-W, E		I think I would like the kind of work a forest ranger does.
86	F	. . .		I am certainly lacking in self-confidence.
136	T	PSY, W, E		I commonly wonder what hidden reason another person may have for doing something nice for me.
176	F	5, PHO	Rn	I do not have a great fear of snakes.
199	F	F		Children should be taught all the main facts of sex.
206	T	F, REL, B-W, E		I am very religious (more than most people).
231	T	5m, E	Rnf	I like to talk about sex.
268	T	9-S, HYP		Something exciting will almost always pull me out of it when I am feeling low.
270	F	2-O, W	Rn	When I leave home I do not worry about whether the door is locked and the windows closed.
281	F	1, 6-O, 8, 0, ORG, CI, W, E		I do not often notice my ears ringing or buzzing.
287	T	. . .		I have very few fears compared to my friends.
289	F	3-S, 4-S, 9-S, E		I am always disgusted with the law when a criminal is freed through the arguments of a smart lawyer.
391	T	W, E		I love to go to dances.
415	T	B-W, E	Rn	If given the chance I would make a good leader of people.
420	T	PSY, CI, B-W, E		I have had some very unusual religious experiences.
435	T	W		Usually I would prefer to work with women.

Table F-4. Content of Race-Related Items by Gender in Psychiatric Samples—continued

Item No. and Direction of Response[a]		Scored Same Way on[b]	Comparison with Other Groups[c]	Content
		Race-Related: Males Only		
467	T	E		I often memorize numbers that are not important (such as automobile licenses, etc.).
505	T	HYP, W, E		I have had periods when I felt so full of pep that sleep did not seem necessary for days at a time.
513	T	W, B-W, E		I think Lincoln was greater than Washington.
515	F	E	Rn	In my home we have always had the ordinary necessities (such as enough food, clothing, etc.).
525	T	PHO, W	Rn	I am made nervous by certain animals.
563	F	FEM		I like adventure stories better than romantic stories.
		Race-Related: Females Only		
10	T	3-O, 7, HEA		There seems to be a lump in my throat much of the time.
16	T	4-O, 6-O, 8, PSY, CI, Rs, E	Rn	I am sure I get a raw deal from life.
24	T	4-O, 6-O, 8, PSY, W, E	Rn	No one seems to understand me.
27	T	F, 6-O, PSY	Rnf	Evil spirits possess me at times.
53	T	F		A minister can cure disease by praying and putting his hand on your head.
59	T	9-O, AUT, Rs, E	Rn	I have often had to take orders from someone who did not know as much as I did.
62	T	1, CI		Parts of my body often have feelings like burning, tingling, crawling, or like "going to sleep."
84	T	4-O, MOR, Rs, E	Rnf	These days I find it hard not to give up hope of amounting to something.
98	T	REL		I believe in the second coming of Christ.
102	F	E		My hardest battles are with myself.
124	T	0, AUT, Rs, B-W, E	Rnf	Most people will use somewhat unfair means to gain profit or an advantage rather than to lose it.

		Race-Related: Females Only		
135	T	Rs, E	Rnf	If I could get into a movie without paying and be sure I was not seen I would probably do it.
147	T	0, Rs, E	Rnf	I have often lost out on things because I couldn't make up my mind soon enough.
170	T	B-W, E		What others think of me does not bother me.
184	T	F, PSY, CI, B-W, E	Rnf	I commonly hear voices without knowing where they come from.
197	T	F, PSY, CI		Someone has been trying to rob me.
213	T	B-W, E		In walking I am very careful to step over sidewalk cracks.
239	T	4-S, 5, FAM, Rs, E	Rn	I have been disappointed in love.
241	T	8, Rs, E	Rn	I dream frequently about things that are best kept to myself.
262	T	. . .		It does not bother me that I am not better looking.
264	T	Rs, B-W, E	Rnf	I am entirely self-confident.
286	T	F		I am never happier than when alone.
293	T	F, 6-O, PSY, CI		Someone has been trying to influence my mind.
295	F	. . .		I liked "Alice in Wonderland" by Lewis Carroll.
319	T	AUT, Rs, E		Most people inwardly dislike putting themselves out to help other people.
330	F	8, ORG, CI		I have never been paralyzed or had any unusual weakness of any of my muscles.
334	T	8, PSY, CI, W	Rnf	Peculiar odors come to me at times.
349	T	7, 8, PSY, CI, W, B-W, E	Rnf	I have strange and peculiar thoughts.
358	T	7, W, E	Rnf	Bad words, often terrible words, come into my mind and I cannot get rid of them.
359	T	7, E		Sometimes some unimportant thought will run through my mind and bother me for days.
364	T	6-O, 8, CI, Rs, B-W, E	Rn	People say insulting and vulgar things about me.
385	T	PHO, W	Rn	Lightning is one of my fears.

Table F-4. Content of Race-Related Items by Gender in Psychiatric Samples—continued

Item No. and Direction of Response[a]		Scored Same Way on[b]	Comparison with Other Groups[c]	Content
		Race-Related: Females Only		
386	T	HYP, W, B-W, E	Rnf	I like to keep people guessing what I'm going to do next.
392	T	PHO		A windstorm terrifies me.
404	T	W, E		People have often misunderstood my intentions when I was trying to put them right and be helpful.
410	T	HOS		I would certainly enjoy beating a crook at his own game.
426	T	HOS, W	Rnf	I have at times had to be rough with people who were rude or annoying.
437	T	AUT, W, E	Rn	It is all right to get around the law if you don't actually break it.
441	F	...		I like tall women.
453	T	SOC	Rn	When I was a child I didn't care to be a member of a crowd or gang.
486	F	HEA	Rnm	I have never noticed blood in my urine.
490	T	REL, B-W	Rnm	I read the Bible several times a week.
507	T	...	Rn	I have frequently worked under people who seem to have things arranged so that they get credit for good work but are able to pass off mistakes onto those under them.
518	T	DEP, W, E		I have often felt guilty because I have pretended to feel more sorry about something than I really was.
532	F	E		I can stand as much pain as others can.
538	T	FEM, E		I think I would like the work of a dressmaker.
541	T	ORG, E		My skin seems to be unusually sensitive to touch.
556	T	W		I am very careful about my manner of dress.
558	T	W		A large number of people are guilty of bad sexual conduct.
560	T	ORG, W	Rn	I am greatly bothered by forgetting where I put things.

APPENDIX G
Data from MMPI Studies of Other Minority Groups

Table G-1. Profile Codes for Subgroups of Wisconsin Freshmen by Religious Denomination

	Males			Females		
Subgroups	***N***	**Code**		***N***	**Code**	
Catholics	469	'78-459 236 10/	-FK/L	346	-984673 0215/	-KF/L
Protestants	994	'58-79 4236 10/	-FK/L	959	-983674 120/5	-KF/L
Jews	283	'5289-473610/	-FK/L	412	-982347601/5	-FK/L
NRIs (No religious identification)	105	'5849-2736 10/	-FK/L	98	'8-469 23701/5	-FK/L

Note: Data are from Bohrnstedt, Borgatta, and Evans (1968).

Table G-2. Profile Codes for Subgroups of West Virginia Church Members

	Male		Female	
Subgroup	**Young**	**Old**	**Young**	**Old**
Conventional Protestants (*N* = 40)	'487-69 32 10/ -FK/L	2'1470 83-69/ 'F-LK/	'64-7 389012/ -FK/L	2'70 31 84-69/ -FLK/
Snake-handling cult members (*N* = 40)	'49 78-62031/ 'F-/LK	'421867-930/ -FLK/	'480-679 231/ 'F-L/K	'4078-61239/ 'F-L/K

Note: Data are from Tellegen, Gerrard, Gerrard, and Butcher (1969).

Table G-3. Profile Codes for Subgroups of North Carolina Prisoners by Religious Denomination

Subgroup	***N***	**Code**	
Baptist	145	'423179-8650/	-FKL/
Catholic	103	'4923-71865/0	-FKL/
Church of God	24	4'27 3689-1 50/	-FLK/
Holiness	46	4'28173-6905/	-FLK/
Methodist	118	'4213 79-6850/	-FLK/
Presbyterian	66	4'2379-16850/	-FKL/

Note: Data are from Panton (1980).

Table G-4. Profile Codes for Subgroups of Indiana Male VA Patients by Religious Denomination

	Thought-disordered			Drug-dependent		
Subgroup	***N***	**Code**		***N***	**Code**	
Catholic	18	8″769′425 13-0/	F′-LK/	18	8427′96135-0/	′F-/KL
Protestant	18	8″724 163′95-0/	F″′-LK/	18	2′4817936-05/	′F-/LK

Note: Data are from Groesch and Davis (1977).

Table G-5. Means, Standard Deviations, and Codes for a Sample of Normal Adult Japanese-Americans

	Males (*N* = 102)		Females (*N* = 100)	
Scale	**Mean**	**S.D.**	**Mean**	**S.D.**
L	45.0	5.9	46.0	7.2
F	56.2	12.7	53.8	9.9
K	50.1	8.5	51.5	9.5
Hs	53.1	10.8	49.0	7.8
D	58.0	11.0	52.9	9.2
Hy	53.8	8.2	49.7	8.6
Pd	54.8	11.5	52.7	10.1
Mf	59.9	9.0	50.2	8.9
Pa	55.0	8.5	53.2	7.9
Pt	58.5	11.1	53.6	8.3
Sc	56.7	13.1	54.3	8.5
Ma	58.4	10.1	54.9	11.7
Si	52.4	9.4	56.4	9.9
A	53.8	10.2	50.2	9.5
R	46.3	9.0	45.7	10.2
Code	-57298 46310/ -FK/L		-0978246 35/1 -FK/L	
Composite of U.S. college students[a]	-95 8743621/		-9348675/12	

Note: Data for the Japanese-American groups are from Abe (1958), those for the male composite profile are from Goodstein (1954), and those for the female composite are from Black (1956).

[a]Scale 0 not included in the profile code; validity code data incomplete.

Table G-6. Means, Standard Deviations, and Codes for Samples of Hawaiian Medical Center Cases

	Somatization Cases							
	Males				Females			
	White (N = 25)		Japanese (N = 25)		White (N = 25)		Japanese (N = 25)	
Scale	Mean	S.D.	Mean	S.D.	Mean	S.D.	Mean	S.D.
L	53.4	10.5	50.2	7.3	51.7	7.4	50.4	7.6
F	63.2	15.2	57.4	10.7	56.8	7.4	57.0	10.0
K	54.4	8.0	55.7	10.3	54.6	11.0	54.2	9.7
Hs	71.2	14.0	75.4	14.2	68.2	12.5	68.4	9.6
D	72.1	14.8	73.9	13.3	65.1	10.5	71.8	13.9
Hy	70.5	11.0	71.3	11.4	71.4	9.5	68.6	6.7
Pd	64.2	13.3	62.6	10.9	63.1	13.9	58.1	13.3
Mf	63.0	8.7	57.1	10.5	48.9	10.8	50.4	8.7
Pa	60.7	15.0	57.7	7.1	59.5	8.9	61.5	10.6
Pt	66.9	13.7	66.0	13.3	59.4	11.6	62.6	9.6
Sc	59.6	20.5	66.6	11.5	63.0	11.4	60.4	12.0
Ma	64.1	29.1	58.4	11.6	58.2	10.1	52.9	11.2
Si	52.2	7.9	55.9	9.8	55.6	11.0	59.1	10.9
Code	213′7495 6-80/		123′874-9650/		3′1248-6790/5		2′31768-0495/	
		′F-KL/		-FKL/		-FKL/		-FKL/

	Neurological Cases							
	Males				Females			
	White (N = 29)		Japanese (N = 13)		White (N = 18)		Japanese (N = 4)	
Scale	Mean	S.D.	Mean	S.D.	Mean	S.D.	Mean	S.D.
L	52.5	9.9	56.4	5.2	48.6	8.5	52.0	4.9
F	59.4	10.8	63.4	17.1	59.7	6.4	62.8	5.5
K	53.9	12.0	56.1	11.2	47.4	5.6	51.3	5.5
Hs	80.0	17.3	81.2	15.2	68.4	14.7	70.0	18.5
D	78.6	16.9	79.3	7.4	69.5	11.5	70.0	3.5
Hy	71.6	14.3	66.6	8.7	61.9	9.9	58.0	6.0
Pd	76.6	17.3	71.5	11.7	65.7	9.4	69.0	11.8
Mf	67.4	11.5	57.7	7.9	46.1	6.3	60.8	13.6
Pa	62.1	9.0	64.8	13.7	59.6	14.2	59.5	15.3
Pt	82.4	21.6	77.3	17.0	70.3	16.5	78.8	18.2
Sc	85.6	21.2	85.9	17.7	68.8	13.5	76.3	16.0
Ma	66.4	14.0	63.5	13.2	58.4	11.5	50.0	8.5
Si	56.5	9.8	57.2	7.4	63.4	9.1	59.5	14.8
Code	871″243′596-0/		81″274′369-50/		7′281403-69/5		7812′4 5-6039/	
		-FKL/		′F-LK/		′F-LK/		′F-LK/

Note: Data are from Tsushima and Onorato (1982).

Table G-7. Means, Standard Deviations, and Codes from a Nationwide Survey of Psychiatric Patients

	Males							
	White (*N* = 36,539)		Black (*N* = 3,350)		Hispanic (*N* = 1,182)		Asian (*N* = 137)	
Scale	**Mean**	**S.D.**	**Mean**	**S.D.**	**Mean**	**S.D.**	**Mean**	**S.D.**
L	49.3	7.9	51.8	8.6	53.5	9.1	51.3	8.2
F	61.9	14.1	67.8	17.5	67.0	17.0	63.5	16.2
K	51.6	9.8	51.0	9.8	51.4	9.8	52.5	8.9
Hs	62.7	16.2	65.9	17.2	67.4	17.4	61.1	14.9
D	70.0	18.0	69.9	16.7	73.2	17.3	69.5	17.9
Hy	64.6	11.9	63.9	13.2	65.2	13.3	62.1	11.2
Pd	67.1	13.3	70.2	12.4	68.5	12.9	63.3	12.6
Mf	62.9	11.1	61.6	9.8	60.9	9.8	61.5	10.9
Pa	62.2	13.1	64.4	16.1	64.3	14.8	61.6	12.1
Pt	67.6	16.3	68.5	15.1	70.4	16.0	65.0	15.4
Sc	68.7	19.1	74.3	20.5	74.9	20.2	68.2	18.8
Ma	61.2	12.1	67.9	12.0	64.5	12.1	59.2	12.3
Si	56.1	12.2	54.9	10.1	56.3	11.1	56.6	11.1
Code	2′87435169-0/ 'F-K/L		84′2791635-0/ 'F-LK/		827′413965-0/ 'F-LK/		'28743651-90/ 'F-KL/	

	Females							
	White (*N* = 38,998)		Black (*N* = 2,819)		Hispanic (*N* = 768)		Asian (*N* = 145)	
Scale	**Mean**	**S.D.**	**Mean**	**S.D.**	**Mean**	**S.D.**	**Mean**	**S.D.**
L	49.8	7.5	50.9	8.0	53.0	9.1	52.8	8.4
F	61.4	11.3	66.3	15.9	66.6	16.1	64.3	15.0
K	51.4	9.2	49.1	9.4	50.8	9.2	54.1	9.2
Hs	61.3	13.4	64.4	13.9	65.6	13.7	59.3	13.4
D	67.5	14.8	67.0	14.2	69.7	14.2	66.6	15.0
Hy	65.7	12.0	65.2	13.1	66.8	12.5	61.4	12.3
Pd	67.2	13.5	69.2	12.9	69.1	14.2	64.8	13.2
Mf	46.1	9.6	51.9	9.9	52.2	10.1	49.5	10.3
Pa	64.1	12.7	65.9	15.2	66.5	14.6	65.3	13.6
Pt	65.4	13.2	65.0	12.8	67.3	13.3	63.5	12.2
Sc	67.6	15.8	71.7	16.7	72.9	16.9	68.2	14.7
Ma	59.1	12.1	64.8	12.3	62.3	12.3	60.3	12.5
Si	59.0	12.1	58.6	10.6	59.4	11.0	58.9	10.5
Code	'8243761-90/5 'F-K/L		8′4263791-05/ 'F-L/K		8′24 73619-05/ 'F-LK/		'82 647 39-10/5 'F-KL/	

Note: Data were compiled by the Roche Psychiatric Service Institute in 1978.

Table G-8. Means, Standard Deviations, and Codes for a Sample of Normal Adult Indians

Scale	Males (*N* = 63)		Females (*N* = 71)	
	Mean	S.D.	Mean	S.D.
L	52.1	7.3	50.5	7.3
F	63.8	14.3	61.4	12.9
K	48.8	9.7	46.3	8.8
Hs	57.9	12.5	52.0	10.5
D	58.1	13.0	55.0	8.3
Hy	53.2	10.3	52.1	10.9
Pd	63.3	12.5	60.9	10.8
Mf	66.9	9.5	57.2	10.4
Pa	62.5	12.6	61.0	12.3
Pt	61.6	11.8	56.3	10.7
Sc	65.3	16.7	60.3	13.0
Ma	65.5	11.2	63.6	13.8
Si	54.5	9.9	57.6	10.8
MAC (Raw)	24.9	6.3	24.9	4.3
(T)	58.7[a]	18.5	64.7	12.6
Code	'598 467-2103/ 'F-L/K		'9648-0572 31/ 'F-L/K	

Note: Data are from LaDue (1982).
[a]T scores for MacAndrew raw scores are prorated from Minnesota normative data.

Table G-9. Means, Standard Deviations, and Codes for White and Indian Students

Scale	Males: White (*N* = 114)		Males: Indian (*N* = 226)		Females: White (*N* = 109)		Females: Indian (*N* = 189)	
	Mean	S.D.	Mean	S.D.	Mean	S.D.	Mean	S.D.
L	47.2	7.3	50.3	8.6	46.8	7.6	47.6	10.3
F	63.0	14.6	72.7	16.0	60.4	16.0	71.8	22.4
K	49.0	8.0	47.6	7.8	48.5	8.5	46.6	8.5
Hs	52.8	10.5	61.1	12.3	50.2	7.6	57.0	10.2
D	54.5	11.2	63.2	12.2	50.4	8.5	58.2	10.0
Hy	54.2	8.2	55.9	8.7	52.4	8.0	55.4	8.8
Pd	58.2	12.2	64.9	14.1	61.2	15.5	65.8	10.7
Mf	54.2	9.4	53.8	8.8	56.8	12.8	61.4	9.5
Pa	58.4	13.0	65.0	18.5	57.8	12.0	63.8	14.5
Pt	39.0	16.2	50.8	14.1	41.2	14.4	50.8	14.4
Sc	46.6	19.8	62.2	19.6	46.3	16.8	60.5	19.1
Ma	59.2	13.4	66.2	12.7	59.2	12.4	64.0	12.4
Si	53.6	9.3	60.1	7.2	56.4	7.8	62.0	6.8
A	54.6	10.8	61.3	9.3	54.3	10.7	59.4	9.4
R	47.4	9.2	47.8	9.8	44.4	9.3	45.0	9.3
Es	44.0	10.8	38.4	9.1	47.3	8.9	41.6	8.2
Code	-964 23501/8:7 'F-/KL		'964 2810-357/ F'-L/K		'4-9650321/87 'F-/KL		'496 058-2137/ F'-/LK	

Note: Data are from Bryde (1966).

Table G-10. Profile Codes for Subgroups of Alaskan University Students

	Males			Females		
	N	Code		*N*	Code	
Native students	51	'78 2-49 63510/	-FL/K	40	'98-47 063512/	-FL/:K
Aleuts	10	7'28 413-60 59/	-FL/K	3	'48 79 03-261/5	-F/LK
Eskimos	25	'78-90425631/	-FL/K	19	'98-47560 312/	-FL/:K
Indians	16	'98-47 256310/	-F/LK	18	'89 4-7036215/	-LF/K
Nonnative (white) students	50	'87-54 932061/	-FKL/	50	'9-48 673012/5	-LK/F
Composite of U.S. college students[a]	5035	-95 8743621/		5014	-9348675/12	

Note: Data for the Alaskan groups are from Herreid and Herreid (1966), those for the male composite profile are from Goodstein (1954), and those for the female composite are from Black (1956).

[a]Scale 0 not included in the profile code; validity code data incomplete.

Table G-11. Means, Standard Deviations, and Codes for Samples of Students Attending a North Carolina Technical Institute

	Males					
	White (*N* = 25)		**Black (*N* = 20)**		**Indian (*N* = 24)**	
Scale	**Mean**	**S.D.**	**Mean**	**S.D.**	**Mean**	**S.D.**
L	51.2	8.0	50.3	8.3	50.6	9.3
F	59.2	14.9	67.8	16.7	65.0	13.7
K	53.4	9.2	48.1	6.7	52.8	7.1
Hs	57.8	12.8	54.3	10.0	60.5	11.5
D	58.0	13.2	57.2	14.8	60.6	10.0
Hy	58.6	8.2	54.6	8.0	58.2	10.5
Pd	63.6	11.9	63.4	10.7	64.9	10.2
Mf	58.2	7.6	57.8	8.8	58.2	7.6
Pa	59.3	12.1	61.1	10.1	59.0	12.6
Pt	59.4	13.9	62.0	11.3	62.2	9.4
Sc	64.0	20.3	74.0	17.1	69.0	17.5
Ma	61.8	12.9	72.1	10.6	61.2	10.6
Si	51.3	9.7	53.6	6.7	54.8	5.5
Code	'849-7635210/ -FKL/		89'476-52 310/ 'F-L/K		'847921-6350/ 'F-KL/	
	Females					
	White (*N* = 36)		**Black (*N* = 32)**		**Indian (*N* = 29)**	
Scale	**Mean**	**S.D.**	**Mean**	**S.D.**	**Mean**	**S.D.**
L	50.3	6.5	49.2	8.4	47.6	7.2
F	59.6	16.3	63.4	16.0	60.4	16.9
K	44.8	7.9	45.6	8.8	48.2	8.7
Hs	50.8	8.2	54.6	10.5	54.8	10.9
D	53.2	8.5	54.8	11.6	56.8	10.4
Hy	52.2	7.8	55.4	9.5	55.8	9.9
Pd	57.9	7.7	62.0	10.5	67.2	10.9
Mf	52.0	9.3	51.0	11.0	50.6	8.3
Pa	55.1	11.1	59.9	12.7	57.8	11.1
Pt	55.8	8.9	59.8	9.6	60.2	9.7
Sc	57.6	12.0	68.2	14.3	63.5	12.2
Ma	59.2	11.2	63.6	12.2	63.2	10.9
Si	61.2	8.7	62.5	10.1	59.8	8.5
Code	'0-948 76 2351/ -FL/K		'8904-67 3215/ 'F-/LK		'489 7-0 62315/ 'F-/KL	

Note: Data are from Bull (1976).

Table G-12. Means, Standard Deviations, and Codes for Three Samples of Male Indian Alcoholics with Comparisons to Other Ethnic Groups

	California		South Dakota				Washington					
	Indian (N = 45)		White (N = 40)		Indian (N = 40)		White (N = 11)		Indian (N = 11)		Hispanic (N = 11)	
Scale	Mean	S.D.	Mean	S.D.	Mean	S.D.	Mean	S.D.	Mean	S.D.	Mean	S.D.
L	49.2	9.0	49.2	6.6	51.6	7.6	50.3	6.6	49.2	3.1	56.0	13.5
F	68.2	11.1	61.4	13.6	60.5	11.1	68.4	21.7	66.4	16.0	63.0	16.0
K	46.6	7.2	50.2	9.8	48.7	9.1	51.0	6.7	47.0	5.3	52.8	11.4
Hs	60.2	(12.1)[a]	58.1	13.5	58.1	14.8	57.2	10.5	61.4	13.3	64.4	15.4
D	69.8	13.9	69.1	17.0	65.2	11.2	59.6	14.6	64.2	12.2	74.7	11.7
Hy	55.9	11.1	58.8	9.2	54.2	11.0	57.6	8.5	55.6	11.8	61.2	11.1
Pd	70.0	(12.1)	70.6	11.5	64.9	10.0	67.2	8.0	64.6	11.9	68.2	8.3
Mf	57.2	6.1	57.3	9.0	51.7	10.4	60.6	8.2	59.8	9.4	58.6	9.0
Pa	61.4	9.9	60.9	11.8	58.7	10.8	57.2	10.1	65.0	11.8	59.3	12.1
Pt	66.9	(12.4)	65.9	11.4	64.3	12.8	57.6	13.5	63.0	12.7	61.6	16.6
Sc	69.6	(11.0)	62.9	12.7	62.2	13.7	62.8	19.4	60.4	9.0	64.0	22.6
Ma	65.0	(10.6)	59.8	10.5	60.8	7.9	65.6	12.4	67.1	10.3	58.8	14.0
Si	60.4	8.3	58.0	11.2	56.8	9.2	55.3	11.3	54.1	9.4	57.2	11.2
MAC (Raw)			26.8	4.4	27.1	2.8	29.3	4.0	28.5	3.7	25.7	4.5
(T)			(63.0)[b]	(12.4)	(63.8)	(7.9)	(70.0)	(11.3)	(67.8)	(10.4)	(59.9)	(12.9)
Code	4'2879601-53/ 'F-/LK		4'2786-93105/ 'F-K/L		'24789-61035/ 'F-L/K		'4985-2 37160/ 'F-KL/		'96427 18-530/ 'F-/LK		2'418 73-6950/ 'F-LK/	

Note: Data are from Kline, Rozynko, Flint, and Roberts (1973) for the California sample; Uecker, Boutilier, and Richardson (1980) for the South Dakota sample; and Page and Bozlee (1982) for the Washington sample.

[a]Standard deviations shown in parentheses are based on uncorrected data.

[b]T scores for MacAndrew raw scores are prorated from Minnesota normative data.

Table G-13. Means, Standard Deviations, and Codes for Samples of Indian Prisoners Compared with Total Prison Populations

	General Prison Populations							
	North Carolina				Canada (Prairie Region)			
	Total (*N* = 2,551)		Indian (*N* = 153)		Total (*N* = 1,460)		Indian (*N* = 298)	
Scale	**Mean**	**S.D.**	**Mean**	**S.D.**	**Mean**	**S.D.**	**Mean**	**S.D.**
L	51.4	8.6	54.5	7.8	52.7	9.1	53.6	9.9
F	57.9	9.2	59.9	9.5	67.4	16.1	71.2	16.2
K	52.5	8.2	52.7	8.1	52.2	10.1	51.1	9.7
Hs	57.1	13.4	58.3	12.9	60.4	14.5	62.0	14.3
D	62.8	11.7	62.7	10.0	65.7	15.3	66.1	14.4
Hy	58.0	9.9	57.0	9.6	60.8	10.8	59.3	11.0
Pd	72.9	10.4	69.4	11.6	74.5	11.9	73.5	11.4
Mf	56.3	8.6	52.8	8.4	58.9	10.4	55.5	9.1
Pa	60.6	11.6	62.3	11.9	64.4	14.0	64.9	14.6
Pt	60.7	11.5	62.0	11.1	65.7	15.0	67.2	14.4
Sc	63.6	13.6	64.5	13.8	71.1	20.2	74.8	20.2
Ma	64.0	10.6	62.4	10.0	66.2	12.4	67.9	12.4
Si	52.5	8.4	54.2	8.4	55.4	11.1	56.0	9.4
Code	4'982 76-3150/		'482967-13 05/		48'927631-50/		84'97261-305/	
		-FKL/		-FLK/		'F-LK/		F'-LK/

	Psychiatric Prison Populations							
	Canada (Pacific Region)				Canada (Prairie Region)			
	Total (*N* = 497)		Indian (*N* = 95)		Total (*N* = 325)		Indian (*N* = 58)	
Scale	**Mean**	**S.D.**	**Mean**	**S.D.**	**Mean**	**S.D.**	**Mean**	**S.D.**
L	52.8	8.3	53.4	7.6	52.9	9.5	53.9	10.4
F	69.3	18.5	78.9	20.1	74.2	19.4	78.5	18.5
K	54.1	10.2	48.6	9.4	51.7	10.8	50.6	10.3
Hs	60.9	14.5	63.9	15.8	63.7	15.9	64.7	14.1
D	67.8	17.4	68.6	15.0	69.5	17.1	68.7	13.0
Hy	62.6	11.0	62.5	12.2	63.8	11.6	61.4	11.4
Pd	77.9	11.2	76.5	10.7	77.6	12.4	77.3	10.6
Mf	63.7	10.8	60.0	10.1	62.5	10.4	58.6	9.0
Pa	67.4	14.9	71.2	13.7	70.3	16.0	69.9	16.3
Pt	68.1	15.1	72.3	12.3	70.7	17.4	72.9	14.8
Sc	74.2	19.6	80.0	18.4	80.4	23.7	85.2	21.5
Ma	65.0	12.5	68.6	12.3	67.6	12.9	69.8	12.3
Si	56.4	12.2	58.6	10.2	58.7	11.9	58.7	9.5
Code	48'726 9531-0/		8"476'29 135-0/		8"476'29315-0/		8"47'69213-05/	
		'F-KL/		F'-L/K		F'-LK/		F'-LK/

Note: Data from North Carolina were provided by Panton (1980; personal communication, 1983); those from the Canadian Prairie Region samples are from Wormith, Borzecki, and Black (1984) and those from the Canadian Pacific Region samples are from Mandelzys (1979) and Mandelzys and Lane (1980).

Table G-14. Means, Standard Deviations, and Codes for a Sample of Indian Patients at a Mental Health Center

	Males (N = 68)		Females (N = 74)	
Scale	**Mean**	**S.D.**	**Mean**	**S.D.**
L	51.1	7.6	50.4	7.5
F	68.8	14.4	73.2	16.4
K	47.0	9.3	47.0	7.1
Hs	59.3	11.9	62.3	12.8
D	67.6	15.5	66.9	12.1
Hy	57.9	10.9	64.2	10.9
Pd	69.4	9.4	76.0	13.4
Mf	56.2	10.9	51.6	10.1
Pa	66.5	14.3	73.0	15.1
Pt	67.4	13.9	69.4	12.0
Sc	71.1	20.0	76.4	16.6
Ma	65.6	11.4	64.6	11.4
Si	58.2	10.2	62.7	9.7
Code	8′42769-1035/ 'F-L/K		846′729301-5/ F′-L/K	

Note: Data are from Pollack and Shore (1980).

Table G-15. Profile Codes for Diagnosed Indian Subgroups

Diagnosis	***N***	**Code**	
Schizophrenia	6	8*64″729′031-/	F″-/LK
Nonpsychotic depression	9	8″64729′310-/	F′-/LK
Situational reaction	17	486′792 03-1/	F′-L/K
Antisocial alcoholism	21	'48 97621-03/	'F-L/K

Note: Data are from Pollack and Shore (1980).

Table G-16. Means, Standard Deviations, and Codes for Matched Samples of Minnesota Psychiatric Inpatients

	Males							
	White (*N* = 60)		Black (*N* = 60)		White (*N* = 17)		Indian (*N* = 17)	
Scale	**Mean**	**S.D.**	**Mean**	**S.D.**	**Mean**	**S.D.**	**Mean**	**S.D.**
L	51.2	10.1	51.3	10.0	48.9	8.9	51.1	6.8
F	70.9	19.2	77.3	24.6	68.4	18.0	67.1	18.8
K	48.9	9.5	49.4	9.4	48.1	10.7	49.6	11.1
Hs	60.7	15.6	62.5	14.8	59.6	12.1	57.8	12.8
D	75.8	20.2	68.3	16.6	64.5	15.1	65.1	18.6
Hy	64.2	12.4	62.4	10.8	61.8	11.4	57.8	13.2
Pd	76.3	13.7	72.9	11.1	68.6	17.1	71.8	13.3
Mf	65.9	11.0	63.2	9.4	59.5	11.5	59.5	12.8
Pa	68.4	13.6	71.8	17.1	62.2	12.6	62.6	14.0
Pt	73.5	16.8	70.9	17.0	68.8	18.3	62.6	12.3
Sc	79.4	22.5	83.7	26.0	75.1	24.0	69.0	18.2
Ma	66.0	13.1	71.6	14.3	67.6	14.7	64.6	16.5
Si	57.3	10.8	53.3	9.1	52.5	10.2	56.6	9.6
Code	8427′69531-0/ F′-L/K		8″4697′2513-0/ F′-L/K		8′749263-150/ ′F-/LK		4′829 67-5130/ ′F-L/K	

	Females							
	White (*N* = 37)		Black (*N* = 37)		White (*N* = 19)		Indian (*N* = 19)	
Scale	**Mean**	**S.D.**	**Mean**	**S.D.**	**Mean**	**S.D.**	**Mean**	**S.D.**
L	49.7	10.6	50.6	10.9	49.2	10.1	49.6	10.4
F	77.1	25.0	95.1	30.8	86.0	33.5	76.4	21.2
K	49.3	11.0	46.7	11.6	52.0	11.3	49.9	12.6
Hs	59.2	13.8	61.5	14.9	55.7	11.4	56.1	10.5
D	66.0	15.3	63.4	13.8	66.4	20.1	62.9	12.4
Hy	63.6	13.1	61.3	13.0	60.2	8.4	60.5	7.5
Pd	71.1	14.6	73.9	14.4	76.8	13.1	73.2	10.3
Mf	48.0	8.2	53.7	9.7	51.9	9.5	50.3	8.1
Pa	72.5	16.3	76.1	15.2	73.2	15.3	70.8	16.6
Pt	65.5	13.9	64.7	12.4	66.0	12.9	64.1	11.0
Sc	75.3	19.6	80.3	17.6	76.4	18.7	70.9	15.4
Ma	67.9	12.7	76.4	12.9	66.1	12.0	69.8	14.9
Si	57.5	11.0	58.6	10.0	59.6	14.9	56.5	11.7
Code	864′9273-10/5 F′-/LK		8″964′7213-05/ F*-L/K		486′297 3-015/ F″-K/L		486′9 723-015/ F′-/KL	

Note: Data are from Butcher, Braswell, and Raney (1983).

Table G-17. Profile Codes for Subgroups of Arizona High School Students

	Males		Females	
	N	Code	*N*	Code
Whites	63	'8974-025631/	68	'84-79630512/
Hispanics	41	'987-0426531/	60	-89407235 61/

Note: Data are from Francis (1964).

Table G-18. Means, Standard Deviations, and Codes for Samples of College Freshmen from the Southwestern United States

	Males				Females			
	White (*N* = 36)		Hispanic (*N* = 36)		White (*N* = 32)		Hispanic (*N* = 32)	
Scale	Mean	S.D.	Mean	S.D.	Mean	S.D.	Mean	S.D.
L	52.1	4.2	53.7	6.5	52.8	3.7	55.9	7.3
F	55.3	7.6	59.2	9.0	56.3	7.5	55.2	6.3
K	52.9	9.2	49.1	10.1	51.9	8.4	51.0	8.7
Hs	51.1	9.1	50.6	9.2	52.1	9.7	50.7	7.1
D	50.3	10.0	51.7	9.1	57.3	14.0	54.5	9.2
Hy	53.3	7.3	52.5	7.9	55.2	10.4	55.3	8.7
Pd	58.6	11.4	56.3	8.9	58.8	11.3	55.8	11.0
Mf	54.2	8.9	53.4	9.1	46.1	9.1	52.5	8.6
Pa	56.6	9.2	54.8	8.8	60.4	11.6	54.7	8.2
Pt	55.8	8.8	60.0	11.6	61.9	13.0	57.2	8.8
Sc	56.9	10.7	61.8	16.8	60.4	11.9	56.0	8.8
Ma	59.8	11.2	64.0	23.3	54.9	11.0	60.0	10.8
Si	50.8	9.5	55.3	9.4	59.1	9.8	54.9	8.8
Code	-94 86753 102/ -FKL/		'987-406 5321/ -FL/K		'768-042391/5 -FLK/		'9-784306251/ -LFK/	

Note: Data are from Reilley and Knight (1970).

Table G-19. Means, Standard Deviations, and Codes for Samples of College Students in Southern California

	Males				Females			
	White (*N* = 22)		Hispanic (*N* = 22)		White (*N* = 17)		Hispanic (*N* = 17)	
Scale	**Mean**	**S.D.**	**Mean**	**S.D.**	**Mean**	**S.D.**	**Mean**	**S.D.**
L	45.9	5.8	49.4	7.1	46.1	5.9	49.3	7.0
F	59.1	11.6	56.0	8.5	53.1	5.2	56.0	8.4
K	53.1	5.8	52.4	5.2	52.2	5.2	53.1	9.7
Hs	51.3	9.8	54.8	9.1	46.7	5.4	52.8	6.9
D	52.8	11.1	58.1	9.1	51.3	6.8	51.5	7.5
Hy	56.0	8.8	57.8	8.9	51.1	5.6	54.2	6.8
Pd	59.1	13.9	59.6	11.0	53.5	10.8	59.8	9.5
Mf	69.2	10.6	61.1	7.2	45.1	8.3	47.6	6.5
Pa	55.2	7.8	51.2	8.4	51.2	8.1	49.8	7.3
Pt	57.5	10.4	58.5	11.2	51.6	7.1	53.8	8.2
Sc	60.4	16.3	61.3	12.3	53.5	7.1	56.9	7.5
Ma	63.6	11.6	60.9	9.1	55.5	8.6	60.2	8.6
Si	48.9	8.4	52.5	6.6	53.9	10.0	55.6	10.4
Code	'598-47 3621/0 -FK/L		'859-4723106/ -FK/L		-9048 7263/15 -FK/L		'9-4 80 3712/65 -FK/L	

Note: Data are from Murphy (1978).

Table G-20. Means, Standard Deviations, and Codes for Samples of Male Heroin Addicts in a Texas VA Hospital

	White (*N* = 161)		Black (*N* = 268)		Hispanic (*N* = 41)	
Scale	**Mean**	**S.D.**	**Mean**	**S.D.**	**Mean**	**S.D.**
L	47.0	6.2	48.6	6.5	51.5	7.6
F	66.2	11.3	63.8	12.0	65.6	11.1
K	48.4	8.1	49.8	8.3	49.8	9.2
Hs	66.7	15.7	67.6	16.6	69.2	15.8
D	75.1	15.5	70.4	15.1	75.5	17.2
Hy	66.1	10.6	64.3	12.1	64.1	11.1
Pd	77.4	11.7	73.5	10.7	73.2	9.7
Mf	61.2	9.9	59.7	9.9	55.0	9.8
Pa	63.3	11.6	61.0	12.8	61.9	11.8
Pt	69.8	14.1	67.2	15.0	70.1	13.5
Sc	71.3	17.4	70.1	18.6	71.2	15.0
Ma	69.5	12.9	70.2	11.4	66.1	11.2
Si	56.9	10.7	53.8	8.6	54.7	9.2
Code	428'79 1365-0/ 'F-/KL		4298'1736-50/ 'F-/KL		2487'1936-50/ 'F-L/K	

Note: Data are from Penk, Robinowitz, Roberts, Dolan, and Atkins (1981b).

Table G-21. Means, Standard Deviations, and Codes for Samples of Short-Term Male Felons in a California Prison

	White (*N* = 396)		Black (*N* = 208)		Hispanic (*N* = 114)	
Scale	**Mean**	**S.D.**	**Mean**	**S.D.**	**Mean**	**S.D.**
L	53.6	8.7	54.6	8.7	55.7	9.1
F	57.4	11.2	60.3	11.8	58.0	10.3
K	54.6	9.1	55.0	8.3	53.2	7.7
Hs	55.7	12.7	57.0	11.9	54.4	9.3
D	61.2	13.5	60.0	11.2	60.0	9.6
Hy	57.2	9.8	56.5	8.8	54.4	7.5
Pd	69.2	11.6	70.1	11.3	66.4	10.7
Mf	60.0	10.2	60.1	9.6	54.9	10.2
Pa	59.7	11.0	59.0	13.4	56.3	10.1
Pt	59.2	13.3	61.1	12.4	57.6	11.3
Sc	58.7	14.7	63.2	14.6	57.5	12.2
Ma	60.1	10.2	63.2	10.8	59.6	11.6
Si	57.8	6.7	56.9	5.6	56.8	5.6
Code	'4295-678031/ -FKL/		4'89 752-6 103/ 'F-KL/		'42-9 7806513/ -FLK/	

Note: Data are from Holland (1979).

Table G-22. Means, Standard Deviations, and Codes for Matched Samples of California Male Misdemeanor Cases

	White (*N* = 36)		Black (*N* = 36)		White (*N* = 32)		Hispanic (*N* = 32)	
Scale	**Mean**	**S.D.**	**Mean**	**S.D.**	**Mean**	**S.D.**	**Mean**	**S.D.**
L	56	10	54	10	54	9	58	8
F	58	12	61	10	62	11	60	14
K	60	10	55	11	54	10	60	9
Hs	58	12	56	15	59	14	62	15
D	62	11	61	12	65	13	66	15
Hy	63	9	57	11	61	11	63	9
Pd	69	12	68	10	71	12	68	13
Mf	58	11	57	11	61	9	58	13
Pa	59	13	59	12	60	12	60	11
Pt	60	13	59	13	61	13	63	13
Sc	63	16	63	14	64	16	67	17
Ma	57	11	65	10	62	15	55	12
Si	51	10	50	8	55	11	51	10
Code	'4382 7-61590/ 'K-FL/		'4982-67 3510/ 'F-KL/		4'28 93576-10/ 'F-LK/		'482 3716-590/ 'FK-L/	

Note: Data are from McCreary and Padilla (1977).

Table G-23. Means, Standard Deviations, and Codes for Samples of Male Patients from Two Texas VA Hospitals

	Medical Hospital Cases					
	White (*N* = 173)		Black (*N* = 99)		Hispanic (*N* = 118)	
Scale	Mean	S.D.	Mean	S.D.	Mean	S.D.
L	48.8	7.9	53.2	9.1	53.2	9.0
F	66.6	18.0	73.9	20.6	75.0	18.7
K	48.1	9.0	48.9	9.7	48.7	9.1
Hs	73.3	17.5	76.1	18.1	76.2	17.8
D	79.4	16.9	75.6	16.7	82.8	16.9
Hy	70.2	11.6	69.7	14.4	71.4	14.0
Pd	70.7	11.7	70.2	12.4	70.6	14.9
Mf	58.4	9.8	60.0	9.1	56.9	10.6
Pa	65.4	13.6	68.1	15.5	70.0	15.2
Pt	73.7	16.6	73.6	15.6	77.0	18.1
Sc	74.8	19.9	80.7	19.9	81.6	22.1
Ma	63.6	13.1	68.1	11.3	66.1	12.6
Si	53.3	12.6	55.9	10.8	55.0	10.0
Code	2871 43′69-50/		8″1274′3 695-0/		28″71 346′9-50/	
	′F-/LK		F′-L/K		F′-L/K	

	Psychiatric Hospital Cases					
	White (*N* = 55)		Black (*N* = 39)		Hispanic (*N* = 34)	
Scale	Mean	S.D.	Mean	S.D.	Mean	S.D.
L	50.2	8.6	51.1	9.7	55.8	10.3
F	76.8	19.9	82.4	21.4	77.5	17.8
K	48.2	10.8	48.3	8.2	49.1	9.0
Hs	71.6	15.6	70.2	15.3	69.8	15.4
D	77.6	16.0	71.9	16.3	77.9	15.7
Hy	68.5	12.1	63.8	12.1	64.6	13.0
Pd	70.3	13.6	72.5	12.8	67.0	12.2
Mf	62.3	7.5	59.9	9.9	57.8	10.1
Pa	69.4	16.0	75.8	15.2	70.3	14.9
Pt	75.3	16.2	71.4	14.6	75.9	14.1
Sc	82.6	18.2	86.3	18.6	81.3	19.4
Ma	64.5	12.9	67.8	10.1	63.2	15.4
Si	61.0	9.9	59.0	7.6	59.2	8.3
Code	8″2714′63950/		8″64271′935-0/		82″76′1439-05/	
	F′-L/K		F‴-L/K		F′-L/K	

Note: Data are from Selters (1973).

Table G-24. Means, Standard Deviations, and Codes for Samples of Psychiatric Outpatients in California

	Males				Females			
	White (*N* = 44)		Hispanic (*N* = 18)		White (*N* = 65)		Hispanic (*N* = 22)	
Scale	Mean (With K)	Mean (No K)	Mean (With K)	Mean (No K)	Mean (With K)	Mean (No K)	Mean (With K)	Mean (No K)
L	48.2		56.6		49.6		40.7	
F	64.6		66.4		67.4		70.2	
K	47.7		53.9		47.7		48.7	
Hs	61.1	61.8	64.3	61.4	60.6	61.3	61.7	61.1
D	71.5		68.9		67.6		68.5	
Hy	63.9		65.7		66.3		62.5	
Pd	75.6	78.2	70.7	67.1	73.9	75.3	72.4	72.9
Mf	66.3		56.7		46.5		49.5	
Pa	68.1		64.6		69.0		65.5	
Pt	71.2	67.0	62.7	55.9	66.6	64.7	66.9	63.7
Sc	73.9	69.0	70.0	59.0	72.4	69.7	74.8	69.9
Ma	66.4	66.0	62.2	58.9	64.8	64.5	65.3	64.5
Si	58.8		52.8		59.5		60.1	
Codes:								
With K	4827′69531-0/ 'F-/LK		48′2 36179-50/ 'F-LK/		48′62739 1-0/5 'F-/LK		84′2769 310-/5 F′-/KL	
No K	42′8675931-0/		′24361-98 570/		4′862 379 1-0/5		4′82 6973 10-/5	

Note: Data are from Plemons (1977).

Table G-25. Means, Standard Deviations, and Codes for Samples of White and Hispanic Psychiatric Patients in a Texas Hospital

	Males				Females			
	White (*N* = 51)		Hispanic (*N* = 38)		White (*N* = 94)		Hispanic (*N* = 57)	
	Mean	S.D.	Mean	S.D.	Mean	S.D.	Mean	S.D.
L	47.9	6.8	52.5	8.2	51.0	7.9	52.3	8.3
F	70.8	13.4	74.0	17.1	70.9	17.7	75.7	17.6
K	45.5	7.0	47.0	7.6	47.2	7.4	45.3	8.3
Hs	67.0	14.0	62.8	12.4	50.0	9.7	59.1	9.3
D	65.1	14.9	70.0	13.5	65.8	13.9	67.5	12.0
Hy	76.7	18.4	78.4	15.6	74.5	14.8	73.7	11.7
Pd	69.8	12.7	63.9	10.8	67.8	13.2	66.2	10.3
Mf	67.7	11.7	66.4	10.7	71.6	13.1	73.7	16.5
Pa	72.9	12.9	73.0	13.3	73.0	13.2	79.4	12.9
Pt	77.0	15.4	76.5	14.3	76.7	13.6	79.8	12.5
Sc	86.8	18.7	90.5	17.5	92.5	16.4	92.4	12.7
Ma	71.6	12.0	70.9	14.6	67.0	13.0	68.1	11.9
Si	73.8	19.9	76.6	15.5	77.6	14.2	81.1	13.4
Code	8″73 069′4512-/ F′-/LK		8*″307692′541-/ F′-L/K		8*″07365′492-1/ F′-L/K		8*0″76 35′924-1/ F′-L/K	

Note: Data are from Hibbs, Kobos, and Gonzalez (1979).

APPENDIX H
T-Score Conversion Tables for the Tri-State and Two-State Samples of Normal Adults

Table H-1. T-Score Conversions for Basic Scales With and Without K Correction (Tri-State Sample: Black Men)

Raw Score	L	F	K	Hs + .5K	D	Hy	Pd + .4K	Mf	Pa	Pt + 1K	Sc + 1K	Ma+ .2K	Si	Hs	Pd	Pt	Sc	Ma	Raw Score
99																			99
98																			98
97																			97
96											120								96
95											119								95
94											118								94
93											117								93
92											116								92
91											115								91
90											114								90
89											113								89
88											112								88
87											111								87
86											110								86
85											109								85
84											108								84
83											107								83
82											105								82
81											104								81
80											103								80
79											102								79
78											101						106		78
77											100						105		77
76											99						104		76
75											98						104		75
74											97						103		74
73											96						102		73
72											95						101		72
71											94						100		71
70											93		110				99		70
69											92		109				98		69

Table H-1. T-Score Conversions for Basic Scales With and Without K Correction (Tri-State Sample: Black Men)—continued

Raw Score	L	F	K	Hs + .5K	D	Hy	Pd + .4K	Mf	Pa	Pt + 1K	Sc + 1K	Ma+ .2K	Si	Hs	Pd	Pt	Sc	Ma	Raw Score
68											91		107				97		68
67											89		106				96		67
66										120	88		104				95		66
65										118	87		103				95		65
64		118								116	86		102				94		64
63		117								115	85		100				93		63
62		116								113	84		99				92		62
61		114								111	83		98				91		61
60		113						119		109	82		96				90		60
59		112						117		107	81		95				89		59
58		111						115		106	80		93				88		58
57		109				118		113		104	79		92				87		57
56		108				116	120	111		102	78		91				86		56
55		107				114	118	109		100	77		89				85		55
54		106				112	116	107		98	76		88				85		54
53		105				110	114	105		97	74		86				84		53
52		103				108	112	103		95	73	116	85				83		52
51		102			118	107	109	101		93	72	114	84				82		51
50		101			115	105	107	99		91	71	112	82		116		81		50
49		100			113	103	105	96		89	70	109	81		114		80		49
48		98			111	101	103	94		87	69	107	80		112	97	79		48
47		97		119	109	99	101	92		86	68	105	79		110	95	78		47
46		96		117	107	97	99	90		84	67	103	77		108	94	77	105	46
45		95		115	104	95	96	88		82	66	101	75		106	93	76	103	45
44		94		113	102	93	94	86		80	65	98	74		104	91	76	101	44
43		92		111	100	92	92	84		78	64	96	73		102	90	75	98	43
42		91		109	98	90	90	82		77	63	94	71		100	89	74	96	42
41		90		106	96	88	88	80		75	62	92	70		98	87	73	94	41
40		89		104	93	86	86	78	116	73	61	90	68		96	86	72	92	40
39		87		102	91	84	83	75	114	71	60	87	67		94	85	71	90	39
38		86		100	89	82	81	73	112	69	58	85	66		91	83	70	88	38

37		85		98	87	80	79	71	110	68	57	83	64		89	82	69	86	37
36		84		96	85	78	77	69	107	66	56	81	63		87	81	68	84	36
35		83		94	82	77	75	67	105	64	55	79	61		85	79	67	82	35
34		81		92	80	75	73	65	103	62	54	76	60		83	78	67	80	34
33		80		90	78	73	70	63	101	60	53	74	59	102	81	77	66	78	33
32		79		87	76	71	68	61	98	59	52	72	57	100	79	75	65	76	32
31		78		85	74	69	66	59	96	57	51	70	56	98	77	74	64	74	31
30		76	83	83	71	67	64	57	94	55	50	68	55	96	75	73	63	72	30
29		75	81	81	69	65	62	55	92	53	49	65	53	94	73	71	62	70	29
28		74	79	79	67	63	60	52	89	51	48	63	52	92	71	70	61	68	28
27		73	77	77	65	62	58	50	87	50	47	61	50	90	69	69	60	66	27
26		72	75	75	63	60	55	48	85	48	46	59	49	88	67	67	59	64	26
25		70	73	73	60	58	53	46	83	46	45	57	48	86	65	66	58	62	25
24		69	71	70	58	56	51	44	80	44	43	54	46	84	63	65	57	60	24
23		68	68	68	56	54	49	42	78	42	42	52	45	82	61	63	57	58	23
22		67	66	66	54	52	47	40	76	41	41	50	43	80	59	62	56	56	22
21		65	64	64	52	50	45	38	73	39	40	48	42	78	57	61	55	54	21
20		64	62	62	49	48	42	36	71	37	39	45	41	76	55	59	54	52	20
19		63	60	60	47	47	40	34	69	35	38	43	39	74	53	58	53	50	19
18		62	58	58	45	45	38	31	67	33	37	41	38	72	50	57	52	48	18
17		61	56	56	43	43	36	29	64	32	36	39	36	70	48	56	51	46	17
16		59	54	54	41	41	34	27	62	30	35	37	35	68	46	54	50	44	16
15	93	58	51	51	38	39	32	25	60	28	34	34	34	66	44	53	49	42	15
14	89	57	49	49	36	37	29	23	58	26	33	32	32	63	42	52	48	40	14
13	84	56	47	47	34	35	27	21	55	24	32	30	31	61	40	50	48	38	13
12	80	54	45	45	32	33	25		53	23	31	28	30	59	38	49	47	35	12
11	76	53	43	43	30	32	23		51	21	30	26	28	57	36	48	46	33	11
10	72	52	41	41	27	30	21		49		29	23	27	55	34	46	45	31	10
9	68	51	39	39	25	28			46		27	21	25	53	32	45	44	29	9
8	64	50	36	37	23	26			44		26		24	51	30	44	43	27	8
7	60	48	34	34	21	24			42		25		23	49	28	42	42	25	7
6	56	47	32	32		22			40		24		21	47	26	41	41	23	6

Table H-1. T-Score Conversions for Basic Scales With and Without K Correction (Tri-State Sample: Black Men)—continued

Raw Score	L	F	K	Hs + .5K	D	Hy	Pd + .4K	Mf	Pa	Pt + 1K	Sc + 1K	Ma+ .2K	Si	Hs	Pd	Pt	Sc	Ma	Raw Score
5	52	46	30	30		20			37		23		20	45	24	40	40	21	5
4	47	45	28	28					35		22			43	22	38	39		4
3	43	43	26	26					33		21			41	20	37	38		3
2	39	42	24	24					31		20			39		36	38		2
1	35	41	22	22					28					37		34	37		1
0	31	40		20					26					35		33	36		0

Table H-2. T-Score Conversions for Basic Scales With and Without K Correction (Tri-State Sample: Black Women)

Raw Score	L	F	K	Hs + .5K	D	Hy	Pd + .4K	Mf	Pa	Pt + 1K	Sc + 1K	Ma+ .2K	Si	Hs	Pd	Pt	Sc	Ma	Raw Score
99											120								99
98											119								98
97											118								97
96											117								96
95											116								95
94											115								94
93											114								93
92											113								92
91											112								91
90											111								90
89											110								89
88											109								88
87											108								87
86											107								86
85											106								85
84											105								84
83											104								83
82											103								82
81											102								81
80											101								80
79											100								79
78											99						101		78
77											98						101		77
76											97						100		76
75											96						99		75
74											95						98		74
73											94						97		73
72											93						96		72
71											92						96		71
70										120	91		104				95		70
69										118	90		103				94		69

Table H-2. T-Score Conversions for Basic Scales With and Without K Correction (Tri-State Sample: Black Women)—continued

Raw Score	L	F	K	Hs + .5K	D	Hy	Pd + .4K	Mf	Pa	Pt + 1K	Sc + 1K	Ma+ .2K	Si	Hs	Pd	Pt	Sc	Ma	Raw Score
68										116	89		102				93		68
67										115	88		100				92		67
66										113	87		99				91		66
65										111	86		98				90		65
64										110	85		96				90		64
63										108	84		95				89		63
62										106	83		94				88		62
61										105	81		92				87		61
60										103	80		91				86		60
59		119				120				101	79		90				85		59
58		118				118				100	78		88				85		58
57		117				116				98	77		87				84		57
56		115			119	114				96	76		86				83		56
55		114			117	112				95	75		84				82		55
54		113			115	111	119			93	74		83				81		54
53		111			113	109	117			91	73		82				80		53
52		110			111	107	115			90	72	118	80				79		52
51		109			109	105	112			88	71	116	79				79		51
50		107			107	103	110			86	70	114	78		117		78		50
49		106			105	101	108			85	69	112	76		115		77		49
48		105		119	103	99	106	21		83	68	110	75		113	89	76		48
47		103		117	101	97	104	24		81	67	107	74		111	88	75		47
46		102		115	99	96	101	26		80	66	105	72		109	87	74	106	46
45		101		113	97	94	99	28		78	65	103	71		107	85	74	104	45
44		99		111	95	92	97	30		76	64	101	70		104	84	73	102	44
43		98		109	93	90	95	33	119	75	63	99	68		102	83	72	100	43
42		97		107	91	88	93	35	117	73	62	97	67		100	82	71	98	42
41		95		105	89	86	90	37	115	71	61	94	66		98	81	70	96	41
40		94		103	87	84	88	40	113	70	60	92	64		96	80	69	94	40
39		92		101	85	83	86	42	110	68	59	90	63		94	78	68	92	39
38		91		98	83	81	84	44	108	66	58	88	62		92	77	68	90	38

37		90		96	81	79	81	47	106	65	57	86	60		90	76	67	88	37
36		88		94	79	77	79	49	104	63	56	83	59		88	75	66	86	36
35		87		92	77	75	77	51	102	61	55	81	58		86	74	65	84	35
34		86		90	75	73	75	53	100	60	54	79	56		84	72	64	82	34
33		84		88	73	71	73	56	98	58	53	77	55	98	82	71	63	80	33
32		83		86	71	70	70	58	95	56	52	75	54	96	80	70	63	78	32
31		82		84	69	68	68	60	93	55	51	72	52	94	78	69	62	76	31
30		80	85	82	67	66	66	63	91	53	50	70	51	92	76	68	61	74	30
29		79	83	80	65	64	64	65	89	51	49	68	50	90	73	66	60	72	29
28		78	81	78	63	62	61	67	87	50	48	66	48	88	71	65	58	70	28
27		76	79	76	61	60	59	69	85	48	47	64	47	86	69	64	58	68	27
26		75	77	74	59	58	57	72	83	46	46	62	46	84	67	63	57	66	26
25		74	75	72	57	57	55	74	80	45	45	59	44	82	65	62	57	64	25
24		72	73	70	55	55	53	76	78	43	44	57	43	80	63	60	56	62	24
23		71	71	67	53	53	50	79	76	41	43	55	42	79	61	59	55	60	23
22		69	68	65	51	51	48	81	74	40	42	53	40	77	59	58	54	58	22
21		68	66	63	48	49	46	83	72	38	41	51	39	75	57	57	53	56	21
20		67	64	61	46	47	44	86	70	36	40	48	38	73	55	56	52	54	20
19		65	62	59	44	45	42	88	68	35	39	46	36	71	53	55	52	52	19
18		64	60	57	42	44	39	90	65	33	38	44	35	69	51	53	51	50	18
17		63	58	55	40	42	37	92	63	31	37	42	34	67	49	52	50	48	17
16		61	56	53	38	40	35	95	61	30	36	40	32	65	47	51	49	46	16
15	95	60	54	51	36	38	33	97	59	28	34	38	31	63	45	50	48	44	15
14	91	59	52	49	34	36	30	99	57	26	33	35	30	61	43	49	47	42	14
13	87	57	50	47	32	34	28	102	55	25	32	33	28	59	40	47	46	40	13
12	82	56	48	45	30	32	26	104	53	23	31	31	27	57	38	46	46	38	12
11	78	55	46	43	28	31	24	106	50	21	30	29	26	55	36	45	45	36	11
10	74	53	44	41	26	29	22	108	48	20	29	27	24	53	34	44	44	34	10
9	70	52	42	39	24	27		111	46		28	24	23	51	32	43	43	32	9
8	66	51	40	36	22	25		113	44		27	22	22	49	30	41	42	30	8
7	62	49	38	34	20	23		115	42		26	20	20	48	28	40	41	28	7

Table H-2. T-Score Conversions for Basic Scales With and Without K Correction (Tri-State Sample: Black Women)

Raw Score	L	F	K	Hs + .5K	D	Hy	Pd + .4K	Mf	Pa	Pt + 1K	Sc + 1K	Ma+ .2K	Si	Hs	Pd	Pt	Sc	Ma	Raw Score
6	58	48	35	32		21		118	40		25			46	26	39	41	26	6
5	54	47	33	30				120	37		24			44	24	38	40	24	5
4	49	45	31	28					35		23			42	22	37	39	22	4
3	45	44	29	26					33		22			40	20	35	38	20	3
2	41	42	27	24					31		21			38		34	37		2
1	37	41	25	22					29		20			36		33	36		1
0	33	40	23	20					27					34		32	35		0

Table H-3. T-Score Conversions for Basic Scales With and Without K Correction (Two-State Sample: White Men)

Raw Score	L	F	K	Hs + .5K	D	Hy	Pd + .4K	Mf	Pa	Pt + 1K	Sc + 1K	Ma + .2K	Si	Hs	Pd	Pt	Sc	Ma	Raw Score
75																			75
74											120								74
73											118								73
72											117								72
71											115								71
70											114		92						70
69											112		91						69
68											111		90				120		68
67											109		89				119		67
66										120	108		88				117		66
65										118	106		87				116		65
64										116	105		86				115		64
63										114	104		85				114		63
62										113	102		84				112		62
61										111	101		83				111		61
60								117		109	99		82				110		60
59								115		107	98		81				109		59
58								113		106	96		81				107		58
57								111		104	95		80				106		57
56								109		102	94		79				105		56
55							119	107		100	92		78				104		55
54					120		117	105		99	91		77				103		54
53					118	119	115	103		97	89		76				101		53
52					116	117	113	101		95	88		75				100		52
51					114	115	111	99		93	86		74				99		51
50					112	113	109	98		92	85		73				98		50
49					110	111	106	96		90	84	118	72				96		49
48					108	108	104	94		88	82	116	71		119	99	95		48
47					106	106	102	92		86	81	114	70		117	98	94		47
46					104	104	100	90		85	79	111	69		115	97	93	115	46
45					102	102	98	88		83	78	109	68		112	95	92	113	45

Table H-3. T-Score Conversions for Basic Scales With and Without K Correction (Two-State Sample: White Men)—continued

Raw Score	L	F	K	Hs + .5K	D	Hy	Pd + .4K	Mf	Pa	Pt + 1K	Sc + 1K	Ma + .2K	Si	Hs	Pd	Pt	Sc	Ma	Raw Score
44					100	100	96	86		81	76	107	67		110	94	90	110	44
43					98	98	94	84		79	75	104	66		108	93	89	108	43
42					96	96	91	82		78	74	102	65		106	91	88	106	42
41				119	94	93	89	80		76	72	100	64		104	90	87	104	41
40				117	92	91	87	78	117	74	71	97	63		102	88	85	101	40
39				114	89	89	85	76	114	72	69	95	62		100	87	84	99	39
38		119		112	87	87	83	75	112	71	68	93	61		98	86	83	97	38
37		117		109	85	85	81	73	110	69	67	90	60		96	84	82	95	37
36		115		107	83	83	79	71	108	67	65	88	59		93	83	81	93	36
35		113		104	81	81	76	69	105	65	64	86	58		91	82	79	90	35
34		111		102	79	79	74	67	103	64	62	83	57		89	80	78	88	34
33		109		99	77	76	72	65	101	62	61	81	56	116	87	79	77	86	33
32		107		97	75	74	70	63	99	60	59	79	55	114	85	77	76	84	32
31		104		94	73	72	68	61	96	58	58	76	54	112	83	76	74	81	31
30		102	78	92	71	70	66	59	94	56	56	74	53	109	81	75	73	79	30
29		100	76	89	69	68	64	57	92	55	55	72	52	107	79	73	72	77	29
28		98	74	87	67	66	61	55	90	53	54	69	51	104	76	72	71	75	28
27		96	72	84	65	64	59	53	87	51	52	67	50	102	74	71	70	73	27
26		94	70	82	63	61	57	52	85	50	51	65	49	100	72	69	68	70	26
25		91	68	79	61	59	55	50	83	48	49	62	48	97	70	68	67	68	25
24		89	66	77	59	58	53	48	81	46	48	60	47	95	68	67	66	66	24
23		87	64	74	57	55	51	46	78	44	46	58	46	92	66	65	65	64	23
22		85	62	72	55	53	49	44	76	43	45	55	45	90	64	64	63	61	22
21		83	60	69	53	51	46	42	74	41	43	53	44	88	62	62	62	59	21
20		81	58	67	51	49	44	40	72	39	42	51	43	85	59	61	61	57	20
19		78	56	64	49	47	42	38	69	37	41	48	42	83	57	60	60	55	19
18		76	54	62	47	44	40	36	67	36	39	46	41	80	55	58	59	53	18
17		74	52	59	45	42	39	34	65	34	38	44	40	78	53	57	57	50	17
16		72	50	57	43	40	36	32	63	32	36	41	39	76	51	56	56	48	16
15	100	70	48	54	41	38	34	30	60	30	35	39	38	73	49	54	55	46	15
14	96	67	46	52	39	36	31	29	58	29	33	37	37	71	47	53	54	44	14
13	93	65	44	49	37	34	29	27	56	27	32	34	36	68	45	51	52	41	13

12	90	63	42	47	35	32	27	25	54	25	31	32	35	66	42	50	51	39	12
11	85	61	40	44	33	30	25	23	51	23	30	30	34	63	40	49	50	37	11
10	80	58	38	42	31	27	23	21	49	22	28	27	33	61	38	47	49	35	10
9	75	56	36	39	29	25	21		47	20	27	25	32	59	36	46	48	33	9
8	70	54	34	37	27	23			45		25	23	31	56	34	45	46	30	8
7	65	52	32	34	25	21			42		24	20	30	54	32	43	45	28	7
6	60	50	30	32	23				40		22		29	51	30	42	44	26	6
5	55	48	28	29	21				38		21		28	49	28	40	43	24	5
4	50	46	26	27					36				27	47	25	39	41	21	4
3	45	44	24	24					33				26	44	23	38	40		3
2	40	41	22	22					31				25	42	21	36	39		2
1	35	39	20						29				24	39		35	38		1
0	30	37							27				23	37		34	37		0

Table H-4. T-Score Conversions for Basic Scales With and Without K Correction (Two-State Sample: White Women)

Raw Score	L	F	K	Hs + .5K	D	Hy	Pd + .4K	Mf	Pa	Pt + 1K	Sc + 1K	Ma + .2K	Si	Hs	Pd	Pt	Sc	Ma	Raw Score
75																			75
74																			74
73																			73
72																			72
71																			71
70													97						70
69											120		96						69
68											118		95						68
67											117		94						67
66										120	115		93						66
65										118	113		92						65
64										117	112		91				119		64
63										115	110		90				118		63
62										113	108		89				117		62
61										111	107		87				116		61
60										109	105		86				114		60
59										107	104		85				113		59
58										106	102		84				112		58
57					119					104	100		83				110		57
56					117	120				102	99		82				109		56
55					115	118				100	97		81				108		55
54					114	116				98	95		80				106		54
53					112	114				97	94		79				105		53
52					110	112	118			95	92		78				104		52
51					108	110	116	20		93	91		77				103		51
50					106	108	114	23		91	89		75				101		50
49					104	106	112	25		89	87		74				100		49
48					102	104	109	27		87	86		73			98	99		48
47					100	101	107	30		86	84		72			97	97		47
46				120	99	99	105	32		84	82	120	71			96	96		46
45				118	97	97	103	34		82	81	117	70			94	95	120	45

44				116	95	95	100	37		80	79	115	69		120	93	93	118	44
43				113	93	93	98	39		78	78	112	68		117	92	92	115	43
42				111	91	91	96	42		76	76	110	67		115	90	91	113	42
41				109	89	89	94	44		75	74	107	66		113	89	90	111	41
40				107	87	87	91	46		73	73	105	65		110	88	88	108	40
39				105	85	85	89	49		71	71	102	63		108	86	87	106	39
38				102	83	83	87	51		69	69	100	62		105	85	86	103	38
37				100	82	80	85	53		67	68	97	61		103	84	84	101	37
36				98	80	78	82	56		65	66	94	60		101	82	83	98	36
35				96	78	76	80	58		64	65	92	59		98	81	82	96	35
34				94	76	74	78	61		62	63	89	58		96	80	81	93	34
33				91	74	72	75	63		60	61	87	57	109	93	78	79	91	33
32				89	72	70	73	65		58	60	84	56	106	91	77	78	89	32
31				87	70	68	71	68		56	58	82	55	104	89	76	77	86	31
30			82	85	68	66	69	70		54	56	79	54	102	86	74	75	84	30
29			80	83	66	64	66	72	118	53	55	76	53	100	84	73	74	81	29
28			77	80	65	61	64	75	114	51	53	74	51	98	81	72	73	79	28
27			74	78	63	59	62	77	111	49	52	71	50	96	79	70	71	76	27
26			72	76	61	57	60	80	107	47	50	69	49	93	77	69	70	74	26
25			70	74	59	55	57	82	104	45	48	66	48	91	74	67	69	71	25
24			68	72	57	53	55	84	100	44	47	64	47	89	72	66	68	69	24
23			66	69	55	51	53	87	97	42	45	61	46	87	70	65	66	67	23
22		118	64	67	53	48	51	89	93	40	44	59	45	85	67	63	65	64	22
21		114	62	65	51	47	48	91	90	38	42	56	44	83	65	62	64	62	21
20		110	60	63	49	45	46	94	86	36	40	54	43	81	62	61	62	59	20
19		107	58	61	48	43	44	96	83	34	39	51	42	78	60	59	61	57	19
18		103	56	59	46	40	42	99	79	33	37	49	40	76	58	58	60	54	18
17		99	54	56	44	38	39	101	75	31	35	46	39	74	55	57	58	52	17
16		95	52	54	42	36	37	103	72	29	34	44	38	72	53	55	57	49	16
15	116	91	50	52	40	34	35	106	68	27	32	41	37	70	50	54	56	47	15
14	110	87	48	50	38	32	33	108	65	25	31	38	36	68	48	53	55	45	14

Table H-4. T-Score Conversions for Basic Scales With and Without K Correction (Two-State Sample: White Women)—continued

Raw Score	L	F	K	Hs + .5K	D	Hy	Pd + .4K	Mf	Pa	Pt + 1K	Sc + 1K	Ma + .2K	Si	Hs	Pd	Pt	Sc	Ma	Raw Score
13	104	83	46	48	36	30	30	110	61	23	29	36	35	65	46	51	53	42	13
12	98	80	44	45	34	28	28	113	58	21	27	33	34	63	43	50	52	40	12
11	92	76	42	43	32	26	26	115	54	20	26	31	33	61	41	49	51	37	11
10	86	72	40	41	30	24	24	117	50		24	28	32	59	38	47	49	35	10
9	80	68	37	39	29	21	21	120	47		22	26	31	57	36	46	48	32	9
8	74	64	35	37	27				44		21	23	30	55	34	45	47	30	8
7	68	61	33	34	25				40			21	29	53	31	43	45	27	7
6	62	57	30	32	23				37				28	50	29	42	44	25	6
5	56	53	28	30	21				33				26	48	26	41	43	23	5
4	50	49	26	28					30				25	46	24	39	42	20	4
3	44	45	24	26					26				24	44	22	38	40		3
2	38	41	22	23					22				23	42		37	39		2
1	32	38	20	21									22	40		35	38		1
0	26	35											21	38		34	36		0

BIBLIOGRAPHY

BIBLIOGRAPHY

Aaronson, B. S. Age and sex influence on MMPI profile peak distribution in an abnormal population. *Journal of Consulting Psychology,* 1958, 22, 203-206.

Abe, S. K. Nisei personality characteristics as measured by the EPPS and MMPI. Doctoral dissertation, University of Utah, 1958. (*Dissertation Abstracts* [*DA*], 1959, 19, 2648)

Abney, M. D. The effect of using separate black and white MMPI norms to compare black and white heroin addicts. Doctoral dissertation, University of Texas at Austin, 1981. (*Dissertation Abstracts International* [*DAI*], 1982, 42B, 2975-2976)

Acosta, F. X., J. Yamamoto, and L. A. Evans. *Effective psychotherapy for low-income and minority patients.* New York: Plenum Press, 1982.

Adebimpe, V. R., J. Gigandet, and E. Harris. MMPI diagnosis of black psychiatric patients. *American Journal of Psychiatry,* 1979, 136, 85-87.

Allen, D. F. (D. A. Azibo). African (black) personality theory, status characteristics theory, and perceived belief similarity: Which is predominant in dominance/reactance behavior? Doctoral dissertation, Washington University, 1983. (*DAI,* 1984, 44B, 3505)

Altus, W. D. "Jewish" names and MMPI items. *Psychological Reports,* 1964, 14, 870.

Altus, W. D., and J. H. Clark. The effect of adjustment patterns upon the intercorrelation of intelligence subtest variables. *Journal of Social Psychology,* 1949, 30, 39-48.

Alvarez, R., ed. *Delivery of services for Latino community mental health.* Monograph No. 2. Los Angeles: UCLA Spanish Speaking Mental Health Research Center, 1975.

Anthony, N. Malingering as role taking. *Journal of Clinical Psychology,* 1976, 32, 32-41.

Arthur, G. An experience in examining an Indian twelfth-grade group with the MMPI. *Mental Hygiene,* 1944, 28, 243-250.

Atkinson, D. R., C. Morten, and D. W. Sue, eds. *Counseling American minorities: A cross-cultural perspective.* Dubuque, Iowa: Wm. C. Brown, 1979.

Ball, J. C. Comparison of MMPI profile differences among Negro-white adolescents. *Journal of Clinical Psychology,* 1960, 16, 304-307.

Ball, J. C. *Social deviancy and adolescent personality: An analytical study with the MMPI.* Lexington: University of Kentucky Press, 1962.

Bamgbose, O., D. Edwards, and S. Johnson. The effects of race and social class on clinical judgment. *Journal of Clinical Psychology,* 1980, 36, 605-609.

Barón, A., ed. *Explorations in Chicano psychology.* New York: Praeger, 1981.

Barron, F. An ego-strength scale which predicts response to psychotherapy. *Journal of Consulting Psychology,* 1953, 17, 327-333. (Also reprinted in Dahlstrom and Dahlstrom, 1980.)

Baughman, E. E. *Black Americans: A psychological analysis.* New York: Academic Press, 1971.

Baughman, E. E., and W. G. Dahlstrom. *Negro and white children: A psychological study in the rural South.* New York: Academic Press, 1968.

Bell, D. A. Racism in American courts: Cause for black disruption or despair? *California Law Review*, 1973, 61, 165-203.

Bennett, J. W., ed. *The new ethnicity: Perspectives from ethnology.* St. Paul: West Publishing Co., 1975.

Bernstein, I. H., L. S. Schoenfeld, and R. M. Costello. Truncated component regression multicollinearity and the MMPI's use in a police officer selection setting. *Multivariate Behavioral Research,* 1982, 17, 99-116.

Berry, J., R. Heaton, and M. Kirby. Neuropsychological assessment of chronic inhalant abusers. Paper presented at the First International Symposium on the Voluntary Inhalation of Industrial Solvents, Mexico City, June 1976.

Bertelson, A. D., P. A. Marks, and G. D. May. MMPI and race: A controlled study. *Journal of Consulting and Clinical Psychology,* 1982, 50, 316-318.

Bier, W. C. A comparative study of a seminary group and four other groups on the MMPI. *Studies in Psychology and Psychiatry from the Catholic University of America,* 1948, 7, 1-107. (Also reprinted in Welsh and Dahlstrom, 1956.)

Black, J. D. MMPI results for fifteen groups of female college students. In G. S. Welsh and W. G. Dahlstrom, eds. *Basic readings on the MMPI in psychology and medicine.* Minneapolis: University of Minnesota Press, 1956.

Blanchard, E. B., J. E. Bassett, and E. Koshland. Psychopathy and delay of gratification. *Criminal Justice and Behavior,* 1977, 4, 265-271.

Bloom, W. Relevant MMPI norms for young adult Air Force trainees. *Journal of Personality Assessment,* 1977, 41, 505-510.

Bohrnstedt, G. W., E. F. Borgatta, and R. R. Evans. Religious affiliation, religiosity, and MMPI scores. *Journal for the Scientific Study of Religion,* 1968, 7, 255-258.

Braucht, G. N. Interactional analysis of suicidal behavior. *Journal of Consulting and Clinical Psychology,* 1979, 47, 653-669.

Brislin, R. W., ed. *Translation: Applications and research.* New York: Gardner, 1976.

Brislin, R. W., W. J. Lonner, and R. M. Thorndike. *Cross-cultural research methods.* New York: Wiley, 1973.

Broen, W. E. Personality correlates of religious attitudes. *Journal of Consulting Psychology,* 1955, 19, 64.

Brown, D. G., and W. L. Lowe. A study of religious beliefs and personality differences in college students. Master's thesis, University of Denver, 1948. (Also in *Journal of Social Psychology,* 1951, 33, 103-129.)

Brown, N. W. An investigation of personality characteristics of Negroes attending a predominantly white university and Negroes attending a black college. Doctoral dissertation, College of William and Mary, 1973. (*DAI,* 1974, 34A, 3980)

Bryde, J. F. *The Sioux Indian student: A study of scholastic failure and personality conflict.* Holy Rosary Mission, Pine Ridge, South Dakota, 1966. (Also: Doctoral dissertation, University of Denver, 1965; *DA,* 1966, 26, 4792.)

Bull, R. W. A tri-racial MMPI study. Master's thesis, University of North Carolina, 1976.

Burke, H. R. Renal patients and their MMPI profiles. *Journal of Psychology,* 1979, 101, 229-236.

Butcher, J. N., B. Ball, and E. Ray. Effects of socioeconomic level on MMPI differences in Negro-white college students. *Journal of Counseling Psychology,* 1964, 11, 83-87.

Butcher, J. N., L. Braswell, and D. Raney. A cross-cultural comparison of American Indian, black, and white inpatients on the MMPI and presenting symptoms. *Journal of Consulting and Clinical Psychology*, 1983, 51, 587-594.

Butcher, J. N., and L. A. Clark. Recent trends in cross-cultural MMPI research and application. In J. N. Butcher, ed. *New developments in the use of the MMPI*. Minneapolis: University of Minnesota Press, 1979.

Butcher, J. N., and R. E. García. Cross-national application of psychological tests. *Personnel and Guidance Journal*, 1978, 56, 472-475.

Butcher, J. N., and P. Pancheri. *A handbook of cross-national MMPI research*. Minneapolis: University of Minnesota Press, 1976.

Cahman, J. A. Personality variables associated with narcotic addiction as measured by the MMPI. Doctoral dissertation, University of Southern California, 1974. (*DAI*, 1974, 35B, 1039.)

Caldwell, M. G. Case analysis method for the personality study of offenders. *Journal of Criminal Law, Criminology, and Police Science*, 1954, 45, 291-298.

Caldwell, M. G. Personality trends in the youthful male offender. *Journal of Criminal Law, Criminology, and Police Science*, 1959, 49, 405-416.

Cameron, P. Personality differences between typical urban Negroes and whites. *Journal of Negro Education*, 1971, 40, 66-75.

Camilli, G., and K. D. Hopkins. Applicability of chi-square 2 × 2 contingency tables with small expected cell frequencies. *Psychological Bulletin*, 1978, 85, 163-167.

Cauce, A. M., and L. I. Jacobson. Implicit and incorrect assumptions concerning the assessment of the Latino in the United States. *American Journal of Community Psychology*, 1980, 8, 571-586.

Chestang, L. W. *Character development in a hostile environment*. Occasional Paper No. 3. School of Social Service Administration, University of Chicago, November 1972.

Christian, W. L., B. R. Burkhart, and M. D. Gynther. Subtle-obvious ratings of MMPI items: New interest in an old concept. *Journal of Consulting and Clinical Psychology*, 1978, 46, 1178-1186.

Clark, C. G., and H. L. Miller. Validation of Gilberstadt and Duker's 8-6 profile type on a black sample. *Psychological Reports*, 1971, 29, 259-264.

Clark, K. B. *Dark ghetto: Dilemmas of social power*. New York: Harper & Row, 1965.

Clemente, F., and W. Sauer. Racial differences in life satisfaction. *Journal of Black Studies*, 1976, 7, 3-10.

Colligan, R. C., D. Osborne, W. M. Swenson, and K. P. Offord. *The MMPI: A contemporary normative study*. New York: Praeger, 1983.

Comstock, B. Psychological measurements in long term inhalant abusers. Paper presented at the First International Symposium on the Voluntary Inhalation of Industrial Solvents, Mexico City, June 1976.

Cooke, G., E. Pogany, and N. G. Johnston. A comparison of blacks and whites committed for evaluation of competency to stand trial on criminal charges. *Journal of Psychiatry and Law*, 1974, 2, 319-337.

Costello, R. M. Racial comparisons on the MMPI. Doctoral dissertation, University of Tennessee, 1971. (*DAI*, 1972, 32B, 4855.)

Costello, R. M. Item level racial differences on the MMPI. *Journal of Social Psychology*, 1973, 91, 161-162.

Costello, R. M. Construction and cross-validation of an MMPI black-white scale. *Journal of Personality Assessment*, 1977, 41, 514-519.

Costello, R. M. Premorbid social competence construct generalizability across ethnic groups: Path analyses with two premorbid social competence components. *Journal of Consulting and Clinical Psychology*, 1978, 48, 1164-1165.

Costello, R. M., H. J. Fine, and B. I. Blau. Racial comparisons on the MMPI. *Journal of Clinical Psychology*, 1973, 29, 63-65.

Costello, R. M., D. W. Tiffany, and R. H. Gier. Methodological issues and racial (black-white) comparisons on the MMPI. *Journal of Consulting and Clinical Psychology*, 1972, 38, 161-168.

Couture, J. E. Alberta Indian youth: A study in Cree and Blood student conflict. Unpublished doctoral dissertation, University of Alberta, 1972.

Cowan, M. A., B. A. Watkins, and W. E. Davis. Level of education, diagnosis and race-related differences in MMPI performance. *Journal of Clinical Psychology*, 1975, 31, 442-444.

Crowne, D. P., and D. Marlowe. A new scale of social desirability independent of psychopathology. *Journal of Consulting Psychology*, 1960, 24, 349-354.

Cuellar, I., L. C. Harris, and R. Jasso. An acculturation scale for Mexican and American normal and clinical populations. *Hispanic Journal of Behavioral Science*, 1980, 2, 199-217.

Dahlstrom, W. G., and L. E. Dahlstrom, eds. *Basic readings on the MMPI: A new selection on personality measurement*. Minneapolis: University of Minnesota Press, 1980.

Dahlstrom, W. G., and G. S. Welsh. *An MMPI handbook*. Minneapolis: University of Minnesota Press, 1960.

Dahlstrom, W. G., G. S. Welsh, and L. E. Dahlstrom. *An MMPI handbook* (Vol. 1). *Clinical interpretation*. Minneapolis: University of Minnesota Press, 1972.

Dahlstrom, W. G., G. S. Welsh, and L. E. Dahlstrom. *An MMPI handbook* (Vol. 2). *Research applications*. Minneapolis: University of Minnesota Press, 1975.

Dana, R. H., R. Hornby, and T. Hoffmann. Local norms for personality assessment of Rosebud Sioux. *White Cloud Journal of American Indian/Alaska Native Mental Health*, 1984, 3, 19-25.

Davis, A., and J. Dollard. *Children of bondage: The personality development of Negro youth in the urban South*. New York: Harper & Row, 1940.

Davis, J. A. Blacks, crime and American culture. *Annals of the American Academy of Political and Social Science*, 1976, 423, 89-98.

Davis, W. E. Race and the differential "power" of the MMPI. *Journal of Personality Assessment*, 1975, 39, 138-140.

Davis, W. E., S. J. Beck, and T. A. Ryan. Race-related and educationally-related MMPI profile differences among hospitalized schizophrenics. *Journal of Clinical Psychology*, 1973, 29, 478-479.

Davis, W. E., and A. P. Gillette. Relationship between patients' responses to objective tests and examiners' characteristics. *Psychological Reports*, 1969, 25, 487-491.

Davis, W. E., and M. H. Jones. Negro versus Caucasian test performance revisited. *Journal of Consulting and Clinical Psychology*, 1974, 42, 675-679.

Dean, K. I. Father absence, feminine identification, and assertive-aggressiveness: A test of compulsive masculinity among institutionalized Negro juvenile delinquents. Doctoral dissertation, Florida State University, 1970. (*DAI*, 1971, 31A, 4912-4913)

Devereux, G. Ethnic identity: Its logical foundations and its dysfunctions. In G. DeVos and L. Romanucci-Ross, eds. *Ethnic identity: Cultural continuities and change*. Palo Alto, Calif.: Mayfield, 1975.

Devries, A. G. Demographic variables and MMPI responses. *Journal of Clinical Psychology*, 1966, 22, 450-452.

Diehl, L. A. The relationship between demographic factors, MMPI scores and the Social Readjustment Rating Scale. Doctoral dissertation, Ohio University, 1977. (*DAI*, 1977, 38B, 2360)

Dodd, J. A retrospective analysis of variables related to duration of treatment in a university psychiatric clinic. *Journal of Nervous and Mental Disease*, 1970, 151, 75-84.

Dohrenwend, B. P., and B. S. Dohrenwend. *Social status and psychological disorder: A causal inquiry*. New York: Wiley, 1969.

Dohrenwend, B. S., and B. P. Dohrenwend, eds. *Stressful life events: Their nature and effects*. New York: Wiley, 1974.

Dolan, M. P., W. R. Roberts, W. E. Penk, R. Robinowitz, and H. G. Atkins. Personality differences among black, white, and Hispanic-American male heroin addicts on MMPI content scales. *Journal of Clinical Psychology*, 1983, 39, 807-813.

Dollard, J. *Caste and class in a Southern town*. New Haven: Yale University Press, 1937.

Draguns, J. G., and L. Phillips. *Culture and psychopathology: The quest for a relationship*. Morristown, N.J.: General Learning Press, 1972.

Dreger, R. M., and K. S. Miller. Comparative psychological studies of Negroes and whites in the United States: 1959-1965. *Psychological Bulletin Monograph Supplement*, 1968, 70 (3, P. 2).

Duberman, L. *Social inequality: Class and caste in America*. Philadelphia: Lippincott, 1976.

Dudley, H. K., E. M. Craig, J. E. Craft, D. M. Sheehan, J. M. Mason, and V. E. Rhoten. The Draw-a-Person Test and young state hospital patients. *Journal of Youth and Adolescence*, 1973, 2, 313-330.

Dvorkin, B. E., ed. *Blacks and mental health in the United States, 1963-1973: A selected annotated bibliography of journal articles*. Washington, D.C.: Howard University Medical-Dental Library, 1974.

Eaton, W. W. *The sociology of mental illness*. New York: Praeger, 1980.

Edinger, J. D., J. B. Bogan, P. H. Harrigan, and M. F. Ellis. Altitude Quotient-IQ discrepancy as an index of personality disorganization among drug offenders. *Journal of Clinical Psychology*, 1975, 31, 575-578.

Edinger, J. D., W. M. Nelson, K. C. Bailey, J. Wallace, and R. Lyman. The utility of Wechsler Adult Intelligence Scale profile analysis with prisoners. *Journal of Clinical Psychology*, 1979, 35, 807-814.

Edwards, A. L. *Manual for the Edwards Personal Preference Schedule* (Rev. ed.). New York: The Psychological Corporation, 1959.

Elion, V. H. The validity of the MMPI as a discriminator of social deviance among black males. *Federal Correctional Institution Research Reports* (Tallahassee, Fla.), 1974 (6, No. 3).

Elion, V. H., and E. I. Megargee. Validity of the MMPI Pd scale among black males. *Journal of Consulting and Clinical Psychology*, 1975, 43, 166-172.

Erdberg, S. P. MMPI differences associated with sex, race, and residence in a southern sample. Doctoral dissertation, University of Alabama, 1969. (*DAI*, 1970, 30B, 5236)

Fillenbaum, G. G., and E. Pfeiffer. The Mini-Mult: A cautionary note. *Journal of Consulting and Clinical Psychology*, 1976, 44, 698-703.

Finney, J. C. Psychiatry and multiculturality in Hawaii. *International Journal of Social Psychiatry*, 1963, 10, 5-11.

Fischer, J. Negroes, whites and rates of mental illness: Reconsideration of a myth. *Psychiatry*, 1969, 32, 428-446.

Fisher, G. The performance of male prisoners on the Marlowe-Crowne Social Desirability scale. II. Differences as a function of race and crime. *Journal of Clinical Psychology*, 1967, 23, 473-475.

Fitch, R. S. Examination of selected MMPI profiles of four groups of Spanish-American and Anglo-American adolescent females. Doctoral dissertation, Baylor University, 1972. (*DAI*, 1973, 33A, 4936)

Fitzpatrick, J. J. Cultural differences, not criminal offenses: A redefinition of types of social behavior. In S. Sylvester, ed. *Politics and crime.* New York: Praeger, 1974.

Flanagan, J., and G. Lewis. Comparison of Negro and white lower class men on the General Aptitude Test battery and the MMPI. *Journal of Social Psychology,* 1969, 78, 289-291.

Fowler, R. D. Computer interpretation of personality tests: The automated psychologist. *Comprehensive Psychiatry,* 1967, 8, 455-467.

Francis, B. S. Culture and sex role as determinants of personality profiles. Master's thesis, University of Arizona, 1964.

Fry, F. D. A study of the personality traits of college students and of state prison inmates as measured by the MMPI. *Journal of Psychology,* 1949, 28, 439-449.

Frye, T. F. An evaluative actuarial study of the MMPI utilizing an Anglo- and Mexican-American sample. Master's thesis, Trinity University, San Antonio, Tex., 1973.

Fuller, C. G., and H. N. Malony. A comparison of English and Spanish (Nuñez) translations of the MMPI. *Journal of Personality Assessment,* 1984, 48, 130-131.

García, R. E. Recent developments of a Spanish language MMPI for Latino populations in the United States. Paper presented at the 18th Annual Symposium on Recent Developments in the Use of the MMPI, Minneapolis, April, 1983.

García, R. E., and A. A. Azán (trans.). *MMPI: Versión Hispana.* Minneapolis: University of Minnesota Press, 1984.

Garside, J. G. A cross-cultural comparison of personality. Doctoral dissertation, Brigham Young University, 1966. (*DA,* 1966, 26, 5864)

Gearing, M. L. The MMPI as a primary differentiator and predictor of behavior in prison: A methodological critique and review of the recent literature. *Psychological Bulletin,* 1979, 86, 929-963.

Genthner, R. W. Differences between black and white patients in the effects of short-term hospitalization. Doctoral dissertation, Kent State University, 1973. (*DAI,* 1973, 34B, 2303)

Genthner, R. W., and J. R. Graham. Effects of short-term public psychiatric hospitalization for both black and white patients. *Journal of Consulting and Clinical Psychology,* 1976, 44, 118-124.

Gilberstadt, H., and J. Duker. *A handbook for clinical and actuarial MMPI interpretation.* Philadelphia: W. B. Saunders, 1965.

Gilbert, D., and J. A. Kahl. *The American class structure: A new synthesis.* Homewood, Ill.: Dorsey, 1982.

Glatt, K. M. An evaluation of the French, Spanish, and German translations of the MMPI. *Acta Psychologica,* 1969, 29, 65-84.

Glenn, N. D. Negro prestige criteria: A case study in the bases of prestige. *American Journal of Sociology,* 1963, 68, 645-657.

Goldberg, D., and P. Huxley. *Mental illness in the community: The pathway to psychiatric care.* London: Tavistock, 1980.

Goldberg, L. R. Diagnosticians vs. diagnostic signs: The diagnosis of psychosis vs. neurosis from the MMPI. *Psychological Monographs,* 1965, 79, (Whole No. 602).

Goldberg, S. D. The use of the MMPI Psychopathic Deviate scale in evaluation of Mexican-American patients: An expanded symbolic interactionalist perspective. Doctoral dissertation, U.S. International University, San Diego, 1980. (*DAI,* 1981, 41B, 4663)

Goldman, V. J. MMPI comparisons of black and white delinquents. Master's thesis, University of North Carolina, 1981.

Goldman, V. J. The MMPI and measurement of aggression in incarcerated male juvenile delinquents. Doctoral dissertation, University of North Carolina, 1984. (*DAI,* 1985, 45B, 2686)

Goldsmith, R., W. Capel, K. Waddell, and G. Stewart. Demographic and sociological implications of addiction in New Orleans: Implications for consideration of treatment modalities. In J. Singh, L. Miller, and H. Lal, eds. *Drug addiction: Clinical and socio-legal aspects*. Mt. Kisco, N.Y.: Futura, 1972.

Goodenough, F. L., and J. E. Anderson. *Experimental child study*. New York: Appleton-Century-Crofts, 1931.

Goodstein, L. D. Regional differences in MMPI responses among male college students. *Journal of Consulting Psychology*, 1954, 18, 437-441. (Also reprinted in Welsh and Dahlstrom, 1956.)

Gottesman, I. I. Biogenetics of race and class. In M. Deutsch, I. Katz, and A. R. Jensen, eds. *Social class, race and psychological development*. New York: Holt, Rinehart & Winston, 1968.

Gottlieb, G., and C. Eisdorfer. Personality patterns of medical out-patients. Unpublished manuscript, Department of Psychiatry, Duke University, 1959.

Graham, J. R. *The MMPI: A practical guide*. New York: Oxford, 1977.

Graham, J. R. Using the MMPI in counseling and psychotherapy. *Clinical notes on the MMPI*. No. 1. Nutley, N.J.: Roche Psychiatric Service Institute, 1979.

Graham, J. R., R. Allon, I. Friedman, and R. S. Lilly. The Ward Evaluation Scale: A factor analytic study. *Journal of Clinical Psychology*, 1971, 27, 118-122.

Graham, J. R., I. Friedman, A. F. Paolino, and R. S. Lilly. An appraisal of the therapeutic value of the mental hospital milieu. *Journal of Community Psychology*, 1974, 2, 153-160.

Graham, J. R., R. S. Lilly, R. Allon, and I. Friedman. Comparison of the factor structures of staff and patient responses on the Ward Evaluation Scale. *Journal of Clinical Psychology*, 1971, 27, 123-128.

Gray-Little, B. The concept of race in personality theory and research. Paper presented at the American Psychological Association convention, Anaheim, Calif., August 1983.

Gray-Little, B., and M. I. Appelbaum. Instrumentality effects in the assessment of racial differences in self-esteem. *Journal of Personality and Social Psychology*, 1979, 37, 1221-1229.

Greene, R. L. *The MMPI: An interpretive manual*. New York: Grune & Stratton, 1980.

Grier, W. H., and P. M. Cobbs. *Black rage*. New York: Basic Books, 1968. (Republished: New York: Bantam, 1969.)

Groesch, S. J., and W. E. Davis. Psychiatric patients' religion and MMPI responses. *Journal of Clinical Psychology*, 1977, 33, 168-171.

Gulliksen, H., and S. S. Wilks. Regression tests for several samples. *Psychometrika*, 1950, 15, 91-114.

Guterman, S. S., ed. *Black psyche: The modal personality patterns of black Americans*. Berkeley, Calif.: Glendessary Press, 1972.

Guzman, D. S. Analysis of Mexican-American and Anglo-American differences on the MMPI. Master's thesis, San Jose State University, 1970.

Gynther, M. D. White norms and black MMPIs: A prescription for discrimination? *Psychological Bulletin*, 1972, 78, 386-402.

Gynther, M. D. Aging and personality. In J. N. Butcher, ed. *New developments in the use of the MMPI*. Minneapolis: University of Minnesota Press, 1979. (a)

Gynther, M. D. Ethnicity and personality: An update. In J. N. Butcher, ed. *New developments in the use of the MMPI*. Minneapolis: University of Minnesota Press, 1979. (b)

Gynther, M. D. Is the MMPI an appropriate assessment device for blacks? *Journal of Black Psychology*, 1981, 7, 67-75.

Gynther, M. D., H. Altman, and I. W. Sletten. Replicated correlates of MMPI two-point code types: The Missouri actuarial system. *Journal of Clinical Psychology*, 1973, 29, 263-289.

Gynther, M. D., H. Altman, and R. W. Warbin. Interpretation of uninterpretable MMPI profiles. *Journal of Consulting and Clinical Psychology*, 1973, 40, 78-83. (a)

Gynther, M. D., H. Altman, and R. W. Warbin. Behavioral correlates for the MMPI 4-9/9-4 code types: A case of the emperor's new clothes. *Journal of Consulting and Clinical Psychology*, 1973, 40, 259-263. (b)

Gynther, M. D., R. D. Fowler, and P. Erdberg. False positives galore: The application of standard MMPI criteria to a rural, isolated Negro sample. *Journal of Clinical Psychology*, 1971, 27, 234-237.

Gynther, M. D., B. G. Gray, and M. E. Strauss. Effects of religious affiliation, religious involvement, and sex on the social desirability ratings of MMPI religion items. *Journal of Consulting and Clinical Psychology*, 1970, 34, 338-342.

Gynther, M. D., and S. B. Green. Accuracy may make a difference, but does a difference make for accuracy? A response to Pritchard and Rosenblatt. *Journal of Consulting and Clinical Psychology*, 1980, 48, 268-272.

Gynther, M. D., D. Lachar, and W. G. Dahlstrom. Are special norms for minorities needed? Development of an MMPI F scale for blacks. *Journal of Consulting and Clinical Psychology*, 1978, 46, 1403-1408.

Gynther, M. D., and J. Ullom. Objections to MMPI items as a function of interpersonal trust, race, and sex. *Journal of Consulting and Clinical Psychology*, 1976, 44, 1020.

Gynther, M. D., and P. H. Witt. Windstorms and important persons: Personality characteristics of black educators. *Journal of Clinical Psychology*, 1976, 32, 613-616.

Haan, N. Coping and defense mechanisms related to personality inventories. *Journal of Consulting Psychology*, 1965, 29, 373-378.

Haertzen, C. A., H. E. Hill, and J. J. Monroe. MMPI scales for differentiating and predicting relapse in alcoholics, opiate addicts, and criminals. *International Journal of the Addictions*, 1968, 3, 91-106.

Haller, J. S. *Outcasts from evolution: Scientific attitudes of racial inferiority, 1859-1900.* Urbana: University of Illinois Press, 1971.

Harris, R. E., and J. C. Lingoes. Subscales for the MMPI: An aid to profile interpretation. Mimeographed materials, Department of Psychiatry, University of California at San Francisco, 1955; corrected version, 1968.

Harrison, R. H., and E. H. Kass. Differences between Negro and white pregnant women on the MMPI. *Journal of Consulting Psychology*, 1967, 31, 454-463.

Harrison, R. H., and E. H. Kass. MMPI correlates of Negro acculturation in a northern city. *Journal of Personality and Social Psychology*, 1968, 10, 262-270.

Hathaway, S. R., and P. F. Briggs. Some normative data on new MMPI scales. *Journal of Clinical Psychology*, 1957, 13, 364-368.

Hathaway, S. R., and J. C. McKinley. A multiphasic personality schedule (Minnesota): I. Construction of the schedule. *Journal of Psychology*, 1940, 10, 249-254. (Also reprinted in Dahlstrom and Dahlstrom, 1980.)

Hathaway, S. R., and E. D. Monachesi. *Adolescent personality and behavior: MMPI patterns of normal, delinquent, dropout, and other outcomes*. Minneapolis: University of Minnesota Press, 1963.

Haven, H. Racial differences on the MMPI O-H (over-controlled hostility) scale. *Federal Correctional Institution Research Reports* (Tallahassee, Fla.), 1969 (l, No. 5).

Hedlund, J. L. MMPI patterns of black and white psychiatric patients. Unpublished materials, Institute of Psychiatry, University of Missouri at St. Louis, 1974.

Hedlund, J. L. MMPI clinical scale correlates. *Journal of Consulting and Clinical Psychology*, 1977, 45, 739-750.

Hendrie, H. C., D. Lachar, and K. Lennox. Personality trait and symptom correlates of life change in a psychiatric population. *Journal of Psychosomatic Research*, 1975, 19, 203-208.

Herl, D. Personality characteristics in a sample of heroin addict methadone maintenance applicants. *British Journal of Addiction*, 1976, 71, 253-259.

Hernandez, C. A., M. J. Haug, and N. N. Wagner, eds. *Chicanos: Social and psychological perspectives* (2nd ed.). St. Louis: C. V. Mosby, 1976.

Herreid, C. F., and J. R. Herreid. Differences in MMPI scores in native and nonnative Alaskans. *Journal of Social Psychology*, 1966, 70, 191-198.

Hibbs, B. J., J. C. Kobos, and J. González. Effects of ethnicity, sex, and age on MMPI profiles. *Psychological Reports*, 1979, 45, 591-597.

Hightower, N. E. Validity of the MacAndrew Alcoholism scale: Racial variations and effects of offender status. Doctoral dissertation, Texas Tech University, 1984. (*DAI*, 1985, 45B, 3336)

Highwater, J. *The primal mind: Vision and reality in Indian America.* New York: Harper & Row, 1981.

Hill, H. E., C. A. Haertzen, and R. Glaser. Personality characteristics of narcotic addicts as indicated by the MMPI. *Journal of General Psychology*, 1960, 62, 127-139.

Hoffmann, T. Personality assessment with native Americans. Paper presented at the Society for Personality Assessment convention, Tampa, March, 1984.

Hoffmann, T., R. H. Dana, and B. Bolton. Measured acculturation and MMPI-168 performance of native American adults. *Journal of Cross-Cultural Psychology*, 1985, 16, 243-256.

Hokanson, J. E., and G. Calden. Negro-white differences on the MMPI. *Journal of Clinical Psychology*, 1960, 16, 32-33.

Holcomb, W. R., and N. A. Adams. Racial influences on intelligence and personality measures of people who commit murder. *Journal of Clinical Psychology*, 1982, 38, 793-796.

Holcomb, W. R., N. A. Adams, and H. M. Ponder. Are separate black and white MMPI norms needed? An IQ-controlled comparison of accused murderers. *Journal of Clinical Psychology*, 1984, 40, 189-192.

Holland, T. R. Ethnic group differences in MMPI profile pattern and factorial structure among adult offenders. *Journal of Personality Assessment*, 1979, 43, 72-77.

Holland, T. R., G. E. Beckett, and M. Levi. Intelligence, personality, and criminal violence: A multivariate analysis. *Journal of Consulting and Clinical Psychology*, 1981, 49, 106-111.

Hollingshead, A. B., and F. C. Redlich. *Social class and mental illness: A community study.* New York: Wiley, 1958.

Holmes, G. R., and R. V. Heckel. Psychotherapy with the first Negro male on one southern university campus: A case study. *Journal of Consulting and Clinical Psychology*, 1970, 34, 297-301.

Holmes, T. H., and R. H. Rahe. The Social Readjustment Rating Scale. *Journal of Psychosomatic Research*, 1967, 11, 213-218.

Honigfeld, G., R. D. Gillis, and J. C. Klett. NOSIE-30: A treatment sensitive ward behavior scale. *Psychological Reports*, 1966, 19, 180-182.

Honigfeld, G., and J. C. Klett. The Nurses' Observation Scale for Inpatient Evaluation: A new scale for measuring improvement in chronic schizophrenia. *Journal of Clinical Psychology*, 1965, 21, 65-71.

Ingram, J. C., P. Marchioni, G. Hill, E. Caraveo-Ramos, and B. McNeil. Recidivism, perceived problem-solving abilities, MMPI characteristics, and violence: A study of black and white incarcerated male adult offenders. *Journal of Clinical Psychology*, 1985, 41, 425-432.

Jackson, F. G. The cross-cultural prediction of psychiatric diagnoses and personality types. Doctoral dissertation, Washington State University, 1978. (*DAI*, 1979, 39B, 4034-4035)

Jacobs, R. A study of drinking behavior and personality characteristics of three ethnic groups. Doctoral dissertation, California School of Professional Psychology, Los Angeles, 1975. (*DAI*, 1976, 36B, 5796)

Jalkanen, R. J. The personality structure of seminarians: The use of available MMPI norms for diagnosis. Master's thesis, Roosevelt University, Chicago, 1955.

Jensen, A. R. *Bias in mental testing.* New York: Free Press, 1980.

Johnson, P. L. Black-white differences on the faking indexes of the MMPI in a prison sample. Doctoral dissertation, Texas Tech University, 1982. (*DAI*, 1983, 43B, 2709)

Johnson, R. L. E. The relation of religious attitudes and selected personality characteristics. Master's thesis, University of Minnesota, 1948.

Jones, E. E. Black-white personality differences: Another look. *Journal of Personality Assessment*, 1978, 42, 244-252.

Jones, E. E., and S. J. Korchin, eds. *Minority mental health.* New York: Praeger, 1982.

Kahgee, S. L., H. R. Miller, and D. L. Streiner. A preliminary investigation of the MMPI performance of native Americans. Paper presented at the 8th International Conference on Personality Assessment, Copenhagen, August, 1983.

Kaiser, H. F. The Varimax criterion for analytic rotation in factor analysis. *Psychometrika*, 1958, 23, 187-200.

Keegan, J. F., and D. Lachar. The MMPI as a predictor of early termination from polydrug abuse treatment. *Journal of Personality Assessment*, 1979, 43, 379-384.

Keeler, M. H., and M. M. Vitols. Migration and schizophrenia in North Carolina Negroes. *American Journal of Orthopsychiatry*, 1963, 33, 554-557.

Kelso, D. R., and C. L. Attneave. *Bibliography of North American Indian mental health.* Westport, Conn.: Greenwood Press, 1981.

Kincannon, J. C. Prediction of the standard MMPI scale scores from 71 items: The Mini-Mult. *Journal of Consulting and Clinical Psychology*, 1968, 32, 319-325.

King, H. F., J. L. Carroll, and G. B. Fuller. Comparison of nonpsychiatric blacks and whites on the MMPI. *Journal of Clinical Psychology*, 1977, 33, 725-728.

Kirk, A., and R. Zucker. Some sociopsychological factors in attempted suicide among urban black males. *Suicide and Life-Threatening Behavior*, 1979, 9, 76-86. (Corrected, 1980, 10, 62.)

Kline, J. A., V. V. Rozynko, G. Flint, and A. C. Roberts. Personality characteristics of male native American alcoholic patients. *International Journal of the Addictions*, 1973, 8, 729-732.

Kline, R. B., D. Lachar, and D. J. Sprague. The Personality Inventory for Children (PIC): An unbiased predictor of cognitive and academic status. *Journal of Pediatric Psychology*, 1985, 10, 461-477.

Klinge, V., and M. E. Strauss. Effects of scoring norms on adolescent psychiatric patients' MMPI profiles. *Journal of Personality Assessment*, 1976, 40, 13-17.

Kosa, J., L. D. Rachiele, and C. O. Schommer. Psychological characteristics of ethnic groups in a college population. *Journal of Psychology*, 1958, 46, 265-275.

Koss, M. P., and J. N. Butcher. A comparison of psychiatric patients' self-report with other sources of clinical information. *Journal of Research in Personality*, 1973, 7, 225-236.

Koss, M. P., J. N. Butcher, and N. Hoffmann. The MMPI critical items: How well do they work? *Journal of Consulting and Clinical Psychology*, 1976, 44, 921-928.

Kramer, M. *Psychiatric services and the changing institutional scene, 1950-1985* (NIMH,

DHEW Publication No. [ADM]77-433). Washington, D.C.: U.S. Government Printing Office, 1977.

Krush, T. P., J. W. Bjork, P. S. Sindell, and J. Nelle. Some thoughts on the formation of personality disorder: Study of an Indian boarding school population. *American Journal of Psychiatry*, 1966, 122, 868-875.

Lachar, D. *The MMPI: Clinical assessment and automated interpretation.* Los Angeles: Western Psychological Services, 1974.

Lachar, D., V. Klinge, and J. L. Grisell. Relative accuracy of automated MMPI narratives generated from adult norms and adolescent norm profiles. *Journal of Consulting and Clinical Psychology*, 1976, 44, 20-24.

Lachar, D., K. Schooff, J. Keegan, and C. Gdowski. Dimensions of polydrug abuse: An MMPI study. In D. R. Wesson, A. S. Carlin, K. M. Adams, and G. C. Beschner, eds. *Polydrug abuse: The results of a national collaborative study.* New York: Academic Press, 1978.

Lachar, D., and J. R. Sharp. Use of parents' MMPIs in the research and evaluation of children: A review of the literature and some new data. In J. N. Butcher, ed. *New developments in the use of the MMPI.* Minneapolis: University of Minnesota Press, 1979.

Lachar, D., and T. A. Wrobel. Validating clinicians' hunches: Construction of a new MMPI critical item set. *Journal of Consulting and Clinical Psychology*, 1979, 47, 277-284.

LaDue, R. A. Standardization of the MMPI for the Colville Indian Reservation. Doctoral dissertation, Washington State University, 1982. (*DAI*, 1983, 43B, 3033)

Lawson, H. H. Psychopathology and attitude toward mental illness of Mexican-American and European-American patients. Doctoral dissertation, University of Arizona, 1979. (*DAI*, 1980, 40B, 3945)

Lawson, H. H., M. W. Kahn, and E. M. Heiman. Psychopathology, treatment outcome and attitude toward mental illness in Mexican American and European patients. *International Journal of Social Psychiatry*, 1982, 28, 20-26.

Lebra, W. P., ed. *Transcultural research in mental health.* Honolulu: University Press of Hawaii, 1972.

Ledwin, A. A comparison between the MMPI-Español and a culturally linguistic revision. Paper presented at the 18th Annual Symposium on Recent Developments in the Use of the MMPI, Minneapolis, April 1983.

Lee, B. L. Demographic variables and the MMPI performance of black college students. Doctoral dissertation, Ball State University, 1978. (*DAI*, 1979, 40B, 922-923)

Leff, J. The cross-cultural study of emotions. *Culture, Medicine, and Psychiatry*, 1977, 1, 317-350.

Leon, G. R., B. Gillum, R. Gillum, and M. Gouze. Personality stability and change over a thirty-year period—middle age to old age. *Journal of Consulting and Clinical Psychology*, 1979, 47, 517-524.

Levinson, B. M. The MMPI in a Jewish traditional setting. *Journal of Genetic Psychology*, 1962, 101, 25-42.

Linn, R. L. Single-group validity, differential validity, and differential prediction. *Journal of Applied Psychology*, 1978, 63, 507-512.

Liske, R., and R. McCormick. MMPI profiles compared for black and white hospitalized veterans. *VA Newsletter for Research in Mental Health and Behavioral Sciences*, 1976, 18, 30-32.

Lockert, E.W., R. E. Dennis, R. C. Cunningham, and A. Kirk. Personality assessments of young American black male homicide perpetrators, assault victims and controls. Paper presented at the 7th International Conference on Personality Assessment, Honolulu, February 1981.

Loehlin, J. C., G. Lindzey, and J. N. Spuhler. *Race differences in intelligence.* San Francisco: Freeman, 1975.

Loper, R. G., M. L. Kammeier, and H. Hoffmann. MMPI characteristics of college freshman males who later became alcoholics. *Journal of Abnormal Psychology,* 1973, 82, 159-162.

Lopreato, J., and L. S. Lewis, eds. *Social stratification.* New York: Harper & Row, 1974.

Lothstein, L. M., and P. Jones. Discriminating violent individuals by means of various psychological tests. *Journal of Personality Assessment,* 1978, 42, 237-243.

Lowe, G. D., and H. E. Hodges. Race and the treatment of alcoholism in a southern state. *Social Problems,* 1972, 20, 240-252.

Lowman, J., and M. D. Galinsky. MMPI profiles in adolescence as indicators of achievement and adjustment in young adulthood. In L. Erlenmeyer-Kimling and N. Miller, eds. *Life-span research on the prediction of psychopathology.* Hillsdale, N.J.: Lawrence Erlbaum Associates, 1986.

Lowman, J., M. D. Galinsky, and B. Gray-Little. *Predicting achievement: A ten-year followup of black and white adolescents.* Chapel Hill, N.C.: Institute for Research in Social Sciences, 1980.

Loya, F., and A. Muñoz. A comparison of the MMPI scales among Anglo, black and Hispanic individuals. Paper presented at the 7th International Conference on Personality Assessment, Honolulu, February 1981.

Luepnitz, R. R., D. L. Randolph, and K. U. Gutsch. Race and socioeconomic status as confounding variables in the accurate diagnosis of alcoholism. *Journal of Clinical Psychology,* 1982, 38, 665-669.

MacAndrew, C. The differentiation of male alcoholic outpatients from nonalcoholic psychiatric outpatients by means of the MMPI. *Quarterly Journal of Studies on Alcohol,* 1965, 26, 238-246.

MacAndrew, C. What the MAC scale tells us about men alcoholics: An interpretive review. *Journal of Studies on Alcohol,* 1981, 42, 604-625.

Malina, R. M. Biological substrata. In K. S. Miller and R. M. Dreger, eds. *Comparative studies of blacks and whites in the United States.* New York: Seminar Press, 1973.

Mandelzys, N. Correlates of offense severity and recidivism probability in a Canadian sample. *Journal of Clinical Psychology,* 1979, 35, 897-907.

Mandelzys, N., and E. B. Lane. The validity of the MMPI as it pertains to Canadian native inmates. *Canadian Journal of Criminology,* 1980, 22, 188-196.

Marken, J. W., and H. T. Hoover. *Bibliography of the Sioux.* Metuchen, N.J.: Scarecrow Press, 1980.

Marks, P. A., W. Seeman, and D. L. Haller. *The actuarial use of the MMPI with adolescents and adults.* Baltimore: Williams and Wilkins, 1974.

Marsella, A. J., K. O. Sanborn, V. Kameoka, L. Shizuru, and J. Brennan. Cross-validation of depression among normal populations of Japanese, Chinese, and Caucasian ancestry. *Journal of Clinical Psychology,* 1975, 31, 281-287.

Martin, C., and R. C. Nichols. Personality and religious belief. *Journal of Social Psychology,* 1962, 56, 3-8.

Martínez, J. L., ed. *Chicano psychology.* New York: Academic Press, 1977.

Mayo, J. A. Utilization of a community mental health center by blacks: Admission to inpatient status. *Journal of Nervous and Mental Disease,* 1974, 158, 202-207.

Mayo, M. A. A comparison of MMPI diagnostic strategies to identify black and white male alcoholics. Doctoral dissertation, Kent State University, 1984. (*DAI,* 1985, 45B, 3340)

McCreary, C., and E. Padilla. MMPI differences among black, Mexican-American, and white male offenders. *Journal of Clinical Psychology,* 1977, 33, 171-177.

McDonald, R. L., and M. D. Gynther. MMPI norms for southern adolescent Negroes. *Journal of Social Psychology,* 1962, 58, 277-282.

McDonald, R. L., and M. D. Gynther. MMPI differences associated with sex, race, and class in two adolescent samples. *Journal of Consulting Psychology*, 1963, 27, 112-116.

McGill, J. C. MMPI score differences among Anglo, black, and Mexican-American welfare recipients. *Journal of Clinical Psychology*, 1980, 36, 147-150.

McGrath, J. H. A comparative study of adolescent drug users, assaulters, and auto thieves. Doctoral dissertation, Rutgers State University, 1967. (*DA*, 1968, 28A, 4290)

McKinley, J. C., and S. R. Hathaway. A multiphasic personality schedule (Minnesota): II. A differential study of hypochondriasis. *Journal of Psychology*, 1940, 10, 255-268. (Also reprinted in Dahlstrom and Dahlstrom, 1980.)

McShane, D. Cross-cultural psychological assessment: Utility for an American Indian tribe. Paper presented at the First International Multi-Ethnic Conference on Assessment, Tampa, March, 1982.

Mead, M., T. Dobzhansky, E. Tobach, and R. E. Light, eds. *Science and the concept of race.* New York: Columbia University Press, 1968.

Meadow, A., D. H. Stoker, and L. A. Zurcher. Sex role and schizophrenia: A cross-cultural study. *The British Journal of Social Psychiatry*, 1967, 1, 250-259.

Meehl, P. E. Theory-testing in psychology and physics: A methodological paradox. *Philosophy of Science*, 1967, 34, 103-115.

Meehl, P. E. High school yearbooks: A reply to Schwarz. *Journal of Abnormal Psychology*, 1971, 77, 143-148.

Middleton, R. Alienation, race, and education. *American Sociological Review*, 1963, 28, 473-477.

Milazzo-Sayre, L. *Admission rates to state and county psychiatric hospitals by age, sex, and race, United States, 1975* (NIMH, Mental Health Statistical Note 140). Washington, D.C.: U.S. Government Printing Office, 1977.

Miller, C., S. C. Knapp, and C. W. Daniels. MMPI study of Negro mental hygiene clinic patients. *Journal of Abnormal Psychology*, 1968, 73, 168-173.

Miller, C., C. Wertz, and S. Counts. Racial differences on the MMPI. *Journal of Clinical Psychology*, 1961, 17, 159-161.

Miller, K. S., and R. M. Dreger, eds. *Comparative studies of blacks and whites in the United States.* New York: Seminar Press, 1973.

Miranda, M., and R. A. Ruiz, eds. *Chicano aging and mental health.* Rockville, Md.: National Institute of Mental Health, 1981.

Mobley, E. L., and S. H. Smith. Some social and economic factors relating to periodontal disease among Negroes. II. Observations on personality traits. *Journal of the American Dental Association*, 1967, 75, 104-110.

Mogar, R. E., W. M. Wilson, and S. T. Helm. Personality subtypes of male and female alcoholic patients. *International Journal of the Addictions*, 1970, 5, 99-113.

Montgomery, G. T., and S. Orozco. Mexican Americans' performance on the MMPI as a function of level of acculturation. *Journal of Clinical Psychology*, 1985, 41, 203-212.

Moore, C. D., and P. J. Handal. Adolescents' MMPI performance, cynicism, estrangement, and personal adjustment as a function of race and sex. *Journal of Clinical Psychology*, 1980, 36, 932-936.

Morris, R. B. Comparison of the MMPI and the Inventario Multifasico de la Personalidad with bilingual subjects. Paper presented at the 18th Annual Symposium on Recent Developments in the Use of the MMPI, Minneapolis, April 1983.

Mosby, D. P. Maternal "identification" and perceived similarity to parents in adolescents as a function of grade placement. Doctoral dissertation, Washington University, 1965. (*DA*, 1966, 26, 6841)

Moss, C. S., R. E. Hosford, W. R. Anderson, and M. Petracca. Personality variables of blacks participating in a prison riot. *Journal of Consulting and Clinical Psychology*, 1977, 45, 505-512.

Most, R. *The development and validation of pre-employment screening indices based on the Behaviordyne Psychodiagnostic Laboratory Service.* Palo Alto, Calif.: Behaviordyne, 1982.

Murphree, H. B., M. J. Karabelas, and L. L. Bryan. Scores of inmates of a federal penitentiary on two scales of the MMPI. *Journal of Clinical Psychology*, 1962, 18, 137-139.

Murphy, J. R. Mexican Americans' performance on the MMPI: As compared with Anglo Americans. Doctoral dissertation, U.S. International University, San Diego, 1978. (*DAI*, 1981, 41B, 3582)

Murray, L., J. Heritage, and W. Holmes. Black-white comparisons of the MMPI Mini-Mult. *Southern Journal of Educational Research*, 1976, 10, 105-114.

National Association for the Advancement of Colored People. *Report on minority testing.* New York: NAACP Special Contribution Fund, 1976.

Nelson, S. E. The development of an indirect, objective measure of social status and its relationship to certain psychiatric syndromes. Doctoral dissertation, University of Minnesota, 1952. (*DA*, 1952, 12, 782)

Neugebauer, R. The reliability of life-event reports. In B. S. Dohrenwend and B. P. Dohrenwend, eds. *Stressful life events and their context.* New York: Prodist, 1981.

Newmark, C. S., L. Gentry, N. Warren, and A. J. Finch. Racial bias in an MMPI index of schizophrenia. *British Journal of Clinical Psychology*, 1981, 20, 215-216.

Newton, F. C-R., E. L. Olmedo, and A. M. Padilla. *Hispanic mental health research: A reference guide.* Berkeley: University of California Press, 1982.

Nies, C. M. Social psychological variables related to family planning among Mexican-American females. Doctoral dissertation, University of Texas at Austin, 1974. (*DAI*, 1974, 35B, 2441)

Nugueras, J. A. The standardization of the MMPI on a selected group of migrant and non-migrant Puerto Rican students. Doctoral dissertation, Pennsylvania State University, 1983. (*DAI*, 1983, 44A, 119)

Ojeda, S. A cross-cultural comparison of MMPI scores of Chicano and Anglo abusive mothers. Master's thesis, San Jose State University, 1980.

Olmedo, E. L. Acculturation: A psychometric perspective. *American Psychologist*, 1979, 34, 1061-1070.

Olmedo, E. L., J. L. Martínez, and S. R. Martínez. Measure of acculturation for Chicano adolescents. *Psychological Reports*, 1978, 42, 159-170.

Olmedo, E. L., and A. M. Padilla. Empirical and construct validation of a measure of acculturation for Mexican Americans. *Journal of Social Psychology*, 1978, 105, 179-187.

Omran, A. R., R. E. Shore, R. A. Markoff, A. Friedhoff, R. E. Albert, H. Barr, W. G. Dahlstrom, and B. S. Pasternack. Follow-up study of patients treated by X-ray epilation for Tinea Capitis: Psychiatric and psychometric evaluation. *American Journal of Public Health*, 1978, 68, 561-567.

Onoda, L. Personality characteristics and attitudes toward achievement among mainland high achieving and underachieving Japanese-American Sanseis. *Journal of Educational Psychology*, 1976, 68, 151-156.

Orozco, S., and G. Montgomery. Mexican Americans' performance on the MMPI as a function of level of acculturation. Paper presented at the Southwestern Psychological Association meetings, Dallas, April 1982.

Overall, J. E., and D. R. Gorham. The Brief Psychiatric Rating Scale. *Psychological Reports*, 1962, 10, 799-812.

Overton, J. R. Postive reinforcement and performance of inmates on the MMPI validity scales. Doctoral dissertation, Memphis State University, 1977. (*DAI*, 1978, 38A, 3962-3963)

Padilla, A. M. *Acculturation: Theory, models and some new findings*. Boulder, CO: Westview Press, 1980.

Padilla, A. M., and P. Aranda. *Latino mental health: Bibliography and abstracts*. Washington, D.C.: U.S. Government Printing Office, 1974.

Padilla, A. M., and R. A. Ruiz. *Latino mental health: A review of literature*. Washington, D.C.: U.S. Government Printing Office, 1973.

Padilla, A. M., and R. A. Ruiz. Personality assessment and test interpretation of Mexican Americans: A critique. *Journal of Personality Assessment*, 1975, 39, 103-109.

Padilla, E. R., E. L. Olmedo, and F. Loya. Acculturation and the MMPI performance of Chicano and Anglo college students. *Hispanic Journal of Behavioral Sciences*, 1982, 4, 451-466.

Page, R. D., and S. Bozlee. A cross-cultural MMPI comparison of alcoholics. *Psychological Reports*, 1982, 50, 639-646.

Pandey, R. E. Personality characteristics of successful, dropout, and probationary black and white university students. *Journal of Counseling Psychology*, 1972, 19, 382-386.

Pando, J. R. Appraisal of various scales of the Spanish version of the Mini-Mult with Spanish Americans. Doctoral dissertation, Adelphi University, 1974. (*DAI*, 1974, 34B, 5688)

Panton, J. H. Inmate personality differences related to recidivism, age and race as measured by the MMPI. *Journal of Correctional Psychology*, 1959, 4, 28-35.

Panton, J. H. An MMPI item content scale to measure religious identification within a state prison population. *Journal of Clinical Psychology*, 1979, 35, 588-591.

Panton, J. H. *Interpretive handbook for the MMPI in correctional classification and diagnostic services* (Rev. ed.). Raleigh, N.C.: Department of Correction, 1980.

Panton, J. H., and R. C. Brisson. Characteristics associated with drug abuse within a state prison population. *Corrective Psychiatry and Journal of Social Therapy*, 1971, 17, 3-33.

Parsons, E. The intercultural setting: Encountering the psychological readjustment needs of black Americans who served in Vietnam. In C. R. Figley, ed. *Trauma: Its consequences and aftermath*. New York: Brunner/Mazel, 1985.

Patalano, F. Personaltiy dimensions of drug abusers who enter a drug-free therapeutic community. *Psychological Reports*, 1978, 42, 1063-1068.

Patterson, E. T., H. L. Charles, W. A. Woodward, W. R. Roberts, and W. E. Penk. Differences in measures of personality and family environment among black and white alcoholics. *Journal of Consulting and Clinical Psychology*, 1981, 49, 1-9.

Pedersen, P., W. Lonner, and J. Draguns, eds. *Counseling across cultures*. Honolulu: University Press of Hawaii, 1976.

Peniston, E. G. The ego strength scale as a predictor of Ute Indian suicide risk. *White Cloud Journal of American Indian/Alaska Native Mental Health*, 1978, 1, 17-19.

Penk, W. E., W. Bell, R. Robinowitz, M. Dolan, J. Black, D. Dorsett, and L. Noriega. Ethnic differences in personality adjustment of black and white male Vietnam combat veterans seeking treatment for substance abuse. In preparation, 1986.

Penk, W. E., A. S. Brown, W. R. Roberts, M. P. Dolan, H. G. Atkins, and R. Robinowitz. Visual memory of black and white male heroin and nonheroin drug users. *Journal of Abnormal Psychology*, 1981, 90, 486-489. (a)

Penk, W. E., W. R. Roberts, R. Robinowitz, M. P. Dolan, H. G. Atkins, and W. A. Woodward. MMPI differences of black and white male polydrug abusers seeking treatment. *Journal of Consulting and Clinical Psychology*, 1982, 50, 463-465.

Penk, W. E., and R. Robinowitz. MMPI differences of black and white drug abusers. *JSAS Catalog of Selected Documents in Psychology*, 1974, 4, 50.

Penk, W. E., R. Robinowitz, R. Kidd, and A. Nisle. Perceived family environments among ethnic groups of compulsive heroin users. *Addictive Behaviors*, 1979, 4, 297-309.

Penk, W. E., R. Robinowitz, W. R. Roberts, M. P. Dolan, and H. G. Atkins. MMPI differences of male Hispanic-American, black, and white heroin addicts. *Journal of Consulting and Clinical Psychology*, 1981, 49, 488-490. (b)

Penk, W. E., R. Robinowitz, W. R. Roberts, F. T. Patterson, M. P. Dolan, and H. G. Atkins. Adjustment differences among male substance abusers varying in degree of combat experience in Vietnam. *Journal of Consulting and Clinical Psychology*, 1981, 49, 426-437. (c)

Penk, W. E., W. A. Woodward, R. Robinowitz, and J. L. Hess. Differences in MMPI scores of black and white compulsive heroin users. *Journal of Abnormal Psychology*, 1978, 87, 505-513.

Penn, M. P. A cross-cultural comparison using MMPI profiles from college students. Master's thesis, University of Arizona, 1963.

Pepper, L. J., and P. N. Strong. Judgmental subscales for the Mf scale of the MMPI. Unpublished materials, Hawaii Department of Health, Honolulu, 1958.

Perlman, M. Social class membership and test-taking attitude. Master's thesis, University of Chicago, 1950.

Persons, R. W., and P. A. Marks. The violent 4-3 MMPI personality type. *Journal of Consulting and Clinical Psychology*, 1971, 36, 189-196.

Peteroy, E. T., and P. E. Pirrello. Comparison of MMPI scales for black and white hospitalized samples. *Psychological Reports*, 1982, 50, 662.

Pine, C. J. Obese and non-obese American Indian and Caucasian performance on the Mini-Mult MMPI and I-E scale. *Journal of Clinical Psychology*, 1983, 39, 251-256.

Plemons, G. A comparison of MMPI scores of Anglo- and Mexican-American psychiatric patients. *Journal of Consulting and Clinical Psychology*, 1977, 45, 149-150.

Plemons, G. The relationship of acculturation to MMPI scores of Mexican American psychiatric outpatients. Unpublished doctoral dissertation, California School of Professional Psychology, 1980.

Pollack, D., and J. H. Shore. Validity of the MMPI with native Americans. *American Journal of Psychiatry*, 1980, 137, 946-950.

Porterfield, L. M. *An examination of the relationship between race and performance in psychological measurement.* Midland, Mich.: Dow Chemical Co., 1964.

Porterfield, L. M. *Negro juvenile delinquent boys: An MMPI study.* Midland, Mich.: Dow Chemical Co., 1967.

Powell, A., and M. Vega. Correlates of adult locus of control. *Psychological Reports*, 1972, 30, 455-460.

Powell, L., H. K. Cameron, C. A. Asbury, and E. H. Johnson. Some characteristics of a special urban educational program. *Journal of Negro Education*, 1975, 44, 361-367.

Powell, L., and E. H. Johnson. The black MMPI profile: Interpretive problems. *Journal of Negro Education*, 1976, 45, 27-36.

Pritchard, D. A., and A. Rosenblatt. Racial bias in the MMPI: A methodological review. *Journal of Consulting and Clinical Psychology*, 1980, 48, 263-267. (a)

Pritchard, D. A., and A. Rosenblatt. Reply to Gynther and Green. *Journal of Consulting and Clinical Psychology*, 1980, 48, 273-274. (b)

Proshansky, H., and P. Newton. The nature and meaning of Negro self-identity. In M. Deutsch, I. Katz, and A. R. Jensen, eds. *Social class, race, and psychological development.* New York: Holt, Rinehart & Winston, 1968.

Quiroga, I. R. The use of a linear discriminant function of MMPI scores in the classification of psychotic and non-psychotic Mexican-American psychiatric patients. Doctoral dissertation, University of Oklahoma, 1972. (*DAI*, 1972, 33B, 448-449)

Quiroga, I. R., and G. Plemons. Cross-cultural comparisons of MMPI profile differences between Mexican-American and Anglo-American psychiatric patients. Unpublished manuscript, 1983.

Ramirez, M. Social responsibilities and failures in psychology: The case of the Mexican-Americans. *Journal of Clinical Child Psychology*, 1971-72, 1, 5-6.

Reilley, R. R., and G. E. Knight. MMPI scores of Mexican-American college students. *Journal of College Student Personnel*, 1970, 11, 419-422.

Ricks, J. H. Local norms—when and why. *Test Service Bulletin*, No. 58. New York: The Psychological Corporation, 1971.

Ritzema, R. J. The effect of demographic variables on the behavioral correlates of MMPI two point code types. Master's thesis, Kent State University, 1974.

Roach, J. L., L. Gross, and O. R. Gursslin, eds. *Social stratification in the United States*. Englewood Cliffs, N.J.: Prentice-Hall, 1969.

Robbins, J. M. Objective versus subjective responses to abortion. *Journal of Consulting and Clinical Psychology*, 1979, 47, 994-995.

Roberts, R. E. Reliability of the CES-D Scale in different ethnic contexts. *Psychiatry Research*, 1980, 2, 125-134.

Robinowitz, R., W. A. Woodward, and W. E. Penk. MMPI comparison of black heroin users volunteering or not volunteering for treatment. *Journal of Consulting and Clinical Psychology*, 1980, 4, 540-542.

Roche Psychiatric Service Institute. Survey of summary statistics on basic MMPI scales of various ethnic groups of mental health clients. Unpublished materials. Nutley, N.J.: RPSI, 1978.

Rosenblatt, A. I. A multivariate analysis of racial differences on the MMPI. Master's thesis, University of Mississippi, 1976.

Rosenblatt, A. I. IQ and race as factors in MMPI profile differences. Doctoral dissertation, University of Mississippi, 1979. (*DAI*, 1980, 40B, 3420)

Rosenblatt, A. I., and D. Pritchard. Moderators of racial differences on the MMPI. *Journal of Consulting and Clinical Psychology*, 1978, 46, 1572-1573.

Rubington, E., and M. S. Weinberg, eds. *Deviance: The interactionist perspective* (2nd ed.). New York: Macmillan, 1973.

Ruiz, R. A. Cultural and historical perspectives in counseling Hispanics. In D. W. Sue, ed. *Counseling the culturally different: Theory and practice*. New York: Wiley, 1981.

Sappington, A., and R. Grizzard. Self-discrimination responses in black school children. *Journal of Personality and Social Psychology*, 1975, 31, 224-231.

Saslow, H. L., and M. J. Harrover. Research on psychosocial adjustment of Indian youth. *American Journal of Psychiatry*, 1968, 125, 224-231.

Schenkel, K. F., and R. H. Hudson. The black man in the world of work: Reclaiming the hard-core unemployed through training. *Professional Psychology*, 1970, 1, 439-443.

Schwab, J. J., R. A. Bell, G. J. Warheit, and R. B. Schwab. *Social order and mental health: The Florida health study*. New York: Brunner/Mazel, 1979.

See, J. J. Insanity proceedings and black-white state hospital admission rate differences. *International Journal of Social Psychiatry*, 1976, 21, 220-228.

See, J. J., and K. S. Miller. Mental health. In K. S. Miller and R. M. Dreger, eds. *Comparative studies of blacks and whites in the United States*. New York: Seminar Press, 1973.

Selters, R. R. An investigation of the relationship between ethnic origin and reactions to the MMPI. Doctoral dissertation, Baylor University, 1973. (*DAI*, 1974, 34B, 5210)

Shaffer, J. W., T. W. Kinlock, and D. N. Nurco. Factor structure of the MMPI-168 in male narcotic addicts. *Journal of Clinical Psychology*, 1982, 38, 656-661.

Shipley, W. C. A self-administering scale for measuring intellectual impairment and deterioration. *Journal of Psychology*, 1940, 9, 371-377.

Shore, J. H., and S. M. Manson. Cross-cultural studies of depression among American Indians and Alaska Natives. *White Cloud Journal of American Indian/Alaska Native Mental Health*, 1981, 2, 5-12.

Shore, R. E. A statistical note on "differential misdiagnosis of blacks and whites by the MMPI." *Journal of Personality Assessment*, 1976, 40, 21-23.

Simpson, G. E., and J. M. Yinger. *Racial and cultural minorities: An analysis of prejudice and discrimination* (4th ed.). New York: Harper & Row, 1972.

Smith, C. P. Behavioral correlates for the MMPI standard F scale and a modified F scale for black and white psychiatric patients. Doctoral dissertation, Kent State University, 1980. (*DAI*, 1980, 41B, 1528)

Smith, C. P., and J. R. Graham. Behavioral correlates for the MMPI standard F scale and for a modified F scale for black and white psychiatric patients. *Journal of Consulting and Clinical Psychology*, 1981, 49, 455-459.

Smith, R. E. Personality configurations of adult male penal populations as revealed by the MMPI. Doctoral dissertation, University of Minnesota, 1955. (*DA*, 1956, 16, 160)

Snowden, L., and P. A. Todman. The psychological assessment of blacks: New and needed developments. In E. E. Jones and S. J. Korchin, eds. *Minority mental health*. New York: Praeger, 1982.

Snyder, D. K., R. B. Kline, and E. C. Podany. Comparison of external correlates of MMPI substance abuse scales across sex and race. *Journal of Consulting and Clinical Psychology*, 1985, 53, 520-525.

Solomon, L. J., D. W. Foy, and B. Nunn. Demographic differences among black and white alcohol abusers. Paper presented at the Southeastern Psychological Association convention, Washington, D.C., 1980.

Soltz, W. H. Comparative study of Negro-white differences on the MMPI and PAS. Doctoral dissertation, University of Missouri, 1970. (*DAI*, 1970, 31B, 3009)

Sowell, T., ed. *Essays and data on American ethnic groups*. Washington, D.C.: Urban Institute, 1978.

Srole, L., T. S. Langner, S. T. Michael, M. K. Opler, and T. A. C. Rennie. *Mental health in the metropolis: The Midtown Study* (Vol. 1). New York: McGraw-Hill, 1962.

Stanton, J. M. Group personality profiles related to aspects of antisocial behavior. *Journal of Criminal Law, Criminology, and Police Science*, 1956, 47, 340-349.

Steinberg, M. D., H. Pardes, D. Bjork, and L. Sporty. Demographic and clinical characteristics of black psychiatric patients in a private general hospital. *Hospital and Community Psychiatry*, 1977, 28, 128-132.

Steinberg, S. *The ethnic myth: Race, ethnicity, and class in America*. New York: Atheneum, 1981.

Strauss, M. E., M. D. Gynther, and J. Wallhermfechtel. Differential misdiagnosis of blacks and whites by the MMPI. *Journal of Personality Assessment*, 1974, 38, 55-60.

Stricker, L. J. Dimensions of social stratification for whites and blacks. *Multivariate Behavioral Research*, 1982, 17, 139-167.

Sue, D. W. (with E. H. Richardson, R. A. Ruiz, and E. J. Smith). *Counseling the culturally different: Theory and practice*. New York: Wiley, 1981.

Sue, S., H. McKinney, D. Allen, and J. Hall. Delivery of community mental health services to black and white clients. *Journal of Consulting and Clinical Psychology*, 1974, 42, 794-801.

Sue, S., and J. K. Morishima. *The mental health of Asian Americans*. San Francisco: Jossey-Bass, 1982.

Sue, S., and D. W. Sue. MMPI comparisons between Asian-American and non-Asian students utilizing a student health psychiatric clinic. *Journal of Counseling Psychology*, 1974, 21, 423-427.

Sundberg, N. D., and L. R. Gonzáles. Cross-cultural and cross- ethnic assessment: Overview and issues. In P. McReynolds, ed. *Advances in psychological assessment* (Vol. 5). San Francisco: Jossey-Bass, 1981.

Sutker, P. B., R. P. Archer, and A. N. Allain. Drug abuse patterns, personality characteristics, and relationships with sex, race, and sensation seeking. *Journal of Consulting and Clinical Psychology*, 1978, 46, 1374-1378.

Sutker, P. B., R. P. Archer, and A. N. Allain. Psychopathology of drug abusers: Sex and ethnic considerations. *International Journal of the Addictions*, 1980, 15, 605-613. (a)

Sutker, P. B., P. J. Brantley, and A. N. Allain. MMPI response patterns and alcohol consumption in DUI offenders. *Journal of Consulting and Clinical Psychology*, 1980, 48, 350-355. (b)

Sutker, P. B., and D. G. Kilpatrick. Personality, biographical, and racial correlates of sexual attitudes and behavior. *Proceedings of the 81st Annual Convention of the American Psychological Association*, 1973, 8, 261-262.

Sutker, P. B., and C. E. Moan. A psychosocial description of penitentiary inmates. *Archives of General Psychiatry*, 1973, 29, 663-667.

Svanum, S., and C. L. Dallas. Alcoholic MMPI types and their relationship to patient characteristics, polydrug abuse, and abstinence following treatment. *Journal of Personality Assessment*, 1981, 45, 278-287.

Swickard, D. L., and B. Spilka. Hostility expression among delinquents of minority and majority groups. *Journal of Consulting Psychology*, 1961, 25, 216-220.

Szapocznik, J., M. H. Scopetta, W. Kurtines, and M. A. Arnalde. Theory and measurement of acculturation. *Interamerican Journal of Psychology*, 1978, 12, 113-130.

Talley, T. A multifaceted inquiry into the personality factors and academic achievement of Indian high school students. Doctoral dissertation, University of South Dakota, 1975. (*DAI*, 1976, 36A, 5063)

Taylor, J. B., M. Carithers, and L. Coyne. MMPI performance, response set, and the "self-concept hypothesis." *Journal of Consulting and Clinical Psychology*, 1976, 44, 351-362. (Also reprinted in Dahlstrom and Dahlstrom, 1980.)

Tellegen, A., N. L. Gerrard, L. B. Gerrard, and J. N. Butcher. Personality characteristics of members of a serpent-handling religious cult. In J. N. Butcher, ed. *MMPI: Research developments and clinical applications.* New York: McGraw-Hill, 1969.

Thomas, A., and S. Sillen. *Racism and psychiatry.* Secaucus, N.J.: Citadel Press, 1972.

Thorndike, R. L. Concepts of culture-fairness. *Journal of Educational Measurement*, 1971, 8, 63-70.

Tsushima, W. T., and V. A. Onorato. Comparison of MMPI scores of white and Japanese-American medical patients. *Journal of Consulting and Clinical Psychology*, 1982, 50, 150-151.

Turner, S. M., and R. T. Jones, eds. *Behavior modification in black populations: Psychosocial issues and empirical findings.* New York: Plenum, 1982.

Uecker, A. E., L. R. Boutilier, and E. H. Richardson. "Indianism" and MMPI scores of men alcoholics. *Journal of Studies on Alcohol*, 1980, 41, 357-362.

Uecker, A. E., L. R. Boutilier, and E. H. Richardson. "Indianism" and the "Richardson Indian Culturalization Test"; a reply to Walker et al. *Journal of Studies on Alcohol*, 1981, 42, 168-171.

Unikel, I. P., and E. B. Blanchard. Psychopathy, race, and delay of gratification by adolescent delinquents. *Journal of Nervous and Mental Disease*, 1973, 156, 57-60.

van den Berghe, P. L. *Race and racism: A comparative perspective.* New York: Wiley, 1967.

Vaughan, R. P. The influence of religious affiliation on the MMPI scales. *Journal of Clinical Psychology*, 1965, 21, 416-417.

Vega, S. The cultural effects upon MMPI responses of industrially injured Mexican and Anglo-American males. Doctoral dissertation, University of Southern California, 1983. (*DAI*, 1984, 44B, 2278)

Velásquez, R. J. The Minnesota Multiphasic Personality Inventory: A guide for methodological investigations with Mexican Americans. A review of the literature. Unpublished manuscript, Harvard University, 1979.

Velásquez, R. J. The Minnesota Multiphasic Personality Inventory (MMPI): a guide for methodological investigations with Chicanos. Paper presented at the Interamerican Congress of Psychology meetings, Quito, Ecuador, July 1983. (a)

Velásquez, R. J. MMPI scores for three different age groups of Mexican American veteran inpatients. Unpublished manuscript, Arizona State University, 1983. (b)

Velásquez, R. J. *An atlas of MMPI group profiles on Mexican Americans.* Los Angeles: UCLA Spanish Speaking Mental Health Research Center, 1984.

Velásquez, R. J. Mexican American-Anglo differences on the MMPI: Does ethnicity or setting make a difference? In preparation, 1986.

Verinis, J. S. Maternal and child pathology in an urban ghetto. *Journal of Clinical Psychology*, 1976, 32, 13-15.

Vernon, S. W., and R. E. Roberts. Use of the SADS-RDC in a tri-ethnic community survey. *Archives of General Psychiatry*, 1982, 39, 47-52.

Vitols, M. M., H. G. Waters, and M. H. Keeler. Hallucinations and delusions in white and Negro schizophrenics. *American Journal of Psychiatry*, 1963, 120, 472-476.

Walker, R. D., F. G. Cohen, and P. S. Walker. "Indianism" and the "Richardson Indian Culturalization Test". *Journal of Studies on Alcohol*, 1981, 42, 163-167.

Walters, G. D. Racial variations on the MacAndrew Alcoholism scale of the MMPI. Doctoral dissertation, Texas Tech University, 1982. (*DAI*, 1983, 43B, 2720)

Walters, G. D., R. L. Greene, and T. B. Jeffrey. Discriminating between alcoholic and nonalcoholic blacks and whites. *Journal of Personality Assessment*, 1984, 48, 486-488.

Walters, G. D., R. L. Greene, T. B. Jeffrey, D. J. Fruzich, and J. J. Haskin. Racial variations on the MacAndrew alcoholism scale of the MMPI. *Journal of Consulting and Clinical Psychology*, 1983, 51, 947-948.

Warheit, G. J., R. A. Bell, J. J. Schwab, and J. M. Buhl. An epidemiologic assessment of mental health problems in the southeastern United States. In M. Weissman, G. Myers, and A. Ross, eds. *Community surveys.* New Brunswick, N.J.: Rutgers University Press, 1984.

Warheit, G. J., C. E. Holzer, and S. A. Arey. Race and mental illness: An epidemiologic update. *Journal of Health and Social Behavior*, 1975, 16, 243-256.

Warheit, G. J., C. E. Holzer, R. A. Bell, and S. A. Arey. Sex, marital status, and mental health: A reappraisal. *Social Forces*, 1976, 55, 459-470.

Warheit, G. J., C. E. Holzer, and J. J. Schwab. An analysis of social class and racial differences in depressive symptomatology: A community study. *Journal of Health and Social Behavior*, 1973, 14, 291-299.

Warner, W. L., M. Meeker, and K. Eells. *Social class in America.* Chicago: Science Research Associates, 1949.

Webb, J. T. Regional and sex differences in MMPI scale high-point frequencies of psychiatric patients. *Journal of Clinical Psychology*, 1971, 27, 483-486.

Weiss, B. L., and D. J. Kupfer. The black patient and research in a community mental health center: Where have all the subjects gone? *American Journal of Psychiatry*, 1974, 131, 415-418.

Weiss, R. W., and S. Russakoff. Relationship of MMPI scores of drug-abusers to personal variables and type of treatment program. *Journal of Psychology*, 1977, 96, 25-29.

Welsh, G. S. An extension of Hathaway's MMPI profile coding system. *Journal of Consulting Psychology*, 1948, 12, 343-344. (Also reprinted in Welsh and Dahlstrom, 1956.)

Welsh, G. S. Factor dimensions A and R. In G. S. Welsh and W. G. Dahlstrom, eds. *Basic readings on the MMPI in psychology and medicine*. Minneapolis: University of Minnesota Press, 1956.

Welsh, G. S., and W. G. Dahlstrom, eds. *Basic readings on the MMPI in psychology and medicine*. Minneapolis: University of Minnesota Press, 1956.

Wendland, M. M. Self-concept development in the Negro adolescent and its relationship to area of residence. Doctoral dissertation, University of North Carolina, 1968. (*DA*, 1969, 29B, 2642)

Wesson, D. R., A. S. Carlin, K. M. Adams, and G. Beschner, eds. *Polydrug abuse: The results of a national collaborative study*. New York: Academic Press, 1978.

Westermeyer, J. Chippewa and majority alcoholism in the Twin Cities: A comparison. *Journal of Nervous and Mental Disease*, 1972, 155, 322-327.

Wexler, H. K., and G. de Leon. The therapeutic community: Multivariate prediction of retention. *American Journal of Drug and Alcohol Abuse*, 1977, 4, 145-151.

White, J. L. *The psychology of blacks: An Afro-American perspective*. Englewood Cliffs, N.J.: Prentice-Hall, 1984.

White, W. G. A psychometric approach for adjusting selected MMPI scale scores obtained by blacks. Doctoral dissertation, University of Missouri, 1974. (*DAI*, 1975, 35B, 4669)

Wiener, D. N. Subtle and obvious keys for the MMPI. *Journal of Consulting Psychology*, 1948, 12, 164-170. (Also reprinted in Welsh and Dahlstrom, 1956.)

Wiggins, J. Substantive dimensions of self-report in the MMPI item pool. *Psychological Monographs*, 1966, 80 (22, whole No. 630). (Also reprinted in part in Dahlstrom and Dahlstrom, 1980.)

Williams, R. M. *Mutual accommodation: Ethnic conflict and cooperation*. Minneapolis: University of Minnesota Press, 1977.

Winslow, R. W., ed. *The emergence of deviant minorities: Social problems and social change*. New Brunswick, N.J.: Transaction Books, 1972.

Witt, P. H., and M. D. Gynther. Another explanation for black-white MMPI differences. *Journal of Clinical Psychology*, 1975, 31, 69-70.

Wormith, J. S., M. Borzecki, and W. H. Black. *Norms and special considerations for MMPI administration with incarcerated native offenders*. Programs Branch User Report No. 1984-15. Ottawa: Ministry of the Solicitor General of Canada, 1984.

Wrobel, T. A., and D. Lachar. Validity of the Wiener Subtle and Obvious scales for the MMPI: Another example of the importance of inventory-item content. *Journal of Consulting and Clinical Psychology*, 1982, 50, 469-470.

Youssef, Z. I. The role of race, sex, hostility, and verbal stimuli in inflicting punishment. *Psychonomic Science*, 1968, 12, 285-286.

Zager, L. D., and E. I. Megargee. Seven MMPI alcohol and drug abuse scales: An empirical investigation of their interrelationships. Convergent and discriminant validity, and degree of racial bias. *Journal of Personality and Social Psychology*, 1981, 40, 532-544.

Zipper, B. The personality and self-concept characteristics of Negro and white delinquent and non-delinquent boys. Doctoral dissertation, University of North Carolina, 1972. (*DAI*, 1973, 34B, 431)

INDEX

INDEX

W. Grant Dahlstrom is professor of psychology at the University of North Carolina, Chapel Hill. He is co-author with Leona E. Dahlstrom of *Basic Readings on the MMPI: A New Selection on Personality Measurement* (Minnesota, 1980).

David Lachar is director of psychology and the clinical psychology residency program at the Institute of Behavioral Medicine (Good Samaritan Medical Center) in Phoenix and is author of *The MMPI: Clinical Assessment and Automated Interpretation* (1974) and other books on child and adolescent personality.

Leona E. Dahlstrom is a clinical psychologist and co-author with W. Grant Dahlstrom and George S. Welsh of the two-volume *MMPI Handbook* (Minnesota, 1972, 1975).